THE BEST TEST PREPARATION FOR THE

GRE

GRADUATE

RECORD

EXAMINATION

IN

LITERATURE IN ENGLISH

Pauline Beard, Ph.D.
Instructor of English
Portland State University
Portland, Oregon

Robert Liftig, Ed.D.
Adjunct Professor of English
Fairfield University
Fairfield, Connecticut

Thomas C. Kennedy, Ph.D.
Professor of English
Washburn University
Topeka, Kansas

James S. Malek, Ph.D.
Chairperson and Professor of English
DePaul University
Chicago, Illinois

Research and Education Association
61 Ethel Road West
Piscataway, New Jersey 08854

The Best Test Preparation for the
GRADUATE RECORD EXAMINATION (GRE)
in LITERATURE IN ENGLISH

REVISED PRINTING, 1992

Printed in the United States of America

Library of Congress Catalog Card Number 91-68593

International Standard Book Number 0-87891-634-2

Research & Education Association
61 Ethel Road West
Piscataway, New Jersey 08854

CONTENTS

PREFACE

This book provides an accurate and complete representation of the Graduate Record Examination Literature in English. The six practice exams are based on the most recently administered GRE Literature in English. Each test is two hours and fifty minutes in length and includes every type of question that can be expected on the actual exam. Following each exam is an answer key with detailed explanations designed to clarify the material for the student. By completing all six exams and studying the explanations that follow, students can discover their strengths and weaknesses and thereby become well-prepared for the actual exam.

ABOUT THE TEST

The Graduate Record Examination (GRE) Literature in English Test is offered four times a year by the Educational Testing Service, under the direction of the Graduate Record Examinations Board. Applicants for graduate school submit GRE test results together with other academic records as part of the highly competitive admission process to graduate school.

The questions for the test are composed by a committee of specialists who are recommended by the Modern Language Association of America, and selected from various undergraduate and graduate faculties. *This test consists of approximately 230 multiple-choice questions. Examinees are allowed 170 minutes to complete the test. There are no breaks - examinees work straight through the entire length of the exam.* Due to the wide diversity of coursework in undergraduate literature programs, not all the material that a student may have studied will be presented on the test. The questions are drawn from all periods of English and American literature, and will also include questions on major foreign writers and the Bible. Knowledge of authors and authors' works is stressed, along with the ability to analyze selections from the following genres:

- drama   - poetry   - short story
- biography   - novel   - history of language
- criticism   - essay

Questions on the GRE Literature in English can be loosely categorized into two divisions:

Interpretive - These questions test the students' ability to distinguish aspects of literature such as voice, tone, mood, theme, literary methods, and style from a given passage of literature (usually an excerpt from a larger work or a short poem).

Factual - These questions are a straightforward testing of specific facts. Students are asked to recall and recognize information regarding: authors and literary works (often based on brief passages written by or about the authors); substance and styles of writing; historical and biographical information; and details such as plot, character, and setting.

The questions are distributed into the following categories with the approximate percentage of total test content for each:

Literary Analysis	(40-55%)
Identification	(20-25%)
Factual Information	(20-25%)
History and Theory of Literary Criticism	(5-10%)

The historical span of information contained on the exam is distributed into the time periods listed below with the approximate percentage of total test content for each:

Literature to 1660 (including Milton)	(25-35%)
English Literature 1660-1925	(30-40%)
American Literature before 1925	(10-15%)
British and American Literature after 1925	(20-25%)
Continental, Classical, and Comparative Literature	(5-10%)

The best way to prepare for this exam is to review your undergraduate program. Because the length and span of the subject is so great, the exam covers knowledge that is standard curriculum for students taking English Literature classes in universities across the country. The Suggested Reading List of Literary Works beginning on page *ix* will also give you an idea of what type of material is covered on the GRE Literature in English. It is essentially impossible to give every conceivable literary work needed to review since the material presented on the exam varies from year to year.

SCORING THE TEST

Each correct answer receives one "raw score" point, each incorrect answer deducts 1/4 of a point, and any omissions should not be counted. Use the formula below to calculate your raw score.

$$\underline{\hspace{2cm}} - (\underline{\hspace{1.5cm}} \times \tfrac{1}{4}) = \underline{\hspace{1.5cm}} \quad \text{(round to nearest whole number)}$$

number right	number wrong	raw score

DO NOT INCLUDE
UNANSWERED QUESTIONS

By using the conversion table on page *viii*, the raw score can be converted to a scaled score, and a percentile ranking can be determined.

While taking these practice tests, it is helpful to observe the same conditions that will be encountered during the actual test administration.

- work in a quiet place, free from distractions and interruptions.

- do not use any reference materials, since these items are not allowed for use during the test.

- work straight through the test. Extra time and short breaks do not occur during the actual exam.

- time yourself accurately, if possible with a watch or clock alarm. Looking up to check the time will act as a distraction (note: watches with alarms are not permitted at the testing center).

- since incorrect answers are penalized ¼ of a point each, and unanswered questions are not counted, it is not a good idea to guess. However, if you are able to eliminate one or more of the answers, guessing may be to your advantage statistically (that is, the odds of choosing the right answer improve).

LITERATURE IN ENGLISH CONVERSION TABLE

TOTAL SCORE

Raw Score	Scaled Score	%*	Raw Score	Scaled Score	%*
227-230	800		107-111	510	42
			103-106	500	39
222-226	790		99-102	490	34
218-221	780		95- 98	480	31
214-217	770		91- 94	470	29
210-213	760		87- 90	460	26
206-209	750		83- 86	450	23
202-205	740	99	79- 82	440	20
198-201	730	99	75- 78	430	18
194-197	720	99	70- 74	420	15
190-193	710	98	66- 69	410	13
185-189	700	97	62- 65	400	11
181-184	690	95	58- 61	390	9
177-180	680	94	54- 57	380	8
173-176	670	92	50- 53	370	7
169-172	660	90	46- 49	360	6
165-168	650	88	42- 45	350	5
161-164	640	86	38- 41	340	4
157-160	630	84	34- 37	330	3
153-156	620	82	29- 33	320	2
148-152	610	79	25- 28	310	2
144-147	600	75	21- 24	300	1
140-143	590	72			
136-139	580	69	17- 20	290	1
132-135	570	64	13- 16	280	1
128-131	560	62	9- 12	270	
124-127	550	57	5- 8	260	
120-123	540	53	1- 4	250	
116-119	530	50	0	240	
112-115	520	47			

*Percent Scoring below the scaled score.

SUGGESTED READING LIST OF LITERARY WORKS

This is a list of literary works mentioned in the test, listed alphabetically by the author's last name. It also includes other works that commonly appear on the GRE Literature in English. This can serve as an outline of suggested reading material. By reading these works for both study and pleasure, your knowledge of literature will broaden.

Adams, Henry. *The Education of Henry Adams*

Addison, Joseph. *The Pleasures of the Imagination*, "Tulips"

Aeres, Jan. *Miss Lonelyhearts*

Aeschylus. *The Libation Bearers, Oresteia*

Algren, Nelson. *The Man with the Golden Arm*

Amis, Kingsley. *Lucky Jim*

Anouilh, Jean. *The Lark*

Aristophanes. *Lysistrata*

Aristotle. *On the Art of Poetry, Poetics*

Arnold, Matthew. "Dover Beach," "The Function of Criticism at the Present Time," "Preface to Poems," "The Scholar Gipsy," "The Study of Poetry," "Thyrsis," "To Marguerite – Continued," "Wordsworth's Grave"

Atwood, Margaret. *Lady Oracle*

Auden, W.H. "In Memory of W.B. Yeats," "Musée des Beaux Arts"

Auerbach, Eric. *Mimesis: The Representation of Reality in Western Literature*

Austen, Jane. *Emma, Northanger Abbey, Pride and Prejudice, Sense and Sensibility*

Baldwin, James. *Go Tell it On the Mountain, Notes of a Native Son*

Baraka, Imamu Amiri (Leroi Jones). "Poem for Half White College Students"

Barth, John. *Lost in the Funhouse*, "The Battle of Maldon"

Beckett, Samuel. *Murphy, Waiting for Godot*

Bede. *Historia Ecclesiastica Gentis Anglorum*

Behan, Brendan. *The Hostage*

Behn, Aphra. *Oroonoko*

Bellow, Saul. *Henderson the Rain King, Seize the Day*

Beowulf

Blair, Robert. "The Grave"

Blake, William. "The Chimney Sweeper," "London," "The Tyger," *A Vision of the Last Judgement*

Boker, George Henry. *Francesca da Rimini*

Booth, Wayne C. *The Rhetoric of Fiction*

Borges, Jorge Luis. *The Garden of Forking Paths*

Boswell, James. *The Life of Samuel Johnson, LL.D.*

Brecht, Bertolt. *The Caucasian Chalk Circle, St. Joan of the Stockyards, The Threepenny Opera*

Brode, Anthony. "Breakfast with Gerard Manley Hopkins"

Brontë, Emily. *Wuthering Heights*

Brooks, Gwendolyn. "We Real Cool"

Browne, Sir Thomas. *Religio Medici*

Browning, Elizabeth Barrett. "Aurora Leigh," *Sonnets from the Portugese*

Browning, Robert. "Andrea Del Sarto," "The Bishop Orders His Tomb at Saint Praxed's Church," "Fra Lippo Lippi," "A Grammarian's Funeral," "The House Holder," "My Last Duchess," "Porphyria's Lover"

Bryant, William Cullen. "The Death of Lincoln"

Bunyan, John. *The Pilgrim's Progress*

Burke, Edmund. *Speech on Conciliation with the Colonies*

Burney, Fanny. *Evelina*

Burns, Robert. "Ae Fond Kiss," "Scots Wha Hae," "Tam o' Shanter," "To a Louse [On Seeing One on a Lady's Bonnet at Church]"

Burton, Robert. *Anatomy of Melancholy*

Butler, Samuel. *Erewhon,* "Hudibras," *The Way of All Flesh*

Byrd, William. *The History of the Dividing Line*

Byron, George Gordon, Lord. *Childe Harold's Pilgrimage, Don Juan, Manfred,* "She Walks in Beauty"

Campion, Thomas. "When to Her Lute Corinna Sings"

Camus, Albert. *The Myth of Sisyphus, The Plague*

Carlyle, Thomas. "Characteristics," *On Heroes and Hero Worship, Portrait of His Contemporaries, Sartor Resartus*

Carroll, Lewis. *Alice's Adventures in Wonderland*

Cather, Willa. *Death Comes to the Archbishop, My Antonia*

Centlivre, Susannah. *A Bold Stroke for a Wife, The Busie Bodie*

Cervantes. *Don Quixote*

Chaucer, Geoffrey. *The Canterbury Tales, Troylus and Criseyde*

Chekov, Anton. *The Cherry Orchard,* "The Darling"

Chopin, Kate. "The Story of an Hour"

Cibber, Colley. *Love's Last Shift*

Coleridge, Samuel Taylor. *Biographia Literaria,* "Christabel," "Frost at Midnight," "On Donne's Poetry," "The Rime of the Ancient Mariner," *Table Talk*

Congreve, William. *The Way of the World*

Conrad, Joseph. *Heart of Darkness, Lord Jim, The Secret Sharer*

Cooper, James Fenimore. *The Deerslayer, The Pioneers*

Cortazar, Julio. *Blow-Up*

Crabbe, George. "The Village"

Crane, Stephen. "The Open Boat," *The Red Badge of Courage*

Cullen, Countee. "From the Dark Tower"

Cumberland, Richard. *The West Indian*

cummings, e.e. "A salesman is an it that stinks Excuse"

Dante Alighieri. *The Divine Comedy I: Inferno, Freedom of the Will*

Declaration of Independence

Defoe, Daniel. *Moll Flanders, Robinson Crusoe*

De Quincey, Thomas. "Confessions of an English Opium Eater"

Dickens, Charles. *Bleak House, David Copperfield, Great Expectations, Hard Times, The Pickwick Papers*

Dickinson, Emily. "The brain is wider than the sky," "I reason, earth is short," "If I can stop one heart from breaking," "That after Horror – that 'twas us"

Donne, John. *An Anatomy of the World [The First Anniversary],* "The Bait," *Devotions Upon Emergent Occasions,* "The Sun Rising," "A Valediction: Forbidding Mourning"

Dos Passos, John (Roderigo). *The Big Money*

Dostoevsky, Fyodor. *Crime and Punishment*

Douglass, Frederick. *The Narrative Life of Frederick Douglass*

Drayton, Michael. "Since there's no help, come let us kiss and part"

Dreiser, Theodore (Herman Albert). *An American Tragedy, Sister Carrie*

Drummond, William. *Notes on Ben Jonson*

Dryden, John. "Absalom and Achitophel," "Alexander's Feast," *All For Love, The Conquest of Granada,* "Epigram on Milton," "Essay of Dramatic Poesy," *An Evening's Love, MacFlecknoe,* "Ode to Mrs. Anne Killigrew," Preface to "Fables Ancient and Modern," "A Song for St. Cecilia's Day, 1687"

Edwards, Jonathan. *Personal Narrative,* "Sinners in the Hands of an Angry God"

Eliot, George. *Adam Bede, Middlemarch, Silas Marner*

Eliot, T.S. "Hamlet and His Problems," "Journey of the Magi," "Little Gidding," "The Love Song of J. Alfred Prufrock," "Tradition and

xiv

Steinbeck, John. *The Grapes of Wrath,* "Tularecito"

Sterne, Laurence. *Tristram Shandy*

Stevens, Wallace. "Anecdote of the Jar"

Stevenson, Robert Louis. *Kidnapped, Strange Case of Dr. Jekyll and Mr. Hyde*

Stoppard, Tom. *Jumpers*

Stowe, Harriet Beecher. *Uncle Tom's Cabin*

Strindberg, August. *Miss Julie*

Stuart, Jesse. *The Thread that Runs So True*

Surrey, Henry Howard, Earl of. "The Soote Season"

Swift, Jonathan. "An Argument Against the Abolishing of Christianity in England," "The Battle of the Books," "Cadenus and Vanessa," "A Description of a City Shower," *Gulliver's Travels,* "A Modest Proposal," "Verses on the Death of Dr. Swift, D.S.P.D., Occasioned by Reading a Maxim in Rochefoucauld"

Synge, John M. *The Playboy of the Western World, The Shadow of the Glen*

Tennyson, Alfred, 1st Baron. "Break, Break, Break," "In Memoriam A.H.H., XCVI," "King Arthur's Order of Chivalry," "The Lady of Shalott," "The Lotos-Eaters," "Mariana," "Songs from the Princess," "Tears, Idle Tears (I Know Not What They Mean)," "To E. FitzGerald," "Ulysses"

Terence. *Andria*

Theocritus. *Idylls*

Thomas, Dylan. "Do Not Go Gentle into That Good Night," "Fern Hill"

Thoreau, Henry David. *Civil Disobedience, Walden*

Thucydides. *History of the Peloponnesian War*

Thurber, James. "The Secret Life of Walter Mitty"

Tolstoy, Leo. *Anna Karenina, War and Peace,* "What is Art?"

Toomer, Jean. "Blood-Burning Moon"

Twain, Mark (Samuel Clemens). *The Adventures of Huckleberry Finn,* "Advice to Youth"

Updike, John. "The Bulgarian Poetess"

Vanbrugh, Sir John. *The Relapse*

Villiers, George, Duke of Buckingham. *The Rehearsal*

Villon, François. "Ballad of Dead Ladies"

Virgil. *The Aeneid, Eclogues*

Voltaire. *Candide*

Vonnegut, Kurt Jr. *Welcome to the Monkey House*

Walker, Alice. "Everyday Use"

Waller, Edmund. "Go Lovely Rose," "Of English Verse," "On a Girdle," "Song"

Warren, Robert Penn. "Blow West wind"

Webster, John. *Duchess of Malfi*

Welty, Eudora. *Delta Wedding,* "Why I Live at the P.O."

Wheatley, Phillis. "On Being Brought from Africa to America"

Whipple, Edwin. *Literature and Life*

White, E.B. "Once More to the Lake"

Whitman, Walt. *Democratic Vistas,* "Pioneers! O Pioneers!," "Song of Myself," "When I Heard the Learn'd Astronomer," "When Lilacs Last in the Dooryard Bloom'd"

"Widsith"

Wilde, Oscar. *The Ballad of Reading Gaol, The Critic as Artist, The Importance of Being Earnest, The Picture of Dorian Gray*

Williams, Tennesee. *Cat on a Hot Tin Roof, The Glass Menagerie, A Streetcar Named Desire*

Williams, William Carlos. "Landscape with the Fall of Icarus," "This is Just to Say"

Wilson, John. *Noctes Ambrosianae of "Blackwood"*

Winstanley, William. *Lives of the Most Famous English Poets*

Winthrop, John. *Journal*

Wollstonecraft, Mary. *A Vindication of the Rights of Woman*

Woolf, Virginia. *The Common Reader,
Mrs. Dalloway, To the Lighthouse*
Woolman, John. *Journal*
Wordsworth, William. *The Excursion,*
"It Is a Beauteous Evening (Calm
and Free)," "My Heart Leaps Up
(When I Behold)," Preface to
Lyrical Ballads, The Prelude, "She
Dwelt among the Untrodden
Ways," "Tintern Abbey," "The
World Is Too Much with Us"
Wright, Richard. *Native Son*
Wycherley, William. *The Country-Wife*
Yeats, William Butler. "Crazy Jane and
the Bishop," "The Dolls," "The
Lake Isle of Innisfree," "Leda and
the Swan," *On a Political Prisoner,*
"Sailing to Byzantium," "When
You Are Old," "The Wild Swans at
Coole"
Young, Edward. "Night-Thoughts"

GRE

LITERATURE in ENGLISH

TEST I

THE GRADUATE RECORD EXAMINATION

LITERATURE in ENGLISH

ANSWER SHEET

1. Ⓐ Ⓑ Ⓒ Ⓓ Ⓔ
2. Ⓐ Ⓑ Ⓒ Ⓓ Ⓔ
3. Ⓐ Ⓑ Ⓒ Ⓓ Ⓔ
4. Ⓐ Ⓑ Ⓒ Ⓓ Ⓔ
5. Ⓐ Ⓑ Ⓒ Ⓓ Ⓔ
6. Ⓐ Ⓑ Ⓒ Ⓓ Ⓔ
7. Ⓐ Ⓑ Ⓒ Ⓓ Ⓔ
8. Ⓐ Ⓑ Ⓒ Ⓓ Ⓔ
9. Ⓐ Ⓑ Ⓒ Ⓓ Ⓔ
10. Ⓐ Ⓑ Ⓒ Ⓓ Ⓔ
11. Ⓐ Ⓑ Ⓒ Ⓓ Ⓔ
12. Ⓐ Ⓑ Ⓒ Ⓓ Ⓔ
13. Ⓐ Ⓑ Ⓒ Ⓓ Ⓔ
14. Ⓐ Ⓑ Ⓒ Ⓓ Ⓔ
15. Ⓐ Ⓑ Ⓒ Ⓓ Ⓔ
16. Ⓐ Ⓑ Ⓒ Ⓓ Ⓔ
17. Ⓐ Ⓑ Ⓒ Ⓓ Ⓔ
18. Ⓐ Ⓑ Ⓒ Ⓓ Ⓔ
19. Ⓐ Ⓑ Ⓒ Ⓓ Ⓔ
20. Ⓐ Ⓑ Ⓒ Ⓓ Ⓔ
21. Ⓐ Ⓑ Ⓒ Ⓓ Ⓔ
22. Ⓐ Ⓑ Ⓒ Ⓓ Ⓔ
23. Ⓐ Ⓑ Ⓒ Ⓓ Ⓔ
24. Ⓐ Ⓑ Ⓒ Ⓓ Ⓔ
25. Ⓐ Ⓑ Ⓒ Ⓓ Ⓔ
26. Ⓐ Ⓑ Ⓒ Ⓓ Ⓔ
27. Ⓐ Ⓑ Ⓒ Ⓓ Ⓔ
28. Ⓐ Ⓑ Ⓒ Ⓓ Ⓔ
29. Ⓐ Ⓑ Ⓒ Ⓓ Ⓔ
30. Ⓐ Ⓑ Ⓒ Ⓓ Ⓔ

31. Ⓐ Ⓑ Ⓒ Ⓓ Ⓔ
32. Ⓐ Ⓑ Ⓒ Ⓓ Ⓔ
33. Ⓐ Ⓑ Ⓒ Ⓓ Ⓔ
34. Ⓐ Ⓑ Ⓒ Ⓓ Ⓔ
35. Ⓐ Ⓑ Ⓒ Ⓓ Ⓔ
36. Ⓐ Ⓑ Ⓒ Ⓓ Ⓔ
37. Ⓐ Ⓑ Ⓒ Ⓓ Ⓔ
38. Ⓐ Ⓑ Ⓒ Ⓓ Ⓔ
39. Ⓐ Ⓑ Ⓒ Ⓓ Ⓔ
40. Ⓐ Ⓑ Ⓒ Ⓓ Ⓔ
41. Ⓐ Ⓑ Ⓒ Ⓓ Ⓔ
42. Ⓐ Ⓑ Ⓒ Ⓓ Ⓔ
43. Ⓐ Ⓑ Ⓒ Ⓓ Ⓔ
44. Ⓐ Ⓑ Ⓒ Ⓓ Ⓔ
45. Ⓐ Ⓑ Ⓒ Ⓓ Ⓔ
46. Ⓐ Ⓑ Ⓒ Ⓓ Ⓔ
47. Ⓐ Ⓑ Ⓒ Ⓓ Ⓔ
48. Ⓐ Ⓑ Ⓒ Ⓓ Ⓔ
49. Ⓐ Ⓑ Ⓒ Ⓓ Ⓔ
50. Ⓐ Ⓑ Ⓒ Ⓓ Ⓔ
51. Ⓐ Ⓑ Ⓒ Ⓓ Ⓔ
52. Ⓐ Ⓑ Ⓒ Ⓓ Ⓔ
53. Ⓐ Ⓑ Ⓒ Ⓓ Ⓔ
54. Ⓐ Ⓑ Ⓒ Ⓓ Ⓔ
55. Ⓐ Ⓑ Ⓒ Ⓓ Ⓔ
56. Ⓐ Ⓑ Ⓒ Ⓓ Ⓔ
57. Ⓐ Ⓑ Ⓒ Ⓓ Ⓔ
58. Ⓐ Ⓑ Ⓒ Ⓓ Ⓔ
59. Ⓐ Ⓑ Ⓒ Ⓓ Ⓔ
60. Ⓐ Ⓑ Ⓒ Ⓓ Ⓔ

61. Ⓐ Ⓑ Ⓒ Ⓓ Ⓔ
62. Ⓐ Ⓑ Ⓒ Ⓓ Ⓔ
63. Ⓐ Ⓑ Ⓒ Ⓓ Ⓔ
64. Ⓐ Ⓑ Ⓒ Ⓓ Ⓔ
65. Ⓐ Ⓑ Ⓒ Ⓓ Ⓔ
66. Ⓐ Ⓑ Ⓒ Ⓓ Ⓔ
67. Ⓐ Ⓑ Ⓒ Ⓓ Ⓔ
68. Ⓐ Ⓑ Ⓒ Ⓓ Ⓔ
69. Ⓐ Ⓑ Ⓒ Ⓓ Ⓔ
70. Ⓐ Ⓑ Ⓒ Ⓓ Ⓔ
71. Ⓐ Ⓑ Ⓒ Ⓓ Ⓔ
72. Ⓐ Ⓑ Ⓒ Ⓓ Ⓔ
73. Ⓐ Ⓑ Ⓒ Ⓓ Ⓔ
74. Ⓐ Ⓑ Ⓒ Ⓓ Ⓔ
75. Ⓐ Ⓑ Ⓒ Ⓓ Ⓔ
76. Ⓐ Ⓑ Ⓒ Ⓓ Ⓔ
77. Ⓐ Ⓑ Ⓒ Ⓓ Ⓔ
78. Ⓐ Ⓑ Ⓒ Ⓓ Ⓔ
79. Ⓐ Ⓑ Ⓒ Ⓓ Ⓔ
80. Ⓐ Ⓑ Ⓒ Ⓓ Ⓔ
81. Ⓐ Ⓑ Ⓒ Ⓓ Ⓔ
82. Ⓐ Ⓑ Ⓒ Ⓓ Ⓔ
83. Ⓐ Ⓑ Ⓒ Ⓓ Ⓔ
84. Ⓐ Ⓑ Ⓒ Ⓓ Ⓔ
85. Ⓐ Ⓑ Ⓒ Ⓓ Ⓔ
86. Ⓐ Ⓑ Ⓒ Ⓓ Ⓔ
87. Ⓐ Ⓑ Ⓒ Ⓓ Ⓔ
88. Ⓐ Ⓑ Ⓒ Ⓓ Ⓔ
89. Ⓐ Ⓑ Ⓒ Ⓓ Ⓔ
90. Ⓐ Ⓑ Ⓒ Ⓓ Ⓔ

91. Ⓐ Ⓑ Ⓒ Ⓓ Ⓔ	121. Ⓐ Ⓑ Ⓒ Ⓓ Ⓔ	151. Ⓐ Ⓑ Ⓒ Ⓓ Ⓔ
92. Ⓐ Ⓑ Ⓒ Ⓓ Ⓔ	122. Ⓐ Ⓑ Ⓒ Ⓓ Ⓔ	152. Ⓐ Ⓑ Ⓒ Ⓓ Ⓔ
93. Ⓐ Ⓑ Ⓒ Ⓓ Ⓔ	123. Ⓐ Ⓑ Ⓒ Ⓓ Ⓔ	153. Ⓐ Ⓑ Ⓒ Ⓓ Ⓔ
94. Ⓐ Ⓑ Ⓒ Ⓓ Ⓔ	124. Ⓐ Ⓑ Ⓒ Ⓓ Ⓔ	154. Ⓐ Ⓑ Ⓒ Ⓓ Ⓔ
95. Ⓐ Ⓑ Ⓒ Ⓓ Ⓔ	125. Ⓐ Ⓑ Ⓒ Ⓓ Ⓔ	155. Ⓐ Ⓑ Ⓒ Ⓓ Ⓔ
96. Ⓐ Ⓑ Ⓒ Ⓓ Ⓔ	126. Ⓐ Ⓑ Ⓒ Ⓓ Ⓔ	156. Ⓐ Ⓑ Ⓒ Ⓓ Ⓔ
97. Ⓐ Ⓑ Ⓒ Ⓓ Ⓔ	127. Ⓐ Ⓑ Ⓒ Ⓓ Ⓔ	157. Ⓐ Ⓑ Ⓒ Ⓓ Ⓔ
98. Ⓐ Ⓑ Ⓒ Ⓓ Ⓔ	128. Ⓐ Ⓑ Ⓒ Ⓓ Ⓔ	158. Ⓐ Ⓑ Ⓒ Ⓓ Ⓔ
99. Ⓐ Ⓑ Ⓒ Ⓓ Ⓔ	129. Ⓐ Ⓑ Ⓒ Ⓓ Ⓔ	159. Ⓐ Ⓑ Ⓒ Ⓓ Ⓔ
100. Ⓐ Ⓑ Ⓒ Ⓓ Ⓔ	130. Ⓐ Ⓑ Ⓒ Ⓓ Ⓔ	160. Ⓐ Ⓑ Ⓒ Ⓓ Ⓔ
101. Ⓐ Ⓑ Ⓒ Ⓓ Ⓔ	131. Ⓐ Ⓑ Ⓒ Ⓓ Ⓔ	161. Ⓐ Ⓑ Ⓒ Ⓓ Ⓔ
102. Ⓐ Ⓑ Ⓒ Ⓓ Ⓔ	132. Ⓐ Ⓑ Ⓒ Ⓓ Ⓔ	162. Ⓐ Ⓑ Ⓒ Ⓓ Ⓔ
103. Ⓐ Ⓑ Ⓒ Ⓓ Ⓔ	133. Ⓐ Ⓑ Ⓒ Ⓓ Ⓔ	163. Ⓐ Ⓑ Ⓒ Ⓓ Ⓔ
104. Ⓐ Ⓑ Ⓒ Ⓓ Ⓔ	134. Ⓐ Ⓑ Ⓒ Ⓓ Ⓔ	164. Ⓐ Ⓑ Ⓒ Ⓓ Ⓔ
105. Ⓐ Ⓑ Ⓒ Ⓓ Ⓔ	135. Ⓐ Ⓑ Ⓒ Ⓓ Ⓔ	165. Ⓐ Ⓑ Ⓒ Ⓓ Ⓔ
106. Ⓐ Ⓑ Ⓒ Ⓓ Ⓔ	136. Ⓐ Ⓑ Ⓒ Ⓓ Ⓔ	166. Ⓐ Ⓑ Ⓒ Ⓓ Ⓔ
107. Ⓐ Ⓑ Ⓒ Ⓓ Ⓔ	137. Ⓐ Ⓑ Ⓒ Ⓓ Ⓔ	167. Ⓐ Ⓑ Ⓒ Ⓓ Ⓔ
108. Ⓐ Ⓑ Ⓒ Ⓓ Ⓔ	138. Ⓐ Ⓑ Ⓒ Ⓓ Ⓔ	168. Ⓐ Ⓑ Ⓒ Ⓓ Ⓔ
109. Ⓐ Ⓑ Ⓒ Ⓓ Ⓔ	139. Ⓐ Ⓑ Ⓒ Ⓓ Ⓔ	169. Ⓐ Ⓑ Ⓒ Ⓓ Ⓔ
110. Ⓐ Ⓑ Ⓒ Ⓓ Ⓔ	140. Ⓐ Ⓑ Ⓒ Ⓓ Ⓔ	170. Ⓐ Ⓑ Ⓒ Ⓓ Ⓔ
111. Ⓐ Ⓑ Ⓒ Ⓓ Ⓔ	141. Ⓐ Ⓑ Ⓒ Ⓓ Ⓔ	171. Ⓐ Ⓑ Ⓒ Ⓓ Ⓔ
112. Ⓐ Ⓑ Ⓒ Ⓓ Ⓔ	142. Ⓐ Ⓑ Ⓒ Ⓓ Ⓔ	172. Ⓐ Ⓑ Ⓒ Ⓓ Ⓔ
113. Ⓐ Ⓑ Ⓒ Ⓓ Ⓔ	143. Ⓐ Ⓑ Ⓒ Ⓓ Ⓔ	173. Ⓐ Ⓑ Ⓒ Ⓓ Ⓔ
114. Ⓐ Ⓑ Ⓒ Ⓓ Ⓔ	144. Ⓐ Ⓑ Ⓒ Ⓓ Ⓔ	174. Ⓐ Ⓑ Ⓒ Ⓓ Ⓔ
115. Ⓐ Ⓑ Ⓒ Ⓓ Ⓔ	145. Ⓐ Ⓑ Ⓒ Ⓓ Ⓔ	175. Ⓐ Ⓑ Ⓒ Ⓓ Ⓔ
116. Ⓐ Ⓑ Ⓒ Ⓓ Ⓔ	146. Ⓐ Ⓑ Ⓒ Ⓓ Ⓔ	176. Ⓐ Ⓑ Ⓒ Ⓓ Ⓔ
117. Ⓐ Ⓑ Ⓒ Ⓓ Ⓔ	147. Ⓐ Ⓑ Ⓒ Ⓓ Ⓔ	177. Ⓐ Ⓑ Ⓒ Ⓓ Ⓔ
118. Ⓐ Ⓑ Ⓒ Ⓓ Ⓔ	148. Ⓐ Ⓑ Ⓒ Ⓓ Ⓔ	178. Ⓐ Ⓑ Ⓒ Ⓓ Ⓔ
119. Ⓐ Ⓑ Ⓒ Ⓓ Ⓔ	149. Ⓐ Ⓑ Ⓒ Ⓓ Ⓔ	179. Ⓐ Ⓑ Ⓒ Ⓓ Ⓔ
120. Ⓐ Ⓑ Ⓒ Ⓓ Ⓔ	150. Ⓐ Ⓑ Ⓒ Ⓓ Ⓔ	180. Ⓐ Ⓑ Ⓒ Ⓓ Ⓔ

181. Ⓐ Ⓑ Ⓒ Ⓓ Ⓔ
182. Ⓐ Ⓑ Ⓒ Ⓓ Ⓔ
183. Ⓐ Ⓑ Ⓒ Ⓓ Ⓔ
184. Ⓐ Ⓑ Ⓒ Ⓓ Ⓔ
185. Ⓐ Ⓑ Ⓒ Ⓓ Ⓔ
186. Ⓐ Ⓑ Ⓒ Ⓓ Ⓔ
187. Ⓐ Ⓑ Ⓒ Ⓓ Ⓔ
188. Ⓐ Ⓑ Ⓒ Ⓓ Ⓔ
189. Ⓐ Ⓑ Ⓒ Ⓓ Ⓔ
190. Ⓐ Ⓑ Ⓒ Ⓓ Ⓔ
191. Ⓐ Ⓑ Ⓒ Ⓓ Ⓔ
192. Ⓐ Ⓑ Ⓒ Ⓓ Ⓔ
193. Ⓐ Ⓑ Ⓒ Ⓓ Ⓔ
194. Ⓐ Ⓑ Ⓒ Ⓓ Ⓔ
195. Ⓐ Ⓑ Ⓒ Ⓓ Ⓔ
196. Ⓐ Ⓑ Ⓒ Ⓓ Ⓔ
197. Ⓐ Ⓑ Ⓒ Ⓓ Ⓔ

198. Ⓐ Ⓑ Ⓒ Ⓓ Ⓔ
199. Ⓐ Ⓑ Ⓒ Ⓓ Ⓔ
200. Ⓐ Ⓑ Ⓒ Ⓓ Ⓔ
201. Ⓐ Ⓑ Ⓒ Ⓓ Ⓔ
202. Ⓐ Ⓑ Ⓒ Ⓓ Ⓔ
203. Ⓐ Ⓑ Ⓒ Ⓓ Ⓔ
204. Ⓐ Ⓑ Ⓒ Ⓓ Ⓔ
205. Ⓐ Ⓑ Ⓒ Ⓓ Ⓔ
206. Ⓐ Ⓑ Ⓒ Ⓓ Ⓔ
207. Ⓐ Ⓑ Ⓒ Ⓓ Ⓔ
208. Ⓐ Ⓑ Ⓒ Ⓓ Ⓔ
209. Ⓐ Ⓑ Ⓒ Ⓓ Ⓔ
210. Ⓐ Ⓑ Ⓒ Ⓓ Ⓔ
211. Ⓐ Ⓑ Ⓒ Ⓓ Ⓔ
212. Ⓐ Ⓑ Ⓒ Ⓓ Ⓔ
213. Ⓐ Ⓑ Ⓒ Ⓓ Ⓔ
214. Ⓐ Ⓑ Ⓒ Ⓓ Ⓔ

215. Ⓐ Ⓑ Ⓒ Ⓓ Ⓔ
216. Ⓐ Ⓑ Ⓒ Ⓓ Ⓔ
217. Ⓐ Ⓑ Ⓒ Ⓓ Ⓔ
218. Ⓐ Ⓑ Ⓒ Ⓓ Ⓔ
219. Ⓐ Ⓑ Ⓒ Ⓓ Ⓔ
220. Ⓐ Ⓑ Ⓒ Ⓓ Ⓔ
221. Ⓐ Ⓑ Ⓒ Ⓓ Ⓔ
222. Ⓐ Ⓑ Ⓒ Ⓓ Ⓔ
223. Ⓐ Ⓑ Ⓒ Ⓓ Ⓔ
224. Ⓐ Ⓑ Ⓒ Ⓓ Ⓔ
225. Ⓐ Ⓑ Ⓒ Ⓓ Ⓔ
226. Ⓐ Ⓑ Ⓒ Ⓓ Ⓔ
227. Ⓐ Ⓑ Ⓒ Ⓓ Ⓔ
228. Ⓐ Ⓑ Ⓒ Ⓓ Ⓔ
229. Ⓐ Ⓑ Ⓒ Ⓓ Ⓔ
230. Ⓐ Ⓑ Ⓒ Ⓓ Ⓔ

GRE LITERATURE IN ENGLISH

TEST I

DIRECTIONS: Choose the best answer for each question and mark the letter of your selection on the corresponding answer sheet.

1. "One must commit oneself to a conjunction with the other – for ever. But it is not selfless – it is a maintaining of the self in mystic balance and integrity – like a star balanced with another star."

    The above description of love is stated by:

    (A) Heathcliff in *Wuthering Heights*

    (B) Birkin in *Women in Love*

    (C) Rochester in *Jane Eyre*

    (D) Stephen Dedalus in *Portrait of an Artist*.

    (E) George Emerson in *A Room with a View*.

Questions 2 – 4 refer to the following passage:

> "Son of heaven and earth,
> Attend: that thou art happy, owe to God;
> That thou continu'st such, owe to thyself,
> That is to thy obedience; therein stand.
> This was that caution giv'n thee; be advised.
> God made thee perfect, not immutable;
> And good he made thee, but to persevere
> He left it in thy power, ordained thy will
> By nature free, not overruled by fate
> Inextricable, or strict necessity;
> Our voluntary service he requires,

Not our necessitated, such with him
Finds no acceptance, nor can find, for how
Can hearts, not free, be tried whether they serve
Willing or no, who will but what they must
By destiny, and can no other choose?
Myself and all th' angelic host that stand
In sight of God enthroned, our happy state
Hold, as you yours, while our obedience holds;
On other surety none; freely we serve,
Because we freely love as in our will
To love or not; in this we stand or fall:
And some are fall'n, to disobedience fall'n,
And so from heav'n to deepest hell; O fall
From what high state of bliss into what woe!"

2. In the above passage the narrator and narratee are:

(A) The Angel Michael and Eve

(B) The Angel Gabriel and Mary

(C) The Angel of Death and Virgil

(D) The Angel Raphael and Adam

(E) The Angel Gabriel and Dante

3. The narrator suggests:

(A) Man's continued happiness depends on God.

(B) Man's continued happiness depends on the angels.

(C) Man cannot change his state.

(D) Man has no free will.

(E) Man must serve God voluntarily.

4. Which of the following best describes the narrator's tone?

(A) Patronizing and didactic

(B) Wise and instructive

(C) Jolly and humorous

(D) Gloomy and bad-tempered

(E) Threatening and vindictive

Questions 5 – 6 refer to the following passage:

Who should come to my lodge this morning but a true Homeric or Paphlagonian man – a Canadian, a wood chopper and post maker, who can hole 50 posts in a day, who made his last supper on a —— which his dog caught.

5.   Whose lodge does the wood chopper visit?

(A) Rosseau's   (D) Homer's

(B) Thoreau's   (E) Frost's

(C) Wordsworth's

6.   Which of the following was the woodman's supper?

(A) A pigeon   (D) A wild boar

(B) A wild turkey   (E) A deer

(C) A woodchuck

Questions 7 – 9 refer to the following stanza:

Heard melodies are sweet, but those unheard
Are sweeter; therefore, ye soft pipes, play on;
Not to the sensual ear, but, more endear'd,
Pipe to the spirit ditties of no tone:
Fair youth, beneath the trees, thou canst not leave
Thy song, nor ever can those trees be bare;
Bold Lover, never, never canst thou kiss,
Though winning near the goal – yet, do not grieve;
She cannot fade, though thou hast not thy bliss,
For ever wilt thou love, and she be fair!

7. Which of the following best describes the theme of this stanza?

(A) Music refreshes the soul.

(B) Youth has every advantage.

(C) Art is immortal.

(D) Imagination enhances life.

(E) Art destroys life.

8. In which literary era was the entire poem written?

(A) Th Elizabethan

(B) The Postmodern

(C) The Romantic

(D) The Victorian

(E) The Modern

9. Which of the following best describes the philosophy of this era?

(A) Delight in the Immortality of Nature bringing man closer to God.

(B) Despair in the failure of man to create the perfect world.

(C) Distrust in the new technology.

(D) Fear of fragmentation in the world as a result of a loss in belief in God.

(E) Triumph in man's ability to overcome nature.

10. "And his mother, still greedy and gallows grim would go on a sorrowful venture; avenge her son's death."

In the above sentence who is the son?

(A) Jesus

(B) Gawain

(C) Isaac

(D) Grendel

(E) Jason

now were getting at it you seem to regard it merely as an experience that will whiten your hair overnight so to speak without altering your appearance at all you wont do it under these conditions it will be a gamble and the strange thing is that man who is conceived by accident and whose every breath is a fresh cast with dice already loaded against him will not face that final man which he knows beforehand he has assuredly to face without essaying expedients ranging all the way from violence to petty chicanery that would not deceive a child until some day in very disgust he risks everything on a single blind turn of a card no man ever does that under the first fury of despair or remorse or bereavement he does it only when he has realized that even the despair or remorse or bereavement is not particularly important to the dark diceman and i temporary and he it is hard believing to think that a love or a sorrow is a bond purchased without design and which matures willynilly and is recalled without warning to be replaced by whatever issues the gods happen to be floating at the time no you will not do that until you come to believe that even she was not quite worth despair perhaps and i i will never do that nobody knows what i know and he i think youd better go on to cambridge right away you might go up into maine for a month you can afford it if you are careful it might be good thing watching pennies has healed more scars than jesus and i suppose i realize that you believe i will realize up there next week or next month and he then you well remember that for you to go to harvard has been your mothers dream since you were born and no compson has ever disappointed a lady

11.   What literary technique does the above passage illustrate?

    (A) Enjambment

    (B) Dream of the unconscious

    (C) Stream of consciousness

    (D) Extended metaphor

    (E) Dislocation of time

12. By what means does the author achieve the effect?

    (A) Poetic language   (D) Lack of meaning

    (B) Use of nuance   (E) Lack of punctuation

    (C) Extended metaphor

13. What is the subject under discussion?

    (A) Coloring one's hair   (D) Courtesy to women

    (B) Killing oneself   (E) Going away to college

    (C) Killing one's dream

14. Which of the following most-closely expresses the main speaker's point of view?

    (A) Life is not worth living.

    (B) Man's life is determined and cannot be altered.

    (C) People let you down and love destroys in the end.

    (D) Man has free will and should exercise it.

    (E) In the game of life man always wins.

15. The author of the passage is

    (A) Thomas Hardy   (D) Kurt Vonnegut, Jr.

    (B) Henry James   (E) William Faulkner

    (C) Theodore Dreiser

16. _____looked vacantly at the richly carpeted floor. A new light was shining upon all the years since her enforced flight. She remembered now a hundred things that indicated as much. She also imagined that he took it on her account. Instead of hatred springing up there was a kind of sorrow generated. Poor fellow! What a thing to have had hanging over his head all the time.

Supply the name that completes the first sentence:

(A) Emma

(D) Carrie

(B) Tess

(E) Maggie

(C) Milly

17.   Come my friends
'Tis not too late to seek a newer world
Push off and sitting well in order smite
The sounding furrows; for my purpose holds
To sail beyond the sunset, and the baths
Of all the Western stars, until I die.

The speaker is:

(A) Achilles

(D) Ishmael

(B) Jason

(E) Ulysses

(C) Ahab

Questions 18 – 22 refer to the following descriptions of plays and characters:

18.   Which describes Ibsen's *A Doll's House*?

19.   Which describes Ibsen's *The Wild Duck*?

20.   Which describes Eugene O'Neill's *The Iceman Cometh*?

(A) Hope's place is the No Chance Saloon, Bedrock Bar, the End of the Line Cafe where five cent whiskey —"cyanide cut with carbolic acid to give it a mellow flavor" — is sold to a collection of down and outers, pimps and whores, by a boozy barman.

(B) He claimed he was not writing a treatise on women's rights but rather advocating the rights of all human beings, and the need for all people to treat each other with mutual respect.

(C) He has suggested that the common man is as capable as a king of experiencing tragedy. His play revolves around the question of whether we feel that this particular common man is "ready to lay down his life" to secure his dignity.

(D) Gina's original illiteracy erupts from the so-called education Hjalmar had given her whenever she is annoyed or embarrassed. Old Ekdar's grammar is affected by consorting with the likes of Pettersen.

(E) His characters never seem to achieve very much. They sit around dreaming of the past or other places, talking of their dreams and bolstering their present day ennui with illusions of the future.

21. What is the main theme of such drama?

(A) The function of truth.

(B) Father and son relationships.

(C) Father and daughter relationships.

(D) The function of revenge.

(E) The function of love.

22. Which best defines the type of drama thus described?

(A) Melodrama

(B) Tragicomedy

(C) Kitchen-sink drama

(D) Realistic Drama

(E) Angry Young Man Drama

23. Moll is a character physically, with hard plump limps that get into bed and pick pockets.

Whose "Moll" does the critic describe?

(A) James Joyce's   (D) Fielding's

(B) Daniel Defoe's   (E) Henry James's

(C) George Eliot's

24. We may divide characters into flat and - - - - -

Complete the same critic's description of character:

(A) Profound   (D) Round

(B) Deep   (E) Stretched

(C) Square

25. This same critic also wrote:

(A) *Lucky Jim*   (D) *To the Lighthouse*

(B) *A Passage to India*   (E) *The Ambassadors*

(C) *Sunlit Dialogues*

Questions 26 – 29 refer to the following passage:

Their society, for instance, is stoic in appearance. They accept such inevitable calamities as death calmly; they eat, sleep and exercise wisely; they believe in universal benevolence as an ideal, and accordingly have no personal ties or attachments. The family is effectively abolished; marriage is arranged by friends as "one of the necessary actions in a reasonable being"; husband and wife like one another, and their children just as much and as little as they like everyone else. Sex is accepted as normal but only for the purpose of procreation. . .They have no curiosity: their language, their arts and sciences are purely functional and restricted to the bare necessities of harmonious social existence.

26. This society features in:

(A) *Animal Farm*   (D) *Gulliver's Travels*

(B) *Slaughterhouse Five* (E) *Brave New World*

(C) *1984*

27. Which best describes such a book?

(A) A Travelogue   (D) A Fable

(B) A Utopia novel   (E) A Satire

(C) An anti-Utopia novel

28. Who lives in the society described?

(A) Midgets   (D) Pigs

(B) Tralfamadorians   (E) Horses

(C) Giants

29. In what age was the book written?

(A) The Elizabethan Age   (D) The Modern Age

(B) The Reformation   (E) The Depression

(C) The Augustan Age

Questions 30 – 33 refer to the opening stanza below:

> Busie old foole, unruly Sunne,
>   Why dost thou thus
> Through windowes, and through curtaines call on us?
> Must to thy motions lovers seasons run?
>   Saucy pedantique wretch, goe chide
>   Late school boyes, and sowre prentices,
> Goe tell Court-huntsmen, that the King will ride,
> Call country ants to harvest offices;
> Love, all alike, no season knowes, nor clyme,
> Nor houres, dayes, months, which are the rags of time.

30.   This impudent address of the sun is:

(A) Anti-heroic   (D) Anti-Miltonic

(B) Anti-Shakesperian   (E) Anti-cleric

(C) Anti-Spenserian

31.   Which is the name for an address to daybreak?

(A) An Ode   (D) An Aubade

(B) An Elegy   (E) A Sestina

(C) A Sonnet

32.   Which best describes the poem's meaning?

(A) The two lovers are all sufficient to each other.

(B) The two lovers prefer the night.

(C) The two lovers want to share their love with the sun.

(D) The two lovers do not want others to know of their love.

(E) The two lovers want the sun to shine forever on their bed.

33.   Which best explains the metaphor of time?

(A) Love is eternal and does not recognize units of time.

(B) Love lasts forever and does not need to be measured in mere fragments of time.

(C) Love does not last forever so there is no point in measuring time.

(D) Measurements of time are useless when trying to hang onto love.

(E) Hours, days, months simply show how love is passing by with time

14

34. There is a far off sound as if out of the sky, the sound of a snapped string, dying away, sad. A stillness falls and there is only the thud of an axe on a tree.

The above stage directions close

(A) *The Master Builder*   (D) *The Tempest*

(B) *Desire Under the Elms*   (E) *The Apple Cart*

(C) *The Cherry Orchard*

Questions 35 – 37 refer to the following lines:

> Do not begrudge us oracles from birds,
>   or any other way of prophesy
>   within your skill; save yourself and the city,
>   save me; redeem the debt of our pollution
>   that lies on us because of this dead man.

35. Who says this and to whom?

(A) Jason to Hercules   (D) Odysseus to the sibyl

(B) Oedipus to Teiresias   (E) Ferdinand to Prospero

(C) Gloucester to Mad Tom

36. Who is the dead man?

(A) King Lear   (D) King Priam

(B) King Alonzo   (E) King Creon

(C) King Laius

37. What happens to the speaker?

(A) He kills his wife.

(B) He kills himself.

(C) He blinds himself.

(D) He is killed in battle.

(E) He kills the fortune-teller.

38. Perhaps it is only a game. Modern women like Sarah exist and I have never understood them.

Sarah exists in

(A) Beckett's *Endgame*

(B) Joyce's *Ulysses*

(C) Dickens's *Great Expectations*

(D) John Fowles' *The French Lieutenant's Woman*

(E) Pynchon's *V*

39. The thing that hath been, it is that which shall be; and that which is done is that which shall be done; and there is no new thing under the sun.

The quote is from

(A) Ecclesiastes   (D) *The Iliad*

(B) *Isaiah*   (E) *The Symposium*

(C) *The Odyssey*

Questions 40 – 42 refer to the following passage:

We picture the world as thick with conquering and elite humanity, but here, with the bugles of the tempest pealing, it was hard to imagine a peopled earth. One viewed the existence of man then as a marvel, and conceded a glamour of wonder to these lice which were caused to cling to a whirling, fire-smitten, ice-locked, disease-stricken, space-lost bulb. One was a coxcombe not to die in it.

40. Which best describes this world-view?

(A) Man's life is futile and farcical

(B) Man is a wonderful creation

(C) Man's life is no more important than an insect's

(D) Man is at the center of the universe

(E) Man's place in the world is to create light

41.   In context which best defines coxcombe?

(A) A conceited fool   (D) A wastrel

(B) A tragic hero   (E) A dandy

(C) A moron

42.   The author of this passage also wrote

(A) *The Stranger*

(B) *Breakfast of Champions*

(C) *The Red Badge of Courage*

(D) *The Crying of Lot 49*

(E) *Tess of the D'Urbervilles*

43.   And round it was upon a hill
                 It made the slovenly wilderness
                 Surround that hill

                 The wilderness rose up to it,
                 And sprawled around, no longer wild.

By "it" the poet means

(A) A blackbird   (D) A plum

(B) Death   (E) Nature

(C) A jar

44.   As to what that exile and that longing for reunion meant, Rieux
       had no idea. But as he walked ahead, jostled on all sides,
       accosted now and then, and gradually made his way into less
       crowded streets, he was thinking it has no importance whether
       such things have or have not a meaning; all we need consider
       is the answer given to men's hope.

What has just ended "that exile?"

(A) The Holocaust   (D) An epidemic

(B) The Russian Revolution   (E) The winter

(C) The French Revolution

45.   What term best describes the author's philosophy?

(A) Determinism   (D) Quietism

(B) Negativism   (E) Nihilism

(C) Existentialism

46.   "The most heterogeneous ideas are yoked by violence to-
      gether."

      Who said this about which sort of poetry?

(A) Bacon on Shakespeare's love sonnets

(B) Dryden on love poetry

(C) Milton on Epic poetry

(D) Samuel Johnson on Metaphysical poetry

(E) Ben Jonson on religious sonnets

47.   There is first of all a succession of phrases in the lives of certain
      generations: youth that passes out into maturity, fortunes that
      meet and clash and reform, hopes that flourish and wane and re-
      appear in other lives, age that sinks and hands on the torch to
      youth again. . .

      The critic Percy Lubbock refers to

(A) *Middlemarch*   (D) *Great Expectations*

(B) *The Sisters*   (E) *War and Peace*

(C) *Crime and Punishment*

48.   Which of the following best defines the term "comedy of manners?"

(A) A play or novel in which strong, moral values are hidden by trite appearances.

(B) A comedy where etiquette is seriously followed.

(C) A play or novel in which etiquette is uproariously parodied.

(D) A play in which odd and witty people make fun of other odd and witty people.

(E) A novel in which unconventional behavior shocks conventional people.

Questions 49 – 51 refer to the works following:

(A) *Ode to Autumn*

(B) Ecclesiastes

(C) *Fern Hill*

(D) *Spring and Fall: To a Young Child*

(E) *Mending Wall*

49.   Which represents the poet and a neighbor as an apple orchard and a pine tree?

50.   Which contains the lines:

Leaves like the things of man, you
With your fresh thoughts care for, can you?

51.   Which is adapted in the following?

To everything
Turn, turn, turn
There is a season
Turn, turn, turn.

52.   The violence of breaking down the door seemed to fill this room with pervading dust. A thin acrid pall as of the tomb seemed to lie everywhere upon the room decked and furnished as for a bridal.

The room is

(A) Miss Emily's in *A Rose for Emily*

(B) Miss Haversham's in *Great Expectations*

(C) Isabel's in *A Portrait of a Lady*

(D) Mrs. Mallard's in *The Story of an Hour*

(E) Bertha Rochester's in *Jane Eyre*

Questions 53 - 56 refer to the following dialogue:

"I realize," the girl said. "Can't we maybe stop talking?"

They sat down at the table and the girl looked across at the dry side of the valley and the man looked at her and at the table.

"You've got to realize," he said, "that I don't want you to do it if you don't want to. I'm perfectly willing to go through with it if it means anything to you."

"Doesn't it mean anything to you? We could get along."

"Of course it does. But I don't want anyone else. And I know it's perfectly simple."

"It's all right for you to say that, but I do know it. . . . Would you do something for me now?"

"I'd do anything for you."

"Would you please please please please please please please stop talking?"

He did not say anything but looked at the bags against the wall of the station. There were labels on them from all the hotels where they had spent nights.

53.   What is the main point of the discussion?

(A) Seduction   (D) Vacation

(B) Abortion   (E) Repetition

(C) Accusation

54. What does the "dry valley" reflect in the relationship?

(A) Dryness

(D) Passion

(B) Finality

(E) Heat

(C) Sterility

55. Which best explains the significance of the details of the bags?

(A) The couple have travelled extensively.

(B) The couple love travelling, not each other.

(C) The couple are on vacation.

(D) The couple have a restless physical relationship.

(E) The couple share their luggage and their emotional love.

56. The author also wrote

(A) *The Blue Hotel*

(B) *Across the River and Into the Trees*

(C) *Catch 22*

(D) *Down and Out in Paris and London*

(E) *Guests of the Nation*

Questions 57 – 58 refer to the following passage:

The plot of such novels usually involved an amazingly virtuous and beautiful heroine in all kinds of terrifying adventures, generally in a foreign land — Italy was popular because of the "banditti." Murders, sadistic villains, old ruins, haunted buildings, long lost children, explanatory documents hidden in secret drawers — all that could shock and horrify the reader were part of the trappings of these novels.

57. The novels referred to are known as

(A) Italian Novels   (D) Naturalistic Novels

(B) Gothic Novels   (E) Detective Novels

(C) Realistic Novels

58. Which of the following is a burlesque of such a novel:

(A) *Northanger Abbey*

(B) *The Mystery of Udolpho*

(C) *The Italian*

(D) *Frankenstein*

(E) *Evelina*

Questions 59 – 62 refer to the following passage:

As to my own part, having turned my thoughts for many years upon this important subject and maturely weighed the several schemes of other projectors, I have always found them grossly mistaken in their computation. It is true a child just dropped from its dam may be supported by her milk for a solar year with little other nourishment, at most not above the value of two shillings, which the mother may certainly get, or the value in scraps, by her lawful occupation of begging; and it is exactly at one year old that I propose to provide for them in such a manner as instead of being a charge upon their parents or the parish, or wanting food and raiment for the rest of their lives, they shall, on the contrary, contribute to the feeding and partly to the clothing of many thousands.

59. The tone of the passage is

(A) Reasonable and mathematical

(B) Angry and threatening

(C) Religious and reverent

(D) Hypocritical and sanctimonious

(E) Mature and sensitive

60. What is the proposal the writer suggests later?

(A) To ship out the nursing mothers to America

(B) To use the babies' hair for thread for weaving

(C) To use the babies' carcasses as meat and soft gloves

(D) To impose a tax on mothers with more than one child

(E) To impose harsh penalties on nursing mothers found begging

61. Which of the following defines such writing?

(A) Realism   (D) Modernism

(B) Satire   (E) Hedonism

(C) Irony

62. A contemporary of the writer was

(A) John Donne   (D) Henry James

(B) Milton   (E) Cyril Tourneur

(C) Henry Fielding

63. As Gregor Samsa awoke one morning from an uneasy dream he found himself transformed into a gigantic insect.

This opening line is

(A) Genet's   (D) Kafka's

(B) Sartre's   (E) Tolstoy's

(C) Ionesco's

> Sir, 'twas not
> Her husband's presence only, called that spot
> Of joy into the Duchess' cheek; perhaps
> Fra Pandolf chanced to say, "Her mantle laps
> Over my lady's wrist too much," or "paint
> Must never hope to reproduce the faint
> Half-flush that dies along her throat." Such stuff
> Was courtesy, she thought, and cause enough
> For calling up that spot of joy. She had
> A heart-how shall I say? – too soon made glad,
> Too easily impressed; she lik'd whate'er
> She looked on, and her looks went everywhere.
> Sir, 'twas all one! My favor at her breast,
> The dropping of the daylight in the West,
> The bough of cherries some officious fool
> Broke in the orchard for her, the white mule
> She rode with round the terrace...........

64.   The poem is an example of

(A) A satiric dialogue   (D) Dramatic irony

(B) A sonnet   (E) A dramatic monologue

(C) A parody

65.   The men are looking at

(A) a statue of a sea horse

(B) a landscape

(C) a portrait

(D) a book of favors

(E) designs for an orchard

66. The speaker reveals himself as

    (A) Proud and egotistical

    (B) Weak and effete

    (C) Angry and inane

    (D) Approving and amiable

    (E) Old and unreasonable

67. The Duchess is revealed as

    (A) one who flirts with all men

    (B) one who takes delight in simple things

    (C) one who knows how beautiful she is and plays on it

    (D) one who delights in rank and jewels

    (E) one who has had many affairs

Questions 68 – 71 refer to the lines below:

<pre>
This fellow's of exceeding honesty,
And knows all qualities, with a learned spirit
Of human dealings. If I do prove her haggard,
Though that her jesses were my dear heartstrings
I'd whistle her off and let her down the wind   5
To prey at fortune. Haply for I am black
And have not those parts of conversation
That chamberers have, or for I am declined
Into the vale of years—yet that's not much—
She's gone. I am abused, and my relief   10
Must be to loathe her. . . . . .
                  Yet 'tis the plague to great ones;
Prerogatived are they less than the base.
'Tis destiny unshunnable, like death.
Even then this forked plague is fated to us   15
When we do quicken. Look where she comes.
</pre>

68. "This fellow" is

    (A) Cassio
    (B) Bassanio
    (C) Mercutio
    (D) Iago
    (E) Horatio

69. Which best defines the metaphor in lines 3–7?

    (A) If I find she is old and deteriorating, I'll lock her up.

    (B) If I find as she gets older she becomes more witch-like, I'll banish her.

    (C) If I find that she is like a hawk gone wild, I'll let her fly free.

    (D) If I find she is like a mare grown old, I'll whistle to her to come to me and love her.

    (E) If I find she is dishonest I'll let her find her own fortune on her own.

70. What is significant about the word "forked" in line 15?

    (A) Split in two – the sign of the devil

    (B) Horned – the sign of the cuckold

    (C) Poisoned – by a contaminated fork

    (D) Deceived – by a liar with a forked-tongue

    (E) Obsessed – with a whore

71. In context, what is the meaning of "quicken" in line 16?

    (A) die
    (B) are born
    (C) fall in love
    (D) fall ill
    (E) rush love too quickly

72. The power of the novel is precisely what made it such a dangerous book in the opinions of most early reviews._____
did not seem to use her power to condemn the action of Edna Pontellier as Flaubert condemned Emma Bovary in the novel to which it is most often compared.

Which author's name completes the passage?

(A) Jane Austen   (D) Kate Chopin

(B) George Eliot   (E) Emily Bronte

(C) George Sand

73. The title of the Shaw play *Arms and the Man* echoes the first lines of

(A) *The Aeneid*   (D) *The Iliad*

(B) *Beowulf*   (E) *The Inferno*

(C) *Paradise Lost*

Questions 74 – 76 refer to the passage below:

And it was at this moment, as I stood there with the rifle in my hands, that I first grasped the hollowness, the futility of the white man's dominion in the East. Here was I, the white man with his gun, standing in front of the unarmed native crowd— seemingly the leading actor of the piece; but in reality I was only an absurd puppet pushed to and fro by the will of those yellow faces behind. I perceived in this moment that when the white man turns tyrant it is his own freedom that he destroys.

74. The white man is

(A) E.M. Forster   (D) Rudyard Kipling

(B) Ernest Hemingway   (E) Frank O'Connor

(C) George Orwell

75.   The incident takes place in

    (A) India   (D) Africa

    (B) Burma   (E) Vietnam

    (C) China

76.   What is the predominant metaphor?

    (A) Metaphor of the hollowman.

    (B) Metaphor of the sea.

    (C) Metaphor of colonialism.

    (D) Metaphor of the journey.

    (E) Metaphor of the stage.

Questions 77 – 79 refer to the poem below:

> We wear the mask that grins and lies
> It hides our cheeks and shades our eyes –
> This debt we pay to human guile;
> With torn and bleeding hearts we smile,
> And mouth with myriad subtleties.   5
>
> Why should the world be over-wise,
> In counting all our tears and sighs?
> Nay, let them only see us while
>   We wear the mask.
>
> We smile, but, O great Christ, our cries   10
> To thee from tortured souls arise.
> We sing, but oh the clay is vile
> Beneath our feet, and long the mile;
> But let the world dream otherwise,
>   We wear the mask!   15

77. Which is the best synonym for "mouth" in line 5?

(A) lips

(D) speak

(B) tongue

(E) laugh

(C) blaspheme

78. Lines 9 – 10 are an example of

(A) inverted syntax

(D) blank verse

(B) onomatopoeia

(E) sprung rhythm

(C) assonance

79. The effect of lines 9 – 10 is

(A) one of anger and hostility toward God.

(B) one of bitterness against God's unfairness.

(C) a railing against the torture God inflicts on men.

(D) a cry of happiness about God's blessings.

(E) a cry from a saddened heart to God.

80. Upon which literary tradition are the names Billy Pilgrim, Goodman Brown, and Willy Loman based?

(A) Pilgrims' stories along a journey as in Chaucer's Tales.

(B) Historical character names as in the Holinshed Chronicles.

(C) Vice and Virtue names as in Medieval Morality Plays.

(D) Famous men's names as in Plutarch's *Lives*.

(E) Concepts and principles as in Aristotle's *Poetics*.

81. Billy Pilgrim, Goodman Brown, Willy Loman — why does the latter prove an exception to the other two?

(A) He is working class.   (D) He is married.

(B) He is old.   (E) He is religious.

(C) He kills himself.

Questions 82 – 83 refer to the criticism below:

The mind receives a myriad impressions — trivial, fantastic, evanescent, or engraved with the sharpness of steel. From all sides they come, an incessant shower of innumerable atoms. . .Life is not a series of gig lamps symmetrically arranged; but a luminous halo, a semi-transparent envelope surrounding us from beginning of consciousness to the end.

82. Which best describes the meaning here in regard to the development of the novel?

(A) The novel should be as fragmented as experience.

(B) The novel's time structure should be linear like life.

(C) The novel's structure should reflect the randomness of experience.

(D) The novel should be free from pattern but must follow conventional life.

(E) The novel should be vague and hazy like a mist, not symmetrically patterned.

83. The author of this passage is

(A) F.R. Leavis   (D) Virginia Woolf

(B) Lionel Trilling   (E) Percy Lubbock

(C) Sartre

84.	But now Fortune, fearing she had acted out of Character, and had inclined too long to the same Side, especially as it was the Right side, hastily turned about: For now goody Brown, — whom Zekiel Brown caressed in his Arms; nor he alone, but half the Parish besides; so famous was she in the Fields of Venus, nor indeed less in those of Mars.

The author employs the technique of

(A) mock heroism

(D) pathetic fallacy

(B) hubris

(E) intentional fallacy

(C) dramatic irony

85.	Who is the "hero" of the work from which the above is excerpted?

(A) Goodman Brown

(D) Hercules

(B) Achilles

(E) Tom Jones

(C) Joseph Andrews

Questions 86 – 87 refer to the parody below:

It is a beauteous morn, opinion grants.
Nothing remains of last night's Summer Formal
Save palms and streamers and the wifely glance
Directed with more watchfulness than normal,
At listless mate who tugs his necktie loose,
Moans, shuns the light and gulps tomato juice.

86.	The poem parodies

(A) Coleridge

(D) Wordsworth

(B) Byron

(E) Dylan Thomas

(C) Frost

87. In the original poem the poet watches his

   (A) Wife   (D) Daughter

   (B) Mother   (E) Sister

   (C) Maid

88. His great speeches on American affairs and his attack on the oppression of India show true historical understanding whereas his profound antipathy to revolution, rather than evolution, leads him to neglect the causes of the French Revolution in horror at its excesses.

   The critic refers to

   (A) Gandhi   (D) Wordsworth

   (B) Thoreau   (E) Burke

   (C) Matthew Arnold

Questions 89 – 91 refer to the speeches that follow:

89. Which lines are spoken by Volpone?

90. Which by Shylock?

91. Which by Falstaff?

(A)   Methinks my moiety, north from Burton here
   In quantity equals not one of yours.

(B) A diamond gone cost me two thousand ducats in Frankfort! The curse never fell on our nation till now; I never felt it till now.

(C)   Let good Antonio look he keep his day,
   Or he shall pay for this.

(D)   Good morning to the day; and next my gold!
   Open the shrine, that I may see my saint.

(E) I would to God thou and I knew where a commodity of good names were to be bought.

92.   Ancient _____ embodied for Yeats the union and subsequent transfiguration, through art, of the body and the holy idea.

Which of the following completes the passage?

(A) Rome   (D) Egypt

(B) Greece   (E) India

(C) Byzantium

Questions 93 – 95 refer to the following passage:

On a table in the middle of the room was a kind of lovely crockery basket that had apples and oranges and peaches and grapes piled up in it which was much redder and yellower and prettier than real ones is but they warn't real because you could see where pieces had got chipped off and showed the white chalk or whatever it was underneath. . . .There was some books too, piled up perfectly exact, on each corner of the table. One was a big family Bible, full of pictures. One was *Pilgrim's Progress*, about a man that left his family it didn't way why. I read considerable in it now and then. The statements was interesting, but tough. Another was "Friendship's Offering," full of beautiful stuff and poetry but I didn't read the poetry.

93.   The narrator of this passage is

(A) David Copperfield   (D) Huckleberry Finn

(B) Dreiser's Carrie   (E) Lambert Strether

(C) Crane's Maggie

94.   Which best explains the significance of the false fruit?

(A) The narrator is starving.

(B) The narrator has never seen fake fruit before, emphasizing the innocence of the character.

(C) The fruit looks amusing and the narrator has a keen sense of humor.

33

(D) The fruit symbolizes the deprivation in the narrator's life.

(E) The fruit symbolizes the false front put up by the family who own it.

95.   Why are the books used ironically here?

(A) The narrator cannot read.

(B) The family are not peace-loving.

(C) The family cannot read.

(D) The narrator loves reading but not poetry.

(E) The family are not pilgrims.

96.   From which country did T.S. Eliot develop his use of symbolism?

(A) England   (D) France

(B) Germany   (E) Egypt

(C) Israel

Questions 97 – 99 refer to the Eliot poetry that follows.

97.   Which is an example of Eliot's symbolism?

98.   Which demonstrates Eliot's poetic paradox?

99.   Which demonstrates Eliot's probing the unconscious for his imagery?

(A)   For I have known them all already, known them all:
         Have known the evenings, mornings, afternoons,
          I have measured out my life in coffee spoons.

(B)   NO! I am not Prince Hamlet, nor was meant to be;
         Am an attendant Lord, one that will do
         To swell a progress, start a scene or two,
         Advise the prince. . .

(C)   I do not know much about gods, but I think that the river
       Is a strong brown God.

(D)   The stair was dark
       Damp, jagged, like an old man's mouth drivelling
            beyond repair,
       Or the toothed gullet of an aged shark.

(E)   What we call the beginning is often the end
       And to make an end is to make a beginning
       The end is where we start from

100.   I hasped the window, I combed his long black hair from his
forehead. I tried to close his eyes — to extinguish if possible, that
frightful life – like gaze of exultation.

    The "I" in this description is

    (A) Little Nell   (D) Nelly Dean

    (B) Maggie Tulliver   (E) Lockwood

    (C) Nick Carraway

101.   A volume of _____'s poems lay before him on the table. He
opened it cautiously with his left hand lest he should waken the child
and began to read the first poem in the book:

       Hushed are the winds and still the evening gloom,
          Not e'en a Zephry wanders through the grove,
       Whilst I return to view my Margaret's tomb
          And scatter flowers on the dust I love.

    He paused. He felt the rhythm of the verse about him in the
room. How melancholy it was! Could he, too, write like that, express
the melancholy of his soul in verse? There were so many things he
wanted to describe; his sensation of a few hours before on Grattan
Bridge for example. . .The child awoke and began to cry.

The volume of poems is written by:

(A) Gerard Manley Hopkins

(B) Wordsworth

(C) Tennyson

(D) Wallace Stevens

(E) Lord Byron

102. The author of the above passage also wrote

(A) *Sons and Lovers*

(B) *To the Lighthouse*

(C) *The Damnation of Theron Ware*

(D) *Ulysses*

(E) *Jude the Obscure*

103. _____ world is not ours, and perhaps we are too neglectful of the graces by which he sets such store. But when a man threatens his young son that spies report to his father on his conduct, and advises him to have affairs only with women of quality, who will combine adultery with polishing his manners, we may well consider him an unpleasant mixture of Polonius and Pandarus.

Whose world is described here?

(A) Richardson's   (D) Sterne's

(B) Addison's   (E) Chesterfield's

(C) Swift's

104. In which literary work does Polonius play a role?

(A) *Oedipus Rex*

(B) *Coriolanus*

(C) *Mourning Becomes Electra*

(D) *Hamlet*

(E) *The Alchemist*

105. In which literary work does Pandarus feature?

(A) *A Midsummer Night's Dream*

(B) Chaucer's *The Miller's Tale*

(C) Chaucer's *Troilus and Criseyde*

(D) Bolt's *A Man For All Seasons*

(E) Eliot's *Murder in the Cathedral*

106. Which best describes a pander's role?

(A) He sacrifices his own interests for other people's.

(B) He acts as a go-between in political matters.

(C) He acts as a liaison in sexual intrigues.

(D) He sends important messages between people.

(E) He flatters people and helps them get on in business.

Questions 107 – 111 refer to the following stanzas:

> And he to me: "The whole shall be made known;
>   Only have patience till we stay our feet
>   On yonder sorrowful shore of Acheron."
>
> Abashed, I dropped my eyes; and, lest unmeet
>   Chatter should vex him, held my tongue, and so
>   Paced on with him, in silence and discreet.

107. "he to me" (line 1) are

    (A) Ulysses to Patroklus   (D) Homer to Odysseus

    (B) God to Adam   (E) Virgil to Dante

    (C) Adam to Eve

108. In context, which best replaces "stay our feet?" (line 2)

    (A) land   (D) slow down

    (B) stop   (E) jump

    (C) stay put

109. Who journeys on the river Acheron?

    (A) The souls of the joyous going to heaven.

    (B) The bodies of soldiers going to rest.

    (C) The souls of unbaptized children going to Limbo.

    (D) The souls of the damned going to Hell.

    (E) The souls of the saved going to Purgatory.

110. Who ferries them across the River Acheron?

    (A) Charybdis   (D) Scylla

    (B) Minos   (E) Charon

    (C) Medusa

111. Which best paraphrases the second stanza?

    (A) Angry, I glared at him, accepted his taunt and continued seething silently.

    (B) Ashamed, I avoided his glance, and in case my useless talking angered him, silently walked by his side.

(C) Embarrassed, I turned away and wanting to meet others, left him standing there silent and angry with me.

(D) Awkward, I looked down and not wanting to anger him further with my chit-chat walked on ahead of him in silence.

(E) Bored, I looked away and thought it was unseemly of me to talk, so walked by his side silently and apart.

Questions 112 – 114 refer to the following dialogue:

"'His last word – to live with'" she insisted. "'Don't you understand I loved him – I loved him – I loved him.'"
I pulled myself together and spoke slowly.
"'The last word he pronounced was – your name.'"

112.   The narrator is

(A) The Director   (D) Edith Summerson

(B) Marlow   (E) Ishmael

(C) Dr. Rieux

113.   The true last words were

(A) "Ah! My angels!"

(B) "I don't complain of none, dear boy."

(C) "The sun. . . the sun."

(D) "The horror – horror."

(E) "Dear old Flo! Master wouldn't hurt you. Come here!"

114.   Which of the following explains why the narrator lies?

(A) The woman is the dead man's wife and the narrator tells what she wants to hear.

(B) The woman is the dead man's mistress who left him for another man.

(C) The woman is the dead man's fiancee who loves flattery.

(D) The woman is the dead man's fiancee who believes in the man's goodness —the narrator knows the man's innate evil.

(E) The dead man had had many affairs – his last words were not this woman's name but another's.

115. The function of the older son is to contrast the father's attitude to him, the loyal steadfast one, and the younger wastrel son. If the father had had only the one son the jubilation of his return would be more understandable. A deep-rooted sibling rivalry perhaps sparks the outcry of the older son.

The above attempts to explain

(A) a parable

(B) a fable

(C) a Freudian premise

(D) a Jungian dream

(E) a Nietzschean view of superman

116. In the above story why does the father rejoice to see the younger son return?

(A) This boy is the father's favorite.

(B) The father cannot tolerate the rivalry between the two boys and teaches the older one a lesson.

(C) The younger son represents the sinner welcomed back into God's forgiveness.

(D) The younger son represents the Oedipal complex which the father has forgiven.

(E) The younger son failed and is now back in the power of the father.

Questions 117 – 119 refer to the two stanzas below excerpted from a longer poem.

I have looked upon those brilliant creatures,
And now my heart is sore.
All's changed since I, hearing at twilight,
The first time on this shore,
The bell-beat of their wings above my head,
Trod with a lighter tread.

Unwearied still, lover by lover,
They paddle in the cold
Companionable streams or climb the air;
Their hearts have not grown old;
Passion or conquest, wander where they will,
Attend upon them still.

117. The poet is

   (A) William Butler Yeats   (D) William Carlos Williams

   (B) George Herbert   (E) Robert Frost

   (C) Emerson

118. The stanzas embody which aspect of the poet's world view?

   (A) That the world is in a constant state of flux which he hates.

   (B) That man can never achieve happiness in this world.

   (C) That man can never be as free and happy as the birds who stay the same always.

   (D) That man needs love and companionship.

   (E) That man changes and grows old but Nature renews herself and appears constant.

119.   "Those brilliant creatures" are

    (A) Peacocks   (D) Geese

    (B) Swans   (E) Doves

    (C) Ducks

Questions 120 – 121 refer to the following dialogue:

    In the meantime let's try and converse calmly, since we're incapable of remaining silent.
    You're right, we're inexhaustible.
    It's so we won't think.
    We have that excuse.
    It's so we won't hear.
    We have our reasons.

120.   The two speakers are

    (A) Ponzo and Lucky   (D) Clov and Hamm

    (B) Molloy and Moran   (E) Biff and Happy

    (C) Vladimir and Estragon

121.   What does the dialogue reveal?

    (A) The two are bored with each other and hide their boredom in idle chatter.

    (B) The characters wish to hide their fear of life by listening to one another.

    (C) The two enjoy chatting to one another.

    (D) The two hope to forget their fear of life by talking.

    (E) The characters are strangers and have nothing vital to say.

122. In this book the hero is just arriving at manhood with the freshness of feeling that belongs to that interesting period of life, and with the power to please that properly characterizes youth. As a consequence he is loved; and, what denotes the real waywardness of humanity, more than it corresponds with theories and moral propositions, he is loved by one full of art, vanity and weakness, and loved principally for his sincerity, his modesty, and his unerring truth and probity.

Which hero does this preface to the novel describe?

(A) Tom Jones   (D) The Reverend Dimsdale

(B) Heathcliff   (E) Theron Ware

(C) The Deerslayer

123. A contemporary of the author of the above preface is

(A) Richardson

(B) Fielding

(C) Edgar Allen Poe

(D) Brockden Brown

(E) Samuel Langhorne Clemens

124. Marlow is terrified of well-bred women, although he has no problem with "females of another class." His shyness – certainly an absurd foible for a young man about town in this day and age – is soon demonstrated when he meets Miss_____.

Supply the name that completes this criticism:

(A) Hardcastle   (D) Andrews

(B) Earnshaw   (E) Teazle

(C) Booby

125. The "day and age" referred to in the above criticism is

(A) The Jacobean Age   (D) The Restoration

(B) The Age of Reason   (E) The Modern Age

(C) The Reformation

126. "An 'Image' is that which presents an intellectual and emotional complex in an instant of time. I use the word 'complex'
rather in the technical sense employed by the newer psycholo-
gists.

The "I" here is

(A) T.S. Eliot   (D) Archibald MacLeish

(B) Wyndham Lewis   (E) Robert Lowell

(C) Ezra Pound

Questions 127 – 129 refer to the passages that follow:

127. Which did Pound write?

128. Which did Robert Lowell write?

129. Which did Archibald MacLeish write?

(A)   There is a moment when we lie
         Bewildered, wakened out of sleep,
         When light and sound and all reply
         That moment time must tame and keep.

(B)   So far for what it's worth
         I have my background;
         And you had your background.

(C)   One dark night,
         my Tudor Ford climbed the hill's skull;
         I watched for love-cars. Lights turned down,
         they lay together, hull to hull,
         where the graveyard shelves on the town. . .

44

(D)   I am moved by fancies that are curled
Around these images and cling:

(E)   I too am a rare
Pattern. As I wander down
The garden paths.

130.   Lady Sneerwell, Mrs. Candour, Sir Oliver Surface, Snake and Careless are all characters from which Restoration play?

(A) *The Beaux Stratagem*   (D) *School for Scandal*

(B) *All for Love*   (E) *Love's Last Shift*

(C) *The Way of the World*

131.   Such names as above are based on which dramatic tradition?

(A) The Greek Chorus   (D) Deus ex machina

(B) The Furies   (E) The Peripeteia

(C) The Humours

132.   Dryden said, "'Tis sufficient to say, according to the proverb, that here is God's plenty."

According to Dryden, where is God's plenty?

(A) In the Bible

(B) In a book of Proverbs

(C) In Dryden's essays

(D) In Chaucer's *Canterbury Tales*

(E) In Shakespeare's History plays

133. He told Hawthorne that his book has been broiled in hell-fire and secretly baptized not in the name of God but in the name of the Devil. He named his tragic hero after the Old Testament ruler who "did more to provoke the Lord God of Israel to anger than all the Kings of Israel that were before him."

This tragic hero is

(A) Ahab   (D) Lucifer

(B) Ishmael   (E) Job

(C) Isaiah

Questions 134 – 138 refer to the following lines taken from a longer poem:

>   Two Handmaids wait the Throne: Alike in Place,
> But diff'ring far in Figure and in Face.
> Here stood Ill-nature like an ancient Maid,
> Her wrinkled Form in Black and White array'd;
> With store of Pray'rs, for Mornings, Nights and Noons, 5
> Her Hand is fill'd; her Bosom with Lampoons.
>
>   There Affectation with a sickly Mien
> Shows in her Cheek the roses of Eighteen,
> Practis'd to Lisp and hang the Head aside,
> Faints into Airs, and languishes with Pride;   10
> On the rich Quilt sinks with becoming Woe,
> Wrapt in a Gown for Sickness and for Show.
> The Fair-ones feel such Maladies as these,
> When each new Night-Dress gives a new Disease.

134. The stanzas are written in

(A) free verse   (D) blank verse

(B) couplets   (E) octosyllabic couplets

(C) heroic couplets

135. Which best paraphrases the second half of line 6?

(A) Her bosom is arrayed with exotic flowers.

(B) Her bosom overflows with political tracts written to flatter a politician.

(C) Her bosom is stuffed with anadromous fishes allegorizing love.

(D) Her bosom is filled with satirical writings which ridicule an enemy.

(E) Her bosom rested against a Grecian lamp.

136. The "Fair-ones" feel such "maladies" (line 13) because

(A) Ladies then never received enough air or exercise and were often sickly but still wanted to look fashionable in bed

(B) The Plague was rampant at this time and fashionable nightdresses were made in which ladies received visitors discreetly

(C) Ladies often received company in their bedrooms, so they became "ill" when they had a new nightdress to show off

(D) The fashion was so highly corseted then ladies often fainted and had to wear loose flowing nightdresses

(E) Fashion was so elaborate then that ladies "fell ill" to avoid seeing people they did not want to see

137. In context, which word best replaces "Mien" in line 7?

(A) Bent (D) Gait

(B) Posture (E) Appearance

(C) Pallor

138. The poet's purpose is

   (A) To vent his misogyny.

   (B) To show male superiority in his day.

   (C) To ridicule the fashionable world of his day.

   (D) To hurt a woman he once loved, who scorned him.

   (E) To take revenge for a trivial trick played on him.

Questions 139 – 140 refer to the following criticism:

What have we in common with these medieval lovers — servants' or
'prisoners' they called themselves — who seem to be always weeping
and always on their knees before ladies of inflexible cruelty?

139. These lovers belong to which tradition?

   (A) The Religion of Love

   (B) Romantic Love

   (C) The Ritual of Love

   (D) Erotic Love

   (E) Courtly Love

140. The tradition begins in

   (A) France   (D) Wales

   (B) Germany   (E) Italy

   (C) Russia

141.   The three main elements of such a love are:

(A) Humility, Courtesy, Adultery

(B) Humility, Sexuality, Adultery

(C) Adultery, Eroticism, Passion

(D) Obedience, Abstinence, Absence

(E) Gallantry, Licentiousness, Feudality

Questions 142 – 145 refer to the following description:

The scene was a plain, bare, monotonous vault of a schoolroom, and the speaker's square forefinger emphasized his observations by under-scoring every sentence with a line on the schoolmaster's sleeve. The emphasis was helped by the speaker's square wall of a forehead, which had his eyebrows for its base, while his eyes found commodious   5
cellarage in two dark caves, overshadowed by the wall. The emphasis was helped by the speaker's mouth, which was wide, thin, and hard set. The emphasis was helped by the speaker's voice, which was inflexible, dry, and dictatorial. The emphasis was helped by the speaker's hair, which bristled on the skirts of his bald head, a plantation of firs to keep   10
the wind from its shining surface, all covered with knobs, like the crust of a plum pie, as if the head had scarcely warehouse-room for the hard facts stored inside. The speaker's square carriage, square legs, square shoulders— nay, his very neckcloth, trained to take him by the throat with an unaccommodating grasp, like a stubborn fact, as it was — all   15
helped the emphasis.

142.   The speaker's name is Mr. Gradgrind – – how does the repeti-tion in the passage add to the name's connotation?

(A) The word "emphasis" repeated adds to the harshness of the name.

(B) The repetition of "speaker" emphasizes how important the name is.

(C) The repeated "square" emphasizes how old-fashioned the speaker is.

(D) The repeated "square" adds to the name by suggesting how harsh reason will grind everyone down.

(E) The repeated "square" suggests how hard facts in schooling will grind down reason and make for nonsense.

143. Which term best describes the author's language?

(A) Descriptive

(D) Symbolic

(B) Allegorical

(E) Prosodic

(C) Metaphorical

144. Which figures of speech do lines 10 – 12 contain?

(A) A metaphor and a simile

(B) Two metaphors

(C) Oxymoron and a simile

(D) Pastoral and a metaphor

(E) Paradox and a simile

145. The author of this passage also wrote:

(A) *The Way of All Flesh*

(B) *Fathers and Sons*

(C) *Villette*

(D) *The Mystery of Edwin Drood*

(E) *Adam Bede*

Questions 146 – 149 refer to the stage directions that follow:

146. Which did Ibsen write?

147. Which did Arthur Miller write?

148.	Which did George Bernard Shaw write?

149.	Which is Absurdist Theater?

(A)	She takes the Captain by the arm and coaxes him down into the chair, where he remains sitting dully. Then she takes the straitjacket and goes behind the chair.

(B)	Same room. Beside the piano the Christmas tree now stands stripped of ornament, burned down candle stubs on its ragged branches.

(C)	The laughter is loud now, and he moves into a brightening area at the left, where THE WOMAN has come from behind the scrim and is standing, putting on her hat, looking into a mirror and laughing.

(D)	The office of the old professor, which also serves as a dining room. To the left, a door opens onto the apartment stairs; upstage, to the right, another door opens onto a corridor of the apartment. Upstage, a little left of center, a window, not very large, with plain curtains; on the outside sill of the window are ordinary potted plants.

(E)	A lady's bedchamber in Bulgaria, in a small town near the Dragoman Pass, late in November in the year 1885. Through an open window with a little balcony a peak of the Balkans, wonderfully white and beautiful in the starlit snow, seems quite close at hand, though it is really far away.

150.	"Well, old chap. . . it do appear that she had settled the most of it, which I mean ter say tied it up on Miss Estella. But she had wrote out a little coddleshell in her own hand a day or two afore the accident, leaving a cool four thousand to Mr. Matthew Pocket."

The speaker is

(A) Joseph in *Wuthering Heights*

(B) Joe Gargery in *Great Expectations*

(C) Mr. Western in *Tom Jones*

(D) Mrs. Malaprop in *The Rivals*

(E) Porfiry in *Crime and Punishment*

151. In context of the above passage, what is the meaning of the word "coddleshell"?

(A) A small bi-valve sea shell

(B) The opening lines of a will

(C) The closing lines of a will

(D) An appendix to a will

(E) A small piece of shell-pink paper attached to a will

Questions 152 – 157 refer to the excerpt of poetry below:

> In all my dreams, before my helpless sight,
> He plunges at me, guttering, choking, drowning.
> If in some smothering dream you too could pace
> Behind the wagon that we flung him in,
> And watch the white eyes writhing in his face,   5
> His hanging face, like a devil's sick of sin;
> If you could hear, at every jolt, the blood
> Come gargling from the froth-corrupted lungs
> Obscene as cancer, bitter as the cud
> Of vile, incurable sores on innocent tongues, —   10
> My friend, you would not tell with such high zest
> To children ardent for some desperate glory,
> The old Lie: Dulce et decorum est
> Pro patria mori

152. The poet dreams of a man who has

    (A) drowned in the English Channel.

    (B) choked to death in the Dresden fire bombing.

    (C) choked to death in a napalm bomb blast.

    (D) drowned in the Pacific in World War Two.

    (E) choked to death in a gas attack in World War One.

153. Which best describes the connotation of "guttering" in line 2?

    (A) A man stumbling into a gutter.

    (B) A flickering candle flame about to go out.

    (C) A choking, gutteral sound.

    (D) A gasping, stuttering sound.

    (E) A bitter sensation in the pit of the stomach.

154. What poetic technique does line 5 demonstrate?

    (A) Assonance   (D) Diction

    (B) Alliteration   (E) Paradox

    (C) Onomatopoeia

155. Which lines demonstrate enjambment?

    (A) lines 1 & 2   (D) lines 2 & 3

    (B) lines 5 & 6   (E) lines 9 & 10

    (C) lines 4 & 5

156. What poetic technique does line 8 demonstrate?

(A) Symbolism   (D) Feminine rhyme

(B) Oxymoron   (E) Slant rhyme

(C) Onomatopoeia

157. Which best captures the tone of the last four lines?

(A) Ironic bitterness

(B) Pompous anger

(C) Righteous indignation

(D) Self-righteous anger

(E) Sad harshness

158. Which three elements best define Post Modernism?

(A) Randomness, Excess, Discontinuity

(B) Flashback, Fragmentation, Humor

(C) Nature, Faith, Solidity

(D) Immorality, Sense of Loss, Meaninglessness

(E) Montage, Metaphor, Absurdity

Questions 159 – 162 refer to the passages that follow:

159. Which did John Stuart Mill write?

160. Which did Matthew Arnold write?

161. Which did Coleridge write?

162. Which did T.S. Eliot write?

(A) Finally, GOOD SENSE is the BODY of poetic genius, FANCY its DRAPERY, MOTION its Life and IMAGI-NATION the soul that is everywhere and in each; and forms all into one graceful and intelligent whole.

(B) They (The Greeks) regarded the whole; we regard the parts.

With them the action predominated over the expression of it; with us the expression predominates over the action.

(C) It is essential that a work of art should be self-consistent, that an artist should consciously or unconsciously draw a circle beyond which he does not trespass: on the other hand, actual life is always the material. . .

(D) What made Wordsworth's poems a medicine for my state of mind, was that they expressed, not mere outward beauty, but states of feeling, and of thought coloured by feeling, under the excitement of beauty.

(E) What can we expect this Aristocracy of Nature to do for us? They are of two kinds: the speculative, speaking or vocal; and the practical or industrial, whose function is silent.

Questions 163 – 166 refer to the following passage:

His head leaned back so far that it rested against the face of a defunct mantelpiece clock, and forom this position his distraught eyes stared down at Daisy, who was sitting, frightened but graceful, on the edge of a stiff chair. . . his lips parted with an abortive attempt at a laugh. Luckily the clock took this moment to tilt dangerously at the pressure of his head, whereupon he turned and caught it with trembling fingers and set it back in its place. . .

"I'm sorry about the clock," he said.
"It's an old clock," I told them idiotically.
I think we all believed for a moment that it had smashed in pieces on the floor.
"We haven't met for several years," said Daisy, her voice as matter-of-fact as it could ever be.
"Five years next November."

55

163. Who narrates this dialogue?

(A) Nick Carraway

(D) The Goat Boy

(B) Ernest Hemingway

(E) Italo Calvino

(C) Ford Maddox Ford

164. What do the details about the "defunct" clock and its falling reveal about these people?

(A) Time is dead as far as these people are concerned.

(B) The narrator is just killing time with these people.

(C) Time has not mattered before but is beginning to matter now as the three become involved in a love triangle.

(D) Time is gradually being destroyed for the two lovers who have been apart for five years.

(E) Time is becoming short as the narrator tries to write the story of these people.

165. Who says the last line and why is the detail important?

(A) The narrator because he has known the couple five years.

(B) The other man because the exact time has been important to him if not to Daisy.

(C) The other man who has hated Daisy for five years and counted the time to revenge himself on her.

(D) The narrator because it seems as if the couple have been there with him for five years.

(E) Daisy's husband who took her away from the other man five years before.

166. The author also wrote

(A) *Nightwood*

(B) *Tender is the Night*

(C) *The Magus*

(D) *A Dance to the Music of Time*

(E) *A Burnt Out Case*

167. Arnold's poem follows a linear progression from moonlit tranquility, through recognition of the loss of faith, to a view of the world as "a darkling plain."

The poem is

(A) *Ode to Immortality*   (D) *Dover Beach*

(B) *Two in the Campagna*   (E) *Endymion*

(C) *Kubla Khan*

168. The horror of proliferation is the theme of _____ . An old couple wait for a crowd of distinguished people to attend a lecture on the lessons the old man wishes to pass on after ninety-five years of existence. The guests come but we see only the frantic activity of the old couple to accommodate their audience. The expected speaker arrives but he is deaf and dumb — he can only gurgle and write meaningless symbols on the blackboard.

The name of the play is

(A) *The Lesson*   (D) *The Chairs*

(B) *The Maids*   (E) *Strange Interlude*

(C) *Endgame*

169. Who is the playwright of the above play and what is its "message?"

(A) Ionesco, the inanity of life and the failure of language

(B) Genet, the blurring of identity between the sexes

(C) Beckett, the desperate futility of life

(D) O'Neill, the mistakes of the past torture the future

(E) Synge, the myths of the past hinder vitality in the present

Questions 170 – 172 refer to the poem that follows:

> I met a traveler from an antique land
> Who said: Two vast and trunkless legs of stone
> Stand in the desert. . .Near them, on the sand,
> Half sunk, a shattered visage lies, whose frown
> And wrinkled lip, and sneer of cold command,   5
> Tell that its sculptor well those passions read
> Which yet survive, stamped on these lifeless things,
> The hand that mocked them, and the heart that fed:
> And on the pedestal these words appear:
> "My name is Ozymandias, king of kings: 10
> Look on my works, ye Mighty and despair!"
> Nothing beside remains. Round the decay
> Of that colossal wreck, boundless and bare
> The lone and level sands stretch far away.

170.   Which most-closely describes the poet's meaning?

(A) The British Empire will one day tumble like the statue Ozymandias built.

(B) The Egyptian Empire was great but it was destroyed by one man's lust for power.

(C) The ruined statue and the sand's reclamation exemplify the futility of man's life on earth.

(D) No man, no matter how great, has the right to set himself up as immortal.

(E) The ruined statue shows that men should not build "graven images" to celebrate their power.

171. What do lines 4 – 7 suggest about Ozymandias?

(A) He was a lifeless old man.

(B) He was conceited and arrogant.

(C) The sculptor captured the man's coldness and arrogance.

(D) The sculptor hated him and so executed a perfect likeness.

(E) The sculptor outlived the model.

172. The poet also wrote

(A) *To a Skylark*

(B) *Cristabel*

(C) *Ode on a Grecian Urn*

(D) *Elegy Written in a Country Churchyard*

(E) *The Magi*

173. Readers feel the same lack of credibility with the too sweet heroine, _____, of *A Room With A View*. Mr. Emerson, her "guardian," guides her into the correct choice of love. Readers grasp the "physical" message of the novel, the scene in the violets and the bathing pool make it clear but the rest of the novel does not support the thesis, especially when the other "guardian," _____, turns out to be on the lovers' side after all!

Complete the passage with the ladies' names:

(A) Lucy Honeychurch and Mrs. Allen

(B) Caroline Abbott and Mrs. Moore

(C) Jordan Baker and Daisy Buchanan

(D) Caroline Abbott and Mrs. Fairfax

(E) Lucy Honeychurch and Miss Bartlett

174. Which of the following words does E.M. Forster use to express the puzzlement of life in most of his novels?

(A) Chaos

(D) Confusion

(B) Riddle

(E) Mayhem

(C) Muddle

Questions 175 – 180 refer to the following lines from a longer poem:

And they, as storms of snow descend to the ground incessant
on a winter's day, when Zeus of the counsels, showing
before men what shafts he possesses, brings on a snowstorm
and stills the winds asleep in the solid drift, enshrouding
the peaks that tower among the mountains and the shoulders out-
        jutting,
and the low lands with their grasses, and the prospering work of men's
        hands,
and the drift falls along the grey sea, the harbours and beaches,
and the surf that breaks against it is stilled, and all things elsewhere
it shrouds from above, with the burden of Zeus' rain heavy upon it;
so numerous and incessant were the stones volleyed from both sides,
some thrown on Trojans, others flung against the Achaians
by Trojans, so the whole length of wall thundered beneath them.

175. Name the poet and work:

(A) Homer's *The Odyssey*

(B) Homer's *The Iliad*

(C) Malory's *Idylls of the King*

(D) Chaucer's *The Knight's Tale*

(E) T.S. Eliot's *Murder in the Cathedral*

176. The city under attack here is

(A) Carthage   (D) Troy

(B) Athens   (E) Rome

(C) Tintagel

177. Who are the Achaians?

(A) The Greeks

(B) The Barbarians

(C) An ancient race of Britons

(D) The Romans

(E) The Goths

178. Who is the hero on each side of the battle?

(A) Beowulf and Hrothgar

(B) Boadicea and Caesar

(C) Jason and Priam

(D) Achilles and Patroklos

(E) Achilles and Hector

179. Which best defines the way the entire simile functions?

(A) The stones come down like snow without causing damage, like snow which hushes, not harms − − the simile works through likeness.

(B) The stones are like snow because they descend in an infinite quantity but the difference between the two, soft and brutal, in reality is a shock − − the simile works through contrast.

(C) The stones are as white as snow and multiply so they look like snowflakes – – the snow-simile works visually.

(D) The stones hurtle down like snow and cause death just as snow deadens all the countryside – – the simile works through likeness.

(E) The stones crash down unlike snow which softens all the countryside – – the simile works through contrast.

180. Which best describes the effect of the snow description?

(A) It shows that men are powerless in the hands of the gods.

(B) It distances the reader from the horror of the battle.

(C) It gives the writer a chance to pause before describing the horrors of the battle.

(D) It universalizes the experience so that the reader can empathize with both sides of the battle.

(E) It adds a serene beauty to what might otherwise be a gruesome scene.

181. Which modern writer uses a similar effect of rain or snow in which work?

(A) Robert Frost in *Stopping by Woods On a Snowy Evening*

(B) T.S. Eliot in *Preludes*

(C) James Joyce in *The Dead*

(D) Robert Creeley in *The Rain*

(E) Sartre in *Nausea*

182.   ... thanks to the limited desire for its company expressed by the
        step-parent, the law of its little life, its being entertained in
        rotation by its father and its mother, wouldn't easily prevail.
        Whereas each of these persons had at first vindictively desired
        to keep it from the other, so at present the remarried relative
        sought now rather to be rid of it – that is to leave it as much as
        possible, and beyond the appointed times and seasons, on the
        hands of the adversary. . .

This is Henry James's preface to which of his novels?

(A) *The American*   (D) *What Maisie Knew*

(B) *The Bostonians*   (E) *The Golden Bowl*

(C) *The Turn of the Screw*

Questions 183 – 186 refer to the excerpted second stanza of a poem
below:

        Now I am a lake. A woman bends over me,
        Searching my reaches for what she really is.
        Then she turns to those liars, the candles or the moon.
        I see her back and reflect it faithfully.
        She rewards me with tears and an agitation of hands.   5
        I am important to her. She comes and goes.
        Each morning it is her face that replaces the darkness.
        In me she has drowned a young girl, and in me an old woman
        Rises toward her day after day, like a terrible fish.

183.   Which best defines the "I" of the initial metaphor?

(A) The lake is a mirror to reflect back the woman's true image
    of herself.

(B) The lake is the mirror to be rewarded for giving back a
    soothing image.

(C) The lake acts as a portrait which flatters the woman.

(D) The lake is too deep to give back a true image so it lies.

(E) The lake waits for the young woman to drown herself in it.

184. Why are candles or the moon liars in line 3?

(A) They give a flattering softening light so the picture they reflect is not "true."

(B) They change so much that the reflection they give back in the mirror can never be true.

(C) They cannot reflect light as a mirror does so there is no image.

(D) Their light is too shadowy or milky to give a good reflection.

(E) The mirror is jealous of their brightness.

185. Which is the closest paraphrase of lines 8 – 9?

(A) The mirror has changed and refuses to give the young woman the reflection she ought to have.

(B) Over time the young girl has grown old with the mirror which reflects the true image of a face now wrinkled and aged.

(C) The woman feels as useless as a fish and thus wishes to drown herself in her rightful milieu, the lake.

(D) The young girl is desperately unhappy like a fish out of water but hates to see this reflected in the mirror.

(E) The mirror has lost its silver backing and reflects only scaled fragments of the young girl.

186. The poet is

(A) Emily Dickinson

(B) Amy Powell

(C) Ted Hughes

(D) Sylvia Plath

(E) Wallace Stevens

187. "When I was writing the *Shadow of the Glen* some years ago, I got more aid than any learning could have given me from a chink in the floor of the old Wicklow house where I was staying, that let me hear what was being said by the several servant girls in the kitchen. This matter I think is of importance, for in countries where the imagination of the people, and the language they use is rich and living, it is possible for a writer to be rich and copious in his words and at the same time to give the reality, which is the root of all poetry, in a comprehensive and natural form."

Who is the "I" in this passage?

(A) James Joyce

(D) Frank O'Connor

(B) John Millington Synge

(E) W.B. Yeats

(C) Sean O'Casey

188. In the above passage which best explains the writer's defense of language?

(A) Writers should be allowed to use any language they like.

(B) Writers should choose only the language of the working people.

(C) Writers should choose only a living, vibrant language because it can express reality.

(D) Writers should use only bright, creative words.

(E) Writers should be allowed to use creative words even if they are "dirty" or in dialect.

Questions 189 – 191 refer to the passages that follow.

189. Which is from *The Sound and the Fury*?

190. Which is from *Go Tell It On The Mountain*?

191. Which is from *Coming Up For Air*?

(A)   "This may be the last time I pray with you,
        This may be the last time I pray with you."

        As they sang they clapped their hands, and John saw
        that Sister McCandless looked about her for a tambou-
        rine.

(B) The sweet corpsy smell, the rustle of Sunday dresses, the
    wheeze of the organ and the roaring voices, the spot of
    light from the hole in the window creeping lowly up the
    nave. . .

(C) She had risen from one of the side seats, and speaking as
    she walked, she moved forward til she stood within the
    altar rail, immediately under the pulpit. The phrases were
    all familiar enough — Jesus a very present help —
    Sprinkled by the blood — but it was as in the case of her
    singing: the words were old; the music was new.

(D) The church had been decorated, with sparse flowers from
    kitchen gardens and hedgerows, and with streamers of
    coloured crepe paper. Above the pulpit hung a battered
    Christmas bell, the accordion sort that collapses. The
    pulpit was empty, though the choir was already in place,
    fanning themselves though it was not warm.

(E) The light of the lamps of the church fell upon an assembly
    of black clothes and white collars, relieved here and there
    by tweeds, on dark mottled pillars of green marble and on
    lugubrious canvasses. The gentlemen sat in the benches,
    having hitched their trousers slightly above their knees
    and laid their hats in security. They sat well back and
    gazed formally at the distant speck of red light which was
    suspended before the high altar.

192.   Anna waits for a "real man" to come down like a deus ex
        machina to heal and help her.

        Whose Anna is this?

        (A) Tolstoy's Anna Karenina

        (B) Arnold Bennet's Anna of the Five Towns

(C) Doris Lessing's in *The Golden Notebook*

(D) Sartre's Anna in *Nausea*

(E) Little Cloud's in *Dubliners*

193. In current usage, the term "deus ex machina" means

(A) a device which descends from the top of the stage to lower a god from the "heavens"

(B) a Puck-like character who causes mischief and complications in the plot.

(C) a character who begins with evil intent but softens as the plot unfolds.

(D) a character who intervenes opportunely to avoid disasters in the plot.

(E) a device for helping other characters descend into the "earth" below stage.

194. She is similar to unlikely writers such as Kafka and Faulkner but what is horrifying about _____ is that she creates terror amidst the hurry and flurry of females as they perform their "duties." In *Delta Wedding* an impetuous girl prepares for her wedding, harrassed and bullied by the people she loves and who love her.

The author's name is

(A) Flannery O'Connor   (D) Joyce Carol Oates

(B) Jane Austen   (E) George Eliot

(C) Eudora Welty

195. The disemboweled are put back together and the dead resurrected. Victims are raped or flogged, or cut into pieces so quickly the readers have no time to sympathize.

The work described is

(A) Vonnegut's *Slaughterhouse–Five*

(B) Gulliver's chapter on the Brobdingnagians

(C) Chaucer's *Miller's Tale*

(D) Margaret Atwood's *The Handmaid's Tale*

(E) Voltaire's *Candide*

196. Identify the famous word or catch phrase from the last work:

(A) "Something will turn up!"

(B) "In the best of possible worlds"

(C) "Snd so on"

(D) "Live!"

(E) "I'm ever so 'umble"

197. Man has ideas that come not through the five senses or the powers of reasoning; but are either the result of direct revelation from God, his immediate inspiration or his immanent presence in the spiritual world.

Which is the term for the philosophy thus outlined?

(A) Pragmatism   (D) Transcendentalism

(B) Humanism   (E) Spiritualism

(C) Behaviorism

Questions 198 – 201 refer to the passages that follow.

198. Which did William James write?

199. Which did Emerson write?

200. Which did Sartre write?

201. Which did Kierkegaard write?

(A) I do not wish to look with sour aspect at the industrious manufacturing village, or the mart of commerce. I love the music of the water wheel; I value the railway; I feel the pride which the sight of a ship inspires; I look on trade and every mechanical craft as education also. But let me discriminate what is precious herein. There is in each of these works an act of invention, an intellectual step, or short series of steps taken; that act or step is the spiritual act; all the rest is mere repetition of the same a thousand times.

(B) I would say that learning to know dread is an adventure which every man has to affront if he would not go to perdition either by not having known dread or by sinking under it. He therefore who has learned rightly to be in dread has learned the most important thing. . . Dread is the possibility of freedom.

(C) Through the process of evolution, human beings have put on sense organs — specialized areas where special types of stimuli are most effective — such as the eye, the ear, the nose, the tongue, the skin and semi-circular canals.

(D) The universe is a system of which the individual members relax their anxieties occasionally, in which the don't care mood is also right for men, and moral holidays in order- - that if I mistake not, is part, at least, of what the Absolute is "known as," that is the great difference in our particular experiences which his being true makes for us, that is his cash value when he is pragmatically interpreted.

(E) Even when I looked at things, I was miles from dreaming that they existed: they looked like scenery to me. I picked them up in my hands, they served me as tools, I foresaw their resistance. But that all happened on the surface. . . all of a sudden, there it was, clear as day: existence had suddenly unveiled itself.

Questions 202 – 206 refer to the passage below:

> I' the Commonwealth I would (by contraries)
> Execute all things: for no kind of traffic
> Would I admit: no name of magistrate:
> Letters should be not known: riches, poverty,
> And use of service, none: contract, succession,   5
> Bourn, bound of land, tilth, vineyard none:
> No use of metal, corn, or wine, or oil:
> No occupation, all men idle, all:
> And women too, but innocent and pure:
> No sovereignty.   10
> · · · · · · · · · ·
> · · · · · · · · · ·
> All things in common Nature should produce
> Without sweat or endeavour: treason, felony,
> Sword, pike, knife, gun, or need of any engine
> Would I not have: but Nature should bring forth
> Of its own kind, all foison, all abundance   15
> To feed my innocent people.

202. The speaker is

(A) a garrulous old fool who talks in riddles.

(B) a garrulous old statesman whose paradoxes describe a utopia.

(C) a wise old counsellor whose riddles advocate an ideal communism.

(D) a sad old politician who is losing his memory.

(E) an interesting old courtier intent on making himself ruler of a commonwealth.

203. In context what do the words bourn, bound and tilth mean in line 6?

(A) Rights of way, acre of land and taxes.

(B) Stream, boundary of land and cultivation.

(C) Valley, acreage and taxes.

(D) Boundaries, rights of property and land cultivation.

(E) Stream, public property rights, and soil.

204. In context what does the word "foison" mean in line 15?

(A) plentiful crop   (D) fish

(B) harvest   (E) fodder

(C) poison

205. This commonwealth contradicts which Bible teaching?

(A) Man should honor his neighbor.

(B) Man produces by the sweat of his brow.

(C) Man should employ his best talents.

(D) God separates the sheep and the goats.

(E) Woman shall bear pain in childbirth.

206. Which author owes a debt to whom for this commonwealth ideal?

(A) Ben Jonson to William Perry

(B) Shakespeare to Montaigne

(C) Voltaire to Rousseau

(D) Pope to Locke

(E) Swift to Hume

Questions 207 – 210 refer to the following passage:

Summertime, oh, summertime, pattern of life indelible, the fade-proof lake, the woods unshatterable, the pasture with the sweetfern and the juniper forever and ever, summer without end; this was the background, and the life along the shore was the design, the cottages with their innocent and tranquil design, their tiny docks with the flagpole and the American flag floating against the white clouds in the blue sky, the little paths over the roots of the trees leading from camp to camp and the paths leading back to the outhouses and the can of lime for sprinkling, and at the souvenir counters at the store the miniature birch-bark canoes and the postcards that showed things looking a little better than they were.

207. As E.B. White recalls a childhood summer, why does he employ one very long sentence?

(A) To highlight the waste he feels now as an old man.

(B) To try to capture the past with a rambling "old man style" not pausing for breath but piling incident on incident.

(C) To give the reader an idea of the haze of the past.

(D) To capture the breathless existence of those summers with so much to see and do.

(E) To capture how excited he was then and how sad he is now reminiscing.

208. Which term best defines the opening three lines?

(A) Oratory   (D) Religious

(B) Rhetoric   (E) Incantation

(C) Celebration

209. Which best explains why the author uses such lines?

(A) To express his joy with those past summers.

(B) To show how important those summers were to him.

(C) To show how deeply moved he is by the remembrance of those summers.

(D) To show how those summers seemed eternal to him then.

(E) To show that the summers work in a healing way for him now.

210. Which best defines the metaphor at work in the last few lines?

(A) The metaphor of the past.

(B) The metaphor of design.

(C) The metaphor of a painting.

(D) The metaphor of summer.

(E) The metaphor of a portrait.

211. The five elements – Awakening, Conflict, Suffering, Tragic Irony, and A Metaphysical Dimension are common to

(A) Tragedy   (D) Play of Ideas

(B) Tragi-Comedy   (E) Social Drama

(C) Black Comedy

212. Which of the following wrote a Revenge Tragedy?

(A) Ben Jonson   (D) Farquhar

(B) Webster   (E) Goldsmith

(C) John Gay

213. Which modern novel incorporates within it a Jacobean Revenge Tragedy?

(A) *The Waterfall*

(B) *One Hundred Years of Solitude*

(C) *The Crying of Lot 49*

(D) *Jalousie*

(E) *The Name of the Rose*

214. He once called her his basil plant; and when she asked for an explanation, said that basil was a plant which had flourished wonderfully on a murdered man's brain.

Which author owes a debt to which poet for this allusion?

(A) Joseph Conrad to Edgar Allen Poe

(B) Graham Greene to Yeats

(C) George Eliot to Keats

(D) George Sand to Tennyson

(E) H.G. Wells to Blake

215. Under his pillow lay the New Testament. He picked it up mechanically. The book belonged to her; it was the same book from which she had read the raising of Lazarus to him. At the beginning of his prison life he had feared that she would drive him frantic with her religion, that she would talk constantly about the gospels, and would force her books on him. But, to his amazement, she had never spoken to him about it, and had not even offered him the New Testament. He had asked for it himself shortly before his illness. He had never opened it till now.

The "he" referred to is

(A) Pierre in *War and Peace*

(B) Jude in *Jude the Obscure*

(C) Raskolnikov in *Crime and Punishment*

(D) Vronsky in *Anna Karenina*

(E) Dick Diver in *Tender is the Night*

216. In the above passage why is the reference to Lazarus important?

    (A) The man has recently found religion and is now a believer like Lazarus.

    (B) The man has ignored God and might be struck down as Lazarus was.

    (C) The man is on death row but may gain a reprieve as Lazarus did.

    (D) The man has recently undergone a form of resurrection of spirit and feels new life as Lazarus did.

    (E) The man has recently been ill and now feels raised from the dead as Lazarus was.

Questions 217 – 218 refer to the author's Preface below:

This middle-class notion about the immobility of the soul was transplanted to the stage, where the middle-class element has always held sway. There a character became synonymous with a gentleman fixed and finished once for all – one who invariably appeared drunk, jolly, sad. And for the purpose of characterization nothing more was needed than some physical deformity like a club-foot, a wooden leg, a red nose; or the person concerned was made to repeat some phrase like "That's capital!" or "Barkis is willin'," or something of that kind.

217. The author is

    (A) stating that characters are drawn too much from the middle-class and that does not mean real-life.

    (B) criticizing playwrights who concentrate on the physical and not the psychological aspects of character.

    (C) suggesting that Naturalist playwrights do not know how to convey realistic characters.

    (D) arguing that characters should not be stock types but show the full range of human variety.

    (E) suggesting that characters should be shown in the process of change.

218. Whose character says "Mr. Barkis is willin'?"

(A) Dickens' in *David Copperfield*

(B) Thackeray's in *Vanity Fair*

(C) Shaw's in *Major Barbara*

(D) Samuel Butler's in *The Way Of All Flesh*

(E) Sterne's in *Tristram Shandy*

219. Chaucer's story describes three rogues who set out to find Death. An old man directs them to a pile of gold florins over which they quarrel and kill one another, thus indeed finding death. However, the greatest irony of the story involves the pilgrim who recounts it.

The tale is

(A) The Merchant's   (D) The Wife of Bath's

(B) The Pardoner's   (E) The Host's

(C) The Miller's

220. Which best describes the irony behind the above story-teller?

(A) He rants against the evils of money but is very wealthy himself.

(B) He preaches against physical love but bears a motto: "Love Conquers All."

(C) He preaches against avarice but has revealed how he himself cheats the common folk out of their money.

(D) He is a successful businessman yet his tale advocates the idle life of the inns.

(E) He preaches against carousing in inns but is a prodigious drinker himself.

Questions 221 – 223 refer to the passages that follow:

221. Which did Virginia Woolf write?

222. Which did V.S. Naipaul write?

223. Which comes from *Sir Gawain and the Green Knight?*

(A) [The] queen, mindful of customs, gold-adorned, greeted the men in the hall; and the noble woman offered the cup first to the keeper of the land. . .

(B) "Put it down there," she said, helping the Swiss girl to place gently before her the huge brown pot in which was the Boeuf en Daube. . . And she peered into the dish, with its shiny walls and its confusion of savoury brown and yellow meats and its bay leaves and its wine, and thought. This will celebrate the occasion. . .

(C) The Professor was not a very strict Hindu — he would take tea, fruit, soda-water, and sweets, whoever cooked them, and vegetables and rice if cooked by a Brahman; but not meat, not cakes lest they contained eggs, and he would not allow anyone else to eat beef: a slice of beef upon a distant plate would wreck his happiness.

(D) Then delicacies and dainties were delivered to the guests,
Fresh food in foison, such freight of full dishes
That space was scarce at the social tables
For the several soups set before them in silver
On the cloth

(E) Leela was taken away and Ganesh was left alone to face the kedgeree-eating ceremony the next morning.
  Still in all his bridegroom's regalia, satin robes, and tasselled crown, he sat down on some blankets in the yard, before the plate of kedgeree. It looked white and unpalatable, and he knew it would be easy to resist any temptation to touch it.

224. Size and time in his dreams mean nothing to him. There is "endless growth and reproduction." He sometimes "seemed to have lived seventy or 100 years" in one night. He was "fixed for centuries" in secret rooms, "buried for a thousand years in stone coffins," doomed to make "everlasting farewells" to those he loved.

These dreams are

(A) Ivan Ilych's as he lies dying

(B) Coleridge's induced by opium

(C) Raskolnikov's after the murders

(D) DeQuincey's induced by opium

(E) Freud's induced by cocaine

Questions 225 – 227 refer to the following lines excerpted from a longer poem:

> Thou then take my brand Excalibur,
> Which was my pride: for thou rememberest how
> In those old days, one summer noon, an arm
> Rose up from out the bosom of the lake,
> Clothed in white samite, mystic, wonderful,   5
> Holding the sword — and how I row'd across
> And took it, and have worn it, like a king:
> And, wheresoever I am sung or told
> In aftertime, this also shall be known.
> But now delay not: take Excalibur,   10
> And fling him far into the middle mere:
> Watch what thou seest, and lightly bring me word.

225. Who is speaking to whom?

(A) King Arthur to Sir Galahad

(B) Sir Gawain to Gringolet

(C) King Arthur to Sir Bedivere

(D) Sir Lancelot to Guinevere

(E) Hrothgar to Beowulf

226. Which best explains the word "samite?" (line 5)

(A) heavily gem-encrusted armor

(B) silver gossamer-like material

(C) highly decorated damask

(D) silk material interwoven with gold and silver thread

(E) simple white muslin interwoven with heraldic devices

227. What happens to the speaker?

(A) He dies and three gloriously apparalled women lead him to the underworld.

(B) The white samite-clad arm draws him down into the Lake of Forgetfulness.

(C) He falls asleep and dreams that a barge drawn by swans takes him away from the battle ground.

(D) A barge with weeping queens on board take him and the other man into the Vale of Avalon.

(E) He dies and a funeral barge with three weeping queens takes him to the island valley of Avalon.

228. The author of the passage is

(A) Wordsworth   (D) John Gardner

(B) Malory   (E) Tennyson

(C) Yeats

Questions 229 – 230 refer to the following passage from an author's letter:

Never in my life have I written anything more difficult than what I am doing now — trivial dialogue . . . I have to portray simultaneously and in the same conversation, five or six characters who speak, several others who are spoken about, the scene, and the whole town. . . and in the midst of all that I have to show a man and woman who are beginning to fall in love with each other.

229. The writer describes which work?

(A) Nadine Gordimer, *A Sport of Nature*

(B) Flauber, *Madame Bovary*

(C) Andre Gide, *The Counterfeiters*

(D) Dickens, *Hard Times*

(E) Boris Pasternak, *Dr. Zhivago*

230. Which scene does the writer eventually choose as a background for the "trivial dialogue"?

(A) An agricultural fair   (D) An opera visit

(B) A Town Hall meeting   (E) A Grand Ball

(C) A dinner party

GRE LITERATURE IN ENGLISH
EXAM I

ANSWER KEY

1.	B	30.	C	59.	A	88.	E
2.	D	31.	D	60.	C	89.	D
3.	E	32.	A	61.	B	90.	B
4.	B	33.	B	62.	C	91.	E
5.	B	34.	C	63.	D	92.	C
6.	C	35.	B	64.	E	93.	D
7.	D	36.	C	65.	C	94.	E
8.	C	37.	C	66.	A	95.	B
9.	A	38.	D	67.	B	96.	D
10.	D	39.	A	68.	D	97.	B
11.	C	40.	C	69.	C	98.	E
12.	E	41.	A	70.	B	99.	D
13.	B	42.	C	71.	B	100.	D
14.	B	43.	C	72.	D	101.	E
15.	E	44.	D	73.	A	102.	D
16.	D	45.	C	74.	C	103.	E
17.	E	46.	D	75.	B	104.	D
18.	B	47.	E	76.	E	105.	C
19.	D	48.	A	77.	D	106.	C
20.	A	49.	E	78.	A	107.	E
21.	A	50.	D	79.	E	108.	A
22.	D	51.	B	80.	C	109.	D
23.	B	52.	A	81.	C	110.	E
24.	D	53.	B	82.	D	111.	B
25.	B	54.	C	83.	D	112.	B
26.	D	55.	D	84.	A	113.	D
27.	E	56.	B	85.	E	114.	D
28.	E	57.	B	86.	D	115.	A
29.	C	58.	A	87.	D	116.	C

GRE LITERATURE IN ENGLISH
EXAM I

117. A	146. B	175. B	204. A
118. E	147. C	176. D	205. B
119. B	148. E	177. A	206. B
120. C	149. D	178. E	207. D
121. D	150. B	179. B	208. E
122. C	151. D	180. D	209. D
123. C	152. E	181. C	210. C
124. A	153. B	182. D	211. A
125. D	154. B	183. A	212. B
126. C	155. E	184. A	213. C
127. B	156. C	185. B	214. C
128. C	157. A	186. D	215. C
129. A	158. A	187. B	216. D
130. D	159. D	188. C	217. D
131. C	160. B	189. D	218. A
132. D	161. A	190. A	219. B
133. A	162. C	191. B	220. C
134. C	163. A	192. C	221. B
135. D	164. D	193. D	222. E
136. C	165. B	194. C	223. D
137. E	166. B	195. E	224. D
138. C	167. D	196. B	225. C
139. E	168. D	197. D	226. D
140. A	169. A	198. D	227. E
141. A	170. C	199. A	228. E
142. E	171. C	200. E	229. B
143. A	172. A	201. B	230. A
144. A	173. E	202. B	
145. D	174. C	203. D	

GRE LITERATURE IN ENGLISH
TEST I

DETAILED EXPLANATIONS
OF ANSWERS

1.   (B)
    D.H. Lawrence believed in a "star-equilibrium" love, with the woman not as a satellite to the male but the two in balance. ("Mino" chapter- *Women in Love*). Consider the alternatives: Heathcliff's love is "of the earth and rocks." Rochester's love is total possession. Stephen's love of the "bird-girl" is of "profane joy." George Emerson's love is "of the body."

2.   (D)
    Raphael tells the story of the Fall of the Angels to Adam in Book V of John Milton's *Paradise Lost*. The first line gives a "clue": "Son of heaven and earth." From context eliminate Michael to Eve and Gabriel to Mary. The Angel of Death does not appear to Virgil. The Angel Gabriel talks to Dante but only to repeat the Annunciation to Mary.

3.   (E)
    The art here is to read the passage intently, eliminating the obvious from context. The angel stresses that continued happiness depends "on thyself," thus eliminating (A) and (B). Man was made "perfect, not immutable" – be careful with Miltonic negative "not unchangeable" – – he can thus change. The angel stresses that man's will is by nature "free."

4.   (B)

Consider carefully the alternatives and eliminate the obviously faulty: the tone is certainly not jolly; it is somewhat gloomy especially in the last lines, but not bad-tempered. It is not vindictive; it could be didactic but not coupled with patronizing – the angel seems willing to be on a level with the man.

5.   (B)

The Canadian wood chopper figures largely in Thoreau's *Walden* as the "true savage." If you do not know the work, consider the other authors – – all loved Nature and the rustic life, but certainly poets like Homer and Frost never mention visitors like the Canadian who symbolizes for Thoreau all that he himself searches for in the simple life.

6.   (C)

Thoreau dwells on the idea of eating various animals not on the usual menu for "civilized" men. The woodchuck that the wood chopper enjoys does not appeal to Thoreau despite his "back to nature self-sufficiency." Considering the alternatives, you would eliminate (D) and (E) as too swift and large for a dog to catch, and (A) and (B) as too agile.

7.   (D)

You should recognize Keats' *Ode on a Grecian Urn*. From this stanza alone, eliminate the other possibilities. Music does refresh the soul but that is not the central point. Youth does have some advantage but not every one. Art is immortal only because the imagination holds the images in time. Nowhere does the stanza say that art destroys life.

8.　　(C)

If you do not know Keats's poem, eliminate the other possibilities by style and tone: the enjambment would be unusual for Elizabethan poetry. The style is too "collected" for the fragmentation of the Postmodern. The tone might be early Victorian but the imagination theme is Romantic. The tone is too uplifting for the Modern.

9.　　(A)

If you know the poem this is simpler. If you are relying on the text alone, go back and read carefully. Nowhere is there a suggestion of despair, distrust or fear. There is an element of triumph but it involves triumph in the imagination. This leaves (A) which sums up the gist of the poem and the philosophy of the era.

10.　　(D)

Beowulf kills Grendel and then must fight the monster's mother. If you do not know the long poem, eliminate by detection of the Middle-English alliteration "greedy and gallows grim," discounting the biblical figures of Jesus and Isaac (even if their mothers had wanted to "avenge" them), and Jason in *The Argonautica*. Gawain does not die within the text.

11.　　(C)

If you have not read *The Sound and the Fury* be aware of the technique placing the reader within the protagonist's brain, here reliving a conversation from the past. Eliminate the poetic term enjambment and the dream notion; the extended metaphor does not sustain the entire passage. Time is dislocated but that is a structural device, not a technique.

12.　　(E)

Neither the poetic language, nor the nuance, nor the extended metaphor of the game of chance achieve the effect of a mind in turmoil.

Certainly there is lack of meaning on first reading, but analyze how that is achieved. The lack of punctuation forces the reader to find the speech rhythms and hence the meaning.

13.   (B)

If you know the novel the answer is clear—Quentin and his father are discussing suicide—if not, eliminate: white hair is mentioned once – as how Mr. Compson thinks his son conceives of death. He mentions the mother's dream of the boy at Harvard but not killing that dream. Courtesy to women and going away to college are evident but not the main point of discussion.

14.   (B)

Even if you know the novel, the speaker's philosophy needs careful thought. The "clue" is given in the metaphor of the game of chance: dice loaded against men. Eliminate (D) and (E): the passage contradicts these. The idea of life not worth living is negated in men hanging on to "expedients" to keep alive. The text does not state that love destroys.

15.   (E)

If you do not know the passage, eliminate the obvious through tone, style or era of writing. Hardy's tone is gloom and doom, but he is too early to use this technique, as was Henry James. Dreiser's sentence structure eliminates him. Vonnegut's zany style and his attitude to death and fate, "so it goes," eliminates him.

16.   (D)

If you do not recognize Dreiser's *Sister Carrie*, eliminate the others: Jane Austen's Emma rarely thinks with pity for anyone nor does anyone take anything on her account; nor for Hardy's Tess of the D'Urbernvilles nor for James' Milly of *Wings of a Dove* or Crane's Maggie or George Eliot's Maggie Tulliver in *Mill on the Floss*.

17.   (E)

If you do not know Tennyson's *Ulysses* which tells of the aged Ulysses setting out with his old crew for a new life, think of the other sailors here, thus eliminating Achilles of *The Iliad*. Jason would have mention of his exciting venture and young crew; Melville's sailors, Ahab and Ishmael, would be described in prose.

18.   (B)

Despite his claim against writing for women's rights, Ibsen's *A Doll's House* with its (in)famous closing of the door at the end, was championed by a number of women's groups in Ibsen's day. Ibsen's comment has been attached to a number of the play's editions and makes the play worth discussing in terms of human equality, not just feminism.

19.   (D)

The names and class distinctions should reveal the play. If you do not recognize them, read the other possibilities and eliminate through those you do know: possibly the Chekhov description (E), and the O'Neill play, (A). In your study of drama, pay close attention to the names of characters as well as the themes of the play.

20.   (A)

All these down-and-out-names are spoken by the protagonist, Hickey, who reveals the lack of hope, futility and total life-despair to these O'Neill characters. If you do not know the play, eliminate by contrasting (A) and (E) – – the O'Neill characters also sit around and talk but the ennui and dream-like aura is not as pronounced as (E) describes.

21.   (A)

Each play has an element of all five answers but O'Neill owes a debt to Ibsen for the "life-lie": a lie hidden in the past which a "crusader" from the past feels he or she must reveal for the "good" of the main protagonists. The trauma, even tragedy, that results makes one deliberate the function of truth in human communication.

22.   (D)

Sometimes the term is Naturalistic, but both terms mean a drama that cuts away the "Fourth Wall" and allows the reader to see into a sitting room, a bar, a "real-life" situation. Answers (A) and (B) are too broad; (C) and (E) too specialized: the drama that flourished in the late 50's – early 60's, mainly in England.

23.   (B)

If you do not recognize E.M. Forster's comment on Defoe's Moll Flanders, eliminate by what you do recognize: James Joyce's character is Molly and not a pick-pocket; George Eliot's heroine is Maggie not Mollie; Fielding's promiscuous village lass is Tom Jones's Moll, never shown picking pockets; Henry James' heroine is Milly.

24.   (D)

A famous criticism from *Aspects of the Novel*, well worth studying, together with Forster's comments on story, plot ("The King died" is a story... "The Queen then died of grief" is a plot) and time structure. He divides famous literary characters into "flat and round" and shows how they function within their particular novel structure.

25.   (B)

If you do not know E.M. Forster as a writer cum critic, eliminate the others: (A) Kingsley Amis writes mainly Science Fiction Criticism; (C) John Gardner concentrated on the morality of fiction. (D) and (E) Virginia Woolf and Henry James, respectively, wrote more on theme and the esoteric value of the novel as Art.

26.   (D)

The Fourth Book of *Gulliver's Travels* describes the Houyhnhnms, the horses who have cancelled all feeling from their lives in favor of Reason, fighting against the Yahoos, feeling carried to the other extreme! Eliminate the others through style – – all too modern for the sentence structure and high seriousness demonstrated here.

27.   (E)

Gulliver's Travels is famous for tricking readers into thinking it is all of these options. It is a travel book – – it satirizes travel accounts well loved in the 18th Century. It describes other societies which appear to be utopias but then are proved not, through satire. The animals would suggest a fable but the satire is stronger than the moral weight fables carry.

28.   (E)

If you do not know the fourth Book, eliminate through what you do know: (A) and (C) the Liliputians and the Brobdingnagians from the same work but with different philosophies from the Houyhnhnms, (B) Vonnegut's little plumbers' friends view death stoically but not so coldly, (D) Orwell's pigs run *Animal Farm* but are more like the Yahoos.

29.   (C)

If you have identified Swift's work correctly, fit him into the correct Age of Reason – the Augustan Age. For (D) and (E) think of Modern pieces that describe such societies – – the style would be less controlled, more fragmented in structure and in thought.

30.   (C)

Whether deliberate or not, Donne mocks the Spenserian poetry so popular in his day, especially the addresses to the Sun. If you do not know Donne's poem, see what you recognize in the other possibilities and cancel out the obvious. (B) is a possibility but the poetry has the same liveliness as Shakespeare's – – the mockery would not be effective enough.

31.   (D)

If you do not know the names of certain types of poems, learn to recognize them. (A) an address often to a "lofty" subject, (B) a lament, (C) 14 lines of poetry with set patterns (Petrarchan, Shakespearian) which should be learned, (E) six stanzas of six lines of poetry in a strict pattern.

32.   (A)

Read the poetry carefully and choose through analysis of context. The lovers do not need the sun to make their love wonderful or complete. There is no mention of non-sharing or preferring the night. If you know the poem, think of the last stanza where the poet admits his love is all worlds to him; thus the sun shines everywhere when shining on their bed.

33.   (B)

The key word is "rags" – – a striking image from Metaphysical Poetry where time is referred to as worthless fragments rather than the all important subject Spenser or Marlowe considered it. The lover claims his love is eternal and has no need to be measured by an inconsequential element like time.

34.   (C)

This last sound is strangely moving on an empty stage. It is integral to the play's meaning: the destruction of the cherry orchard means the destruction of the way of life of the characters. If you do not know the play, think of the endings of the others: they all involve people on stage, at the very end, giving meaningful speeches before the curtain falls.

35.   (B)

If you do not recognize Sophocles' play, analyze through context. "Oracles" and "prophecy" narrow the choice to (D), (E), (B). The sybil would have no need of other prophecies to save themselves. Do the characters in (C) & (D) refer to prophecies or a city or a dead king? Recognize them as Shakespeare's characters and the style is not correct.

36.   (C)

If you have established the speaker as Oedipus (and discounted the Shakespeare characters) think of the Sophocles story: the "dead king" is his father whom he killed, thus fulfilling the prophecy at his birth. King Priam was King of the Greeks dealing with the "Helen Problem." Creon was Jocasta's brother who becomes king after Oedipus blinds himself.

37.   (C)

As Teiresias prophesies, Oedipus wanders in darkness. After learning that he has killed his father and had children by his mother, Oedipus blinds himself with a brooch. Jocasta hangs herself.

38.   (D)

The two key words are "modern" and of course "Sarah" – John Fowles' mysterious heroine. Eliminate the Dickens novel then because of the "modern," and the others because of the names of the heroines or lack of heroines. Pynchon's *V* has a number of women's names – – Rachel, Esther, Victoria, but no Sarah.

39.   (A)

If you do not recognize the Bible passage, eliminate the others through style and content particularly (C) and (D) which would be more poetic, dealing with specific subjects. (E) is a dialogue and is much clearer in its expression, without the technique of paradox. Isaiah also has its own content and distinctive style.

40.   (C)

This is one of Crane's most famous passages which reflects his realistic world view. If you do not know Crane, look carefully at the harshness of the middle sentence, with the hyphenated adjectives. The word "licc" comes across very bitterly. Through context, eliminate the other possibilities as too gentle and trivial.

41.   (A)

If you do not know the word through Chaucer and Shakespeare studies, eliminate the others through the context. The bitter tone must accompany an equally bitter noun. Think of Chaucer's tale of Chanticleer, and the word carries connotations of both foolishness and arrogance. The other possibilities do not capture the almost sneering tone of the last sentence.

42.   (C)

Thomas Hardy does have a passage similar to this where Tess and a companion toil like insects across a field, but here the sentence structure is too short and cryptic for Hardy. (B) and (D), Vonnegut and Pynchon, would be much lighter and more humorous. The opposite would be true for (A); Camus' tone and style are darker than Crane's.

43.   (C)

Anecdote of a Jar by Wallace Stevens is well known for the central position of an inconsequential object. He does the same for blackbirds but not just one. (B) Death and (E) Nature are too general. William Carlos Williams wrote a poem about plums, but again, not just one, and not with such an important status in the poem.

44.   (D)

  The key words are "exile" and the name Rieux. If you have read *The Plague* by Albert Camus you will recall the exile was caused by bubonic plague. Rieux is the doctor who survives the epidemic and learns about existence in the process. If you are unfamiliar with the work, think of other works that deal with periods of exile and what causes them, which will limit your choice.

45.   (C)

  Again if you know Camus, the philosophy will follow naturally. Both *The Plague* and *The Stranger* show men battling the problems of existence. From the context of the passage, gather the idea that the character is deeply meditating on the notion of life's meaning and the possibility of hope, and this should lead you to eliminate the other negative choices.

46.   (D)

  This is the most famous criticism of Metaphysical poetry such as that of Donne (the pair of compasses illustrates the point). If you do not know the author, eliminate by thinking of the types of poetry listed, none of which have particularly "violent" images. Do not be confused by Jonson/Johnson—the former wrote at approximately the same time as Donne—but does not comment on religious poetry.

47.   (E)

  Percy Lubbock's *Craft of Fiction* is an important piece of criticism still. He deals with the "big" novels such as *Middlemarch*, but here the context gives the answer: youth and age, generation to generation. Analyze the other works and realize that only *War and Peace* has this sweep of time — - the others lock into one generation.

48.   (A)

Oscar Wilde's plays are famous for this type of comedy. If you do not know the term or the type of play or novel think of the choices. (B) is too specific. (C) could be applied to many works. (D) is a possibility but again could be applied to most comedies, as (E) could be applied to many novels. Novels of Jane Austen and E.M. Forster perfectly define the term.

49.   (E)

Frost's famous poem outlines his neighbor's efforts to keep a wall between them. Frost's image captures the poet as a genial, nature loving, integral-to-nature-man, as "fertile" and adaptable as an apple tree. The neighbor is as trenchant, solid and unchanging as the pine tree. He insists on rebuilding the wall between them.

50.   (D)

Gerard Manley Hopkins' poetry is easily recognizable for its "sprung rhythm," a counterpoint to the normal English rhythm. If you do not recognize the title, go back to the poetry -- the second line should reveal the difference from the usual in poetry, and indeed from the example in 51.

51.   (B)

Ecclesiastes lends itself into being adapted to various poems and songs because of its rhythms and paradoxes. *Ode to Autumn* and *Fern Hill* are equally as rhythmic but without the same resonance of meaning – one dealing with death of a season, the other the death of youth.

52.   (A)

If you do not know this climactic scene in Faulkner's short story, eliminate the others: Chopin's Mrs. Mallard comes down from her room to die. Mr. Rochester opens Bertha Rochester's cell to show Jane Eyre and the wedding guests the "bride" he is forced to live with; Miss Haversham's whole house is a tomb; Isabel Archer looks into the tiny room that symbolizes her husband's world.

53.   (B)

If you do not recognize Hemingway's *Hills like White Elephants*, analyze the passage carefully: what is it the male thinks is so easy and the female is so reluctant to discuss? – – not simply (A) or (D). There is accusation and repetition but they are not the main point of the discussion.

54.   (C)

Simply from context, the word sums up the relationship gathered from the desultory conversation, a relationship without love, commitment or understanding between the man and the woman. When an author as sparse in description as Hemingway includes a detail such as this, you know it is there for a specific reason.

55.   (D)

Two key elements help here: the amount of labels on the luggage and the point of the <u>nights</u> spent together, not days or vacations or weeks, but specifically nights. The word "nights" suggests a purely physical relationship which can be gathered from the conversation also, and the labels suggest the restlessness of a couple constantly packing bags and moving on.

56.   (B)

You may recongize the dry Hemingway style in the dialogue between male and female. Crane's *Blue Hotel* has little dialogue between men and women. *Catch 22's* style is totally different. *Down and Out* has narrative of travels with few relationships delineated; Frank O'Connor's tale deals with loyalties between men.

57.   (B)

If you do not know the Gothic novel, eliminate through analyzing the other types of novels. None of the other choices has the specific listing of details, particularly the second sentence opening list. Some of the choices may have elements of the Gothic but cannot be correctly called Gothic if lacking the main "ingredients."

58.   (A)

Parodies and burlesques grow out of serious novels, poems or plays. Jane Austen used Udolpho in her novel (the two "heroines" and "hero" discuss the plot) to poke fun at the type and show the nature of real evil in the world. The other choices here have elements of the Gothic but none makes a burlesque like Austen's.

59.   (A)

The trick of Swift in his *Modest Proposal* is to convince the reader he is a reasonable man who has done research into the problem of the poor. The other suggestions are not relevant to this passage -- if you know the whole tract leave it at a distance to analyze this particular piece of information.

60.   (C)

If you know the whole document, you will know the exact proposal for the starving Irish under consideration. If not, read the passage carefully to see in which direction the writer is heading. (A), (D) and (E) would be financially crippling in the implementation, and imagine the collection time for suggestion (B)!

61.   (B)
Swift is famous for his satirical writing, especially this piece which original readers took very seriously, outraged at the suggestion of eating babies. The other suggestions can be eliminated by referring again to context: certainly not realistic, too harsh for irony, too serious and calm for Modernism, and certainly too unpleasant for hedonism.

62.   (C)
This is a good test if you know the author, and, more importantly, can place him/her in the correct era. Think of how early (A), (B) and (E) were writing, and how much later and in a much softer style is Henry James. Think of works by Fielding in a similar vein, poking fun at the Establishment-Mock-Heroic, yet with serious consideration of the plight of the poor.

63.   (D)
In your reading be very aware of opening and closing lines in whatever genre. Kafka's famous opener from *Metamorphosis* sets symbol and theme for the entire work. All the other possibilities involve striking writers, but Genet and Ionesco are primarily play-wrights, and Sartre and Tolstoy have less dramatic starting points.

64.   (E)
Browning perfected the technique of the Dramatic Monologue, a poem in which a speaker addresses a silent listener – – not to be confused with the soliloquy in which the speaker addresses thin air, a thinking-aloud process. If you are not familiar with the form, eliminate through what you recognize; none of the others applies.

65.   (C)

If you do not know the poem *My Last Duchess* and the situation (showing a portrait of the dead Duchess to an ambassador for the next duchess!), catch the clue in the lines 3–4 about the paint and the painter and the subject of the painting, not a landscape, designs or a book, but a portrait of the lady under discussion. Later the two men look at the sea horse sculpture.

66.   (A)

Again read closely and analyze through tone. What is the Duke saying about the lady? He disliked her simply because she enjoyed simple earthly pleasures which, he suggests, he does not. His tone is not weak, certainly, nor is it angry; it is not approving nor is it unreasonable; there is an element of both pride and egoism.

67.   (B)

A good Dramatic Monologue reveals as much about the subject as the speaker. The lady is revealed as sweet and pleasure loving — — enjoying the simpler things of life. There is no hint here, or in the rest of the poem that she is flirtatious, licentious, avaricious or interested in rank — — yet her husband has her executed, as revealed later in the poem.

68.   (D)

Othello has just listened to Iago's hints about Desdemona's infidelity, and his pleas to "Beware jealousy!" Pay close attention to Shakespearian names which can sound similar: (A) is the courtier accused of sleeping with Desdemona; (B) Bassanio from *The Merchant of Venice*; (C) Mercutio from *Romeo and Juliet*; and (E) Horatio from *Hamlet*.

69. (C)

Most Shakespeare editions give a detailed explanation of this metaphor which would need no explanation for the Elizabethans: a haggard is a partly trained hawk gone wild. The jesses are straps which attach the hawk to the trainer's wrist. If Desdemona is unfaithful, like a hawk gone wild, then Othello will release her and allow her freedom.

70. (B)

Horns were supposedly the sign of a man whose wife was unfaithful. Othello is beginning to believe Iago's lies about Desdemona's adultery; he is being cuckolded. Later when she wishes to bind Othello's head for a headache, he insists the handkerchief (the handkerchief which is so vital to the plot) is too small, i.e. the horns are beginning to grow!

71. (B)

If you are not familiar with the word, think of the religious phrase the "quick and dead" – – the living and the dead. In context, derive the meaning: great ones are susceptible to adulterous affairs – – they are as inevitable as death – – as soon as they are born. Thus Othello makes the contrast between the living and the dead.

72. (D)

Kate Chopin is well known for her short stories. Her main novel, *The Awakening* is less favored but well worth reading for its similar theme to *Madame Bovary* but with more sympathy for the heroine. A feminist novel written in the late 1800's. . . if you do not know the novel think of the heroines of the authors listed here. None of them relates to Flaubert's character.

73.   (A)

Shaw's play parodies the Greek concept of heroism in battle and gallantry to women. The so-called hero Sergius is brave in battle but weak in life. The so-called coward Bluntchi runs away from battle but is morally brave. Think of the first lines of the epics listed and eliminate those whose contexts do not fit Shaw's title.

74.   (C)

In *Shooting an Elephant*, Orwell crystallizes all the conflicts and fears involved in colonialism. The other writers listed write on colonialism, but none was so directly and personally involved as Orwell, nor expresses himself with such feeling. Orwell served as a policeman in Burma.

75.   (B)

If you know the passage and Orwell's life, the answer is clear. If not, read the passage for "clues." "Dominion in the East" rules out (C), (D) and (E) (the rifle shows the era for the latter). The yellow faces and the white man's uneasiness rules out India — — very little of the literature in this age shows white men uneasy with their roles in India.

76.   (E)

Again, read the passage closely. Hollowness is mentioned and a sea of faces but not as metaphors. There is no mention of a journey. Colonialism is the theme. He does refer to "leading actor of the piece" and later "an absurd puppet" — — terms to do with the stage.

77.   (D)

The subject continues from the word "smile" in line 4, "We smile with torn and bleeding hearts and we <u>mouth</u> with myriad subtleties." So the synonym should involve a verb of speech, thus eliminating (A) and (B). The tone of the stanza is too gentle for (C). Laugh is too close to smile in context, which leaves the simple verb "speak."

78.   (A)

This perhaps seems too simple, but the whole poem is based on a simple song-like structure. Think of the usual English syntax: "We smile, but O, Great Christ, our cries <u>arise</u> from tortured souls <u>to thee</u>." None of the other possibilities listed appear in the poem. If possible read aloud and the inversion becomes very clear.

79.   (E)

Again, reading aloud cancels out (A), (B) and (C) – – there is little effect of hostility or anger. The poet is not praising God for His blessings; rather he is lamenting the bitter sadness of life which human beings hide behind a smiling mask. The use of commas in line 10 accentuates the idea of a heart crying out in distress.

80.   (C)

The Medieval writers or singers frequently names their characters for the vices or virtues they displayed, so that the simple country folk watching a play would identify a character immediately. Later this devise became more sophisticated. Thus Everyman represents every human being. John Bunyon's Christian, in *Pilgrim's Progress*, is every Christian.

81.   (C)

The three men have 2 of 3 aspects in common – – Billy Pilgrim is getting old, in fact ages terribly in the war. Goodman Brown is young still. They are all working class in the sense that they have to work for a living. Although the other two may wish they were dead, only Willy Loman kills himself.

82.   (C)

This is a famous statement on the novel in *The Common Reader* by Virginia Woolf who recommends that novels not be straight, linear, A to B chronologies, but reflect the randomness of life's experience.

Woolf experimented in Stream of Consciousness writing which shows not fragmentation but life-like accounts of how life is passed in the brain.

83.   (D)

If you do not know Woolf's criticism, she is well worth reading. Woolf deals with large concepts in a readable fashion. Think of the critics here you do know: Leavis, Trilling and Lubbock, the main names in criticism of the novel, tend to write on specific works with attention to the text. Sartre deals mainly with time and Existentialism.

84.   (A)

Henry Fielding pokes fun at society in the Age of Reason (or the Augustan Age named after Augustus who brought culture to his age), for worshipping all aspects of Greek life. The "battle," not between great Greek heroes but a simple village girl and her neighbors, bears allusions to Venus and Mars which should provide clues for your answer.

85.   (E)

Do not be misled by "Goody Brown," a nickname for a good wife, nor get caught up by the Heroic/Epic style and choose Hercules or Achilles. Distinguish between Fielding's other mock-heroic novel, *Joseph Andrews*, which not only mocked the epic, but also Richardson's *Pamela*, whose heroine Fielding claimed as Joseph Andrew's sister!

86.   (D)

The poet is parodying Wordsworth's "It is a beauteous evening," written after experiencing a transcendental moment with his daughter. Here the poet "lowers the tone" as the wife watches the husband with a hang-over. You may recognize the original poem for the parody but not the poet. Think of famous poems by the other poets listed and eliminate.

87.   (D)

Wordsworth's poem particularly extolls the innocence of his child as they walk together in the twilight, the favorite time for the Romantics. The relationship is tender, holy, the emotions linked to the tranquility of the evening – – in direct contrast to the relationship and the time of day parodied in the modern version.

88.   (E)

All the writers listed were opposed to revolution – – Gandhi even acknowledging a debt to Thoreau, but Wordsworth and Burke particularly wrote about the French Revolution. Wordsworth does not neglect to ponder the causes. Burke was so horrified at the way the Revolution was conducted that he turned away from analyzing its roots.

89.   (D)

The famous opening lines of Jonson's play, spoken by Volpone himself, make a sacriligious parody of the prayer to God at the opening of a new day. If you are not familiar with the play, analyze the style and tone of the other possibilities, all to do with money or possessions. Distinguish the Shakespearian style from the Jonsonian.

90.   (B)

Do not be confused with Salonio's speech (C) where Antonio's debt to Shylock is directly mentioned. In *The Merchant of Venice*, Shylock's speeches are frequently in the normal speech patterns of conversation, not in blank verse or rhyme. Salonio, as a friend of the rich merchant Antonio, maintains the speech patterns of the upper-class.

91.   (E)

Again, to establish a character of the lower class, Shakespeare gives Falstaff the speech patterns of prose, unlike Hotspur's speech (A).

Notice when Prince Hal speaks to Falstaff he adopts the lower class speech. When he talks to his peers he reverts to blank verse. In this speech Falstaff begins the wish-process for a change of identity.

92.   (C)

For a number of poets, Byzantium embodies the Golden Age, civilization and richness. Yeats elaborated one stage further and endowed it with a holiness which, as the comment suggests, makes for a transfiguration of the body's spirituality and physicality. Think of the options and poems associated with them – Byzantium is the only choice.

93.   (D)

If you do not recognize the speech patterns of Huck Finn, start eliminating through the names you do know: (A) David Copperfield's tone and style of speech are much more elevated as Strether's is (E) and he is not the narrator, nor are Carrie and Maggie, (B) and (C), whose speech patterns are as colloquial but not as harsh.

94.   (E)

If you recognize the passage, you will recognize the Grangerford house. On the surface the family is orderly and civilized, yet underneath the surface lies a hypocrisy: the morbidity of the dead young girl obsessed with death when alive, the feuding with the Shepherdsons for thirty years. They are not what they seem, just like the fake fruit.

95.   (B)

Look closely at the titles of the books: The Bible, *Pilgrim's Progress,* "Friendship's Offering," and the fact they are piled up exactly, i.e. never read! Even if you do not know the family and their feuding, the titles suggest an irony, and the other possibilities can be eliminated in context.

96.   (D)

   As you study T.S. Eliot's poetry, have a clear idea of his debt to Baudelaire specifically and the French Symbolists in general. He was an Anglophile, but do not be confused over his love for a country and his debt for his inspiration and style. He refers to ancient civilizations such as (C) and (E) but the symbolism is distinctly French-derived.

97.   (B)

   Frequently Eliot's symbolism can be detected only in the poem seen as an integral whole. In *Prufrock* the allusions to characters from the past, characters such as Lazarus and John the Baptist and here, Hamlet, become central symbols for the poem. Do not be confused with (C) from *The Dry Salvages* which personifies the river as a god.

98.   (E)

   Little Gidding shows the poet wrestling with words and meaning and returning exactly where he began, to begin all over again, a process the poet saw as part of the life cycle of man. The entire opening movement of the poem builds upon poetic paradox: "We die with the dying: We are born with the dead."

99.   (D)

   Eliot writes of worlds in despair, fragmented, ruined – – the imagery for such worlds demands delving into the sub-conscious, the night-world of dreams and nightmares. Often the probing produces surrealistic images of madness, debris, waste and, of course, drought, as in *The Waste Land*. Here the nightmare image prevails.

100.   (D)

   Nelly Dean tells Lockwood how she found Heathcliff and tended to his corpse which seemd to exult in death. If you do not know Emily Bronte's *Wuthering Heights*, think of death secenes you do know:

eliminate (A) and (B): Little Nell and Maggie Tulliver die, not their narrators. Nick Carraway finds Gatsby's body but does not tend the corpse.

101. (E)
Lord Byron's poems mean a great deal to the protagonist, Little Cloud. Trapped in a non-Romantic setting, he yearns for the profound loves and exotic adventures of Byron. If you do not know the poetry excerpt in Joyce's short story, eliminate (A), (C), and (D) through style, then try to recall a Wordsworth poem addressed to Margaret.

102. (D)
Again if you do not know the piece, eliminate through style. (A) is a possibility considering D.H. Lawrence's short stories but not this particular novel. (B) and (C) are too modern for the style depicted here, and Hardy's style too distinct to be confused with Joyce. Do not neglect Joyce's short stories which are well worth studying.

103. (E)
Lord Chesterfield wrote letters to his son, letters which seem outrageous in some parts to modern readers, but give an interesting insight into the lifestyles of the age. His world was Richardson's and Fielding's who fictionalize the time's mores. Addison and Chesterton developed the essay and epistolary art.

104. (D)
Do not neglect minor figures in your Shakespeare studies. Polonius is famous not only for his advice to Laertes about borrowing and women, but also to Ophelia about how to handle men. His attitudes reflect the hypocrisy, the "rottenness" in the State of Denmark.

105.　(C)

Pandarus features slightly in *The Iliad*, but Chaucer develops the character into a scoundrel to whom readers react differently. He does "procure" Criseyde for Troilus but also brings humor and fun to the story, querying whether Troilus is a man or a mouse in his virginal attitude to women.

106.　(C)

There is an element of all these possibilities in the definition but the main point of a pander's role is the sexual dimension. You can pander to someone's wants and desires by giving in too easily, but the true role involves procuring the sexual favors of one human being for another.

107.　(E)

Virgil is conducting Dante to Hell, Canto III, *Inferno*, lines 76–81. If you do not know Dante then eliminate through style: the Bible and *Paradise Lost* would be in more elevated language. Homer never engages in conversation with Odysseus. This passage establishes the relationship between Master and Disciple, something none of the other works develop.

108.　(A)

Derive the meaning from the reading. The two are obviously about to cross a river even if you do not know the name of the river into Hell. The word "shore" is your clue. The active verb (E) is too energetic for the tone of the passage. The others do not capture the idea of getting out of a boat and putting one's feet on dry land.

109.　(D)

If you do not know Dante or the mythical terms for the journey to Hell, eliminate through context: the words "sorrowful shore" eliminate (A) and (E). As Virgil is taking Dante, neither a soldier nor a child, eliminate (B) and (C). The passage suggests that we all have the potential to cross the river into Hell.

110. (E)

Again if you do not know the mythology, eliminate from names you may recognize through other readings. (A) and (D) are the sea monsters from *The Odyssey*. Minos, not to be confused with the minotaur, is the Judge in Hell. Medusa is the monster with the hair of serpents that break off and multiply.

111. (B)

The key to understanding the passage are the words "abashed" and "unmeet," and deriving from the context the relationship between Master and Disciple, the Leader and the Led. The paraphrase should capture the shame and the humility on the part of the narrator. Eliminate the options that suggest anger on the narrator's part.

112. (B)

Death scenes are very important in novels and plays. These last words from Kurtz in *Heart of Darkness* are perhaps the most well known as they reveal the dying man's whole personality. (A) is from the same novel. Dr. Rieux in *The Plague* has too many victims for him to recall last words. (D) and (E) come close to death but do not narrate last words.

113. (D)

Kurtz's last words reveal the innate evil of the man and the Hell which is receiving him. (A) is Balzac's Old Goriot thinking of his daughters to the end. (B) Dickens's Magwitch from *Great Expectations*, (C) Osvald from Ibsen's *Ghosts* before sinking into insanity, and (E) Flory to the dog he shoots before killing himself, in Orwell's *Burmese Days*.

114.   (D)

You need to know the plot for the relationship between the fiancee and Kurtz. Marlow cannot reveal to a good, innocent woman the horrifying evil of the man she loved. The man's last words would instantly reveal that Kurtz was not thinking of her or any human thing at that moment, but slipping into evil as horrifying as that which he had perpetrated on earth.

115.   (A)

Do not neglect the simplest of stories from the Bible – – the Parables, and from folklore – – the Fables. This parable does raise some interesting psychological points – especially the role of the older son – the stalwart believer who never deviates from love of God but who sees sinners more feted than he is.

116.   (C)

The Parable of the Prodigal Son illustrates one of the central premises of Christianity: that sinners will be forgiven and welcomed back, more loved than before, into God's fold. If you do not know the parable, some of the other possibilities could be considered but there is always a deeper meaning to the seemingly simple stories.

117.   (A)

The poem is well known among Yeats'work. If you do not know it, analyze the style of the verse and contrast it with the other poets listed. (B) George Herbert was a religious poet in Donne's era. The rest are "Nature Poets" but write about nature in a more philosophical manner, concentrating on the fate and patterns of human life.

118.   (E)

A favourite theme of Yeats, and the Romantic poets, Coleridge and Wordsworth, was the constancy of nature. The birds come back each year as if they were the same birds. Trees seem to die each year but come back, as if resurrected, in the Spring, a feat which man cannot achieve.

119.   (B)

There are clues in the stanzas even if you do not know the poem: peacocks and doves do not "paddle in the cold/Companionable streams;" ducks and geese seem infinitely less ethereal than swans, and think of the well-known poem of Yeats, *Leda and the Swan,* a bird of interest to him.

120.   (C)

Vladimir and Estragon feature in the play *Waiting for Godot,* frequently performed these days and well worth reading. The other characters are also from Beckett's works with the exception of Biff and Happy, who sound like Beckett people but in fact are Arthur Miller's from *Death of a Salesman.*

121.   (D)

If you know the play, be careful distinguishing between (B) and (D). The characters do not listen to each other, which is one of Beckett's main points about the lack of human communication in the modern age. Eliminate (A) because the boredom is not apparent here. Eliminate (E) as the feeling is strong that they know each other well and can relax with one another.

122.   (C)

In the preface to *The Deerslayer,* Fenimore Cooper sets the story behind the strange attraction of Judith for his hero. If you do not know the story, analyze the other heroes and "plug into" the relationship described. (A), (B) and (D) do not fit the description of the hero. (E) begins well but no Judith exists in the story.

123. (C)

Although he lived for a shorter span than Cooper, Edgar Allen Poe (1809–1849) writes at approximately the same time. Brockden Brown, often considered the first American novelist, was much earlier as were Richardson and Fielding in England. (E) Mark Twain comes later. While studying specific authors be aware of their time and contemporaries.

124. (A)

Do not confuse Goldsmith's Marlow with Conrad's – – different genres and different literary periods. *She Stoops to Conquer* is a Restoration Comedy, frequently performed and very amusing to read. Analyze the other choices: (B) is Catherine's name from *Wuthering Heights*. (C) and (D), Booby and Andrews, are from *Joseph Andrews* and, (E) is Teazle is from *The Rivals*.

125. (D)

A late play in the Restoration period, *She Stoops to Conquer* has softened some of the outright farce of the true Restoration play, like a Congreve, or a Wycherley play. There is more fun in Goldsmith and Sheridan and less cruelty than in the earlier plays, but the period is still considered Restoration.

126. (C)

Ezra Pound's explanations of Modern Poetry and his work within the movement are worth studying. A number of writers including T.S. Eliot owe debts to him not only for influence but also for personal friendship and help in publishing. The other poets/critics listed rarely express themselves quite so clearly or so emphatically.

127.   (B)

Much of Pound's writing is complex and difficult to grasp on first reading because of the internalized symbolism as in T.S. Eliot's case. However, often as in this excerpt, a cryptic tone comes across which reflects the man's approach to life: a modern take-me-for-what-I-am-attitude which antagonized even his friends.

128.   (C)

Do not confuse with Amy Lowell's work (E) who was influenced by Pound and the French symbolists; her internalizing of images can make for difficult reading. Robert Lowell is more straightforward in the imagery and verse patterns. The picture here of the "hill-skull" and the graveyard extending the metaphor is typical of Lowell, along with his love and death images.

129.   (A)

MacLeish deals with similar subjects as Pound's, especially in thinking about time and its complexity. However, in the poetry itself MacLeish's verse patterns are less "modern." MacLeish tends to favor old rhyme schemes playing variations upon old patterns in a much more controlled and open way than Pound and his followers tended to do.

130.   (D)

The Sheridan play stands out from the others which are all early Restoration plays. Sheridan places more symbolic weight on his characters' names. His famous Mrs. Malaprop gave birth to the word "malapropism." Like Goldsmith's, Sheridan's plays tone down the cruelty of the early plays and become semi-realistic comedies.

131.   (C)

The Humours developed from the Morality Plays where the characters took on the attributes of their names, often associated with sins: Sloth, Gluttony, etc. Ben Jonson developed the technique for attributes of personality — — Sheridan polished it so that without seeing the play we know that Lady Sneerwell will be a snob and Snake not to be trusted.

132.   (D)

Dryden's criticism is frequently neglected but he does have interesting insights, and writes in clear, succinct prose. Eliminate the obvious from (A), (B) and (C), especially the latter where he would hardly praise his own work so lavishly, and think of the range and diversity in Chaucer's tales versus Shakespeare's history plays.

133.   (A)

If you do not know Biblical names, ponder the "he" talking to Hawthorne. Eliminate Isaiah and Job as non-tragic figures not involved with someone who knew Hawthorne. Lucifer in Milton's hands became a tragic figure, but Milton lived centuries before Hawthorne. Ishmael was not an Old Testament ruler, which leaves Melville's tragic hero, Ahab.

134.   (C)

Alexander Pope took the Heroic Couplet to new heights, splitting the lines at the caesura, developing a 2 by 5 stress rather than the plodding iambic or octosyllabic line. If you do not know the poem or the poet's technique, cancel out the obvious (A) and (D) and distinguish between the different types of couplets.

135.   (D)

The key word here is in fact omitted but in context mentally add the verb "filled." Your vocabulary should include the word lampoon, especially if you have studied this era when the lampoon was a very popular means of attacking one's enemy.

136.   (C)

(A) and (B) are possibilities but from the context analyze why the "Fair Ones" become ill in the first place. Capture the tone of the poetry and the mockery behind it. There were plenty of reasons for women to fall ill in Pope's day but in this case, the advent of a new nightdress that they could show off in their rooms provoked diseases.

137.   (E)

Again your working vocabulary should help you but the meaning can be gauged from the stanzas. If possible read aloud and fit each word into the sentence. (C) is a possibility but why use two words that mean the same? (D) suggests movement with Affectation is not demonstrating in Pope's mock heroic presentation of emblems.

138.   (C)

The last lines provide the clue if you do not know the whole poem which was written to ridicule two families quarrelling over a trivial incident: the theft of a lock of hair. Pope in *The Rape of the Lock* builds the incident into a ridiculous Epic, mocking the epic traditions and more importantly, the foolishness of society around him.

139.   (E)

C.S. Lewis' book *The Allegory of Love* sets out clearly and interestingly the type of love enjoyed by the knights of the Middle Ages. If you do not know the work it is worth studying, but here think of examples such as *Le Roman de La Rose* and *Sir Gawain and the Green Knight* and the type of love practiced in these poems.

140.   (A)

Lewis describes how the tradition grew out of the Troubador poetry in the eleventh century in Languedoc. He then shows the continuity from the Provencal love song through the love poetry of the Middle Ages, through Petrarch to the modern day. Eliminate (B) and (C) whose early poetry tells of war not love, and (D) and (E) who develop song rather than poetry.

141. (A)
The original description reveals some of the elements of the Courtly love tradition if you are unfamiliar with it. Again think of the poetry of the time that reflects the love or legends such as the love between Guinevere and Lancelot. The husband is not as important as other rivals, male humility is stressed, and sexuality is down-played "off-stage."

142. (E)
The key is to look carefully at the name and its connotations. There is a harshness but the "grinding" down sound gives a motion also. There is a notion of wearing down, reducing, and in the end the passage suggests a nonsense process behind the name. If you know the novel *Hard Times* then the philosophy of the speaker adds to the passage.

143. (A)
If you recognize Dickens as the author you will know his reputation for purely descriptive writing: adjective piled upon adjective in a balanced structure. There is no allegorical writing here. Metaphorical writing exists, but that term does not encompass the language in use, nor does symbolic, although symbols are at work. Prosodic refers to a particular type of verse – not in use here.

144. (A)
The speaker's hair is likened to a plantation of firs but the author does not use the words "like" or "as" – the figure of speech is a metaphor. However, Dickens then follows the notion with the idea of the speaker's head looking like the crust of a plum pie – a simile. Know the terms for figures of speech for poetry as well as prose.

145.   (D)

Hard Times is a lesser known Dickens novel instructive in its criticism of England's educational system. You might surmise from the description that the author is Charles Dickens. If you are not aware of his unfinished novel *The Mystery of Edwin Drood*, analyze those you know: (A) Samuel Butler, (B) Turgenev, (C) Charlotte Bronte and (E) George Eliot, and recall if this passage derives from these.

146.   (B)

You should recognize Ibsen's directions for *A Doll's House*. Christmas plays an integral part in the play – – the jollity of the season, the children's gifts and laughter all contrast with the internal trauma Nora experiences. If you do not know the play think of the alternative choices, none of which includes Christmas.

147.   (C)

THE WOMAN plays an important part in the climax of the play *Death of a Salesman* when Willy Loman relives the scene of Biff finding out about his father's affair – – the shock that changes the father/son relationship. Again, if the play is unfamiliar, analyze the alternatives – – the stage directions in Arthur Miller's play are unique in their use of the past.

148.   (E)

Shaw is renowned for the fully detailed stage directions which add to the realism of the plays. You may recognize the Bulgarian setting for *Arms and the Man*. If not, the pure wealth of detail should lead you to think of Shaw. In your study of drama take careful note of the different style of stage directions.

149. (D)

This may puzzle you if you do not know Ionesco's play *The Lesson*, the key for which is the detail, "the office of the old professor." The directions are totally straight; the play itself becomes more and more absurd until the professor kills the student and the maid lets in another victim. Do not be confused with (A), the dark drama of Strindberg's *The Father*.

150. (B)

The grammar would suggest a lower class character, a servant perhaps like (A) Joseph or a rough diamond squire like (C) Mr. Western. However, the names Estella and Matthew Pocket should reveal *Great Expectations*. If you do not know the book, think of the choices, none of which contain an Estella nor Matthew Pocket.

151. (D)

Joe Gargery is a veritable Mr. Malaprop. The word meant is very similar in sound to "coddleshell" – a codicil (D) not a cockleshell (A). Read the passage closely and eliminate why he should be talking about (A) in the context of a will or why shell-pink paper would be attached to an official document. Your working vocabulary should sift the rest.

152. (E)

If you know Wilfred Owen's famous World War I poem, *Dulce et Decorum*, the answer is straightforward. If not, eliminate the drownings (A) and (D), because the man is thrown onto the wagon still alive and choking. He would have burned to death after choking in the Dresden fire-storm, and been blown to pieces after a napalm bomb attack.

153.   (B)

The participle "guttering" is interesting with the connotation of a candle guttering, about to go out, and the gutteral sound the man makes as his lungs disintegrate. The adjective "smothering" describing dream takes on another dimension as one thinks of the dying man also smothering – the association is passed from the dream to the dreamer.

154.   (B)

Review terms for poetic techniques, especially when they sound alike as (A) and (B) do. Assonance is the repetition of the vowel sounds; alliteration repats the consonants as in watch white writhing. (C) Onomatopoeia is the sound of the action i.e. "oozing," (D) diction is the broad term for the choice and use of words and (E) paradox sets up a shocking contrast that may be true.

155.   (E)

Enjambment means the flow or continuation of the sentence from one line of poetry into the next, in rhyme, blank verse or in couplets. This poem has a number of lines that use this technique to capture the effect of the speaking voice talking at a high speed with intense emotion.

156.   (C)

Again, analyze the use of technique. (C) means the action is captured in the sound – – one can hear the man dying. The poem is built on sensory images rather than on symbolism, (A). Oxymoron involves incongruous terms (B). Feminine rhyme has the final syllable unstressed. Slant rhyme is an imperfect rhyme, e.g., slow/law.

157. (A)

The poet captures an anti-war bitterness and an irony when he considers how the tradition has been handed down to children, a belief that it is sweet and glorious to die for one's country. The First World War soldiers found death in the trenches sickening and horrifying. The other possibilities are too harsh for the tone.

158. (A)

Post Modernism is becoming more widely understood, both as a means of literature and criticism, since the work of such writers cum critics as David Lodge simplifies the jargon and explains the philosophies of early proponents such as Jacques Derrida. The other choices have elements of Post Modernism, but often one element counteracts another as in (B) Humor.

159. (D)

Mill wrote this after a period of illness when he came to realize that his childhood education (learning Greek at the age of three) repressed all feeling; the over-developed mind had not produced a totally round, integrated human being. He turns now to the appreciation of beauty and art. His writings are neglected but are useful for showing the shift from reason to imagination.

160. (B)

Hellenism became part of Matthew Arnold's world-view and produced a very important essay. Look at Arnold's essays as well as his poetry for excellent insights into the thinking of the nineteenth century, especially in regard to education and England's relationship with America.

161.   (A)

Read Coleridge's *Biographia Literaria* for his thoughts on the mind and imagination. Like Mill, Coleridge sees magic, almost mystical healing powers in the imagination. Recognize work by Coleridge in this field by the key words Imagination and Fancy always capitalized. The criticism aids in the understanding of Coleridge's poetry.

162.   (C)

Even if you do not know T.S. Eliot's essays (the most important mentions the "objective correlative" in his criticism on *Hamlet*), you will recognize the calm, balanced tone of the prose. Contrast with (E), the strident almost querulous tone of Carlyle. Key concerns for Eliot are the integrity of the writer, and writing as a state of art.

163.   (A)

Nick Carraway, the most intriguing of narrators, simply relates the dialogue between Gatsby and Daisy. If you do not know *The Great Gatsby*, or recall this particular passage, think of the other narrators listed: (B) and (C) do not involve themselves as narrators as (D) sometimes does. (E), Barth's Giles or George relates stranger dialogues than this.

164.   (D)

It is as if the stopped clock is smashed to pieces as the time between the lovers' meetings is gradually being destroyed. Gatsby and Daisy should have married five years ago; the time between has been wasted time emotionally, if not financially for Gatsby who builds his empire to regain the only woman he has ever loved.

165. (B)

The other man, of course, is Gatsby who has counted the minutes in a classically Romantic way since losing Daisy, and has put his time to "good" use in building a fortune. From the tone of the conversation the other choices can be eliminated, especially (E), Tom Buchanan, who is not mentioned here and indeed knows nothing of the meeting.

166. (B)

If you recognize *The Great Gatsby* and know Scott Fitzgerald's work, this is straightforward. If not, think of the authors of these novels involving time: (A) Djuna Barnes, (C) John Fowles, (D) Anthony Powell, (E) Graham Greene, and eliminate by those you do know.

167. (D)

Even if you do not know the poem, the phrase "darkling plain" should resurrect the association of *Dover Beach* where a love-regret develops into a world-view. Analyze the other titles and decide if any of them have the progression described, or, decide which poet wrote which poem: (A) Wordsworth, (B) Browning, (C) Coleridge, (E) Keats.

168. (D)

If you do not recognize the play from the description, analyze the others for what you do recognize. None of the other involves the characters mentioned here, although all except (E) have only two or three characters. *The Chairs* has only three, but the impression is given of hundreds as the chairs on stage multiply and audience noise grows.

169. (A)

Ionesco deals with the lack of communication he observes between modern human beings. Even if you do not know the play, the description would give you the central point: the old man wishes to pass on what he has learned in ninety-five years of life – the point is there is no message. In Ionesco's view we are all deaf mutes and can no longer communicate.

170.   (C)

The poet meditates on not only the destruction of empires, but on man's status on earth – – the futility of countries building empires or men building statues to themselves because in time all vestiges of man's stay on earth will be hidden, as if by the sands of time. Ozymandias spoke truer than he knew when instructing "Look on my works. . . and despair!"

171.   (C)

The face of the mammoth statue still retains the frown, wrinkled lip and sneer of command of the ruler – – all words that suggest coldness and arrogance. The poet reveals nothing about the sculptor's attitude to his model other than he captured the likeness well. Read the three lines carefully so that you capture the adjectives and the sculptor's role.

172.   (A)

If you do not know the poet, Shelley, go through the choices to analyze which you do know: (B) Coleridge, (C) Keats, (D) Gray, (E) T. S. Eliot. Then go one stage further and think of the range of the poets and whether *Ozymandias* belongs to that poet. This tests whether you can recognize the poet's range. In this case the two poems are in direct contrast.

173.   (E)

If you do not know *A Room With A View*, eliminate from the choices of heroines and chaperones (A) the right heroine, the wrong chaperone – Mrs. Allen is from Austen's *Northanger Abbey*, (B) Caroline Abbott from Forster's *Where Angels Fear to Tread* and Mrs. Moore of *A Passage to India*, (C) from *The Great Gatsby*, (D) Mrs. Fairfax is from *Jane Eyre*.

174.   (C)

You need to know Forster's works for this word, repeated in *A Room With A View* and featured in his novels and short stories. However, recalling the humanism of Forster you would discount the strength of (A) and (E), and the exaggeration of (B) and (D). The author wishes human beings simply "to connect" and "muddle" gets in the way.

175.   (B)

If you do not know the work you might be confused by the choices which all involve war-like passages. However, if you read the passage closely and detect the long Heroic simile you will narrow the choice to (A) and (B). Think then of *The Odyssey's* tales, all much lighter in tone than *The Iliad*, even when death is involved.

176.   (D)

Having established that *The Iliad* is the work, the city is obvious, especially when backed up by the idea of the city under siege, and the Trojans involved. None of the other cities have such a history written in such a way. Tintagel has never been proven as King Arthur's city for example. Carthage is associated with Aeneas and Dido.

177.   (A)

Even without knowledge of this particular text and the name for the Greeks, you will recall the war between Greece and Troy for a hundred years starting with the abduction of Helen by Paris. The others, except perhaps the Romans, do not figure in large eloquent pieces of description such as this nor did they worship Zeus, a clue from the passage itself.

178.   (E)

Again if you are not sure of the battle, analyze the choices: (A) are on the same side, (B) Boadicea, a British heroine, fights the Romans, not one particular hero, (C), Jason lived in the generation prior to Priam, (D) Achilles and Patroklos were dearest friends – the death of the latter restores Achilles to the battle where he cruelly slaughters Hector.

179. (B)

Frequently a Homeric simile will begin describing one aspect and after its lengthy run, end up with a totally different focus. The effect is still striking. Here the first image is of the softness of snow but the last lines contrast that softness with the image of "stones volleyed," "thrown," "flung" and the idea of the noise of the stones as "thunder."

180. (D)

There are elements of each choice that are viable but the main effect of the snow causing a haze over the works of man and bringing all into uniformity universalizes the scene. The armies then could be any armies; the soldiers are all men. Homer's listeners felt, and today's readers feel for humanity in the struggle.

181. (C)

Perhaps the most famous of Joyce's stories captures the same effect at its close. Snow is falling over all of Ireland but the effect is universal. We feel not simply for the protagonists but for humanity. The other choices deal with similar effects of rain or snow but do not move into the realm of universalizing an experience.

182. (D)

The main character is unique in James' work in that she is a child, and the narrative unique in the art of the novel because the events are seen through a child's consciousness. The idea came from a real case where the child became a shuttle-cock between changing sets of parents. If you do not know the novel, analyze those familiar to you – none centers around one child.

183. (A)

Sylvia Plath's *The Mirror* begins with the woman's mirror at home "speaking." In the second stanza there is still a mirror but this time the woman sees her reflection in a lake, another mirror refusing to give an untrue image of the woman. She can destroy that image by agitating the water. You do not need to know the poem to derive the meaning from context.

184.   (A)
Once you have established the metaphor of the lake as mirror and the fact that the woman does not want her real, true image, you will derive the meaning of the "liars," the soft, flattering lights that people use so that they can hide the wrinkles and the sagging flesh of the aging face.

185.   (B)
The mirror refuses, indeed is incapable of, reflecting the young girl who has "gone down" with age in the mirror. It must show the truth, the aging woman with her disappointments and scaling, old wrinkled skin. The other choices are too harsh: (C) and (D), impossible (A), or not substantiated from the text, (E).

186.   (D)
The poet is obviously a woman. It would take an ingenious male poet to capture the woman's feelings at aging — — eliminate (C) and (E). Emily Dickinson's style is distinctive; her poetry instantly recognized by structure alone. Amy Powell's would contain repeated symbolism.

187.   (B)
The title *Shadow of the Glen* or the content of the passage should reveal the playwright, for Synge was involved with the Abbey Theater group who wanted to revitalize the Irish language and prove that natural speech was suitable for the stage. Analyze the other Irish names listed, the body of work of each and whether the passage's title fits.

188.   (C)

You do not need to know Synge's theories. Derive the meaning from the passage. If he learned from listening to Wicklow servant girls, then obviously he was interested in the speech and rhythms of the simple country folk. He adds a rider for the use of the language if that language is "rich and copious," not "bright" or "dirty."

189.   (D)

This scene in the last section of *The Sound and the Fury* is crucial to the whole structure. Here Dilsey recognizes the "first and the last" of the Compson family and time, symbolized by the Christmas bell even though the time is Easter: birth and resurrection. If you do not know the passage, the heat and the sparseness of the scene would suggest a Southern, Faulknerian church.

190.   (A)

The names may well reveal the novel. If not, the song, the audience participation and the tambourine would reveal the church as James Baldwin's. The stiff, deathly church scenes in (B) and (E) would discount them. (C) is a possibility, but the refrains from the hymns establish a white Presbyterian service from *The Fall of Theron Ware*.

191.   (B)

George Bowling reminisces about his childhood church in passages replete with memories. Time has given the church scene an aura of mystery. If you do not know the Orwell novel, you may confuse the scene with (E) from James Joyce's *Grace* but that church is established as very proper -- the way the men are dressed and the "high altar" -- not an Orwellian church scene.

192.   (C)

Increasingly popular, Lessing's novel is well worth studying. If you do not know the work, think of the other "Annas" listed: (D) and (E) are in fact "Annies" so they can be eliminated. If you know the other two, you know they did not want or wait for a deus ex machina in their lives; they handled their own destinies.

193.   (D)

The key words here are "current usage." The original term was used for a device in the theater that was lowered from the top of the stage as if a god were entering the drama to manipulate the turn of events. In current usage the term is found in criticism of all genres, for one who turns around imminent disaster.

194.   (C)

The title and brief description should reveal the author. If you are not familiar with the work, the comparison with Faulkner and Kafka would immediately cancel the choices (B) and (E). Then think of the body of work of (A) and (C) and fit the title into that body, or think of how they might resemble Faulkner and Kafka.

195.   (E)

Some of the choices can be eliminated immediately if you do not recognize the work from the description. (C) is full of coarse mishaps and (D) has disembowelings and floggings but never resurrection. (B) is more magical with Gulliver in the land of the giants, but as with the magic quality of (A), real life prevails and we do sympathize with the victims.

196.   (B)

If you have identified the work correctly, you will recall Pangloss' statement. If unsure, identify the other choices: (A) McCawber is in *David Copperfield*, (C) the narrator in *Slaughterhouse-Five*, (D) Lambert Strether in *The Ambassadors*, (E) Uriah Heep in *David Copperfield*.

127

197.　(D)

You may not recognize Emerson's work on *Nature*, but the New England Transcendentalists had a certain turn of phrase that identifies them with the basic elements of their belief. In this passage, the notion of an extra sense, an inspiration from outside the body, links immediately to transcendentalism. The premise does not apply to the other choices.

198.　(D)

William James wrote a number of brilliant essays but is best remembered for his work on Pragmatism. The passage delineates some part of his philosophy and the word "pragmatically" is the key word here. Like that of his brother Henry, William James' prose is convoluted, the sentences longer than the modern norm — — another key to identification.

199.　(A)

The Transcendentalists were criticized for their withdrawal from society and seemingly effete approach to life. This is Emerson's defence, stressing the fact that he does not criticize progress or technology; he is not a "back to nature" hermit. But he does add the proviso that technology comes from an outside source that transcends the work of man.

200.　(E)

If you know Sartre's *Nausea* you will recognize Roquentin's sudden awareness of existence. If not you may be confused with (B) from Soren Kierkegaard's essay on *Dread*. Both men considered dread or "angst" as necessary to man, but Sartre balances his existentialism with a greater belief in man's power to overcome the dread, to live in full awareness and acceptance of man's sorrow.

201.   (B)

Kierkegaard pinpoints the isolation of modern man, aware of an awesome dread in his life but unable to come to terms with it. Kierkegaard believed that only through knowing dread can a being achieve freedom to be an individual in an increasingly mechanized mob -- not to be confused with (D), the behaviorist philosophy, which maintained that the body alone could adapt to a better way of life.

202.   (B)

You should recognize Gonzalo's ideal Commonwealth from *The Tempest*. He is garrulous and not particularly smart but wise enough to know when to cheer up the king and when to leave him alone. The utopia he describes is ridiculed by the other courtiers but it does have some good points, without advocating an ideal communism.

203.   (D)

Most Shakespeare texts explicate this passage clearly. If you do not know the passage, slip in each of the possibilities with close regard to the rest of the paradozes, i.e. "tilth" may sound close to taxes -- certainly Gonzalo does not want these, but the word means land cultivation. He is not against streams but against boundaries (bourn).

204.   (A)

From context gather the gist of the passage. Gonzalo may mean simply harvest (B) or fodder (E) but in this utopia the crops would be abundant. In (D) you may be confused with the French word poisson-fish, but it does not fit the utopia context, nor does the similar sounding name poison (C), which no doubt Gonzalo would disallow on his island.

205.   (B)

Gonzalo's utopia suggests that all the goodness and riches would be achieved without any effort on the part of the inhabitants (thus not an ideal communism) which counteracts the Biblical teaching of man having to work for his living, from which developed the Protestant work ethic. None of the other choices are mentioned in the context of this passage.

206. (B)

Shakespeare read widely and borrowed extensively. He follows closely Montaigne's essay *Of the Cannibals* for Gonzalo's utopia. If you have identified *The Tempest* correctly you can eliminate choices (A), (C), (D) and (E).

207. (D)

The general effect of the long sentence and the piling up of detail one after the other, separated only by the comma, is to create a breathlessness. (B) is a possibility but the vigor and excitement is not the rambling of an old man, nor is there a haze over the writing (C) but rather an immediacy. The passage does not suggest waste or sadness, (A) and (E).

208. (E)

There is a rhetoric here which is religious; there is celebration and the whole effect is of someone reading aloud in an oratorical fashion. However, the specific oratory is the incantation of a psalm or prayer. If possible read aloud and the repetition of "for ever and ever (world) without end (Amen)" comes over very clearly.

209. (D)

The author looks back on those summers as if they would never end – – the feeling one often has as a child. The other choices have some validity, but the point is the eternity of childhood summers captured by the incantation of a prayer. If you know the essay, the author returning to the same place with his son perpetuates the endless circle of time.

210. (C)

The key words are "background" and "design": all the other details fill in the painting. Once the metaphor is established, return to line 1 and pick up the "fadeproof" idea, the lake in the painting's background never fading (a Keatsian notion). The photographs are not true pictures because they embellish. White's painting holds the truth within it.

211. (A)

The choices involving comedy can be cut out immediately. (D) and (E) are possibilities but the Suffering in the five elements is too strong a term for this type of drama, and very often Tragic Irony is not developed. Tragedy specifically carries the Metaphysical Dimension which separates it from the other types within the genre.

212. (B)

Webster is most famous for *The Duchess of Malfi*, perhaps the darkest of all the Jacobean Revenge Tragedies. If you do not know the playwright, think of the plays in the body of work of the other choices. All of them are renowned for their light comedies, particularly Gay and Farquhar, both of whom have had plays turned into operas.

213. (C)

Thomas Pynchon deftly manipulates a Jacobean revenge plot within his own plot of the Trystero. If you do not know the novel, think of the other choices and analyze if the authors use the other genre. (D) and (E) might be possibilities but those works deal with the darkness of a man's possessiveness of his wife and a "detective story" within a monastery.

214. (C)

Identify first of all the author of the piece. All the writers are capable of morbidity such as this, but here Dr. Lydgate refers to his trivial wife Rosamond who has destroyed his integrity, in George Eliot's masterpiece *Middlemarch*. The allusion is to Keats's *Isabella or the Pot of Basil*. If you know one of the works, the other will fall into place.

215. (C)

If you do not know the novel, the keywords are "prison life." Analyze the other choices deliberating if those characters ever went to prison or experienced "rebirth." Without knowing the novel, think how the title alone suggests that the protagonist is punished, and the most famous of such protagonists is Raskolnikov.

216. (D)

Without knowing the novel or perhaps not recognizing the passage, read how the passage reveals that the man has been ill, but there is neither exultation at being raised from the dead as Lazarus experienced in the New Testament parable, nor a religious conversion. You need to know the parable and eliminate the choices that cannot be given from the text.

217. (D)

Strindberg's preface to *Miss Julie* holds a wealth of criticism on drama techniques as well as an insight into the playwright's methods. He criticizes the practice of writers simply pursuing stock characters and not attending to the range of human qualities. Even if you have not read the preface, the context will show the way the playwright thinks.

218. (A)

Stock characters produce stock phrases and Dickens has a full appreciation of how a stock character works. If you do not recognize the courting cry of Mr. Barkis, then analyze the other choices. None of the other works, despite their importance and possibility for stock characters, have produced a phrase that is instantly recognizable.

219. (B)

It is difficult to learn all the plots of the pilgrims' tales but the main ones are worth studying closely. Some of the pilgrims have distinct personalities which Chaucer plays on and develops along with the tales. Read closely the description here and analyze which pilgrim tells which tale and which ones have a certain irony behind their story.

220. (C)
The Pardoner's story outrages the pilgrims because he has just revealed how he dupes country folk into believing pigs' bones are the relics of Christ, and makes a fortune out of duplicity. Yet his story's conclusion warns against avarice, stressing the fact that "money is the root of all evil." The other tales are fun but without this depth of irony.

221. (B)
Literary meals are very important, bringing together characters, or functioning as prologues to climaxes, disasters, or simply as celebrations. Here Mrs. Ramsey serves her beautiful stew with her family and friends gatthered around her, each character revealing his or her thoughts. The wistful style of the passage distinguishes it from the other choices.

222. (F)
You may know (C) from Forster's *A Passage to India* better than (E) from Naipaul's first novel *The Mystic Masseur*. Now living in England, the Jamaican contemporary writer once lived in India. (C) shows the planning for the picnic before the incident in the caves, crucial to the plot. The only other "Indian" choice is (E) the "hero's" wedding meal.

223. (D)
The choice between (A) and (D) may seem difficult if you do not know the poems, but the key word "hall" should reveal the meeting hall of Hrothgar's manor in *Beowulf*. The alliteration and verse arrangement should reveal the Gawain poem. This meal is especially important as the Green Knight delivers his challenge at the Christmas feast.

224. (D)

De Quincey is not widely read but his thoughts as an Opium Eater are fascinating. If you do not know this work, analyze the choices: Ivan Ilych does not reveal his dreams. Coleridge's dreams were sexually oriented and *Kubla Khan* was allegedly drug-inspired. Raskolnikov's dreams are less specific but more terrifying.

225. (C)

If you do not know the poem *Morte D'Arthur*, and the story of King Arthur bidding Sir Bedivere three times to throw away the sword, then recall the legend. Eliminate (B), Gawain talking to his horse, and (E), misplaced characters. (C) Sir Lancelot did not carry Excalibur. Sir Galahad died before King Arthur on beholding the Grail.

226. (D)

Mystical materials such as samite are crucial to legends and epics. Think of Penelope's and the Lady of Shalott's webs. If you do not know the word, eliminate (A) the heavy armour and (E) the heraldic devices – – illustrations show the material as pure and soft without decoration, glistening as silk does, especially inset with gold and silver.

227. (E)

It is helpful to know the poem but the choices can be narrowed from thinking again of the legend, which often remains in our consciousness from childhood. Eliminate (A) and (B) – – King Arthur goes to neither place. Eliminate (C) as no battleground is mentioned in the poetry here. Eliminate (D) as Bedivere outlives King Arthur.

228. (E)

Tennyson followed closely the work of Malory's *Morte D'Arthur*, planning eventually to write twelve books for an "Arthurian Epic." If you do not know the poet's achievement here, eliminate Wordsworth and Yeats who did not work on this legend, and John Gardner who adapted the legend of Beowulf into a novel, *Grendel*.

229.   (B)
This excerpt from a letter shows Flaubert grappling with the scene famous for its interweaving of distinct consciousnesses, conversations, and the backdrop of mundanity for a passionate life. The last two lines provide the central keys: the man and the woman are Rodolphe Boulanger and Emma Bovary. None of the other choices contains such an impressive scene.

230.   (A)
Nothing could be more mundane than this background. Nothing could be more striking, nor more hilarious than the lovers' conversation intertwined with speeches about pigs and manures. The other possibilities would not provide such an impressive contrast nor show what the writer desires in his letter.

GRE

LITERATURE in ENGLISH

TEST II

THE GRADUATE RECORD EXAMINATION

LITERATURE in ENGLISH

ANSWER SHEET

1. Ⓐ Ⓑ Ⓒ Ⓓ Ⓔ	31. Ⓐ Ⓑ Ⓒ Ⓓ Ⓔ	61. Ⓐ Ⓑ Ⓒ Ⓓ Ⓔ
2. Ⓐ Ⓑ Ⓒ Ⓓ Ⓔ	32. Ⓐ Ⓑ Ⓒ Ⓓ Ⓔ	62. Ⓐ Ⓑ Ⓒ Ⓓ Ⓔ
3. Ⓐ Ⓑ Ⓒ Ⓓ Ⓔ	33. Ⓐ Ⓑ Ⓒ Ⓓ Ⓔ	63. Ⓐ Ⓑ Ⓒ Ⓓ Ⓔ
4. Ⓐ Ⓑ Ⓒ Ⓓ Ⓔ	34. Ⓐ Ⓑ Ⓒ Ⓓ Ⓔ	64. Ⓐ Ⓑ Ⓒ Ⓓ Ⓔ
5. Ⓐ Ⓑ Ⓒ Ⓓ Ⓔ	35. Ⓐ Ⓑ Ⓒ Ⓓ Ⓔ	65. Ⓐ Ⓑ Ⓒ Ⓓ Ⓔ
6. Ⓐ Ⓑ Ⓒ Ⓓ Ⓔ	36. Ⓐ Ⓑ Ⓒ Ⓓ Ⓔ	66. Ⓐ Ⓑ Ⓒ Ⓓ Ⓔ
7. Ⓐ Ⓑ Ⓒ Ⓓ Ⓔ	37. Ⓐ Ⓑ Ⓒ Ⓓ Ⓔ	67. Ⓐ Ⓑ Ⓒ Ⓓ Ⓔ
8. Ⓐ Ⓑ Ⓒ Ⓓ Ⓔ	38. Ⓐ Ⓑ Ⓒ Ⓓ Ⓔ	68. Ⓐ Ⓑ Ⓒ Ⓓ Ⓔ
9. Ⓐ Ⓑ Ⓒ Ⓓ Ⓔ	39. Ⓐ Ⓑ Ⓒ Ⓓ Ⓔ	69. Ⓐ Ⓑ Ⓒ Ⓓ Ⓔ
10. Ⓐ Ⓑ Ⓒ Ⓓ Ⓔ	40. Ⓐ Ⓑ Ⓒ Ⓓ Ⓔ	70. Ⓐ Ⓑ Ⓒ Ⓓ Ⓔ
11. Ⓐ Ⓑ Ⓒ Ⓓ Ⓔ	41. Ⓐ Ⓑ Ⓒ Ⓓ Ⓔ	71. Ⓐ Ⓑ Ⓒ Ⓓ Ⓔ
12. Ⓐ Ⓑ Ⓒ Ⓓ Ⓔ	42. Ⓐ Ⓑ Ⓒ Ⓓ Ⓔ	72. Ⓐ Ⓑ Ⓒ Ⓓ Ⓔ
13. Ⓐ Ⓑ Ⓒ Ⓓ Ⓔ	43. Ⓐ Ⓑ Ⓒ Ⓓ Ⓔ	73. Ⓐ Ⓑ Ⓒ Ⓓ Ⓔ
14. Ⓐ Ⓑ Ⓒ Ⓓ Ⓔ	44. Ⓐ Ⓑ Ⓒ Ⓓ Ⓔ	74. Ⓐ Ⓑ Ⓒ Ⓓ Ⓔ
15. Ⓐ Ⓑ Ⓒ Ⓓ Ⓔ	45. Ⓐ Ⓑ Ⓒ Ⓓ Ⓔ	75. Ⓐ Ⓑ Ⓒ Ⓓ Ⓔ
16. Ⓐ Ⓑ Ⓒ Ⓓ Ⓔ	46. Ⓐ Ⓑ Ⓒ Ⓓ Ⓔ	76. Ⓐ Ⓑ Ⓒ Ⓓ Ⓔ
17. Ⓐ Ⓑ Ⓒ Ⓓ Ⓔ	47. Ⓐ Ⓑ Ⓒ Ⓓ Ⓔ	77. Ⓐ Ⓑ Ⓒ Ⓓ Ⓔ
18. Ⓐ Ⓑ Ⓒ Ⓓ Ⓔ	48. Ⓐ Ⓑ Ⓒ Ⓓ Ⓔ	78. Ⓐ Ⓑ Ⓒ Ⓓ Ⓔ
19. Ⓐ Ⓑ Ⓒ Ⓓ Ⓔ	49. Ⓐ Ⓑ Ⓒ Ⓓ Ⓔ	79. Ⓐ Ⓑ Ⓒ Ⓓ Ⓔ
20. Ⓐ Ⓑ Ⓒ Ⓓ Ⓔ	50. Ⓐ Ⓑ Ⓒ Ⓓ Ⓔ	80. Ⓐ Ⓑ Ⓒ Ⓓ Ⓔ
21. Ⓐ Ⓑ Ⓒ Ⓓ Ⓔ	51. Ⓐ Ⓑ Ⓒ Ⓓ Ⓔ	81. Ⓐ Ⓑ Ⓒ Ⓓ Ⓔ
22. Ⓐ Ⓑ Ⓒ Ⓓ Ⓔ	52. Ⓐ Ⓑ Ⓒ Ⓓ Ⓔ	82. Ⓐ Ⓑ Ⓒ Ⓓ Ⓔ
23. Ⓐ Ⓑ Ⓒ Ⓓ Ⓔ	53. Ⓐ Ⓑ Ⓒ Ⓓ Ⓔ	83. Ⓐ Ⓑ Ⓒ Ⓓ Ⓔ
24. Ⓐ Ⓑ Ⓒ Ⓓ Ⓔ	54. Ⓐ Ⓑ Ⓒ Ⓓ Ⓔ	84. Ⓐ Ⓑ Ⓒ Ⓓ Ⓔ
25. Ⓐ Ⓑ Ⓒ Ⓓ Ⓔ	55. Ⓐ Ⓑ Ⓒ Ⓓ Ⓔ	85. Ⓐ Ⓑ Ⓒ Ⓓ Ⓔ
26. Ⓐ Ⓑ Ⓒ Ⓓ Ⓔ	56. Ⓐ Ⓑ Ⓒ Ⓓ Ⓔ	86. Ⓐ Ⓑ Ⓒ Ⓓ Ⓔ
27. Ⓐ Ⓑ Ⓒ Ⓓ Ⓔ	57. Ⓐ Ⓑ Ⓒ Ⓓ Ⓔ	87. Ⓐ Ⓑ Ⓒ Ⓓ Ⓔ
28. Ⓐ Ⓑ Ⓒ Ⓓ Ⓔ	58. Ⓐ Ⓑ Ⓒ Ⓓ Ⓔ	88. Ⓐ Ⓑ Ⓒ Ⓓ Ⓔ
29. Ⓐ Ⓑ Ⓒ Ⓓ Ⓔ	59. Ⓐ Ⓑ Ⓒ Ⓓ Ⓔ	89. Ⓐ Ⓑ Ⓒ Ⓓ Ⓔ
30. Ⓐ Ⓑ Ⓒ Ⓓ Ⓔ	60. Ⓐ Ⓑ Ⓒ Ⓓ Ⓔ	90. Ⓐ Ⓑ Ⓒ Ⓓ Ⓔ

91. Ⓐ Ⓑ Ⓒ Ⓓ Ⓔ
92. Ⓐ Ⓑ Ⓒ Ⓓ Ⓔ
93. Ⓐ Ⓑ Ⓒ Ⓓ Ⓔ
94. Ⓐ Ⓑ Ⓒ Ⓓ Ⓔ
95. Ⓐ Ⓑ Ⓒ Ⓓ Ⓔ
96. Ⓐ Ⓑ Ⓒ Ⓓ Ⓔ
97. Ⓐ Ⓑ Ⓒ Ⓓ Ⓔ
98. Ⓐ Ⓑ Ⓒ Ⓓ Ⓔ
99. Ⓐ Ⓑ Ⓒ Ⓓ Ⓔ
100. Ⓐ Ⓑ Ⓒ Ⓓ Ⓔ
101. Ⓐ Ⓑ Ⓒ Ⓓ Ⓔ
102. Ⓐ Ⓑ Ⓒ Ⓓ Ⓔ
103. Ⓐ Ⓑ Ⓒ Ⓓ Ⓔ
104. Ⓐ Ⓑ Ⓒ Ⓓ Ⓔ
105. Ⓐ Ⓑ Ⓒ Ⓓ Ⓔ
106. Ⓐ Ⓑ Ⓒ Ⓓ Ⓔ
107. Ⓐ Ⓑ Ⓒ Ⓓ Ⓔ
108. Ⓐ Ⓑ Ⓒ Ⓓ Ⓔ
109. Ⓐ Ⓑ Ⓒ Ⓓ Ⓔ
110. Ⓐ Ⓑ Ⓒ Ⓓ Ⓔ
111. Ⓐ Ⓑ Ⓒ Ⓓ Ⓔ
112. Ⓐ Ⓑ Ⓒ Ⓓ Ⓔ
113. Ⓐ Ⓑ Ⓒ Ⓓ Ⓔ
114. Ⓐ Ⓑ Ⓒ Ⓓ Ⓔ
115. Ⓐ Ⓑ Ⓒ Ⓓ Ⓔ
116. Ⓐ Ⓑ Ⓒ Ⓓ Ⓔ
117. Ⓐ Ⓑ Ⓒ Ⓓ Ⓔ
118. Ⓐ Ⓑ Ⓒ Ⓓ Ⓔ
119. Ⓐ Ⓑ Ⓒ Ⓓ Ⓔ
120. Ⓐ Ⓑ Ⓒ Ⓓ Ⓔ

121. Ⓐ Ⓑ Ⓒ Ⓓ Ⓔ
122. Ⓐ Ⓑ Ⓒ Ⓓ Ⓔ
123. Ⓐ Ⓑ Ⓒ Ⓓ Ⓔ
124. Ⓐ Ⓑ Ⓒ Ⓓ Ⓔ
125. Ⓐ Ⓑ Ⓒ Ⓓ Ⓔ
126. Ⓐ Ⓑ Ⓒ Ⓓ Ⓔ
127. Ⓐ Ⓑ Ⓒ Ⓓ Ⓔ
128. Ⓐ Ⓑ Ⓒ Ⓓ Ⓔ
129. Ⓐ Ⓑ Ⓒ Ⓓ Ⓔ
130. Ⓐ Ⓑ Ⓒ Ⓓ Ⓔ
131. Ⓐ Ⓑ Ⓒ Ⓓ Ⓔ
132. Ⓐ Ⓑ Ⓒ Ⓓ Ⓔ
133. Ⓐ Ⓑ Ⓒ Ⓓ Ⓔ
134. Ⓐ Ⓑ Ⓒ Ⓓ Ⓔ
135. Ⓐ Ⓑ Ⓒ Ⓓ Ⓔ
136. Ⓐ Ⓑ Ⓒ Ⓓ Ⓔ
137. Ⓐ Ⓑ Ⓒ Ⓓ Ⓔ
138. Ⓐ Ⓑ Ⓒ Ⓓ Ⓔ
139. Ⓐ Ⓑ Ⓒ Ⓓ Ⓔ
140. Ⓐ Ⓑ Ⓒ Ⓓ Ⓔ
141. Ⓐ Ⓑ Ⓒ Ⓓ Ⓔ
142. Ⓐ Ⓑ Ⓒ Ⓓ Ⓔ
143. Ⓐ Ⓑ Ⓒ Ⓓ Ⓔ
144. Ⓐ Ⓑ Ⓒ Ⓓ Ⓔ
145. Ⓐ Ⓑ Ⓒ Ⓓ Ⓔ
146. Ⓐ Ⓑ Ⓒ Ⓓ Ⓔ
147. Ⓐ Ⓑ Ⓒ Ⓓ Ⓔ
148. Ⓐ Ⓑ Ⓒ Ⓓ Ⓔ
149. Ⓐ Ⓑ Ⓒ Ⓓ Ⓔ
150. Ⓐ Ⓑ Ⓒ Ⓓ Ⓔ

151. Ⓐ Ⓑ Ⓒ Ⓓ Ⓔ
152. Ⓐ Ⓑ Ⓒ Ⓓ Ⓔ
153. Ⓐ Ⓑ Ⓒ Ⓓ Ⓔ
154. Ⓐ Ⓑ Ⓒ Ⓓ Ⓔ
155. Ⓐ Ⓑ Ⓒ Ⓓ Ⓔ
156. Ⓐ Ⓑ Ⓒ Ⓓ Ⓔ
157. Ⓐ Ⓑ Ⓒ Ⓓ Ⓔ
158. Ⓐ Ⓑ Ⓒ Ⓓ Ⓔ
159. Ⓐ Ⓑ Ⓒ Ⓓ Ⓔ
160. Ⓐ Ⓑ Ⓒ Ⓓ Ⓔ
161. Ⓐ Ⓑ Ⓒ Ⓓ Ⓔ
162. Ⓐ Ⓑ Ⓒ Ⓓ Ⓔ
163. Ⓐ Ⓑ Ⓒ Ⓓ Ⓔ
164. Ⓐ Ⓑ Ⓒ Ⓓ Ⓔ
165. Ⓐ Ⓑ Ⓒ Ⓓ Ⓔ
166. Ⓐ Ⓑ Ⓒ Ⓓ Ⓔ
167. Ⓐ Ⓑ Ⓒ Ⓓ Ⓔ
168. Ⓐ Ⓑ Ⓒ Ⓓ Ⓔ
169. Ⓐ Ⓑ Ⓒ Ⓓ Ⓔ
170. Ⓐ Ⓑ Ⓒ Ⓓ Ⓔ
171. Ⓐ Ⓑ Ⓒ Ⓓ Ⓔ
172. Ⓐ Ⓑ Ⓒ Ⓓ Ⓔ
173. Ⓐ Ⓑ Ⓒ Ⓓ Ⓔ
174. Ⓐ Ⓑ Ⓒ Ⓓ Ⓔ
175. Ⓐ Ⓑ Ⓒ Ⓓ Ⓔ
176. Ⓐ Ⓑ Ⓒ Ⓓ Ⓔ
177. Ⓐ Ⓑ Ⓒ Ⓓ Ⓔ
178. Ⓐ Ⓑ Ⓒ Ⓓ Ⓔ
179. Ⓐ Ⓑ Ⓒ Ⓓ Ⓔ
180. Ⓐ Ⓑ Ⓒ Ⓓ Ⓔ

181. Ⓐ Ⓑ Ⓒ Ⓓ Ⓔ
182. Ⓐ Ⓑ Ⓒ Ⓓ Ⓔ
183. Ⓐ Ⓑ Ⓒ Ⓓ Ⓔ
184. Ⓐ Ⓑ Ⓒ Ⓓ Ⓔ
185. Ⓐ Ⓑ Ⓒ Ⓓ Ⓔ
186. Ⓐ Ⓑ Ⓒ Ⓓ Ⓔ
187. Ⓐ Ⓑ Ⓒ Ⓓ Ⓔ
188. Ⓐ Ⓑ Ⓒ Ⓓ Ⓔ
189. Ⓐ Ⓑ Ⓒ Ⓓ Ⓔ
190. Ⓐ Ⓑ Ⓒ Ⓓ Ⓔ
191. Ⓐ Ⓑ Ⓒ Ⓓ Ⓔ
192. Ⓐ Ⓑ Ⓒ Ⓓ Ⓔ
193. Ⓐ Ⓑ Ⓒ Ⓓ Ⓔ
194. Ⓐ Ⓑ Ⓒ Ⓓ Ⓔ
195. Ⓐ Ⓑ Ⓒ Ⓓ Ⓔ
196. Ⓐ Ⓑ Ⓒ Ⓓ Ⓔ
197. Ⓐ Ⓑ Ⓒ Ⓓ Ⓔ

198. Ⓐ Ⓑ Ⓒ Ⓓ Ⓔ
199. Ⓐ Ⓑ Ⓒ Ⓓ Ⓔ
200. Ⓐ Ⓑ Ⓒ Ⓓ Ⓔ
201. Ⓐ Ⓑ Ⓒ Ⓓ Ⓔ
202. Ⓐ Ⓑ Ⓒ Ⓓ Ⓔ
203. Ⓐ Ⓑ Ⓒ Ⓓ Ⓔ
204. Ⓐ Ⓑ Ⓒ Ⓓ Ⓔ
205. Ⓐ Ⓑ Ⓒ Ⓓ Ⓔ
206. Ⓐ Ⓑ Ⓒ Ⓓ Ⓔ
207. Ⓐ Ⓑ Ⓒ Ⓓ Ⓔ
208. Ⓐ Ⓑ Ⓒ Ⓓ Ⓔ
209. Ⓐ Ⓑ Ⓒ Ⓓ Ⓔ
210. Ⓐ Ⓑ Ⓒ Ⓓ Ⓔ
211. Ⓐ Ⓑ Ⓒ Ⓓ Ⓔ
212. Ⓐ Ⓑ Ⓒ Ⓓ Ⓔ
213. Ⓐ Ⓑ Ⓒ Ⓓ Ⓔ
214. Ⓐ Ⓑ Ⓒ Ⓓ Ⓔ

215. Ⓐ Ⓑ Ⓒ Ⓓ Ⓔ
216. Ⓐ Ⓑ Ⓒ Ⓓ Ⓔ
217. Ⓐ Ⓑ Ⓒ Ⓓ Ⓔ
218. Ⓐ Ⓑ Ⓒ Ⓓ Ⓔ
219. Ⓐ Ⓑ Ⓒ Ⓓ Ⓔ
220. Ⓐ Ⓑ Ⓒ Ⓓ Ⓔ
221. Ⓐ Ⓑ Ⓒ Ⓓ Ⓔ
222. Ⓐ Ⓑ Ⓒ Ⓓ Ⓔ
223. Ⓐ Ⓑ Ⓒ Ⓓ Ⓔ
224. Ⓐ Ⓑ Ⓒ Ⓓ Ⓔ
225. Ⓐ Ⓑ Ⓒ Ⓓ Ⓔ
226. Ⓐ Ⓑ Ⓒ Ⓓ Ⓔ
227. Ⓐ Ⓑ Ⓒ Ⓓ Ⓔ
228. Ⓐ Ⓑ Ⓒ Ⓓ Ⓔ
229. Ⓐ Ⓑ Ⓒ Ⓓ Ⓔ
230. Ⓐ Ⓑ Ⓒ Ⓓ Ⓔ

GRE LITERATURE
IN ENGLISH

TEST II

DIRECTIONS: Choose the best answer for each question and mark the letter of your selection on the corresponding answer sheet

Questions 1-3 refer to the excerpts below.

1.   Which refers to Donne?

2.   Which refers to Wordsworth?

3.   Which refers to Swift?

    (A) As for his works in verse and prose,
         I own myself no judge of those;
         Nor can I tell what critics thought 'im:
         But this I know, all people bought 'em,
         As with a moral view designed
         To cure the vices of mankind.

    (B) With_____, whose muse on dromedary trots,
         Wreathe iron pokers into truelove knots;
         Rhyme's sturdy cripple, fancy's maze and clue,
         Wit's forge and fire-blast, meaning's press and screw.

    (C) Standing aloof in giant ignorance,
           Of thee I hear and of the Cyclades,
         As one who sits ashore and longs perchance
           To visit dolphin-coral in deep seas.
         So thou wast blind!--but then the veil was rent;
           For Jove uncurtained Heaven to let thee live,
         And Neptune made for thee a spumy tent,
           And Pan made sing for thee his forest-hive;. . .

(D) In honored poverty thy voice did weave
     Songs consecrate to truth and liberty,--
     Deserting these, thou leavest me to grieve,
     Thus having been, that thou should cease to be.

(E) Sheeplike, unsociable reptilian, two
     hell-divers splattered squawking on the water,
     loons devolving to a monochrome.
     You honored nature,

     helpless, elemental creature.
     The black stump of your hand
     just touched the waters under the earth
     and left them quickened with your name. . . .

4.   Her work "represents a romanticism *in extremis,* made pub-
        lic with grotesque clarity. Her poetry has been praised as a
        supreme example of the confessional mode in modern litera-
        ture and disparaged as the "longest suicide note ever written."
        The subject of some of it is her parents, who are treated unsym-
        pathetically ('Daddy, daddy, you bastard, I'm through"). She
        wrote an autobiographical novel about personality distintegra-
        tion, and committed suicide.

        This passage describes

        (A) Virginia Woolf   (D) Sylvia Plath

        (B) Elizabeth Bishop   (E) Adrienne Rich

        (C) Anne Sexton

Questions 5-7 refer to the following poems.

5.   Which contains the following lines?

        And we are here as on a darkling plain
        Swept with confused alarms of struggle and flight
        Where ignorant armies clash by night.

6. Which is a carpe diem poem?

7. Which is a literary ballad?

   (A) *Dover Beach*

   (B) *Lines Composed a Few Miles Above Tintern Abbey*

   (C) *La Belle Dame sans Merci*

   (D) *Break, Break, Break*

   (E) *To the Virgins, to Make Much of Time*

8. The phrase "graveyard school" designates a group of eighteenth-century British poets who wrote long poems on death and immortality. The works of all of the following are associated with the graveyard school EXCEPT

   (A) Thomas Parnell   (D) James Thompson

   (B) Robert Blair   (E) Thomas Gray

   (C) Edward Young

9. The influence of the graveyard school was first reflected in America in which of the following?

   (A) Michael Wigglesworth's *The Day of Doom*

   (B) Edward Taylor's *A Fig for Thee Oh! Death*

   (C) Phillis Wheatley's *An Hymn to the Evening*

   (D) Philip Freneau's *The House of Night*

   (E) Longfellow's *The Jewish Cemetery at Newport*

10. All of the following are sonnet sequences EXCEPT

    (A) Sidney's *Astrophel and Stella*

    (B) Spencer's *Amoretti*

    (C) Tennyson's *In Memoriam*

(D) D. G. Rossetti's *House of Life*

(E) William Ellery Leonard's *Two Lives*

Questions 11–13

> A shudder in the loins engenders there
> The broken wall, the burning roof and tower
> And Agamemnon dead.
>   Being so caught up,
> So mastered by the brute blood of the air,   5
> Did she put on his knowledge with his power
> Before the indifferent beak could let her drop?

11. Agamemnon was

    (A) killed in battle in the Trojan War

    (B) killed by Circe while accompanying Odysseus home from the Trojan War

    (C) murdered by his son Orestes

    (D) murdered by his wife Clytemnestra

    (E) pierced by an arrow shot by Artemis

12. "His" (line six) refers to

    (A) Agamemnon   (D) Apollo

    (B) Priam   (E) Zeus

    (C) Orestes

13. The author of this passage is

    (A) Byron   (D) Yeats

    (B) Keats   (E) T. S. Eliot

    (C) Tennyson

Questions 14–16 refer to the excerpts below.

14. Which is spoken by Shaw's Barbara?

15. Which is spoken by Wilde's Lady Bracknell?

16. Which is spoken by Congreve's Millamant?

(A) Come to dinner when I please, dine in my dressing-room when I'm out of humor, without giving a reason. To have my closet inviolate; to be sole empress of my teatable, which you must never presume to approach without first asking leave. And lastly, wherever I am, you shall always knock at the door before you come in. These articles subscribed, if I continue to endure you a little longer, I may by degrees dwindle into a wife.

(B) What business have you, miss, with *preference* and *aversion*? They don't become a young woman; and you ought to know, that as both always wear off, 'tis safest in matrimony to begin with a little *aversion*. I am sure I hated your poor dear uncle before marriage as if he'd been a black-a-moor—and yet, miss, you are sensible what a wife I made!—and when it pleased heav'n to release me from him, 'tis unknown what tears I shed!

(C) I don't believe in that anymore. I believe that, before all else, I'm a human being, no less than you--or anyway, I ought to try to become one. I know the majority thinks you're right, Torvald, and plenty of books agree with you, too. But I can't go on believing what the majority says, or what's written in books. I have to think over these things myself and try to understand them.

(D) I should have given you up and married the man who accepted it. After all, my dear old mother has more sense than any of you. I felt like her when I saw this place--felt that I must have it--that never, never, never could I let it go; only she thought it was the houses and the kitchen ranges and the linen and china, when it was really all the human souls to be saved; not weak souls in starved bodies, sobbing with gratitude for a scrap of bread and treacle, but fullfed, quarrelsome, snobbish, uppish creatures, all standing on their little rights and dignities, and thinking that my father ought to be greatly obliged to them for making so much money for him--and so he ought. That is where salvation is really wanted...I have got rid of the bribe of heaven.

(E) I confess I feel somewhat bewildered by what you have just told me. To be born, or at any rate bred, in a handbag, whether it had handles or not, seems to me to display a contempt for the ordinary decencies of family life that remind me of the worst excesses of the French Revolution. And I presume you know what that unfortunate movement led to? As for the particular locality in which the handbag was found, a cloakroom at a railway station might serve to conceal a social indiscretion--has probably, indeed, been used for that purpose before now--but it could could hardly be regarded as an assured basis for a recognized position in good society.

Questions 17–19

ROSALIND Well, in her person I say I will not have you.

ORLANDO   Then in mine own person I die.

ROSALIND No, faith, die by attorney. The poor world is almost six thousand years old, and in all this time there was not any man died in his own person, videlicet, in a love-cause. Troilus had his brains dash'd out with a Grecian club; yet he did what he could to die before, and he is one of the 5
patterns of love. Leander he would have liv'd many a fair year, though Hero had turn'd nun, if it had not been for a hot midsummer night; for, good youth, he went but forth to wash him in the Hellespont and being taken with the cramp was drown'd; and the foolish chroniclers of that age found

17.   In line one, "by attorney" means

(A) of natural causes   (D) by someone else's hand

(B) of old age   (E) in a courtroom

(C) by proxy

18. Rosalind's account of Leander's death

(A) is more accurate than that given by historians of Leander's day

(B) is intended to undercut romantic idealism

(C) is an exception to the general point she is making, the "exception that proves the rule"

(D) outlines a pattern of chivalric behavior that she wishes Orlando to emulate

(E) is intended to reinforce Orlando's current mode of behavior

19. These lines are from

(A) *As You Like It*

(B) *Every Man in his Humour*

(C) *The Way of the World*

(D) *Much Ado about Nothing*

(E) *The Rivals*

Questions 20-22

The poet is the sayer, the namer, and represents beauty. He is a sovereign and stands on the centre. For the world is not painted or adorned, but is from the beginning beautiful; and God has not made some beautiful things, but Beauty is the creator of the universe...

For poetry was all written before time was, and whenever we are so finely organized that we can penetrate into that region where the air is music, we hear those primordial warblings and attempt to write them down, but we lose ever and anon a word or a verse and substitute something of our own, and thus miswrite the poem. The men of more delicate ear write down these cadences more faithfully, and these transcripts, though imperfect, become the songs of the nations. For nature is as truly beautiful as it is good, or as it is reasonable, and must as much appcar as it must be done, or be known.

20. The author of this passage is a spokesman of

(A) naturalism   (D) realism

(B) aestheticism   (E) surrealism

(C) transcendentalism

21. The second paragraph contains ideas associated with

(A) optimism   (D) nihilism

(B) materialism   (E) existentialism

(C) utilitarianism

22. The author of this passage is also the author of

(A) *The Raven*   (D) *Self-Reliance*

(B) *Walden*   (E) *Biographia Literaria*

(C) *On Liberty*

23. To say "He was not unmindful" when one means that "He gave careful attention" is to employ

(A) inversion   (D) epanodos

(B) litotes   (E) hyperbole

(C) zeugma

Questions 24-28

> But Lord Crist, whan that it remembreth me
> Upon my youthe and on my jolitee,
> It tikleth me aboute myn herte roote – –
> Unto this day it dooth myn herte boote
> That I have had my world as in my time.
> But age, allas, that al wol envenime,
> Hath me biraft my beautee and my pith--
> Lat go, farewel, the devel go therwith!

5

146

The flour is goon, ther is namore to telle:
The bren as I best can now moste I selle;
But it to be right merye wol I fonde.   10

24.   What is the meaning of "envenime" in line six?

(A) enlighten   (D) poison

(B) perfect   (E) delight

(C) envy

25.   In the metaphor in lines nine and ten, what is compared to what?

(A) The speaker's body to the seed husk of cereal grain

(B) The speaker's beauty to faded flowers

(C) The speaker's body to cereal grain ready for harvesting

(D) The speaker's beauty to flour that has gone bad

(E) The speaker's body to flowers that are now difficult to sell

26.   Which of the following best expresses the speaker's attitude toward past experience? The speaker

(A) tries not to think about the past

(B) would like to do a number of things differently if given the chance

(C) feels pleasure in recalling good times past

(D) feels guilt for some previous flings

(E) regrets numerous missed opportunities

27.   The speaker might best be described as

(A) a romantic   (D) a Pollyanna

(B) a misanthrope   (E) a pragmatist

(C) an idealist

28. The speaker is

(A) Alison in *The Miller's Tale*

(B) the Prioress

(C) the Wife of Bath

(D) the Pardoner

(E) Griselda in *The Clerk's Tale*

Questions 29-33

His adherence to general nature has exposed him to the censure of criticks, who form their judgments upon narrower principles. Dennis and Rhymer think his Romans not sufficiently Roman; and Voltaire censures his kings as not completely royal. Dennis is offended, that Menenius, a senator of Rome, should play the buffoon; and Voltaire perhaps thinks decency violated when the Danish Usurper is represented as a drunkard. But our poet always makes nature predominate over accident; and if he preserves the essential character, is not very careful of distinctions superinduced and adventitious. His story requires Romans or kings, but he thinks only on men. He knew that Rome, like every other city, had men of all dispositions; and wanting a buffoon, he went into the senate-house for that which the senate-house would certainly have afforded him. He was inclined to shew an usurper and a murderer not only odious but despicable, he therefore added drunkenness to his other qualities, knowing that kings love wine like other men, and that wine exerts its natural power upon kings. These are the petty cavils of petty minds; a poet overlooks the casual distinction of country and condition, as a painter, satisfied with the figure, neglects the drapery.

29. The writer under discussion is

(A) Sophocles   (D) Dryden

(B) Milton   (E) Spencer

(C) Shakespeare

148

30.   "Superinduced and adventitious" (line ten) means

(A) additional and chance, not inherent

(B) superficial and hazardous, not certain

(C) careless and unnatural, not innate

(D) unclear and indefinite, not carefully considered

(E) basic and essential, not accidental

31.   Which of the following best describes the writer's use of
       Dennis, Rhymer, and Voltaire in this passage?

(A) He agrees with most of their criticism, but says it derives
     from narrower principles than he is using in this essay.

(B) He finds greater merit in Voltaire's criticism than in that of
     Rhymer and Dennis.

(C) He admires all three as critics, but respectfully differs with
     them on these matters.

(D) He finds greater merit in the criticism of Rhymer and
     Dennis than in Voltaire's.

(E) He believes the criticism of all three is trivial and mis-
     guided.

32.   Which of the following best expresses the critical principle on
       which the author's specific arguments are based?

(A) The poet, like the painter, must not neglect finishing
     touches, the "drapery" that particularizes the individual.

(B) The poet must be aware of cultural differences and
     changing fashions in order to portray them accurately.

(C) The poet should focus his efforts on the accurate represen-
     tation of universal truths and characteristics, on general
     nature common to all ages and places.

(D) The poet is a product of his own time and place, is best
     acquainted with it, and must therefore depict its unique
     characteristics in order to leave an accurate account for
     future generations.

(E) Particular manners and eccentricities best define human individuality; hence the poet should concentrate on a just representation of these.

33. The author of this passage is

(A) Sidney

(D) Poe

(B) Johnson

(E) Ruskin

(C) Shelley

Questions 34-36 refer to the excerpts below.

34. Which is the "I" of Poe's *The Cask of Amontillado*?

35. Which is the "I" of Joyce's *Araby*?

36. Which is the "I" of Eudora Welty's *Why I Live at the P.O*?

(A) My family are naturally the main people in China Grove, and if they prefer to vanish from the face of the earth, for all the mail they get or the mail they write, why, I'm not going to open my mouth. Some of the folks here in town are taking up for me and some turned against me. I know which is which. There are always people who will quit buying stamps just to get on the right side of Pappa-Daddy.

But here I am, and here I'll stay. I want the world to know I'm happy.

And if Stella-Rondo should come to me this minute, on bended knees, and *attempt* to explain the incidents of her life with Mr. Whitaker, I'd simply put my fingers in both my ears and refuse to listen.

(B) In walks these three girls in nothing but bathing suits. I'm in the third checkout slot, with my back to the door, so I don't see them until they're over by the bread. The one that caught my eye first was the one in the plaid green two-piece. She was a chunky kid, with a good tan and a sweet broad soft-looking can with those two crescents of

white just under it, where the sun never seems to hit, at the top of the backs of her legs. I stood there with my hand on a box of HiHo crackers trying to remember if I rang it up or not. I ring it up again and the customer starts giving me hell. She's one of these cash-register-watchers, a witch about fifty with rouge on her cheekbones, and no eye brows, and I know it made her day to trip me up. She'd been watching cash registers for fifty years and probably never seen a mistake before.

(C)   I kept on creeping just the same, but I looked at him over my shoulder.

"I've got out at last," said I, "in spite of you and Jane. And I've pulled off most of the paper, so you can't put me back!"

Now why should that man have fainted? But he did, and right across my path by the wall, so that I had to creep over him every time!

(D) No answer still. I thrust a torch through the remaining aperture and let it fall within. There came forth in return only a jingling of the bells. My heart grew sick--on account of the dampness of the catacombs. I hastened to make an end of my labor. I forced the last stone into its position; I plastered it up. Against the new masonry I re-erected the old rampart of bones. For the half a century no mortal has disturbed them. *In pace requiescat*!

(E)   I lingered before her stall, though I knew my stay was useless, to make my interest in her wares seem the more real. Then I turned away slowly and walked down the middle of the bazaar. I allowed the two pennies to fall against the sixpence in my pocket. I heard a voice call from one end of the gallery that the light was out. The upper part of the hall was now completely dark.

Gazing up into the darkness I saw myself as a creature driven and derided by vanity; and my eyes burned with anguish and anger.

Questions 37-39 refer to the excerpts below.

37. Which is spoken by Jaques?

38. Which is spoken by Falstaff?

39. Which is spoken by Caliban?

(A) Slanders, sir; for the satirical rogue says here that old men
    have grey beards, that their faces are wrinkled, their eyes
    purging thick amber and plum-tree gum, and that they
    have a plentiful lack of wit, together with most weak
    hams. All which, sir, though I most powerfully and
    potently believe, yet I hold it not honesty to have it thus
    set down, for yourself, sir, shall grow old as I am, if like
    a crab you could go backward.

(B)   All the world's a stage,
    And all the men and women merely players.
    They have their exits and their entrances,
    And one man in his time plays many parts,
    His acts being seven ages. At first the infant,
    Mewling and puking in the nurse's arms . . .
                                  Last scene of all,
    That ends this strange eventful history,
    Is second childishness and mere oblivion,
    Sans teeth, sans eyes, sans taste, sans every thing.

(C) Our revels now are ended. These our actors,
    As I foretold you, were all spirits and
    Are melted into air, into thin air;
    And, like the baseless fabric of this vision,
    The cloud-capp'd tow'rs, the gorgeous palaces,
    The solemn temples, the great globe itself,
    Yea, all which it inherit, shall dissolve
    And, like this insubstantial pageant faded,
    Leave not a rack behind. We are such stuff
    As dreams are made on, and our little life
    Is rounded with a sleep.

(D) You taught me language, and my profit on 't
    Is, I know how to curse. The red plague rid you
    For learning me your language!

(E) I'll starve ere I'll rob a foot further. An 'twere not as good a deed as drink to turn true man and to leave these rogues, I am the veriest varlet that ever chew'd with a tooth. Eight yards of uneven ground is threescore and ten miles afoot with me, and the stony-hearted villains know it well enough.   A plague upon it when thieves cannot be true one to another!

Questions 40-42 refer to the descriptions below.

40.   Which describes heroic drama?

41.   Which describes a dumb show?

42.   Which describes the masque?

(A) A form of Italian low comedy in which the actors, who usually performed conventional or stock parts, such as the "pantaloon," improvised their dialogue, though a plot or scenario was provided them.

(B) An elaborate form of court entertainment, combining poetic drama, music, song, dance, elegant costuming, and stage spectacle. The plot was usually slight, and chiefly mythological and allegorical. The characters were played by ladies and gentlemen of the court, including royalty. The play concluded with a dance of players, who removed their masks and took members of the audience for partners.

(C) Developed in England during the Restoration, it was characterized by excessive spectacle, violent emotional conflicts in the main characters, extravagant bombastic dialogue, and epic personages as chief characters. It was usually set in a distant land, and its hero was torn between love and honor.

(D) An episode of pantomime introduced into a spoken play. It was common in Elizabethan drama, in which it was used in imitation of Seneca. An example is the miming of the banishment of the Duchess and her family in *The Duchess of Malfi.*

153

(E) A form made popular on the Elizabethan stage by Thomas Kyd, whose *Spanish Tragedy* is an early example of the type. It is largely Senecan in its inspiration and technique. The theme is vengeance carried out by a father for a son or vice versa. A common trait is the sensational use of horrors, such as murders on stage and exhibitions of dead bodies.

43. All of the following are pastoral elegies EXCEPT

(A) Milton's *Lycidas*

(B) Johnson's *The Vanity of Human Wishes*

(C) the November eclogue of Spencer's *The Shepheardes Calendar*

(D) Shelley's *Adonais*

(E) Arnold's *Thyrsis*

44. _____ grew out of several convergent ideas, of which the antipathy to Italian opera was but one: an even more cogent one was the satirizing of the court circle by comparing it with the underworld.

Which of the following correctly completes the line above?

(A) *Tamburlaine, Part I*   (D) *The Beggar's Opera*

(B) *The Duchess of Malfi*   (E) *She Stoops to Conquer*

(C) *Venice Preserved*

Questions 45-47

DORIMANT You were talking of play, madam. Pray, what may be your stint?

HARRIET A little harmless discourse in public walks, or at most an appointment in a box, barefaced, at the playhouse: you are for masks and private meetings, where women engage for all they are worth, I hear.

DORIMANT I have been used to deep play, but I can make one at small game when I like my gamester well.

HARRIET And be so unconcerned you'll ha' no pleasure in't.

DORIMANT When there is a considerable sum to be won, the hope of drawing people in makes every trifle considerable.

45.   In this exchange, meaning is conveyed through

(A) classical allusions   (D) direct statement

(B) invective   (E) dramatic irony

(C) an extended metaphor

46.   Which of the following best captures the meaning of Dorimant's second speech?

(A) Although he prefers to gamble for large sums, he can be content playing for lower stakes if the game is sufficiently interesting.

(B) Although he has been accustomed to sexual conquest, he can settle for less if he likes his partner well enough.

(C) He is competent at all kinds of games, whether serious or frivolous.

(D) Although he prefers serious games, he is willing to play less serious ones if he likes his partner well enough.

(E) He prefers many sexual partners, but can be content with one if she is sufficiently interesting.

47.   The dialogue is characteristic of

(A) Elizabethan comedy of humours

(B) heroic drama

(C) Restoration comedy

(D) eighteenth-century sentimental comedy

(E) theater of the absurd

Questions 48-50 refer to the pairings below.

48. Which use unintrusive or impersonal narration?

49. Which use fallible or unreliable narrators?

50. Which use self-conscious narrators?

(A) Sterne's *Tristram Shandy* and Proust's *Remembrance of Things Past*

(B) Hardy's *The Mayor of Casterbridge* and Forster's *Howards End*

(C) Lardner's *Haircut* and Faulkner's *The Sound and the Fury*

(D) Hemingway's *The Killers* and *A Clean Well-Lighted Place*

(E) Tolstoy's *The Death of Ivan Ilych* and Hawthorne's *The Scarlet Letter*

Questions 51-54

We shall not always plant while others reap
The golden increment of bursting fruit,
Not always countenance, abject and mute,
That lesser men should hold their brothers cheap;
Not everlastingly while others sleep   5
Shall we beguile their limbs with mellow flute,
Not always bend to some more subtle brute;
We were not made eternally to weep.

The night whose sable breast relieves the stark
White stars is no less lovely being dark,   10
And there are buds that cannot bloom at all

In light, but crumple, piteous, and fall;
So in the dark we hide the heart that bleeds,
And wait, and tend our agonizing seeds.

51.   The poem differs in form from the usual pattern of a Petrarchan sonnet in that

(A) a shift in the thought process occurs at the beginning of line nine
(B) it contains an octave and a sestet rather than three quatrains and a couplet

(C) it contains more than five rhymes

(D) the sestet contains three couplets

(E) the octave contains eight lines

52.   Which of the following most accurately states the burden of the octave?

(A) It protests the elevation of inferior men to high public office while more able men go unrecognized.

(B) It predicts that the oppressed will not forever be oppressed.

(C) It expresses a desire for the redistribution of wealth.

(D) It is a plea for violent revolution.

(E) It predicts that the abolition of slavery will be followed by years of more subtle oppression.

53.   Which of the following most accurately expresses the idea contained in lines nine and ten?

(A) The armies of darkness will eventually overwhelm the armies of light.

(B) The darkness of night threatens to obliterate starlight.

(C) The night would be lovelier without stars.

(D) The white stars are lovely in spite of the darkness of night.

(E) Black is beautiful.

157

54. Countée Cullen, the author of this poem, was one of the more notable writers of the

(A) Harlem Renaissance

(B) poetic movement known as Imagism

(C) Aesthetic Movement

(D) fin de siécle

(E) Age of Sensibility

Questions 55 – 57 refer to the excerpts below.

55. Which was written by Henry Fielding?

56. Which was written by D.H. Lawrence?

57. Which was written by E.M. Forster?

(A) But if you pick up a novel, you realize immediately that infinity is just a handle to this self-same jug of a body of mine; while as for knowing, if I find my finger in the fire, I know that fire burns, with a knowledge so emphatic and vital, it leaves Nirvana merely a conjecture. Oh, yes, my body, me alive, *knows*, and knows intensely. And as for the sum of all knowledge, it can't be anything more than an accumulation of all the things I know in the body, and you, dear reader, know in the body.

(B) Now a comic Romance is a comic Epic-Poem in Prose; differing from Comedy, as the serious Epic from Tragedy: its Action being more extended and comprehensive; containing a much larger Circle of Incidents, and introducing a greater Variety of Characters. It differs from the serious Romance in its Fable and Action, in this; that as in the one these are grave and solemn, so in the other they are light and ridiculous: it differs in its Characters, by introducing Persons of inferiour Rank, and consequently of inferiour Manners, whereas the grave Romance, sets the highest before us; lastly in its Sentiments and Diction; by preserving the Ludicrous instead of the Sublime.

(C) There is one point at which the moral sense and the artistic sense lie very near together; that is in the light of the very obvious truth that the deepest quality of a work of art will always be the quality of the mind of the producer. In proportion as that intelligence is fine will the novel, the picture, the statue partake of the substance of beauty and truth. To be constituted of such elements is, to my vision, to have purpose enough. No good novel will ever proceed from a superficial mind; that seems to me an axiom which, for the artist in fiction, will cover all needful moral ground: if the youthful aspirant take it to heart it will illuminate for him many of the mysteries of "purpose."

(D) Fiction — — if it at all aspires to be art — — appeals to temperament. And in truth it must be, like painting, like music, like all art, the appeal of one temperament to all the other innumerable temperaments whose subtle and resistless power endows passing events with their true meaning, and creates the moral, the emotional atmosphere of the place and time. Such an appeal, to be effective, must be an impression conveyed through the senses; and, in fact, it cannot be made in any other way, because temperament, whether individual or collective, is not amenable to persuasion. All art, therefore, appeals primarily to the senses, and the artistic aim when expressing itself in written words must also make its appeal through the senses, if its high desire is to reach the secret spring of responsive emotions.

(E) Yes, oh, dear, yes — — the novel tells a story. That is the fundamental aspect without which it could not exist. That is the highest factor common to all novels, and I wish that it was not so, that it could be something different--melody, or perception of truth, not this low atavistic form.

Questions 58-60

"Ah yes, a new journal might be worth trying. There was one advertised in the *Times Literary Supplement* a little while ago. Paton or some such name the editor fellow was called. You might have a go at him, now that it doesn't seem as if any of the more established reviews have got room for your... effort. Let's see now; what's the exact title you've given it?"

Dixon looked out of the window at the fields wheeling past, bright green after a wet April. It wasn't the double-exposure effect of the last half minute's talk that had dumbfounded him, for such incidents formed the staple material of Welch colloquies; it was the prospect of reciting the title of the article he'd written. It was a perfect title, in that it crystallised the article's niggling mindlessness, its funereal parade of yawn-enforcing facts, the pseudo-light it threw upon non-problems. Dixon had read, or begun to read, dozens like it, but his own seemed worse than most in its air of being convinced of its own usefulness and significance. "In considering this strangely neglected topic," it began. This what neglected topic? This strangely what topic? This strangely neglected what? His thinking all this without having defiled and set fire to the typescript only made him appear to himself as more of a hypocrite and fool. "Let's see," he echoed Welch in a pretended effort of memory: "Oh yes; *The economic influence of the developments in shipbuilding techniques, 1450 to 1485*. After all, that's what it's ..."

58.   This passage satirizes

(A) pedantic government reports

(B) yellow journalism

(C) writers who stoop to plagiarism

(D) trivial academic scholarship

(E) historians

59. Which of the following best describes the narrative technique used in this excerpt?

(A) The author uses Dixon as a kind of narrator, though in third person; events are filtered through Dixon's consciousness by means of an inside view.

(B) The author uses omniscient third person narration; events are seen from the points of view of both Welch and Dixon although we learn more about Dixon.

(C) The author uses an objective point of view, neither commenting on nor judging events.

(D) The author maximizes distance between Dixon and the reader, thereby reducing our sympathy for Dixon.

(E) The author uses first person narration in which the narrator is a primary agent in the action.

60. The author of this passage is

(A) Jack Kerouac　　　　(D) Kingsley Amis

(B) Woody Allen　　　　(E) Ken Kesey

(C) Joyce Cary

61. One of the chief tenets of Aestheticism (or the "Aesthetic Movement") is that

(A) any work of art is essentially utilitarian, and that its "reality" must be defined by reference to objects outside the work

(B) art is the highest value among man's works because it is self-sufficient and has no aim other than its own perfection

(C) art increases in value in direct proportion to the degree to which it reflects current and redeeming social values

(D) art will achieve perfection when artists pay equal attention to beauty and utility

(E) organic form is superior to artifice because the former refers to the real world whereas the latter does not

62. In a universe deprived of illusions and light, man feels an alien. His is an irremediable exile . . . This divorce between man and his life, the actor and his setting, truly constitutes the feeling of Absurdity.

Works influenced by this outlook have been written by

(A) Chekhov and Tolstoy   (D) Turgenev and Lermontov

(B) Ibsen and Silone   (E) Doctorow and Malamud

(C) Camus and Ionesco

63. The term "negative capability" was introduced by

(A) Dryden   (D) Keats

(B) Coleridge   (E) Hazlitt

(C) Johnson

64. We real cool. We
Left school. We

Lurk late. We
Strike straight. We

Sing sin. We
Thin gin. We

Jazz June. We
Die soon.

The author is

(A) Countée Cullen   (D) Richard Wilbur

(B) Langston Hughes   (E) Joyce Carol Oates

(C) Gwendolyn Brooks

65.   This work is an early instance of the propagandist novel and the
       novel of crime and its detection. Its intent is to illustrate "the
       tyranny and perfidiousness exercised by the powerful members
       of the community against those who are less privileged than
       themselves." This novel's author was an atheist who believed
       that rational creatures can live harmoniously without laws and
       institutions, married Mary Wollstonecraft, and also wrote
       Enquiry concerning Political Justice.

       The work described above is

       (A) *Moll Flanders*   (D) *Humphrey Clinker*

       (B) *Caleb Williams*   (E) *Tristram Shandy*

       (C) *Pamela*

Questions 66-78. For each of the following passages, identify the
author or the work. Base your decision on the content and style of each
passage.

66.   From hence, ye Beauties, undeceiv'd
       Know, one false step is ne'er retriev'd,
            And be with caution bold.
       Not all that tempts your wand'ring eyes
       And heedless hearts, is lawful prize;
            Nor all, that glitters, gold.

(A) Sir Walter Raleigh   (D) Thomas Gray

(B) Richard Lovelace   (E) William Blake

(C) Jonathan Swift

67.   "And what in the world, my dear, did you mean by it?"--that
        sound, as at the touch of a spring, rang out as the first effect of
        Fanny's speech. It broke upon the two women's absorption with
        a sharpness almost equal to the smash of the crystal, for the door
        of the room had been opened by the Prince without their taking
        heed. He had apparently had time, moreover, to catch the
        conclusion of Fanny's act; his eyes attached themselves,
        through the large space allowing just there, as happened, a free
        view, to the shining fragments at this lady's feet. His question
        had been addressed to his wife, but he moved his eyes imme-
        diately afterwards to those of her visitor, whose own then held
        them in a manner of which neither party had been capable,
        doubtless, for mute penetration, since the hour spent by him in
        Cadogan Place on the eve of his marriage and the afternoon of
        Charlotte's reappearance. Something now again became pos-
        sible for these communicants, under the intensity of their pres-
        sure, something that took up that tale and that might have been
        a redemption of pledges then exchanged.

        (A) Jane Austen   (D) W. M. Thackeray

        (B) Edith Wharton   (E) Henry James

        (C) George Eliot

68.   [He] believed in the green light, the orgiastic future that year by
        year recedes before us. It eluded us then, but that's no matter-
        -tomorrow we will run faster, stretch out our arms farther . . .
         And one fine morning--
            So we beat on, boats against the current, borne back cease-
        lessly into the past.

        (A) Melville   (D) Faulkner

        (B) Dreiser   (E) Porter

        (C) Fitzgerald

164

69.   I reason, Earth is short--
And Anguish--absolute--
And many hurt,
But, what of that? . . .

I reason, that in Heaven--
Somehow, it will be even--
Some new Equation, given--
But, what of that?

(A) Emily Dickinson

(B) Walt Whitman

(C) Ezra Pound

(D) Wallace Stevens

(E) Dorothy Parker

70.   He looked down at the tangled wet hair, the wild, bare, animal
shoulders. He was amazed, bewildered, and afraid. He had
never thought of loving her. He had never wanted to love her.
When he rescued her and restored her, he was a doctor, and she
was a patient. He had had no single personal thought of her.
Nay, this introduction of the personal element was very dis-
tasteful to him, a violation of his professional honor. It was
horrible to have her there embracing his knees. It was horrible.
He revolted from it, violently. And yet--and yet--he had not the
power to break away.

(A) James Fennimore Cooper's *The Last of the Mohicans*

(B) Emily Bronte's *Wuthering Heights*

(C) D. H. Lawrence's *The Horse Dealer's Daughter*

(D) Ernest Hemingway's *The Short Happy Life of Francis
Macomber*

(E) Graham Greene's *The End of the Affair*

71.   In Dublin a week later, that would be September 19th, Neary
minus his whiskers was recognized by a former pupil called
Wylie, in the General Post Office contemplating from behind
the statue of Cuchulain. Neary had bared his head, as though the
holy ground meant something to him. Suddenly he flung aside

his hat, sprang forward, seized the dying hero by the thighs and began to dash his head against his buttocks, such as they are.

(A) Jonathan Swift

(D) Samuel Beckett

(B) James Joyce

(E) J.P. Donleavy

(C) Dylan Thomas

72. I have upset the poor man, he thought. Bishops, just like the very poor and the uneducated, should be treated with a special prudence.

Whispers were to be heard from the passage outside his door. Then the key turned in the lock. So I am a prisoner, he thought, like Cervantes.

(A) Mark Twain

(D) John Steinbeck

(B) Graham Greene

(E) Jorge Luis Borges

(C) Gabriel Garcia Marquez

73. I said to Hanson, as I recall, "We're two of a kind. Smolak was cast off and I am an Ishmael, tool." As I lay in the stable, I would think about Dick's death and about my father. But most of the time I lived not with horses but with Smolak, and this poor creature and I were very close. So before pigs ever came on my horizon, I received a deep impression from a bear. So if corporeal things are an image of the spiritual and visible objects are renderings of invisible ones, and if Smolak and I were outcasts together, two humorists before the crowd, but brothers in our souls--I enbeared by him, and he probably humanized by me--I didn't come to the pigs as a tabula rasa. It only stands to reason. Something deep already was inscribed on me. In the end, I wonder if Dahfu would have found this out for himself.

(A) Faulkner's *Absalom, Absalom!*

(B) Wright's *Native Son*

(C) Malamud's *The Assistant*

(D) Bellow's *Henderson the Rain King*

(E) Heller's *Catch-22*

166

74. She tried to go on with her letter, reminding herself that she was only an elderly woman who had got up too early in the morning and journeyed too far, that the despair creeping over her was merely her despair, her personal weakness, and that even if she got a sunstroke and went mad the rest of the world would go on. But suddenly, at the edge of her mind, Religion appeared, poor little talkative Christianity, and she knew that all its divine words from "Let there be Light" to "It is finished" only amounted to "boum." Then she was terrified over an area larger than usual; the universe, never comprehensible to her intellect, offered no repose to her soul, the mood of the last two months took definite form at last, and she realized that she didn't want to write to her children, didn't want to communicate with anyone, not even with God.

(A) D. H. Lawrence   (D) Virginia Woolf

(B) Joseph Conrad   (E) Graham Greene

(C) E. M. Forster

75. No matter: she was not happy, and never had been. Why was life so unsatisfying? Why did everything she leaned on in stantly crumble into dust? . . . But if somewhere there existed a strong, handsome man with a valorous, passionate and refined nature, a poet's soul in the form of an angel, a lyre with strings of bronze intoning elegiac nuptial songs to the heavens, why was it not possible that she might meet him some day? No, it would never happen! Besides, nothing was worth seeking-- everything was a lie! Each smile hid a yawn of boredom, each joy a curse, each pleasure its own disgust; and the sweetest kisses only left on one's lips a hopeless longing for a higher ecstasy.

(A) Zola   (D) Maupassant

(B) Proust   (E) Anatole France

(C) Flaubert

76. If you really want to hear about it, the first thing you'll really want to know is where I was born, and what my lousy childhood was like, and how my parents were occupied and all before they had me, and all that David Copperfield kind of crap.

(A) Cheever's *The Wapshot Chronicle*

(B) Salinger's *The Catcher in the Rye*

(C) Roth's *Goodbye, Columbus*

(D) Amis' *Lucky Jim*

(E) Bellow's *Herzog*

77. O impotence of mind in body strong!
But what is strength without a double share
Of wisdom? Vast, unwieldy, burdensome,
Proudly secure, yet liable to fall
By weakest subtleties; not made to rule,
But to subserve where wisdom bears command.
God, when he gave me strength, to show withal,
How slight the gift was, hung it in my hair.

(A) *Everyman*   (D) *Samson Agonistes*

(B) *Doctor Faustus*   (E) *All for Love*

(C) *King Lear*

78. . . . ah yes I know them well who was the first person in the universe before there was anybody that made it all who ah that they dont know neither do I so there you are they might as well try to stop the sun from rising tomorrow the sun shines for you he said the day we were lying among the rhododendrons on Howth head in the grey tweed suit and his straw hat the day I got him to propose to me yes first I gave him the bit of seedcake out of my mouth and it was leapyear like now yes 16 years ago my God after that long kiss I near lost my breath yes he said I was a flower of the mountain . . .

168

(A) Thomas Hardy   (D) Arnold Bennett

(B) Aldous Huxley   (E) Evelyn Waugh

(C) James Joyce

Questions 79-81 refer to the excerpts below.

79.   Which is an example of objective narration?

80.   Which is an example of metafiction?

81.   Which is an example of euphuism?

(A) It'll never be known how this has to be told, in the first person or in the second, using the third person plural or continually inventing modes that will serve for nothing. If one might say: I will see the moon rose, or: we hurt me at the back of my eyes, and especially: you the blond woman was the clouds that race before my your his our yours their faces. What the hell.

(B) The question held her a minute, and while she waited, with her eyes on him, she put out a grasping hand to his arm, in the flesh of which he felt her answer distinctly enough registered. Thus she gave him, standing off a little, the firmest, longest, deepest injunction he had ever received from her. "Nothing--in spite of everything--*will* happen. Nothing *has* happened. Nothing *is* happening."

(C) The fourth day out, I think (we were then working down the east side of the Gulf of Siam, tack for tack, in light winds and smooth water)--the fourth day, I say, of this miserable juggling with the unavoidable, as we sat at our evening meal, that man, whose slightest movement I dreaded, after putting down the dishes ran up on deck busily. This could not be dangerous. Presently he came down again; and then it appeared that he had remembered a coat of mine which I had thrown over a rail to dry after having been wetted in a shower which had passed over the ship in the afternoon.

(D) I see now that as the fish Scolopidus in the flood Araris at the waxing of the Moon is as white as the driven snow, and at the waning as black as the burnt coal, so [X], which at the first encreasing of our familiarity, was very zealous, is now at the last cast become most faithless.

(E) He did not say anything but looked at the bags against the wall of the station. There were labels on them from all the hotels where they had spent nights.

"But I don't want you to," he said. "I don't care anything about it."

"I'll scream," the girl said.

The woman came out through the curtains with two glasses of beer and put them down on the damp felt pads. "The train comes in five minutes," she said.

82.   "No one who had ever seen [X] in her infancy would have supposed her born to be an heroine. Her situation in life, the character of her father and mother, her own person and disposition, were all equally against her."

These sentences are the first in

(A) *Emma*   (D) *Mansfield Park*

(B) *Pride and Prejudice*   (E) *Northanger Abbey*

(C) *Sense and Sensibility*

83.   A central theme in many of his novels is man's struggle against the neutral force that rules the universe, a force that is indifferent to man's suffering. This theme is frequently joined to an examination of life's ironies and love's disappointments. One of his novels deals with an intelligent and sensitive girl of humble origins driven to murder and hence to death by hanging by a series of bitterly ironic circumstances and events. Another chronicles the destruction of a villager whose intellectual ambitions are thwarted by his sensuality and by circumstances.

This passage describes

(A) D. H. Lawrence

(D) Evelyn Waugh

(B) Thomas Hardy

(E) Charles Dickens

(C) Joseph Conrad

Questions 84-86

Where's Héloise, the learned nun,
　　　For whose sake Abeillard, I ween,
Lost manhood and put priesthood on?
　　　(From Love he won such dule and teen!)
　　　And where, I pray you, is the queen
Who willed that Buridan should steer
　　　Sewed in a sack's mouth down the Seine?
But where are the snows of yesteryear?

84. This poem is structured around

(A) incremental repetition

(B) mock heroic conventions

(C) the "loathly lady"/beautiful princess motif

(D) the carpe diem motif

(E) the ubi sunt motif

85. Line three refers to the fact that Pierre Abelard

(A) became a monk in order to avoid corrupting Héloise,
who was a nun

(B) gave up a promising career at court because he was in love
with Heloise, whom he could never marry

(C) turned from the masculine pursuits of knighthood, such as
warfare, to the less vigorous pursuits of theology after
falling in love

(D) became a monk after Heloise's uncle had him emasculated

(E) became a priest after falling in love with Heloise because he wanted to be as spiritually similar to her as possible

86. The poem's poignancy derives largely from the author's awareness of

(A) the transitory, almost illusory, nature of all earthly beauty

(B) the futility of political intrigue

(C) the foolishness of theological quarrels

(D) the problem of evil in the world

(E) endless cycles of death and renewal

Questions 87-89

--I am a gentleman in a dustcoat trying
To make you hear. Your ears are soft and small
And listen to an old man not at all,
They want the young men's whispering and sighing.
But see the roses on your trellis dying
And hear the spectral singing of the moon;
For I must have my lovely lady soon,
I am a gentleman in a dustcoat trying.

--I am a lady young in beauty waiting
Until my truelove comes, and then we kiss.
But what grey man among the vines is this
Whose words are dry and faint as in a dream?
Back from my trellis, Sir, before I scream!
I am a lady young in beauty waiting.

87. The speaker of the first eight lines can best be identified as

(A) the girl's father

(B) an elderly suitor the young lady has rejected

(C) death

(D) nature

(E) Father Time

88. The young lady's naive romanticism is best indicated by which of the following words or phrases?

(A) beauty waiting

(B) truelove

(C) dream

(D) trellis

(E) scream

89. The form of this poem can best be described as a variation of a

(A) Pindaric ode

(B) Horatian ode

(C) Petrarchan sonnet

(D) Shakespearean sonnet

(E) villanelle

Questions 90-92 refer to the excerpts below.

90. Which is an example of a periodic sentence?

91. Which is an example of an oxymoron?

92. Which is an example of pathetic fallacy?

(A) He will tell you the names of the principal favourites, repeat the shrewd sayings of a man of quality, whisper an intrigue that is not yet blown upon by common fame; or, if the sphere of his observations is a little larger than ordinary, will perhaps enter into all the incidents, turns, and revolutions in a game of ombre.

(B) To write the Life of him who excelled all mankind in writing the lives of others, and who, whether we consider his extraordinary endowments, or his various works, has been equalled by few in any age, is an arduous, and may be reckoned in me a presumptuous task.

(C) The one red leaf, the last of its clan,
   That dances as often as dance it can.

(D) O Death in life, the days that are no more.

(E) When Nerves were too delicately spun to bear the rude
   Shakes and Jostlings which we meet with in this transitory world, Nature gave way; She sunk and died a Martyr
   to Excessive Sensibility.

Questions 93-96

About suffering they were never wrong,
The Old Masters: how well they understood
Its human position; how it takes place
While someone else is eating or opening a window or just
          walking dully along;
How, when the aged are reverently, passionately waiting   5
For the miraculous birth, there always must be
Children who did not specially want it to happen, skating
On a pond at the edge of the wood:
They never forgot
That even the dreadful martyrdom must run its course   10
Anyhow in a corner, some untidy spot
Where the dogs go on with their doggy life and the torturer's
          horse
Scratches its innocent behind on a tree.

In Brueghel's *Icarus*, for instance: how everything turns away
Quite leisurely from the disaster; the plowman may   15
Have heard the splash, the forsaken cry,
But for him it was not an important failure; the sun shone
As it had to on the white legs disappearing into the green
Water; and the expensive delicate ship that must have seen
Something amazing, a boy falling out of the sky,   20
Had somewhere to get to and sailed calmly on.

93. Which of the following best describes the relationship of the second stanza to the first?

(A) The second stanza continues the development of the general idea advanced in stanza one.

(B) The second stanza proposes a general idea based on the specific examples in stanza one.

(C) The second stanza provides a specific example of the general idea advanced in stanza one.

(D) The second stanza proposes a general idea that contrasts with the general idea advanced in stanza one.

(E) The second stanza uses a specific instance to contradict the general idea advanced in stanza one.

94. What do the children in the first stanza have in common with the plowman in the second stanza?

(A) Both refuse to take responsibility for their actions.

(B) Both believe they are powerless to influence human history.

(C) They are used as examples of one of man's greatest strengths--the ability to carry on in the face of disaster.

(D) Both are indifferent to extraordinary events.

(E) Both would like to take part in the world around them, but realize the futility of any action they might take.

95. Auden uses dogs and a horse (line twelve) chiefly to illustrate

(A) obliviousness to suffering

(B) man's superior rationality in comparison to the animal world

(C) the moral superiority of animals to man because of the former's greater innocence

175

(D) the untidiness of nature

(E) the necessity of suffering in daily life

96. Another poem dealing with Brueghel's *Icarus* was written by

(A) Hart Crane

(B) T. S. Eliot

(C) Wallace Stevens

(D) Marianne Moore

(E) William Carlos Williams

Questions 97-98

My mistress' eyes are nothing like the sun;
Coral is far more red than her lips' red:
If snow be white, why then her breasts are dun;
If hairs be white, black wires grow on her head.

97. In these lines, the author is satirizing the use of which of the following by other Elizabethan sonneteers?

(A) hackneyed Petrarchan conceits

(B) encomia

(C) rhymed quatrains

(D) obscure metaphysical conceits

(E) love as the subject of sonnets

98. The author of these line is

(A) Wyatt

(B) Sidney

(C) Raleigh

(D) Marlowe

(E) Shakespeare

Questions 99-100

. . . a kind of discordia concors; a combination of dissimilar images, or discovery of occult resemblances in things apparently unlike . . . .The most heterogeneous ideas are yoked by violence together; nature and art are ransacked for illustrations, comparisons, and allusions . . . but the reader commonly thinks his improvement dearly bought, and, though he sometimes admires, is seldom pleased.

99.   The author is discussing

   (A) the pathetic fallacy   (D) heroic drama

   (B) Renaissance pastoral poetry   (E) Hudibrastic poetry

   (C) metaphysical wit

100.   The author of this passage is

   (A) Swift   (D) Dryden

   (B) Pope   (E) Johnson

   (C) Addison

101.   The conclusion of Bertolt Brecht's *Threepenny Opera*, in which Macheath is suddenly and unexpectedly reprieved, parodies the abuse of which literary device?

   (A) Anagnorisis   (D) Deus ex machina

   (B) Bombast   (E) Pathetic fallacy

   (C) Comic relief

102. An epithalamium might appropriately be sung

(A) at a coronation   (D) at any church service

(B) at a funeral   (E) on New Year's Eve

(C) at a wedding

103. He lived amidst th' untrodden ways,
     To Rydal Lake that lead,
A bard whom there were none to praise,
     And very few to read.

These lines parody the first stanza of a poem by

(A) Herrick   (D) Arnold

(B) Pope   (E) Yeats

(C) Wordsworth

104. Joan of Arc has been the subject of dramas by all of the following EXCEPT

(A) Giraudoux   (D) Brecht

(B) Anouilh   (E) Shaw

(C) Schiller

105. "Sentimental" is sometimes used to describe works that celebrate man's natural benevolence and seek to evoke tears for the sufferings of the virtuous or innocent.

Examples of sentimental works are

(A) Henry Fielding's *Tom Jones* and Sir George Etherege's *The Man of Mode*

(B) Samuel Richardson's *Clarissa* and Henry Fielding's *The Tragedy of Tragedies, or Tom Thumb*

(C) Fanny Burney's *Evelina* and John Gay's *The Beggar's Opera*

(D) Jane Austen's *Emma* and Thomas Otway's *Venice Preserved*

(E) Henry Mackenzie's *The Man of Feeling* and Sir Richard Steele's *The Conscious Lovers*

106. _____ published epic poems and verse fragments that were purported to be translations from the Gaelic of a poet called _____.Although these works were greatly admired for their romantic, melancholy spirit and for their exotic rhythm, their authenticity was doubted by Dr. Johnson and others. Subsequent research has shown that these works are a combination of liberally edited traditional Gaelic poems and passages written by their publisher.

Which of the following correctly completes the first sentence above?

(A) Sir Walter Scott . . . Eyrbiggia

(B) James Boswell . . . Temora

(C) David Hume . . . Cuthullin

(D) Henry Mackenzie . . . Fingal

(E) James Macpherson . . . Ossian

Questions 107-108

I intend to let Lady Danvers see no farther of my papers, than to her own angry letter to her brother; for I would not have her see my reflections upon it; and she'll know, down to that place, all that's necessary for her curiosity, as to my sufferings, and the stratagems used against me, and the honest part I have been enabled to act: And I hope, when she has read them all, she will be quite reconciled: for she will see it is all God Almighty's doings; and that a gentleman of his parts and knowledge was not to be drawn in by such a poor young body as me. . .

And so, with my humble duty to you both, and my dear
Mr. B----'s kind remembrance, I rest
Your ever-dutiful and gratefully happy Daughter.

107.   The excerpt is from

(A) a picaresque novel   (D) an epistolary novel

(B) a novella   (E) an historical novel

(C) a Gothic novel

108.   The author of this passage is

(A) Defoe   (D) Smollett

(B) Richardson   (E) Sterne

(C) Fielding

Questions 109-110

"The new anesthetizer is giving away!" shouted an intern.
"There is no one in the East who know how to fix it!"
"Quiet, man!" said ____, in a low, cool voice. He sprang to
the machine, which was now going pocketa-pocketa-queep-
pocketa-queep. He began fingering delicately a row of glistening dials. "Give me a fountain pen!" he snapped. Someone handed him a fountain pen. He pulled a faulty piston out
of the machine and inserted the pen in its place. "That will
hold for ten minutes," he said. "Get on with the operation."
A nurse hurried over and whispered to Renshaw, and ____
saw the man turn pale. "Coreopsis has set in," said Renshaw
nervously. "If you would take over,____?" ____ looked at
him and at the craven figure of Benbow, who drank, and at
the grave, uncertain faces of the two great specialists. "If
you wish," he said. They slipped a white gown on him; he

adjusted a mask and drew on thin gloves; nurses handed him shining . . .

"Back it up, Mac Look out for that Buick!"
_____ jammed on the brakes. "Wrong lane, Mac," said the parking-lot attendant, looking at _____ closely. "Gee. Yeh," muttered _____. He began cautiously to back out of the lane marked Exit Only. "Leave her sit there," said the attendant. "I'll put her away."

109. Which of the following names correctly completes this excerpt?

(A) Augie March   (D) Gregor Samsa

(B) Holden Caulfield   (E) Alibi Ike

(C) Walter Mitty

110. Which of the following best describes the story's narrative strategy? The narrator

(A) contrasts the protagonist's real and fantasy lives for comic effect

(B) uses prolonged inside views to illustrate the inadequacy of others in the world the protagonist is forced to live in

(C) contrasts the protagonist's sensitivity and intellectual superiority with the boorishness and brutality of others

(D) uses understatement to convey his moral indignation at the protagonist's excesses

(E) contrasts appearance and reality in appealing to the sentimental nature of his readers, who are expected to weep for the protagonist's excesses

111. *Widsith* deals with the life of

(A) a Celtic king

(B) an Anglo-Saxon scop

(C) an Arthurian knight

(D) an early Christian missionary

(E) a Norman courtier

112. "Courage is the instrument by which the hero realizes himself. 'Fate often saves an undoomed man when his courage is good,' says _____ in his account of his swimming match: that is, if Fate has not entirely doomed a man in advance, courage is the quality that can perhaps influence Fate against its natural tendency to doom him now. . . . Doom, of course, ultimately claims him, but not until he has fulfilled to its limits the pagan ideal of a heroic life."

Which of the following correctly completes the second sentence?

(A) Cuchulian

(D) Bcowulf

(B) Odysseus

(E) Achilles

(C) Hrothgar

113. Scrious over my cereals I broke one breakfast my fast
     With something-to-read searching retinas retained by print
  on a packet;
     Sprung rhythm sprang, and I found (the mind fact-mining
  at last)
     An influence Father-[X]-fathered on the copy-writing
  racket

These lines parody the style of (the"X" in line four)

(A) Robinson Jeffers

(D) Gerard Manley Hopkins

(B) H[ilda] D[oolittle]

(E) Hart Crane

(C) Edna St. Vincent Millay

114. I chopped down the house that you had been saving to live
    in next summer.
    I am sorry, but it was morning, and I had nothing to do
      and its wooden beams were so inviting. . . .

    I gave away the money that you had been saving to live on
      for the next ten years.
    The man who asked for it was shabby
      and the firm March wind on the porch was so juicy and
      cold.

These two stanzas are from a poem entitled "Variations on a
Theme by ____"

(A) Emily Dickinson   (D) Wallace Stevens

(B) William Carlos Williams   (E) Robert Lowell

(C) Archibald MacLeish

115. Gramercy, Good Deeds! Now may I true friends see.
    They have forsaken me every one--
    I loved them better than my Good Deeds alone.
    Knowledge, will you forsake me also?

These lines are from

(A) *The Knight of the Burning Pestle*

(B) *Everyman*

(C) *The Faerie Queene*

(D) *The Brome Play of Abraham and Isaac*

(E) *Volpone*

Questions 116-118 refer to the excerpts below.

116. Which is by William Blake?

183

117. Which is by James Baldwin?

118. Which is by Oscar Wilde?

(A) So no wonder that in certain cities of America, in New York of course, and New Orleans, in Chicago and San Francisco and Los Angeles, in such American cities as Paris and Mexico, D.F., this particular part of a generation was attracted to what the Negro had to offer. In such places as Greenwich Village, a menage-a-trois was completed--the bohemian and the juvenile delin quent came face-to-face with the Negro, and the hipster was a fact in American life. If marijuana was the wedding ring, the child was the language of Hip for its argot gave expression to the abstract states of feeling which all could share, at least all who were Hip.

(B) The day of my father's funeral had also been my nineteenth birthday. As we drove him to the graveyard, the spoils of injustice, anarchy, discontent, and hatred were all around us. It seemed to me that God himself had devised, to mark my father's end, the most sustained and brutally dissonant of codas. And it seemed to me, too, that the violence which rose all about us as my father left the world had been devised as a corrective for the pride of his eldest son. I had declined to believe in that apocalypse which had been central to my father's vision; very well, life seemed to be saying, here is something that will certainly pass for an apocalypse until the real thing comes along.

(C) The Last Judgment is an Overwhelming of Bad Art & Science. Mental Things are alone Real; what is Called Corporeal Nobody Knows of its dwelling Place; it is in Fallacy & its Existence an Imposture. Where is the Existence Out of Mind or Thought? Where is it but in the Mind of a Fool? . . . "What," it will be Questioned,

"When the Sun rises do you not see a round Disk of fire somewhat like a Guinea?" O no no, I see an Innumerable company of the Heavenly host crying "Holy Holy Holy is the Lord God Almighty." I question not my Corporeal or Vegetative Eye any more than I would Question a Window concerning a Sight. I look thro it & not with it.

(D) I am not sure when the word "Gothic" was first generically applied to the architecture of the North; but I presume that whatever the date of its original usage, it was intended to imply reproach, and express the barbaric character of the nations among whom that architecture arose. It never implied that they were literally of Gothic lineage, far less that their architecture had been originally invented by the Goths themselves; but it did imply that they and their buildings together exhibited a degree of sternness and rudeness, which, in contradistinction to the character of Southern and Eastern nations, appeared like a perpetual reflection of thecontrast between the Goth and the Roman in their first encounter.

(E) It is the spectator, and not life, that art really mirrors. Diversity of opinion about a work of art shows that the work is new, complex, and vital.

When critics disagree the artist is in accord with himself.

We can forgive a man for making a useful thing as long as he does not admire it. The only excuse for making a useless thing is that one admires it intensely.

All art is quite useless.

Questions 119-123

If all the world and love were young,
And truth in every shepherd's tongue,
These pretty pleasures might me move
To live with thee and be thy love.

Time drives the flocks from field to fold   5
When rivers rage and rocks grow cold,
And Philomel becometh dumb;
The rest complains of cares to come.

The flowers do fade, and wanton fields
To wayward winter reckoning yields;   10
A honey tongue, a heart of gall,
Is fancy's spring, but sorrow's fall.

119. These lines are from a poem (*The Nymph's Reply to the Shepherd*) by _____, in reply to a poem (*The Passionate Shepherd to His Love*) by _____. Which of the following correctly completes the preceding sentence?

(A) Shakespeare . . . Surrey

(B) Raleigh . . . Marlowe

(C) Marvell . . . Spenser

(D) Waller . . . Lovelace

(E) Jonson . . . Herrick

120. The nymph asserts that the idyllic world portrayed by the shepherd is

(A) unrealistic, ignoring changes that come with the passage of time, harsh aspects of pastoral life, and such things as the need to provide for old age

(B) no longer viable because time has brought about societal and economic changes that make pastoral life virtually impossible

(C) tempting and possible, but not sufficiently enticing because she does not trust this shepherd

(D) not appealing because such a pastoral life leads ultimately to a rustication and regret that she does not intend to experience

(E) acceptable to the young, but not to her because she is no
longer young

121. Philomela (line seven) was

(A) the goddess of the fields and hence of fertility

(B) a minor deity associated with rural locations and sometimes associated with pastoral poetry

(C) turned into a nightingale or swallow but unable to sing
because she betrayed her mate

(D) a country girl who was abandoned by her lover after having
been seduced by him

(E) a maiden whose tongue was cut out by her sister's husband
so she could not reveal that he raped her

122. Which of the following best expresses the idea contained in
lines eleven and twelve?

(A) Spring is a time of plenty, but fall is a time of want.

(B) Submitting to fancy's sweet talk will eventually lead to
remorse or bitterness.

(C) We may think spring is a time of happiness, but experience
teaches us it contains an equal portion of sorrow.

(D) Spring fills the heart with thoughts of love and the ability
to express them, but they eventually fade.

(E) Although fancy rules the heart, sorrow follows a fall from
virtue.

123. Another response to *The Passionate Shepherd to His Love*,
entitled *The Bait*, was written by

187

(A) John Skelton   (D) George Herbert

(B) Michael Drayton   (E) Sir John Suckling

(C) John Donne

Questions 124-126

When I heard the learn'd astronomer
When the proofs, the figures, were ranged in columns before
    me,
When I was shown the charts and diagrams, to add, divide, and
    measure them,
When I sitting heard the astronomer where he lectured with
    much applause in the lecture-room,
How soon unaccountable I became tired and sick,   5
Till rising and gliding out I wander'd off by myself,
In the mystical moist night-air, and from time to time,
Look'd up in perfect silence at the stars.

124.   All of the following oppositions or contrasts are present in the
poem EXCEPT

(A) applause/silence

(B) scientific analysis/mysticism

(C) mathematical certainty/error

(D) light/dark

(E) group/individual

125.   Which of the following words has more than one meaning in
context?

(A) Figures (line 2)   (D) Mystical (line 7)

(B) Measure (line 3)   (E) Perfect (line 8)

(C) Applause (line 4)

126. The author of the poem above is

    (A) Emerson   (D) Whitman

    (B) James Russell Lowell   (E) Frost

    (C) Sandburg

Questions 127-130

> Men are but children of a larger growth;
> Our appetites as apt to change as theirs,
> And full as craving too, and full as vain;
> And yet the soul, shut up in her dark room,
> Viewing so clear abroad, at home sees nothing;   5
> But, like a mole in earth, busy and blind,
> Works all her folly up, and casts it outward
> To the world's open view: thus I discovered,
> And blamed the love of ruined Antony;
> Yet wish that I were he, to be so ruined.   10

127. "Her" in line seven refers to

    (A) Cleopatra   (D) lust or passion

    (B) soul   (E) appetite

    (C) mole

128. Dolabella has "discovered" Antony's love primarily because

    (A) he has used stealth to observe Antony in the latter's unguarded moments

    (B) he has observed Antony in two perspectives, from afar and up close

    (C) he has had the advantage of viewing him from "abroad", which has given him the emotional detachment necessary for objective analysis

(D) Antony's increasing vanity has aroused Dolabella's suspicions

(E) Antony's "soul" has revealed it to him

129. Dolabella's attitude toward Antony can best be described as one of

(A) unqualified admiration

(B) compassionate understanding

(C) bitter disillusionment

(D) moral condemnation

(E) self-congratulatory superiority

130. This passage is from

(A) Shakespeare's *Antony and Cleopatra*

(B) Shakespeare's *Julius Caesar*

(C) Samuel Daniel's *Cleopatra*

(D) Dryden's *All for Love*

(E) Shaw's *Caesar and Cleopatra*

Questions 131-136

Cou'd our first Father, at his toilsome Plough,
Thorns in his Path, and Labour on his Brow,
Cloath'd only in a rude, unpolish'd Skin;
Cou'd he, a vain, fantastick Nymph have seen,
In all her Airs, in all her Antick Graces;   5

Her various Fashions, and more various Faces;
How had it pos'd that Skill, which late Assign'd
Just Appellations to each sev'ral Kind,
A right Idea of the Sight to frame,
T' have guest from what new Element she came,   10
T' have hit the wavering Form, or giv'n this Thing a Name.

131. "Father" in line one refers to

(A) God

(D) Satan

(B) time

(E) George Washington

(C) Adam

132. "Pos'd" in line seven means

(A) perplexed

(D) undermined

(B) possessed

(E) contradicted

(C) positioned

133. The tone of the poem can best be described as

(A) nostalgic

(D) prayerful

(B) angry

(E) jocose

(C) solemn

134.. "Frame" in line nine is closest in meaning to

(A) recall

(D) enclose

(B) analyze

(E) devise falsely

(C) formulate

135. "Skill" (line seven) refers to the ability to

(A) solve puzzles from slight clues

(B) interpret the ways of God to man

(C) recognize the presence of incorporeal beings

(D) deduce valid conclusions from premises

(E) name things appropriately

136. "Thing" in the last line refers to

(A) Skill

(D) Nymph

(B) Appelation

(E) Idea

(C) Element

Questions 137-139 refer to the descriptions below.

137. Which describes John Ford's *'Tis Pity She's a Whore?*

138. Which describes Tennesee Williams' *A Streetcar Named Desire?*

139. Which describes Eugene O'Neill's *The Hairy Ape?*

(A) Militant in its pride in the middle-class, this prose tragedy recounts the downfall and eventual execution of a naive apprentice who is seduced by a more experienced woman who leads him to embezzle from his employer and finally to murder his uncle to satisfy her greed. The play is overtly didactic; its author defined the end of tragedy as "the exciting of the passions in order to the correcting such of them as are criminal, either in their nature, or through their excess."

(B) This play deals with a statesman and saint whose individualism, spirituality, and wit help him preserve his "adamantine sense of his own self" while struggling with political forces that ultimately destroy him. His refusal to compromise costs him his life, but establishes him as a man of strong character and integrity. The author uses the device of the Common Man to address the audience directly and to comment on the action of the play.

(C) This play deals with the incestuous love of brother and sister (Giovanni and Annabella). The pregnant Annabella marries one of her suitors, but refuses to name her lover after her pregnancy is discovered . Giovanni eventually stabs Annabella to forestall her husband's vengeance after the latter learns the identity of Annabella's lover. The husband and Giovanni are both killed in the final scene of the play. Like other plays by the same author, this work is marked by its powerful portrayal of melancholy and despair.

(D) This expressionist play deals with the perversion of human strength by technological progress. Its protagonist, a stupid and brutal stoker on a transatlantic liner, is a study in dehumanization, literally subservient to machines. His growing discontent and ineffectual rebellion end when he is crushed to death by a beast he has liberated in a zoo. The author's work has been criticized for its social pleading, but praised for its depiction of the suffering of common men and for its probing of the psychology of alienation.

(E) This play's heroine has "always depended on the kindness of strangers." Horrified by the contrast between her idealized vision of life at their former family estate and the squalid surroundings of her sister's home and her brother-in-law's crudity, she relies on liquor and self-delusions about her age, beauty, and former suitors in trying to cope with an uncongenial present. She is eventually raped by her brother-in-law and committed to a mental institution. The author's plays include a number of then-controversial subjects, such as castration, drug addiction, homosexuality, nymphomania, and cannibalism.

Questions 140-142 refer to the excerpts below.

140.   Which is by Ambrose Philips?

141.   Which is by George Crabbe?

142.   Which is by Robert Burns?

(A) O zummer clote! when the brook's a-slidén
          So slow an' smooth down his zedgy bed,
      Upon thy broad leaves so seäfe a-ridén
          The water's top wi' thy yoller head.
                  By black run'd allers,
                  An' weedy shallers
      Thee then dost float, goolden zummer clote!

(B) O come, my Love! Nor think th' Employment mean,
The Dams to milk, and little Lambkins wean;
To drive a-Field by Morn the fat'ning Ewes,
E'er the warm Sun drinks up the cooly Dews.
How would the Crook beseem thy beauteous Hand!
How would my Younglins round thee gazing stand!

(C)   O Tam! hadst thou but been sae wise
As ta'en thy ain wife Kate's advice!
She tauld thee weel thou was a skellum,
A bletherin', blusterin', drunken blellum . . .
She prophesied that, late or soon,
Thou would be found deep drowned in Doon;
Or catched wi' warlocks in the mirk
By Alloway's auld haunted kirk.

(D) Of all the Girls that are so smart,
There's none like pretty Sally;
She is the darling of my Heart,
& She lives in our alley;
There is no Lady in the Land
Is half so sweet as Sally;
She is the darling of my Heart,
& She lives in our alley.

(E) Yes, thus the Muses sing of happy swains,
Because the Muses never knew their pains:
They boast their peasants' pipes, but peasants now
Resign their pipes and plod behind the plough;
And few amid the rural-tribe have time
To number syllables and play with rhyme.

Questions 143-145 refer to the excerpts below.

143.   Which is spoken by Iago?

144.   Which is spoken by Enobarbus?

145.   Which is spoken by Coriolanus?

(A) You should account me the more virtuous that I have not
been common in my love. I will, sir, flatter my sworn
brother, the people, to earn a dearer estimation of them;
'tis a condition they account gentle. And since the wisdom
of their choice is rather to have my hat than my heart,
I will practice the insinuating nod and be off to them most
counterfeitly; that is, sir, I will counterfeit the bewitch-
ment of some popular man and give it bountiful to the
desirers.

(B) I cannot tell what you and other men
Think of this life; but, for my single self,
I had as lief not be as live to be
In awe of such a thing as I myself.

(C) If it were done when 'tis done, then 'twere well
It were done quickly. If th' assassination
Could trammel up the consequence, and catch
With his surcease success, that but this blow
Might be the be-all and the end-all-here,
But here, upon this bank and shoal of time,
We'd jump the life to come.

(D) Virtue? A fig! 'Tis in ourselves that we are thus, or thus. Our
bodies are our gardens, to the which our wills are
gardeners; so that if we will plant nettles or sow lettuce,
set hyssop and weed up thyme, supply it with one gender
of herbs or distract it with many--either to have it sterile
with idleness or manured with industry--why, the power
and corrigible authority of this lies in our wills.

(E) Now he'll outstare the lightning. To be furious
Is to be frighted out of fear, and in that mood
The dove will peck the estridge; and I see still
A diminution in our captain's brain
Restores his heart. When valor preys on reason,
It eats the sword it fights with. I will seek
Some way to leave him.

Questions 146-151

A doll in the doll-maker's house
Looks at the cradle and bawls:
"That is an insult to us."
But the oldest of all the dolls,
Who had seen, being kept for show,   5
Generations of his sort,
Out-screams the whole shelf: "Although
There's not a man can report
Evil of this place,
The man and the woman bring   10
Hither, to our disgrace,
A noisy and filthy thing."
Hearing him groan and stretch
The doll-maker's wife is aware
Her husband has heard the wretch   15
And crouched by the arm of his chair,
She murmurs into his ear,
Head upon shoulder leant:
"My dear, my dear, O dear,
It was an accident."   20

146. The oldest doll's objections metaphorically point primarily to a contrast between

(A) good and evil

(B) life and art

(C) happiness and sorrow

(D) permanence and impermanence

(E) single life and married life

147. The doll-maker can best be seen as a metaphor for:

(A) the destructive effects of time on all men's lives

(B) the vanity of all earthly striving

(C) the artist who must live in the real world but create idealized objects

(D) the henpecked husband

(E) man's essential loneliness and isolation

148. The author of this poem also wrote

(A) *'Ah, Are You Digging on My Grave?'*

(B) *Sailing to Byzantium*

(C) *Ode to the West Wind*

(D) *Fern Hill*

(E) *The British Museum Reading Room*

Questions 149-151

As though to breathe were life! Life piled on life
Were all too little, and of one to me
Little remains; but every hour is saved
From that eternal silence, something more,
A bringer of new things; and vile it were
For some three suns to store and hoard myself . . .

This is my son, mine own Telemachus,
To whom I leave the scepter and the isle--
Well-loved of me, discerning to fulfill
This labor, by slow prudence to make mild
A rugged people, and through soft degrees
Subdue them to the useful and the good.
Most blameless is he, centered in the sphere
Of common duties, decent not to fail
In offices of tenderness, and pay
Meet adoration to my household gods,
When I am gone. He works his work, I mine.

149. Which of the following best describes the portrait of Telemachus that emerges? He is

(A) an ambitious man anxious for his father's throne

(B) a hypocrite

(C) a virtuous, dutiful, loving son and strong leader of men

(D) a potential tyrant who will abuse his authority

(E) an able administrator but unexciting man

150. The speaker expresses

(A) fear of death

(B) a desire for additional experience

(C) a belief in immortality

(D) a need for solitary meditation

(E) a desire for death

151. The author of this passage is

(A) Coleridge   (D) Browning

(B) Keats   (E) Arnold

(C) Tennyson

Questions 152-155 refer to the excerpts below.

152. Which is the "I" of Defoe's *Moll Flanders* ?

153. Which is the "I" of Margaret Atwood's *Lady Oracle* ?

154. Which is the "I" of Sterne's *Tristram Shandy* ?

155. Which is the "I" of Cather's *My Antonia* ?

(A) I had only to close my eyes to hear the rumbling of the wagons in the dark, and to be again overcome by that obliterating strangeness. The feelings of that night were so near that I could reach out and touch them with my hand. I had the sense of coming home to myself, and of having found out what a little circle man's experience is. For [her] and for me, this had been the road of Destiny; had taken us to those early accidents of fortune which predetermined for us all that we can ever be. Now I understood that the same road was to bring us together again. Whatever we had missed, we possessed together the precious, the incommunicable past.

(B) Something quite remote from anything the builders intended has come out of their work, and out of the fierce little human tragedy in which I played; something none of us thought about at the time: a small red flame--a beaten-copper lamp of deplorable design, relit before the beaten-copper doors of a tabernacle; the flame which the old knights saw from their tombs, which they saw put out; that flame burns again for other soldiers, far from home, farther, in heart, than Acre or Jerusalem. It could not have been lit but for the builders and the tragedians, and there I found it this morning, burning anew among the old stones.

(C) It must be observ'd, that when the old Wretch, my Brother (Husband) was dead, I then freely gave my Husband an Account of all that Affair, and of this Cousin, as I had call'd him before, being my own Son by that mistaken unhappy Match: He was perfectly easy in the Account, and told me he should have been as easy if the old Man, as we call'd him, had been alive; for, said he, it was no Fault of yours, nor of his; it was a Mistake impossible to be prevented; he only reproach'd him with desiring me to conceal it, and to live with him as a Wife, after I knew that he was my Brother, that, he said, was a vile part.

(D) I planned my death carefully; unlike my life, which meandered along from one thing to another, despite my feeble attempts to control it. My life had a tendency to spread, to get flabby, to scroll and festoon like the frame of a baroque mirror, which came from following the line of least resistance. I wanted my death, by contrast, to be neat and simple, understated, even a little severe, like a

199

Quaker church or the basic black dress with a single
strand of pearls much praised by fashion magazines when
I was fifteen. . . . At first I thought I'd managed it.

(E) In the beginning of the last chapter, I inform'd you exactly
when I born;--but I did not inform you, *how*. No; that particular was reserved entirely for a chapter by itself;--be-
sides, Sir, as you and I are in a manner perfect strangers to
each other, it would not have been proper to have let you
into too many circumstances relating to myself all at
once.--You must have a little patience. I have undertaken,
you see, to write not only my life, but my opinions also;
hoping and expecting that your knowledge of my character, and of what kind of a mortal I am, by the one, would
give you a better relish for the other.

Questions 156-157

I on my horse, and Love on me doth try
  Our horsemanships, while by strange work I prove
  A horseman to my horse, a horse to Love;
  And now man's wrongs in me, poor beast, descry.

156. The poet's portrayal of "Love" in this stanza is an example of

(A) personification   (D) apostrophe

(B) metonymy   (E) dead metaphor

(C) synecdoche

157. "Horsemanships" in line two is plural because

(A) love rides the speaker while the speaker rides his horse

(B) the speaker has committed more than one wrong

(C) love exercises many forms of control over the speaker

(D) love controls him better than he controls love

(E) love appears in many forms

Questions 158-159

"I didn't want to kill!" Bigger shouted."But what I killed for, I *am*! It must've been pretty deep in me to make me kill! I must have felt it awful hard to murder. . . .What I killed for must've been good! Bigger's voice was full of frenzied anguish. "It must have been good. When a man kills, it's for something . . I didn't know I was really alive in this world until I felt things hard enough to kill for 'em. . . .It's the truth, Mr. Max. I can say it now, 'cause I'm going to die. I know what I'm saying real good and I know how it sounds. But I'm all right. I feel all right when I look at it that way. . . ."

158.   The preceding passage best supports which of the following statements?

(A) Bigger is an embodiment of the chief tenets of existential-ist philosophy.

(B) Bigger has achieved self-identity through violence.

(C) Like Iago, Bigger is driven by motive, but there is also an inexplicable reality behind his rational exterior.

(D) Ultimately, Bigger ends where he began, understanding little of the world around him and even less of himself.

(E) Bigger now realizes that his acts have been impulsive and therefore meaningless.

159.   The passage is from

(A) James Baldwin's *Another Country*

(B) Ralph Ellison's *Invisible Man*

(C) Norman Mailer's *The Armies of the Night*

(D) Richard Wright's *Native Son*

(E) James Dickey's *Deliverance*

160. Which two poets wrote long poems to "justify the ways of God to men" and to "vindicate the ways of God to man"?

(A) Longfellow and Emerson

(B) Milton and Wordsworth

(C) Emerson and Wordsworth

(D) Milton and Pope

(E) Longfellow and Pope

Questions 161-163 refer to the poems below.

161. Which is a dramatic monologue?

162. Which is a villanelle?

163 Which contains the following lines?

> A thing of beauty is a joy forever
> Its loveliness increases; it will never
> Pass into nothingness; . . .

(A) *Do Not Go Gentle Into That Good Night*

(B) *Ode: Intimations of Immortality*

(C) *Endymion*

(D) *Porphyria's Lover*

(E) *Ozymandias*

Questions 164-166

[His] mother had charged him to return with his shield or upon it. Or perchance he was some Achilles, who had nourished his wrath apart, and had now come to avenge or rescue his Patroclus. He saw this unequal combat from afar,--for the blacks were nearly twice the size of the red,--he drew near with rapid pace till he stood on his guard within half an inch of the combatants; then, watching his opportunity, he sprang upon the black warrior, and commenced his operations near the root of his right fore leg, leaving the foe to select among his own members; and so there were three united for life, as if a new kind

202

of attraction had been invented which put all other locks and cements to shame. I should not have wondered by this time to find that they had their respective musical bands stationed on some eminent chip, and playing their national airs the while, to excite the slow and cheer the dying combatants. I was myself excited somewhat even as if they had been men. The more you think of it, the less the difference.

164. The combatants are

(A) Greeks   (D) dogs

(B) Americans   (E) ants

(C) French

165. Patroclus was

(A) the husband of Helen of Troy

(B) the king of Troy

(C) once Achilles' friend, but killed Achilles after the two quarrelled

(D) Achilles' friend, killed in the Trojan War

(E) Achilles' son

166. The author of this passage is

(A) Benjamin Franklin   (D) Henry David Thoreau

(B) Washington Irving   (E) Oliver Wendell Holmes

(C) Nathaniel Hawthorne

Questions 167-169 refer to the works below.

167. Which is an example of Menippean satire?

168. Which is a confession?

203

169. Which is a polemic?

   (A) Sir Thomas Brown's *Religio Medici*

   (B) John Locke's *Essay Concerning Human Understanding*

   (C) Robert Burton's *Anatomy of Melancholy*

   (D) John Milton's *Areopagitica*

   (E) Ben Johnson's *Timber*

Questions 170-171

   "The roman á clef is a novel in which the reader is expected to identify, within the apparent fiction, actual people or events. One example is _____, whose characters are entertaining caricatures of such contemporary literary figures as Coleridge, Byron, and Shelley. A more recent instance is _____, in which we find, under fictional names, well-known people of the twenties, such as the novelist D. H. Lawrence, the critic Middleton Murry, and the right-wing political extremist, Oswald Mosely."

170. Which correctly completes the second sentence?

   (A) William Harrison Ainsworth's *The Tower of London*

   (B) Benjamin Disraeli's *Vivian Grey*

   (C) John Gibson Lockhart's *Adam Blair*

   (D) James Morier's *Hajji Baba in London*

   (E) Thomas Love Peacock's *Nightmare Abbey*

171. Which correctly completes the third sentence?

   (A) Aldous Huxley's *Point Counter Point*

   (B) H. G. Well's *Tono-Bungay*

   (C) Arnold Bennett's *The Old Wives' Tale*

   (D) Dorothy Richardson's *Pilgrimage*

   (E) Somerset Maugham's *Of Human Bondage*

Questions 172-173

[He] had been a subordinate clerk in the Dead Letter Office at Washington, from which he had been suddenly removed by a change in the administration. When I think over this rumour, hardly can I express the emotions which seize me. Dead letters! does it not sound like dead men? . . . Sometimes from out the folded paper the pale clerk takes a ring--the finger it was meant for, perhaps, moulders in the grave, a bank-note sent in swiftest charity--he whom it would relieve, nor eats nor hungers any more; pardon for those who died despairing; hope for those who died unhoping; good tidings for those who died stifled by unrelieved calamities. On errands of life, these letters speed to death.

172.   Dead letters serve as a metaphor for

(A) government inefficiency

(B) the protagonist's existence

(C) governmental indifference to the suffering of its citizens

(D) man's inhumanity to man

(E) the protagonist's family

173.   The author of the passage above is also the author of

(A) *Benito Cereno*

(B) *The Red Badge of Courage*

(C) *Ethan Frome*

(D) *The Fall of the House of Usher*

(E) *The House of the Seven Gables*

Questions 174-175

O our Scots nobles were richt laith
    To weet their cork-heeled shoon

But lang owre a' the play were played
   Their hats they swam aboon.

O lang, lang may their ladies sit,   5
   Wi' their fans into their hand,
Or e'er they see Sir Patrick Spens
   Come sailing the the land.

174. Which of the following best expresses the meaning of lines three and four? The Scots nobles

(A) drowned

(B) refused to go

(C) changed their minds in the middle of the voyage

(D) mutinied

(E) jumped overboard and swam to shore

175. This excerpt is from

(A) a sixteenth-century broadside ballad

(B) a mock epic

(C) a Middle English lyric

(D) a medieval popular ballad

(E) a seventeenth-century elegy

176. The _____ was a medieval form: a short comic or satiric tale in verse that deals realistically with middle-class or lower-class characters and that revels in the obscene and ribald.

Which of the following correctly completes the definition above?

(A) parable   (D) allegory

(B) beast fable   (E) exemplum

(C) fabliau

Questions 177-179 refer to the excerpts below.

177. Which is by Swift?

178. Which is by Carlyle?

179. Which is by Cardinal Newman?

(A) This process of training, by which the intellect, instead of being formed or sacrificed to some particular or accidental purpose, some specific trade or profession, or study or science, is disciplined for its own sake, for the perception of its own proper object, and for its own highest culture, is called Liberal Education; and though there is no one in whom it is carried as far as is conceivable, or whose intellect would be a pattern of what intellects should be made, yet there is scarcely anyone but may gain an idea of what real training is, and at least look towards it, and make its true scope and result, not something else, his standard of excellence; . . . And to set forth the right standard, and to train according to it, and to help forward all students toward it according to their various capacities, this I conceive to be the business of a University.

(B) To every one of us the world was once as fresh and new as to Adam. And then, long before we were susceptible of any other mode of instruction, Nature took us in hand, and every minute of waking life brought its educational influence, shaping our actions into rough accordance with Nature's laws, so that we might not be ended untimely by too gross disobedience. . . . And Nature is still continuing her patient education of us in that great university, the universe, of which we are all members.

(C) However, without venturing into the abstruse, or too eagerly asking Why and How, in things were our answer must needs prove, in great part, an echo of the question, let us be content to remark farther, in the merely historical way, how that Aphorism of the bodily Physician holds good in quite other departments. Of the Soul, with her activities, we shall find it no less true than of the Body: nay, cry the Spiritualists, is not that very division of the unity,

Man, into a dualism of Soul and Body, itself the symptom of disease; as, perhaps, your frightful theory of Materialism of his being but a Body, and therefore, at least, once more a unity, may be the paroxysm which was critical, and the beginning of cure! But omitting this, we observe with confidence enough, that the truly strong mind view it as Intellect, as Morality, or under any other aspect, is nowise the mind, acquainted with its strength; that here as before the sign of health is Unconsciousness.

(D) Since therefore the knowledge and survey of vice is in this world so necessary to the constituting of human virtue, and the scanning of error to the confirmation of truth, how can we more safely, and with less danger, scout into the regions of sin and falsity than by reading all manner of tractates and hearing all manner of reason? And this is the benefit which may be had of books promiscuously read.

(E) And to urge another argument of a parallel nature: if Christianity were once abolished, how could the freethinkers, the strong reasoners, and the men of profound learning, be able to find another subject so calculated in all points whereon to display their abilities? . . . We are daily complaining of the great decline of wit among us, and would we take away the greatest, perhaps the only, topic we have left? Who would ever have suspected Asgil for a wit, or Toland for a philosopher, if the inexhaustible stock of Christianity had not been at hand to provide them with materials?

180. The British had possessed the country so completely. Their withdrawal was so irrevocable. And to me even after many months something of fantasy remained attached to all the reminders of their presence. I had grown up in a British colony and it might have been expected that much would have been familiar to me. But England was at least as many-faceted as India. England, as it expressed itself in Trinidad, was not the England I had lived in; and neither of these countries could be related to the England that was the source of so much that I now saw about me.

208

The author of this passage is

(A) E. M. Forster

(D) Nadine Gordimer

(B) Rudyard Kipling

(E) Doris Lessing

(C) V. S. Naipaul

Questions 181-183

That was when people had begun to feel really sorry for her.
People in our town, remembering how old lady Wyatt, her
great-aunt, had gone completely crazy at last, believed that the
Griersons held themselves a little too high for what they really
were. None of the young men were quite good enough for Miss
Emily and such. We had long thought of them as a tableau, Miss
Emily a slender figure in white in the background, her father a
spraddled silhouette in the foreground, his back to her and
clutching a horsewhip, the two of them framed by the back-
flung front door. So when she got to be thirty and was still
single, we were not pleased exactly, but vindicated; even with
insanity in the family she wouldn't have turned down all of her
chances if they had really materialized.

181. The attitude of the townspeople toward Miss Emily is best
described as one of

(A) disdain tempered by understanding

(B) compassion mixed with self-congratulation

(C) condescension and moral superiority

(D) obsequiousness combined with self-righteousness

(E) pity tinged with envy

182. The tableau chiefly suggests

(A) that Miss Emily was an abused child

(B) the social pretentiousness of Emily's family

(C) the domineering and overly-protective nature of Emily's
father

(D) Miss Emily's purity and her father's stern morality

(E) that the Griersons successfully protected themselves from the ravages of passing time

183. The author of this passage is

(A) Katherine Anne Porter

(B) Stephen Crane

(C) Eudora Welty

(D) Flannery O'Connor

(E) William Faulkner

184. A subtype of the Bildungsroman is the Künstlerroman, which represents the development of a novelist or other artist into the stage of maturity in which he recognizes his artistic destiny and achieves mastery of his artistic self. Instances of this type include

(A) Proust's *Remembrance of Things Past* and Gide's *The Counterfeiters*

(B) Mann's *Death in Venice* and Joyce's *Dubliners*

(C) Cervantes' *Don Quixote* and Koestler's *Darkness at Noon*

(D) Balzac's *Père Goriot* and Hugo's *Les Misérables*

(E) Gogol's *Dead Souls* and Lermontov's *And Quiet Flows the Don*

Questions 185-187

Then, by God, in the very doorway, she fell on her knees and began praying, and after looking at her for a minute or two Noble did the same by the fireplace. I pushed my way out past her and left them at it. I stood at the door, watching the stars and listening to the shrieking of the birds dying out over the bogs. It is so strange what you feel at times like that you can't describe it. Noble says he saw everything ten times the size, as though there were nothing in the whole world but that little patch of bog with the two Englishmen stiffening into it, but with me it was as if the patch of bog where the Englishmen were was a million miles away, and even Noble and the old woman, mumbling behind me, and the birds and the bloody stars were all far away, and I was somehow very small and very lost and lonely like a child astray in the snow. And anything that happpened to me afterwards, I never felt the same about again.

185. The narrator's final image of himself suggests

(A) exhilaration at feeling aligned with nature

(B) joy in recognizing man's centrality in the cosmos

(C) remorse at not being able to join Noble and the old woman in prayer

(D) sorrow in recognizing man's essential isolation and loneliness

(E) depression after recognizing God's indifference to man's suffering

186. The passage is from

(A) Frank O'Connor's *Guests of the Nation*

(B) Joyce's *Clay*

(C) Sherwood Anderson's *I'm a Fool*

(D) Katherine Anne Porter's *Flowering Judas*

(E) Toni Cade Bambara's *The Lesson*

187. Two other stories that deal with loss of innocence are

(A) Kafka's *The Metamorphosis* and Alice Walker's *Everyday Use*

(B) Dorothy Parker's *You Were Perfectly Fine* and Thurber's *The Secret Life of Walter Mitty*

(C) Hawthorne's *My Kinsman, Major Molineux* and Doris Lessing's *Sunrise on the Veld*

(D) Kate Chopin's *The Story of an Hour* and Tillie Olsen's *I Stand Here Ironing*

(E) John Cheever's *The Swimmer* and Kurt Vonnegut's *Harrison Bergeron*

Questions 188-190

This new theatrical movement was sparked by the violent reaction of young people against the stereotyping processes of mass civilization, the regimentation of the welfare state, and the anxieties of the atomic age. It exploded in 1956 in _____ the first of the naturalistic "kitchen-sink" dramas, in which the young hero hurls invectives at class distinctions, patriotism, suburban boredom, and his mother-in-law. Similarly, the most cherished patriotic tenets of the Irish establishment were mocked in 1958 in_____. At almost the same time, the influence of the Theatre of the Absurd showed clearly in _____ and many others. These plays depicted man's cosmic absurdity, his inability to communicate with his fellows, and his fears and loneliness.

188. Which correctly completes the second sentence?

(A) Christopher Fry's *The Lady's Not for Burning*

(B) Edward Albee's *The American Dream*

(C) T. S. Eliot's *The Cocktail Party*

(D) John Osborne's *Look Back in Anger*

(E) Tom Stoppard's *Rosencrantz and Guildenstern Are Dead*

189. Which correctly completes the third sentence?

(A) Brendan Behan's *The Hostage*

(B) Sean O'Casey's *Shadow of a Gunman*

(C) Shaw's *Arms and the Man*

(D) John Millington Synge's *The Playboy of the Western World*

(E) John Arden's *Armstrong's Last Goodbye*

190. Which correctly completes the fourth sentence?

(A) Alan Ayckbourn's *Absurd Person Singular*

(B) Noel Coward's *Private Lives*

(C) Harold Pinter's *The Caretaker*

(D) Frederick Lonsdale's *On Approval*

(E) Robert Bolt's *A Man for All Seasons*

Questions 191-193

The soote season, that bud and bloom forth brings,
With green hath clad the hill and eke the vale;
The nightingale with feathers new she sings;
The turtle to her make hath told her tale.
Summer is come, for every spray now springs;   5

The hart hath hung his old head on the pale;
The buck in brake his winter coat he flings,
The fishes float with new repairéd scale;
The adder all her slough away she slings,
The swift swallow pursueth the fliés small;   10
The busy bee her honey now she mings.
Winter is worn, that was the flowers' bale.
And thus I see among these pleasant things,
Each care decays, and yet my sorrow springs.

191. The author of this sonnet is

(A) Skelton   (D) Spenser

(B) Surrey   (E) Nashe

(C) Sidney

192. The central contrast in the poem is between

(A) activity and inactivity

(B) summer and winter

(C) change and permanence

(D) nature's happiness and the speaker's state of mind

(E) nature's wasted energy and the speaker's self-control

193. This sonnet, like those of many other Renaissance poets, draws its inspiration from the poetry of

(A) Sappho   (D) Petrarch

(B) Ovid   (E) Homer

(C) Tasso

194. "There, sir! An attack upon my language! What do you think of that?--an aspersion upon my parts of speech! Was ever such a brute! Sure if I reprehend anything in this world, it is the use of my oracular tongue, and a nice derangement of epitaphs!"

The speaker of the passage above is

(A) Mistress Quickly in *Henry IV, Part I*

(B) Lady Wishfort in *The Way of the World*

(C) Kate Hardcastle in *She Stoops to Conquer*

(D) Mrs. Malaprop in *The Rivals*

(E) Lady Bracknell in *The Importance of Being Earnest*

Questions 195-198

Margaret greeted her lord with peculiar tenderness on the morrow. Mature as he was, she might yet be able to help him to the building of the rainbow bridge that should connect the prose in us with the passion.

Without it we are meaningless fragments, half monks, half beasts, unconnected arches that have never joined into a man. With it love is born, and alights on the highest curve, glowing against the grey, sober against the fire. Happy the man who sees from either aspect the glory of these outspread wings. The roads of his soul lie clear, and he and his friends shall find easy going.

It was hard going in the roads of Mr. Wilcox's soul. From boyhood on he had neglected them. "I am not a man who bothers about my own inside," Outwardly he was cheerful, reliable, and brave; but within, all had reverted to chaos, ruled so far as it was ruled at all, by an incomplete asceticism. Whether as a boy, husband, widower, he had always the sneaking belief that bodily passion is bad, a belief that is desirable only when held passionately. Religion had confirmed him. The words that were read aloud on Sunday to him and to other respectable men were the words that had once kindled the souls of St. Catherine and St. Francis into a white-hot hatred of the carnal. He could not be as the saint and love the Infinite with a seraphic ardour, but he could be a little ashamed of loving a wife.

195. In the first paragraph, "prose" can best be said to be associated with

(A) monks and beasts   (D) grey and fire

(B) monks and grey   (E) beasts and grey

(C) passion and fire

196. According to the narrator, Mr. Wilcox's greatest fault is

(A) the chaotic nature of his inner life

(B) an inadequate education

(C) his lack of religious convictions

(D) his willingness to marry without loving his wife

(E) his occasional lapses from cheerfulness, reliability, and courage

197. Which of the following statements best expresses the narrator's attitude toward carnality?

(A) Sexual desire is incompatible with marital love.

(B) Sexual desire necessarily leads to guilt or shame.

(C) If man cannot attain a "white-hot hatred of the carnal," he should at least strive for an incomplete asceticism.

(D) Absolute hatred of sexual desire is preferable to an incomplete asceticism

(E) Spiritual wholeness is possible only when bodily passion is suppressed.

198. The author of the passage above is

(A) E. M. Forster   (D) Arnold Bennett

(B) W. M. Thackeray   (E) Virginia Woolf

(C) Aldous Huxley

Questions 199-204

The cod-piece that will house
    Before the head has any,
The head and he shall louse;
    So beggars marry many.
The man that makes his toe   5
    What he his heart should make
Shall of a corn cry woe,
    And turn his sleep to wake.

199. In line one, "cod-piece" is used to mean

(A) article of clothing covering the male genitalia

(B) fish

(C) wise man

(D) penis

(E) beggar

216

200. The sense of line two is retained and clarified by substituting which of the following for "any"?

(A) a hat

(D) learned to reason

(B) mastered the heart

(E) gained control of the senses

(C) a house

201. The first three lines can best be paraphrased by which of the following?

(A) The man who fathers children before he has a house can expect penury.

(B) The man who spends money foolishly will become a beggar.

(C) Promiscuous, unthinking sexual activity will ruin the lives of others.

(D) When lust and reason pull in different directions, man always allows lust to rule.

(E) Man's sexual appetites mature before he is capable of reasoning.

202. Which is the best paraphrase of line four?

(A) Hence beggars marry more than once

(B) To enable many beggars to marry

(C) Consequently many women prefer beggars

(D) Thus marriage makes many men beggars

(E) Which is why there are so many married beggars

203. Which of the following best expresses the sense of the last four lines? The man who

(A) elevates what is base over what is noble can expect misery and wakefulness

(B) allows his heart to influence business decisions will lose all he owns

(C) wanders aimlessly rather than settling down mistakenly subordinates reason to sentiment

(D) bases his actions on uncritical benevolence rather than on self-interest will regret it later

(E) deserts his family will never be able to repair the damage done to his own heart

204. How has King Lear made the last four lines applicable to himself? He has

(A) not paid sufficient attention to the poor while king

(B) chosen to run away rather than confront his daughters directly

(C) turned his back on Kent even though he knows Kent loves him and is loyal

(D) relinquished his crown when there was no need to do so

(E) given precedence to Goneril and Regan above Cordelia

Questions 205-208 refer to the passages below.

205. Which describes Aristophanes' *Lysistrata* ?

206. Which describes Sophocles' *Antigone* ?

207. Which describes Moliere's *Tartuffe* ?

208. Which describes Euripides' *Medea* ?

(A) Forced to choose between loyalty to family and loyalty to a new king, who is also her uncle, the heroine chooses the former and duty to what she calls the laws of the gods rather than the laws of the state.

(B) This play satirizes both religious hypocrisy and fraudulence, and also makes fun of the obsessive fanaticism and gullibility of those who allow themselves to be victimized by the greedy and self-serving.

(C) The heroine decides to leave her husband and to achieve self-realization after she discovers that his position in society is more important to him than her love and their mutual respect.

(D) This play asks its audience to make love not war. The women of the play try to bring an end to a war that threatens their city by refusing to have sexual relations with their men as long as the latter continue the war.

(E) Deserted by her husband for another woman, the protagonist seeks revenge by killing their two children and the "other woman."

Questions 209-211

This is the excellent foppery of the world, that when
    we are sick in fortune--
often the surfeits of our own behavior--we make
    guilty of our disasters the sun,
the moon, and stars, as if we were villains on
    necessity, fools by heavenly
compulsion, knaves, thieves, and treachers
    by spherical predominance, drunkards,
liars, and adulterers by an enforc'd obedience   5
    of planetary influence, and all that
we are evil in, by a divine thrusting on. An
    admirable evasion of whoremaster
man, to lay his goatish disposition on the charge
    of a star! My father compounded
with my mother under the Dragon's Tail, and my
    nativity was under Ursa Major, so that
it follows I am rought and lecherous. Fut, I should
    have been that I am, had the
maidenliest star in the firmament twinkled on my   10
    bastardizing.

209. "Foppery" (line one) can best be understood to mean

   (A) finery
   (B) appearance
   (C) habit
   (D) condition
   (E) foolishness

210. "Goatish" (line seven) means

   (A) sluggish
   (B) irrational
   (C) lecherous
   (D) fickle
   (E) irresponsible

211. Which of the following statements is LEAST accurate? The speaker

   (A) believes man shapes his own character

   (B) believes man tries to blame his mistakes on something other than himself

   (C) has little or no belief in Providence

   (D) believes in astrological determinism

   (E) believes that man's misfortunes are often the result of his own excessive behavior

Questions 212-216

I am poor brother Lippo, by your leave!
You need not clap your torches to my face.
Zooks, what's to blame? you think you see a monk!
What 't is past midnight, and you go the rounds,
And here you catch me at an alley's end   5
Where sportive ladies leave their doors ajar?
The Carmine's my cloister: hunt it up,
Do,--harry out, if you must show your zeal,
Whatever rat, there, haps on his wrong hole,

And nip each softling of a wee white mouse,　　10
Weke, weke, that's crept to keep him company!
Aha, you know your betters! Then, you'll take
Your hand away that's fiddling on my throat,
And please to know me likewise. Who am I?
Why, one, sir, who is lodging with a friend　　15
Three streets off--he's a certain . . . how d' ye call?
Master-- a . . . Cosimo of the Medici,
I' the house that caps the corner. Boh! you were best!
Remember and tell me, the day you're hanged,
How you affected such a gullet's-gripe!　　20
But you, sir, it concerns you that your knaves
Pick up a manner nor discredit you: . . .

212.　　The poem is set in

(A)　medieval Rome

(B)　early Renaissance Florence

(C)　medieval Spain

(D)　early Renaissance Naples

(E)　nineteenth-century Milan

213.　　The opening scene takes place after midnight in an area

(A)　infested by rats

(B)　adjacent to the Carmelite cloister where Lippo Lippi lives

(C)　in the city's main business district

(D)　in front of the Medici palace

(E)　that contains houses of prostitution

214.　　To whom is Lippo Lippi speaking when he says "Boh! you were best?"

(A)　the policeman (or watchman) who handled him most roughly (line 18)

(B)　the most aggressive of the ruffians or thieves who have accosted him

(C) the officer in charge of the police patrol

(D) the leader of the ruffians

(E) the respectable-looking friend who has rescued him

215. What causes the men who have stopped him to treat him more gently?

(A) They feel compassion for his situation

(B) The effectiveness of his rhetorical self-defense

(C) The arrival of his friend

(D) His mention of his connection to the Medici

(E) He has embarrassed them by stressing his weakness and their greatly superior strength

216. To whom is Lippo Lippi speaking in line twenty-one ("But you, sir")?

(A) the policeman who handled him most roughly

(B) the most aggressive of the ruffians

(C) the officer in charge of the police patrol

(D) the leader of the ruffians

(E) the respectable-looking friend who has rescued him

Questions 217-219

Shall I compare thee to a summer's day?
Thou art more lovely and more temperate:
Rough winds do shake the darling buds of May,
And summer's lease hath all too short a date;
Sometime too hot the eye of heaven shines,   5
And often is his gold complexion dimm'd;
And every fair from fair sometimes declines,
By chance or nature's changing course untrimm'd:

But thy eternal summer shall not fade
Nor lose possession of that fair thou ow'st;   10
Nor shall Death brag thou wand'rest in his shade,
When in eternal lines to time thou grow'st;
So long as men can breathe or eyes can see,
So long lives this, and this gives life to thee.

217. According to the speaker, death will be unable to "brag thou wand'rest in his shade" because

(A) the beloved is like summer, which returns each year

(B) the beloved is like summer, which is sunny, not shady

(C) death releases the beloved into eternal life

(D) the beloved, partaking of the earth's natural cycles, will be remembered each summer

(E) the beloved derives life from this poem for as long as it is read

218. The greatest shift in thought process in the poem occurs at the beginning of line

(A) three   (D) eleven

(B) five   (E) thirteen

(C) nine

219. The primary theme of the poem is

(A) the permanence of poetry

(B) the beauty of the beloved

(C) the disappointments of summer

(D) the unreliability of nature

(E) the impermanence of love

Questions 220-221

Proud of their weakness, however, they must always be protected, guarded from care, and all the rough toils that dignify the mind.--If this be the fiat of fate, if they will make themselves insignificant and contemptible, sweetly to waste "life away," let them not expect to be valued when their beauty fades, for it is the fate of the fairest flowers to be admired and pulled to pieces by the careless hand that plucked them. In how many ways do I wish, from the purest benevolence, to impress this truth on my sex; yet I fear that they will not listen to a truth that dear bought experience has brought home to many an agitated bosom, nor willingly resign the privileges of rank and sex for the privileges of humanity, to which those have no claim who do not discharge its duties.

220. Which of the following statements best expresses the "truth" the author wishes to impress upon her sex?

(A) Women must subordinate household pursuits to careers to achieve full humanity.

(B) Women must preserve their beauty as long as possible because they lose their power when it fades.

(C) Men are the natural antagonists of women; hence women must substitute reasoned judgment for naive trust.

(D) To achieve full humanity, women must be willing to give up the arbitrary power of beauty.

(E) Women face more natural obstacles than men; hence they must not allow socially-conditioned roles to add to those obstacles.

221. The author of this passage is

(A) Lady Mary Wortley Montagu

(B) Mary Wollstonecraft

(C) Mary Shelley

(D) Kate Chopin

(E) Virginia Woolf

Questions 222-230. Identify the author of each of the following passages. Base your decision on the content and style of each passage.

222.　　. . . but we must remain firm in our conviction that hymns to the gods and praises of famous men are the only poetry which ought to be admitted into our State. For if you go beyond this and allow the honeyed muse to enter, either in epic or lyric verse, not law and the reason of mankind, which by common consent have ever been deemed best, but pleasure and pain will be the rulers in our State

　　(A) Plato　　　　　　　(D) Quintilian

　　(B) Aristotle　　　　　(E) Boethius

　　(C) Horace

223.　　Strong sense, united to delicate sentiment, improved by practice, perfected by comparison, and cleared of all prejudice, can alone entitle critics to this valuable character; and the joint verdict of such, wherever they are to be found, is the true standard of taste and beauty.

　　(A) Reynolds　　　　　(D) D. G. Rossetti

　　(B) Hume　　　　　　(E) Mill

　　(C) Hazlitt

224.　　The best means would be, my friend, to gain, first of all, clear knowledge and appreciation of the true sublime. The enterprise is, however, an arduous one. For the judgment of style is the last and crowning fruit of long experience. None the less, if I must speak in the way of precept, it is not impossible perhaps to acquire discrimination in these matters by attention to some such hints as those which follow.

　　(A) Quintilian　　　　(D) Cicero

　　(B) Longinus　　　　　(E) Dionysius of Halicarnassus

　　(C) Demetrius

225. I have said that poetry is the spontaneous overflow of powerful feelings: it takes its origin from emotion recollected in tranquility: the emotion is contemplated till, by a species of reaction, the tranquility gradually disappears, and an emotion, kindred to that which was before the subject of contemplation, is gradually produced, and does itself actually exist in the mind.

(A) Wordsworth

(B) Coleridge

(C) Carlyle

(D) Arnold

(E) Pater

226. In general, the impossible must be justified by reference to artistic requirements, or to the higher reality, or to received opinion. With respect to the requirements of art, a probable impossiblility is to be preferred to a thing improbable and yet possible.

(A) Scaliger

(B) Horace

(C) Cicero

(D) Longinus

(E) Aristotle

227. So that sith the ever-praise-worthy Poesie, is full of vertue-breeding delightfulness, and voyde of no gyfte, that ought to be in the noble name of learning: sith the blames laid against it, are either false, or feeble: sith the cause why it is not esteeemed in Englande, is the fault of Poet-apes, not Poets: sith lastly, our tongue is most fit to honor Poesie, and to bee honored by Poesie, I conjure you all, that have had the evill lucke to reade this incke-wasting toy of mine, even in the name of the nyne Muses, no more to scorne the sacred misteries of Poesie.

(A) Milton

(B) Hobbes

(C) Sidney

(D) Ben Jonson

(E) Thomas De Quincey

228.   First follow Nature, and your judgment frame
By her just standard, which is still the same:
Unerring Nature! still divinely bright,
One clear, unchang'd, and universal light,
Life, force, and beauty, must to all impart,
At once the source, and end, and test of art.

(A) Dryden   (D) Shelley

(B) Pope   (E) Ruskin

(C) Poe

229.   The only way of expressing emotion in the form of art is by
finding an "objective correlative;" in other words, a set of
objects, a situation, a chain of events which shall be the formula
of that <u>particular</u> emotion; such that when the external facts,
which must terminate in sensory experience, are given, the
emotion is immediately evoked.

(A) Auden   (D) John Crowe Ransom

(B) T. S. Eliot   (E) Robert Penn Warren

(C) Stephen Spender

230.   "The business of a poet," said Imlac, "is to examine, not the
individual, but the species; to remark general properties and
large appearances; he does not number the streaks of the tulip,
or describe the different shades in the verdure of the forest."

(A) Dryden   (D) Lamb

(B) Edward Young   (E) Wilde

(C) Johnson

GRE LITERATURE IN ENGLISH
EXAM II

ANSWER KEY

1.	B	30.	A	59.	A	88.	B
2.	D	31.	E	60.	D	89.	C
3.	A	32.	C	61.	B	90.	B
4.	D	33.	B	62.	C	91.	D
5.	A	34.	D	63.	D	92.	C
6.	E	35.	E	64.	C	93.	C
7.	C	36.	A	65.	B	94.	D
8.	D	37.	B	66.	D	95.	A
9.	D	38.	E	67.	E	96.	E
10.	C	39.	D	68.	C	97.	A
11.	D	40.	C	69.	A	98.	E
12.	E	41.	D	70.	C	99.	C
13.	D	42.	B	71.	D	100.	E
14.	D	43.	B	72.	B	101.	D
15.	E	44.	D	73.	D	102.	C
16.	A	45.	C	74.	C	103.	C
17.	C	46.	B	75.	C	104.	A
18.	B	47.	C	76.	B	105.	E
19.	A	48.	D	77.	D	106.	E
20.	C	49.	C	78.	C	107.	D
21.	A	50.	A	79.	E	108.	B
22.	D	51.	D	80.	A	109.	C
23.	B	52.	B	81.	D	110.	A
24.	D	53.	E	82.	E	111.	B
25.	A	54.	A	83.	B	112.	D
26.	C	55.	B	84.	E	113.	D
27.	E	56.	A	85.	D	114.	B
28.	C	57.	E	86.	A	115.	B
29.	C	58.	D	87.	C	116.	C

GRE LITERATURE IN ENGLISH
EXAM II

ANSWER KEY

117.	B	146.	B	175.	D	204.	E
118.	E	147.	C	176.	C	205.	D
119.	B	148.	B	177.	E	206.	A
120.	A	149.	E	178.	C	207.	B
121.	E	150.	B	179.	A	208.	E
122.	B	151.	C	180.	C	209.	E
123.	C	152.	C	181.	B	210.	C
124.	C	153.	D	182.	C	211.	D
125.	E	154.	E	183.	E	212.	B
126.	D	155.	A	184.	A	213.	E
127.	B	156.	A	185.	D	214.	A
128.	E	157.	A	186.	A	215.	D
129.	B	158.	B	187.	C	216.	C
130.	D	159.	D	188.	D	217.	E
131.	C	160.	D	189.	A	218.	C
132.	A	161.	D	190.	C	219.	A
133.	E	162.	A	191.	B	220.	D
134.	C	163.	C	192.	D	221.	B
135.	E	164.	E	193.	D	222.	A
136.	D	165.	D	194.	D	223.	B
137.	C	166.	D	195.	B	224.	B
138.	E	167.	C	196.	A	225.	A
139.	D	168.	A	197.	D	226.	E
140.	B	169.	D	198.	A	227.	C
141.	E	170.	E	199.	D	228.	B
142.	C	171.	A	200.	C	229.	B
143.	D	172.	B	201.	A	230.	C
144.	E	173.	A	202.	E		
145.	A	174.	A	203.	A		

GRE LITERATURE IN ENGLISH
TEST II

DETAILED EXPLANATIONS
OF ANSWERS

1.   (B)
This is Coleridge's four-line poem, *On Donne's Poetry*. Donne had not been popular during the eighteenth century. Coleridge's terse commentary reveals his admiration, albeit qualified, for Donne's mastery of the metaphysical style.

2.   (D)
This is from Shelley's *To Wordsworth*, in which Shelley expresses his disillusionment with Wordsworth's abandonment of the liberal social causes that he formerly supported in his poetry.

3.   (A)
This is Swift's comment on himself in *Verses on the Death of Dr. Swift*, in which he says he wrote in order to correct man's folly.

4.   (D)
Plath's autobiographical novel, *The Bell Jar*, relates experiences from her early adult life, including a period of intense psychiatric therapy. "Daddy, you bastard, I'm through" is from a poem entitled *Daddy*, one of several that expose the attitudes and personalities of her German father and Austrian mother.

5.   (A)

These are concluding lines from Matthew Arnold's *Dover Beach*, in which the poet contrasts pleasing appearances (of both world and sea) with harsher realities.

6.   (E)

Herrick's poem, like many others that have a "seize the day" motif, emphasizes that life is short and time is fleeting in urging the pursuit of present pleasure. The auditors of carpe diem poems are often reluctant virgins.

7.   (C)

Coleridge's poem is an example of narrative poems written by "lettered" poets in deliberate imitation of the form and spirit of popular ballads.

8.   (D)

Parnell's *Night-Piece on Death* , Blair's *The Grave* , Young's *Night-Thoughts*, and Gray's *Elegy Written in a Country Churchyard* are all associated with the graveyard school. Parnell is an early exemplar or forerunner, Gray's *Elegy* is the most famous poem produced by the group, and the poems of Blair and Young are perhaps most typical of the graveyard school.

9.   (D)

Freneau's poem (1779) is the first significant American poem to deal with the abstract subject of death. Its conventions derive directly from the English "Graveyard Poets."

10.   (C)

The poems in *In Memoriam* form a sequence, but they are not sonnets.

11. (D)

Agamemnon was murdered by his wife Clytemnestra and her lover Aegisthus upon his return from Troy, and his murder was later avenged by his son Orestes.

12. (E)

In Greek mythology, Zeus visited Leda in the form of a swan. The offspring of their union were Helen and Clytemnestra.

13. (D)

These are the final lines from William Butler Yeats' *Leda and the Swan*.

14. (D)

This passage is from Shaw's *Major Barbara*. Barbara has turned from the Salvation Army to the saving of another order of souls.

15. (E)

This is Lady Bracknell's reaction, in *The Importance of Being Earnest*, to the news that Jack's first home was a handbag in a railroad station.

16. (A)

This is from the "marriage contract" scene in Congreve's *The Way of the World*, in which Millamant establishes conditions of her marriage to Mirabel. Her demands underscore the desire of heroines in the Restoration comedy of manners to maintain independence and individuality after marriage.

17.   (C)

Rosalind urges Orlando to hire someone else to die in his place rather than die himself from unrequited love. In the world's history, Rosalind says, no man has ever died for love.

18.   (B)

Rosalind's account of Leander's death is highly anti-romantic; in her account, Leander drowned from a cramp after going to cool off on a hot summer evening in the Hellespont, not while swimming across it to visit Hero, as other accounts claim.

19.   (A)

The dialogue is from Shakespeare's *As You Like It*, set in the Forest of Arden.

20.   (C)

The passage reflects such transcendental notions as the presence of truths that are beyond the reach of man's limited senses, the usefulness of intuition as a guide to universal truth, and nature as an image in which the divine can be perceived.

21.   (A)

Emerson's belief that God is all-loving and all-pervading underlies his assertions that nature is "beautiful" and "good" in the second paragraph.

22.   (D)

This excerpt is from *The Poet* (1844). He wrote *Self-Reliance*, his celebration of individualism, somewhat earlier. Emerson is perhaps the leading spokesman of transcendentalism in America.

23.   (B)

Litotes is a form of understatement in which something is affirmed by stating the negative of its opposite. Used frequently as a form of ironic expression, litotes was also a characteristic figure of speech in Old English poetry.

24.   (D)

Age poisons all, including the speaker, whose beauty has been taken from her by the passage of time.

25.   (A)

Her "pith" has been taken by age; the flour is gone, leaving her only the "bran," the seed husk, which she will now sell as best she can.

26.   (C)

Unto this day, she says, it makes her heart glad that she had her fling earlier in life. When she thinks about her "youthe" and "jolitee," it does her "herte boote" (heart good).

27.   (E)

Although she is not happy about losing her beauty, she accepts the ravages of time, realistically appraises what she has left (and what its value might be if marketed properly), and is determined to make the most of what she has.

28.   (C)

The Wife of Bath gives this account of herself in the prologue to her tale in Chaucer's *The Canterbury Tales*.

29.   (C)

A general critical precept underlying the essay is the author's belief that "nothing can please many, and please long, but just representations of general nature." Shakespeare has pleased many and pleased long; the reason, according to the author is that Shakespeare is the preeminent painter of general nature.

30.   (A)

Shakespeare is always careful to preserve the essential characteristics of men, the author says, but is less careful with additional and chance distinctions (that is, characteristics that are accidental, deriving merely from social position or place of abode, as opposed to those that derive from nature and are inherent). This is less a criticism of Shakespeare than an assertion that he gave more attention to what is important than to what is unimportant.

31.   (E)

All concentrate on "accident" rather than "nature"; hence they focus on the unimportant at the expense of the significant. Consequently, the author says their objections are "the petty cavils of petty minds."

32.   (C)

Since the differences between men are "casual," Shakespeare rightly focuses on the universal rather than the specific. Like the artist who "neglects the drapery," Shakespeare ignores the inessentials of nationality and custom.

33.   (B)

The passage is from Johnson's Preface to his edition (in eight volumes) of Shakespeare's plays. The Preface has been praised highly; a later Shakespearean editor called it "perhaps the finest composition in our language."

34.   (D)

Poe's narrator, Montresor, finishes building a tomb containing his living "friend", Fortunato, in the catacombs under Montresor's residence. Montresor lures Fortunato there on the pretext of looking at a cask of amontillado, but then chains him to a wall inside a vault.

35.   (E)

This is the scene of the boy's epiphany at the bazaar in *Araby*. His romantic idealism shattered, the narrator's fall from innocence is accompanied by a painful awareness of the "emptiness" of the world and of the foolishness of his romantic expectations.

36.   (A)

The passage reflects the youthful determination and distinctive voice of Welty's narrator, who moves to the post office to "get even" with her family.

37.   (B)

This is Jaques' melancholy portrait of the stages of man's life in *As You Like It*.

38.   (E)

The portly Falstaff complains of having to walk any distance, and vows to give up theft if thieves cannot be true to one another. The passage is from *Henry IV, Part I*.

39.   (D)

This is Caliban's reply to Miranda, who has tried to "civilize" the savage by, among other things, teaching him speech, in *The Tempest*.

40.   (C)

Heroic drama derives from an attempt to combine tragedy and the epic. An example of heroic drama is Dryden's *The Conquest of Granada*.

41.   (D)

Another well-known dumb show is the preliminary episode, summarizing the action to come, of the play-within-a-play in *Hamlet*.

42.   (B)

The masque was developed in Renaissance Italy and flourished in England during the reigns of Elizabeth I, James I, and Charles I. The masque drew upon some of the finest artistic talent of the time, including scripts by Ben Jonson and stage machinery by Inigo Jones. Productions were lavish and costly; the form was literally the sport of kings and queens until the Puritan triumph in 1642.

43.   (B)

An elegy is a formal and sustained poetic lament for the dead. The pastoral elegy is a species of the elegy that represents both the mourner and the one he mourns as shepherds. The pastoral elegy developed elaborate conventions, including an invocation of the muses, nature joining in the mourning for the dead shepherd, a procession of appropriate mourners, a closing consolation, and so forth. Johnson's poem is a meditation on, as the title makes clear, the futility of ambition that leads to discontent; it is not a pastoral elegy.

44.   (D)

John Gay's *The Beggar's Opera* was the first and best of eighteenth-century ballad operas, a form established in part to compete with Italian opera, which was growing in popularity in London. Gay set his lyrics to familiar ballads and peopled his work with underworld figures whose dialogue draws attention to parallels between the court and the underworld.

45. (C)
 This exchange between the hero and heroine of Sir George Etherege's *The Man of Mode* is typical of many such exchanges in the Restoration comedy of manners. Its meaning depends on the audience's recognition of the speakers' use of an extended metaphor, which is sometimes similar to metaphysical wit. The two seem to be speaking of one thing, but meaning refers to something else. In this instance Dorimant and Harriet appear to be talking about gaming; in fact, Harriet lets Dorimant know that she will engage in innocent diversions but will not submit to him sexually. Each tests the other to see what the terms and conditions of their relationship might be.

46. (B)
 Dorimant lets Harriet know that he can be content with less than sexual conquest (meaning depends on a pun in "deep play") if he likes his partner well enough; implicit in his remark is the notion that he does like Harriet well enough.

47. (C)
 The exchange is characteristic of the wit present in the battle of the sexes in the Restoration comedy of manners. Such exchanges are based on extended conceits, often with sexual undertones. One of the yardsticks by which a character's "worth" is measured in Restoration comedy is the ability to handle language, which is a reflection of social grace, intellect, and the ability to manipulate others. The most admirable use language as a form of power, rather than being controlled by language. Wit in this sense is not a primary virtue in the other choices offered (for example, the language of heroic drama is noted for bombast; that of sentimental comedy avoids sexual innuendo).

48. (D)
 Hemingway uses so-called impersonal narration in both stories; that is, the narrator reports or "shows" the action in dramatic scenes,

without commenting or judging. These Hemingway stories are extreme examples of the use of the unintrusive narrator, who tells us nothing of the inner feelings or motives of characters.

49.　(C)

Fallible or unreliable narrators are those whose interpretations and evaluations of the events they narrate are based on norms (or values or beliefs) that differ from those of the author. The reader is expected to share the norms of the author, not those of the narrator. Unreliablity, may be based on moral obtuseness or corruption, excessive innocence, stupidity, oversophistication, or other factors that distance the narrator from the author and reader. Lardner and Faulkner made use of such narrators.

50.　(A)

Sterne and Proust use narrators who are aware that they are composing works of art and take readers into their confidence, commenting on various problems of composition, either seriously (as in Proust) or for comic purposes (as in Sterne).

51.　(D)

The sonnet adheres to Petrarchan form in the octave (rhyming abbaabba), but differs from it in the sestet by introducing couplets rather than the usual rhyme scheme (cdecde or some variant, such as cdccdc). In other ways it adheres to the conventions of the Petrarchan sonnet--a shift of thought occurs at the beginning of the sestet, and it contains no more than five rhymes.

52.　(B)

Countée Cullen, a black poet, predicts that the oppressed will not always be oppressed, will not always plant what others reap, will not always "beguile" the limbs of the oppressor "with mellow flute" while the oppressor sleeps. The oppressed, he says, were not made to weep eternally.

53.   (E)
The night is "no less lovely" being black; in fact the blackness of the night "relieves the stark white stars," giving them a loveliness they would not have without blackness.

54.   (A)
The "Harlem Renaissance" denotes a period of literary achievement in the 1920's in Harlem, a section of upper Manhattan. Other writers of the period include Langston Hughes and Jean Toomer.

55.   (B)
This is Fielding's definition of the comic romance, as distinct from comedy and from the serious romance, in his Preface to *Joseph Andrews*.

56.   (A)
This is from Lawrence's *Why the Novel Matters*. The passage reflects Lawrence's belief that one <u>knows</u> only through the body, and his assertion that the novelist understands this, while parsons, philosphers, and scientists may not.

57.   (E)
In *Aspects of the Novel*, Forster says that although all novels tell stories, story-telling is not the novelist's greatest achievement.

58.   (D)

Dixon pokes fun at mindless, insignificant academic scholarship; aware of the limited value of such work, he persists in order to keep his university teaching position.

59.   (A)

Although the novel is related in third person narration, events are seen through Dixon's eyes. It is his perspective on other characters and action that shapes the reader's responses. Although Dixon evokes considerable laughter at his own expense, he is treated sympathetically by the author.

60.   (D)

The passage is from Kingsley Amis' comic novel, *Lucky Jim*.

61.   (B)

The Aesthetic Movement was a European phenomenon of the latter nineteenth century. Its rallying cry became "art for art's sake."

62.   (C)

The passage is from *The Myth of Sisyphus*, by the existentialist writer Albert Camus. Eugene Ionesco is a leading writer of the drama of the absurd.

63.   (D)

The term was used by Keats to describe the objective, impersonal aspect of Shakespeare, and has subsequently been used to denote an artist's ability to avoid expressing his own personality in his work.

64.   (C)

Gwendolyn Brooks' poem *We Real Cool*, subtitled *The Pool Players. Seven at the Golden Shovel*. Brooks has spent most of her life in the Chicago area. She is the first black writer to win a Pulitzer Prize.

65.   (B)

The novel described is William Godwin's *Caleb Williams*. While employed as a secretary, Caleb realizes that his employer has committed a murder. The novel argues strongly for various social reforms, emphasizing especially the need for legal reform.

66.   (D)

The concluding stanza of Thomas Gray's comic (sometimes called "mock-heroic") poem, *Ode on the Death of a Favourite Cat, Drowned in a Tub of Gold Fishes*.

67.   (E)

The passage, in typical Jamesian style, is from *The Golden Bowl*. The scene occurs immediately after Fanny Assingham has broken the golden bowl. The husband and wife are Amerigo (the Prince) and Maggie.

68.   (C)

These are the concluding lines of Fitzgerald's *The Great Gatsby*. The "he" is Gatsby, whose pursuit of a vision destroys him; the passage emphasizes the influence of the past on man's attempts to shape the future.

69.   (A)

The lines given are two of the three stanzas from Dickinson's *I reason, Earth is short*, reflecting the style and thematic concerns of much of her poetry.

70.   (C)

Lawrence's protagonist is more "refined," more sensitive, articulate, and intellectual, than the rough, strongly-feeling. inarticulate townspeople where he serves as a doctor. The passage emphasizes the irrational nature and power of love, which is stronger than the protagonist's rational will.

71.   (D)

This passage is from Beckett's novel *Murphy*, which deals with Murphy's humorous and tragic search for self. The author draws on Gaelic legend in Murphy's quest for self-identity. The work is written in Beckett's highly individual style, and is set in both Dublin and London.

72.   (B)

The passage is from Graham Greene's *Monsignor Quixote*, whose protagonist is the spiritual and literal heir of Cervantes' hero. The novel is in the tradition of Cervantes, dealing with the adventures of Monsignor Quixote, whose unpriestly behavior leads to difficulties with his bishop.

73.   (D)

Henderson feels kinship with Smolak, a circus bear; both are outsiders, "humorists before the crowd." Henderson's relationship with Smolak is important in Henderson's efforts to identify and accept self.

74.   (C)

The passage is from E. M. Forster's *A Passage to India*. It relates the aftermath of Mrs. Moore's nihilistic experience in the Marabar caves, an experience that undermines her "grip on life."

75. (C)

This passage is from Flaubert's *Madame Bovary*. The passage reflects Emma's disillusionment as well as her persistent romantic illusions.

76. (B)

This is the vivid, vernacular narrative voice of Holden Caulfield at the beginning of Salinger's *The Catcher in the Rye*.

77. (D)

The passage is from Milton's *Samson Agonistes*. Samson is reflecting on the relative importance of his gift of strength from God. The last line alludes to the fact that the seat of Samson's strength is his hair, which Dalila has cut, thereby depriving him of his strength.

78. (C)

This excerpt is from Molly Bloom's long interior monologue, related in stream of consciousness, that concludes Joyce's *Ulysses*.

79. (F)

This passage, from Hemingway's *Hills Like White Elephants*, uses an unintrusive, impersonal ("objective") narrator; that is, the narrator "shows" the action in dramatic scenes, without introducing his own comments or judgements.

80. (A)

Metafiction explores or questions the nature and conventions of fiction itself; the elements of fiction are taken not as givens but as problematic. This example is from Julio Córtazar's *Blow-Up*.

81. (D)

Euphuism is a formal and elaborate prose style whose name derives from John Lyly's *Euphues: The Anatomy of Wit* (1578). The style contains moral maxims, relies on balanced and antithetical constructions, makes use of elaborate patterns of alliteration and assonance, and displays fondness for long similes and allusions to mythological figures and the habits of legendary animals. This example is from Lyly's *Euphues;* the [X] in the passage is Euphues.

82.   (E)

Jane Austen's patronizing description of Catherine Morland, the heroine of *Northanger Abbey*. Plain and unimpressive, Catherine only gradually wins our admiration.

83.   (B)

The two novels alluded to are *Tess of the D'Urbervilles* and *Jude the Obscure*.

84.   (E)

A number of poems from the Middle Ages are concerned with beauty that must die. An important element of these poems is the ubi sunt motif, from the Latin sentence, Ubi sunt qui ante nos fuerunt? ("Where are they who before us were?"). This stanza is the second in Francois Villon's *The Ballad of Dead Ladies*; the ubi sunt motif is stated directly in the last line ("Where are the snows of yesteryear?").

85.   (D)

Héloise and Abelard are famous lovers whose relationship has been the subject of many literary works. Abelard was a scholastic philospher and theologian; Héloise was his student. They were secretly married to avoid hindering Abelard's advancement in the church. After Héloise's uncle took revenge, Abelard became a monk and Héloise a nun. Abelard lived from 1079 to 1142.

86.   (A)

All of the beautiful ladies of the past are dead, gone like the snows of yesteryear. Medieval poems like Villon's combine an appreciation for the world's beauty with an awareness of the transitory nature of that beauty, which is nearly illusory when viewed against the background of eternity. In asking the ubi sunt question, the poet calls to mind life's splendor, but the grim and inevitable answer poignantly reminds the reader how short-lived that splendor is.

87.   (C)
John Crowe Ransom's *Piazza Piece* is a modern "death and the maiden" poem. Although the young lady believes she is waiting for love, the speaker in the octave, with broader perspective, asserts that she is really waiting for death. He must "have my lovely lady soon"; the images he uses (dying roses; "spectral singing of the moon") reinforce the idea of death's presence.

88.   (B)
"Truelove" conveys not an individual, but an idea of a romantic type. Making "truelove" one word rather than two underscores the young lady's naive expectations.

89.   (C)
It is closer to a Petrarchan sonnet than to a Shakespearean sonnet in its structure (octave/sestet rather than three quatrains and a couplet) and in its rhyme scheme, although it differs slightly from the conventional rhyme scheme of a Petrarchan sonnet in the octave and more radically in the sestet.

90.   (B)
A periodic sentence withholds syntactic closure; that is, it is composed so that the completion of the sense is suspended until the end of the sentence. The effect tends to be formal or oratorical. This example is from Boswell's *Life of Samuel Johnson.*

91.   (D)
An oxymoron is a paradox that combines terms that ordinarily are contraries, as in this example from Tennyson.

92.   (C)
The pathetic fallacy signifies giving human capacities and feelings to natural objects, such as the dancing leaf in Coleridge's *Christabel.*

93.   (C)

Everything turning away from Icarus' fall in stanza two provides a specific example of the general idea (indifference to suffering or to the extraordinary) advanced in stanza one; similarly, Brueghel's painting is a specific instance of Auden's generalization about the Old Masters' understanding the human position of suffering.

94.   (D)

The children are indifferent to the miraculous birth and the plowman is indifferent to the fall of Icarus.

95.   (A)

The dogs and horse are oblivious to suffering; we might think that the world should take notice of something as dreadful as martyrdom, but in fact daily life continues unaffected.

96.   (E)

William Carlos Williams' *Landscape with the Fall of Icarus* also deals with this legend.

97.   (A)

While novel and effective in Petrarch, the types of figures used by him became tired and conventional in love poems written by his imitators. Shakespeare satirizes some of the standard objects used for similes by Elizabethan sonneteers in this sonnet.

98.   (E)

This is a stanza from Shakespeare's Sonnet 130.

99.   (C)

This is Johnson's unsympathetic description of metaphysical wit in his *Life of Cowley*.

100.   (E)

Johnson's *Life of Cowley*.

101.   (D)

The term is Latin for a "god from a machine," from the practice of some Greek playwrights of ending plays with a god lowered on stage in a machine to resolve the work's complication. The phrase is now used to mean any improbable or forced plot resolution.

102.   (C)

An epithalamium is a song or a song or poem written to celebrate a wedding. The form was used by many ancient Greek and Roman poets; one of the most famous English marriage hymns is Spencer's *Epithalamion*, written to celebrate his own marriage.

103.   (C)

It parodies Wordsworth's *She Dwelt Among the Untrodden Ways*.

104.   (A)

Anouilh's *The Lark*, Schiller's *The Maid of Orleans*, Brecht's *St. Joan of the Stockyards*, and Shaw's *Saint Joan* all deal with Joan of Arc.

105.   (E)

Mackenzie's novel is an eighteenth-century sentimental tear-jerker; Steele's play is among the earliet and most influential eighteenth-century sentimental comedies.

106.   (E)

Macpherson was an obscure Scottish schoolteacher who Ossianic "translations" attracted a great deal of attention, especially in Germany, where they contributed to romantic stirrings, and in Scotland, where they evoked national pride.   In one sense, Macpherson's works are forgeries in that he wrote some of the material himself and altered fragments of Gaelic verse; on the other hand, they are based on traditional Gaelic poems and are partly authentic.

107. (D)

This is an excerpt from one of the heroine's letters to her parents, filled with her usual self-justifications in discussing her behavior toward "Mr. B." and others.

108. (B)

The excerpt is from Richardson's *Pamela*.

109. (C)

The excerpt is from James Thurber's *The Secret Life of Walter Mitty*.

110. (A)

Much of the story's mirth derives from Thurber's interweaving of Mitty's fantasy and real lives. In the former, Mitty imagines himself heroic and influential or famous in whatever role he plays; in the latter, he is timid, hen-pecked, and ineffectual.

111. (B)

The seventh-century English poem deals with an Anglo-Saxon court poet named Widsith. The scop's functions are somewhat similar to those of the poet laureate of later times.

112. (D)

Beowulf explores this statement by its hero. He uses his strength to test fate, and extends courage to its outer limits. Fate ultimately controls men's lives, but it can be influenced by heroism, as Beowulf's life illustrates.

113. (D)

This stanza is from Anthony Brode's *Breakfast with Gerard Manley Hopkins* in which he parodies Hopkins' sprung rhythm.

114. (B)

These are two of the four stanzas in Kenneth Koch's *Variations on a Theme by William Carlos Williams*. The "theme" is Williams' *This is*

Just to Say ("I have eaten/the plums/that were in/the icebox...").

115.   (B)
Everyman is the best surviving example of a medieval morality play. The play is an allegory that dramatizes the moral struggle of all Christians and teaches that man can take with him from this world only what he has given and nothing that he has received. In this play, the allegorical significance of each actor is defined by his name (Knowledge, Beauty, Strength, Good Deeds, and so on).

116.   (C)
This excerpt is from Blake's *A Vision of the Last Judgement* and deals with the relationship between imaginative vision and the corporeal eye. Reality is defined in relation to the visionary (mental), not in relation to "corporeal" being.

117.   (B)
This excerpt is from the beginning of Baldwin's *Notes of a Native Son*, and deals with the death of Baldwin's father.

118.   (E)
This is from the Preface to *The Picture of Dorian Gray*, and contains Wilde's characteristically witty remarks about the uselessness of art.

119.   (B)
Raleigh and Marlowe.

120.   (A)
The nymph's reply denies the accuracy of the shepherd's portrait of an idyllic rustic existence in a land of plenty and eternal spring. Her reply emphasizes changes that come with the passage of time, the harshness of winter, and the need to be aware of and to plan for such conditions.

121.   (E)

In Greek mythology, after Philomela was raped and her tongue cut out by her brother-in-law, Philomela was turned into a swallow (in some accounts, a nightingale; "Philomel" is the allusive name often given to the nightingale in English poetry). The nymph's mention of Philomel draws attention to the brutal aspects of love, in contrast to the romantic vision of the shepherd.

122.   (B)

"Honey tongue" is associated with "fancy's spring" and "heart of gall" is associated with "sorrow's fall." Listening to fancy's sweet talk in the spring will later result in bitterness or remorse ("gall").

123.   (C)
John Donne.

124.   (C)

The lecture is associated with applause, scientific analysis, light, and crowds, in contrast to the speaker's solitary contemplation of the stars, associated with silence, mysticism, darkness, and individuality. A contrast between mathematical certainty and error is not present in the poem; while mathematical certainty might be associated with the astronomer's lecture, the speaker would not associate "error" with his silent contemplation of the heavens.

125.   (E)

Perfect is used in the sense of "complete" silence, but also suggests "perfection" (the welcome silence that allows for wonder after the noise of the lecture-hall).

126.   (D)
   Whitman's *When I Heard the Learn'd Astronomer* implicitly celebrates nature's mystical qualities and the individual's solitary communion with nature.

127.   (B)
   The soul, like a mole, casts its folly out of its tunnel for all the world to see. The soul may be perceptive in viewing others, but fails to see its own folly.

128.   (E)
   "Thus I discovered" continues the analogy of the soul and the mole. Antony's soul has revealed its folly to plain view, and Dolabella has seen it.

129.   (B)
   Although Dolabella once blamed Antony's love for Cleopatra, he now wishes he were Antony "to be so ruined" (that is, he knows that Antony's love has ruined him, but understands, even approves of, the reasons Antony persists in his ruin).

130.   (D)
   The passage is from Dryden's *All for Love*, written in conscious imitation of Shakespeare's style.

131.   (C)
   This short, humorous poem, *Adam Pos'd*, is by Anne Finch (1661-1720), Countess of Winchilsea. Finch imagines that Adam would have had difficulty identifying and naming a vain, affected eighteenth-century coquette, having seen nothing like her in the natural world. "Father" refers to Adam.

132. (A)

The nymph's appearance would have perplexed Adam's ability to identify and name things.

133. (E)

The poem makes fun of the affected behavior and appearance of the coquette.

134. (C)

Adam would have difficulty formulating the right idea of what he is seeing.

135. (E)

The reference is to Genesis 2:19-20, Adam's naming of species.

136. (D)

The wavering form, the "Thing," is the Nymph of line four.

137. (C)

Ford's play was published in 1633.

138. (E)

William's masterpiece is frequently produced.

139.   (D)

O'Neill's protagonist, Yank, is in fact crushed to death by an ape, the only creature with whom he now feels kinship. He frees the ape to help him wreak destruction, but of course fails in this final act of rebellion.

140.   (B)

From *The First Pastoral*. Philips published six pastorals; his use of Theocritus' realistic manner rather than Virgil's more idealized mode caused a minor controversy in the eighteenth century.

141.   (E)

From Crabbe's *The Village* (1783), in which Crabbe debunks pastoral poetry.

142.   (C)

Burns' *Tam o' Shanter* is a mock-heroic treatment of folk material. The poem was written for a book on Scottish antiquities; its events are recounted in a broad Scottish folk dialect.

143.   (D)

Iago's expression of his belief that man's will controls his character and body, not some external force, is found in the first act of *Othello*.

144.   (E)

Believing that Antony's valor has become irrational and foolhardy, Enobarbus decides to abandon him (in *Antony and Cleopatra*), a decision that he will later regret and that will be the cause of Enobarbus' self-loathing.

145.   (A)

Coriolanus' speech reflecting his distaste for seeking popular approval to govern is from the second act of *Coriolanus*.

146.   (B)

The lifeless perfection of the dolls (they are not "filthy") contrasts with the filth and the noise of a real, living human child. Both are small and human in form, but the dolls are the product of art.

147.   (C)

The poem gives us a glimpse of two different realms, art and life, both "inhabited" by the doll-maker. Both make demands on the artist as art comes into conflict with the real world.

148.   (B)

Yeats is the author of both *The Dolls* and *Sailing to Byzantium*.

149.   (E)

Unlike his father, Telemachus has the patience and prudence to rule "a rugged people" effectively, but he also lacks Ulysses' heroism and sense of adventure.

150.   (B)

The elderly Ulysses plans to set sail in search of additional experience for its own sake and to test further his will. He cannot be content merely "to breathe," and plans to use fully the little time left to him.

151.   (C)
The passage is from Tennyson's dramatic monologue, *Ulysses*.

152.   (C)
Defoe's Moll, near the end of the novel, explains how she handled the difficult task of telling her current husband that she had been married to her brother and had borne him a son.

153.   (D)
Atwood's heroine, a compulsive maker of fantasies, begins the novel with her greatest fantasy.

154.   (E)
Sterne's self-conscious narrator takes the reader into his confidence, addressing him familiarly and explaining how he will proceed as narrator.

155.   (A)
Jim Burden, Cather's narrator, returns to the scene of his and Antonia's childhood in Nebraska at the end of the novel; the passage stresses the extent to which life's early circumstances and experiences shape adult destinies.

156.   (A)
In these lines from a sonnet by Sidney, love is personified (i.e. an abstraction given human attributes.

157.   (A)
If the speaker rides his horse, he in turn is ridden by love ("a horse to

Love"), which controls him as completely as he controls his horse.

158. (B)

Bigger asserts his identity ("I am") only after committing murder, and defines his identity through acts of violence. Unlike Max, who attempts to "explain" Bigger in terms of class struggle, Bigger attaches individual (not class) meaning to his acts. He does not see himself as a sociological phenomenon or an illustration of communist doctrine, but as someone who has been awakened to a sense of self only after exercising personal control of others, however violent.

159. (D)

The passage is from the conclusion of *Native Son*.

160. (D)

Milton's *Paradise Lost* attempts to "justify the ways of God to men" and Pope's *An Essay on Man* seeks to "vindicate the ways of man to God."

161. (D)

Browning's *Porphyria's Lover* is a dramatic monologue delivered by a deranged speaker who has strangled Porphyria, whose only crime has been acts of kindness to the speaker.

162. (A)

The villanelle consists of five tercets and a quatrain, all on two rhymes; it also systematically repeats the first and third lines of the first tercet. Thomas' poem is surprising for its depth of emotion conveyed in such an elaborate, self-conscious stanzaic form.

163. (C)
These famous lines are from Book I of Keats' *Endymion*.

164. (E)
The author is describing a battle between red and black ants in his woodpile; he unflatteringly compares man's militaristic tendencies or behavior to the behavior of the ants.

165. (D)
Patroclus, Achilles' friend, was killed in the Trojan War while Achilles sulked. The latter then returns to battle to avenge Patroclus' death.

166. (D)
The passage is from *Walden* .

167. (C)
Menippean satire is a type of indirect satire named after the Greek cynic Menippus. It deals with mental attitudes rather than with fully realized characters and is a miscellaneous form held together by a loosely constructed narrative. In longer works, such as Burton's Anatomy

168.　(A)

Confession is a form of autobiography that gives an intellectualized account of intensely personal and introverted experiences. Burton's *Religio Medici* is a confession of Christian faith qualified by a general scepticism.

169.　(D)

A polemic is a vigorously argumentative work on a controversial subject. *Areopagitica*, addressed to the "Lords and Commons of England," attacks censorship and supports "the liberty of unlicensed printing" of books.

170.　(E)

Peacock's novel appeared in 1818. His portraits of Coleridge and Wordsworth are unflattering; Shelley, who was not offended by Peacock's portrayal, said that Peacock's "fine wit makes such a wound, the knife is lost in it."

171.　(A)

Point Counter Point was published in 1928.

172.　(B)

As the narrator says, dead letters sound like "dead men," especially Bartleby, whose hopeless and ineffectual life has been a kind of death-in-life.

173.　(A)

Melville wrote *Benito Cereno* as well as *Bartleby, the Scrivener*.

174. (A)
Lines three and four tell us that long before this action was completed, their hats swam above them (that is, the men drowned).

175. (D)
The excerpt is from one of the best of the medieval popular ballads, *Sir Patrick Spens*.

176. (C)
The fabliau was popular in France in the twelfth and thirteenth centuries and in England during the fourteenth century. Chaucer's *The Miller's Tale* is a fabliau.

177. (E)
Swift attacks, through satire, favorite targets in *An Argument Against the Abolishing of Christianity in England*.

178. (C)
In his *Characteristics*, Carlyle discusses self-consciousness, which he regards as modern man's most characteristic symptom of diseased mind and spirit.

179. (A)
This is part of Newman's discussion of the nature and value of liberal education in his *The Idea of a University*.

180. (C)
Naipaul grew up in Trinidad, but visited India, the country his family had left two generations earlier.

181. (B)

The townspeople feel sorry for Miss Emily (the narrator consistently displays a compassionate understanding of her position in society), but their compassion is tempered by self-congratulation about being right that she had not received numerous marriage proposals (that is, they feel vindicated in their belief that "the Griersons held themselves a little too high for what they really were").

182. (C)

The horse-whip is to drive away Miss Emily's suitors while Miss Emily stands behind him; she is thus both protected and dominated by her father.

183. (E)

The story is Faulkner's *A Rose for Emily*.

184. (A)

The novels of both Proust and Gide deal with the maturation of the artist.

185. (D)

Having unwillingly participated in the execution of the two English prisoners and having thus "disturbed the hidden powers" that value brotherhood more than duty to country, the young narrator feels "small and lost and lonely like a child astray in the snow"; moreover, his loss of innocence and recognition of isolation and loneliness are permanent (he can never feel the same about "anything that happened to me afterwards").

186.   (A)
The passage is from the conclusion of O'Connor's story.

187.   (C)
Hawthorne's Robin encounters evil and Lessing's boy experiences helplessness while observing a dying buck being devoured by ants. Both experiences fundamentally change the way in which each protagonist views the world.

188.   (D)
John Osborne's *Look Back in Anger*.

189.   (A)
Brendan Behan's *The Hostage*.

190.   (C)
Theater of the Absurd had already developed in France under the leadership of Beckett and Ionesco.

191.   (B)
Surrey's sonnets, while similar in subject matter, differ from those of Wyatt in establishing a form (three quatrains and a couplet) that has become known as the "English" sonnet.

192.   (D)
The poet gives us a catalogue of the pleasant activities of the "soote season" ("sweet season"; spring) in order to contrast nature's happiness with his increasing sorrow.

193.   (D)

This poem is Surrey's adaptation of a Petrarchan sonnet, to which it owes its subject matter. Unrequited love is a common subject in poems imitative of Petrarch.

194.   (D)

Famous for her misuse of words, Mrs. Malaprop has given her name to the English language as the term (malapropism) designating the humorous misapplication of a word, usually the use of a word sounding somewhat like the one intended but ludicrously wrong in context ("reprehend" for "apprehend", for example).

195.   (B)

The narrator urges the building of a rainbow bridge that connects the two sides of man's being, his "prosaic" half and his "passionate" half, in order to achieve wholeness. If man consists only of "prose," he becomes a monk and is "grey"; if he consists only of "passion," he becomes a "beast," an uncontrolled fire. When the two are connected, man achieves wholeness as opposed to complete self-denial or un-bridled lust. The narrator associates "passion" with "beasts" and "fire," while associating "prose with "monks" and "grey."

196.   (A)

The narrator says that Mr. Wilcox, while appearing reliable and brave on the outside, has never examined his inner life--his motives, beliefs, feelings. Having failed to engage in self-examination and self-criticism, his attitudes toward such matters as personal relations and sexual desire are muddled.

197.   (D)

Although the narrator argues for the wholeness that comes from connecting passion (including sexual desire) with prose, he also asserts that the absolute rejection of carnality is preferable to Mr. Wilcox's incomplete asceticism, which leads him to be ashamed of loving his wife. One can say that the narrator most admires the man who successfully builds a rainbow bridge and is thus complete, but one can also admire the saints' complete rejection of carnality because it is based on absolute conviction, whereas Mr. Wilcox's view of sexual desire lacks conviction and prevents him from achieving fully satisfying personal relationships. The narrator believes that sexual desire is fully compatible with marital love, need not be guilt-ridden, and is an important part of spiritual wholeness.

198.　(A)

The passage is from Forster's *Howards End*, which affirms the primacy of human relations, as opposed to the life of "telegrams and anger."

199.　(D)

In this line, "cod-piece" stands for what it covers.

200.　(C)

The line means "before he has a house for his head."

201.　(A)

The first two lines can be restated thus: If man houses his sexual organ (that is, engages in sexual intercourse that will produce children) before he has a house for his head (that is, before he owns a house). The addition of the third line completes the thought--can surely expect penury (more literally, will become a louse-infested vagabond).

202.　(E)

Many men _do_ father children before having a house, which is why there are so many married beggars. It is not marriage that makes men beggars, but the failure to provide economic security before satisfying sexual desire.

203. (A)

The man who elevates the base toe over the noble heart can expect misery (will develop a "corn" on his heart) and sleeplessness.

204. (E)

He has elevated the base Goneril and Regan over the noble Cordelia.

205. (D)

Aristophanes' play addressed actual conditions. War with Sparta threatened the fabric of Athenian life. Aristophanes' comic solution might have had as good a chance as any other to stop the war.

206. (A)

Creon has only recently been crowned, so Antigone's refusal to abide by his decree forbidding the burial of one of her brothers constitutes a challenge, from his point of view, to his authority. He sees the conflict as one between duty to family and duty to state, with the latter taking priority. Antigone broadens the terms of the conflict, appealing to the laws of the gods, which require burial of the dead and which take priority over the laws of the state.

207. (B)

Tartuffe is one of the best-known works of the French neoclassical theater. It relies on satire, brilliant dialogue and characterization, and the ingenuity of its plot to achieve its effects.

208. (E)

Euripides' material is drawn from Greek mythology, but reshaped to underscore the contrast between Medea's powerful character and the relatively weak Jason. The play is especially remarkable for its characterization of Medea, whose acts repel and whose strength and sense of betrayal attract audiences.

209.   (E)

The speaker is Edmund in *King Lear*. Edmund says that men blame the sun, the moon, and the stars when things go wrong, when in fact man's disasters result from his own character and behavior. This tendency to claim that we cannot control what we are or what we do, to claim that we are what we are because of some external influence or necessity, is "the excellent foppery" (foolishness) of the world, designed to avoid responsibility for the consequences of one's own actions.

210.   (C)

Edmund says that he would have been lecherous regardless of the constellations in ascendance at his birth.

211.   (D)

Edmund has no belief in the influence of the stars, sun, and moon on man's life and character.

212.   (B)

Browning's poem, *Fra Lippo Lippi*, is set at the beginning of the Renaissance in Italy, at a time when medieval attitudes were beginning to give way to a greater appreciation of earthly pleasures. Lippo Lippi was a Florentine painter and friar, who lived from 1406 to 1469; the Medici were a powerful banking family and virtual rulers of Florence.

213.   (E)

Lippo Lippi is caught in an alley where "sportive ladies" (i.e., prostitutes) leave their doors ajar (to welcome business).

214.   (A)

After the grip on his throat has been relaxed, Lippo Lippi says to the policeman who had held him by the throat that he was "best" (i.e. most thorough in carrying out his role).

215. (D)
See #212 above. Lippo Lippi's patron was extremely influential; hence Lippo Lippi's mention of his connection with the Medici causes the police to treat him with greater deference.

216. (C)
Lippo Lippi suggests to the officer in charge of the patrol that he must be concerned about the manner in which his subordinates behave because their behavior will reflect on him.

217. (E)
"This," in line fourteen, refers to this poem, and it is this poem that gives life to the beloved as long as the poem survives and is read. The beloved's "eternal summer" will fade, when that eternal summer is conceived in physical terms, because time destroys all youth and beauty, but the beloved's eternal summer has been preserved in this poem and is thus no longer subject to the ravages of time.

218. (C)
The first two quatrains compare the beloved to a summer's day, emphasizing the imperfection and changeability of summer. Line nine introduces the chief thought of the poem that will be developed through line fourteen--the notion that the beloved's beauty can triumph over time by being captured in poetry. The first eight lines emphasize impermanence; the last six emphasize permanence. The final couplet completes the thought begun in line nine.

219. (A)
Although the sonnet appears at the beginning to be an elaborate compliment that compares the beloved favorably to a summer's day, it

uses that comparison to make a larger point about the permanence of poetry, one vehicle that allows man to triumph over death and time. The poem moves steadily from the beauty of the beloved to a stronger preoccupation with the power of poetry.

220. (D)
The author argues that women who depend entirely on beauty for power must expect to lose their power when beauty fades. Hence full humanity must result from such things as independent reasoning. The author is not advocating abolishing the roles of daughters, wives, and mothers, but rather building different foundations for those roles.

221. (B)
The passage is from Mary Wollstonecraft's *A Vindication of the Rights of Woman*.

222. (A)
The passage is from Plato's *Republic*, in which he disallows epic and lyric poetry a place in his Utopian state

223. (B)
This is Hume's definition of the standard of taste in his essay, *Of the Standard of Taste*.

224. (B)
The passage is from Longinus' *On the Sublime*, the source of much later discussion of the sublime in the arts, especially in the eighteenth century.

225. (A)
This is Wordsworth's famous definition of poetry in his Preface to the *Lyrical Ballads*.

226. (E)

The passage is from Aristotle's *Poetics*. Aristotle is here arguing that a probable impossibility is preferable to a possible improbability in art--that is, things that are impossible in the real world can be made probable in art because every work establishes its own laws of probability. Questions of probability must be answered with reference to the world of the work of art, not with reference to the real world. Something that may be possible in the real world may be improbable in a given art work, and that improbable possibility is less desirable than something impossible in the real world that has been made probable in an art work.

227. (C)

This is from Sidney's *An Apologie for Poetrie*, in which he affirms its delightfulness and instructiveness, and defends it against the misguided objections of its detractors.

228. (B)

This excerpt is from Pope's *An Essay on Criticism*. This particular passage contains Pope's well-known assertion that nature is the source, end, and test of art.

229. (B)

This is Eliot's definition of the "objective correlative," a term that was picked up, somewhat to Eliot's surprise, by later critics. The passage is from Eliot's essay, *Hamlet and His Problems*, in which Eliot examines what he believes are the artistic flaws of Shakespeare's play.

230. (C)

The passage is from Johnson's *Rasselas*. Imlac, here a mouth piece for Johnson, explains that the poet is to strive for the just representation of general nature, to seek to depict that which is universal; he should not concentrate on particular nature, on those eccentricities or peculiarities that distinguish the individual from the species. If he focuses on particular nature, he will not have universal appeal, and his work will not stand the test of time.

GRE

LITERATURE in ENGLISH

TEST III

THE GRADUATE RECORD EXAMINATION

LITERATURE in ENGLISH

ANSWER SHEET

1. Ⓐ Ⓑ Ⓒ Ⓓ Ⓔ
2. Ⓐ Ⓑ Ⓒ Ⓓ Ⓔ
3. Ⓐ Ⓑ Ⓒ Ⓓ Ⓔ
4. Ⓐ Ⓑ Ⓒ Ⓓ Ⓔ
5. Ⓐ Ⓑ Ⓒ Ⓓ Ⓔ
6. Ⓐ Ⓑ Ⓒ Ⓓ Ⓔ
7. Ⓐ Ⓑ Ⓒ Ⓓ Ⓔ
8. Ⓐ Ⓑ Ⓒ Ⓓ Ⓔ
9. Ⓐ Ⓑ Ⓒ Ⓓ Ⓔ
10. Ⓐ Ⓑ Ⓒ Ⓓ Ⓔ
11. Ⓐ Ⓑ Ⓒ Ⓓ Ⓔ
12. Ⓐ Ⓑ Ⓒ Ⓓ Ⓔ
13. Ⓐ Ⓑ Ⓒ Ⓓ Ⓔ
14. Ⓐ Ⓑ Ⓒ Ⓓ Ⓔ
15. Ⓐ Ⓑ Ⓒ Ⓓ Ⓔ
16. Ⓐ Ⓑ Ⓒ Ⓓ Ⓔ
17. Ⓐ Ⓑ Ⓒ Ⓓ Ⓔ
18. Ⓐ Ⓑ Ⓒ Ⓓ Ⓔ
19. Ⓐ Ⓑ Ⓒ Ⓓ Ⓔ
20. Ⓐ Ⓑ Ⓒ Ⓓ Ⓔ
21. Ⓐ Ⓑ Ⓒ Ⓓ Ⓔ
22. Ⓐ Ⓑ Ⓒ Ⓓ Ⓔ
23. Ⓐ Ⓑ Ⓒ Ⓓ Ⓔ
24. Ⓐ Ⓑ Ⓒ Ⓓ Ⓔ
25. Ⓐ Ⓑ Ⓒ Ⓓ Ⓔ
26. Ⓐ Ⓑ Ⓒ Ⓓ Ⓔ
27. Ⓐ Ⓑ Ⓒ Ⓓ Ⓔ
28. Ⓐ Ⓑ Ⓒ Ⓓ Ⓔ
29. Ⓐ Ⓑ Ⓒ Ⓓ Ⓔ
30. Ⓐ Ⓑ Ⓒ Ⓓ Ⓔ

31. Ⓐ Ⓑ Ⓒ Ⓓ Ⓔ
32. Ⓐ Ⓑ Ⓒ Ⓓ Ⓔ
33. Ⓐ Ⓑ Ⓒ Ⓓ Ⓔ
34. Ⓐ Ⓑ Ⓒ Ⓓ Ⓔ
35. Ⓐ Ⓑ Ⓒ Ⓓ Ⓔ
36. Ⓐ Ⓑ Ⓒ Ⓓ Ⓔ
37. Ⓐ Ⓑ Ⓒ Ⓓ Ⓔ
38. Ⓐ Ⓑ Ⓒ Ⓓ Ⓔ
39. Ⓐ Ⓑ Ⓒ Ⓓ Ⓔ
40. Ⓐ Ⓑ Ⓒ Ⓓ Ⓔ
41. Ⓐ Ⓑ Ⓒ Ⓓ Ⓔ
42. Ⓐ Ⓑ Ⓒ Ⓓ Ⓔ
43. Ⓐ Ⓑ Ⓒ Ⓓ Ⓔ
44. Ⓐ Ⓑ Ⓒ Ⓓ Ⓔ
45. Ⓐ Ⓑ Ⓒ Ⓓ Ⓔ
46. Ⓐ Ⓑ Ⓒ Ⓓ Ⓔ
47. Ⓐ Ⓑ Ⓒ Ⓓ Ⓔ
48. Ⓐ Ⓑ Ⓒ Ⓓ Ⓔ
49. Ⓐ Ⓑ Ⓒ Ⓓ Ⓔ
50. Ⓐ Ⓑ Ⓒ Ⓓ Ⓔ
51. Ⓐ Ⓑ Ⓒ Ⓓ Ⓔ
52. Ⓐ Ⓑ Ⓒ Ⓓ Ⓔ
53. Ⓐ Ⓑ Ⓒ Ⓓ Ⓔ
54. Ⓐ Ⓑ Ⓒ Ⓓ Ⓔ
55. Ⓐ Ⓑ Ⓒ Ⓓ Ⓔ
56. Ⓐ Ⓑ Ⓒ Ⓓ Ⓔ
57. Ⓐ Ⓑ Ⓒ Ⓓ Ⓔ
58. Ⓐ Ⓑ Ⓒ Ⓓ Ⓔ
59. Ⓐ Ⓑ Ⓒ Ⓓ Ⓔ
60. Ⓐ Ⓑ Ⓒ Ⓓ Ⓔ

61. Ⓐ Ⓑ Ⓒ Ⓓ Ⓔ
62. Ⓐ Ⓑ Ⓒ Ⓓ Ⓔ
63. Ⓐ Ⓑ Ⓒ Ⓓ Ⓔ
64. Ⓐ Ⓑ Ⓒ Ⓓ Ⓔ
65. Ⓐ Ⓑ Ⓒ Ⓓ Ⓔ
66. Ⓐ Ⓑ Ⓒ Ⓓ Ⓔ
67. Ⓐ Ⓑ Ⓒ Ⓓ Ⓔ
68. Ⓐ Ⓑ Ⓒ Ⓓ Ⓔ
69. Ⓐ Ⓑ Ⓒ Ⓓ Ⓔ
70. Ⓐ Ⓑ Ⓒ Ⓓ Ⓔ
71. Ⓐ Ⓑ Ⓒ Ⓓ Ⓔ
72. Ⓐ Ⓑ Ⓒ Ⓓ Ⓔ
73. Ⓐ Ⓑ Ⓒ Ⓓ Ⓔ
74. Ⓐ Ⓑ Ⓒ Ⓓ Ⓔ
75. Ⓐ Ⓑ Ⓒ Ⓓ Ⓔ
76. Ⓐ Ⓑ Ⓒ Ⓓ Ⓔ
77. Ⓐ Ⓑ Ⓒ Ⓓ Ⓔ
78. Ⓐ Ⓑ Ⓒ Ⓓ Ⓔ
79. Ⓐ Ⓑ Ⓒ Ⓓ Ⓔ
80. Ⓐ Ⓑ Ⓒ Ⓓ Ⓔ
81. Ⓐ Ⓑ Ⓒ Ⓓ Ⓔ
82. Ⓐ Ⓑ Ⓒ Ⓓ Ⓔ
83. Ⓐ Ⓑ Ⓒ Ⓓ Ⓔ
84. Ⓐ Ⓑ Ⓒ Ⓓ Ⓔ
85. Ⓐ Ⓑ Ⓒ Ⓓ Ⓔ
86. Ⓐ Ⓑ Ⓒ Ⓓ Ⓔ
87. Ⓐ Ⓑ Ⓒ Ⓓ Ⓔ
88. Ⓐ Ⓑ Ⓒ Ⓓ Ⓔ
89. Ⓐ Ⓑ Ⓒ Ⓓ Ⓔ
90. Ⓐ Ⓑ Ⓒ Ⓓ Ⓔ

91. Ⓐ Ⓑ Ⓒ Ⓓ Ⓔ
92. Ⓐ Ⓑ Ⓒ Ⓓ Ⓔ
93. Ⓐ Ⓑ Ⓒ Ⓓ Ⓔ
94. Ⓐ Ⓑ Ⓒ Ⓓ Ⓔ
95. Ⓐ Ⓑ Ⓒ Ⓓ Ⓔ
96. Ⓐ Ⓑ Ⓒ Ⓓ Ⓔ
97. Ⓐ Ⓑ Ⓒ Ⓓ Ⓔ
98. Ⓐ Ⓑ Ⓒ Ⓓ Ⓔ
99. Ⓐ Ⓑ Ⓒ Ⓓ Ⓔ
100. Ⓐ Ⓑ Ⓒ Ⓓ Ⓔ
101. Ⓐ Ⓑ Ⓒ Ⓓ Ⓔ
102. Ⓐ Ⓑ Ⓒ Ⓓ Ⓔ
103. Ⓐ Ⓑ Ⓒ Ⓓ Ⓔ
104. Ⓐ Ⓑ Ⓒ Ⓓ Ⓔ
105. Ⓐ Ⓑ Ⓒ Ⓓ Ⓔ
106. Ⓐ Ⓑ Ⓒ Ⓓ Ⓔ
107. Ⓐ Ⓑ Ⓒ Ⓓ Ⓔ
108. Ⓐ Ⓑ Ⓒ Ⓓ Ⓔ
109. Ⓐ Ⓑ Ⓒ Ⓓ Ⓔ
110. Ⓐ Ⓑ Ⓒ Ⓓ Ⓔ
111. Ⓐ Ⓑ Ⓒ Ⓓ Ⓔ
112. Ⓐ Ⓑ Ⓒ Ⓓ Ⓔ
113. Ⓐ Ⓑ Ⓒ Ⓓ Ⓔ
114. Ⓐ Ⓑ Ⓒ Ⓓ Ⓔ
115. Ⓐ Ⓑ Ⓒ Ⓓ Ⓔ
116. Ⓐ Ⓑ Ⓒ Ⓓ Ⓔ
117. Ⓐ Ⓑ Ⓒ Ⓓ Ⓔ
118. Ⓐ Ⓑ Ⓒ Ⓓ Ⓔ
119. Ⓐ Ⓑ Ⓒ Ⓓ Ⓔ
120. Ⓐ Ⓑ Ⓒ Ⓓ Ⓔ

121. Ⓐ Ⓑ Ⓒ Ⓓ Ⓔ
122. Ⓐ Ⓑ Ⓒ Ⓓ Ⓔ
123. Ⓐ Ⓑ Ⓒ Ⓓ Ⓔ
124. Ⓐ Ⓑ Ⓒ Ⓓ Ⓔ
125. Ⓐ Ⓑ Ⓒ Ⓓ Ⓔ
126. Ⓐ Ⓑ Ⓒ Ⓓ Ⓔ
127. Ⓐ Ⓑ Ⓒ Ⓓ Ⓔ
128. Ⓐ Ⓑ Ⓒ Ⓓ Ⓔ
129. Ⓐ Ⓑ Ⓒ Ⓓ Ⓔ
130. Ⓐ Ⓑ Ⓒ Ⓓ Ⓔ
131. Ⓐ Ⓑ Ⓒ Ⓓ Ⓔ
132. Ⓐ Ⓑ Ⓒ Ⓓ Ⓔ
133. Ⓐ Ⓑ Ⓒ Ⓓ Ⓔ
134. Ⓐ Ⓑ Ⓒ Ⓓ Ⓔ
135. Ⓐ Ⓑ Ⓒ Ⓓ Ⓔ
136. Ⓐ Ⓑ Ⓒ Ⓓ Ⓔ
137. Ⓐ Ⓑ Ⓒ Ⓓ Ⓔ
138. Ⓐ Ⓑ Ⓒ Ⓓ Ⓔ
139. Ⓐ Ⓑ Ⓒ Ⓓ Ⓔ
140. Ⓐ Ⓑ Ⓒ Ⓓ Ⓔ
141. Ⓐ Ⓑ Ⓒ Ⓓ Ⓔ
142. Ⓐ Ⓑ Ⓒ Ⓓ Ⓔ
143. Ⓐ Ⓑ Ⓒ Ⓓ Ⓔ
144. Ⓐ Ⓑ Ⓒ Ⓓ Ⓔ
145. Ⓐ Ⓑ Ⓒ Ⓓ Ⓔ
146. Ⓐ Ⓑ Ⓒ Ⓓ Ⓔ
147. Ⓐ Ⓑ Ⓒ Ⓓ Ⓔ
148. Ⓐ Ⓑ Ⓒ Ⓓ Ⓔ
149. Ⓐ Ⓑ Ⓒ Ⓓ Ⓔ
150. Ⓐ Ⓑ Ⓒ Ⓓ Ⓔ

151. Ⓐ Ⓑ Ⓒ Ⓓ Ⓔ
152. Ⓐ Ⓑ Ⓒ Ⓓ Ⓔ
153. Ⓐ Ⓑ Ⓒ Ⓓ Ⓔ
154. Ⓐ Ⓑ Ⓒ Ⓓ Ⓔ
155. Ⓐ Ⓑ Ⓒ Ⓓ Ⓔ
156. Ⓐ Ⓑ Ⓒ Ⓓ Ⓔ
157. Ⓐ Ⓑ Ⓒ Ⓓ Ⓔ
158. Ⓐ Ⓑ Ⓒ Ⓓ Ⓔ
159. Ⓐ Ⓑ Ⓒ Ⓓ Ⓔ
160. Ⓐ Ⓑ Ⓒ Ⓓ Ⓔ
161. Ⓐ Ⓑ Ⓒ Ⓓ Ⓔ
162. Ⓐ Ⓑ Ⓒ Ⓓ Ⓔ
163. Ⓐ Ⓑ Ⓒ Ⓓ Ⓔ
164. Ⓐ Ⓑ Ⓒ Ⓓ Ⓔ
165. Ⓐ Ⓑ Ⓒ Ⓓ Ⓔ
166. Ⓐ Ⓑ Ⓒ Ⓓ Ⓔ
167. Ⓐ Ⓑ Ⓒ Ⓓ Ⓔ
168. Ⓐ Ⓑ Ⓒ Ⓓ Ⓔ
169. Ⓐ Ⓑ Ⓒ Ⓓ Ⓔ
170. Ⓐ Ⓑ Ⓒ Ⓓ Ⓔ
171. Ⓐ Ⓑ Ⓒ Ⓓ Ⓔ
172. Ⓐ Ⓑ Ⓒ Ⓓ Ⓔ
173. Ⓐ Ⓑ Ⓒ Ⓓ Ⓔ
174. Ⓐ Ⓑ Ⓒ Ⓓ Ⓔ
175. Ⓐ Ⓑ Ⓒ Ⓓ Ⓔ
176. Ⓐ Ⓑ Ⓒ Ⓓ Ⓔ
177. Ⓐ Ⓑ Ⓒ Ⓓ Ⓔ
178. Ⓐ Ⓑ Ⓒ Ⓓ Ⓔ
179. Ⓐ Ⓑ Ⓒ Ⓓ Ⓔ
180. Ⓐ Ⓑ Ⓒ Ⓓ Ⓔ

181. Ⓐ Ⓑ Ⓒ Ⓓ Ⓔ
182. Ⓐ Ⓑ Ⓒ Ⓓ Ⓔ
183. Ⓐ Ⓑ Ⓒ Ⓓ Ⓔ
184. Ⓐ Ⓑ Ⓒ Ⓓ Ⓔ
185. Ⓐ Ⓑ Ⓒ Ⓓ Ⓔ
186. Ⓐ Ⓑ Ⓒ Ⓓ Ⓔ
187. Ⓐ Ⓑ Ⓒ Ⓓ Ⓔ
188. Ⓐ Ⓑ Ⓒ Ⓓ Ⓔ
189. Ⓐ Ⓑ Ⓒ Ⓓ Ⓔ
190. Ⓐ Ⓑ Ⓒ Ⓓ Ⓔ
191. Ⓐ Ⓑ Ⓒ Ⓓ Ⓔ
192. Ⓐ Ⓑ Ⓒ Ⓓ Ⓔ
193. Ⓐ Ⓑ Ⓒ Ⓓ Ⓔ
194. Ⓐ Ⓑ Ⓒ Ⓓ Ⓔ
195. Ⓐ Ⓑ Ⓒ Ⓓ Ⓔ
196. Ⓐ Ⓑ Ⓒ Ⓓ Ⓔ
197. Ⓐ Ⓑ Ⓒ Ⓓ Ⓔ

198. Ⓐ Ⓑ Ⓒ Ⓓ Ⓔ
199. Ⓐ Ⓑ Ⓒ Ⓓ Ⓔ
200. Ⓐ Ⓑ Ⓒ Ⓓ Ⓔ
201. Ⓐ Ⓑ Ⓒ Ⓓ Ⓔ
202. Ⓐ Ⓑ Ⓒ Ⓓ Ⓔ
203. Ⓐ Ⓑ Ⓒ Ⓓ Ⓔ
204. Ⓐ Ⓑ Ⓒ Ⓓ Ⓔ
205. Ⓐ Ⓑ Ⓒ Ⓓ Ⓔ
206. Ⓐ Ⓑ Ⓒ Ⓓ Ⓔ
207. Ⓐ Ⓑ Ⓒ Ⓓ Ⓔ
208. Ⓐ Ⓑ Ⓒ Ⓓ Ⓔ
209. Ⓐ Ⓑ Ⓒ Ⓓ Ⓔ
210. Ⓐ Ⓑ Ⓒ Ⓓ Ⓔ
211. Ⓐ Ⓑ Ⓒ Ⓓ Ⓔ
212. Ⓐ Ⓑ Ⓒ Ⓓ Ⓔ
213. Ⓐ Ⓑ Ⓒ Ⓓ Ⓔ
214. Ⓐ Ⓑ Ⓒ Ⓓ Ⓔ

215. Ⓐ Ⓑ Ⓒ Ⓓ Ⓔ
216. Ⓐ Ⓑ Ⓒ Ⓓ Ⓔ
217. Ⓐ Ⓑ Ⓒ Ⓓ Ⓔ
218. Ⓐ Ⓑ Ⓒ Ⓓ Ⓔ
219. Ⓐ Ⓑ Ⓒ Ⓓ Ⓔ
220. Ⓐ Ⓑ Ⓒ Ⓓ Ⓔ
221. Ⓐ Ⓑ Ⓒ Ⓓ Ⓔ
222. Ⓐ Ⓑ Ⓒ Ⓓ Ⓔ
223. Ⓐ Ⓑ Ⓒ Ⓓ Ⓔ
224. Ⓐ Ⓑ Ⓒ Ⓓ Ⓔ
225. Ⓐ Ⓑ Ⓒ Ⓓ Ⓔ
226. Ⓐ Ⓑ Ⓒ Ⓓ Ⓔ
227. Ⓐ Ⓑ Ⓒ Ⓓ Ⓔ
228. Ⓐ Ⓑ Ⓒ Ⓓ Ⓔ
229. Ⓐ Ⓑ Ⓒ Ⓓ Ⓔ
230. Ⓐ Ⓑ Ⓒ Ⓓ Ⓔ

GRE LITERATURE
IN ENGLISH

TEST III

Directions: Choose the best answer for each question and mark the letter
of your selection on the corresponding answer sheet.

Questions 1 – 3 refer to the excerpts below.

1. Which refers to Milton?

2. Which refers to Chaucer?

3. Which refers to Spenser?

(A) Discouraged, scorned, his writings vilified,
Poorly – poor man – he lived; poorly – poor man – he
died.

(B) His fame is gone out like a candle in a snuff and his memory
will always stink, which might have lived in honorable re-
pute, had he not been a notorious traitor, and most impi-
ously and villainously belied that blessed martyr, King
Charles I.

(C) The character and service of this gentleman are sufficient
to put all those men called kings to shame. While they are
receiving from the sweat and labors of mankind a prodi-
gality of pay . . . he is rendering every service in his
power, and refusing every pecuniary reward.

(D) His manly cheerfulness is especially delicious to me in my
old age. How exquisitely tender he is, and yet how perfectly free from the least touch of sickly melancholy or
morbid drooping.

(E) (His) muse is at once indecent and ugly, lascivious and
gawky, lubricious and coarse.

4.   I still think of _____ as I thought when I first read him, that he is a superior poet to Milton; that he runs neck and neck with Homer; and that none but Shakespeare has gone decidedly beyond him.

Which of the following correctly completes the sentence above?

(A) Jonson   (D) Ovid

(B) Spenser   (E) Dante

(C) Catallus

5.   The basic tenet of Existentialism is that

(A) nothing exists but what is imagined.

(B) meaning is determined by the imagination.

(C) existence is the significant fact, but it has no intrinsic meaning.

(D) meaning is established by general agreement.

(E) agreement as to significance is the only true existence.

6.   ". . .handsome, clever, and rich, with a comfortable home and happy disposition seemed to unite some of the best blessings of existence; and had lived nearly twenty-one years in the world with very little to distress or vex her."

The sentence completed above describes

(A) Flaubert's *Madame Bovary*

(B) Austen's *Emma*

(C) Cather's *Antonia*

(D) Dickens' *Agnes Wakefield*

(E) Fitzgerald's *Daisy*

Ae Fond Kiss

Ae fond kiss, and then we sever!
Ae farewell, and then forever!
Deep in heart-wrung tears I'll pledge thee,
Warring sighs and groans I'll wage thee.
Who shall say that Fortune grieves him
While the star of hope she leaves him?
Me, nae cheerfu' twinkle lights me;
Dark despair around benights me.

I'll ne'er blame my partial fancy,
Nothing could resist my Nancy:
but to see her was to love her;
Love but her, and love forever.
Had we never lov'd sae kindly,
Had we never lov'd sae blindly,
Never met – or never parted –
We had ne'er been broken-hearted.

Fare thee weel, thou first and fairest!
Fare Thee weel, thou best and dearest!
Thine be ilka joy and treasure,
Peace, enjoyment, love, and pleasure!
Ae fond kiss, and then we sever;
Ae farewell, alas, forever!
Deep in heart-wrung tears I'll pledge thee,
Warring sighs and groans I'll wage thee!

7.   In the first stanza the poet implies that

(A) his love has left him a glimmer of hope that she will return to him

(B) his love gives him no hope that she will return to him

(C) their separation was unexpected

(D) their separation was expected

(E) their heart-break was of little consequence.

8.   Which of the following most closely restates the poet's view of his affair with Nancy?

(A) Their love was unavoidable, as was their heartbreak.

(B) They could have avoided falling in love, but once done, they could not have avoided the heartbreak.

(C) If it wasn't for his "partial fancy" he could have avoided both love and heartbreak.

(D) He holds himself to blame for falling in love with her.

(E) He holds Nancy to blame for their tragic affair.

9.   This poem is written in

(A) Chaucerian English   (D) Scots Dialect

(B) Spenserian English   (E) Standard English

(C) West Country Dialect

10.   The school of poetry known as "Fleshly" is associated with

(A) Dickinson   (D) Swinburne

(B) Wordsworth   (E) Wilde

(C) Whitman

11.   "I was taught to think, and I was willing to believe, that genius was not a bawd, that virtue was not a mask, that liberty was not a name, that love had its seat in the human heart. Now I would care little if these words were struck out of the dictionary, or if I had never heard them. They are become to my ears a mockery and a dream."

The "I" in the passage above is

(A) Dashiel Hammett   (D) Franz Kafka

(B) T.S. Eliot   (E) R.L. Stevenson

(C) William Hazlitt

12. I go out the East Gate –
    There are girls like clouds.
    Though (many) as clouds,
    None absorbs my thoughts.
    White robe, grey kerchief
    She delights my heart.

    I go out the Gate Tower –
    There are girls like reeds.
    Though (many) as reeds,
    None detains my thoughts.
    White robe and madder,
    She can delight me.

    This selection is characterized by

    (A) Iamb   (D) personification

    (B) dactyl-troche   (E) irreducible denominators

    (C) repetition and variation

13. This poem is an example of

    (A) Elegiaic poetry   (D) Chinese folk poetry

    (B) Post Modern Imagism   (E) Homeric Ode

    (C) Japanese Haiku

14. Which of the following is from the *Magna Carta*?

15. Which of the following is from the *Declaration of Independence*?

16. Which of the following is from *The Mayflower Compact*?

17. Which of the following is from *The Republic*?

(A) They in their humble address have freely declared that it is much on their hearts (if they may be permitted) to hold forth a lively experiment, that a most flourishing civil State may stand and best be maintained, and that among our English subjects, with a full liberty in religious concernments. . .

(B) What reason, then, remains for preferring justice to the extreme of injustice, when common belief and the best authorities promise us the fulfillment of our desires in this life and the next, if only we conceal our ill-doing under a veneer of decent behaviour?

(C) We have granted, moreover, to all free men of our kingdom, for us and our heirs forever, all the liberties written below to be had and holden by themselves and their heirs from us and our heirs.

(D) We whose names are underwritten, the loyall subjects of our dread soveraigne Lord, King James, by ye grace of God, of Great Britaine, Franc, and Ireland king, defender of ye faith. . .

(E) We have Petitioned for Redress in the most humble terms: Our repeated Petitions have been answered only by repeated injury. A Prince, whose character is thus marked by every act which may define a Tyrant, is unfit to be the ruler of a free people.

Questions 18 – 21 refer to the following passage.

Build thee more stately mansions, O my soul,
    As the swift seasons roll: —
    Leave thy low-vaulted past.
    Let each new temple, nobler than the last,
    Shut thee from heaven with a dome more vast,
    Till thou at length art free,
Leaving thine outgrown shell by life's unresting sea.

18. The excerpt above expresses sentiments typical of

    (A) the Age of Enlightenment

    (B) the New England Renaissance

    (C) the Fin de Siecle

    (D) the Classic Revival

    (E) the Cavalier Poets

19. The soul is compared here to

    (A) a molting shellfish   (D) a church builder

    (B) the ocean   (E) a monastery

    (C) a home builder

20. The "thee" to whom the poet refers is

    (A) his God   (D) his soul

    (B) his Church   (E) his body

    (C) Nature

21. This poem was written by

    (A) Edgar Allen Poe

    (B) Oliver Wendell Holmes

    (C) John Greenleaf Whittier

    (D) Henry Wadsworth Longfellow

    (E) William Ellery Channing

Questions 22 – 24 refer to the following passage.

And Julia's voice was lost, except in sighs,
    Until too late for useful conversation;
The tears were gushing from her gentle eyes,
    I wish, indeed, they had not had occasion;
But who, alas, can love, and then be wise?
    Not that remorse did not oppose temptation:
A little still she strove, and much repented,
    And whispering "I will ne'er consent" – consented.

22.   The tone of this stanza can best be described as

    (A) paenic   (D) half-serious

    (B) congratulatory   (E) cynical

    (C) oxymoronic

23.   The poem is written in

    (A) Trochaic pentameter   (D) Rhopalic verse

    (B) Ottava Rima   (E) Rime riche

    (C) Versi sciolti

24.   The selection is taken from

    (A) *Childe Harold's Pilgrimage*

    (B) *The Rape of the Lock*

    (C) *Don Juan*

    (D) *Byzantium*

    (E) *Cynara*

25. Ah, happy, happy boughs! that cannot shed
         Your leaves, nor ever bid the Spring adieu;
     And happy melodist, unwearied,
         Forever piping song forever new;
     More happy love! more happy, happy love!
         Forever warm and still to be enjoyed,
             Forever panting, and forever young;
     All breathing human passion far above,
         That leaves a heart high-sorrowful and cloyed,
             A burning forehead, and a parching tongue.

This selection demonstrates craftsmanship similar to that of

(A) Shakespeare   (D) Wordsworth

(B) Rossetti   (E) Milton

(C) Browning

Questions 26 – 28 refer to the descriptions below.

26. Which describes tragedy?

27. Which describes comedy?

28. Which describes satire?

(A) . . . a monumental chapter in the history of human egotism.

(B) The debauching of virgins and the amours of strumpets...

(C) . . . a sort of glass wherein beholders do generally discover
        everybody's face but their own, which is the chief reason
        for that kind reception it meets with in the world.

(D) . . . an imitation of an action that is serious, complete, and
        of a certain magnitude, effecting, through pity and fear,
        the proper katharsis, or purgation, of emotions.

(E) (It) is finer and more philosophical than history; for (it)
        expresses the universal, and history only the particular.

Questions 29 – 31 refer to the following poem.

In Reading gaol by Reading town
     There is a pit of shame,
And in it lies a wretched man
     Eaten by teeth of flame,
In a burning winding-sheet he lies,
     And his grave has got no name.

And there, till Christ call forth the dead,
     In silence let him lie:
No need to waste the foolish tear,
     Or heave the windy sigh:
The man had killed the thing he loved,
     And so he had to die.

And all men kill the thing they love,
     By all let this be heard,
Some do it with a bitter look,
     Some with a flattering word,
The coward does it with a kiss,
     The brave man with a sword!

29.   The connection developed in this poem is one between

    (A) the murderer and the brave man

    (B) the murderer's corpse and the objects of love

    (C) the murderer and all men

    (D) resurrection through Christ and insensitivity

    (E) Reading gaol and the pit of shame

30.   The author implies that brutalizing others

    (A) will cause physical death

    (B) will cause spiritual death

    (C) shows a brave man to be a coward

(D) is a result of Original Sin

(E) is a cause for being sent to Hell

31. The poem was written by

(A) Thomas Hardy

(B) Vachel Lindsay

(C) Samuel Taylor Coleridge

(D) Wilfred Owen

(E) Oscar Wilde

32. The Beowulf utterances, "Wa–la–wa, Wa–la–wa," and the American Indian "Nyah–eh–wa, Nyah–eh–wa," are considered by poets to be

(A) Synecdoches

(B) Pararhymes

(C) Poesias lyricas

(D) Parallel refrains

(E) Tone-colors

33. Which of the following is from Dryden's description of the work of the poet?

(A) . . . is like that of a curious gunsmith or watchmaker: the iron or silver is not his own, but they are the least part of that which gives the value; the price lies wholly in the workmanship.

(B) . . . a mixture of work touched with intense and individual power with work of almost no character at all.

(C) the grand cure for all the maladies and miseries that ever beset mankind, – honest work, which you intend getting done.

(D) ... let him ask no other blessedness. He has a work, a life-purpose; he has found it, and will follow it.

(E) ... keeps at bay the three great evils: boredom, vice, and need.

34. He had, to a morbid excess, that desire to rise which is vulgarly called ambition, but no wish for the esteem or the love of his species; only the hard wish to succeed – not shine nor serve – succeed, that he might have the right to despise a world which galled his self-conceit.

The writer referred to here is

(A) Walt Whitman

(B) Ezra Pound

(C) Ralph Waldo Emerson

(D) Edgar Allen Poe

(E) Ernest Hemingway

Questions 35 – 38 refer to poems listed below, all written by Alexander Pope.

35. Which poem describes a lady who is:

> As some fond virgin, whom her mother's care
> Drags from the town to wholesome country air,
> Just when she learns to roll a melting eye,
> And hear a spark, yet think no danger nigh;

36. Which poem refers to "Belinda" as a pseudonym?

37. Which poem contains the lines:

> Nothing so true as what you once let fall,
> "Most women have no characters at all."
> Master too soft a lasting mark to bear,
> And best distinguished by black, brown, or fair.

38.   From which poem is the following lover's message?

Dear fatal name! rest ever unrevealed,
Nor pass these lips in holy silence sealed.
Hide it, my heart, within that close disguise,
Where mixed with God's, his loved idea lies.

(A) *Epistle to Miss Blount*   (D) *To a Lady*

(B) *Eloisa to Abelard*   (E) *Rape of the Lock*

(C) *Essay On Man*

Questions 39 – 40 refer to the following passage.

For a long time she leaned forward, playing cow-poker with
Peter against Uncle Karl and Mother and watching for the first sign of
Ocean City. At nearly the same instant, picnic ground and Ocean City
standpipe hove into view; an Amoco filling station on their side of the
road cost Mother and Uncle Karl fifty cows and the game; Magda
bounced back, clapping her right hand on Mother's right arm; Ambrose
moved clear "in the nick of time."

At this rate our hero, at this rate our protagonist will remain in the
funhouse forever. Narrative ordinarily consists of alternating dramatization and summarization. One symptom of nervous tension, paradoxically, is repeated and violent yawning; neither Peter nor Magda
nor Uncle Karl nor Mother reacted in this manner. Although they were
no longer small children, Peter and Ambrose were each given a dollar
to spend on boardwalk amusements in addition to what money of their
own they'd brought along. Magda too, though she protested she had
ample spending money. The boys' mother made a little scene out of
distributing the bills; she pretended that her sons and Magda were small
children and cautioned them not to spend the sum too quickly or in one
place. Magda promised with a merry laugh and, having both hands free,
took the bill with her left. Peter laughed also and pledged in a falsetto
to be a good boy. His imitation of a child was not clever. The boys'
father was tall and thin, balding, fair-complexioned. Assertions of that

sort are not effective; the reader may acknowledge the proposition, but. We should be much farther along than we are; something has gone wrong; not much of this preliminary rambling seems relevant. Yet everyone begins in the same place; how is it that most go along without difficulty but a few lose their way?

39.   Which is <u>NOT</u> an effect of the narrator's commentaries on the story?

(A) The juxtaposition of the action with a critical analysis of the techniques used sheds light on the various strategies available to an author.

(B) The reader is drawn into the story; he or she moves from detatched observer to a confidante of the narrator.

(C) The discourses on technique provide a formal tone for the passage as a whole.

(D) The narrator's comments force a severing of the classical concept of the unities.

(E) The narrator's comments provide humorous commentary on the applications of literary criticism.

40.   A technique used throughout the passage is

(A) non sequitur   (D) hubris

(B) enjambment   (E) pathetic fallacy

(C) inverted syntax

41.   I believe Shakespeare was not a whit more intelligible in his own day than he is now to an educated man, except for a few local allusions of no consequence. He is of no age – nor of any religion, or party, or profession. The body and substance of his works came out of the unfathomable depths of his own oceanic mind: his observation and reading, which was considerable, supplied him with the drapery of his figures.

In this passage, S.T. Coleridge is answering the central question:

(A) What was the origin of Shakespeare's drama?

(B) What political alignment can we assign to Shakespeare?

(C) Why are his plays difficult for the modern reader to understand?

(D) Are Shakespeare's plays as comprehensible now as they were when they were written?

(E) What role do local allusions play in understanding Shakespeare's plays?

Oedipus Tyrannus, the *Alchemist*, and *Tom Jones* (are) the three most perfect plots ever planned. And how charming, how wholesome, Fielding always is! To take him up after Richardson is like emerging from a sick room heated by stoves into an open lawn, on a breezy day in May.

42.   In this statement, Coleridge is commenting upon Fielding's ability as a

(A) realist   (D) master of characterization

(B) moralist   (E) master of composition

(C) master of wit

43.   The soul to love created prone and free,
        Is mobile to all objects of delight
        When roused by pleasure to activity.
    From something real your perceptive sight
        Shapes forth an image and displays in you
        So as to make the spirit turn to it;
    And if, so turning, she incline thereto,
        That inclination is love, is nature's bent
        Through pleasure striking root in you anew.

The passage above best identifies the aesthetic philosophy of:

(A) Ovid

(B) Virgil

(C) Herodotus

(D) Sappho

(E) Plato

Let not young souls be smothered out before
They do quaint deeds and fully flaunt their pride.
It is the world's one crime its babes grow dull,
Its poor are ox-like, limp, and leaden-eyed.
Not that they starve, but starve so dreamlessly,
Not that they sow, but that they seldom reap,
Not that they serve, but have no gods to serve;
Not that they die, but that they die like sheep.

44. The poet's message may best be paraphrased:

(A) False pride is the greatest sin of mankind.

(B) Youth is often wasted on the young.

(C) Mankind does not do God's bidding.

(D) Man allows human misery when he can prevent it.

(E) People do not fully engage themselves in life's tragedies.

45. The poem was written by

(A) Wilfred Owen

(B) Vachel Lindsay

(C) Edna St. Vincent Millay

(D) Carl Sandburg

(E) Robert Lowell

Questions 46 – 47 refer to the following passage.

Let us make an image of the soul, an ideal image of the soul, like the composite creations of ancient mythology, such as the Chimera or Scylla or Cerberus; and there are many others to which two or more different natures are said to grow into one.

46. The writer's central admission is that

    (A) the soul does not exist without man's suppositions.

    (B) ideal images are composites of different natures.

    (C) mythical figures never existed.

    (D) images take on a life of their own after one imagines them.

    (E) concepts of the soul can best be found in ancient mythol
        ogy.

47. The writer's reference point may best be described as

    (A) Platonic   (D) Gnostic

    (B) Aristotelian   (E) Organic

    (C) Christian

Questions 48 – 50 refer to the following passage.

> Cuddie, for shame, hold up thy heavye head,
> And let us cast with what delight to chace,
> And weary thys long lingring Phoebus race.
> Whilome thou want the shephcards laddes to leade,
> In rymes, in ridles, and in bydding base: 5
> Now they in thee, and thou in sleepe art dead.

48. The poet uses archaic language

    (A) out of homage to Chaucer.

    (B) to reinforce Classical allusions.

    (C) to insure proper "ryme."

    (D) to reflect the language of the time at which he writes.

    (E) to reinforce the Biblical nature of his story.

49. Lines two and three may be paraphrased:

(A) let us consider how much delight there is in winning.

(B) let us see how much good it is to run a race.

(C) let us see with what happiness Phoebus races.

(D) let us see how we may pass the day pleasantly.

(E) let us see how races help us rush the lingering day.

50. This poem was written by

(A) Geoffrey Chaucer   (D) Christopher Marlowe

(B) Dante   (E) Edmund Spenser

(C) Caedmon

51. "An insult conveyed in the form of a compliment," is a playful definition of

(A) Synecdoche   (D) Periapetia

(B) Irony   (E) the pathetic fallacy

(C) Hyperbole

52. A newly invented metaphor assists thought by evoking a visual image, while on the other hand a metaphor which is technically "dead" (eg. iron resolution) has in effect reverted to being an ordinary word and can generally be used without loss of vividness. But in between these two classes there is a huge dump of worn-out metaphors which have lost all evocative power and are merely used because they save people the trouble of inventing phrases for themselves.

In this passage, George Orwell is talking about

(A) vivid metaphors   (D) invented phrases

(B) ordinary words   (E) dying metaphors

(C) powers of evocation

Questions 53–55 refer to the following poem.

> She that but little patience knew,
> From childhood on, had now so much
> A gray gull lost its fear and flew
> Down to her cell and there alit,
> And from her fingers ate its bit.
>
> Did she in touching that lone wing
> Recall the years before her mind
> Became a bitter, an abstract thing,
> Her thought some popular enmity:
> Blind and leader of the blind
> Drinking the foul ditch where they lie?
>
> When long ago I saw her ride
> Under Ben Bulben to the meet,
> The beauty of her countryside
> With all youth's lonely wildness stirred,
> She seemed to have grown clean and sweet
> Like any rock-bred, sea-borne bird:
>
> Sea-borne, or balanced on the air
> When first it sprang out of the nest
> Upon some lofty rock to stare
> Upon the cloudy canopy,
> While under its storm-beaten breast
> Cried out the hollows of the sea.

53.   The "she" (line 1) in this poem is

(A) the poet's daughter

(B) a murderess

(C) a political prisoner

(D) a temptress

(E) the poet's wife

54.   The poem contrasts the

(A) woman before she became embittered, to the time afterward.

(B) poet's idealization of the woman and her true nature.

(C) the "sea-borne" bird to the "gray gull."

(D) "the beauty of her countryside" to the "lofty rock."

(E) "popular enmity" to the "little patience" of her youth.

55.   The poem was written by

(A) Wallace Stevens   (D) William Yeats

(B) Gertrude Stein   (E) Robert Frost

(C) John Keats

Questions 56 – 57 refer to the following passage.

I fretted the other night at the hotel at the stranger who broke into my chamber after midnight, claiming to share it. But after his lamp had smoked the chamber full and I had turned round to the wall in despair, the man blew out his lamp, knelt down at his bedside, and made in low whisper a long earnest prayer. Then was the relation entirely changed between us. I fretted no more, but respected and liked him.

56.   Which of the following passages was also written by the author of the passage quoted above?

(A) Yesterday I weeded out violets from the iris bed. The iris was being choked by thick bunches of roots, so much like fruit under the earth. I found one single very fragrant violet and some small autumn crocuses.

(B) I had a couple of close ones during this show. On the way in, my platoon was evidently silhouetted against the night sky, and was fired on four times at a range of maybe 300 yards by an eighty-eight.

(C) When summer opens, I see how fast it matures, and fear it will be short; but after the heats of July and August, I am reconciled, like one who has had his swing, to the cool of autumn. So will it be with the coming of death.

(D) While taking my noon walk today, I had more morbid thoughts. What is it about death that bothers me so much? Probably the hours. Melnick says the soul is immortal and lives on after the body drops away, but if my soul exists without my body I am convinced all my clothes ill be too loose-fitting.

(E) As the least drop of wine tinges the whole goblet, so the least particle of truth colors our whole life. It is never isolated, or simply added as treasure to our stock. When any real progress is made, we unlearn and learn anew what we thought we knew before.

57.   The author of the initial passage quoted above is

(A) Henry David Thoreau

(B) Ralph Waldo Emerson

(C) Oliver Wendell Holmes

(D) Francis Parkman

(E) William Byrd

Questions 58 – 60 refer to the excerpts below.

58.   Which of the following is from Rodin's *Art In Life*?

59.   Which of the following is from Shelley's *A Creative Influence*?

60. Which of the following is from Ruskin's *The Society of Books*?

(A) Since human nature remains constant in its essential traits, it is to be expected that certain experiences should be fairly common and recurrent among all human beings.

(B) It is at once the center and circumference of knowledge. It is as the odor and the color of the rose to the texture of the elements which compose it.

(C) A lovely landscape does not appeal only by the agreeable sensations that it inspires, but by the ideas that it awakens. The lines and the colors do not move you in themselves, but by the profound meaning that it awakens.

(D) According to the sincerity of our desire that our friends may be true and our companions wise, and in proportion to the earnestness and discretion with which we choose both, will be the general chances of our happiness and usefulness.

(E) Last night I went to a wide place on the Kilkarton road to listen to some Irish songs. The voices melted into the twilight and were mixed into the trees, and when I thought of the words they too melted away, and were mixed with the generations of men.

Questions 61 – 63 refer to the following passage.

But sires, by cause I am a burel man,
At my biginning first I you beseeche
Have me excused of my rude speeche.
I lerned nevere retorike, certain:
Thing that I speke it moot be bare and plain;   5

61. The character speaking in this Chaucer tale is

(A) The Knight   (D) The Franklin

(B) Chanticleer   (E) The Friar

(C) The Miller

62. Which of the following has two syllables when the lines are properly read aloud?

   (A) rude (line 3)   (D) excused (line 3)

   (B) moot (line 5)   (E) speke (line 5)

   (C) bare (line 5)

63. The word "burel" (line 1) may best be interpreted as meaning

   (A) slovenly   (D) sophisticated

   (B) pugnacious   (E) brutal

   (C) uneducated

Questions 64 – 66 refer to the following.

Peregrine.   Sir, I am grieved I bring you worse disaster:
        The gentleman you met at the port today,
        That told you, he was newly arrived –

Sir Politic. Ay, was. A fugitive punk?

Peregrine.   No sir, a spy set on you;
        And he has made relation to the senate
        That you professed to him to have a plot
        To sell the state of Venice to the Turk.

64. The "gentleman" referred to here is

   (A) Candide   (D) Shylock

   (B) Corbaccio   (E) Ernest

   (C) Peregrine

65. The play from which this excerpt is drawn is entitled

   (A) *The Duchess of Malfi*   (D) *Rasselas*

   (B) *Volpone*   (E) *The Secular Masque*

   (C) *Everyman*

66. What's Hecuba to him, or he to Hecuba,
   That he should weep for her? What would he do,
   Had he the motive and the cue for passion
   That I have? He would drown the stage with tears
   And cleave the general ear with horrid speech;
   Make mad the guilty and appal the free,
   Confound the ignorant, and amaze indeed
   The very faculties of eyes and ears.

   The speaker is

   (A) Coriolanus   (D) Paulina

   (B) Miranda   (E) Hamlet

   (C) Antony

Questions 67 – 76. For each of the following passages, identify the author or the work. Base your decision on the content and style of each passage.

67. My worthy booksellers and friends, Messieurs Dilly in the
   Poultry, at whose hospitable and well-covered table I have seen
   a greater number of literary men than at any other, except that
   of Sir Joshua Reynolds, had invited me to meet Mr. Wilkes. .

   (A) Pepys   (D) Franklin

   (B) Johnson   (E) Burke

   (C) Boswell

68. The commonwealth of learning is not at this time without master-builders, whose mighty designs in advancing the sciences will leave lasting monuments to the admiration of posterity: but every one must not hope to be a Boyle or a Sydenham; and in an age that produces such masters as the great Huygenius, and the incomparable Mr. Newton.

(A) Pope

(B) Locke

(C) Ruskin

(D) Burke

(E) Smith

69. Everyone will be conscious of a likeness here to Wordsworth; and if Wordsworth did great things with this nobly plain manner, we must remember, what indeed he himself would always have been forward to acknolwedge, that Burns used it before him.

(A) Coleridge

(B) Goethe

(C) Dryden

(D) Newman

(E) Arnold

70. But we may agree to all this, and yet strongly dissent from the assumption that literature alone is competent to supply this knowledge. After having learnt all that Greek, Roman, and Eastern antiquity have thought and said, and all that modern literature has to tell us, it is not self-evident that we have laid a sufficiently broad and deep foundation. . .

(A) Wilde's *The Critic as Artist*.

(B) Pater's *The Renaissance*.

(C) Arnold's *Preface to Poems*.

(D) Huxley's *Science and Culture*.

(E) Lawrence's *Etruscan Places*.

71. What we mean by "aristocracy" is merely the richer part of the community, that live in the tallest houses, drive real carriages, (not "kerridges,") ked-glove their hands, and French-bonnet their ladies' heads, give parties where the persons who call them by the above title are not invited, and have a provokingly easy way of dressing. . .

(A) Thoreau's *Walden*.

(B) Emerson's *Nature*.

(C) Hawthorne's *The Artist of the Beautiful*.

(D) Holmes' *Elsie Venner*.

(E) Wharton's *The Custom of the Country*.

72. A more secret, sweet, and overpowering beauty appears to man when his heart and mind open to the sentiment of virtue. Then instantly he is instructed in what is above him. He learns that his being is without bound; that, to the good, to the perfect, he is born, low as he now lies in evil and weakness.

(A) Thoreau   (D) Lincoln

(B) Freneau   (E) Emerson

(C) Poe

73. Oh, slow to smite and swift to spare,
    Gentle and merciful and just!
Who, in the fear of God, didst bear
    The sword of power, a nation's trust!

(A) Bryant   (D) Dickinson

(B) Hardy   (E) Poe

(C) Whitman

74.   . . . performs its secret ministry,
        Unhelped by any wind. The owlet's cry
        Came loud – and hark, again! loud as before.

   (A) Arnold's *Dover Beach*

   (B) Coleridge's *Frost At Midnight*

   (C) Blake's *The Echoing Green*

   (D) Emerson's *Uriel*

   (E) Frost's *Mowing*

75.   Good Heavens! What liberties have I been taking with one of
        the potentates of the earth, and the man on whose conduct more
        important consequences depend than on that of any other
        historical personage of the century!

   (A) Poe   (D) Jefferson

   (B) E.B. White   (E) Emerson

   (C) Hawthorne

76.   I was first of all the kings who drew
        The knighthood-errant of this realm and all
        The realms together under me, their Head,
        In that fair Order of my Table Round

   (A) Tennyson   (D) Marlowe

   (B) Mansfield   (E) Arnold

   (C) Poe

77.   In 1943 _____ said the problem of the times was the
        decay in the belief in personal immortality. Several French
        novelists had turned existentialist and several English novelists
        Catholic (possibly the same reaction), while he himself, like
        many of the more likeable writers, had adopted a hardy
        Humanist's masculine skepticism.

Edward Hoagland is speaking here of

(A) Jean-Paul Sartre   (D) George Orwell

(B) William Golding   (E) Nathaniel West

(C) Ernest Hemingway

Questions 78 – 79 refer to the following.

Love_____, she alone is free;
She can teach ye how to climb
Higher than the sphery chime:
Or, if _____ feeble were,
Heaven itself would stoop to her.

78. Which repeated word will complete the poem?

(A) Comus   (D) Virtue

(B) Venus   (E) Truth

(C) Beauty

79. The author of this poem is

(A) Pope   (D) James Legge

(B) Dryden   (E) Jonson

(C) Milton

80. Privat prayer, suche as men secreitlie offer onto God by thame selves, requyres no speciall place; althocht that Jesus Chryst commandeth when we pray to enter into out chamber, and to clois the dur, and sa to pray secretlie unto our Father.

The passage above is written in a dialect similar to that of

(A) Chaucer   (D) Burns

(B) Beowulf   (E) Shakespeare

(C) Grendel

Questions 81 – 83 refer to the excerpts below.

81.   Which of the following refers to Shakespeare?

82.   Which of the following refers to Jonson?

83.   Which of the following refers to Marlowe?

(A) He redeemed his vices with his virtues. There was ever more in him to be praised than to be pardoned.

(B) (He) was happy in his buskin Muse –
Alas, unhappy in his life and end:
Pity it is that wit so ill should dwell,
Wit lent from Heaven, but vices sent from Hell.

(C) As Helen was to the Trojans, so has that man been to this republic – the cause of war, the cause of mischief, the cause of ruin.

(D) He is a great lover and praiser of himself; a contemner and scorner of others; given rather to lose a friend than a jest . . .

(E) I am persuaded that, had (he) applied to poetry, he would have made a very fine epic poem.

84.   Whenever we read the obscene stories, the voluptuous de baucheries, the cruel and tortuous executions, the unrelenting vindictiveness, with which more than half (of it) is filled, it would be more consistent that we call it the work of a demon . . . It is a history of wickedness that has served to corrupt and brutalize mankind.

In this passage

(A) Mencken is discussing Shakespeare's plays

(B) Poe is discussing Chaucer

(C) Shaw is discussing *The Book of the Dead*

(D) Paine is discussing the Bible

(E) Trilling is discussing *The Way of All Flesh*

Questions 85 – 87 refer to the descriptions below.

85.   Which describes John Galsworthy?

86.   Which describes Thomas Hardy?

87.   Which describes Edgar Allen Poe?

(A) His wild love for Jesus is mixed with perverse and poison-
ous hate of Jesus: his moral hostility to the devil is mixed
with secret worship of the devil.

(B) For though (he) consciously made the younger betrayer a
plebian and an imposter, unconsciously, with the supreme justice of the artist, he made him the same as de
Stancy, a true aristocrat, or as Fitzpiers, or Troy.

(C) . . . he chose to sentimentalise and glorify the most doggy
sort of sex. Setting out to satirise the Forsytes, he glorifies
the anti, who is one worse.

(D) His Mr. Ashenden is also an elderly author, who becomes
an agent in the British Secret Service during the War.

(E) The absence of real central or impulsive being in himself
leaves him inordinately, mechanically sensitive to
sounds and effect, associations of sounds, associations
of rhyme . . .

Question 88 – 90 refer to the excepts below.

88.   Which of the following is from *As You Like It*?

89.   Which of the following is from *Henry VI*?

302

90. Which of the following is from *Macbeth*?

(A) Nothing in his life became him like the leaving of it.

(B) What is pomp, rule, reign, but earth and dust?
And, live we how we can, yet die we must.

(C) Were kisses all the joys of bed, one woman would another wed.

(D) By Heaven, it is as proper to our age to cast beyond ourselves in our opinions as it is common for the younger sort to lack discretion.

(E) The fool doth think he is wise, but the wise man knows himself to be a fool.

Questions 91 – 94 refer to the passages below.

91. Which of the following is a parody of Twain?

92. Which of the following is a parody of Salinger?

93. Which of the following is a parody of Nathaniel West?

94. Which of the following is a parody of Camus?

(A) Dear Scottish Lady, – Your problems are quite easily solved. The root cause of chronic sleep-walking is nervous tension, so please relax and above all avoid fretting about domestic matters.

(B) But you know – I felt kinda sorry for the guy. I get like that sometimes – and when he spoke, I was damn near bawling. I really was.

(C) As they walked on, she smelled good. She smells good, thought Perley. But that's all right, I add good. And when we get to Schrafft's, I'll order from the menu, which I like very much indeed.

303

(D) I keep hoping for some dark horse to gallop over the horizon, eyes ablaze and mane slick as snake juice. I keep hoping, but I remember to say hello to the Senator when he nods my way. A body can't be too careful these days, and can't have too many friends.

(E) Stayed in bed reading *The Ecstasy of Indifference* by Claude who plays on the left wing. Got half way through but couldn't be bothered to finish it.

Questions 95 – 97 refer to the excerpts below.

95.   Which "I" is Sinclair Lewis?

96.   Which "I" is T.S. Eliot?

97.   Which "I" is William Dean Howells?

(A) I had fallen in love at first sight with the whole place – she herself was probably so used to it that she didn't know the impression it was capable of making on a stranger – and I had felt it really a case to risk something.

(B) I say judged, not amputated, by them; not judged to be as good as, or worse or better than, the dead; and certainly not judged by the canons of dead critics.

(C) I would beseech the literary critics of our country to disabuse themselves of the mischievous notion that they are essential to the progress of literature in the way critics have vainly imagined.

(D) I can't help it, I'm crazy about thoroughbred horses. I've always been that way. When I was ten years old and saw I was going to be big and couldn't be a rider I was so sorry I nearly died.

(E) But I liked to hear him talk – it made my work, when not interrupting it, less mechanical, less special.

Questions 98 – 100 refer to the following selection.

> Unreal City,
> Under the brown fog of a winter dawn,
> A crowd flowed over London Bridge, so many,
> I had not thought death had undone so many.
> Sighs, short and infrequent, were exhaled,
> And each man fixed his eyes before his feet.
> Flowed up the hill and down King William Street . . .

98.   The description of the city is similar to one found in the writings of

(A) Flaubert   (D) Shakespeare

(B) Dante   (E) Ovid

(C) Baudelaire

99.   The poets reference to sighs is cited by him as derived from

(A) *La Dame Sans Merci*   (D) *The Inferno*

(B) *Faustus*   (E) *Prometheus Unbound*

(C) *Don Juan*

100.   The author of the poem is

(A) John Dos Passos   (D) Gwendolyn Brooks

(B) Theodore Roethke   (E) William Carlos Williams

(C) T.S. Eliot

Questions 101 – 103 refer to the following.

> Vanity, saity the preacher, vanity!
> Draw round my bed: is Anselm keeping back?
> Nephews – sons mine . . . ah God, I know not! Well –
> She, men would have to be your mother once,
> Old Gandolf envied me, so fair she was!

101. The excerpt above is an example of

(A) Decalogue

(B) Stream of Consciousness

(C) Discursive Argument

(D) Dramatic Monologue

(E) Expressive Mode

102. The first line is an allusion to

(A) Shakespeare

(B) Thackeray's *Vanity Fair*

(C) Shelley's *Ozymandias*

(D) The Old Testament

(E) *Pilgrim's Progress*

103. The poem was written by

(A) Christina Rosetti   (D) Oscar Wilde

(B) Charles Swinburne   (E) Matthew Arnold

(C) Robert Browning

Questions 104 – 107 refer to the parodies below.

104. Which of the following is a parody of Romantic Literature?

105. Which of the following is a parody of Realistic Writing?

106. Which of the following is a parody of Existential Writing?

107. Which of the following is a parody of Stream of Consciousness?

(A) Went to the beach with Marie. Very hot. Saw cripple
     kicking mangy dog. I wondered whether to stop the
     cripple and talk to him about happiness and money. I
     wondered whether to kill him or not, but didn't really feel
     in the mood for that. Perhaps tomorrow, after a swim.

(B) Wait; no; what I said was not enough for him to leave the
     house on; it must have been the blurted inscrutable chance
     confirmation of something he already knew, and was half
     able to assess, either out of the blown fact of boyhood or
     pure male divination or both.

(C) He sat watching, even from his distant perch, the fire
     sweeping down the bra'hill, and across the wild green
     lawn, and ever closer to their poor abode. How brightly it
     flared! How keenly he relished the hum and then the roar
     of it as it swept ever closer!

(D) The little hollow was green.
     The Thing was pulpy white. Its eyes were white. It
     had blackish-yellow lips. It was beautifully spotted with
     red, like tomato stains on a rolled napkin.

(E) It is also the effect of our perpetual masqueradings and
     disguisings, effect of which Edgar more than most had in
     the past days been made to feel the force, to induce in us
     wavering uncertainties, unstable though golden as the re-
     flexion of the sun on running water. . .

Questions 108 – 109 refer to the following.

What is a man, if his chief good and market of his time be but
to sleep and feed? A beast, no more. Sure he that made us with such
large discourse, looking before and after, gave us not that capability
and godlike reason to fust in us unused.

108. The speaker is arguing that

(A) Unconscious impulses destroy mankind's potential for greatness.

(B) Man can never be more than a beast who sleeps and feeds.

(C) Because of Original Sin, humanity lost any potential to transcend their bestial natures.

(D) God intended mankind to be more than mere beasts; our minds are proof of that.

(E) Money causes an obsession with physical gratification, causing people to ignore their higher mental faculties.

109. This speech was given by

(A) Falstaff   (D) Miranda

(B) Caesar   (E) Beatrice

(C) Hamlet

Questions 110 – 111 refer to the following.

Come, seeling night, scarf up the tender eye of pitiful day; and with thy bloody and invisible hand cancel and tear to pieces that great bond which keeps me pale! – Light thickens; and the crow makes wing to rocky wood; good things of day begin to droop and drowse; whiles night's black agents to their prey do rouse.

110. The "prey" referred to in this passage are

(A) Night's hands.

(B) The birds of Night.

(C) Dreams

(D) Daylight's fading rays

(E) Living creatures

111. The passage is taken from

(A) *Measure for Measure*   (D) *Macbeth*

(B) *Cymbeline*   (E) *King Lear*

(C) *Henry V*

Brutus: Fates, we will know your pleasures: that we shall die, we know;   'tis but the time and drawing days out, that men stand upon.

Cassius: Why, he that cuts off twenty years of life, cuts off so many years of fearing death.

Brutus: Grant that, and then is death a benefit.

112. Brutus' sentiments are best paraphrased:

(A) It is better to die young and brave than old and cowardly.

(B) Only the old know that their death is certain.

(C) A youth of 20 fears death more than an older man.

(D) Cowards die many times before their deaths.

(E) Death benefits those who have grown old in spirit.

For form is not a personal thing like style. It is impersonal like logic. And just as the school of _____ was logical in its expressions, so it seems the school of Flaubert is, as it were, logical in its aesthetic form.

113. Which of the following correctly completes the quote?

(A) Whitman   (D) Chaucer

(B) Mallory   (E) T.S. Eliot

(C) Pope

Questions 114 – 117 refer to the following.

As I went down the hill along the wall
There was a gate I had leaned at for the view
And had just turned from when I first saw you
As you came up the hill. We met. But all
We did that day was mingle great and small   5
Footprints in summer dust as if we drew
The figure of our being less than two
But more than one as yet. Your parasol
Pointed the decimal off with one deep thrust.
And all the time we talked you seemed to see   10
Something down there to smile at in the dust.
(Oh, it was without prejudice to me!)
Afterward I went past what you had passed
Before we met and you what I had passed.

114.   The first eight lines are similar in rhyme scheme to

(A) the Shakespearean sonnet

(B) the Spenserian sonnet

(C) the Dantean sonnet

(D) the Petrarchan sonnet

(E) the Rosettian sonnet

115.   "Less than two but more than one as yet" (line 7) refers to

(A) the lovers' shadows in the dust.

(B) the tracing of the parasol in the dust.

(C) the time before the lovers' relationship broke apart.

(D) the time before the two lovers had fully committed themselves to each other.

(E) the time before they met.

116.   The heroic couplet reinforces the idea that

    (A) the lovers had met by accident.

    (B) it was love at first sight.

    (C) their footsteps were left in the sands of time.

    (D) their first parting was painful.

    (E) the relationship was bound to end unhappily.

117.   This poem was written by

    (A) Vachel Lindsay

    (B) Edna St. Vincent Millay

    (C) Robert Frost

    (D) Lord Byron

    (E) Elizabeth Barrett Browning

       Come you spirits
That tend on mortal thoughts, unsex me here;
And fill me, from the crown to the toe, topfull
Of direst cruelty! Make thick my blood,
Stop up the access and passage to remorse,
That no compunctious visitings of nature
Shake my fell purpose, nor keep peace between
The effect and it!

118.   These lines are spoken by

    (A) Cleopatra   (D) Volumnia

    (B) Tatiana   (E) Viola

    (C) Lady Macbeth

Questions 119 – 122 refer to the passages below.

119. Which is by Faulkner?

120. Which is by D.H. Lawrence?

121. Which is by Fitzgerald?

122. Which is by Kafka?

(A) They made no response, but I was used to silent company and went on with my work, only a little disconcerted – even though exhilarated by the sense that this was at least the ideal thing – at not having got rid of them after all.

(B) During these last decades the interest in professional fasting has markedly diminished. It used to pay very well to stage such great performances under one's own management, but today that is quite impossible. We live in a different world now. At one time the whole town took a lively interest in the hunger artist; from day to day of his fast the excitement mounted; everybody wanted to see him at least once a day; there were people who bought season tickets for the last few days and sat from morning till night in front of his small barred cage; even in the nighttime there were visiting hours, when the whole effect was heightened by torch flares;

(C) He was still trembling when he reached the street, but a walk down the Rue Bonaparte to the quais set him up, and as he crossed the Seine, fresh and new by the quai lamps, he felt exultant.

(D) The boy watched that too. He watched it for the next two years from that moment when Boon touched Lion's head and then knelt beside him, feeling the bones and muscles, the power.

(E) And so the house came to be haunted by the unspoken phrase: *There must be more money! There must be more money!* The children could hear it all the time, though nobody said it aloud. they heard it at Chrstimas, when the expensive and splendid toys filled the nursery. Behind the shining modern rocking-horse, behind the smart doll's house, a voice would start whispering: "There *must* be more money! There *must* be more money!" And the chil

dren would stop playing, to listen for a moment. They
would look into each other's eyes, to see if they had all
heard. And each one saw in the eyes of the other two that
they too had heard. "There *must* be more money! There
must be more money!"

Questions 123 – 124 refer to the following.

Mother.   I know, dear, but don't say it's ridiculous, because the
papers were full of it; I don't know about New York, but there
was half a page about a man missing even longer than Larry, and
he turned up from Burma.

Chris.   He couldn't have wanted to come home very badly. Mom.

Mother. Don't be so smart.

Chris.   You can have a helluva time in Burma.

123.   In this exchange above, Chris is

    (A) concerned with providing information.

    (B) concerned with ridiculing his mother's false beliefs.

    (C) using humor to bring his mother back to reality.

    (D) arguing for greater freedom for himself at home.

    (E) defending Larry's recent excuses for not returning.

124.   This excerpt is from

    (A) *Tea and Sympathy*

    (B) *The Rose Tattoo*

    (C) *Incident At Vichy*

    (D) *All My Sons*

    (E) *The Caucasian Chalk Circle*

125. It may displease the lord of the Heatho-Bards and each thane of that people when he goes in the hall with the woman, the noble sons of the Danes, her retainers, are feasted.

This passage is from

(A) *Eric's Saga*

(B) *Macbeth*

(C) *Sir Gawain and the Green Knight*

(D) *Beowulf*

(E) *Hamlet*

126. A lovere and a lusty bacheler,
With lokkes crulle ans they were laid in presse.
Of twenty yeer of age he was, I gesse.

The character described above is

(A) the Franklin

(B) the Yeoman

(C) The Squire

(D) the Knight

(E) the Monk

Questions 127 – 129 refer to the following passage.

In the first place, as he is the father of English poetry, I hold him in the same degree of veneration as the Grecians held Homer, or the Romans _____. He is a perpetual fountain of good sense; learned in all sciences; and therefore, speaks properly on all subjects.

127. The "he" referred to in the first sentence is

(A) Shakespeare

(B) Caedmon

(C) Dryden

(D) Chaucer

(E) The Venerable Bede

128. Which of the following best completes the first sentence?

(A) Ovid

(D) Horatio

(B) Catallus

(E) Virgil

(C) Cicero

129. The passage was written by

(A) Samuel Johnson

(D) Ben Jonson

(B) John Dryden

(E) Jonathan Swift

(C) G.B. Shaw

Questions 130 – 133 refer to the following.

Some guide the course of wandering orbs on high,
Or roll the planets through the boundless sky.
Some less refined, beneath the moon's pale light
Pursue the stars that shoot athwart the night,
Or suck the mists in grosser air below,
Or dip their pinions in the painted bow,
Or brew fierce tempests on the wintry main,
Or o'er the glebe distill the kindly rain.

130. "Some" in the first line refers to

(A) human professions

(B) the pantheon of gods

(C) the tasks assigned to the spheres

(D) the links in the Great Chain of Being

(E) nature's cycles

131. The poet here uses the technique of

(A) discourse

(D) extrapolation

(B) specification

(E) extirpation

(C) cataloguing

315

132. "Glebe" in the last line can best be interpreted as meaning

    (A) faces of the people   (D) cultivated fields

    (B) mountain crags   (E) oceans' beaches

    (C) desert sands

133. This excerpt is from

    (A) Congreve's *Love for Love*

    (B) Bacon's *Novum Organum*

    (C) Pope's *Rape of the Lock*

    (D) Lovelace's *To Althea*

    (E) Milton's *Paradise Lost*

Questions 134 – 136 refer to the following passage.

The first of these characters has struck every observer, native and foreign. In place of the discordant local dialects of all the other major countries, including England, we have a general Volkssprache for the whole nation, and if it is conditioned at all it is only by minor differences in punctuation and vocabulary, and by the linguistic struggles of various groups of newcomers.

134. The "first character" that the author notes is

    (A) the tendency of American English to develop into different dialects.

    (B) the tendency for different American dialects to coalesce into one.

    (C) the general uniformity of American English throughout the country.

    (D) the tendency of immigrants to alter American pronunciation.

    (E) the general inability of scholars to identify Standard American English.

135. The author implies that

    (A) immigrants are a threat to the linguistic integrity of American English.

    (B) immigrants have no influence on the general accent.

    (C) immigrants have a minor influence on linguistic aspects.

    (D) immigrants have traditionally altered American speech.

    (E) only in spoken English do immigrants have an influence.

136. This passage was written by

    (A) H.L. Mencken   (D) James Michener

    (B) J.C. Furnas   (E) William Safire

    (C) T.S. Eliot

137. Thou youngest virgin-daughter of the skies,
     Made in the last promotion of the blest,
     Whose palms, new plucked from paradise
     In spreading branches more sublimely rise

     Introductory lines such as these would appear most appropriately in

    (A) an Ode   (D) an Epitaph

    (B) an Elegy   (E) a Song

    (C) an Encomium

Questions 138 – 140 refer to the following.

    Ye who listen with credulity to the whispers of fancy, and pursue with eagerness the phantoms of hope; who expect that age will perform the promises of youth, and that the deficiencies of the present day will be supplied by the morrow – attend to the history of Rasselas, prince of _____.

138. This opening paragraph suggests that the "history" the author is about to relate will be a

    (A) parable

    (B) Biblical allusion

    (C) philosophical fable

    (D) paradoxical roman a clef

    (E) totological summary

139. The passage above is most appropriately completed with the proper noun

    (A) Arabia   (D) Polonia

    (B) Egypt   (E) Abyssinia

    (C) Ethiopia

140. The passage above was written by

    (A) William Congreve   (D) James Boswell

    (B) Jonathan Swift   (E) Thomas Gray

    (C) Samuel Johnson

141. I say that democracy can never prove itself beyond cavil, until it founds and luxuriantly grows its own forms of art, poems, schools, theology, displacing all that exists, or that has been produced anywhere in the past, under opposite influences.

    The narrator in this passage is

    (A) John Ruskin   (D) Walt Whitman

    (B) Henry Newman   (E) H.L.Mencken

    (C) Abraham Lincoln

142. The point of view and the manner are not self-sprung in him, he caught them of others; and he had not the free and abundant use of them. But whereas Addison and Pope never had the use of them (he) had the use of them at times.

The poet referred to here is

(A) Congreve

(B) Noyes

(C) Tennyson

(D) Gray

(E) Burns

Questions 143 – 144 refer to the following passage.

(He) was not without what talkers call wit, and there were touches of prickly sarcasm in him, contemptuous enough of the world and its idols and popular dignitaries; he had traits even of poetic humour: but in general he seemed deficient in laughter; or indeed in sympathy for concrete human things either on the sunny or on the stormy side.

143. The poet being referred to here is

(A) Wordsworth

(B) Blake

(C) Coleridge

(D) Hopkins

(E) Hume

144. This passage appears in

(A) Arnold's *The Study of Poetry*

(B) Carlyle's *Portrait of His Contemporaries*

(C) Johnson's *The Preface to Shakespeare*

(D) Huxley's *Agnosticism and Christianity*

(E) Ruskin's *Sartor Resartus*

Questions 145 – 147 refer to the following passage.

The poet of whose works I have undertaken the revision may now begin to assume the dignity of an ancient and claim the privilege of established fame and prescriptive veneration. He has long outlived his century, the term commonly fixed as the test of literary merit.

145. Who first set down the "test" to which the author refers?

(A) Plato

(B) Aristotle

(C) Virgil

(D) Horace

(E) Pythagoras

146. The poet the author is speaking of is

(A) Christopher Marlowe

(B) Geoffrey Chaucer

(C) William Shakespeare

(D) Dante

(E) Sir Walter Raleigh

147. The author of the passage above is

(A) William Wordsworth

(B) Thomas Gray

(C) Matthew Arnold

(D) Samuel Johnson

(E) Jonathan Swift

148. Adam walked round by the rick-yard, at present empty of ricks, to the little wooden gate leading into the garden — once the well-tended kitchen-garden of a manor house; now, but for the handsome brick wall with stone coping that ran along one side of it . . . a true farmhouse garden.

The author of this passage is

(A) Jane Austen

(B) George Eliot

(C) Charles Dickens

(D) Thomas Hardy

(E) Jack London

Questions 149 – 150 refer to the following passage.

Who cares whether Mr. Ruskin's views on Turner are sound or not? What does it matter? That mighty and majestic prose of his, so fervid and so fiery colored in its noble eloquence, so rich in its elaborate symphonic music, so sure and certain at its best, in subtle choice of word and epithet, is at least as great a work of art as any of those wonderful sunsets that bleach or rot on their corrupted canvases in England's Gallery . . .

149.   The author is arguing that

(A) criticism is irrelevant to the purity of art.

(B) criticism is independent to the quality of art.

(C) criticism is equal with art as a form of art.

(D) artists should not be bounded by what critics say about them.

(E) critics should not be held to account for what they say about art.

150.   The author of this passage is

(A) Matthew Arnold   (D) Oscar Wilde

(B) Henry Newman   (E) G.B. Shaw

(C) Walter Pater

Questions 151 – 153 refer to the following.

Look in my face; my name is Might-have-been;
I am also called No-more, Too-late, Farewell;
Unto thine ear I hold the dead-sea-shell
Cast up thy Life's foam–fretted feet between;
Unto thine eyes the glass where that is seen   5

Which had Life's form and Love's, but by my spell
Is now a shaken shadow intolerable,
Of ultimate things unuttered the frail screen.
Mark me, how still I am! But should there dart
One moment through thy soul the soft surprise   10
Of that winged Peace which lulls the breath of sighs, –
Then shalt thou see me smile, and turn apart
Thy visage to mine ambush at thy heart
Sleepless with cold commemorative eyes.

151.   One poetic device that is repeated throughout this poem is

(A) personification   (D) allegory

(B) assonance   (E) onomatopoeia

(C) alliteration

152.   The poet is

(A) appealing to his lover to be more attentive

(B) regretting a loss of love

(C) announcing his reluctance to proceed further with the
     affair

(D) explaining his wish for some response to his overtures of
     love

(E) appealing to his former lover for a resurrection of their
     romance

153.   The author of this poem is

(A) Browning   (D) Rossetti

(B) Tennyson   (E) W.S. Gilbert

(C) Donne

Questions 154 – 155 refer to the following.

> Have the elder races halted?
> Do they droop and end their lesson, wearied over there beyond the seas?
> We take up the task eternal, and the burden and the lesson,
> Pioneers! O pioneers!

154. The "elder races" cited here refer to

(A) The Ancient Greeks

(B) The Ancient Romans

(C) The Contemporary Europeans

(D) Pre-historic Man

(E) First Century Christians

155. This poem was written by

(A) John Greenleaf Whittier

(B) Ralph Waldo Emerson

(C) Walt Whitman

(D) Alfred Noyes

(E) Ellery Channing

156. The gradual removal of these suspicions at length led me to the experimentum crucis, which was this: I took two boards, and placed one of them close behind the prism at the window, so that the light might pass through a small hole made in it for thepurpose and fall on the other board . . .

This is an account of an experiment conducted by

(A) Benjamin Franklin   (D) Jonathan Edwards

(B) Leonardo da Vinci   (E) Isaac Newton

(C) Joseph Priestly

Questions 157 – 159 refer to the following passage.

He had before served me a scurvy trick, which set the Queen laughing, although at the same time she were heartily vexed, and would have immediately cashiered him, if I had not been so generous as to intercede. Her Majesty had taken a marrow bone upon her plate, and after knocking out the marrow, placed the bone again in the dish, erect as it stood before; the dwarf watching his opportunity, while Glumdalclitch was gone to the sideboard . . .

157. The passage above is an account of

(A) a descent into Hades

(B) a voyage to Brobdingag

(C) the arrival in Wonderland

(D) an introduction to Utopia

(E) an expedition in *Journey to the Center of the Earth*

158. "Cashiered" is best interpreted as meaning

(A) paid off   (D) ridiculed

(B) executed   (E) rewarded

(C) dismissed

159. The passage was written by

(A) Lewis Carroll   (D) Jules Verne

(B) Isasac Asimov   (E) H.G. Wells

(C) Jonathan Swift

Questions 160 – 162 refer to the following.

Ever such is time, which takes in trust
Our youth, our joys, and all we have,
And pays us but with age and dust,
Who in the dark and silent grave
When we have wandered all our ways
Shuts up the story of our days,
And from which earth, and grave, and dust
The Lord shall raise me up, I trust.

160.   This poem is best described as

    (A) an Elegy   (D) a Epitaph

    (B) a Pastoral   (E) an Encomium

    (C) a Psalm

161.   In this poem three forces battle each other; they are

    (A) youth, time, and death

    (B) trust, time, and the Lord

    (C) joy, death, and dust

    (D) youth, age, and death

    (E) life, death, and the Lord

162.   The poem was written by

    (A) Shakespeare   (D) Lovelace

    (B) Spenser   (E) Daniel

    (C) Raleigh

Questions 163 – 165 refer to the following.

When to her lute Corinna sings,
Her voice revives the leaden strings,
And doth in highest notes appear
As any challenged echo clear;
But when she doth of mourning speak
Ev'n with her sighs the strings do break.

And as her lute doth live or die,
Led by her passion, so must I:
For when of pleasure she doth sing,
My thoughts enjoy a sudden spring,
But if she doth of sorrow speak,
Ev'n from my heart the strings do break.

163. A controlling poetic device in the first stanza is

   (A) onomatopoeia   (D) personification

   (B) chiasmus   (E) synecdoche

   (C) alliteration

164. A poetic device that ties the second stanza to the first is

   (A) irony   (D) allusion

   (B) metaphor   (E) personification

   (C) meter

165. The author of this poem is

   (A) Thomas Campion   (D) John Suckling

   (B) Samuel Daniel   (E) Robert Southwell

   (C) Richard Lovelace

Questions 166 – 167 refer to the following passage.

We are to regard _____ as the puissant and glorious founder, _____as the splendid high priest, of our age of prose and reason, of our excellent and indispensable eighteenth century. For the purposes of their mission, and destiny their poetry, like their prose, is admirable.

166. The first writer referred to here is

(A) Arnold

(D) Dryden

(B) Congreve

(E) Milton

(C) Malory

167. The second writer referred to here is

(A) Pope

(D) Congreve

(B) Dryden

(E) Malory

(C) Milton

168. His name in that new life leaped into characters before his eyes and to it there followed a mental sensation of an undefined face or colour of a face. The colour faded and became strong like a changing glow of pallid brick red.

The character being described here is

(A) Eliot's Silas Marner

(B) Austen's Frank Churchill

(C) Dickens' Martin Chuzzlewit

(D) Verne's Captain Nemo

(E) Joyce's Rev. Stephen Dedalus, S.J.

169. For no very intelligible reason, Mr. Lucas had hurried ahead of his party. He was perhaps reaching the age at

which independence becomes valuable, because it is so soon to be lost. Tired of attention and consideration, he liked breaking away from the younger members, to ride by himself, and to dismount unassisted.

This passage is taken from

(A) *The Road to Colonus*

(B) *To the Lighthouse*

(C) *Far From the Madding Crowd*

(D) *The Open Window*

(E) *The House of Mirth*

Questions 170 – 171 refer to the following passage.

And that's what you learn, when you're a novelist. And that's what you are very liable not to know, if you're a parson, or a philosopher, or a scientist, or a stupid person. If you're a parson, you talk about souls in heaven. If you're a novelist, you know that paradise is in the palm of your hand, and on the end of your nose, because both are alive; and alive, and man alive, which is more than you can say, for certain, of paradise.

170. The author of this passage has learned

(A) that parsons are not qualified to talk about heaven.

(B) that paradise is the realm of the philosopher.

(C) that what you hold in your hand is all that is real.

(D) that whatever else might be true, he himself is alive.

(E) that stupidity and belief in paradise go hand in hand.

171. The author of this passage is also the author of

(A) *The Mayor of Casterbridge*

(B) *To the Lighthouse*

(C) *The Great Gatsby*

(D) *Sons and Lovers*

(E) *To Your Scattered Bodies Go*

172. My family originated in a village in the mountains of Leon, where Nature was kinder to them than Fortune, although in those poor villages my father was reputed to be a rich man, and indeed, he would have been if he had been as skillful in preserving his estate as he was in spending it.

The character here describing his family's history is

(A) David Copperfield   (D) Don Quixote

(B) Huckleberry Finn   (E) Jean Valjean

(C) Tess

173. Levin laid his brother on his back, sat down beside him and, hardly daring to breathe, gazed at his face. The dying man lay with closed eyes but the muscles of his forehead twitched every now and then, as with one thinking deeply and intently.

This passage is from

(A) *The Cossacks*   (D) *Fathers and Sons*

(B) *War and Peace*   (E) *Crime and Punishment*

(C) *Anna Karenina*

Questions 174 – 175 refer to the following.

"In contrast to Newton and Schopenhauer, your ancestor did not believe in a uniform, absolute time. He believed in an infinite series of times, in a growing, dizzying net of divergent, convergent and parallel times. This network of times which approached one another, forked, broke off, or were unaware of one another for centuries,

329

embraces *all* possibilities of time. We do not exist in the majority of these times; in some you exist, and not I; in others, I, and not you; in others, both of us. In the present one, which a favorable fate has granted me, you have arrived at my house; in another, while crossing the garden, you found me dead; in still another, I utter these same words, but I am a mistake, a ghost."

"In every one," I pronounced, not without a tremble to my voice, "I am grateful to you and revere you for your re-creation of the garden of Ts'ui Pen,"

"Not in all," he murmured with a smile. "Time forks perpetually toward innumerable futures. In one of them I am your enemy."

174.	The tone of the passage is:

(A) threatening

(B) gloomy

(C) sarcastic

(D) patronizing

(E) instructive

175.	The author of this passage is

(A) Jorge Luis Borges

(B) John Barth

(C) Samuel Beckett

(D) Kurt Vonnegut

(E) Margaret Atwood

Questions 176 – 179 refer to the following excerpts.

176.	Which is by Aldous Huxley?

177.	Which is by Flannery O'Connor?

178.	Which is by F. Scott Fitzgerald?

179.	Which is by John Updike?

(A) The chairman spoke in Bulgarian, musically, at length. There was polite laughter. Nobody translated for Bech. The professorial type, his hair like a flazen toupee, jerked forward.

(B) The old woman and her daughter were sitting on their porch when Mr. Shiftlet came up their road for the first time. The old woman slid to the edge of her chair and leaned forward, shading her eyes from the piercing sunset with her hand.

(C) Inert, Sebastian abandoned himself to the tenderness which at ordinary times he would never allow her to express, and in the very act of self-abandonment found a certain isolation. Suddenly and irrelevantly, it came into his mind that this was one of the situations he had always looked forward to in his dream of a love affair with Mary Esdaile — or whatever other name one chose to give the dark-haired mistress of his imagination.

(D) As I watched him he adjusted himself a little, visibly. His hand took hold of hers, and as she said something low in his ear he turned toward her with a rush of emotion. I think that voice held him most, with its fluctuating, feverish warmth, because it couldn't be over-dreamed — that voice was a deathless song.

(E) Lem hesitated only long enough to take a firm purchase on his store teeth, then dashed into the path of the horses. With great strength and agility, he grasped their bridles and dragged them to a rearing halt, a few feet from the astounded and thoroughly frightened pair.

180.　　　　　He above the rest
In shape and gesture proudly eminent,
Stood like a tower. His form had yet not lost
All his original brightness, nor appeared
Less then Archangel ruined, and the excess
Of glory obscured: as when the sun new-risen
Looks through the horizontal misty air

This is a description of

(A) Prometheus　　　(D) Satan

(B) Kubla Khan　　　(E) Gabriel

(C) Abu Ben Adem

Questions 181 – 182 refer to the following passage.

There was something in his physiognomy extremely singular, and that cannot easily be defined. It bore the traces of many passions, which seemed to have fixed the features they no longer animated. An habitual gloom and severity prevailed over the deep lines of his countenance; and his eyes were so piercing that they seemed to penetrate, at a single glance, into the hearts of men, and to read their most secret thoughts; few persons could support their scrutiny or even endure to meet them twice.

181. This is a classic description of

(A) The Existential Hero   (D) The Satanic Hero

(B) The Anti-Hero   (E) The Psaltic Hero

(C) The Byronic Hero

182. The passage quoted above was written by

(A) Samuel Coleridge   (D) Lord Byron

(B) Ann Radcliffe   (E) Albert Camus

(C) Matthew Arnold

Questions 183 – 186 refer to the following excerpt.

Let us begin and carry up this corpse,
    Singing together.
Leave we the common crofts, the vulgar thorpes
    Each in its tether
Sleeping safe on the bosom of the plain,   5
    Cared for till cock-crow:
Look out if yonder be not day again
    Rimming the rock-row!
That's the appropriate country: there, man's thought,
    Rarer, intenser,   10
Self-gathered for an outbreak, as it ought,
    Chafes in the censer.

183. The verse is characterized by a style that might best be described as

(A) pastoral   (D) charged

(B) lyrical   (E) strained

(C) harsh

184. "Thorpes" (line 3) might best be interpreted as meaning

(A) corrals   (D) villages

(B) stagnant pools   (E) citadels

(C) mountain sides

185. The tone of this poem is characterized by a contrast between

(A) the life of the corpse bearers and the lifelessness of the corpse.

(B) the low nature of the "common crofts" and the loftiness of the mountain tops.

(C) the night of death and the dawning with the cock-crow.

(D) intense idealistic thought and the realities of the earth.

(E) the sleeping crofts and the outbreak of singing.

186. This excerpt was written by

(A) Tennyson   (D) Christina Rossetti

(B) Coleridge   (E) Shelley

(C) Browning

Questions 187 – 189 refer to the following.

There comes Emerson first, whose rich words, every one,
Are like gold nails in temples to hang trophies on,
Whose prose is grand verse, while his verse, the Lord knows,
Is some of it pr–No, 'tis not even prose;

I'm speaking of metres; some poems have welled
From those rare depths of should that have ne'er been excelled;
They're not epics, but that doesn't matter a pin,
In creating, the only hard thing's to begin:

187.   The reference to "nails in temples" in the second line is

    (A) an allusion to the New Testament

    (B) an allusion to Greek fable

    (C) an allusion to the Seven Cities of Cibola

    (D) an allusion to the Old Testament

    (E) an allusion to Milton's *Lysistrata*

188.   This excerpt is similar to

    (A) An elegy   (D) An encomium

    (B) A paen   (E) A satire

    (C) A contemporanium

189.   This poem was written by

    (A) Henry David Thoreau   (D) Walt Whitman

    (B) William Cullen Bryant   (E) John Greenleaf Whittier

    (C) James Russell Lowell

Questions 190–193 refer to the following.

Prince.   Where shall we take a purse tomorrow, Jack?

Falstaff. Zounds, where thou wilt, lad; I'll make one; and I do not,
call me villain and baffle me.

Prince.   I see a good amendment of life in thee – from praying to purse-taking.

Falstaff.   Why, Hal, 'tis my vocation, Hal; 'tis no sin for a man to labor in his vocation.

Poins! Now shall we know if Gadshill have set a match. O, if men were to be saved by merit, what hole in hell were hot enough for him? This is the most omnipotent villain that ever cried "stand" to a true man.

190.   "Baffle" in the second speech can best be interpreted as meaning

(A) confound   (D) disgrace

(B) command   (E) beat

(C) reprimand

191.   The characters are planning

(A) to enter a monastery.

(B) to change their lives dramatically.

(C) to call a meeting of their fellows.

(D) to commit a robbery.

(E) to appoint a new leader.

192.   "Zounds" can best be interpreted as meaning

(A) Go!   (D) Jesus' wounds!

(B) By God!   (E) I am astonished!

(C) A swoon take me!

193.   This excerpt is from

(A) *The Merchant of Venice*

(B) *Henry VI, I*

(C) *Troilus and Cressida*

(D) *Richard II*

(E) *Henry IV, I*

Questions 194 – 197 refer to the excerpts about aesthetics below.

194.   Which is by Walter Pater?

195.   Which is by John Ruskin?

196.   Which is by John Henry Newman?

197.   Which is by John Stuart Mill?

(A) And now, reader, look round this English room of yours, about which you have been proud so often, because the work of it was so good and strong, and the ornaments of it so finished. Examine again all those accurate moldings, and perfect polishings, and unerring adjustments of the seasoned wood and tempered steel.

(B) That, however, the word "poetry" imports something quite peculiar in its nature; something which may exist in what is called prose as well as in verse; something which does not even require the instrument of words, but can speak through the other audible symbols called musical sounds, and even through the visible ones . . .

(C) One of the most beautiful passages of Rousseau is that in the sixth book of the "Confessions," where he describes the awakening in him of the literary sense. An undefinable taint of death had clung always about him, and now in early manhood he believed himself smitten by mortal disease.

(D) And first, the initial doctrine of the infallible teacher must
be an emphatic protest against the existing state of man
kind. Man had rebelled against his Maker. It was this that
caused the divine interposition: and the first act of the
divinely accredited messenger must be to proclaim it.

(E) O mighty poet! Thy works are not as those of other men,
simply and merely great works of art, but are also like the
phenomena of nature, like the sun and the sea, the stars
and the flowers, like frost and snow . . .

Questions 198 – 200 refer to the excerpts below.

198.   Which is spoken by Browning's Fra Lippo Lippi?

199.   Which is spoken by Tennyson's Mariana?

200.   Which is spoken by Rosetti's Blessed Damozel?

(A)   I was not sorrowful, I could not weep,
And all my memories were put to sleep.

(B)   She only said, "My life is dreary,
He cometh not," she said;
She said, "I am aweary, aweary,
I would that I were dead!"

(C)   Zooks, are we pilchards, that they sweep the streets
And count fair prize what comes into their net?
He's Judas to a tittle, that man is!

(D)   If I should die, think only this of me,
That there's some corner of a foreign field
That is forever England. There shall be

(E)   "We two," she said, "will seek the groves
Where the lady Mary is,

337

With her five handmaidens, whose names
Are five sweet symphonies,
Cecily, Gertrude, Magdalen,
Margaret, and Rosalys.

Questions 201 – 202 refer to the following.

Rather than love, than money, than fame, give me truth. I sat at a table where were rich food and wine in abundance, and obsequious attendance, but sincerity and truth were not; and I went away hungry from the inhospitable board. The hospitality was as cold as the ices. I thought there was no need of ice to freeze them.

201. The reference to "ices" (line 4) refers to both

(A) the lack of hospitality and the indifference to truth.

(B) the dessert and ice needed to keep it cold.

(C) the lack of hospitality, the dessert, and the ice needed to keep it cold.

(D) the cold pursuit of truth and the lack of hospitality.

(E) the weather from which the author is escaping and the lack of hospitality.

202. This passage was written by

(A) Emerson   (D) Thoreau

(B) Melville   (E) Channing

(C) Whitman

Questions 203 – 204 refer to the following.

To conclude, then, there is no occupation concerned with the management of social affairs which belongs either to woman or to man, as such. Natural gifts are to be found here and there in both creatures alike; and every occupation is open to both, so far as their natures are concerned, though woman is for all purposes the weaker.

203. The writer is arguing here for

   (A) the equality of women.

   (B) the inequality of women to men.

   (C) the equality of women in occupations.

   (D) the equality of women in the management of social affairs.

   (E) the inequality of the nature of women to that of men.

204. The author of this passage is

   (A) Germaine Greer   (D) Plato

   (B) Jonathan Edwards   (E) Oscar Wilde

   (C) Jane Austen

Questions 205 – 207 refer to the following excerpt.

The Sea of Faith
Was once, too, at the full and round earth's shore
Lay like the folds of a bright girdle furled.
But now I only hear
Its melancholy long, withdrawing roar,   5
Retreating, to the breath
Of the night wind, down the vast edges drear
And naked shingles of the world.

205. The reference to the "folds of a bright girdle furled" (line 3)
     compares the sea to

   (A) folds of bright clothing

   (B) a pennant

   (C) an undergarment

   (D) loose flesh

   (E) an encompassing shore

206. The poet's tone and imagery attempts to imitate

    (A) the ebbing of the tide

    (B) the lapping of the waves at high tide

    (C) a full, pounding tide

    (D) a neap tide

    (E) a red tide

207. The author of this poem is

    (A) Charles Swinburne   (D) Matthew Arnold

    (B) John Keats   (E) Alfred Tennyson

    (C) Percy Shelley

Questions 208 – 209 refer to the following excerpt.

If you will aid me in this enterprise,
Then draw your weapons and be resolute;
If not, depart. Here will Benvolio die,
But_____'s death shall quit my infamy.

208. This quote is properly completed with the name

    (A) Macbeth   (D) Martino

    (B) Romeo   (E) Carolus

    (C) Faustus

209. The excerpt was written by

    (A) Ben Jonson   (D) Thomas Campion

    (B) Christopher Marlowe   (E) Robert Herrick

    (C) William Shakespeare

Questions 210 – 212 refer to the following excerpt.

_____.   (Dropping his familiarity and speaking with freezing politeness) If our conversation is to continue, Louka, you will please remember that a gentleman does not discuss the conduct of the lady he is engaged to with her maid.

Louka: It's so hard to know what a gentleman considers right. I thought from your trying to kiss me that you had given up being so particular.

210.   The unidentified speaker above is

(A) Volpone   (D) Sergius

(B) Candide   (E) Hyperion

(C) Mercutio

211.   The comic force of this interchange hinges on the use of the word

(A) gentleman   (D) right

(B) particular   (E) conduct

(C) maid

212.   The play from which this excerpt is taken is

(A) *She Stoops to Conquer*

(B) *Measure for Measure*

(C) *Arms and the Man*

(D) *The Comedy of Errors*

(E) *Sunday in The Park With George*

213. _____ had a syncophantish, but a sincere admiration of the genius, erudition and virtue of Ursa-Major, and in recording the noble growlings of the Great Bear, thought not of his own Scotch snivel.

The quote above concerns a biography written by

(A) Ben Johnson

(D) James Boswell

(B) Ben Franklin

(E) Edward Fitzgerald

(C) John Milton

Questions 214 – 216. For each of the following passages, identify the author or the work. Base your decision on the content and style of each passage.

214. It is only by the exercise of reason that man can discover God. Take away that reason and he would be incapable of under standing anything; and, in this case, it would be just as consistent to read even in a book called the Bible to a horse as to a man. How then is it that those people pretend to reject reason?

(A) John Locke

(D) Thomas Paine

(B) Bertrand Russell

(E) John Stuart Mill

(C) Benjamin Franklin

215. On the isles's lone beach they paid him in silver for their passage out, the stranger having declined to carry them at all except upon that condition; though willing to take every means to insure the due fulfillment of his promise.

(A) Joseph Conrad

(D) Samuel Johnson

(B) Herman Melville

(E) Robert Louis Stevenson

(C) Richard Dana

216. Far other, however, was the truly fashionable gentleman of those days – his dress, which served for both morning and evening, street and drawing-room, was a linsey-woolsey coat, made, perhaps, by the fair hands of the mistress of his affections. . .

(A) Washington Irving   (D) Bret Harte

(B) Samuel Clemens   (E) Hart Crane

(C) Stephen Crane

Questions 217 – 219 refer to the following excerpt.

Wha for Scotland's king and law
Freedom's sword will strongly draw,
Freeman stand, or freeman fa',
      Let him follow me!

By Oppression's woes and pains,
By your sons in servile chains,
We will drain our dearest veins,
      But they shall be free!

Lay the proud usurpers low!
Tyrants fall in every foe!
Liberty's in every blow!
      Let us do or die!

217. The poet imagines that these words were spoken by

(A) Robert Emmett   (D) Robert Bruce

(B) Macduff   (E) Athelred

(C) Edward II

218. The excerpt might best be termed

(A) a rallying cry to the speaker's troops

(B) a response in defiance of a challenge

(C) a soliloquy by a doomed soldier

(D) a rebel leader's appeal to desert

(E) an appeal to the populace for soldiers

219. This excerpt was written by

   (A) Thomas Day

   (B) Dylan Thomas

   (C) William Butler Yeats

   (D) Robert Burns

   (E) Thomas Clancy

Questions 220 – 223 refer to the following.

> Yet once more, O ye laurels, and once more
> Ye myrtles brown, with ivy never sere,
> I come to pluck your berries harsh and crude,
> And with forced fingers rude,
> Shatter your leaves before the mellowing year.   5
> Bitter constraint and sad occasion dear,
> Compels me to disturb your season due;
> For_____ is dead, dead ere his prime,
> Young_____, and hath not left his peer.

220. This excerpt might best be described as a

   (A) Dramatic dialogue

   (B) Elegy

   (C) Monody

   (D) Epic

   (E) Colloquy

221. The use of the word "crude" in the third line indicates that

   (A) the speaker will be rough as he harvests the berries

   (B) the berries are of low quality

   (C) the words which the poet sings are primitive ones

   (D) the berries are not yet ripe

   (E) there are bitter truths he will reveal

222. The repeated name which best completes this excerpt is

(A) Angelica

(D) Lycidas

(B) Valentine

(E) Prometheus

(C) Lysistrata

223. The author of this poem is

(A) William Shakespeare

(D) John Milton

(B) John Donne

(E) Alexander Pope

(C) John Dryden

224. Hail to thee, blithe Spirit!
    Bird thou never wert,
  That from Heaven, or near it,
    Pourest thy full heart
In profuse strains of unpremeditated art.

These lines are written by the same poet who wrote

(A) *In Memorium*

(B) *Whispers of Immortality*

(C) *The Hound of Heaven*

(D) *The Rainbow*

(E) *Ode to the West Wind*

Questions 225 – 228 refer to the following excerpt.

        Hear me recreant!
On thine allegiance, hear me!
Since thou hast sought to make us break our vow,
Which we durst never yet, and with strained pride
To come between our sentence and our power,
Which nor our nature nor our place can bear,

Our potency made good, take thy reward.
Five days we do allot thee, or provision.
To shield thee from diseases of the world;
And on the sixth to turn thy hated back
Upon our kingdom: if, on the tenth day following,
Thy banished trunk be found in our dominions,
The moment is thy death. Away! by Jupiter,
This shall not be revoked.

225. The speaker is telling the recreant

(A) that he is condemned to death

(B) that he is condemned to prison

(C) that he is being exiled

(D) that he is to be rewarded

(E) that he is to be condemned by the entire country

226. The most appropriate contextual interpretation of the word "recreant" (line 1) is

(A) one who commits evil deeds

(B) one who does not do his duty

(C) one who has recreated the truth to his own liking

(D) a blackguard

(E) a traitor

227. This excerpt is from

(A) *Julius Caesar*

(B) *Romeo and Juliet*

(C) *Richard II*

(D) *King Lear*

(E) *Much Ado About Nothing*

Questions 228 – 230 refer to the following excerpt.

When that rich soul which to her heaven is gone,
Whom all do celebrate who know they have one
(for who is sure he hath a soul, unless
It see, and judge, and follow worthiness,
And by deeds praise it? He who doth not this,   5
May lodge an inmate soul, but 'tis not his);
When that queen ended here her progress time,
And, as to her standing house, to heaven did climb,
Where, loath to make the saints attend her long,
She's now a part both of the choir and song   10

228.   Line 9 indicates that the subject of the poem

(A) was always considerate

(B) was always in a hurry

(C) never received the attention she deserved

(D) lived an eventful life

(E) died early

229.   The poem might best be described as

(A) an invocation to the Muse

(B) a declaration of love

(C) a commemorative

(D) an epigram

(E) an encomium

230.   The poem was written by

(A) John Donne   (D) John Milton

(B) John Dryden   (E) Sir Francis Bacon

(C) Ben Jonson

GRE LITERATURE IN ENGLISH
EXAM III

ANSWER KEY

1.	B	30.	B	59.	B	88.	E
2.	D	31.	E	60.	D	89.	B
3.	A	32.	D	61.	D	90.	A
4.	E	33.	A	62.	E	91.	D
5.	C	34.	D	63.	C	92.	B
6.	B	35.	A	64.	C	93.	A
7.	B	36.	E	65.	B	94.	E
8.	A	37.	D	66.	E	95.	D
9.	D	38.	B	67.	C	96.	B
10.	D	39.	C	68.	B	97.	C
11.	C	40.	A	69.	E	98.	C
12.	C	41.	D	70.	D	99.	D
13.	D	42.	E	71.	D	100.	C
14.	C	43.	B	72.	E	101.	D
15.	E	44.	E	73.	A	102.	D
16.	D	45.	B	74.	B	103.	C
17.	B	46.	B	75.	C	104.	C
18.	B	47.	A	76.	A	105.	D
19.	A	48.	A	77.	D	106.	A
20.	D	49.	D	78.	D	107.	B
21.	B	50.	E	79.	C	108.	D
22.	D	51.	B	80.	D	109.	C
23.	B	52.	E	81.	A	110.	E
24.	C	53.	C	82.	D	111.	D
25.	D	54.	A	83.	B	112.	D
26.	D	55.	D	84.	D	113.	C
27.	B	56.	C	85.	C	114.	D
28.	C	57.	B	86.	B	115.	D
29.	C	58.	C	87.	E	116.	B

GRE LITERATURE IN ENGLISH
EXAM III

ANSWER KEY

117.	C	146.	C	175.	A	204.	D
118.	C	147.	D	176.	C	205.	A
119.	D	148.	B	177.	B	206.	A
120.	E	149.	C	178.	D	207.	D
121.	C	150.	D	179.	A	208.	C
122.	B	151.	C	180.	D	209.	B
123.	C	152.	E	181.	C	210.	D
124.	D	153.	D	182.	B	211.	D
125.	D	154.	C	183.	C	212.	C
126.	C	155.	C	184.	D	213.	D
127.	D	156.	E	185.	D	214.	D
128.	D	157.	B	186.	C	215.	B
129.	B	158.	C	187.	D	216.	A
130.	D	159.	C	188.	B	217.	D
131.	C	160.	D	189.	C	218.	A
132.	D	161.	B	190.	D	219.	D
133.	C	162.	C	191.	D	220.	C
134.	C	163.	D	192.	D	221.	D
135.	C	164.	B	193.	E	222.	D
136.	A	165.	A	194.	C	223.	D
137.	A	166.	D	195.	A	224.	E
138.	C	167.	A	196.	D	225.	C
139.	E	168.	E	197.	B	226.	E
140.	C	169.	A	198.	C	227.	D
141.	D	170.	D	199.	B	228.	E
142.	D	171.	D	200.	E	229.	C
143.	C	172.	D	201.	D	230.	A
144.	B	173.	C	202.	D		
145.	D	174.	E	203.	D		

GRE LITERATURE IN ENGLISH
EXAM III

DETAILED EXPLANATIONS
OF ANSWERS

1.   (B)
Winstanley from *Lives of the Most Famous English Poets*, 1687. Milton, archetypal Puritan that he was, is most likely the target of this invective.

2.   (D)
Coleridge in *Table Talk*, 1834. An excellent statement on the vibrancy of the Chaucerian tongue – the quality that has kept his writing alive through the centuries.

3.   (A)
Fletcher in *The Purple Island*, 1633. Serious vilification was not a problem for the other authors listed.

4.   (E)
Macaulay, in letter to T.F. Ellis, 1834. Dante's writing, distant at this time by 500 years, had long been recognized by English academics. Remember also, the infatuation of the English Romantics (ca. 1830) with Italian culture.

5.   (C)
   This is close to Sartre, and to his borrowing from Descartes: "I think, therefore, I exist." Meaning is determined by our actions, not from some intrinsic force.

6.   (B)
   From *Emma*. Austen's attention to domestic details is evident here.

7.   (B)
   The poet implies that she has NOT left him any hope, because: "dark despair around benights me." Before this he states that no one would grieve as long as there was some hope – some star of light – but "nae cheerfu' twinkle lights" him at all.

8.   (A)
   The poet presents a somewhat unexpected and sympathetic view of their affair. He could not have avoided falling in love with Nancy, for "nothing could resist my Nancy," and he therefore does not blame himself (his "partial fancy"). The heartbreak was inevitable, or so is the implication.

9.   (D)
   The poem is written by Robert Burns, the popularizer of "the Guid Scots Tongue." It does not strain at archaism, as does Spenser's poetry; nor is its rhyme dependent on ancient Germanic pronunciations, as is Chaucer's.

10.   (D)
   The title of an Essay by Buchanan (1871) which criticized Swinburne, Morris, and Rosetti for praising each others' work as part of their "Mutual Admiration School." Swinburne, of course, had often been criticized for a decadent and pronounced attention to sensuality.

11. (C)

From *On the Pleasure of Hating*, 1821. A fine critical intellect at work here should be a clue, as well as a hatred for hyprocrisy.

12. (C)

The similes, in this excerpt, are not personifications, nor is the rhythm either (A) or (B). (E) refers to an obscure characteristic of Indian poetry, leaving (C) – which is evident from a quick scan.

13. (D)

Repetition from stanza to stanza is characteristic of folk poetry the world over: this particular selection is Chinese.

14. (C)

The listing of liberties is a clue.

15. (E)

Note that "Petition for Redress" is a thematic clue.

16. (D)

The reign of James I is a clue to historical placement.

17. (B)

The Greek love of Classical Argument is evident here in phrasing.

18. (B)

The dedication to self-improvement and attention to the details of nature are typical elements in this period. The Biblical syntax bespeaks the poet's Puritan progenitors.

19. (A)

The soul is compared to a molting shellfish – as the living organism grows ever-larger vaults and domes with which to enclose its expanding flesh, and leaving the old shell behind on the sand.

20. (D)

The poet directly addresses his soul (in Line 1) and continues in this manner throughout.

21. (B)

From *The Chambered Nautilus* – a classic New England contemplation of the higher responses possible in human nature.

22. (D)

The poet himself described it as "the half-serious rhyme."

Qualifiers such as "not that," and "indeed," contribute to this tone, as does the rather clipped rhyme in this stanza.

23. (B)

Having 8 iambic lines rhyming abababcc.

24. (C)

From Byron. Typical of the poet's interest in women, romance, and romantic conquest.

25.   (D)
From Keat's *Ode to a Grecian Urn*. Keats' poetry is placed on a level with Wordsworth's in demonstrating the best Romantic craftsmanship.

26.   (D)
From Aristotle in *Poetics*.

27.   (B)
From Lactantius in *Divinae Institutiones*.

28.   (C)
From Swift in *The Battle of the Books*. A satirical tone, almost to the point of being comic, is typical of the author's posture.

29.   (C)
The basic connection developed in this poem is between the murderer and "all men." Just as the murderer had killed the thing he loved, so do all men, usually in much more subtle ways.

30.   (B)
Though the wretched man is eaten by "teeth of flame" in the "pit of shame," it is a spiritual Hell that is more likely to engulf the insensitive person while he and his victim are alive. "All men kill the thing they love," but the instruments of death range from "a sword" to "a flattering word."

31.   (E)
From *The Ballad of Reading Gaol*.

32. (D)

Based in tense emotion, they are considered to represent the most elemental lyrical nature of poetry, and, because of the repetition, they are considered refrains.

33. (A)

From *An Evening's Love*. There is a curious connection here between this description and that of "The Clockwork Universe," another 17th Century approach to the understanding of the mysteries of creation: one with which Dryden was very familiar.

34. (D)

From Poe's obituary in the *New York Tribune*, 1849. Poe was known as morbid even in his own time. What is less well known to contemporary readers was his professional life: important editorships won and lost, and power in literary circles wielded, at times, in a formative and forceful manner.

35. (A)

The tone of an epistle is honored here.

36. (E)

While pseudonyms were standard, the satire "Rape," required special attention to anonymity.

37. (D)

Dryden is quoting the surprising words of the lady.

38.   (B)

In reference to the tragic love affair, "fatal" here is an important clue.

39.   (C)

While the interruptions can be formal in tone, they add humor to the passage. Barth both illustrates and parodies the conventions of the short story in "Lost in the Funhouse."

40.   (A)

Transitions such as "Narrative ordinarily consists of alternating dramatization and summarization. One symptom of nervous tension, paradoxically, is repeated and violent yawning. . ." are clearly not following a discernibly logical order. None of the other choices are appropriate here.

41.   (D)

From *Table Talk*. It is precisely because Coleridge believes Shakespeare's writings are not based in locale, political affiliation, or religious identification that he considers the Bard's works to have been equally understandable to both Shakespeare's educated contemporaries and the succeeding generations of readers.

42.   (E)

From *Table Talk*. The introductory line is: "What a master of composition Fielding was!" The following lines support this statement.

43.   (B)

From "Virgil To Dante" in Dante's *Freedom of the Will*. Virgil's aesthetic philosophy had a strong influence on the Early Renaissance.

44. (E)

The poet is encouraging his fellows to "do quaint deeds and fully flaunt their pride," despite painful situations like poverty and death.

45. (B)

From *The Leaden Eyed*. Lindsay's poetic forcefulness through repetition is evident here.

46. (B)

This is the author's central point. The supposition is that an ideal image of the soul can be constructed.

47. (A)

From Plato's *The Beast and the God in Man*. Implicit here is that reality and the ideal differ significantly, since reality is a vague reflection of the ideal – a key Platonic point.

48. (A)

In this poem, "the god of shepherds" is named Tityrus, really Chaucer, to whom he wishes to pay homage.

49. (D)

The Goddess Phoebus is associated with the passage of the day – a clue here to the paraphrase.

50. (E)

From *The Shepheardes Calender*. Pastoral elements and archaisms (sometime criticized as being forced – as opposed to Chaucer's poetry) are strong indications. Translations of Dante are rarely so obscure in syntax.

51.   (B)

From Whipple in *Literature and Life*. Note how the definition, if converted into representative dialogue, would be a clearly ironical statement.

52.   (E)

From *Dying Metaphors* in *Politics and the English Language*.

Orwell makes a distinction between "technically dead" words, which are "ordinary," and "worn-out," and dying metaphors, which lie between expressions that are newly-invented and those that have become ordinary.

53.   (C)

From *On a Political Prisoner*. The word "cell" in the first stanza is not the only clue. "Bitterness," an abundance of time, "popular enmity," "blind and leader of the blind" all contrast with the freedom of the bird of her youth.

54.   (A)

The poet's central question is whether the woman recalled the "years before her mind/Became a bitter, an abstract thing?" He wonders if the feeding bird has caused this recollection – as the poet remembers her.

55.   (D)

Note the typical Yeatsean lyrical voyage between the exuberant expansiveness of nature (lofty rock/cloudy canopy), and the detailed particularness (ate its bit).

56.   (C)

Note the didactic nature of each passage. Both passages lay out an analogy from real-life experience, then advance questions or implicating statements which point to moral lessons.

57.   (B)

From his *Journal*. Remember that the author was a minister. This helps explain the moral tone and didactic nature, even of this diary entry.

58.   (C)

"Lines," "colors," "landscape," and the almost textual feel of this short passage should give a clue to the identity of the selection's sculptor-author.

59.   (B)

This selection offers a portrait of words of sensation, as you would expect from the great Romantic.

60.   (D)

"Proportion" is here the key word to this great aesthetician's musings.

61.   (D)

Curiously, Chaucer's language, like the Franklin's, has been praised for its directness, its "bare and plain" talk. It is this characteristic, among others, that sets Chaucer aside from his more florid contemporaries.

62.   (E)

Pronounced, "spek – eh."

63.   (C)

Uneducated – this is reinforced by the rest of the passage.

64.   (C)

This is a matter of simple recall.

65.   (B)

By Ben Jonson, 1606.

66.   (E)

From Act II ii.

67.   (C)

From *The Life of Samuel Johnson, L.L.D*. The detailed, accurate, almost note-taking quality should be a clue to the famous biographer's authorship.

68.   (B)

From *An Essay Concerning Human Understanding*. The political and philosophical scope of the author's concerns should give a clue to its origin.

69.   (E)

From *Wordsworth*. The eye of the literary critic is obviously at work. References locate the piece more precisely as to time.

70.   (D)

Huxley, *Science and Culture*.

71.   (D)

Social knowledge and critical commentary are emphasized in this short passage. These are qualities that make authorship by most of the other choices doubtful.

72.   (E)

From *Divinity School Address*. Puritanical origin (evil and weak man) and New England Renaissance belief in the unbounded moral potential of man should be clues here.

73.   (A)

From *The Death of Lincoln*. Written for New York City's Arrangements Committee to honor Lincoln as his casket was brought to the City by train on its way to Springfield, Ill., shortly after his assassination.

74.   (B)

Note the similarity in syntax to *The Rime of the Ancient Mariner*.

75. (C)

While the exuberance at the beginning of the passaage may seem out of character, the historical concern, and concentration on individual psychology are characteristic of Hawthorne.

76. (A)

From *King Arthur's Order of Chivalry*. Tennyson had a particular interest in knighthood and the "glorious" days of the Middle Ages.

77. (D)

From *The Problem of the Golden Rule*. Orwell's humanism indicates the eventual emergence of individualism and re-establishment of personal dignity even in the face of overwhelming despotism – as "anonymous" as it might turn out to be (ie. *1984*).

78. (D)

Morality was seen as a guiding factor in 17th Century England – during which century it was written, as indicated by the language of this poem.

79. (C)

From *Comus*. Note the clean, short, almost epigramic tone.

80. (D)

Though written two hundred years before, the passage shows obvious elements of Scots (althocht/dur, etc.). Pronounciation indicates the presence of heavy "r."

81.   (A)

From Jonson's *Discoveries*. The alliterate "p" bespeaks the author's poetic talents.

82.   (D)

From Drummond's *Notes on Ben Jonson*. Jonson was not the most popular among his fellow "public" writers.

83.   (B)

From *The Return from Parnassus*. Marlowe, the reknowned tragedian, whose life reflected the themes of his works.

84.   (D)

From *The Age of Reason*. The author means there's to be something surprising in his viewpoint – even shocking. Paine, of course, was never one to strive for popularity by advancing traditional views, and his "Unitarian" orientation toward rationality and against iconoclasm are evidenced in this passage.

85.   (C)

From Lawrence's *John Galsworthy*. Obvious question in clue: Who wrote the *Forsyte Saga*?

86.   (B)

From Lawrence's *Thomas Hardy*. Hardy's ability to ennoble the common man is what impresses D.H. Lawrence here.

87.   (E)

From Lawrence's *Edgar Allen Poe*. A look at Poe's poem *The Bells* is evidence of the descriptive accuracy of this passage.

88.   (E)

V.i. The play's technique, based on disguise and deception, is reflected in this famous quote.

89.   (B)

V.ii. The tragic Shakespearean commentary on political power filtered through the disappointment of a fallen historical figure is reflected here.

90.   (A)

I.iv. Well known direct reference to Macbeth.

91.   (D)

Silverman from *Pro Malo Publico*. Usage such as "a body" is a clue to the satirist attempt to imitate Clemens' style.

92.   (B)

Hopkins from *The Grand Old Duke Of York*. From an exceptionally comic exaggeration of Salinger's style – as is easily found in Holden Caufield's casual and qualified speaking in *The Catcher In The Rye*.

93.   (A)

Jan Aeres from *Miss Lonelyhearts*. The diary nature of West's famous work, and the "prissy" quality of the advice is imitated here.

94.   (E)

Pellman in *Diary of a Stranger*. The internal joke, while not characteristic of Camus, makes the piece illustrative of the stranger's cold indifference to the universe that surrounds him.

95.   (D)

From *I Want to Know Why*. The crisp "modern American" quality to the writing is indicative of Lewis' literary gifts.

96.   (B)

From *Tradition and the Individual Talent*. Eliot, the precise critic, is seen in this small excerpt.

97.   (C)

From *Criticism and Fiction*. The 19th Century writer did not feel awkward with "beseech," and his message to the first or second generation of American critics as they start "anew" also places the time.

98.   (C)

In *Fleurs de Mal*: "Swarming city, city filled with dreams / Where the ghost in full daylight hails the passerby."

99.   (D)

IV, 25–27. Heathen who uttered "sighs, which caused the eternal air to tremble."

100.   (C)

From *The Wasteland*, Lines 60–65.

101. (D)
One person speaking in a poetic form. The self-questioning emphasizes the monologic nature of the passage.

102. (D)
See Ecclesiastes i.2.

103. (C)
From *The Bishop Orders His Tomb*. Dramatic monologue is characteristic of many of Browning's finest works.

104. (C)
Parody of Sir Walter Scott by Raffel. The vivid descriptions and the
Scots "bra" are clues.

105. (D)
Parody of Stephen Crane by Frank Norris. Details of color placed
within otherwise stark sentence structure is indicative of a "Naturalistic" writer like Crane.

106. (A)
Parody of Albert Camus by Pellman. Cruelty, indifference, and in-
congruity – classic elements of *The Stranger*.

107. (B)
Parody of William Faulkner by Peter DeVries. Popular American
writer DeVries imitates Faulkner's Stream of Consciousness technique.

108. (D)
Its main thrust is to reinforce the denial in the first sentence that man is not just a beast.

109. (C)
IV.v. The Prince of Denmark wrestles with the meaning of life and the purpose of humanity in the famous play, even as the lofty thinker wrestles with his own base and murderous impulses.

110. (E)
The passage speaks of the coming of death (night). The agents of death prey on living creatures and kill them.

111. (D)
III.ii. Shakespeare's command of the language indicates a character's need to slough off mortal fears and call up courage to face difficult deeds.

112. (D)
Cassius is playing Devil's advocate.

113. (C)
From Lawrence's *Thomas Mann*. Pope, author of "Whatever is, is right," is considered the true believer in 17th century logical methods.

114. (D)
The octave of the Petrarchan sonnet reads abbaabba.

115.   (D)

The traditional metaphor for marriage (or in contemporary parlance – commitment) is two people becoming one. The speaker is recalling their first meeting, remembering it as the first momentous step toward their union.

116.   (B)

A classic romantic image is of two who love each other so much that they worship the ground the other walks on. Here, each is retracing the other's steps, thinking about the other as they pass along the path.

117.   (C)

From *Meeting and Passing*. Hills, walls, and footprints, as well as the typical lilt of Frostian poetry, indicate its origin.

118.   (C)

Lady Macbeth's famous "unsex me" speech is in I.v. This speech exemplifies the horrible swiftness of the play and the commitment to unnatural activity.

119.   (D)

The ability to project a child's vision into his sentences is typical of much of Faulkner's work, including the best of *The Sound and the Fury*, as well as this excerpt from "The Bear."

120.   (E)

The haunting refrain and the rocking-horse are important elements of Lawrence's *The Rocking-Horse Winner*.

121.   (C)

Fitzgerald's Paris expatriate setting – indicated both by the place names and seeming name dropping match this excerpt from *Babylon Revisited* to the author.

122.   (B)

This is the famous opening to Kafka's *A Hunger Artist*.

123.   (C)

Chris is frustrated by his mother's belief in the fantasy that Larry will be found alive.

124.   (D)

Domestic arguments symbolizing greater issues is typical of Miller's work. Here, in what Miller used as practice for his later *Death of a Salesman* mother and son argue for possession of memories and over Chris' effort to marry Larry's old girlfriend, Annie.

125.   (D)

In reference to the Danish occupation of England circa 800 A.D.

126.   (C)

Chaucer describes the squire in the Prologue.

127.   (D)

Often described as the "Father of English Poetry." Sciences at this time also referred to geography and the study of human nature.

128. (D)

We are looking for a Roman "generalist" – a poet as well as a sage.

129. (B)

From *Preface to Fables Ancient and Modern.* Horatio's emphasis on good sense is in sympathy with Dryden's own philosophical tendencies.

130. (D)

The passage begins: "Ye know the spheres and various tasks assigned. . ." The items in the passage are the spheres' tasks.

131. (C)

More than just listing, cataloguing is generally employed to achieve a desired emotional effect.

132. (D)

Rain, to be "kindly," needs to fall on that which needs it, i.e. cultivated fields.

133. (C)

Pope's *Rape of the Lock.*

134. (C)

These words are taken from the preceding paragraph; "Volkssprache" – people's language – reinforces the point.

135. (C)
   Immigrants can "condition" American pronunciation and vocabulary.

   It is of interest that one of the prime conditionings is the addition of vocabulary (single words and expressions) – often associated with food from the countries of immigrant origin.

136. (A)
   From *The American Language*. A particular interest of Mencken was the influence of immigrants (such as in his own family's German background) on American English.

137. (A)
   Taken from Dryden's *Ode to Mrs. Anne Killigrew*. Direct address is typical of Ode introductions.

138. (C)
   A type of fiction that was popularized and inspired by the *Arabian Nights*.

139. (E)
   The answer is found in the title of the selection: *The History of Rasselas, Prince of Abyssinia*.

140. (C)
   From *The History of Rasselas, Prince of Abyssinia*.

141.   (D)

From *Democratic Vistas*. The theme, word usage, and American optimism about American prospects are clues.

142.   (D)

From Arnold's *The Study of Poetry*. Gray was early noted as being an imitator, or perhaps better put, a popularizer of others' techniques.

143.   (C)

Though seemingly heavy-handed, a brief recollection of *The Rime of the Ancient Mariner* will reinforce Coleridge's dour memory.

144.   (B)

The key question here should be: "Which of these is a contemporary work of criticism?"

145.   (D)

From *Epistles* II.1.

146.   (C)

From *The Preface to Shakespeare*. After half a millenium, debates on the greatness of Shakespeare – where they have ever existed – have now almost passed from the critical scene.

147.   (D)

Johnson writes a century and a half after Shakespeare's death.

148. (B)
From *Adam Bede*, although the minute attention to domestic details is characteristic of Austen as well.

149. (C)
Ruskin's prose, the author says, should be looked at as an art form itself.

150. (D)
From *The Critic as Artist*. Wilde uses a typical tone of chatty debate and forceful impressionistic language.

151. (C)
Prominent among the devices employed here is the repetition of initial sound: "foam-fretted feet" (Line 4), "shaken shadow" (Line 7), "soul the soft surprise" (Line 10).

152. (E)
The poet's relationship has been called (presumably by his lover) "no-more," but he does not accept this. He only looks for a sign of hope (a "dart through thy soul"), and then, he tells her, he will smile again.

153. (D)
From *A Superscription*. Note especially Rosetti's fine use of metaphor.

154. (C)
The poet, commenting on the new American mission, refers to the "Old World."

155. (C)

From *Pioneers! O Pioneers!* Free verse and patriotic theme – amplified by frequent use of exclamation marks are clues to origin.

156. (E)

From *Light and Colors*, a famous account of a well-known experiment in optics by one of the greatest scientists of the Enlightenment.

157. (B)

The proper name "Glumdalclitch" and the quasi-reportorial tone of the passage are clues to this tale of adventure.

158. (C)

The dwarf, a seeming supplicant to the Queen, would have been dismissed – "cashiered" still retains most of its original meaning.

159. (C)

From *Gulliver's Travels*.

160. (D)

Entitled *The Author's Epitaph, Made by Himself.* Note the heavy beat, the morbid imagery, and the barely hopeful tone.

161. (B)

Time takes in trust (and delivers death); only the Lord can undo the process.

162. (C)
Supposed to have been written on the eve of his beheading in the Tower of London, although this has from time to time been contested.

163. (D)
Corinna sings to her lute and the strings are resurrected. Her voice has powers of resurrection and, by extension, death.

164. (B)
When, in the last line, the poet compares his heart to the strings breaking on a lute, he directly ties the second stanza to the first where Corinna's sighs break her lute's strings.

165. (A)
From *When to Her Lute Corinna Sings*, 1601. Note the noble and respectful tone of the 17th Century.

166. (D)
Dryden is considered the founder of then-contemporary poetry by his immediate descendants.

167. (A)
Pope is immediately associated with *The Age of Reason*.

168. (E)
From *A Portrait of the Artist as a Young Man*. Note Joyce's simple but powerful descriptive terms.

169. (A)

By E. M. Forster. Note the enormous amount of "information" contained within the prose while at the same time the syntax remains tight. Indicative of Forster and others of the early 20th Century.

170. (D)

Immediately preceeding this passage, the author said, "And whatever is me alive is me." Blood and bones are in his hand, and he can see that if he cuts his hand open – proof positive of life.

171. (D)

From Lawrence's *Why the Novel Matters*. Lawrence's use of repetition "alive ... alive ... alive" and the nature of these repetitions mark this passage as uniquely his.

172. (D)

From Cervantes. The haplessness described in the father is about to devolve upon the son.

173. (C)

Levin's response to an intensity of feeling is about to be tested – a favorite theme of the author.

174. (E)

Although the stream of time bears infinite tones, this passage has only one. The possibility of enmity exists but the passage is mostly concerned with describing Ts' ui Pên's idea of time.

175. (A)
From *The Garden of Forking Paths*.

176. (C)
From *Time Must Have A Stop*. Note the analytic and precise description, indicative of a scientific mind at work.

177. (B)
From *The Life You Save May Be Your Own*.

178. (D)
From *The Great Gatsby*. The lush description of Daisy's voice ("fluctuating, feverish," "deathless song") is a clue.

179. (A)
From *The Bulgarian Poetess*. Politeness and decorum (as would be found in a meeting) are a thin haze over more serious and tumultuous concerns of civilization.

180. (D)
From *Paradise Lost I*. The idea of Satan as a ruined Archangel is strange to many who would rather view evil as always separate from good.

181. (C)
From *The Italian Villain*. The portraits of Lord Byron often included in anthologies are said by many to show these same features – the Byronic hero is as much based on the man as his work.

182. (B)
A reading of Radcliffe's passage while viewing Byron portraits is a lesson in her descriptive powers.

183. (C)
The use of consonance (corpse, carry, cock-crow) and the use of short words in awkward forms (rarer, intenser) contributes to the harsh sound.

184. (D)
Especially evident along side "crofts" (small, farmed tracts of land).

185. (D)
The common nature of the details provided contrast with the hint that the corpse belongs in a rare (also "thin" as air) atmosphere.

186. (C)
From *A Grammarian's Funeral*, – the passage demonstrates that Browning was a master of more lyrical forms as well as the free verse of his dramatic monologues.

187. (D)
From *Ecclesiastes XII* – referring to the "words of the wise."

188. (B)
A choral song in honor of a great person.

189. (C)

From *A Fable for Cities*. A rather chatty example of this 19th Century New Englander's admiration for his fellows.

190. (D)

From a method of disgrace for knights: to be hung upside down by the heels.

191. (D)

Clues are "Gadshill," a notorious hill outside London where robberies took place; taking a purse; and the command "stand" — as in "Stand and deliver! Your money or your life."

192. (D)

Also interpreted as "God's wounds!"

193. (E)

From I.ii.

194. (C)

From Pater's *The Renaissance*. The master of aesthetic studies demonstrates his talent by his choice of diction.

195. (A)

From Ruskin's *The Stones of Venice*. Awareness is the central theme in Ruskin's aesthetic lexicon, which is reflected in his orders to the reader.

196. (D)

From Newman's *Apologia Pro Vita Sua*. The Cardinal's religious studies influence his writing.

197. (B)

From Mill's *What Is Poetry*? Mills' searching and inquisitive mind touched on many subjects and is reflected in his prose.

198. (C)

Look for Browning's particularly convincing dramatic style which matches diction to imagined personality.

199. (B)

Tennyson's lyrical sense gives an almost haunting beauty to these few lines.

200. (E)

Ever concerned with love, Rossetti weaves an image of goddesses, music, and seduction.

201. (D)

The play on the word "ices" is a triple entendre. "Ices" in the 19th Century was dessert, a term used like today's "as cold as ice," and an obvious reference to a lack of hospitality.

202. (D)

From *Walden*. Note the diarist's attention to detail mixed with Thoreau's perhaps over-high expectations for his fellow man.

203.   (D)
The author is specific in the argument – not just in occupations, but in type.

204.   (D)
It is easy to let the references toward equality obscure the notation that women are weaker, but the passage is 2500 years old. From *The Republic* by Plato – believe it or not!

205.   (A)
Since undergarments cannot be furled and a pennant is inconsistent with the ocean imagery, fields of bright clothing is the most logical answer.

206.   (A)
The sea is retreating. It leaves behind "naked shingles" – the rocky shore.

207.   (D)
From *Dover Beach*.

208.   (C)
While a character named Benvolio appears in Shakespeare, this passage does not.

209.   (B)
From *Doctor Faustus*, IV, iii.

210. (D)

Louka's oft-repeated retort to Sergius.

211. (D)

"The dramatic situation itself contributes to the comedy, but the word "right," coming as it does in response to a plausible – if hypocritical – statement by Sergius, and before Louka's biting comment that she "thought... you had given up being so particular," – acts as a pivot point for the comic scene's full emotional delivery.

212. (C)

By G.B. Shaw.

213. (D)

John Wilson, from *Noctes Ambrosianae*, 1822. This piece of vitriole, of course, refers to the Scottist Boswell's admiration for Samuel Johnson – The Great Bear.

214. (D)

From *The Age of Reason*. Paine's own biting logic is evident in this quote – from the famous and aptly entitled work of the British expatriot and American revolutionary.

215. (B)

From *The Encantadas*. Melville's love of the exotic detail, yet awareness of the larger dynamics is evidenced here.

216. (A)

From *The Golden Reign of Wouter Van Twiller*. Irving, the social historian, knew how to manipulate precise descriptive terms (linsey-woolsey) and quaint modifiers (the fair hands of his mistress) to spin a tale of bygone days.

217. (D)

At the Battle of Bannockburn, 1314. One of Scotland's greatest heroes – often recalled by Scots in the century following the Battle of Culloden.

218. (A)

This is evident from the high rhetoric and sense of imminent bloodshed. The final cry to "do or die" is a final appeal.

219. (D)

From *Scots, Wha Hae*, the unofficial national anthem of Scotland.

220. (C)

The poet himself subtitles it this way. Monody is a song sung in Greek drama by a single voice.

221. (D)

This parallels the premature taking of life – the berries were plucked too early and the human life was taken before its time.

222. (D)

The prematurely fallen hero here was really the poet's college friend, Edward King, who drowned in the Irish Sea in 1637.

223.   (D)

From *Lycidas*. Termed "probably the most perfect piece of pure literature in existence," by Arthur Machen in 1923.

224.   (E)

The short stanza is from Shelley's *To A Skylark*. "Ode" begins: "O wild West Wind, thou breath of Autumn's being . . ." Notice the similarity of address and lofty verbiage.

225.   (C)

"Banished" is the key here.

226.   (E)

If "miscreant" is "misbeliever," then, "recreant" resembles "rebeliever" - or someone who has turned on previous commitments.

227.   (D)

The royal "we," the unwillingness to reconsider the order and the obsession with the nature of his power are indicative of Lear.

228.   (E)

"Attend" here means "await." Taken in context, emphasizes her short "time on earth."

229.   (C)

This was written to commemorate the death of Elizabeth Drury, a 14 year old girl.

230.   (A)
From *An Anatomy of the World*, 1611. The artful use of many rhymed couplets while avoiding monotony is indicative of Dryden's poetic genius.

GRE

LITERATURE in ENGLISH

TEST IV

THE GRADUATE RECORD EXAMINATION

LITERATURE in ENGLISH

ANSWER SHEET

1. Ⓐ Ⓑ Ⓒ Ⓓ Ⓔ
2. Ⓐ Ⓑ Ⓒ Ⓓ Ⓔ
3. Ⓐ Ⓑ Ⓒ Ⓓ Ⓔ
4. Ⓐ Ⓑ Ⓒ Ⓓ Ⓔ
5. Ⓐ Ⓑ Ⓒ Ⓓ Ⓔ
6. Ⓐ Ⓑ Ⓒ Ⓓ Ⓔ
7. Ⓐ Ⓑ Ⓒ Ⓓ Ⓔ
8. Ⓐ Ⓑ Ⓒ Ⓓ Ⓔ
9. Ⓐ Ⓑ Ⓒ Ⓓ Ⓔ
10. Ⓐ Ⓑ Ⓒ Ⓓ Ⓔ
11. Ⓐ Ⓑ Ⓒ Ⓓ Ⓔ
12. Ⓐ Ⓑ Ⓒ Ⓓ Ⓔ
13. Ⓐ Ⓑ Ⓒ Ⓓ Ⓔ
14. Ⓐ Ⓑ Ⓒ Ⓓ Ⓔ
15. Ⓐ Ⓑ Ⓒ Ⓓ Ⓔ
16. Ⓐ Ⓑ Ⓒ Ⓓ Ⓔ
17. Ⓐ Ⓑ Ⓒ Ⓓ Ⓔ
18. Ⓐ Ⓑ Ⓒ Ⓓ Ⓔ
19. Ⓐ Ⓑ Ⓒ Ⓓ Ⓔ
20. Ⓐ Ⓑ Ⓒ Ⓓ Ⓔ
21. Ⓐ Ⓑ Ⓒ Ⓓ Ⓔ
22. Ⓐ Ⓑ Ⓒ Ⓓ Ⓔ
23. Ⓐ Ⓑ Ⓒ Ⓓ Ⓔ
24. Ⓐ Ⓑ Ⓒ Ⓓ Ⓔ
25. Ⓐ Ⓑ Ⓒ Ⓓ Ⓔ
26. Ⓐ Ⓑ Ⓒ Ⓓ Ⓔ
27. Ⓐ Ⓑ Ⓒ Ⓓ Ⓔ
28. Ⓐ Ⓑ Ⓒ Ⓓ Ⓔ
29. Ⓐ Ⓑ Ⓒ Ⓓ Ⓔ
30. Ⓐ Ⓑ Ⓒ Ⓓ Ⓔ

31. Ⓐ Ⓑ Ⓒ Ⓓ Ⓔ
32. Ⓐ Ⓑ Ⓒ Ⓓ Ⓔ
33. Ⓐ Ⓑ Ⓒ Ⓓ Ⓔ
34. Ⓐ Ⓑ Ⓒ Ⓓ Ⓔ
35. Ⓐ Ⓑ Ⓒ Ⓓ Ⓔ
36. Ⓐ Ⓑ Ⓒ Ⓓ Ⓔ
37. Ⓐ Ⓑ Ⓒ Ⓓ Ⓔ
38. Ⓐ Ⓑ Ⓒ Ⓓ Ⓔ
39. Ⓐ Ⓑ Ⓒ Ⓓ Ⓔ
40. Ⓐ Ⓑ Ⓒ Ⓓ Ⓔ
41. Ⓐ Ⓑ Ⓒ Ⓓ Ⓔ
42. Ⓐ Ⓑ Ⓒ Ⓓ Ⓔ
43. Ⓐ Ⓑ Ⓒ Ⓓ Ⓔ
44. Ⓐ Ⓑ Ⓒ Ⓓ Ⓔ
45. Ⓐ Ⓑ Ⓒ Ⓓ Ⓔ
46. Ⓐ Ⓑ Ⓒ Ⓓ Ⓔ
47. Ⓐ Ⓑ Ⓒ Ⓓ Ⓔ
48. Ⓐ Ⓑ Ⓒ Ⓓ Ⓔ
49. Ⓐ Ⓑ Ⓒ Ⓓ Ⓔ
50. Ⓐ Ⓑ Ⓒ Ⓓ Ⓔ
51. Ⓐ Ⓑ Ⓒ Ⓓ Ⓔ
52. Ⓐ Ⓑ Ⓒ Ⓓ Ⓔ
53. Ⓐ Ⓑ Ⓒ Ⓓ Ⓔ
54. Ⓐ Ⓑ Ⓒ Ⓓ Ⓔ
55. Ⓐ Ⓑ Ⓒ Ⓓ Ⓔ
56. Ⓐ Ⓑ Ⓒ Ⓓ Ⓔ
57. Ⓐ Ⓑ Ⓒ Ⓓ Ⓔ
58. Ⓐ Ⓑ Ⓒ Ⓓ Ⓔ
59. Ⓐ Ⓑ Ⓒ Ⓓ Ⓔ
60. Ⓐ Ⓑ Ⓒ Ⓓ Ⓔ

61. Ⓐ Ⓑ Ⓒ Ⓓ Ⓔ
62. Ⓐ Ⓑ Ⓒ Ⓓ Ⓔ
63. Ⓐ Ⓑ Ⓒ Ⓓ Ⓔ
64. Ⓐ Ⓑ Ⓒ Ⓓ Ⓔ
65. Ⓐ Ⓑ Ⓒ Ⓓ Ⓔ
66. Ⓐ Ⓑ Ⓒ Ⓓ Ⓔ
67. Ⓐ Ⓑ Ⓒ Ⓓ Ⓔ
68. Ⓐ Ⓑ Ⓒ Ⓓ Ⓔ
69. Ⓐ Ⓑ Ⓒ Ⓓ Ⓔ
70. Ⓐ Ⓑ Ⓒ Ⓓ Ⓔ
71. Ⓐ Ⓑ Ⓒ Ⓓ Ⓔ
72. Ⓐ Ⓑ Ⓒ Ⓓ Ⓔ
73. Ⓐ Ⓑ Ⓒ Ⓓ Ⓔ
74. Ⓐ Ⓑ Ⓒ Ⓓ Ⓔ
75. Ⓐ Ⓑ Ⓒ Ⓓ Ⓔ
76. Ⓐ Ⓑ Ⓒ Ⓓ Ⓔ
77. Ⓐ Ⓑ Ⓒ Ⓓ Ⓔ
78. Ⓐ Ⓑ Ⓒ Ⓓ Ⓔ
79. Ⓐ Ⓑ Ⓒ Ⓓ Ⓔ
80. Ⓐ Ⓑ Ⓒ Ⓓ Ⓔ
81. Ⓐ Ⓑ Ⓒ Ⓓ Ⓔ
82. Ⓐ Ⓑ Ⓒ Ⓓ Ⓔ
83. Ⓐ Ⓑ Ⓒ Ⓓ Ⓔ
84. Ⓐ Ⓑ Ⓒ Ⓓ Ⓔ
85. Ⓐ Ⓑ Ⓒ Ⓓ Ⓔ
86. Ⓐ Ⓑ Ⓒ Ⓓ Ⓔ
87. Ⓐ Ⓑ Ⓒ Ⓓ Ⓕ
88. Ⓐ Ⓑ Ⓒ Ⓓ Ⓔ
89. Ⓐ Ⓑ Ⓒ Ⓓ Ⓔ
90. Ⓐ Ⓑ Ⓒ Ⓓ Ⓔ

91. Ⓐ Ⓑ Ⓒ Ⓓ Ⓔ
92. Ⓐ Ⓑ Ⓒ Ⓓ Ⓔ
93. Ⓐ Ⓑ Ⓒ Ⓓ Ⓔ
94. Ⓐ Ⓑ Ⓒ Ⓓ Ⓔ
95. Ⓐ Ⓑ Ⓒ Ⓓ Ⓔ
96. Ⓐ Ⓑ Ⓒ Ⓓ Ⓔ
97. Ⓐ Ⓑ Ⓒ Ⓓ Ⓔ
98. Ⓐ Ⓑ Ⓒ Ⓓ Ⓔ
99. Ⓐ Ⓑ Ⓒ Ⓓ Ⓔ
100. Ⓐ Ⓑ Ⓒ Ⓓ Ⓔ
101. Ⓐ Ⓑ Ⓒ Ⓓ Ⓔ
102. Ⓐ Ⓑ Ⓒ Ⓓ Ⓔ
103. Ⓐ Ⓑ Ⓒ Ⓓ Ⓔ
104. Ⓐ Ⓑ Ⓒ Ⓓ Ⓔ
105. Ⓐ Ⓑ Ⓒ Ⓓ Ⓔ
106. Ⓐ Ⓑ Ⓒ Ⓓ Ⓔ
107. Ⓐ Ⓑ Ⓒ Ⓓ Ⓔ
108. Ⓐ Ⓑ Ⓒ Ⓓ Ⓔ
109. Ⓐ Ⓑ Ⓒ Ⓓ Ⓔ
110. Ⓐ Ⓑ Ⓒ Ⓓ Ⓔ
111. Ⓐ Ⓑ Ⓒ Ⓓ Ⓔ
112. Ⓐ Ⓑ Ⓒ Ⓓ Ⓔ
113. Ⓐ Ⓑ Ⓒ Ⓓ Ⓔ
114. Ⓐ Ⓑ Ⓒ Ⓓ Ⓔ
115. Ⓐ Ⓑ Ⓒ Ⓓ Ⓔ
116. Ⓐ Ⓑ Ⓒ Ⓓ Ⓔ
117. Ⓐ Ⓑ Ⓒ Ⓓ Ⓔ
118. Ⓐ Ⓑ Ⓒ Ⓓ Ⓔ
119. Ⓐ Ⓑ Ⓒ Ⓓ Ⓔ
120. Ⓐ Ⓑ Ⓒ Ⓓ Ⓔ

121. Ⓐ Ⓑ Ⓒ Ⓓ Ⓔ
122. Ⓐ Ⓑ Ⓒ Ⓓ Ⓔ
123. Ⓐ Ⓑ Ⓒ Ⓓ Ⓔ
124. Ⓐ Ⓑ Ⓒ Ⓓ Ⓔ
125. Ⓐ Ⓑ Ⓒ Ⓓ Ⓔ
126. Ⓐ Ⓑ Ⓒ Ⓓ Ⓔ
127. Ⓐ Ⓑ Ⓒ Ⓓ Ⓔ
128. Ⓐ Ⓑ Ⓒ Ⓓ Ⓔ
129. Ⓐ Ⓑ Ⓒ Ⓓ Ⓔ
130. Ⓐ Ⓑ Ⓒ Ⓓ Ⓔ
131. Ⓐ Ⓑ Ⓒ Ⓓ Ⓔ
132. Ⓐ Ⓑ Ⓒ Ⓓ Ⓔ
133. Ⓐ Ⓑ Ⓒ Ⓓ Ⓔ
134. Ⓐ Ⓑ Ⓒ Ⓓ Ⓔ
135. Ⓐ Ⓑ Ⓒ Ⓓ Ⓔ
136. Ⓐ Ⓑ Ⓒ Ⓓ Ⓔ
137. Ⓐ Ⓑ Ⓒ Ⓓ Ⓔ
138. Ⓐ Ⓑ Ⓒ Ⓓ Ⓔ
139. Ⓐ Ⓑ Ⓒ Ⓓ Ⓔ
140. Ⓐ Ⓑ Ⓒ Ⓓ Ⓔ
141. Ⓐ Ⓑ Ⓒ Ⓓ Ⓔ
142. Ⓐ Ⓑ Ⓒ Ⓓ Ⓔ
143. Ⓐ Ⓑ Ⓒ Ⓓ Ⓔ
144. Ⓐ Ⓑ Ⓒ Ⓓ Ⓔ
145. Ⓐ Ⓑ Ⓒ Ⓓ Ⓔ
146. Ⓐ Ⓑ Ⓒ Ⓓ Ⓔ
147. Ⓐ Ⓑ Ⓒ Ⓓ Ⓔ
148. Ⓐ Ⓑ Ⓒ Ⓓ Ⓔ
149. Ⓐ Ⓑ Ⓒ Ⓓ Ⓔ
150. Ⓐ Ⓑ Ⓒ Ⓓ Ⓔ

151. Ⓐ Ⓑ Ⓒ Ⓓ Ⓔ
152. Ⓐ Ⓑ Ⓒ Ⓓ Ⓔ
153. Ⓐ Ⓑ Ⓒ Ⓓ Ⓔ
154. Ⓐ Ⓑ Ⓒ Ⓓ Ⓔ
155. Ⓐ Ⓑ Ⓒ Ⓓ Ⓔ
156. Ⓐ Ⓑ Ⓒ Ⓓ Ⓔ
157. Ⓐ Ⓑ Ⓒ Ⓓ Ⓔ
158. Ⓐ Ⓑ Ⓒ Ⓓ Ⓔ
159. Ⓐ Ⓑ Ⓒ Ⓓ Ⓔ
160. Ⓐ Ⓑ Ⓒ Ⓓ Ⓔ
161. Ⓐ Ⓑ Ⓒ Ⓓ Ⓔ
162. Ⓐ Ⓑ Ⓒ Ⓓ Ⓔ
163. Ⓐ Ⓑ Ⓒ Ⓓ Ⓔ
164. Ⓐ Ⓑ Ⓒ Ⓓ Ⓔ
165. Ⓐ Ⓑ Ⓒ Ⓓ Ⓔ
166. Ⓐ Ⓑ Ⓒ Ⓓ Ⓔ
167. Ⓐ Ⓑ Ⓒ Ⓓ Ⓔ
168. Ⓐ Ⓑ Ⓒ Ⓓ Ⓔ
169. Ⓐ Ⓑ Ⓒ Ⓓ Ⓔ
170. Ⓐ Ⓑ Ⓒ Ⓓ Ⓔ
171. Ⓐ Ⓑ Ⓒ Ⓓ Ⓔ
172. Ⓐ Ⓑ Ⓒ Ⓓ Ⓔ
173. Ⓐ Ⓑ Ⓒ Ⓓ Ⓔ
174. Ⓐ Ⓑ Ⓒ Ⓓ Ⓔ
175. Ⓐ Ⓑ Ⓒ Ⓓ Ⓔ
176. Ⓐ Ⓑ Ⓒ Ⓓ Ⓔ
177. Ⓐ Ⓑ Ⓒ Ⓓ Ⓔ
178. Ⓐ Ⓑ Ⓒ Ⓓ Ⓔ
179. Ⓐ Ⓑ Ⓒ Ⓓ Ⓔ
180. Ⓐ Ⓑ Ⓒ Ⓓ Ⓔ

181. Ⓐ Ⓑ Ⓒ Ⓓ Ⓔ
182. Ⓐ Ⓑ Ⓒ Ⓓ Ⓔ
183. Ⓐ Ⓑ Ⓒ Ⓓ Ⓔ
184. Ⓐ Ⓑ Ⓒ Ⓓ Ⓔ
185. Ⓐ Ⓑ Ⓒ Ⓓ Ⓔ
186. Ⓐ Ⓑ Ⓒ Ⓓ Ⓔ
187. Ⓐ Ⓑ Ⓒ Ⓓ Ⓔ
188. Ⓐ Ⓑ Ⓒ Ⓓ Ⓔ
189. Ⓐ Ⓑ Ⓒ Ⓓ Ⓔ
190. Ⓐ Ⓑ Ⓒ Ⓓ Ⓔ
191. Ⓐ Ⓑ Ⓒ Ⓓ Ⓔ
192. Ⓐ Ⓑ Ⓒ Ⓓ Ⓔ
193. Ⓐ Ⓑ Ⓒ Ⓓ Ⓔ
194. Ⓐ Ⓑ Ⓒ Ⓓ Ⓔ
195. Ⓐ Ⓑ Ⓒ Ⓓ Ⓔ
196. Ⓐ Ⓑ Ⓒ Ⓓ Ⓔ
197. Ⓐ Ⓑ Ⓒ Ⓓ Ⓔ

198. Ⓐ Ⓑ Ⓒ Ⓓ Ⓔ
199. Ⓐ Ⓑ Ⓒ Ⓓ Ⓔ
200. Ⓐ Ⓑ Ⓒ Ⓓ Ⓔ
201. Ⓐ Ⓑ Ⓒ Ⓓ Ⓔ
202. Ⓐ Ⓑ Ⓒ Ⓓ Ⓔ
203. Ⓐ Ⓑ Ⓒ Ⓓ Ⓔ
204. Ⓐ Ⓑ Ⓒ Ⓓ Ⓔ
205. Ⓐ Ⓑ Ⓒ Ⓓ Ⓔ
206. Ⓐ Ⓑ Ⓒ Ⓓ Ⓔ
207. Ⓐ Ⓑ Ⓒ Ⓓ Ⓔ
208. Ⓐ Ⓑ Ⓒ Ⓓ Ⓔ
209. Ⓐ Ⓑ Ⓒ Ⓓ Ⓔ
210. Ⓐ Ⓑ Ⓒ Ⓓ Ⓔ
211. Ⓐ Ⓑ Ⓒ Ⓓ Ⓔ
212. Ⓐ Ⓑ Ⓒ Ⓓ Ⓔ
213. Ⓐ Ⓑ Ⓒ Ⓓ Ⓔ
214. Ⓐ Ⓑ Ⓒ Ⓓ Ⓔ

215. Ⓐ Ⓑ Ⓒ Ⓓ Ⓔ
216. Ⓐ Ⓑ Ⓒ Ⓓ Ⓔ
217. Ⓐ Ⓑ Ⓒ Ⓓ Ⓔ
218. Ⓐ Ⓑ Ⓒ Ⓓ Ⓔ
219. Ⓐ Ⓑ Ⓒ Ⓓ Ⓔ
220. Ⓐ Ⓑ Ⓒ Ⓓ Ⓔ
221. Ⓐ Ⓑ Ⓒ Ⓓ Ⓔ
222. Ⓐ Ⓑ Ⓒ Ⓓ Ⓔ
223. Ⓐ Ⓑ Ⓒ Ⓓ Ⓔ
224. Ⓐ Ⓑ Ⓒ Ⓓ Ⓔ
225. Ⓐ Ⓑ Ⓒ Ⓓ Ⓔ
226. Ⓐ Ⓑ Ⓒ Ⓓ Ⓔ
227. Ⓐ Ⓑ Ⓒ Ⓓ Ⓔ
228. Ⓐ Ⓑ Ⓒ Ⓓ Ⓔ
229. Ⓐ Ⓑ Ⓒ Ⓓ Ⓔ
230. Ⓐ Ⓑ Ⓒ Ⓓ Ⓔ

GRE LITERATURE IN ENGLISH

TEST IV

DIRECTIONS: Choose the best answer for each question and mark the letter of your selection on the corresponding answer sheet.

Questions 1-3 refer to the excerpts below.

1.   In which one does Auden refer to Yeats?

2.   In which one does Pound refer to Whitman?

3.   In which one does Dryden refer to Milton?

(A)   He listeneth to the lark,
Whose song comes with the sunshine through the dark
Of painted glass in leaden lattice bound;
He listeneth and he laugheth at the sound,
Then writeth in a book like any clerk.

He is the poet of the dawn,...

(B) ...the great poetical observer of men, who
in every age is born to record and eternize
its acts. This he does as a master, as a father,
and superior, who looks down on their little follies
from the Emperor to the Miller; sometimes with severity, oftener with joke and sport.

(C) You were silly like us: your gift survived it all;
The parish of rich women, physical decay,
Yourself: mad Ireland hurt you into poetry.

(D) Three poets in three distant ages born,
Greece, Italy, and England did adorn.
The first in loftiness of thought surpass'd,
The next in majesty, in both the last:
The force of Nature could no farther go;
To make a third, she join'd the former two.

(E) I have detested you long enough.
   I come to you as a grown child
   Who has had a pig-headed father;
   I am old enough now to make friends.
   It was you that broke the new wood,
   Now is a time for carving.
   We have one sap and one root--
   Let there be commerce between us.

4. "We find less talk of life as an exercise in endurance,
   and of death in a hopeless cause; and we hear more of life
   as a seeking and a journeying."
        --R.W. Southern, *The Making of the Middle Ages*
           p. 222

   Which of the following pairs of literary works would best serve
   as examples for the above contrast:

   (A) *The Knight's Tale* and *The Miller's Tale*.

   (B) *The Divine Comedy* and *The Decameron*.

   (C) *The Seafarer* and *The Wanderer*.

   (D) *King Horn* and *Sir Orfeo*.

   (E) *Beowulf* and *Sir Gawain and the Green Knight*.

5. "The object of the imitation is not only a complete
   action but such as stir up pity and fear, and this is
   best achieved when the events are unexpectedly inter-
   connected. This, more than what happens accidentally
   and by chance, will arouse wonder."
                         --Aristotle, *Poetics*

   On the basis of the above observation, Aristotle might
   be expected to object most strongly to which of the following?

   (A) Hardy's *The Return of the Native*.

   (B) Shakespeare's *Macbeth*.

(C) Steinbeck's *The Grapes of Wrath.*

(D) O'Neill's *Long Day's Journey into Night.*

(E) Ibsen's *The Wild Duck.*

6.   "I labor to portray in Arthur before he
was king the image of a brave knight perfected in
the twelve private moral virtues as Aristotle hath
devised."

Identify the author of the above quote and work he refers to:

(A) Malory, *Le Morte D'Arthur.*

(B) Spenser, *The Faerie Queene.*

(C) T.H. White, *The Once and Future King.*

(D) Chaucer, *The Knight's Tale.*

(E) Chretien de Troyes, *The Knight of the Cart.*

7.   "The concentration of attention upon matter-of-fact is
the supremacy of the desert. Any approach to such triumph
bestows on learning a fugitive, and a cloistered virtue,..."
                --Alfred North Whitehead, *Modes of Thought*

In the above passage, Whitehead borrows a phrase from:

(A) Mill's *On Liberty*

(B) Milton's *Areopagitica*

(C) Thoreau's *Civil Disobedience*

(D) Aristotle's *Ethics*

(E) Rousseau's *The Social Contract*

Questions 8-11

And I said his opinion was good:

What shold he study and make himselven wood

Upon a book in cloistre alway to pure

Or swinken with his handes and laboure

As Austin bit? How shall the world be served?

Let Austin have his swink to him reserved!

8. Because of the vowel shift in the 15th century, Chaucer's pronunciation of "how" and "be" in line 5 would be closest to the modern pronunciation of

(A) "who" and "buy."

(B) "hoe" and "bay."

(C) "Hah" and "bah."

(D) "hoe" and "buy."

(E) "who" and "bay."

9. In this passage, Chaucer is describing

(A) the Parson.

(B) the Pardoner.

(C) the Monk.

(D) the Clerk.

(E) the Friar.

10. The language of the passage is

(A) Old English

(B) Middle English

(C) Welsh

(D) Elizabethan English

(E) Anglo-Saxon

11. In context, the passage could best be described as

(A) ridiculing hypocrisy.

(B) anti-intellectual.

(C) attacking religion.

(D) a Protestant attack on Catholicism.

(E) an expression of Lollardism.

Questions 12-13

Dream Deferred

What happens to a dream deferred?

> Does it dry up
> like a raisin in the sun?
> Or fester like a sore--
> And then run?
> Does it stink like rotten meat?
> Or crust and sugar over --
> like a syrupy sweet?
>
> Maybe it just sags
> like a heavy load.
>
> Or does it explode?

12. The principle rhetorical device used in this poem is

(A) antithesis

(B) irony

(C) simile

(D) personification

(E) understatement

13.   The topic of the poem is:

   (A) Freudian dream theory.

   (B) adolescent frustration.

   (C) pollution of Nature.

   (D) the transience of love.

   (E) the consequences of racism.

Questions 14-16

in Just-
spring   when the world is mud-
luscious the little
lame balloonman

whistles   far   and wee

and eddieand bill come
running from marbles and
piracies and it's
spring

when the world is puddle-wonderful
the queer
old balloonman whistles
far   and   wee
and bettyandisabel come dancing

from hop-scotch and jump-rope and

it's
spring
and
          the

                goat-footed

balloonMan   whistles
far
and
wee

14.   The versification of the poem would be best classified as:

   (A) iambic pentameter

   (B) blank verse

   (C) ballad stanza

   (D) sprung rhythm

   (E) free verse

15.   The description of the balloonman recalls which of the following from Greek mythology?

   (A) The Cyclops

   (B) The Gorgons

   (C) Hermes

   (D) Eros

   (E) Pan

16. The tone is best described as

   (A) elegiac

   (B) sarcastic

   (C) laudatory

   (D) whimsical

   (E) devotional

Questions 17-19 refer to the excerpts below.

17. In which excerpt is the "I" character Huckleberry Finn?

18. In which excerpt is the "I" character David Balfour?

19. In which excerpt is the "I" character Benjy Compson?

(A) Down-stairs we came out through the first-floor dining-room to the street. A waiter went for a taxi. It was hot and bright. Up the street was a little square with trees and grass where there were taxis parked. A taxi came up the street, the waiter hanging out at the side. I tipped him and told the driver where to drive, and got in beside Brett. The driver started up the street. I settled back. Brett moved closer to me. We sat close against each other. O put my arm around her and she rested against me comfortably. It was very hot and bright, and the houses looked sharply white. We turned out onto the Gran Via.

(B) Through the fence, between the curling flower spaces, I could see them hitting. They were coming toward where the flag was and I went along the fence. Luster was hunting in the grass by the flower tree. They took the flag out, and they were hitting. Then they put the flag back and they went to the table, and he hit and the other hit. Then they went on, and I went along the fence. Luster came away from the flower tree and we went along the fence and they stopped and we stopped and I looked through the fence while Luster was hunting in the grass.

(C) Well, I got a good going-over in the morning, from old Miss Watson, on account of my clothes; but the widow she didn't scold, but only cleaned off the grease and clay and looked so sorry that I thought I would behave a while if I could. Then Miss Watson she took me in the closet and prayed but nothing come of it.

(D) The tower, I should have said, was square; and in every corner the step was made of a great stone of a different shape, to join the flights. Well, I had come close to one

396

of these turns, when, feeling forward as usual, my hand slipped upon an edge and found nothing but emptiness beyond it. The stair had been carried no higher; to set a stranger mounting it in the darkness was to send him straight to his death;...

E) For a long time I used to go to bed early. Sometimes, when I had put out my candle, my eyes would close so quickly that I had not even time to say "I'm going to sleep." And half an hour later the thought that it was time to go to sleep would awaken me; I would try to put away the book which, I imagined, was still in my hands, and to blow out the light; I had been thinking all the time, while I was asleep, of what I had just been reading, but my thoughts had run into a channel of their own, until I myself seemed actually to have become the subject of my book: a church, a quartet, the rivalry between Francois I and Charles V. This impression would persist for some moments after I was awake; it did not disturb my mind, but it lay like scales upon my eyes and prevented them from registering the fact that the candle was no longer burning.

Questions 20-23

He answered, "I don't know how to sing; for that was the reason I left the entertainment and came out to this place, because I couldn't sing." The other who talked to him replied, "All the same, you shall sing for me." "What must I sing?" he asked. "Sing the beginning of created things!" said the other. Hereupon he at once began to sing verses which he had never heard before, to the praise of God the creator.

Bede, *Historia Ecclesiastica Gentis Anglorum*

20.   The singer in the above passage is

A) Beowulf

B) Sir Gawain

(C) Caedmon

(D) Chaucer

(E) Dante

21. The song referred to above as praising God the creator was originally in what language?

(A) Middle English

(B) Latin

(C) Anglo-Saxon

(D) Hebrew

(E) Anglo-Norman

22. The versification of the song was:

(A) alliterative

(B) iambic pentameter

(C) ballad stanza

(D) free verse

(E) heroic couplets

23. The passage itself could best be classified as an example of

(A) epic simile

(B) comic relief

(C) classical allusion

(D) mock epic

(E) dream vision

Questions 24-26

It is quite impossible, said Drachmann, that a light covering of dust should have the effect which is repeatedly attributed to it in the play. In itself, it is not a very important point, but there it is; Sophocles put it there, and we would like to know why. Since the habits of animals and birds of prey are not matters of   5 specialized knowledge, Sophocles is inviting his audience to accept something that they would all recognize to be contrary to ordinary experience. In naturalistic drama, a contrivance of this kind would be no more than a confession that the dramatist had got himself into a difficulty, and could not escape except by   10 a miracle. Drachmann's error was that he thought he was dealing with a Pinero.

H.D.F. Kitto *Form and Meaning in Drama*

24.   The "light covering of dust" (line 1-2) refers to

(A) the burial of Oedipus at the end of *Oedipus at Colonus*.

(B) the burial of Polyneices by Antigone in *Antigone*.

(C) the riddle of the sphinx in *Oedipus the King*.

(D) the execution of Antigone by Creon in *Antigone*.

(E) the response of the Delphic oracle in *Oedipus the King*.

25.   The best definition of "naturalistic" (line 8) would be

(A) finding inspiration in nature.

(B) assuming that scientific laws are adequate to account for all phenomena.

(C) based on principles of economic determinism.

(D) concerned with an accurate representation of human nature.

(E) pantheistic.

26.   For specific examples from a work by Pinero, the author might refer to

(A) *Mrs. Warren's Profession*

(B) *The Three Sisters*

(C) *The Second Mrs. Tanqueray*

(D) *Hedda Gabler*

(E) *The Rivals*

Questions 27-28

THE LAKE ISLE

O God, O Venus, O Mercury, patron of thieves,
Give me in due time, I beseech you, a little tobacco-shop
With the little bright boxes
     piled up neatly upon the shelves
And the loose fragrant cavendish
     and the shag,
And the bright Virginia
     loose under the bright glass cases,
And a pair of scales not too greasy,
And the whores dropping in for a word or two in passing,
For a flip word, and to tidy their hair a bit.

O God, O Venus, O Mercury, patron of thieves,
Lend me a little tobacco-shop,
     or install me in any profession
Save this damned profession of writing,
     where one needs one's brains all the time.

27. The title of the poem

    (A) refers to the place where the poem was written.

    (B) refers to the birth of Venus.

    (C) refers to a poem by W.B. Yeats.

    (D) refers to a brand of tobacco.

    (E) refers to the place where the poet like to go on vacation.

28. The poem might be classified as

   (A) Petrarchan

   (B) Romantic

   (C) Anti-Petrarchan

   (D) Anti-Romantic

   (E) Pre-Raphaelite

Questions 29-30

The end then of learning is to repair the ruins of our first parents by regaining to know God aright and out of that knowledge to love Him, to imitate Him, to be like Him,...

29. The passage is from

   (A) St. Augustine's *The City of God*

   (B) More's *Utopia*

   (C) Mill's *On Liberty*

   (D) Dewey's *Experience and Education*

   (E) Milton's *On Education*

30. The metaphor "repair the ruins" depends for its meaning on

   (A) Freud's theory of the Oedipal Complex.

   (B) The etymology of "ruin" which is derived from Latin "ruo, ruere," meaning "to fall."

   (C) knowledge about archeological sites.

   (D) reference to the tearing down of medieval churches by Protestants during the Reformation.

   (E) reference to Greek and Roman temples.

Questions 31-33

Of the young Sir Willoughby, her word was brief; and there was
the merit of it on a day when he was hearing from sunrise to the
setting of the moon salutes in his honour, songs of praise and
Ciceronian eulogy. Rich, handsome, courteous, generous, lord
of the Hall, the feast, and the dance, he excited his guests of both 5
sexes to a holiday of flattery. And, says Mrs. Mountstuart,
while grand phrases were mouthing round about him: *"You see
he has a leg."*

31.   The passage is from

    (A) Hardy's *Jude the Obscure*

    (B) Dickens' *David Copperfield*

    (C) Thackery's *Vanity Fair*

    (D) Fielding's *Tom Jones*

    (E) Meredith's *The Egoist*

32.   In the context, "Ciceronian" (line 4) means characterized by

    (A) self-sacrifice and patriotism.

    (B) stoic self-discipline.

    (C) interest in politics.

    (D) degenerate Roman sensuality.

    (E) empty rhetorical formulas.

33.   The passage could best be described as

    (A) melodramatic.

    (B) satiric.

    (C) lyric.

(D) mock epic.

(E) allegorical.

Questions 34-35

In this progressive unmasking of himself the audience sees the
hero as his own destroyer, as the detective who discovers the
criminal to be himself. The closer he comes to his imminent
downfall, the higher his stature. The true tragic grandeur comes
when he and the audience recognize that he must bear full moral   5
responsibility for his life and acts. To expiate his crimes he first calls
for his sword to kill himself. Then in a moment of bitter irony he seizes
his wife Jocasta's golden pin and pierces his eyeballs...

                              --William Fleming *Arts and Ideas*

34.   The character described above is:

(A) King Lear

(B) Everyman

(C) Oedipus

(D) Hamlet

(E) Orestes

35.   "Irony" (line 8) means

(A) sarcasm

(B) depression

(C) oxymoron

(D) reversal

(E) fate

36.   Sailor, can you hear
The Pequod's sea wings, beating landward, fall
 Headlong and break on our Atlantic wall
Off 'Sconset, where the yawing S-boats splash
The bellbuoy,...
                         --Robert Lowell, *The Quaker Graveyard*
                                    in Nantucket

In the above lines Lowell alludes to

(A) the Biblical story of Jonah

(B) Homer's *Odyssey*

(C) Sinbad

(D) Melville's *Moby Dick*

(E) Shakespearc's *The Tempest*

37.   Which of the following plays by Eugene O'Neill could best be
       described as autobiographical?

(A) *The Iceman Cometh*

(B) *Long Day's Journey into Night*

(C) *Marco Millions*

(D) *The Great God Brown*

(E) *The Hairy Ape*

38.   Which of the following plays by Eugene O'Neill is based on the
       myth of Hippolytus?

(A) *Mourning Becomes Electra*

(B) *Moon for the Misbegotten*

(C) *Strange Interlude*

(D) *Desire Under the Elms*

(E) *The Emperor Jones*

Questions 39-40

39. Hog Butcher for the World,
Tool Maker, Stacker of Wheat,
Player with Railroads and the Nation's Freight Handler;
Stormy, husky, brawling,
City of the Big Shoulders:

40. Yet ours is no work-a-day only. No
other provides so many recreations for the spirit
--contests and sacrifices all the year round, and
beauty in our public buildings to cheer the heart
and delight the eye day by day. Moreover, the
city is so large and powerful that all the wealth
of all the world flows in to her,...

Identify each of the above cities:

(A) Athens

(B) Chicago

(C) New York

(D) Paris

(E) London

41. Eastern guard tower
glints in sunset; convicts rest
like lizards on rocks.

In the above poem by Ethridge Knight, which of the following
features is essential to the poem's classification as a haiku?

(A) Reference to one of the four directions of the compass, east.

(B) The simile, in this case a comparison of convicts to lizards.

(C) Alliteration: "guard" and "glints," "rest" and "rocks,"
"like" and "lizards."

(D) The use of animals to satirize human behavior.

(E) The alternation of five-, seven-, and five-syllable lines.

Questions 42-44

42.   The fog comes
on little cat feet.

It sits looking
over harbor and city
on silent haunches
and then moves on.

43.   The yellow fog that rubs its back upon the window-panes,
The yellow smoke that rubs its muzzle on the window-panes,
Licked its tongue into the corners of the evening,
Lingered upon the pools that stand in drains,
Let fall upon its back the soot that falls from chimneys,
Slipped by the terrace, made a sudden leap,
And seeing that it was a soft October night,
Curled once about the house, and fell asleep.

44.   Fog everywhere. fog up the river, where it flows among
green aits and meadows; fog down the river, where it rolls
defiled among the tiers of shipping, and the waterside
pollutants of a great (and dirty) city. Fog on the Essex
marshes, fog on the Kentish heights. Fog creeping into the
cabooses of collier-brigs; fog lying out on the yards, and
hovering in the rigging of great ships; fog dropping on the
gunwales of barges and small boats.

Identify the authors of the above descriptive passages:

(A) Charles Dickens   (D) Robert Frost

(B) Ernest Hemingway   (E) Carl Sandburg

(C) T.S. Eliot

45. In reading which of the following novels would it be most appropriate to consider characterization from a Freudian point of view?

(A) Dickens' *A Tale of Two Cities*

(B) Fielding's *Tom Jones*

(C) Thackery's *Vanity Fair*

(D) Lawrence's *Sons and Lovers*

(E) Steinbeck's *Of Mice and Men*

46. The phrase "nature red in tooth and claw" is from

(A) Wordsowrth's *Tintern Abbey*

(B) Tennyson's *In Memoriam A.H.H.*

(C) Blake's *The Marriage of Heaven and Hell*

(D) Yeats' *Sailing to Byzantium*

(E) T.S. Eliot's *The Waste Land*

Questions 47-49

A man can hold land if he can just eat and pay taxes; he can do that.

Yes, he can do that until his crops fail one day and he has to borrow money from the bank.

But – – you see, a bank or a company can't do that, because those creatures don't breathe air, don't eat side-meat. They breathe profits; they eat the interest on money. If they don't get it, they die the way you die without air, without side-meat.

> Steinbeck, *Grapes of Wrath*

47. The repetition of "he can do that" and the use of the second person pronoun

(A) are errors in grammar, showing the speaker is illiterate.

(B) are colloquial.

(C) represent dialect.

(D) are ironic, showing that the author is actually ridiculing the ideas being expressed.

(E) are stylistic devices that add emphasis.

48. Events referred to in the passage are associated with what historical period?

(A) The economic depression of the 1930's.

(B) The frontier in the 19th century.

(C) the gold rush in California.

(D) Slavery in the ante-bellum south.

(E) The pre-revolutionary colonies.

49. The ideas underlying the test show the influence of

(A) Henry David Thoreau   (D) Sigmund Freud

(B) Rousseau   (E) John Stuart Mill

(C) Karl Marx

Question 50

It is unlikely that any readers will recall working out such principles in the course of learning English; in fact, few speakers will claim that they are even aware of knowing such principles. Yet their ability to judge "words" such as those cited above as English or not can only be explained by the assumption that speakers of English possess this type of knowledge. In other words, this suggests that we have knowledge about our native tongue of which we are not conscious. Like Moliere's M. Jourdain, we all speak prose, but we are totally unaware of doing so.

- - Halle, "The Rules of Language,"
Language: Introductory Readings

50.   The play to which Halle alludes ridicules

(A) Pre-Socratic philosophy

(B) Medieval scholasticism

(C) Utilitarianism

(D) middle-class desire for education

(E) progressive education

51.   But I may not stand, mine head works so. Ah Sir Launcelot,
said King Arthur, this day have I sore missed thee: alas,
that ever I was against thee, for now have I my death, whereof
Sir Gawaine me warned in my dream. Then Sir Lucan took up
the king the one part, and Sir Bedivere the other part, and
in the lifting the king swooned; and Sir Lucan fell in a swoon
with the lift, that the part of his guts fell out of his body,
and therewith the noble knight's heart brast.
                                     - - Malory, *Le Morte D'Arthur*

In context, the above passage could best be classified as

(A) an example of verbal irony.

(B) mock epic.

(C) a tragic and heroic passage from a romance.

(D) estates satire.

(E) a parody of medieval literature.

Questions 52-54 refer to the excerpts below.

52.   Which passage is from Conrad's *Lord Jim*?

53.   Which passage is from Melville's *Moby Dick*?

54.   Which passage is from Crane's *The Open Boat*?

(A) Tuesday, Sept. 8th. This was my first day's duty on board the ship; and though a sailor's life is a sailor's life wherever it may be, yet I found everything very different here from the customs of the brig Pilgrim. After all hands were called, at daybreak, three minutes and a half were allowed for every man to dress and come on deck, and if any were longer than that, they were sure to be overhauled by the mate, who was always on deck, and making himself heard all over the ship.

(B) The harpoon was darted; the stricken whale flew forward; with igniting velocity the line ran through the groove - - ran foul. Ahab stooped to clear it; he did clear it; but the flying turn caught him round the neck, and voicelessly as Turkish mutes bowstring their victims, he was shot out of the boat, ere the crew knew he was gone.

(C) "The shadow prowling amongst the graves of butterflies laughed boisterously.

"'Yes! Very funny the terrible thing is. A man that is born falls into a dream like a man who falls into the sea. If he tries to climb out into the air as inexperienced people endeavour to do, he drowns - - *nicht wahr*? No! I tell you! The way is to the destructive element submit yourself, and with the exertions of your hands and feet in the water make the deep, deep sea keep you up. . .' "

(D) What became of my Companions in the Boat, as well as those who escaped on the Rock, or were left in the Vessel, I cannot tell; but conclude they were all lost. For my own Part, I swam as Fortune directed me, and was pushed forward by Wind and Tide. I often let my Legs drop, and could feel no Bottom; But when I was almost gone, and able to struggle no longer, I found myself within my Depth; and by this Time the Storm was much abated. The Declivity was so small, that I walked near a Mile before I got to the Shore, which I conjectured was about Eight O'Clock in the Evening. I then advanced forward near half a Mile, but could not discover any Sign of Houses or Inhabitants; at least I was in so weak a Condition, that I did not observe them. I was extremely tired, and with that, and the Heat of the Weather, and about half a Pint of Brandy that I drank as I left the Ship, I found my self much inclined to sleep. I lay down on the Grass, which was very short and soft; where I slept sounder than ever I remember to have done in my Life, and as I reckoned, above Nine Hours; for when I awaked, it was just Day-light. I attempted to rise, but was not able to stir: For as I happened to lie on my Back, I found my Arms and Legs were strongly fastened on each Side to the Ground; and my Hair, which was long and thick, tied down in the same Manner.

(E) None of them knew the color of the sky. Their eyes glanced level, and were fastened upon the waves that swept toward them. These waves were of the hue of slate, save for the tops, which were of foaming white, and all of the men knew the colors of the sea. The horizon narrowed and widened, and dipped and rose, and at all times its edge was jagged with waves that seemed thrust up in points like rocks.

Many a man out to have a bathtub larger than the boat which here rode upon the sea. These waves were most wrongfully and barbarously abrupt and tall, and each froth-top was a problem in small-boat navigation.

55.   Now, as there is an infinity of possible universes in the ideas of God, and as only one of them can exist, there must be a sufficient reason for the choice of God, which determines him to select one rather than another.

And this reason can be found in the fitness, or in the degrees of perfection that these worlds contain, each possible world having a right to claim existence in proportion to the measure of perfection which it possesses.

The idea expressed above is most directly ridiculed in

(A) Aristophanes' *The Clouds*

(B) Swift's *Gulliver's Travels*

(C) Voltaire's *Candide*

(D) Moliere's *Tartuffe*

(E) Oscar Wilde's *The Importance of Being Earnest*

56. "The excursus upon the origin of Odysseus' scar
is not basically different from the many passages in which
a newly introduced character, or even a newly
appearing object or implement, though it be in the thick
of battle, is described as to its nature and origin."

- - - Auerbach, *Mimesis*

Although the above statement refers to Homer's *Odyssey*, the
idea, if applied to English literature, could best be illustrated
with examples from

(A) Shakespeare's *King Lear*

(B) Spenser's *The Faerie Queene*

(C) Chaucer's *Miller's Tale*

(D) *Sir Gawain and the Green Knight*

(E) *Beowulf*

Questions 57-59

57. Which of the following passages is an example of anachronism?

58. Which of the following passages is an example of a self-
consciously archaic style?

59. Which of the following passages is the author's representation
of a geographical or ethnic dialect which is not his own?

(A) Whilom ther was dwelling at Oxenforde
A riche gnof that gestes heeld to boorde,
And of his craft he was a carpenter.
With him ther was dwelling a poore scoler,
Hadde lerned art, but al his fantasye
Was turned for to lere astrologye, . . .

412

(B) A gentle Knight was pricking on the plaine,
    Ycaldd in mightie armes and silver shielde,
    Wherein old dints of deepe woundes did remaine,
    The cruell markes of many' a bloody fielde;

(C) Now hast thou but one bare hour to live
    And then thou must be damned perpetually!
    Stand still, you ever-moving spheres of heaven,
    That time may cease and midnight never come;
    Fair Nature's eye, rise, rise again, and make
    Perpetual day;

(D) *Mac.* By Crish, la! tish ill done: the work ish give
    over, the trumpet sound the retreat. By my hand, I
    swear, and my father's soul, the work ish till done;
    it ish gove over: I would have blowed up the town, so
    Crish save me, la! in an hour: O tish ill done, tish
    ill done; by my hand, tish ill done!

    Flu. Captain Macmorris, I beseech you now, will you
    voutsafe me, look you, a few disputations with
    you, as partly touching or concerning the disciplines of
    the war, the Roman wars, in the way of argument, look
    you,
    and friendly communication; partly to satisfy my opinion,
    and partly for the satisfaction, look you, of my mind, as
    touching the direction of the military discipline; that is
    the point.

    Jamy. It sall be very gud, gud feith, gud captains bath:
    and I sall quit you with gud leve, as I may pick occasion:
    that sall I, marry.

(E) But we sely shepherds that walkis on the moor
    In faith we are nearhandis out of the door
    No wonder, as it standis, if we be poor,
    For the tilth of our landis lyis fallow on the floor,
            As ye ken.
        We are so hamid,
        For-taxid and ramid,
        We are made hand-tamid
            With these gentlery-men.

Questions 60-61

> In Brueghel's *Icarus*, for instance: how everything turns away
> Quite leisurely from the disaster; the ploughman may
> Have heard the splash, the forsaken cry,
> But for him it was not an important failure;
>
> - - Auden

60. The Greek myth referred to above is the source also for the name of a central character in

   (A) Joyce's *A Portrait of the Artist as a Young Man*

   (B) Shaw's *Man and Superman*

   (C) Shaw's *Pygmalion*

   (D) O'Neill's *Mourning Becomes Electra*

   (E) Chaucer's *Knight's Tale*

61. Auden's theme can best be paraphrased as

   (A) Only someone educated in the classics would recognize an allusion to Greek mythology.

   (B) The archetypes of mythology are universal.

   (C) In their immediate context, heroic events often seem insignificant.

   (D) The tragic hero is punished for trying to go beyond human limitations.

   (E) True happiness lies in attending to the business of everyday life, instead of trying to be a hero.

Questions 62-64

62. I have said that poetry is the spontaneous overflow of powerful feelings: it takes its origin from emotion recollected in tranquility;. . .

63.   Poetry therefore is an art of imitation, for so Aristotle termeth it in the word *mimesis*, that is to say, a representing, counterfeiting, or figuring-forth- - to speak metaphorically, a speaking picture; with this end, to teach and delight.

64.   It begins in delight and ends in wisdom. The figure is the same for love. No one can really hold that the ecstasy should be static and stand still in one place. It begins in delight, it inclines to the impulse, it assumes direction with the first line laid down, it runs a course of lucky events, and ends in a clarification of life - - not necessarily a great clarification, such as sects and cults are founded on, but in a momentary stay against confusion.

Identify the authors of the above definitions of poetry:

(A) T.S. Eliot   (D) Robert Frost

(B) William Wordsworth   (E) Dr. Samuel Johnson

(C) Sir Philip Sidney

Questions 65-67

65.   I had not a dispute but a disquisition, with Dilke on various subjects; several things dove-tailed in my mind, and at once it struck me what quality went to form a Man of Achievement, especially in Literature, and which Shakespeare possessed so enormously — I mean Negative Capability, that is, when a man is capable of being in uncertainties, mysteries, doubts, without any irritable reaching after fact and reason. . .

66.   So to see Lear acted, – – to see an old man tottering about the stage with a walking-stick, turned out of doors by his daughters in a rainy night, has nothing in it but what is painful and disgusting. We want to take him into shelter and relieve him. This is all the feeling which the acting of Lear ever produced in me. But the Lear of Shakespeare cannot be acted.

67. His first defect is that to which may be imparted most of the evil in books or in men. He sacrifices virtue to convenience and is so much more careful to please than to instruct that he seems to write without any moral purpose.

The above statements about Shakespeare are made by:

(A) Dr. Samuel Johnson   (D) Charles Lamb

(B) John Keats   (E) T.S. Eliot

(C) Coleridge

68. The epilogue to Tolstoy's *War and Peace* is

(A) an essay about the nature of art.

(B) an argument in favor of historical determinism.

(C) an argument in favor of freeing the serfs.

(D) an essay showing the importance of military strategy.

(E) an argument supporting the significance of heroic action.

69. Which of the following works best exemplifies "courtly love?"

(A) *Beowulf*

(B) Chaucer's *Troilus and Criseyde*

(C) Shakespeare's *Henry IV Part 2*

(D) Milton's *Paradise Lost*

(E) Pope's *Rape of the Lock*

70. Which of the following best exemplifies allegory?

(A) Chaucer's *Reeve's Tale*

(B) Shakespeare's *Richard II*

(C) Milton's *Samson Agonistes*

(D) Spenser's *The Faerie Queene*

(E) Wycherley's *The Country Wife*

71. Which of the following poets did <u>NOT</u> write sonnets?

(A) Robert Frost

(B) Edna St. Vincent Millay

(C) John Milton

(D) John Donne

(E) Alexander Pope

Questions 72-74

Do not go gentle into that good night,
Old age should burn and rave at close of day;
Rage, rage against the dying of the light.

Though wise men at their end know dark is right,
Because their words had forked no lightning they   5
Do not go gentle into that good night.

Good men, the last wave by, crying how bright
Their frail deeds might have danced in a green bay,
Rage, rage against the dying of the light.

Wild men who caught and sang the sun in flight,   10
And learn, too late, they grieved it on its way,
Do not go gentle into that good night.

Grave men, near death, who see with blinding sight
Blind eyes could blaze like meteors and be gay,
Rage, rage against the dying of the light.   15

And you, my father, there on the sad height,
Curse, bless, me now with your fierce tears, I pray.
Do not go gentle into that good night.
Rage, rage against the dying of the light.

72. The poem is an example of a

    (A) villanelle.   (D) rondeau.

    (B) sestina.   (E) triolet.

    (C) sonnet.

73. The theme of the poem can best be paraphrased as

    (A) the good man dies peacefully because he has faith in divine justice.

    (B) everyone is afraid of dying because no one really knows anything about the afterlife.

    (C) although one naturally tends to fear death, it is pointless to do so because death is inevitable.

    (D) since death is inevitable, the only thing to do is to try to live a good life.

    (E) the fact of death makes life seem more precious.

74. The rhetorical term illustrated by (line 16), "And you, my father. . ."

    (A) synecdoche   (D) litotes

    (B) metonymy   (E) simile

    (C) apostrophe

Questions 75-76

Our two souls, therefore, which are one,
    Though I must go, endure not yet
A breach, but an expansion,
    Like gold to airy thinness beat.

75. The versification of the above lines may be described as

(A) iambic pentameter (D) Alexandrine

(B) iambic tetrameter (E) alliterative

(C) blank verse

76. The passage is from a poem by

(A) Donne (D) Ben Jonson

(B) Keats (E) Tennyson

(C) Chaucer

Questions 77-79 refer to the excerpts below.

77. Which passage is by John Stuart Mill?

78. Which passage is by Thomas Hobbes?

79. Which passage is by Henry David Thoreau?

(A) In a democracy you must have seen how men condemned to death or exile stay on and go about in public, and no one takes any more notice than he would of a spirit that walked invisible. There is so much tolerance and superiority to petty considerations; such contempt for all those fine principles we laid down in founding our common wealth, as when we said that only a very exceptional nature could turn out a good man, if he had not played as a child among things of beauty and given himself only to creditable pursuits. A democracy tramples all such notions under foot; with a magnificent indifference to the sort of life a man has led before he enters politics, it will promote to honour anyone who merely calls himself the people's friend.

(B) Thus, in imagination, individuals seem freer under dominance of the bourgeoisie than before, because their conditions of life seem accidental; in reality, of course, they are less free, because they are more subjected to the violence of things. The difference from the estate comes out particularly in the antagonism between the bourgeoisie and the proletariat.

419

(C) A wise man will not leave the right to the mercy of chance, nor wish it to prevail through the power of the majority. There is but little virtue in the action of masses of men. When the majority shall at length vote for the abolition of slavery, it will be because they are indifferent to slavery, or because there is but little slavery left to be abolished by their vote. *They* will then be the only slaves. Only *his* vote can hasten the abolition of slavery who asserts his own freedom by his vote.

(D) The object of this Essay is to assert one very simple principle, as entitled to govern absolutely the dealings of society with the individual in the way of compulsion and control, whether the means used be physical force in the form of legal penalties, or the moral coercion of public opinion. That principle is, that the sole end for which mankind are warranted, individually or collectively, in interfering with the liberty of action of any of their number, is self-protection.

(E) Hereby it is manifest, that during the time men live without a common Power to keep them all in awe, they are in that condition which is called Warre; and such a warre, as is of every man, against every man.

Questions 80-82

The world is too much with us; late and soon,
Getting and spending, we lay waste our powers:
Little we see in Nature that is ours;
We have given our hearts away, a sordid boon!
This Sea that bares her bosom to the moon;   5
The winds that will be howling at all hours,
And are up-gathered now like sleeping flowers;
For this, for everything, we are out of tune;
It moves us not. – – Great God! I'd rather be
A Pagan suckled in a creed outworn;   10
So might I, standing on this pleasant lea,
Have glimpses that would make me less forlorn;
Have sight of Proteus rising from the sea;

Or hear old Triton blow his wreathed horn.

80. The author of the poem is

(A) Spenser   (D) Keats

(B) Milton   (E) Yeats

(C) Wordsworth

81. The poem can best be classified as

(A) Petrarchan   (D) pantheist

(B) Anti-Petrarchan   (E) satirical

(C) Deist

82. An understanding of the last two lines is helped most by the knowledge that

(A) the adjective "protean," meaning "variable," is derived from "Proteus."

(B) the prefix "tri-" means "three."

(C) the prefix "pro-" means "for."

(D) Proteus and Triton are seagods from classical mythology.

(E) Menelaus tells about an encounter with Proteus in Homer's *Odyssey*.

Questions 83-85

Let me not to the marriage of true minds
Admit impediments; love is not love
Which alters when it alteration finds,
Or bends with the remover to remove.
O, no, it is an ever-fixed mark   5
That looks on tempests and is never shaken;
It is the star to every wand'ring bark,
Whose worth's unknown, although his height be taken.

421

Love's not Time's fool, though rosy lips and cheeks
Within his bending sickle's compass come;   10
Love alters not with his brief hours and weeks,
But bears it out even to the edge of doom.
  If this be error and upon me proved,
  I never writ, nor no man ever loved.

83.   "Impediment" (line 2) refers to

   (A) a barrier or wall that channels water.

   (B) a military barricade.

   (C) a legal restriction.

   (D) encumbering baggage or equipment.

   (E) a speech obstruction, a stammer or stutter.

84.   "Mark" (line 5) refers to

   (A) a navigational beacon.

   (B) wrinkles or scars on the face.

   (C) writing.

   (D) a distinguishing trait or quality.

   (E) a rating, an assessment of merit or ability.

85.   The sonnet was written in the

   (A) 15th century   (D) 18th century

   (B) 16th century   (E) 19th century

   (C) 17th century

Questions 86-88 refer to the excerpts below

86. Which passage is by Jonathan Swift?

87. Which passage is by Dr. Samuel Johnson?

88. Which passage is by Laurence Sterne?

(A) I would not give a groat for that man's knowledge in pencraft who does not understand this, – – That the best plain narrative in the world, tacked very close to the last spirited apostrophe to my uncle Toby, – – would have felt both cold and vapid upon the reader's palate; – – therefore I forthwith put an end to the chapter, – – though I was in the middle of my story.

(B) We shall conclude this chapter by a melancholy truth which obtrudes itself on the reluctant mind; that even admitting, without hesitation or inquiry, all that history has recorded or devotion has feigned on the subject of martyrdoms, it must still be acknowledged that the Christians, in the course of their intestine dissensions, have inflicted far greater severities on each other than they had experienced from the zeal of infidels.

(C) Thus fell Jonathan Wild the GREAT, by a death as glorious as his life had been, and which was so truly agreeable to it that the latter must have been deplorably maimed and imperfect without the former; a death which hath been alone wanting to complete the characters of several ancient and modern heroes, whose histories would then have been read with much greater pleasure by the wisest in all ages.

(D) The other, was a Scheme for entirely abolishing all Words whatsoever: And this was urged as a great Advantage in Point of Health as well as Brevity. For, it is plain, that every Word we speak is in some Degree a Diminuition of our Lungs by Corrosion; and consequently contributes to the shortening of our Lives. An Expedient was therefore offered, that since Words are only Names for Things, it would be more convenient for all Men to carry about them, such Things as were necessary to express the particular Business they are to discourse on.

(E) "The business of a poet," said Imlac, "is to examine not the individual but the species; to remark general properties and large appearances. He does not number the streaks of the tulip, or describe the different shades in the verdure of the forest. He is to exhibit in his portraits of nature such prominent and striking features as recall the original to every mind; and must neglect the minuter discriminations, which one may have remarked and another have neglected, for those characteristics which are alike obvious to viligance and carelessness."

Questions 89-91

89.   "My love for Heathcliff resembles the eternal rocks beneath – – a source of little visible delight, but necessary. Nelly, I *am* Heathcliff. . ."

90.   "I am Madam Bovary."

91.   They reckon ill who leave me out;
        When me they fly, I am the wings;

Identify the speaking voice in each of the above passages:

(A) Gustave Flaubert   (D) Anna Karenina

(B) Catherine Earnshaw   (E) Antoine de St.-Exupery

(C) Brahma

Questions 92-94

THE WINDHOVER
        TO CHRIST OUR LORD
I caught this morning morning's minion, king-
    dom of daylight's dauphin, dapple-dawn-drawn Falcon, in his riding
    Of the rolling level underneath him steady air, and striding
High there, how he rung upon the rein of a wimpling wing
In his ecstasy! then off, off forth on swing,   5

424

As a skate's heel sweeps smooth on a bow-bend: the hurl and gliding
  Rebuffed the big wind. My heart in hiding
Stirred for a bird, – – the achieve of, the mastery of the thing!

Brute beauty and valour and act, oh, air, pride, plume, here
  Buckle! AND the fire that breaks from thee then, a billion   10
Times told lovelier, more dangerous, O my chevalier!

  No wonder of it: sheer plod makes plough down sillion
Shine, and blue-bleak embers, ah my dear,
  Fall, gall themselves, and gash gold-vermillion.

92.   The central comparison unifying the poem as a whole is

       (A) between the falcon and a skate's heel in line six.

       (B) between the falcon and the shining earth of a ploughed
            field.

       (C) between the intense beauty of nature and the even more
            intense beauty of God.

       (D) between the soaring falcon and the poet's heart in line
            seven.

       (E) between the outer world of nature and the inner world of
            the poet's imagination.

93.   Throughout the poem, the poet makes ample use of

       (A) allusions to classical mythology

       (B) verbal irony

       (C) personification

       (D) alliteration

       (E) puns

94.   The tone of the poem could best be characterized as

(A) ecstatic   (D) witty

(B) sarcastic   (E) reticent

(C) melancholy

Questions 95-97

Which of the following novels could best be described as

95.   epistolary?

96.   stream of consciousness?

97.   picaresque?

    (A) Cervantes' *Don Quixote*

    (B) Richardson's *Pamela*

    (C) Dickens' *Great Expectations*

    (D) Joyce's *Ulysses*

    (E) Steinbeck's *Of Mice and Men*

Questions 98-100

Which of the following plays is an example of

98.   Restoration Comedy?

99.   Elizabethan Tragedy?

100.   Theater of the Absurd?

    (A) Congreve's *The Way of the World*

    (B) Goldsmith's *She Stoops to Conquer*

    (C) Marlowe's *Doctor Faustus*

    (D) Beckett's *Waiting for Godot*

    (E) Shaw's *Major Barbara*

101. Human sacrifice is a theme in

(A) *Oedipus Rex* by Sophocles

(B) *Antigone* by Sophocles

(C) *The Eumenides* by Aeschylus

(D) *Iphigenia in Aulis* by Euripides

(E) *The Dead* by James Joyce

Questions 102-104 refer to the following poems.

102. Which one is about the author's childhood?

103. Which one expresses a philosophy that might best be classified as Deist?

104. Which one contains the lines:

Oh! lift me as a wave, a leaf, a cloud!
I fall upon the thorns of life! I bleed!

(A) *The Second Coming*

(B) *Ode to the West Wind*

(C) *Fern Hill*

(D) *An Essay on Man*

(E) *Il Penseroso*

Questions 105-107 refer to the scenes described below.

105. Which is the setting for O'Neill's *The Iceman Cometh*?

106. Which is the setting for Williams' *The Glass Menagerie*?

107. Which is the setting for Miller's *The Crucible*?

(A) A bus station

(B) A bar room

(C) A Mississippi plantation

(D) Salem, Massachusetts

(E) An apartment in St. Louis

Questions 108-110 refer to the passages below.

108. Which speaker is Desdemona?

109. Which speaker is Juliet?

110. Which speaker is Cordelia?

(A)   O, these men, these men!
Dost thou in conscience think, – – tell me, Emilia, – –
That there be women do abuse their husbands
In such gross kind?

(B) Unhappy that I am, I cannot heave
My heart into my mouth: I love your majesty
According to my bond; nor more nor less.

(C)   I have given suck, and know
How tender 'tis to love the babe that milks me:
I would, while it was smiling in my face,
Have pluck'd my nipple from his boneless gums,
And dash'd the brains out, had I sworn as you
Have done to this.

(D) O, what a noble mind is here o'er-thrown!
The courtier's, soldier's, scholar's, eye, tongue, sword;
The expectancy and rose of the fair state,
The glass of fashion and the mould of form,
The observed of all observers, quite, quite down!

(E) Now, by Saint Peter's Church and Peter too,
He shall not make me there a joyful bride.
I wonder at this haste; that I must wed
Ere he, that should be husband, comes to woo.

Questions 111-113

Let observation, with extensive view,
Survey mankind, from China to Peru;
Remark each anxious toil, each eager strife,

And watch the busy scenes of crowded life;
Then say how hope and fear, desire and hate,   5
O'erspread with snares the clouded maze of fate,
Where wav'ring man, betrayed by vent'rous pride
To tread the dreary paths without a guide,
As treach'rous phantoms in the mist delude,
Shuns fancied ills, or chases airy good.   10
How rarely reason guides the stubborn choice,
Rules the bold hand, or prompts the suppliant voice;
How nations sink, by darling schemes oppressed,
When vengeance listens to the fool's request.

       – from Dr. Samuel Johnson, *The Vanity of
Human Wishes*

111.   The passage above is from a poem that Johnson wrote as an
adaptation of a work by which of the following classical poets?

    (A) Ovid   (D) Juvenal

    (B) Virgil   (E) Homer

    (C) Horace

112.   Which of the following statements best summarizes the theme
that Johnson expresses in these fourteen lines?

    (A) Because human beings are governed by pride instead of
reason, they create many problems for themselves.

    (B) Placing too much faith in human reason leads to tragedy.

    (C) Most of the problems that humanity faces are the result of
archaic social institutions and outmoded customs.

    (D) In China and Peru, human progress is being held back by
religious superstition, while, by implication, England is
moving ahead economically because it is governed rationally.

    (E) Although there are many problems in the world, through
education and technological progress, we will be able to
find solutions for these problems.

113. The break in line ten between "ills," and "or" is referred to as

(A) enjambment   (D) ellipsis

(B) a troche   (E) a cesura

(C) elision

Questions 114-116

The scene harks back to the fabliaux in its superficial features, but it is more broadly meaningful than any scene in that literature. In the context of the *Prologue's* doctrinal material, we behold not only a magnificently natural creature in domestic squabble; she is also the embodiment of experience ripping out the pages of the book of authority, and of militant feminism fetching traditional masculine domination a healthy blow on the cheek. The symbolism of her position could not have been made secure without the naturalistic style whereby Chaucer creates and then protects it.

Charles Muscatine, *Chaucer and the French Tradition*

114. The character referred to above is

(A) Criseyde in *Troilus and Criseyde*

(B) Alisoun in *The Miller's Tale*

(C) Emelye in *The Knight's Tale*

(D) May in *The Merchant's Tale*

(E) *The Wife of Bath*

115. For an example of a fabliau that illustrates the point Muscatine makes in the first sentence, one might refer to

(A) *The Pardoner's Tale*

(B) *The Nun's Priest's Tale*

(C) *The Reeve's Tale*

(D) *The Monk's Tale*

(E) *The Knight's Tal*

116. The "doctrinal material" referred to in Muscatine's second sentence includes allusions to the writings of

   (A) St. Paul and St. Jerome

   (B) St. Thomas Aquinas

   (C) St. Anselm

   (D) Boethius

   (E) Aristotle and Plato

117. "Art for art's sake" best characterizes the esthetic philosophy of

   (A) Plato   (D) Alexander Pope

   (B) Oscar Wilde   (E) Horace

   (C) T.S. Eliot

118. The most rigorous defense of the unities of time, place and action is to be found in

   (A) Antonin Artaud's *The Theater and its Double*

   (B) Dr. Samuel Johnson's *Preface to Shakespeare*

   (C) Dryden's *An Essay of Dramatic Poesy*

   (D) T.S. Eliot's *Tradition and the Individual Talent*

   (E) Sir Philip Sidney's *The Defense of Poesy*

119. For a comprehensive definition of "archetype," one would best turn to the writings of

   (A) Plato   (D) Carl G. Jung

   (B) Aristotle   (E) Samuel Coleridge

   (C) T.S. Elliot

> So passeth, in the passing of a day,
> Of mortal life the leaf, the bud, the flower;
> No more doth flourish, after first decay,
> That erst was sought to deck both bed and bower
> Of many a lady and many a paramour: 5
> Gather therefore the rose, whilst yet is prime,
> For soon comes age, that will her pride deflower:
> Gather the rose of love, whilst yet is time,
> Whilst loving thou mayest loved be with equal crime.

120. The theme of the passage can be classified as

    (A) appearance and reality

    (B) *deus ex machina*

    (C) *in media res*

    (D) Platonic love

    (E) *carpe diem*

121. The versification in the final line can best be classified as:

    (A) iambic hexameter   (D) free verse

    (B) iambic pentameter   (E) alliterative verse

    (C) blank verse

Questions 122-124

> Thou, nature, art my goddess; to thy law
> My services are bound. Wherefore should I
> Stand in the plague of custom, and permit
> The curiosity of nations to deprive me,
> For that I am some twelve or fourteen moonshines   5
> Lag of a brother? Why bastard? wherefore base?
> When my dimensions are as well compact,

My mind as generous, and my shape as true,
As honest madam's issue? Why brand they us
With base? with baseness? bastardy? base, base?   10
Who, in the lusty stealth of nature, take
More composition and fierce quality
Than doth, within a dull, stale, tired bed,
Go to the creating a whole tribe of fops,
Got 'tween asleep and wake? Well, then,   15
Legitimate Edgar, I must have your land;

122.   The above passage, taken in context, is an example of

(A) a dramatic monologue by Robert Browning.

(B) an eclogue.

(C) the use of a persona in the Anglo-Saxon elegiac tradition.

(D) Elizabethan soliloquy

(E) a mock-epic invocation.

123.   The theme of the passage can best be paraphrased as

(A) illegitimate children are the responsibility of the society as
a whole and should be cared for by the state.

(B) it is perfectly acceptable for men to have adulturous affairs,
but not for women.

(C) the rights of inheritance are imposed by artificial and
unnatural customs.

(D) adultery and the consequent illegitimate offspring are
violations of the natural order of society.

(E) lechery is one of the consequences of humanity's alienation
from God.

124.   The speaker could best be classified as

(A) Machiavellian   (D) a personification

(B) an anti-hero   (E) the protagonist

(C) a foil

Questions 125-127 refer to the excerpts below.

125. In which passage does E.M. Forster discuss his writing?

126. In which passage does William Faulkner discuss his writing?

127. In which passage does George Bernard Shaw discuss his writing?

(A) Then, as a final act of restoration, I settled for a while at Chapala to work on a play called "The Poker Night," which later became "A Streetcar Named Desire." It is only in his work that an artist can find reality and satisfaction, for the actual world is less intense than the world of his invention and consequently his life, without recourse to violent disorder, does not seem very substantial. The right condition for his is that in which his work is not only convenient but unavoidable.

(B) It will now be proper to answer an obvious question, namely, Why, professing these opinions, have I written in verse? To this, in addition to such answer as is included in what has been already said, I reply, in the first place, Because, however I may have restricted myself, there is still left open to me what confessedly constitutes the most valuable object of all writing, whether in prose or verse — – the great and universal passions of men, the most general and interesting of their occupations, and the entire world of nature before me – – to supply endless combinations of forms and imagery.

(C) To get back to the Salvation Army with the knowledge that even the Salvationists themselves are not saved yet; that poverty is not blessed, but a most damnable sin; and that when General Booth chose Blood and Fire for the emblem of Salvation instead of the Cross, he was perhaps better inspired than he knew: such knowledge, for the daughter of Andrew Undershaft, will clearly lead to something hopefuller than distributing bread and treacle at the expense of Bodger.

(D) Sometimes technique charges in and takes command of the dream before the writer himself can get his hands on it. That is *tour de force* and the finished work is simply a matter of fitting bricks neatly together, since the writer knows probably every single word right to the end before he puts the first one down. This happened with *As I Lay Dying*. It was not easy. No honest work is. It was simple in that all the material was already at hand. It took me just about six weeks in the spare time from a twelve-hour-a-day job at manual labor. I simply imagined a group of people and subjected them to the simple universal natural catastrophes, which are flood and fire, with a simple natural motive to give direction to their progress.

(E) Place is more important than time in this matter. Let me tell you a little more about *A Passage to India*. I had a great deal of difficulty with the novel, and thought I would never finish it. I began it in 1912, and then came the war. I took it with me when I returned to India in 1921, but found what I had written wasn't India at all. It was like sticking a photograph on a picture. However, I couldn't *write* it when I was in India. When I got away, I could get on with it.

Questions 128-130

128. My love is lyke to yse, and I to fyre;
     how comes it then that this her cold so great
     is not dissolv'd through my so hot desyre,
     but harder growes the more I her intreat?

129. A dungeon horrible, on all sides round,
     As one great furnace flamed; yet from those flames
     No light; but rather darkness visible
     Served only to discover sights of woe, . . .

130. "Doth God exact day labor, light denied?"
     I fondly ask; but Patience, to prevent
     That murmur, soon replies: "God doth not need
     Either man's work or his own gifts; who best
     Bear his mild yoke, they serve him best. . ."

Each of the above passages illustrates which of the following:

(A) oxymoron

(D) non sequitur

(B) synesthesia

(E) personification

(C) antithesis

131. My mistress' eyes are nothing like the sun;
coral is far more red than her lips' red;
If snow be white, why then her breasts are dun;
If hairs be wires, black wires grow on her head.

This passage could best be classified as

(A) Petrarchan

(D) mock epic

(B) Anti-Petrarchan

(E) surreal

(C) Romantic

Questions 132-134

132. All through the starlit night, with open eyes,
he pondered what he had heard about his father,
until at his bedside grey-eyed Athena
towered and said:
    "The brave thing now, Telemakhos,
would be to end this journey far from home..."

133. If in his study he hath so much care
To hang all old strange things, let his wife beware.

134. As when two rams, stirred with ambitious pride,
Fight for the rule of the rich fleeced flock,
their horned fronts so fierce on either side
Do meet, that with the terror of the shock
Astonied both, stand senseless as a block,
Forgetful of the hanging victory:
So stood these twain, ...

Each passage above provides an example of which of the following terms?

(A) epithalamion

(D) epilogue

(B) epithet

(E) epigram

(C) epic simile

Questions 135-137

135. pastoral elegy

136. dramatic monologue

137. mock epic

For each of the above classifications, choose the appropriate example:

(A) Pope's *The Rape of the Lock*

(B) Pope's *An Essay on Man*

(C) Browning's *My Last Duchess*

(D) Milton's *Lycidas*

(E) Milton's *Paradise Lost*

Questions 138-140

138. Break, break, break,
    On thy cold gray stones, O sea!
And I would that my tongue could utter
    The thoughts that arise in me.

139. Tyger! Tyger! burning bright
In the forests of the night,
What immortal hand or eye
Could frame thy fearful symmetry?

140. The brain is wider than the sky,
            For, put them side by side,
      The one the other will include
            With ease, and you beside.

      Identify the author of each quatrain.

      (A) Emily Dickinson   (D) William Blake

      (B) William Shakespeare   (E) Alfred, Lord Tennyson

      (C) John Dryden

141. The relationship between Orestes and Pylades is most nearly
      parallel to which of the following relationships?

      (A) Hal and Falstaff

      (B) Don Quixote and Sancho

      (C) Troilus and Pandarus

      (D) Hamlet and Horatio

      (E) Mr. Bloom and Stephan Dedalus

142. The Baroque is a style following the Renaissance, character-
      ized by content by intense religious experience, personal
      emotion, and expressiveness, and characterized in form by
      vitality, movement, and magnificence.

      Which of the following literary works would best illustrate the
      Baroque as defined above?

      (A) Chaucer's *The Canterbury Tales*

      (B) Ben Jonson's *Volpone*

      (C) Milton's *Paradise Lost*

      (D) Pope's *An Essay on Man*

      (E) Wordsworth's *The Prelude*

> Much have I travell'd in the realms of gold,
>   And many goodly states and kingdoms seen;
>   Round many western islands have I been
> Which bards in fealty to Apollo hold,
> Oft of one wide expanse had I been told   5
>   That deep-brow'd Homer ruled as his demesne;
>   Yet did I never breathe its pure serene
> Till I heard Chapman speak out loud and bold:
> Then felt I like some watcher of the skies
>   When a new planet swims into his ken;   10
> Or like stout Cortez when with eagle eyes
>   He star'd at the Pacific — — and all his men
> Look'd at each other with a wild surmise — —
>   Silent, upon a peak in Darien.

143.   The words "fealty" (line 4) and "demesne" (line 6) establish a metaphor derived from

(A) Ancient Greek city states.

(B) Plato's *Republic*.

(C) Aristotle's *Politics*.

(D) medieval feudalism

(E) Rousseau's *The Social Contract*.

144.   Apollo is referred to in line 4 because he is

(A) the sun god.

(B) the god of medicine.

(C) the god of poetry and music.

(D) the god of reason and order opposed, according to Nietzsche, to Diounysus, the god of wine and the irrational.

(E) the god who, in Homer's *Odyssey*, befriends the hero and helps him reach home.

145. In line 11, Keats apparently misidentifies the discoverer of the Pacific Ocean. An error of this sort is an example of

(A) the intentional fallacy.   (D) poetic justice.

(B) the pathetic fallacy.   (E) Romantic irony.

(C) poetic license.

Questions 146-148 refer to the following excerpts.

146. Which excerpt is by Robert Frost?

147. Which excerpt is by Jonathan Edwards?

148. Which excerpt is by Dr. Samuel Johnson?

(A) I found a dimpled spider, fat and white,

On a white heal-all, holding up a moth

Like a white piece of satin cloth – –

Assorted characters of death and blight. . .

(B) There is a spider, too, in the bathroom, of uncertain lineage, bulbous at the abdomen and drab, whose six-inch mess of web works, works somehow, works miraculously, to keep her alive and me amazed. The web is in a corner behind the toilet, connecting tile wall to tile wall. The house is new, the bathroom immaculate, save for the spider, her web, and the sixteen or so corpses she's tossed to the floor.

(C) The person of Pope is well known not to have been formed by the nices model. He has, in his account of the "Little Club," compared himself to a spider. . .

(D) The God that holds you over the pit of hell, much as one holds a spider, or some loathsome insect, over the fire, abhors you and is dreadfully provoked. . .

(E) Blasted with sighs, and surrounded with tears,
    Hither I come to seek the spring,
    And at mine eyes, and at mine ears,
Receive such balms as else cure everything;
    But oh, self-traitor, I do bring
The spider love, which transubstantiates all, . . .

149.　Altogether the scene was somewhat peculiar, at least to Captain Delano, nor, as he saw the two thus postured, could he resist the vagary, that in the black he saw a headsman, and in the white a man at the block. But this was one of those antic conceits, appearing and vanishing in a breath, from which, perhaps, the best regulated mind is not always free.

　　　　　　　　　　－－ Melville, *Benito Cereno*

As illustrated in the passage quoted above, Melville creates irony in *Benito Cereno* by using which of the following narrative techniques?

(A) Omniscient third-person narration.

(B) Limited third-person point of view.

(C) First person narration.

(D) Stream of consciousness.

(E) Allegorical personification.

150.　In the plan and cross section of Chartres cathedral the number 3 is all-pervasive. There are the triple entrance portals. The facade rises in three steps from the level of the doorways, through the intermediate story, to the rising towers intended to elevate the thoughts of the worshipers and direct their aspirations heavenward. In the interior there are the three corresponding levels, beginning with the nave arcade, the triforium gallery, and the windowed clerestory.

　　　　　　　　　　－－ William Fleming *Arts and Ideas*

Which of the following literary works exhibits a number symbolism in its structure most nearly similar to that described above in the architecture of Chartres cathedral?

(A) Dante's *Divine Comedy*

(B) Chaucer's *The Canterbury Tales*

(C) Milton's *Paradise Lost*

(D) *Beowulf*

(E) Boccaccio's *The Decameron*

Questions 151-152

TWO RIVERS

Thy summer voice, Musketaquit,
Repeats the music of the rain;
But sweeter rivers pulsing flit
Through thee, as thou through Concord Plain.

Thou in thy narrow banks are pent: 5
The stream I love unbounded goes
Through flood and sea and firmament;
Through light, through life, it forward flows.

I see the inundation sweet,
I hear the spending of the stream   10
Through years, through men, through Nature fleet,
Through love and thought, through power and dream.

Musketaquit, a goblin strong,
Of shard and flint makes jewels gay;
They lose their grief who hear his song,   15
And where he winds is the day of day.

So forth and brighter fares my stream, — —
Who drink it shall not thirst again;
No darkness stains its equal gleam,
And ages drop in it like rain.   20

151.   In the poem, the poet

(A) contrasts a minor, local river, now known as the Concord,
with a much larger river, probably the Mississippi.

(B) compares Nature and Art, and argues for the superiority of
the latter because the imagination is not restricted by
reality.

(C) contrasts the tawdry and materialistic present with a heroic past.

(D) contrasts a river of Nature with a mystical and spiritual river.

(E) contrasts a minor, local river, now known as the Concord, with a river from Greek mythology.

152. In the final quatrain, the poet uses which of the following?

(A) An allusion to a verse from the New Testament.

(B) Synesthesia.

(C) Irony.

(D) Satire.

(E) Double entendre.

153. The corrupt world is the final clue to the meaning of the Fool. He is not of tragic scope. He affirms the dignity of man neither as animal nor angelic reason. Nor has he the ennobling weakness of compassion. He remains a figure of pathos because he is so helpless— — helplessly immobilized by a handy-dandy of opposites neither of which he can choose. Nor will he admit of any third ground, the possibility that knavishness might not be an ultimate, that wisdom might be redeemable, that society might be capable of re-birth. He does not survive his own grim laughter, and disappears for that reason.

Danby, *The Fool and Handy-Dandy*.

The author of the above passage discusses a problem of interpretation in

(A) Chaucer's *The Miller's Tale*.

(B) Marlowe's *The Jew of Malta*.

(C) Jonson's *Volpone*.

(D) Shakespeare's *King Lear*.

(E) Webster's *The Duchess of Malfi*.

154. "Neo-classicism is characterized by clarity of statement, by objectivity, reason and tolerance in attitude, and by balance and symmetry in form."

Which of the following would best illustrate this definition?

(A) Blake's *Jerusalem*

(B) Pope's *An Essay on Criticism*

(C) Donne's *The Ecstasy*

(D) Smart's *A Song to David*

(E) Traherne's *Wonder*

155. By contrast, a Greek temple or even a Romanesque abbey is a completed whole, and in both the observer's eye eventually can come to rest. The appeal of the Gothic lies in the very restlessness that prevents this sense of completion. The observer is caught and swept up in the general stream of movement and from the initial impulse gets the desire to continue it. The completion, however, can only be in the imagination, since there were, in fact, no finished cathedrals.

William Fleming, *Arts and Ideas*

Which of the following literary works comes closest to illustrating the structural esthetic ascribed in the above passage to the Gothic cathedral?

(A) Dante's *The Divine Comedy*

(B) Chaucer's *The Canterbury Tales*

(C) Milton's *Paradise Lost*

(D) Boccaccio's *The Decameron*

(E) Shakespeare's *Hamlet*

Questions 156-158

156. In which of the following works is tuberculosis important?

157. In which of the following works is smallpox important?

158. In which of the following works is cancer important?

(A) Williams' *Cat on a Hot Tin Roof*.

(B) Mann's *The Magic Mountain*.

(C) Dickens' *Bleak House*.

(D) Sartre's *No Exit*.

(E) Kafka's *The Trial*.

Questions 159-160

Neither a borrower nor a lender be,
For loan oft loses both itself and friend,
And borrowing dulls th 'edge of husbandry.
This above all, to thine own self be true,
And it must follow as the night the day
Thou canst not then be false to any man.

159. What is happening in the above passage?

(A) Hamlet, at the conclusion of the play, is summing up the
significance of the tragedy, drawing a moral.

(B) Portia is lecturing Shylock in the trial scene.

(C) Polonius is giving advice to his son before Laertes returns
to France.

(D) Henry IV, shortly before his death, is giving advice to his
son, Prince Hal.

(E) Iago is giving hypocritical advice to Othello.

160. The versification in the above passage could best be classified as

(A) free verse   (D) terza rima

(B) blank verse   (E) heroic couplets

(C) alliterative verse

Questions 161-163

161. And I had done a hellish thing,
And it would work 'em woe:
For all averred, I had killed the bird
That made the breeze to blow.

162. Thou wast not born for death, immortal Bird!
No hungry generations tread thee down;
The voice I hear this passing night was heard
In ancient days by emperor and clown:

163. Hail to thee, blithe Spirit! – –
Bird thou never wert! – –
That from Heaven, or near it,
Pourest thy full heart
In profuse strains of unpremeditated art.

Identify the birds in the above passages:

(A) a nightingale.   (D) a raven.

(B) an eagle.   (E) a skylark.

(C) an albatross.

Questions 164-165

Some to conceit alone their taste confine,
And glitt'ring thoughts struck out at ev'ry line;
Pleased with a work where nothing's just or fit,
One glaring chaos and wild heap of wit.

Poets, like painters, thus unskilled to trace   5
The naked nature and the living grace,
With gold and jewels cover ev'ry part,
And hide with ornament their want of art.

164.   In the first line, "conceit" refers to

(A) pride   (D) abstraction

(B) narcissism   (E) metaphor

(C) hyperbole

165.   The poetry referred to in the above passage might best be
classified as

(A) mock heroic   (D) Victorian

(B) Romantic   (E) allegorical

(C) metaphysical

166.   "Others have assumed that since he was a rebel against the
monarchy of the Stuarts he must also have been a rebel against
the monarchy of God and secretly of the devil's party. At the
very least, there is felt to be a disquieting contrast between re-
publicanism for the earth and royalism for Heaven."

                                              - C.S. Lewis

The above passage refers to

(A) Milton's *Paradise Lost*

(B) Marlowe's *Doctor Faustus*

(C) Spenser's *The Faerie Queene*

(D) Shakespeare's *Richard II*

(E) Blake's *Jerusalem*

167. "The Reeve was a sclendre colerik man;"

The meaning of "colerik" in the above line is derived from

(A) medieval astrology.

(B) alchemy.

(C) the theory of the four humors.

(D) an allegorical interpretation of a Biblical passage.

(E) Plato's theory of the soul.

168. In The Divine Comedy, Dante is guided through Hell by

(A) St. Augustine (D) Ovid

(B) St. Jerome (E) Virgil

(C) Beatrice

Questions 169-171

169. Roland Barthes

170. Cleanth Brooks

171. Stanley Fish

Pair each of the above critics with the corresponding school of criticism with which they are associated.

(A) formalism

(B) reader-response criticism

(C) psychoanalytical criticism

(D) the New Criticism

(E) deconstruction

172. The measure is <u>English</u> Heroic Verse without Rime, as that of <u>Homer</u> in <u>Greek</u>, and of <u>Virgil</u> in <u>Latin</u>; Rime being no necessary Adjunct or true Ornament of Poem or good Verse, in longer Works especially, but the Invention of a barbarous Age, to set off wretched matter and lame Meter; grac't indeed since by the use of some famous modern Poets, carried away by Custom, but much to thir own vexation, hindrance, and constraint to express many things otherwise, and for the most part worse than else they would have exprest them.

In the above passage

(A) Milton defends his use of blank verse in *Paradise Lost*.

(B) Marlowe defends his use of blank verse in *Tamburlaine Part I*.

(C) Ezra Pound defends his use of free verse in *The Cantos*.

(D) John Dryden discusses his translation of Virgil's *Aeneid*.

(E) Edmund Spenser discusses versification in *The Faerie Queene*.

173. "One of those writers, of whom there are not a great many in any literature, who have discovered a new way of writing, valid not only for themselves but for others. I should place him. . . as one of those rare writers who have brought their language up to date."

– – T.S. Eliot

In the above passage Eliot is referring to

(A) Mark Twain   (D) Geoffrey Chaucer

(B) James Joyce   (E) Edmund Spenser

(C) William Shakespeare

Questions 174-175

Batter my heart, three-personed God; for you
As yet but knock, breathe, shine, and seek to mend;
That I may rise, and stand, o'erthrow me, and bend
Your force, to break, blow, burn, and make me new.

I, like an usurped town, to another due,   5
Labor to admit you, but Oh, to no end,
Reason your viceroy in me, me should defend,
But is captived, and proves weak or untrue.
Yet dearly I love you, and would be loved fain,   10
But am betrothed unto your enemy:
Divorce me, untie, or break that knot again,
Take me to you, imprison me, for I
Except you enthral me, never shall be free,
Nor ever chaste, except you ravish me.

174.   The best paraphrase of the second quatrain (lines 5-8) would
       be:

       (A) If I acted rationally, I would do what is right, but my mind
           is overpowered by evil motives.

       (B) I am in love with another woman, but I am not willing to
           admit it.

       (C) If the government were more rational in its policies,
           ordinary citizens wouldn't become traitors.

       (D) Religion is one of the principal causes of conflict in the
           world.

       (E) This town, London, is now controlled by the Puritans.

175.   The "enemy" in line 10 is

       (A) Satan.

       (B) Spain, a country with which England was at war.

       (C) the Anglican Church.

       (D) the poet's rival.

       (E) the poet's wife.

176. Since a prince must know how to use the character of beasts, he should pick for imitation the fox and the lion. As the lion cannot protect himself from traps, and the fox cannot defend himself from wolves, you have to be a fox in order to be wary of traps, and a lion to overawe the wolves. Those who try to live by the lion alone are badly mistaken. Thus a prince cannot and should not keep his word when to do so would go against his interest, or when the reasons that made him pledge it no longer apply. Doubtless if all men were good, this rule would be bad; but since they are a sad lot, and keep no faith with you, you in turn are under no obligation to keep it with them.

This text would serve most appropriately as a point of reference for

(A) Shakespeare's *Henry IV Part 2*

(B) Milton's *Paradise Lost*

(C) Chaucer's *Troilus and Criseyde*

(D) Wordsworth's *The Prelude*

(E) Joyce's *Ulysses*

Questions 177-179

177. Faulkner's *The Sound and the Fury*

178. Hemingway's *For Whom the Bell Tolls*

179. Huxley's *Brave New World*

The above titles are derived from lines from which of the following works?

(A) Donne's *Devotions*

(B) Shakespeare's *Macbeth*

(C) Bunyon's *Pilgrim's Progress*

(D) Milton's *Paradise Lost*

(E) Shakespeare's *The Tempest*

Questions 180-181

JANET WAKING

Beautifully Janet slept
Till it was deeply morning. She woke then
And thought about her dainty-feathered hen,
To see how it had kept.

One kiss she gave her mother.   5
Only a small one gave she to her daddy
Who would have kissed each curl of his shining baby;
No kiss at all for her brother.

"Old Chucky, old Chucky!" she cried,
Running across the world upon the grass   10
To Chucky's house, and listening. But alas,
Her Chucky had died.

It was a transmogrifying bee
Came droning down on Chucky's old bald head
And sat and put the poison. It scarcely bled,   15
But how exceedingly

And purply did the knot
Swell with the venom and communicate
Its rigor! Now the poor comb stood up straight
But Chucky did not.   20

So there was Janet
Kneeling on the wet grass, crying her brown hen
(Translated far beyond the daughters of men)
To rise and walk upon it.

And weeping fast as she had breath   25
Janet implored us, "Wake her from her sleep!"
And would not be instructed in how deep
Was the forgetful kingdom of death.

452

180. "Transmogrifying" (line 13) means

   (A) changing into a bizarre or fantastic form; rendering ridiculous.

   (B) changing from a material to a spiritual form

   (C) translating from one language to another.

   (D) reincarnating, changing from one form of life to another.

   (E) increasing in entropy, becoming more random.

181. In the context of the whole poem, the opening line implies

   (A) Janet had been up late the night before.

   (B) Janet should have been up and about earlier doing her chores and taking care of her pet.

   (C) Janet was an innocent child with no knowledge of death.

   (D) Janet was a spoiled, rich child who was allowed to sleep in.

   (E) The whole story may have been just a dream that Janet had.

182. Which of the following literary works was originally published in serial form?

   (A) Chaucer's *The Canterbury Tales*

   (B) Dickens' *David Copperfield*

   (C) Hemingway's *The Sun Also Rises*

   (D) Faulkner's *Light in August*

   (E) Pope's *The Rape of the Lock*

183. Which of the following poets reported seeing, as a child, a tree full of angels?

   (A) Geoffrey Chaucer   (D) William Blake

   (B) William Shakespeare   (E) William Wordsworth

   (C) John Milton

When my love swears that she is made of truth
I do believe her, though I know she lies,
That she might think me some untutored youth,
Unlearned in the world's false subtleties.
Thus vainly thinking that she thinks me young.   5
Although she knows my days are past the best,
Simply I credit her false-speaking tongue;
On both sides thus is simple truth suppressed.
But wherefore says she not she is unjust?
And wherefore say not I that I am old?   10
O, love's best habit is in seeming trust,
And age in love loves not to have years told.
    Therefore I lie with her and she with me,
    And in our faults by lies we flattered be.

184. An editor's footnote to line 13 reads: 13 *lie with* i.e. lie to (with *double entendre*). The footnote implies

(A) that line 13 contains a misprint and that "with" was probably originally "to."

(B) that the meaning of "lie with" has changed and that what the poet originally meant is closer to what we would mean today by "lie to."

(C) that the poet is using the phrase metaphorically, not literally.

(D) that "lie with" is a pun with intentional ambiguity.

(E) that the poet was being intentionally obscure.

185. In order for the rhythm of line 4 to be consistant with the metrical pattern in the rest of the poem

(A) "Unlearned" must be read as three syllables.

(B) the silent "e" at the end of "false" must be pronouned.

(C) "subtleties" must be pronounced as two syllables.

(D) "subtleties" must be pronounced as four syllables.

(E) the words "in the" must be counted as one unstressed syllable.

186. Which of the following features is essential in classifying this poem as a sonnet?

(A) It ends with a rhymed couplet.

(B) It is about erotic love.

(C) The first twelve lines are divided into four quatrains.

(D) The tone of the poem is witty and ironic.

(E) The poem has fourteen lines.

187. "What is honor? A word. What is that word honor? Air – – a trim reckoning! Who hath it? He that dies a Wednesday. Doth he feel it? No. Doth he hear it? No. 'Tis insensible then? Yea, to the dead. But will it not live with the living? No. Why? Detraction will not suffer it. Therefore I'll none of it. Honor is a mere scutcheon – – and so ends my catechism."

The philosophical position that Falstaff assumes in the above speech might best be classified as

(A) stoicism   (D) neo-Platonism

(B) the Donatist heresy (E) nominalism

(C) Calvinism

188. For a theory of tragedy as the "catharsis" of emotions, one should read:

(A) Sidney, *Defence of Poesie*

(B) Tolstoy, *What Is Art?*

(C) Aristotle, *Poetics*

(D) Freud, *The Psychopathology of Everyday Life*

(E) A.C. Bradley, *Shakespearean Tragedy*

189. In Jane Austen's *Sense and Sensibility*, "sense" refers to

(A) any one of the faculties of perception, sight, hearing, taste, smell, feeling, as the basis for empirical knowledge.

(B) sensuousness.

(C) sensuality.

(D) a practical reasonable regard for one's own self-interest.

(E) esthetic appreciation transcending moral conventions.

190. "Beauty is truth, truth beauty," – – that is all
  Ye know on earth, and all ye need to know."

Critics have disagreed as to exactly what "ye" refers to in the poem. Which of the following are possible solutions?

(A) Either the nightingale or the poet.

(B) Either the nightingale or humanity.

(C) Either the urn or humanity.

(D) Either the rose or the woman the poet loves

(E) Either the rose or humanity.

191. Which of the following is a satire of religious hypocrisy?

(A) Moliere's *Tartuffe*

(B) Jonson's *Volpone*

(C) Wycherley's *The Country Wife*

(D) Aristophanes' *The Clouds*

(E) Sheridan's *The Rivals*

192. Synge's *The Playboy of the Western World* is written in

    (A) Gaelic   (D) Welsh

    (B) Old English   (E) Erse

    (C) Irish English

193. Which of the following works was not written in the author's native language:

    (A) Dante's *Divine Comedy*

    (B) Conrad's *Lord Jim*

    (C) Dostoevsky's *Crime and Punishment*

    (D) Chaucer's *The Canterbury Tales*

    (E) Thackery's *Vanity Fair*

194. For a view of the human condition as totally absurd, one should read

    (A) Tolstoy   (D) Dante

    (B) Zola   (E) Virgil

    (C) Kafka

195. For examples of Romanticism, one should read

    (A) Milton   (D) Steinbeck

    (B) Moliere   (E) Beckett

    (C) Goethe

196. "... false wit chiefly consists in the resemblance and congruity sometimes of single letters, as in anagrams, chronograms, lipograms, and acrostics; sometimes of syllables, as in echoes and doggerel rhymes; sometimes of words, as in puns and quibbles; and sometimes of whole sentences or poems, cast into the figures of eggs, axes, or altars:..."

        -- Addison: (Wit: True, False, Mixed) *The Spectator*

One could illustrate Addison's last example from the poems of

(A) Edmund Spenser   (D) John Donne

(B) Robert Herrick   (E) William Shakespeare

(C) George Herbert

197. Which of the following could be classified as a Cavalier poet?

(A) Ben Jonson   (D) Richard Lovelace

(B) Geoffrey Chaucer   (E) John Dryden

(C) John Milton

198. Shakespeare's four plays, *Pericles*, *Cymbeline*, *The Winter's Tale*, and *The Tempest* are traditionally classified as

(A) tragedies   (D) satires

(B) comedies   (E) romances

(C) histories

199. Which of the following is an example of a masque?

(A) Ben Jonson's *Volpone*

(B) *Everyman*

(C) Milton's *Comus*

(D) Shakespeare's *As You Like It*

(E) Congreve's *The Way of the World*

200. "I am commencing an undertaking, hitherto without precedent, and which will never find an imitator. I desire to set before my fellows the likeness of a man in all the truth of nature, and that man myself."

The author is

(A) St. Augustine   (D) Pepys

(B) Cellini   (E) Freud

(C) Rousseau

201.   "... and then I asked him with my eyes to ask again yes and then
he asked me would I yes to say yes my mountain flower and first
I put my arms around him yes and drew him down to me so he
could feel my breasts all perfume yes and his heart going like
mad and yes I said yes I will Yes"

The speaker in the above passage is

(A) Emma Bovary   (D) Molly Bloom

(B) Anna Karenina   (E) Becky Sharp

(C) Catherine Earnshaw

202.   "A poem should not mean
            But be."

The idea expressed in these lines is typical of poetry that is
characterized as

(A) Elizabethan   (D) Victorian

(B) neo-classical   (E) Modern

(C) Romantic

203.   In Sheridan's *The School for Scandal*, "sentiment" refers to

(A) intense religious emotion.

(B) erotic love.

(C) esthetic refinement.

(D) a hypocritical statement of a moral platitude.

(E) appreciation of nature.

Questions 204-205

"I have been assured by a very knowing American of my acquaintance in London, that a young healthy child, well nursed, is, at a year old, a most delicious, nourishing, and wholesome food, whether stewed, roasted, baked, or boiled; and I make no doubt that it will equally serve in a fricasee or a ragout."

204.   The author of the above passage is

(A) Chaucer   (D) Wordsworth

(B) Milton   (E) Tennyson

(C) Swift

205.   The passage is an example of

(A) allegory   (D) litotes

(B) simile   (E) apostrophe

(C) irony

206.   O wad some Pow'r the giftie gie us
        To see oursels as others see us!

The above lines are written in

(A) Old English   (D) Gaelic

(B) Middle English   (E) Celtic

(C) Scottish English

207.   To find an example of a kenning, one should read

(A) *The Seafarer*   (D) *Gulliver's Travels*

(B) *King Lear*   (E) *Walden*

(C) *Samson Agonistes*

208. An alternation of heroic and comic scenes is typical of the drama of which of the following playwrights?

(A) Sophocles

(D) Dryden

(B) Racine

(E) Congreve

(C) Shakespeare

Questions 209-211

Although Shakespeare, Milton, and Chaucer are often listed as the greatest English poets, not everyone has considered them above reproach. From the list below of five poet-critics identify:

209. Which one considered Chaucer of lesser stature because he lacked "high seriousness"?

210. Which one said that Milton's *Paradise Lost* "is one of the books which the reader admires and lays down, and forgets to take up again. None ever wished it longer than it is"?

211. Which one said of *Hamlet* that "So far from being Shakespeare's masterpiece, the play is most certainly an artistic failure"?

(A) John Dryden

(D) Samuel Taylor Coleridge

(B) Dr. Samuel Johnson

(E) Matthew Arnold

(C) T. S. Eliot

212. Shakespeare wrote *Macbeth* in response to

(A) the ascension to the throne of England of James I.

(B) the death of Elizabeth I.

(C) the execution of Charles I.

(D) the defeat of the Spanish Armada.

(E) the execution of Mary, Queen of Scots.

Avenge O Lord thy slaughter'd Saints, whose bones
  Lie sacatter'd on the Alpin mountains cold,
  Ev'n them who kept thy truth so pure of old
  When all our Fathers worship't Stocks and Stones,
Forget not: in thy book record their groanes   5
  Who were thy Sheep and in their antient Fold
  Slayn by the bloody Piemontese that roll'd
  Mother with Infant down the Rocks. Their moans
The Vales redoubl'd to the Hills, and they
  To Heav'n. Their martyr'd blood and ashes sow
O're all th'Italian fields where still doth sway
The triple Tyrant: that from these may grow
  A hunder'd-fold, who having learnt thy way
  Early may fly the Babylonian wo.

213. The "slaughter'd saints" in line 1 are

   (A) Protestants massacred by Catholics

   (B) Catholics massacred by Protestants

   (C) Christians massacred by Moslems

   (D) Christians massacred by Romans

   (E) innocent civilians killed in the Napoleonic Wars

214. Lines 8-10, "Their moans/ The Vales redoubl'd to the Hills, and
      they/ To Heav'n," illustrates

   (A) irony   (D) enjambment

   (B) synesthesia   (E) sprung rhythm

   (C) litotes

My heart leaps up when I behold
   A rainbow in the sky:
So was it when my life began;
So is it now I am a man;
So be it when I shall grow old,   5
   Or let me die!
The Child is father of the Man;
And I could wish my days to be
Bound each to each by natural piety.

215.   The best paraphrase for line 7 ("The Child is father of the Man")
is

   (A) Children do not realize it, but they grow up to be parents
themselves and have to discipline their own children.

   (B) Parents have difficulty communicating with their children
because the children lack experience.

   (C) Children have difficulty communicating with their parents
because adults tend to be set in their ways.

   (D) The personality of the adult is determined by the experiences he or she had as a child.

   (E) The experiences of the child are determined by the adult
society in which he or she grows up.

216.   By "natural piety" (line 9) the poet means

   (A) the appreciation of nature.

   (B) the recognition of the rainbow as the biblical symbol of
God's covenant with Noah and his descendants.

   (C) the worship of God through the study of His Creation.

   (D) the belief that the universe is a mechanical device like a
clock, created by God but then allowed to run on its own
without further intervention.

   (E) the worship of gods and goddesses personifying natural
forces and phenomena.

217. "In 1773, ten years after he first saw Johnson and nearly ten after its foundation, he was somewhat grudgingly admitted, on Johnson's insistence, to the Literary Club. The reluctance of some of its members is understandable. Before the appearance of his great work, few people suspected his quality. It was also in 1773 that he guided Johnson on a three months' tour of Scotland and its Western Islands."

— — Hazelton Spencer, *et. al.*, *British Literature*, Vol. 1

The person referred to in the passage is

(A) Robert Burns

(D) James Boswell

(B) Edward Gibbon

(E) Thomas Gray

(C) Oliver Goldsmith

Questions 218-220 refer to the following excerpts.

218. Which passage was written by Ernest Hemingway?

219. Which passage was written by William Faulkner?

220. Which passage was written by James Joyce?

(A) It was as if the boy had already divined what his senses and intellect had not encompassed yet: that doomed wilderness whose edges were being constantly and punily gnawed at by men with plows and axes who feared it because it was wilderness, men myriad and nameless even to one another in the land where the old bear had earned a name, and through which ran not even a mortal beast but an anachronism indomitable and invincible out of the old wild life which the little puny humans swarmed and hacked at in a fury of abhorence and fear like pygmies about the ankles of a drowsing elephant; — — the older bear, solitary, indomitable, and alone; widowed childless and absolved of mortality — — old Priam reft of his old wife and outlived all his sons.

(B) The old man still had two drinks of water in the bottle and he used half of one after he had eaten the shrimps. The skiff was sailing well considering the handicaps and he steered with the tiller under his arm. He could see the fish and he had only to look at his hands and feel his back against the stern to know that his had truly happened and was not a dream. At one time when he was feeling so badly toward the end, he had thought perhaps it was a dream. Then when he had seen the fish come out of the water and hang motionless in the sky before he fell, he was sure there was some great strangeness and he could not believe it. Then he could not see well, although now he saw as well as ever.

(C) "This – yer Smiley had a mare – – the boys called her the fifteen-minute nag, but that was only in fun, you know, because of course she was faster than that – – and he used to win money on that horse, for all she was so slow and always had the asthma, or the distemper, or the con-sumption, or something of that kind. They used to give her two or three hundred yards' start, and then pass her under way; but always at the fag end of the race she'd get excited and desperate like, and come cavoting and strad-dling up, and scattering her legs around limber, some-times in the air, and sometimes out to one side among the fences, and kicking up m-o-r-e dust and raising m-o-r-e racket with her coughing and sneezing and blowing her nose — and always fetch up at the stand just about a neck ahead, as near as you could cipher it down.

(D) Nippers, the second on my list, was a whiskered, sallow, and, upon the whole, rather piratical-looking young man of about five and twenty. I always deemed him the victim of two evil powers – - ambition and indigestion. The am-bition was evinced by a certain impatience of the duties of a mere copyist – –an unwarrantable usurpation of strictly professional affairs, such as the original draw-ing up of legal documents. The indigestion seemed beto-kened in an occasional nervous testiness and grinning ir-ritability, causing the teeth to audibly grind together over mistakes committed in copying; unnecessary maledictions, hissed, rather than spoken, in the heat of business; and especially by a continual discontent with the height of the table where he worked.

(E) A few light taps upon the pane made him turn to the window. It had begun to snow again. He watched sleepily the flakes, silver and dark, falling obliquely against the lamplight. The time had come for him to set out on his journey westward. Yes, the newspapers were right: snow was general all over Ireland.It was falling on every part of the dark central plain, on the treeless hills, falling upon the bog of Allen and, farther westward, softly falling into the dark mutinous Shannon waves. It was falling, too, upon every part of the lonely churchyard on the hill where Michael Furey lay buried. It lay thickly drifted on the crooked crosses and headstones, on the spears of the little gate, on the barren thorns. His soul swooned slowly as he heard the snow falling faintly through the universe and fainly falling, like the descent of their last end, upon all the living and the dead.

221. Which of the following works could best be characterized as existentialist?

(A) Tolstoy's *War and Peace*

(B) Milton's *Paradise Lost*

(C) Sartre's *No Exit*

(D) Dante's *The Divine Comedy*

(E) Marlow's *Doctor Faustus*

222. Which of the following works would be an example of the alliterative revival?

(A) *Pearl*

(B) *The Faerie Queene*

(C) *The Duchess of Malfi*

(D) *Lycidas*

(E) *The Country Wife*

Questions 223 - 224

> If it were done when'tis done, then 'twere well
> It was done quickly: if the assassination
> Could trammel up the consequence, and catch
> With his surcease success; that but this blow
> Might be the be-all and the end-all here,   5
> We'd jump the life to come.

223. The author of the above lines is

(A) Chaucer

(B) Spenser

(C) Shakespeare

(D) Milton

(E) Wordsworth

224. In the above context, "success" (line 4) means

(A) victory

(B) wealth

(C) fame

(D) the act or process of becoming entitled as a legal beneficiary to the property of a deceased person

(E) any result or outcome

225. "Better to reign in hell, than serve in heav'n."
The above line summarizes the point of view of

(A) John Milton

(B) Satan in Milton's *Paradise Lost*

(C) Dr. Faustus in Marlow's *Dr. Faustus*

(D) Machiavelli

(E) Othello in Shakespeare's *Othello*

Questions 226 - 227

The Sea of Faith
Was once, too, at the full, and round earth's shore
Lay like folds of a bright girdle furled.
But now I only hear
Its melancholy, long, withdrawing roar,   5
Retreating, to the breath
Of the night-wind, down the vast edges drear
And naked shingles of the world.

226. The author of the above lines is

(A) Arnold

(B) Hopkins

(C) Keats

(D) Blake

(E) Dryden

227. The author compares a withdrawing wave of the ocean to

(A) a general loss of religious faith.

(B) his personal loss of religious faith.

(C) a loss of trust between himself and someone he loves.

(D) a loss of self-confidence, of faith in himself.

(E) a general decrease in patriotism.

Questions 228 - 230

228. Quoth the Raven, "Nevermore."

229. For the rain it raineth every day.

230. That all the woods may answer and your echo ring!

Identify the authors of the above refrains.

(A) William Wordsworth

(B) Edgar Allan Poe

(C) William Shakespeare

(D) Edmund Spenser

(E) Alfred Lord Tennyson

GRE LITERATURE IN ENGLISH
EXAM IV

ANSWER KEY

1.	C	39.	B	77.	D
2.	E	40.	A	78.	D
3.	D	41.	E	79.	C
4.	E	42.	E	80.	C
5.	A	43.	C	81.	D
6.	B	44.	A	82.	D
7.	B	45.	D	83.	C
8.	E	46.	B	84.	A
9.	C	47.	B	85.	B
10.	B	48.	A	86.	D
11.	A	49.	C	87.	E
12.	C	50.	D	88.	A
13.	E	51.	C	89.	B
14.	E	52.	C	90.	A
15.	E	53.	B	91.	C
16.	D	54.	E	92.	C
17.	C	55.	C	93.	D
18.	D	56.	E	94.	A
19.	B	57.	E	95.	B
20.	C	58.	B	96.	D
21.	C	59.	D	97.	A
22.	A	60.	A	98.	A
23.	E	61.	C	99.	C
24.	B	62.	B	100.	D
25.	B	63.	C	101.	D
26.	C	64.	D	102.	C
27.	C	65.	B	103.	D
28.	D	66.	D	104.	B
29.	E	67.	A	105.	B
30.	B	68.	B	106.	E
31.	E	69.	B	107.	D
32.	E	70.	D	108.	A
33.	B	71.	E	109.	E
34.	C	72.	A	110.	B
35.	D	73.	E	111.	D
36.	D	74.	C	112.	A
37.	B	75.	B	113.	E
38.	D	76.	A	114.	E

GRE LITERATURE IN ENGLISH TEST IV

115.	C	154.	B	193.	B
116.	A	155.	B	194.	C
117.	B	156.	B	195.	C
118.	C	157.	C	196.	C
119.	D	158.	A	197.	D
120.	E	159.	C	198.	E
121.	A	160.	B	199.	C
122.	D	161.	C	200.	C
123.	C	162.	A	201.	D
124.	A	163.	E	202.	E
125.	E	164.	E	203.	D
126.	D	165.	C	204.	C
127.	C	166.	A	205.	C
128.	C	167.	C	206.	C
129.	A	168.	E	207.	A
130.	E	169.	E	208.	C
131.	B	170.	D	209.	E
132.	B	171.	B	210.	B
133.	E	172.	A	211.	C
134.	C	173.	A	212.	A
135.	D	174.	A	213.	A
136.	C	175.	A	214.	D
137.	A	176.	A	215.	D
138.	E	177.	B	216.	A
139.	D	178.	A	217.	D
140.	A	179.	E	218.	B
141.	D	180.	A	219.	A
142.	C	181.	C	220.	E
143.	D	182.	B	221.	C
144.	C	183.	D	222.	A
145.	C	184.	D	223.	C
146.	A	185.	A	224.	E
147.	D	186.	E	225.	B
148.	C	187.	E	226.	A
149.	B	188.	C	227.	A
150.	A	189.	D	228.	B
151.	D	190.	C	229.	C
152.	A	191.	A	230.	D
153.	D	192.	C		

GRE LITERATURE IN ENGLISH
TEST IV

DETAILED EXPLANATIONS
OF ANSWERS

1.   (C)

Auden's sytle is typically ironic. He delates the image of the poet, referring to him as "silly." This would be typical of modern poets in general. It might refer to Yeats's Irish patriotism, his Romanticism, and his ideas about history and mythology. Nevertheless, the silliness is "like us" in that, for Auden, this sense of the anti-heroic is something universally human. The poet achieves greatness in his art, in spite of himself, his ego, his fellow countrymen. Again, it is ironic that the insanity of Irish politics, "mad" Ireland, actually causes great art.

2.   (E)

Pound is establishing a relationship here in his own mind between the modern and the Romantic. He sees both an opposition and a connection between himself and Whitman. Whitman is the "pioneer" in Pound's metaphor, the Romantic 19th-century poet who broke new ground, writing in free verse, writing about everyday experiences, taking his images from the comtemporary world. Pound sees himself as the craftsman, taking this rough material and making works of art. Pound is thus also opposing the "classical" and the "Romantic."

3.   (D)

Dryden writes in an epigrammatic style typical of the neo-classicism of the late 16th and early 17th centuries. The lines are end-stopped, the meter is regular. Dryden writes in iambic pentameter with rhymed couplets. The style has the balance and symmetry of neo-classicism. The content is also neo-classical: the subject matter is art itself. The references are to Homer and Virgil, the great poets of classical Greece and Rome. That Dryden places Milton in their company shows his own tolerance and open-mindedness, since Milton has been a champion of the defeated Puritan cause. Even though Dryden wrote after the Restoration, he appreciated Milton's greatness. Answers (A) and (B) are Longfellow and Blake, respectively, on Chaucer.

4.   (E)

Southern is making a distinction here between the romance as the typical genre of the later Middle Ages and the epic as the typical genre of the Dark Ages. *The Knight's Tale* and *The Miller's Tale* would offer a contrast of romance with, not epic, but *fabliau* a genre that follows the romance and parodies it. Answer (B) would again contrast the fabliau, this time the stories of *The Decameron,* not with a romance, but with Dante's elaborate alleorical poem *The Divine Comedy.* Answer (C) compares two poems that are quite similar, both Anglo-Saxon elegiac poems from the Dark Ages. Answer (D) pairs again two very similar poems, both short middle English romances. Only answer (E) fits Southern's comparison. Only in answer (E) do we have an epic from the Dark Ages, *Beowulf,* and a romance from the later Middle Ages, *Sir Gawin and the Green Knight.* In *Beowulf* we have the celebration of endurance as the hero defeats Grendel and we have death in a hopeless cause when he is killed by the dragon. In contrast, Sir Gawain's quest to fulfill his pledge to the Green Knight is an example of the "seeking" and "journeying" for adventure and self-knowledge that is typical of the romance.

5.   (A)

Hardy is *The Return of the Native* constructs a tragic story based to a large extent on coincidental events. This stands in contrast to the plays by Shakespeare and O'Neill in which tragedy is determined more by character. It also stands in contrast with the novel by Steinbeck and the play by Ibsen in which tragedy is determined more by economic and social factors.

6.   (B)

The passage is from Spenser's letter to Raleigh, introducing *The Faerie Queene.* Although Arthur is not really a major character in any of the books of *The Faerie Queen,* he does appear in each book as a Christ-figure and personification of perfection. Each of the twelve virtues was to be the subject of a separate book, but Spenser never completed the project, leaving only the first six books, and some fragments. As for Malory's *Le Morte d'Arthur,* it is a more literal Arthurian romance with all of the usual knights and many, many episodes, but without the philosophical and allegorical content of Spenser's neo-Platonic work. White's 20th-century version is again focused directly on Arthur and tends to be typically modern in its emphasis on psychological development. Chaucer's *Knight's Tale* is not Arthurian at all, but is set in Ancient Greece. Chretien's *The Knight of The Cart* is a perfect example of medival romance, but it is primarily focused on the adventures of Lancelot, and like Marlory's work, it is not self-consciously allegorical and philosophical like Spencer.

7.   (B)
The phrase "cloister virtue" is from Milton's *Areopagitica* in which he argues against censorship because it deprives the public of the freedom and responsibility of choosing good over evil, a freedom that Milton felt to be necessary for true virtue. The notion of a "cloistered virtue" is thus, to Milton, a contradiction, since it implies ignorance of evil, and not the exercise of free choice. The essays by Mill and Rousseau are concerned with the rights of individuals and minorities in a democracy. Thoreau argues for disobeying immoral laws, even in a democracy. Aristotle establishes the basis of morality in moderation between evil extremes. Milton's argument and phrasing is characterized by its theological context.

8.   (E)
The vowel shift in the 15th-century changed stressed vowels upward and changed the highest vowels to diphthongs. This the diphthong in modern English "how" was pronounced by Chaucer like the high back vowel in modern English "who." In addition, the high front vowel in modern English, "be," was pronounced by Chaucer like the middle front vowel of modern English "bay.

9.   (C)
The character that Chaucer describes in this passage in the Monk. Medieval monks lived in cloisters, labored with their hands in raising their own food, and studied and copied theological and other texts. In contrast, the parson lived and worked among the people, the pardoner and friar travelled from place to place, and the clerk was a scholar who studied and wrote, but who would not have worked with his hands.

10.   (B)

The language of the text is 14th century Middle English, the English spoken during the later Middle Ages. Anglo-Saxon and Old English are the same thing, the form of English, essentially a dialect of Old Germanic, brought to Britain by the Anglo-Saxons and spoken in Britian during the Dark Ages from the Anglo-Saxon invasion until, roughly, the Norman Conquest. Elizabethan English is the form of Early Modern English spoken in England during the reign of Elizabeth I at the end of the 16th century.

11.   (A)

The object of the satire in the passage is the traditional topic of hypocrisy. Chaucer exposes the gap between what a monk is supposed to be, ideally, and what this monk actually is in practice. The passage is not intellectual, because Chaucer implies that the monk ought to be in the monastery studying. The passage is not anti-religious because in ridiculing hyprocrisy, Chaucer reaffirms traditional religious values. Chaucer wrote prior to the Reformation and, therefore, was not expressing an explicity Protestant view. As for Lollardism, Chaucer is not, at least in this passage, explicitly addressing the dispute concerning the publication of an English Bible or other issue of importance to Wycliff. The subject of the satire in this particular passage is more literary and traditional than that. It is part of a classical literary tradition satirizing hyprocrisy in general.

12.   (C)

A simile is an explicit comparision using the words "like" or "as." In this poem, "like a raisin," "like a sore," "like rotten meat," "like a syrupy sweet," and "like a heavy load," are all similes. This device is the organizing principle of the poem. Antithesis is the juxtaposition of opposites. Irony is meaning one thing while saying the opposite, as in "What a nice day!" when it is raining. Personification is a character representing an abstraction. Understatement is a form of emphasis that implies more by saying less, as in "He wasn't a bad fighter," for someone who defeats every opponent. None of these other rhetorical devices is used in the particular poem.

13. (E)

On the face of it, the poem might be about Freudian dream theory or adolescent frustration. There is no obvious way of determining what sort of dream is implied in the first line. There seems no particular reason, however, to read the poem as referring to pollution or nature or the transience of love. To read this as a statement about racism requires knowledge that the poet, Langston Hughes, is one of the foremost black poets of American literature and that Hughes often wrote on the topic of racism.

14. (E)

Iambic pentameter would require lines of ten syllables with alternating unstressed and stressed syllables. Blank verse would be iambic pentameter without rhyme. A ballad stanza would be a quatrain rhyming ABCB. Sprung rythm is a somewhat eccentric meter devised by Hopkins, basically iambic pentameter with numerous substitutions created longer and irregular lines. Since the poem has neither meter nor rhyme, it is best classified as free verse.

15. (E)

The iconography "goat-footed" suggests Pan, a Greek nature god. The cyclops were one-eyed monsters encountered by Odysseus. The Gorgons were women with snakes for hair. Looking at them turned the beholder to stone. Hermes, the messenger of the gods, more winged sandals. Eros was the Greek form of Cupid and is associated with a bow and arrow. The association in this poem of the balloonman with Pan suggests a spirit of Nature appropriate to the theme of seasonal rebirth.

16. (D)

An elegiac tone would express sorrow at the death of a loved one or with respect to some other profound loss. The emphasis would be on the transcience of worldly things. A sarcastic tone would be typical of satire. One might expect sarcasm if the poet were ridiculing politicians, pedants, quacks, hypocrites or other traditional targets of satire. A laudatory tone would be appropriate to a poem praising the deeds or virtues of exemplary individuals, those who have exhibited great courage in war or in other stressful situations. A devotional tone would be appropriate to a religious poem in which the poet expresses personal religious feeling or relates religious experiences. This poem is not theological or patriotic or satirical. It is not about death. The tone is rather playful, which is appropriate for a very positive statement about children and spring. It is thus best described as whimsical.

17.   (C)

The speaking voice of Mark Twain's hero, Huckleberry Finn, is characterized by colloquial diction and syntax. The themes of "good behavior," discipline and religion are also typical. Huck resists the civilizing influences of Miss Watson and the widow. The author implies that if Huck is to be influenced at all, it will be more through the positive and gentle approach of the widow than through the more rigid approach of Miss Watson. Through his own voice, Huck reveals himself to be a character of genuine and spontaneous virtue, a nature neither refined nor corrupted by civilization.

18.   (D)

David Balfour, the hero of Robert Louis Stevenson's *Kidnapped,* recounts early in the novel the attempt of his uncle to murder him. The avaricious uncle wants the estate for himself and tries to do away with his nephew. The winding stairway leading to nothingness is a vivid image of the danger, excitement and adventure encountered by young Balfour in the course of the novel. He survives, of course, to claim his rightful inheritance, but not before additional dangerous episodes.

19.   (B)

Benjy is the idiot brother in William Faulkner's *The Sound and the Fury*. The first part of the novel is told from his point of view. This accounts for the extremely concrete descriptions. Benjy is incapable of any abstract formulations and makes no connections whatsoever. He is very fond of the old pasture which has been sold off for a golf course. In the excerpt, he is staring through the fence at people playing golf. He describes what he sees without apparently understanding what it means.

Excerpt (A) is from the conclusion of Hemingway's *The Sun Also Rises*. The "I" character, Jake, is a somewhat cynical American who works as a newspaper correspondent in Europe. Neither Huck, David, nor Benjy is an adult; none of them would take a taxi with a girl friend named Brett. Excerpt (E) is the opening of Marcel Proust's *Remembrance of Things Past*. The relatively long sentences are typical of Proust's style. The intense preoccupation with the details of the speaker's mental states is typical of the novel throughout. Neither David, Huck, nor Benjy are so completely introspective.

20.   (C)

Both Beowulf and Sir Gawain are characters in major medieval works. Beowulf fights Grendel, Grendel's mother, and a dragon. Sir Gawain seeks the Green Knight in order to fulfill a bargain with him. Neither Beowulf nor Gawain are known for their singing. Chaucer and Dante are major medieval authors. Dante wrote *The Divine Comedy*, Chaucer *The Canterbury Tales*. Again, neither was inspired to sing. The Answer is Caedmon.

21.   (C)

Although Bede wrote in Latin, the spoken language at the time was Anglo-Saxon. This was the language in which Caedmon composed his hymns. Hebrew would be the language of the Old Testament, but even that text would be known not in Hebrew, but in St. Jerome's Latin translation. Middle English was not spoken in England until after the Norman Conquest (1066) and Anglo-Norman was the dialect of medieval French Spoken in England by the Norman aristocracy.

22.   (A)

Like other early Germanic and Anglo-Saxon poetry, Caedmon's hymn is alliterative. The tradition of iambic pentameter in English does not start until the late Middle Ages, for example, Chaucer's *The Canterbury Tales*. Ballad stanza is typical of the Scottish border ballads from the late medieval period. Free verse is characteristic of 20th century poetry, and heroic couplets are typical of 18th century poetry.

23.   (E)

Like *The Dream of the Rood*, and a number of other medieval works, the passage from Bede could be classified as a dream vision. Caedmon, after leaving the hall, falls asleep and is visited by an angel in a dream. When he wakes up, he returns and sings the songs as instructed by the angel. An epic simile is an extended comparison as found in Homer's *Iliad* and *Odyssey* and as imitated by Virgil in Latin or by Spenser or Milton in English. Comic relief might best be illustrated by the interlude scenes in Marlowe's *Doctor Faustus* or other Elizabethan drama, when lower class characters parody the activities of the heroic characters. Classical allusions are references to Greek and Roman mythology, characteristic of Reniassance literature. A mock epic is a work that imitates epic form while dealing with commonplace topics for humorous effect. An example would be Pope's *The Rape of the Lock*.

24.   (B)

The reference is to the burial of Polyneices by his sister, Antigone, an action that she undertakes in violation of Creon's edict in Sophocles' *Antigone*. Oedious was not buried, or more precisely the manner of his death in *Oedipus at Colonus* was a mystery. Antigone was not, in fact, executed by Creon, although the execution planned was one of entombment. She hung herself. Neither the sphinx nor the oracle in *Oedipus the King* refer to the burial of Polyneices or any other "light covering of dust."

25.   (B)

Kitto characterizes Drachman's reading of Sophocles as one that assumes that the dramatic events are meant to follow the natural laws of cause and effect without any supernatural intervention. "Finding inspiration in nature" would be a form of Romanticism as in the poetry of Worsdworth. Economic Determinism refers to the ideas of Karl Marx that economic circumstances, particularly the modes of production and the conflicts of classes, determine all social relationships and intellectual positions. "An accurate representation of human nature," would depend on one's assumptions about human nature. It would be based on some theory of psychology (Plato's theory of the soul, Freud's theory of the unconscious). Finally, pantheism is the worship of nature and could either refer to Romanticism again or else could refer to the worship of gods that personify natural forces as in Greek and Roman mythology. "Naturalism" as used by Kitto is associated with late 19th-century literature. It follows Realism and precedes Modernism. It is characterized by the assumption that literature should present an objective and "scientific" analysis of human experience.

26.   (C)
The Second Mrs. Tanqueray is a play by Pinero about a woman who, after being a mistress for several upper-class gentlemen, tries to gain acceptance and respectability through marriage, but is driven to suicide by social prejudice. Shaw's *Mrs. Warren's Profession* was in part a response to this play, implying that Pinero's treatment of the subject was melodramatic and sentimental. *Mrs. Warren's Profession* is a comedy about prostituion that deals with the topic from a Marxist point of view, and does so with wit and satire. *The Rivals* is a comedy by the late 18th-century playwright, Richard Sheridan. Like other comedies of the period, it is witty, satirical, and it reconciles individual love with aristocratic and family duty. *The Three Sisters* and *Hedda Gabler* are tragic dramas by Chekov and Ibsen, respectively. They are examples of early modern drama. They emphasize psychological analysis of characterization and the importance of social and economic context.

27.   (C)
This poem by Ezra Pound is a parody of a poem by W.B. Yeats entitled *The Lake Isle of Innisfree*. In his poem, Yeats remembers a little island in a lake near where he grew up and his dream of living there in a little cottage in imitation of Thoreau in *Walden*.

28.   (D)
In his parody of Yeats, Pound substitutes an urban and middle class setting, a tobacco shop, for the island. He implies that Yeat's desire to run off to an island is a form of escapism. From Pound's point of view, poetry is not to be found by escaping into nature. Instead, it is a craft, an art, requiring hard work and discipline. In comparison, running a tobacco shop seems like an escape. The emphasis on art as craft rather than inspiration, the references to art as the subject matter, and the invocation of classical gods and goddesses are all features of Pound's classicism. In making fun of Yeats' desire to escape into nature, Pound is anti-Romantic.

29.   (E)

The passage is from Milton's *On Education*. It is characteristic of Milton in that it provides a theological basis for his ideas about education. Humanity is alienated from God and it is the aim of education to direct humanity back to God. Although St. Augustine and More would share similar views, their works are not specifically about education. Mill addresses the limits on social control of individual freedom. His views are not theological and are not directly related to education. Dewey writes about education, but not from a traditional theological viewpoint.

30.   (B)

The use of "ruin" in this context is characteristic of Milton's style. The Latin root means "fall" and Milton's phrase, "the ruins of our first parents" becomes the "fall" in a theological sense, alienation from God as a result of the eating of the apple in the Garden of Eden. Milton frequently uses English words derived from Latin with the Latin meaning adding a second, usually literal level to the text.

31.   (E)

Sir Willoughby, the vain young aristocrat, is the central character in Meredith's *The Egoist*.

32.   (E)

Whatever reputation imperial Rome might have had for degenerate sensuality, Cicero embodied the republican virtues of patriotism, stoicism and dedication to politics. In this context, however, the term "Ciceronian" refers to the neo-classical rhetorical traditions and thus empty rhetorical formulas used on formal occasions.

33.   (B)

The passage is satiric, in that it ridicules contemporary social behavior. Melodramatic would describe a plot with an exaggerated sense of seriousness. Lyric would describe a short poem expressing personal emotions. Mock epic would be satire of ordinary contemporary events in the form of a heroic epic. While this passage is also satire, it lacks the epic form that characterizes mock epic. Allegorical refers to a text in which there is a second level of symbolic meaning.

34.   (C)

The hero who seeks self-knowledge only to find that he has killed his own father and married his own mother is Oedipus. Lear and Hamlet are Shakesperian heroes. Lear divides his kingdom between two of his daughters, disowning the third, only to be rejected by the daughters he favored. Hamlet revenges the murder of his father. Everyman is the protagnonist of a medieval allegory about death. Orestes, the hero of a Greek trilogy by Aeschylus, revenges the murder of his father. Although all of these heroes may seek some form of self-knowledge, Oedipus blinds himself with his wife's pin.

35.   (D)

Sarcasm is a particular statement expressing ridicule with a tone of voice often implying irony. Depression is a particular state of mind. Oxymoron is a self-contradiction. Fate is the concept that the future is already determined. Although "irony" can have a variety of meanings, in this case the irony is referring to irony of plot, that is, reversal. The blinding is particularly ironic in that Oedipus, when at last he "sees" the truth, chooses not to see.

36.   (D)

The Pequod is Ahab's ship in which he pursues the white whale in Melville's Novel, *Moby Dick*.

37.   (B)

The family in *Long Day's Journey into Night* is based to a large extent on O'Neill's own family. There are many parallels: the father who was an actor, the tragic mother, the two brothers.

38.   (D)

O'Neill used the myth of Hippolytus as the basis for *Desire Under the Elms*. In the myth, Phaedra falls in love with her stepson, is rejected by him, accuses him of trying to seduce her and then commits suicide. Believing the false accusation, the husband, Theseus, curses his son, Hippolytus, resulting in the son's death. O'Neill modernized the story, placing it in rural New England in order to have classical tragedy in a modern colloquial form.

39.   (B)

These are the opening lines of Carl Sandburg's *Chicago*. He celebrates the modern city's energy, industry, productivity. It is a very positive statement about the city. He sees it as a center of life and creativity. The poem is full of the concrete imagery typical of modern poetry. Sandburg uses colloquial diction and free verse.

40.   (A)

This passage is from Pericles' funeral oration as represented in Thucydides' history of the Peloponnesian War. Pericles praises Athens and urges the Athenians to continue the fight to defend their city.

41.   (E)

The haiku is a Japanese verse form that cannot be exactly duplicated in English. However, the feature that is most consistently imitated in English translations of haiku and in original English poems classified as haiku, is the alternation of a syllabic meter: five, seven, five. Beyond that, the haiku also requires concrete nature imagery and simplicity of statement with a minimum of comment. The nature imagery usually implies a particular season. A reference to a particular direction is not required. The simile, an explicit comparison of convicts to lizards, is a feature typical of European poetry and not actually characteristic of the haiku. Alliteration is a principle of versification in medieval Germanic poetry. It is not essential to the haiku. Knight uses it effectively, but not systematically. The use of animals to satirize human behavior is a classical tradition, and perhaps a universal literary genre. It is not, however, characteristic of the haiku.

42.   (E)

The first comparison of fog to a cat is by Carl Sandburg. The poem is typical of Sandburg's free-verse style and of his celebration of urban imagery.

43.   (C)

The lines are from T.S. Eliot's The Lovesong of J. Alfred Prufrock. The scene sets the mood for Prufrock's journey out into the night to an evening party at which he would meet a woman he is in love with. Eliot uses repetition and occasional rhyme. The effect is psychological, an atmosphere of obscurity and uncertainty that coincides with Profrock's own inner insecurity.

44.   (A)

This is the opening passage of the novel *Bleak House* by Charles Dickens. The fog is a characteristic feature of London. The style of the passage is noteworthy because of its sentence fragments (especially the sequence of present participles), used to paint a scene, a visual and spatial world existing at the same time, seemingly in a timeless and unchanging state. The fog may function as a symbol of the general obscurity and obfuscation in society, especially in the legal profession, which is satirized in the novel.

45.   (D)

Of the novels listed, Lawrence's is the one in which characterization would most appropriately be considered from a psychological or Freudian point of view. In the other novels, characterization is defined largely in terms of moral choices made within a social or economic context. Lawrence is also concerned with the effect of the social and economic context of characters, but more than the authors, Lawrence considers unconscious psychological motivations. Lawrence is particularly interested in the repression of sexual energy and its consequences, a typical Freudian theme. Lawrence analyzes relations between male and female characters and between parent and child in terms of this repression.

46.   (B)

The phrase is from Tennyson's *In Memoriam A.H.H.* The phrase reflects the Victorian concern with a changing view of nature, particularly the effect of the writings of Charles Darwin. Nature is not a peaceful subject of contemplation as in the poetry of Wordsworth. On the other hand, although "tooth and claw" is a figure of speech, it is not a symbol as it might be in the poetry of Blake, Yeats or Eliot. Tennyson refers to the literal violence of nature.

47.   (B)

The repetitions and the use of the second person pronoun suggest the language of ordinary conversation. Thus, they are colloquial. They are questions of style, not grammar. They do not reflect one way or the other on literacy, the ability to read and write. Both literate and illiterate speakers use a colloquial style in conversation. They are not characteristic features of a particular dialect, either geographic, ethnic, or socio-economic. The author is affirming the ideas being expressed, not ridiculing them. Thus, there is no irony. They are not specifically for emphasis. The language suggests a conversation in which the economic conditions are being discussed.

48.   (A)

The passage refers to the economic depression of the 1930's during which farmers in Oklahoma and elsewhere lost their land and moved to California looking for work.

49.   (C)

The passage reveals the influence of Marx. Specifically, it implies economic determinism, that human behavior is the product of economic factors, and class conflict, that an individual's point of view depends on his place in the economic system. Thoreau was a liberal individualist and anti-slavery moralist. He was interested in economic factors mainly in so far as he could be as independent as possible from them. Rosseau believed that human nature was corrupted by civilization and was concerned with protecting the individual from the tyranny of the majority. He was not particularly concerned with economic factors. Freud developed the theory of the unconscious and was concerned with psychology, not economics. Mill was a 19th century liberal particularly concerned with the rights of the individual.

50.   (D)

The play, Molier's *Le Bourgeois Gentilhomme*, ridicules, from an aristocratic point of view, middle class aspirations, especially the middle class desire to become educated and acquire culture. The satire is directed in part at the middle class hero, M. Jourdain, but in large measure as well at the pedants, scholars and charaltans who take advantage of him.

51. (C)

The context is Malory's 15th century prose romance, *Le Morte D'Arthur*. The passage is from the description of the death of King Arthur near the end of the work. In context, then, it is a perfectly straightforward tragic and heroic passage from a medieval romance. It is not an example of irony because there is no gap between what is said and what is meant. It is not mock epic because it deals with an heroic past, not with everyday contemporary events. It is not estates satire because it does not ridicule representatives of various classes and professions. Finally, it is not a parody of medieval literature, but rather it is the genuine item.

52. (C)

This passage is from Conrad's *Lord Jim*. The quotes within quotes are typical of Conrad's narrative style, which often consists of stories within stories. Here, a secondary character, Stein, is presenting one of the central philosophical principles of the novel, summed up in a metaphor of surviving at sea by relaxing and floating rather than struggling.

53. (B)

This passage is from Melville's *Moby Dick*. Ahab is the whaling captain obsessed with hunting the white whale in order to get revenge for the loss of a leg. At this particular moment near the end of the novel, a harpoon has been thrown at Moby Dick and the line from the harpoon has pulled Ahab overboard.

54. (E)

This passage is from Crane's *The Open Boat*. These are the opening paragraphs of the story. Crane presents the situations as seen by the four men in the boat. Their ship has sunk and they are trying to reach shore. The restricted point of view places the reader in the boat.

Passage (A) is from Dana's *Two Years Before the Mast*, an autobiographical account of Dana's experience as a young man on board a merchant vessel sailing from Boston around Cape Horn to California in the 19th century. Dana was particularly concerned to document the working conditions of the ordinary seaman. Passage (D) is from

Swift's satirical work, *Gulliver's Travels*. The shipwrecked hero, Lemuel Gulliver, has just arrived in Lilliput, and while he was sleeping the Lilliputians have tethered his limbs and hair.

55.   (C)

The passage given is from Leibniz's *Monadology*. It sums up his belief that this world is "the best of all possible worlds." That view is expressly ridiculed in Voltaire's *Candide* in the character of Pangloss.

56.   (E)

In this passage, Auerbach discusses a feature of epic style: the tendency to identify every character, every object even, in terms of history, both its past history and its future destiny. The same stylistic feature can be found in the English epic *Beowulf*. As in the *Odyssey*, characters are introduced in terms of their family lineage. Digressions explain the origin of a sword of the destiny of a mead hall. As in the *Odyssey*, there is a continual opening up of the story and no attempt to create suspense by withholding information concerning the ultimate fate of anyone. In contrast, in *Sir Gawain and the Green Knight*, a romance from the 14th century, meaning is determined not by history, but by symbolism, by imbuing characters and objects with a special significance, symbolic colors like red and green, symbolic plants like the holly, symbolic images like the five-pointed star. In Chaucer's *Miller's Tale*, characters are described in terms of their nature, but not in terms of history. Meaning in the fabliau depends to a large extent on the implicit contrast with the serious romance genre, the juxtaposition with the *Knight's Tale*. In Spenser's Renaissance allegory, *The Faerie Queene*, symbolism becomes, if anything, more self-conscious, more complex. As for Shakespeare, although he often uses history for subject matter, the dramas have a classical balance of symbolism and realism. In none of these other works is there the continual insistence on history, the continual digression or epithet that ties each character and object into the web of time. This feature is characteristic of the epic.

57.   (E)

An anachronism is a reference to something out of place in history. The most obvious example of an anachronism is in the passage from

The Second Shepherds' Play. The shepherds are portrayed as if they lived, not in Palestine at the time of Christ, but as if they lived in medieval England. This may in part be attributed to a general lack of historicity in medieval literature. In addition, it shows the underlying assumption that events like the birth of Christ transcend time and are eternally present. In any case, the complaint about bad treatment at the hands of the aristocracy refers to contemporary rather than historical conditions.

58.   (B)
Since all of the passages are archaic by modern standards, it is difficult to recognize language that is purposefully archaic in terms of its own contemporary audience. This is, however, a stylistic feature of the poetry of Edmund Spenser. It is illustrated by the past participle "ycladd" in the second line of the first book of *The Faerie Queene*. The past participle prefix "y-" was no longer used in the 16th century. Spenser was accused by Ben Jonson of creating his own language in his attempts to imitate the language of the past.

59.   (D)
The imitation of geographical and ethnic dialects is in the conversation between the Irish, Welsh, and Scottish officers from Shakespeare's *Henry V*. Shakespeare uses dialect for comic effect, appealing to his English audience and ridiculing the non-English varieties of English.

60.   (A)
Auden is referring to the myth of Dadalus. In the myth, Dadalus and his son, Icarus, escape from Crete by attaching feathers to their arms with wax. With the feathers, they are able to fly. Not heeding his father's warning, Icarus flies too near the sun, the wax melts, and he falls into the sea and drowns. Joyce refers to the myth by naming the central character in his semi-autobiographical novel, Stephen Dedalus. Shaw's *Man and Superman* is based on the story of Don Juan. Shaw's *Pygmalion* uses the Greek myth of the sculptor whose work of art comes alive for the title. O'Neill's *Mourning Becomes Electra* is a modern adaptation of the *Oresteia*. Chaucer's *Knight's Tale* includes references to classical gods and goddesses. None of these works, however, refers to the myth of Dedalus.

61.   (C)

Auden uses examples of famous paintings to show how great artists portrayed heroic events. He finds that great artist juxtaposed tragic suffering with the indifference of the immediate context. In this case, the ploughman is busy with his work and is indifferent to the fate of Icarus. The point is not that the ploughman lacks education. It is his indifference, not his lack of knowledge, that determines his reaction. The image of Icarus falling from the sky may or may not be universal. In some respects, he does fit the pattern of the hero who reaches beyond human limitations. These are not, however, questions that concern Auden in this particular poem. Nor does he concern himself with the relative happiness of the ploughman in contrast to Icarus. The theme is the apparent insignificance of heroic action in its immediate context.

62.   (B)

The emphasis on spontaneity, emotion, and memory is typical of Romantic poets, especially Wordsworth. The whole process of re-membering a past emotion is well illustrated in his poem *I Wandered Lonely as a Cloud*. This passage is from Wordsworth's "Preface" to *Lyrical Ballads*.

63.   (C)

The sentence sums up the poetic philosophy of Sir Philip Sidney. It is from Sidney's *Defense of Poesy*. With the explicit reference to Aristotle and the implicit reference to Horace ("teach and delight"), the sentence shows the classical influence typical of the Renaissance. Sidney founds his argument on accepted and traditional authorities from Greek and Roman sources. The point of view is distinct from Wordsworth's also in its emphasis on didacticism and mimesis rather than on personal emotional expression.

64.   (D)

The statement is typically modern. Frost starts with the emphasis on personal emotion and in this we see a strong link with the Romantics of the 19th century. There is an analytical detachment, however, not typical of Romanticism. Emotional experience is discussed in psycho-logical, even biological, terms. It is also not an end in itself, but leads to an intellectual understanding, a "clarification." The significance of

this understanding is not insisted on, but rather deflated. It is not "great." It is at best "momentary." Frost places poetry within the larger context of physics: a world of entropy, of increasing randomness.

65.   (B)

This statement by John Keats is from his letters. As a Romantic poet, Keats responds favorably to the elements of Romanticism that he finds in Shakespeare, especially a tolerance of ambiguity. The approval of "mysteries" and the disapproval of "fact and reason" is typical of Romanticism and is in part a reaction against 18th century neo-classicism.

66.   (D)

The point of view is that of another 19th century Romantic, Charles Lamb. He prefers a Shakespeare of the imagination to an actual production of Shakespeare. The play that he imagines when he reads the text is always superior to any staged performance. This emphasis on the superiority of the imagination over physical reality is typical of Romanticism.

67.   (A)

Dr. Johnson's criticism of Shakespeare is that the plays lack a clear moral purpose. He objects to fictions in which evil triumphs and good goes unrewarded. This point of view is diametrically opposed to that of Keats. While Keats, the Romantic, celebrates the ambiguity in Shakespeare, Johnson, a typical 18th century neo-classicist, decries the lack of clear moral statement.

68.   (B)

At the end of his novel, Tolstoy appends a long essay, his "epilogue," in which he argues against the importance of individual action in historical events. He cites examples of generals who knew little or nothing of what was actually happening in the confusion of a battle. The argument is anti-Romantic in that it eliminates the contribution of the individual hero, the heroic personality. The argument also under-cuts the classical emphasis on aristocratic leadership. It is, in effect, an argument for historical determinism, for the importance of impersonal forces in shaping the course of history, forces beyond the control of the individual will.

69.   (B)

The term "courtly love" refers to the medieval tradition of a knight's worship of a lady, expressed in feudal and religious metaphors. A good example would be the relationship depicted in Chaucer's romance, *Troilus and Criseyde*. In *Beowulf*, women are not the object of worship or of literary cults. In Shakespeare's *Henry IV Part 2*, the focus is on the relationship between Hal and Falstaff, not courtly love, although there is some parody of romance in the scenes involving Falstaff and Doll Tearsheet. It is a minor element and the relationship is the opposite of "courtly." Milton's *Paradise Lost* deals with the relationship between the sexes before and after the fall. The approach is theological, but not medieval. Pope's *Rape of the Lock* ridicules the behavior of both sexes in contemporary society.

70.   (D)

Allegory is an extended metaphorical narrative with characters that are personifications. Spenser's work is allegorical throughout. Chaucer's *Reeve's Tale* is a fabliau, a short, humorous, "realistic" story about students tricking a miller and sleeping with his wife and daughter. The characters are not personifications and the narrative is not an extended metaphor. Shakespeare's *Richard II* uses metaphor and symbolism throughout but as figures of speech. The story itself is based on historical events. Milton's *Samson Agonistes* is based on the Biblical story of Samson, with parallels to Milton's own blindness. Wycherley's *The Country Wife* is a Restoration Comedy satirizing contemporary society. Although characters in the other works might be said to personify certain virtues and vices, only in *The Faerie Queene* is the narrative metaphorical throughout in a consistant and systematic fashion.

71.   (E)

Sonnet writing in England started in the Renaissance and continued through the first part of the 17th century. Both Donne and Milton wrote sonnets. The sonnet was associated with the densely metaphorical style of the Renaissance. After the Restoration, this style fell out of fashion and poets stopped writing sonnets. This hiatus lasted about 150 years until the Romantic period. Wordsworth and Keats wrote sonnets and the practice continued on into the first half of the 20th century. Both Robert Frost and Edna St. Vincent Millay wrote sonnets. Thus the poet who did *not* write sonnets was Alexander Pope, living in the eighteenth century when the form was out of fashion.

72.   (A)

The poem is a villanelle, The form is chacterized by having just two rhymes through nineteen lines, with three-line stanzas rhyming ABA throughout, and with the first and third lines of the first stanza repeated as refrains as the last lines of alternating stanzas and both lines repeated at the end of the last stanza. A sestina, in contrast, does not use rhyme. Instead it has six-line stanzas with the same six words ending each line in alternating order throughout the stanzas. An example would be Ezra Pound's *Sestina: Altaforte*. The sonnet is a fourteen-line rhymed lyric, usually in iambic pentameter, and consisting of two quatrains and a sestet, or three quatrains and a couplet. The rondeau and triolet are shorter forms with refrains and strict rhyme schemes.

73.   (E)

The idea that the good die peacefully is exactly the cliche that the poem contradicts. Fear of the unknown is the theme of Hamlet's "To be or not to be" soliloquy, but not of this poem which focuses on regrets about this life, not anxieties about the next. Stoic resignation is not the theme of the poem. If anything, the poet urges just the opposite: life never seems so valuable as when you face the possibility of losing it.

74.   (C)

Synecdoche and metonymy are forms of metaphor. Synecdoche uses the part for the whole ("All *hands* on deck") and metonymy uses something associated with the subject ("According to *the White House*,..."). Litotes means understatement and a simile is an explicit comparison. The rhetorical form in question, direct address of an imaginary or absent person, is referred to as apostrophe.

75.   (B)

The verse is iambic tetrameter. Each line consists of eight syllables alternating unstressed and stressed. Each pair of syllables constitutes a foot. The pattern on unstressed syllable followed by stressed syllable is an iamb. Since there are four of these in each line, it is iambic tetrameter. If there were ten syllables in each line, making five iambs, it would be iambic pentameter. If the poem had meter, but lacked rhyme, it would be blank verse. A line with twelve syllables, typically iambic hexameter, would be an Alexandrine. Alliterative poetry has varying number of syllables in each line, but typically has four stressed syllables with a repetition of the initial sound in the first three of these.

76. (A)

The stanza is from *A Valediction: Forbidding Mourning* by John Donne. The unusual and original comparison of the separated souls to beaten gold is typical of 17th century metaphysical poetry in general, and of Donne's poetry in particular. Chaucer writes in Middle English and typically in iambic pentameter and uses proverbs more than similes. He tends also to write narrative rather than lyric poetry. Ben Jonson, a contemporary of Donne's, wrote in a plainer, more straight-forward neo-classical style. Both Keats and Tennyson, as is typical of 19th century poets, use more nature imagery and focus more on evoking moods and feelings. This particular detachment, analyzing a psychological situation from a theological point of view, is particularly typical of Donne.

77. (D)

This is Mill's statement of his thesis in his essay *On Liberty*. As a 19th century liberal, Mill was particularly concerned with protecting the individual from the tyranny of the majority, especially with regard to behavior that is essentially harmless to others.

78. (E)

In this statement from *Leviathan*, Hobbes sums up his philosophy of human nature: that is essentially rapacious and requires the restraint of law to make it social.

79. (C)

This statement is from Thoreau's *On Civil Disobedience*. He is justifying civil disobedience in a democracy. He recognizes the opposing argument that, in a democracy, one perhaps should try to convince a majority to change an unjust law instead of going ahead and disobeying on one's own. Thoreau argues that one's own individual morality takes precedence over the virtue of the system.

Passage (A) is from Plato's *Republic*. It shows Plato's antipathy for democratic government. He sees it as an intermediate stage between oligarchy and despotism, and he views it as corresponding to a personality lacking in self-discipline. Passage (B) is from *The German Ideology* by Karl Marx and Frederick Engels. In the passage, Marx and

Engels express the view that freedom under capitalism is an illusion because individuals are controlled by economic, material constraints.

80.   (C)

The sonnet is by William Wordsworth. The other poets wrote sonnets, but not on this theme. Spenser wrote a sequence of Petrarchan love sonnets, the *Amoretti*. Like Petrarch's sonnets, they are addressed to a woman the poet is in love with, and they have the metaphors and other rhetorical features typical of Renaissance love poetry. Milton wrote a number of sonnets on personal and theological themes. He did not write about nature per se, which was in any case not an object of worship for Milton. He did use many classical allusions, but he never expresses nostalgia for Greek or Roman mythology. Keats would be the closest to Wordsworth in style and outlook, and he also used nature imagery profusely, but he often wrote about art as well: the Elgin marbles, reading Homer in translation, dreaming about the poems he would like to write himself. Yeats started as a Romantic lyricist, but in his mature style became more of a symbolist.

81.   (D)

In so far as the poem expresses a worship of nature, or at least a nostalgia for the worship of nature, it could be classified as pantheist. A Petrarchan poem would be, for example, a typical Renaissance sonnet imitating the style of Petrarch. An Anti-Petrarchan poem would be one that parodied the Petrarchan style. A deist poem would be one like Pope's *An Essay on Man* expressing a belief in God, but rejecting or ignoring other theological notions such as the fall, the trinity, the redemption. A satirical poem would be one ridiculing contemporary society. Wordsworth does criticize contemporary society, but with a serious, even somewhat desperate tone. It is not the playful or bitter ridicule of satire.

82.   (D)

The important point in the last two lines is that Proteus and Triton are sea gods. Wordsworth conjectures that a pantheist religion would make possible a more intense enjoyment of nature. The modern meaning of "protean" (variable) derives from the ability of the sea god, Proteus, to change shape. This is illustrated in the account Menelaus tells Telemachos of his encounter with Proteus. Wordsworth is not concerned here with the modern meaning of "protean", the episode from the *Odyssey* or with the meanings of the prefixes "pro" and "tri".

83.   (C)

In the first two lines, Shakespeare uses a phrase from the marriage service. In this context "impediments" refers to legal restrictions that might keep the marriage from taking place, such as, for example, a previous marriage that is still in effect. The word "impediment" can have other meanings, (a barrier, a barricade, a stammer) but none of these are relevant to this poem. The meaning here is determined by the metaphor ("marriage of true minds") and the reference to the marriage service.

84.   (A)

In this context, "mark" refers to a manmade aid to navigation. A typical example form the Elizabethan period would be a pile of stones onshore by which one could determine one's position at sea. Although "mark" could have numerous other meanings, the navigational metaphor is continued throughout the quatrain.

85.   (B)

Shakespeare wrote his sonnets in the 1590's. Thus, they are dated at the end of the 16th century. The 15th century is still for the most part the Middle Ages in England. Shakespeare was not born yet and no one was writing sonnets in English. Shakespeare lived on into the 17th century and continued to write plays, but not sonnets. During the 18th century, the neoclassical period, sonnet writing went out of style altogether. The Romantic poets of the 19th century wrote sonnets but they tended to write about nature and they did not use the complicated metaphors characteristic of Renaissance poetry.

86.   (D)

The passage is from Part III of Swift's *Gulliver's Travels*: "A Voyage to Laputa, etc." Swift is here satirizing philosophical views about language, particularly nominalism, the view that abstract ideas are mere words. He inverts this in the notion that words are merely the names of material objects.

87.   (E)
  The passage is from Dr. Johnson's *The History of Rasselas, Prince of Abyssinia*. Johnson expresses the neo-classical credo that art should express general truths, not the individual or particular experience.

88.   (A)
  Uncle Toby is a major character in Sterne's *Tristram Shandy*. The passage also illustrates salient features of Sterne's style: his digressions and the self-conscious address of the reader by the author concerning the writing of the novel. The author presents himself as being in the process of creating the novel.

  Passage (B) is from Edward Gibbon's *The History of the Decline and Fall of the Roman Empire*. Gibbon here reflects with typical detachment on the irony of history, particularly the history of religion. In this instance, he sees irony in the fact that more Christians were killed by fellow-Christians than by non-Christians. Passage (C) is from Henry Field's *Jonathan Wild*. The author comments on the appropriateness of the hero's demise, and on the endings of plots and lives generally. The implication is that many so-called heroes deserved to be hanged.

89.   (B)
  The speaker is Catherine Earnshaw in Emily Bronte's *Wuthering Heights*. The subject matter of the novel is the obsessive love between Catherine and Heathcliff.

90.   (A)
  The speaker is Flaubert. Asked who he had modeled the heroine of his novel *Madame Bovary* on, Flaubert replied, "Madame Bovary? C'est moi." (I am Madame Bovary.) The author suggests, in effect, that he draws on his own experiences, his own feelings, his own personality, to create his characters.

91.   (C)
  The speaker is Brahma in Ralph Waldo Emerson's poem, *Brahma*. Brahma is the supreme spirit in Hindu theology. Emerson is reaching beyond the limits of the traditional religious beliefs of his own culture. To do this, he finds significance in the philosphy and mythology of oriental religions.

92.   (C)

The central comparison organizing the poem as a whole is between the beauty of nature, illustrated by the falcon and by the ploughed field, and the even greater beauty of God, referred to as "my chevalier," in line eleven. The identity of "my chevalier" is given in the dedication after the title: "To Christ Our Lord." There is a comparison between the falcon and a skate in line six, but this does not unify the poem as a whole. The poet does not compare the falcon with the shining earth, but merely gives the image of the ploughed earth as an additional example. The poet's heart stirs in line eight, but there is no explicit or implicit comparison between the falcon and the heart. The inner world of the poet's imagination is not a topic, as such, of the poem. The images are from nature, not from the imagination. They are perhaps transformed through the poet's vision, but they remain external to the poet. The comparison is not between nature outside the poet and his imagination within, but between a nature and a God both external to the poet.

93.   (D)

The poet uses abundant alliteration in every line of the poem. Alliteration is the repetition of consonants, especially initial consonants. We have, for example, a repetition of "m" in line one, a repetition of "d" in line two, a repetition of "st" in line three and so on. There are no explicit references in the poem to classical mythology. There is no verbal irony, no gap between what the poet says and what he means. The falcon is an example of the beauty of nature, but it is a literal falcon, not a personification of an abstraction. The poet uses words throughout in a literal and unambiguous way. There are no puns.

94.   (A)

The tone of the poem could best be described as ecstatic. The poet expresses an intense enjoyment of the beauty of nature. Through the poem, the poet tries to communicate this energy and intensity. Sarcasm is a tone of voice associated with bitter irony and ridicule. In contrast, this poem is entirely positive; there is no sarcasm. A melancholy tone would be appropriate to a poem expressing depression or regret. A witty tone suggests a poet interested in word play and clever metaphors. In this case, the poet is completley serious. Although the style may suggest a poet who is trying to express something beyond the powers of expression, the poet is not reticent. He does not hold back.

In contrast, the words seem to spill forth overflowing the strict limits of iambic pentameter implied by the sonnet form.

95.   (B)

Richardson's *Pamela* is epistolary in that the novel consists of letters written by the heroine. The action of the novel, such as the seduction of Pamela, takes place between the letters and is revealed through references to the action in the letters. The device creates a limited point of view.

96.   (D)

The term "stream of consciousness" is derived from the theories of Sigmund Freud. It refers to the random associations of thoughts and memories during ordinary experience. It formed the basis for Freud's psychoanalytical technique by which a patient was asked to free associate until repressed memories were recovered. As a literary term, it describes the style of James Joyce in *Ulysses* in which the author represents the associations and scattered thoughts of his characters during their moment to moment experiences.

97.   (A)

"Picaresque" describes a narrative like Cervantes' *Don Quixote* in which a comic hero has a series of adventures (or misadventures). There are numerous digressions, stories within stories, and the main principle of unity is the identity of the central hero. The novel is, in effect, the stringing together of many short episodes, all with the same hero. In addition, there may be a vague notion of a quest holding the novel together, but the effect is satirical rather than heroic.

98.   (A)

The term "Restoration Comedy" refers to those plays written in the period directly following the 1660 restoration of the Stuart monarchy. The comedies, like Congreve's *The Way of the World*, were cynical and satirical, and reflected the reaction against the Puritan Commonwealth. Goldsmith's *She Stoops to Conquer* is an 18th century comedy written about 100 years later. The late 18th century comedies have some of the same satiric qualities as the Restoration comedies, but they are less cynical. Shaw's *Major Barbara* is a modern comedy in much the same satiric tradition as the other two, but with a Marxist point of view.

99.   (C)

"Elizabethan" refers to literature from the latter part of the 16th century, the reign of Elizabeth I. Marlowe's *Doctor Faustus* is a tragedy from this period. Marlowe pioneered the development of dramatic blank verse.

100.   (D)

Beckett, an Irish writer who lived in Paris and wrote in French, broke with the "realistic" tradition of modern drama. His play *Waiting for Godot* is a prime example of 20th century theater of the absurd. There is no plot as such and no attempt to imitate "real" experience. Throughout the play two bums are waiting for a character named Godot who never shows up. There is an implication that this absurd situation is a metaphor for the general human condition.

101.   (D)

Human sacrifice is a theme in *Iphigenia in Aulis* by Euripides. In this play, Agamemnon sacrifices his daughter, Iphigenia, in order to propitiate Artemis and gain favorable winds for the Greek fleet setting sail for Troy. The murder of their daughter becomes an issue between Agamemnon and his wife, Clytemnestra, throughout the Mycenian legend. Revenge for the sacrifice is part of Clytemnesta's motivation in murdering Agamemnon when he returns from Troy. The other Greek plays deal with various forms of murder, death and execution, but not with human sacrifice per se. The story *The Dead* by James Joyce depicts contemporary life in modern Ireland and is the last story in his collection, *Dubliners*.

102.   (C)

Fern Hill by Dylan Thomas describes the carefree days of the poet's childhood growing up in rural Wales, as he remembers that freedom from the adult perspective of lost innocence.

103.   (D)

A Deist philosophy is expressed in Alexander Pope's verse essay, *An Essay on Man*. The poem is a statement of 18th century philosophical beliefs that God created a world that operates by natural law without the necessity of further intervention. The poem expresses a belief in God the creator, but is notably lacking in any references to such traditional Christian beliefs as the fall, the incarnation, the redemption, the second coming, or the last judgment.

104.   (B)

The lines are from Shelley's *Ode to the West Wind*. The lines exemplify the histrionic exaggeration that characterizes some Romantic poetry. The poet invokes the west wind, from which he hopes for inspiration.

105.   (B)

O'Neill's *The Iceman Cometh* takes place in a bar room. The characters in the bar are persuaded to test their fantasies, to live out their pipe dreams, in order to free themselves form self-delusion. The result, however, is that in losing these illusions, they lose the only sustaining hope in their lives and find themselves totally demoralized.

106.   (E)

William's *The Glass Menagerie* takes place in an apartment in St. Louis where the hero lives with his mother and sister. The sister, Laura, has a collection of tiny glass animals, the "glass menagerie," that she plays with. The play involves the mother's unsuccessful attempt to find a husband for the daughter, and it ends with the hero's decision to leave the family and strike out on his own. the situation is loosely autobiographical.

107.   (D)

Miller's *The Crucible* describes the witch trials of colonial Salem, Massachusetts. Miller uses the trials as an analogy for the anti-Communist Congressional investigations of the early 1950's.

108.   (A)

Desdemona is discussing infidelity with her maid, Emilia, who is also Iago's wife. She is reacting to Othello's jealousy. Neither she nor Emilia knows that the jealousy is the result of Iago's plot. Desdemona, the ingenue heroine, finds infidelity unthinkable. Neither she nor

Emilia, her foil, takes a somewhat more practical and worldly view of it.

109.   (E)

Juliet is reacting to the news that her parents have arranged a marriage for her to the County Paris. She is already secretly married to Romeo and he has been banished for the murder of her cousin, Tybalt.

110.   (B)

Cordelia is refusing to flatter her father as her two sisters have done. It is this refusal to flatter Lear that causes the king to disown Coredelia, and divide the kingdom between the two sisters.

111.   (D)

Johnson's poem is an example of satire. Of the five classical poets, the one associated with this genre is Juvenal. Ovid wrote *Metamorphoses*, a collection of myths, and *The Art of Love*, among other major works. He is generally associated with erotic poetry, not satire. Homer and Virgil wrote epics. Virgil also wrote eclogues and Horace wrote odes.   The satirical genre appealed to 18th century neo-classical writers. In writing satire, Johnson turned to a classical model, Juvenal, and adapted Juvenal's *Tenth Satire*, replacing classical examples with modern ones.

112.   (A)

In these lines, Johnson sets pride in opposition to reason, and notes that it is by following pride that humanity creates many problems for itself. There is no indication that mankind ever uses too much reason. Johnson rather laments the infrequency with which humanity follows reason. These problems are the result, not of institutions and customs, but of human nature itself. The problems are not limited to China and Peru. The phrase "from China to Peru" implies that this condition is utterly universal and includes the whole world. There is no indication in this passage that humanity can change this condition through education or technology.

113.   (E)

The correct term for the break is "cesura." The artful variation of this cesura is considered one of the important technical problems in the writing of 18th century rhymed couplets. Enjambment refers to the running of the syntactic unit beyond the end of the line, so that the sentence continues through the rhyme and on into the next line. A troche is a metrical foot with two syllables, the first stressed and the second unstressed. An elision is the leaving out of an unstressed vowel or syllable so that the line fits the meter. Ellipsis is the leaving out of words or phrases that are understood or implied in context.

114.   (E)

The reference is to the Wife of Bath. Muscatine refers to the *Wife of Bath's Prologue* in which the Wife of Bath presents a history of her five marriages and gives her views on the relationship between the sexes. In her fifth marriage, she ripped up her husband's book, which gave examples of wicked wives and this lead to a fight between husband and wife. Muscatine sees these actions as symbolic of the conflict between experience and authority, between feminism and masculine domination.

115.   (C)

The Reeve's Tale is an example of a fabliau. *The Pardoner's Tale* consists of a sermon, the "spiel" used by the Pardoner to sell pardons, illustrated by a moral exemplum, the story of the three revelers who kill each other over the gold that they find. *The Nun's Priest's Tale* is an animal fable. *The Monk's Tale* is a series of "tragedies," each one an example of the fall of a great person. *The Knight's Tale* is a romance.

116.   (A)

In the *Wife of Bath's Prologue* there are many allusions to the writings of St. Paul and St. Jerome, especially with regard to the virtue of virginity. The wife defends her own life, her many marriages, and her acknowledged lecherousness, against what she perceives as implied theological criticism.

117.   (B)

"Art for art's sake" was the esthetic philosophy of Oscar Wilde. It is typical of modern art generally, except when a particular philosophy, such as Freudianism or Marxism, dominates the art. The others, Plato, Eliot, Pope, and Horace, all embrace some degree of didacticism. Plato argued in *The Republic* that the arts must serve a moral purpose or be excluded from society. Eliot believed that art should be subordinate to religion. Horace articulated the classifical belief that art must "teach and delight." Pope followed Horace in his neo-classicism.

118.   (C)

A rigorous defense of the unities is to be found in Dryden's *An Essay of Dratic Poesy*. Dryden is writing from a later 17th century neo-classical point of view. Artaud's essay is a somewhat incoherent manifesto of the theater of the absurd and has nothing to do with unities. Johnson defends Shakespeare's violations of the unities of time and place and argues that they are articifical notions of no real importance in the drama. Neither Eliot nor Sidney are particularly concerned with drama or with dramatic unities.

119.   (D)

The "archetype" is one of the central concepts in the writings of Carl G. Jung. Jung was a disciple of Freud, who broke with Freud when Jung developed his theory of the collective unconscious. Jung believed that myths and dreams were closely related. He believed in a common source of dream material throughout the human race. Jung referred to the figures of dream and myth shared by humanity as "archetypes."

120.   (E)

The theme of the passage is "carpe diem," Latin for "grab the day." It means, in effect, enjoy life while you can. Appearance and reality would refer to a siutation in which the truth of the matter is not what it seems to be. Such a theme usually involves some form of disillusionment or recognition. "Deus ex machina" means "a god from a machine" and refers to the tendency in some classical Greek drama to end the work with the appearance of a god coming down out of the heavens with the help of stage machinery. This term is now extended to any articifical and spectacular conclusion that does not really follow naturally or inevitably from the story. "In media res" means "in the middle of things" and refers to the narrative strategy of starting the story in the middle and then having the beginning told as a flashback or story within a story. Platonic love refers to spiritual, as opposed to physical, love.

121.　(A)

The final line is iambic hexameter in that it has twelve syllables divided into six feet, each foot consisting of an unstressed syllable followed by a stress syllable, that is, an iamb. The first eight lines are iambic pentameter; that is, they have ten, not twelve, syllables, divided into five, not six, iambs.

122.　(D)

The passage is an example of an Elizabethan soliloquy, a speech delivered by a character alone on the stage, talking to the audience. In this case it is Edmund from Shakespeare's *King Lear*. Browning's monologues are poems in which a character, not the poet himself, speaks throughout. An eclogue is a pastoral poem in which the poet speaks through the voice of a shepherd, or often through a dialogue between two shepherds. In the Anglo-Saxon elegies, *The Seafarer* and *The Wanderer*, a speaking voice bewails the loss of comrades and the transcience of all things. In a mock-epic invocation the poet uses the formulas of epic style for comic effect.

123.　(C)

Edmund argues in this soliloquy that the rights of inheritance are imposed by artificial and unnatural customs. He opposes Nature to custom. According to Nature, he is just as much his father's son as is his legitimate brother Edgar. In taking Nature as his goddess, Edmund is justifying his plot to get rid of his brother and claim the inheritance for himself.

124.　(A)

The speaker is Machiavellian in that he plots immoral political action for his own well being and without regard for moral considerations. An anti-hero is a somewhat comic figure who has a heroic role but lacks heroic stature. Bloom in Joyce's *Ulysses* would be an example. A foil is a character who sets off the heroic character by being more practical. An example would be Emilia (to Desdemona) in Shakespeare's *Othello*. A personification is a character who represents an abstraction, like Good Deeds in *Everyman*. The protagonist is the hero or heroine of a drama or narrative, the character who is trying to accomplish something or who takes a stand for moral values. An example would be Antigone in Sophocles' *Antigone*.

125. (E)

In this passage, E.M. Forster is discussing his novel, *A Passage to India*. The statement is from an interview in *The Paris Review*. Forster discusses the effect of place on the writing process. He found that he could not complete his novel about India while he was still in India. His creativity was hindered by the sense of contrast between the real world he experienced everyday and the fictitious world of the novel. Nevertheless, as soon as he left India, he was able to complete the novel. Once the subject matter was a memory, once it no longer impinged immediately on his daily experience, he could continue creating his ficitonal India.

126. (D)

In this passage, William Faulkner discusses the writing of his novel, *As I Lay Dying*. This statement is also from an interview in *The Paris Review*. Faulker is discussing the writing process. In this case, the novel occurred to him as a fully formed idea and his task was simply to put it together.

127. (C)

The passage is from Shaw's Preface to *Major Barbara*. Shaw wrote prefaces to many of his plays discussing in detail the characters, the plots and the themes of the plays. These prefaces are obviously directed to the reader of the play rather than to the theater audience. In this passage, Shaw discusses the changing ideas of "the daughter of Andrew Undershaft," that is to say, Barbara herself.

Passage (A) is from *The Catastrophe of Success* by Tennessee Williams. Williams discusses the difficulties he had with writing once he had become famous. Passage (B) is from William Wordsworth's *Preface to Lyrical Ballads*.

128. (C)

In this quatrain from a sonnet by Spenser, the poet uses antithesis: a contrast of words or phrases with opposite meanings, emphasized by parallel structure. Here there are several such opposites: "yse" and "fyre," "cold" and "hot," and "dissolv'd" and "harder grows." All of these are metaphors for the opposition between the poet's desire and his love's disdain.

129. (A)

In these lines from Milton's *Paradise Lost*, the poet uses an oxymoron: "darkness visible." An oxymoron is the paradoxical juxtaposition of words that normally contradict each other. In this case "darkness" and "visible" would seem to be contradictory. Milton thus suggests that there arc states and conditions in the world that are beyond our imagination and that seem paradoxical because they are beyond our experience.

130. (E)

In these lines from a sonnet by Milton, the poet uses personification, a character that embodies an abstract concept. In this case, the virtue Patience is personified and speaks to the poet. The Term "synesthesia" refers to the mixing of physical senses as, for example, if a sound recalled or were described in terms of a color. The phrase "non sequitur" means "it does not follow" and it designates any statement that does not follow logically from whatever preceded it.

131. (B)

These lines from Shakespeare's sonnet 130 could best be classified as anti-Petrarchan. The term indicates a reversal of the Petrarchan conventions. Petrarch perfected the rhetoric of the love sonnet, especially a repetoire of comparisons for describing his beloved Laura. These particular metaphors and other rhetorical devices were much imitated by Renaissance poets, DuBellay and Ronsard in France, Wyatt and Spenser in England, among others. Wyatt's sonnets are in effect translations of Petrarch's into English. The comparisons typically praise the physical and spiritual perfections of the woman. What Shakespeare does is to reverse this convention: he calls attention to the absurdity of the comparisons. The sonnet is not Petrarchan because it denies rather than reaffirms the tradition. It is not Romantic, as that would suggest a sonnet about nature. It is not mock epic: that would be a poem in which the rhetorical formulas of the epic, an invocation, heroic epithets, epic similes, and so on, are applied to everyday, trivial, contemporary events. It is not surreal: this term applies to modern poetry and art in which imagery is juxtaposed in a way to suggest the irrational and the sub-conscious. Shakespeare's reversal of the Petrarchan conventions is a rational, self-conscious display of wit.

132. (B)

In these lines from Homer's *Odyssey*, "grey-eyed" is an epithet, a short descriptive word or phrase repeatedly associated with a particular character or other object. The use of an epithet is typical of epic style.

133. (E)

This couplet by John Donne is an epigram: a short, witty poem with a snappy ending.

134. (C)

These lines from Spenser's *The Faerie Queene* illustrate the epic simile, an extended comparison that stands as a set piece within the epic. Such similes are typical of Homer's style and were imitated by Virgil, Spenser, and Milton among others.

135. (D)

Milton's *Lycidas* is a pastoral elegy. "Elegy" is a term for a poem lamenting someone's death. Milton's poem is pastoral in that he assumes the role of a shepherd and he uses both the classical and Biblical pastoral traditions: both the shepherd as poet and the shepherd as clergy.

136. (C)

Browning's *My Last Duchess* is a dramatic monologue. The entire poem is cast in the speaking voice of a particular character: the Duke of Ferrara. The Duke seems to be addressing someone whom he is showing around his palace. Thus the poem itself seems to be a statement by a character in a dramatic situation, as if it were a passage from a verse drama.

137.   (A)

Pope's *The Rape of the Lock* is a mock epic, a poem that uses the formulas of serious epic juxtaposed with everyday common place subject matter in order to heighten the satiric effect. In this case the subject is a practaical joke, the cutting of a lock of hair. Pope intensifies his ridicule of the topic by presenting it as if it were of epic significance.

138.   (E)

The first quatrain is by Tennyson. Among its stylistic characteristics are the importance placed on sound as an element of poetry, and the use of sound to evoke an intense and universal emotion. These qualities are typical of Victorian poetry and are a continuation of elements of Romanticism.

139.   (D)

This is the first quatrain from William Blake's poem *The Tyger* in *Songs of Experience*. *The Tyger* corresponds to a similar poem in *Songs of Innocence* addressed to a lamb. It is typical of Blake's poetry that the tiger becomes a symbol of the destructive forces of nature and human nature that may seem, at least at first sight, to be evil.

140.   (A)

This is the first quatrain from a poem by Emily Dickinson. The predilection for an inner world of thought and reflection, ("the brain"), over nature, ("the sky"), is typical of Dickinson.

141.   (D)

Orestes and Pylades are characters from *The Libation Bearers* by Aeschylus. In that play Orestes avenges the death of his father by murdering his mother and her lover. Pylades, his friend and partner, has only one line in the whole play. The relationship that is most nearly parallel is that between Hamlet and Horatio. Hamlet is also called upon to avenge his father's death. To do so, he murders his own uncle, his mother's second husband. Horatio, Hamlet's friend, is a man of few words. Hal is a heroic character, but he is not avenging his father's death. His friend Falstaff is a comic foil and hardly a silent partner. Don Quixote is mock-heroic rather than heroic and Sancho is his servant, not a friend on an equal social basis. Like Falstaff, Sancho is a comic foil. Troilus and Pandarus are friends, but Pandarus is older and he acts as a go-between in arranging the affair between Troilus and Criseyde. That is not Pylades' role. Bloom and Stephen Dedalus represent middle aged and adolescent points of view, respectively. They are not of the same generation and neither is involved in a revenge plot.

142. (C)

The literary work that would best illustrate this definition of the Baroque would be Milton's *Paradise Lost*. Milton wrote the poem in the middle of the 17th century at the end of the English Renaissance. The focus on religious subject matter is typically Baroque. The magnificence of Milton's ornate rhetoric is also typically Baroque. Chaucer's *The Canterbury Tales* is a late medieval work. Although there is religious subject matter, the style is plainer and more straight-forward. It is less ornate and there is less emphasis on intense religious emotion. Ben Jonson's *Volpone* is an example of Renaissance neo-classicism. It is moral, but not particularly theological. It is didactic, but provokes laughter and reflection rather than intense religious emotion. Pope's *An Essay on Man* is a continuation of neo-classicism into the 18th century. It is to some extent a reaction against the Baroque in its balanced couplets, its rational consideration of philosophical questions, and its Deist theology. Wordsworth's *The Prelude* is a Romantic text describing the cultivation of an esthetic sensitivity to nature through childhood experiences. Although intensity of emotion is evoked, the subject matter is more psychological than theological and the style is relatively plain.

143. (D)

"Fealty" and "demesne" are terms derived from medieval feudalism. "Fealty" is the loyalty pledge by a subject to a lord in the feudal system. "Demesne" refers to the land controlled by an individual within the feudal system. In this sonnet, the poet, John Keats, uses "fealty" to refer to the loyalty of the poet to his art as represented by Apollo, the Greek god of, among other things, poetry. Keats uses "demesne" to refer to the poet's works. This metaphor of poetry as land is extended in the general metaphor of the poem, in which reading is discussed as a form of travelling and exploring.

144.   (C)

Apollo functions in the poem as the god of poetry and music. He is also a sun god and god of medicine, but these functions are not relevant to this poem in which Keats is concerned with reading a translation of Homer. Nietzsche did use Apollo as a symbol of reason and order, but this is also irrelevant to Keats' poem. As for Apollo's role in Homer's *Odyssey*, it was Athena, not Apollo, who befriended the hero.

145.   (C)

Balboa, not Cortez, discovered the Pacific. This sort of error in fact is referred to as poetic license, implying that it is minor detail irrelevant to the overall effect of the poem. The intentional fallacy occurs when the reader focuses on what an author supposedly meant to say rather than on what he actually did say. The pathetic fallacy is the author's use of nature to heighten emotional intensity, as for example, a sudden thunderstorm during a murder scene. Poetic justice refers to the rewarding of good and the punishing of bad characaters in the outcome of a narrative. Romantic irony is the undercutting of artistic illusion by the self-conscious intrusion of the artist revealing himself as creator. Examples would be Sterne's *Tristram Shandy* and Byron's *Don Juan*.

146.   (A)

This is the opening quatrain from Robert Frost's sonnet, *Design*. Features that are typical of Frost's style are the detailed observation of nature, the detached and ironic reflections on those observations, and the traditional meter and rhyme scheme.

147.   (D)

The passage is form Jonathan Edwards' sermon *Sinners in the Hands of an Angry God*. Edwards was an 18th century American Protestant theologian. He was part of an 18th century religious revival known as the Great Awakening.

148.   (C)

This description of the person of Alexander Pope is from Samuel Johnson's *The Life of Pope* from *The Lives of the Most Eminent English Poets*. In his fifty-two essays on individual poets, Johnson combines biographical details and literary criticism.

Passage (B) is from Annie Dillard's essay, *The Death of a Moth*.

Passage (E) is from John Donne's poem, *Twickenham Garden*.

149.　(B)

Melville uses a limited third-person point of view to create a gap between what we know and what is actually happening in the narrative. By limiting the reader's view of events to that of Captain Delano, Melville leads us through an experience of misunderstanding and recognition. We share in Captain Delano's observations and intuitions and we share his uncertainty. We actively participate with Captain Delano in trying to make sense out of the observations. In the end we are forced to reevalue our own assumptions. This gap between what is actually happening and what we are aware of is a form of irony.

150.　(A)

Of these works of literature, the one that makes the most elaborate use of number symbolism, especially of the number three, is Dante's *Divine Comedy*. The work is divided into three books: Hell, Purgatory, and Heaven. Each book consists of thirty-three cantos with one introductory canto to make an even hundred. The cantos are written in terza rima, three-line stanzas with an interlacing rhyme scheme: ABA BCB CDC...etc.

151.　(D)

The poet, Ralph Waldo Emerson, contrasts a river of Nature, as it happens, a minor, local river, known as the Concord, with a mystical and spiritual river. He gives the Concord its American Indian name: Musketaquit. The mystical and spiritual river that "goes/Through flood and sea and firmament..." is an image of the underlying spiritual reality central to the beliefs of the 19th century New England transcendalists.

152.　(A)

In the final quatrain, Emerson uses an allusion to a verse from the New Testament. The reference is to John 4:14 "Whosever drinketh of the water that I shall give him shall never thirst."

511

153. (D)

In this passage, Danby discusses the character of the fool in Shakespeare's *King Lear*. In particular, Danby considers the disappearance of the fool from the play after Act III. He explains this disappearance in thematic terms.

154. (B)

The poem that would best illustrate this definition of neo-classicism is Pope's *An Essay on Criticism*. Donne's *The Ecstasy* is characterized by metaphorical density and complexity of statement rather than by clarity of statement. Blake's *Jerusalem* is characterized by a complex personal symbolism, rather than clarity of statement. Smart's *A Song to David* and Traherne's *Wonder* both express intense personal religious emotion, not objectivity and reason. Blake's and Smart's poems have long lines of varying lengths, not balance and symmetry of form.

155. (B)

Among the works of literature listed, the one that comes closest to illustrating the esthetic ascribed to the Gothic cathedral is *The Canterbury Tales* by Chaucer. Like the cathedral, Chaucer's collection of tales is an unfinished work. It has a beginning and an end, but it is unfinished from within. In this way it points, like the cathedral, beyond itself from the finite to the infinite. This idea is expressed in the other works, but in *The Canterbury Tales*, Chaucer expresses the idea through the structure of the work.

156. (B)

Tuberculosis is important in Thomas Mann's *The Magic Mountain*. The novel takes place at a tuberculosis sanitorium and the major characters are tuberculosis patients.

157. (C)

Smallpox is important in *Bleak House* by Charles Dickens. The heroine gets small pox, but in spite of her scarred face, she is happily united with the hero at the end of the novel, showing the triumph of spiritual over physical values.

158.   (A)

Cancer is important in *Cat on a Hot Tin Roof*. In the play by Tennessee Williams, Big Daddy is dying of cancer. Part of the conflict between father and son stems from the father's refusal to admit the truth about his condition.

159.   (C)

In these lines form Shakespeare's *Hamlet*, Polonius is giving advice to his son before Laertes returns to France. Polonius is somehwat pedantic and comic. Thus, there is an element of irony in having these truisms mouthed by a foolish character.

160.   (B)

Blank verse is typical of Elizabethan drama. Blank verse is poetry with meter (specifically iambic pentameter), but without rhyme. Shakespeare uses it particularly in heroic, upper class scenes. For comic, lower class scenes, he typically uses prose.

161.   (C)

This quatrain is from Coleridge's *The Rime of the Ancient Mariner*. The bird in question is the albatross killed by the Ancient Mariner.

162.   (A)

These lines are from *Ode to a Nightingale* by John Keats. Listening to the nightingale's song at night, Keats contemplates death, but comes to the conclusion that intense enjoyment of nature is reserved for the living.

163.   (E)

These are the opening lines of Shelley's *To a Skylark*. Shelley envies the skylark's intensity and purity of expression.

164.   (E)

"Conceit" in the first line refers to metaphor. The word is related to "concept" and originally meant "idea." As used in the Renaissance with regard to poetry, it refers to a fanciful or witty idea or expression. In these lines from *An Essay on Criticism*, Pope is referring disparagingly to the densely metaphorical style of 17th century poetry. He particularly objects to the originality and oddness of the comparisons. This meaning of "conceit" is now archaic. The modern sense of the word, "a high opinion of oneself," had a separate development from the same original meaning of "idea."

165. (C)

The poetry that Pope is referring to and that he dislikes is often classified as metaphysical. The term designates a body of 17th century poetry characterized by a densely metaphorical style. The metaphors themselves are often strikingly original. The term "metaphysical" refers to the theological and religious concerns that form the typical subject matter of this poetry.

166. (A)

C.S. Lewis is discussing John Milton and specifically referring to Milton's description of Heaven in *Paradise Lost*. Lewis goes on to defend Milton's views as consistent. According to Lewis, Milton opposes royalism on Earth because it is a worship of human authority. In contrast, Milton accepts "royalism for Heaven," as Lewis puts it, because God deserves our loyalty and worship.

167. (C)

In this line from the General Prologue of Chaucer's *The Canterbury Tales*, "colerik" means having an abundance of choler, one of the four humors. The theory of the four humors was a medieval theory of physiology and psychology, according to which health, moods, and personality are determined by variations in and mixtures of the four bodily fluids, blood, phlegm, choler or black bile.

168. (E)

Dante is guided through Hell by Virgil. In the Middle Ages, Virgil was considered to be the foremost of classical writers. The Greek language and Greek literature were not widely known in western Europe during the Middle Ages. Among Latin authors, Virgil was revered for his high seriousness and patriotism. His works were read as allegorized foreshadowings and prophesies of Christianity. Ovid's works were perceived as less serious, more licentious, and he was more popular in the Renaissance. Beatrice is the woman who inspires Dante and who guides him in Heaven. It is appropriate that his guide in Hell should be pre-Christian.

169.   (E)

Roland Barthes is a major figure in deconstructionism. This school of criticism traces its philosophical origins back to the linguistic theories of Saussure. In particular, deconstruction applies to literary criticism, the linguistic notion that the meaning of a word depends in part on the implied contrast betweeen the word and other words that might be used in its place.

170.   (D)

Cleanth Brooks was a major figure in the New Criticism. This school of criticism was closely associated with modern literature. Among other things, New Criticism emphasized the importance of the text independent of any historical or biographical consideration.

171.   (B)

Stanley Fish is one of the principal propnents of reader-response criticism. This school of criticism focusses attention on the unfolding experiences of the reader in the course of his/her encounter with the work of literature.

172.   (A)

The passage is from a prefatory note to Milton's *Paradise Lost*. The note is entitled "Verse." In the note, Milton justifies his use of blank verse in the epic with the argument that Greek and Latin poets did not use rhyme.

173.   (A)

Eliot refers here to Mark Twain's use of colloquial language, the language of everyday conversation. Shakespeare used colloquial language, especially in comic scenes, but in this respect he was not really different from other Elizabethan dramatists. Both Chaucer and

Shakespeare used language that was contemporary, but it was not this particular characteristic that distinguished them from other writers. Spenser, on the other hand, used an archaic style. His language was just the opposite of "up-to-date." James Joyce pioneered the style of "stream of consciousness." The language was colloquial and the style was imitated. It was not the language itself, however, that was unusual, but the idea of presenting characterization through the free association of thoughts. It led to the highly idiosyncratic style of *Finnegan's Wake*, a synthetic style unlike anything else. Eliot's point then is not appropriate to Joyce, Shakespeare, Chaucer, or Spenser. It applies to Mark Twain, because Twain bridged the gap between current style and what was considered in 19th century America to be "literary" language. Mark Twain violated the notion of correct literary language by making literature out of ordinary language. Other writers had done this before, but in the 19th century it came as a shock to many readers. It was in this sense that he brought his language, that is to say, the accepted literary language, "up-to-date."

174.   (A)

The poem is organized around a sequence of metaphors. The metaphor in the second quatrain compares the poet to a town that is governed by usurping power. The rightful governor is God. As his representative, God has given the poet reason. The poet's reason, however, has not proved strong enough or loyal enough to defend the poet against evil. Thus the best paraphrase is that the poet's mind is "overpowered by evil motives." The particular evil is not specified. It is not necessarily adultery or love with another woman. The political references in the poem are all part of the metaphor. The poet is not referring to political policies, or to London or any other town. The poet expresses his need for God's help, not any dissatisfaction with organized religion or any concern over religion as a cause of conflict.

175.   (A)

In the sestet, the poet continues with a metaphor comparing himself to a bride about to marry someone she does not love, someone referred to as "your enemy" in line 10. Since, from the first line on, the poem is addressed directly to God, "your" means "God's." Thus the enemy is God's enemy Satan, not the enemy of England in a war. The poet, John Donne, converted to the Anglican church and became a famous preacher. He would not have considered the Anglican church to be

God's enemy; in any case, the poem is not about conflicts between religions. It is not a poem about a rival poet. The marriage in the sestet is metaphorical and thus does not refer to the poet's literal marriage.

176.   (A)

The passage from Machiavelli's *The Prince* would serve most appropriately as a point of reference for Shakespeare's *Henry IV Part 2*. In *Henry IV Part 1*, Prince Hal has shown himself to be a lion in defeating Hotspur and the other rebels. In *Henry IV Part 2*, Hal's younger brother, Prince John, demonstrates the value of playing the fox when he outwits another group of rebels. Shakespeare argues, like Machiavelli, that in an evil world there may be good uses for devious means.

177.   (B)

Faulkner's title is a phrase from a soliloquy by Macbeth in Shakespeare's tragedy. After he learns of Lady Macbeth's suicide, the hero sounds a note of despair, saying that life is a "tale told by idiot, full of sound and fury, signifying nothing." The first section of Faulkner's novel is written in first person stream of consciousness narration from the point of view of Benjy, who is retarded.

178.   (A)

Hemingway's title is taken from a phrase in Donne's *Devotions*. Hemingway quotes the extended passage, "No man is an island..." Donne's text is a series of meditations written while the 17th century poet and theologian was sick with the plague. The particular occasion for the meditating in question was the hearing of a funeral bell tolling for someone else's death. Donne argues that all humanity is interrelated and that the death of another only serves to remind each of us of our common fate. Hemingway's novel is about the death of an American fighting in the Spanish Civil War. He uses Donne's text as a point of reference for humanism, for human emphathy, and for its sense of the interrelatedness of the human family.

179.   (E)

Huxley's title is taken from Shakespeare's *The Tempest*. The phrase is uttered by the ingenue heroine Miranda when she sees all the shipwrecked characters for the first time. She has been raised by her father in isolation on a remote island and she views humanity for the first time. She is very impressed. The line is comic in context because we know that these characters are rather ordinary in many ways, but at the same time Miranda suggests that ordinary humanity is in itself a marvelous creation. Huxley turns this around a bit, using the phrase to refer to a future world, an artificial Utopia lacking the hardships and suffering that challenge us in this world.

180.   (A)

In this poem by John Crowe Ransom, the word "transmogrifying" in line 13 means "changing into a bizarre or fantastic form, rendering ridiculous." The bee sting has changed the appearance of the rooster adding a purple welt to his head that makes the comb stand up straight. From an objective point of view this appearance is bizarre, fantastic, and ridiculous. The contrast between the limpness of the body and comb is also bizarre. This point of view is, however, in contrast with the attitude of the character in the poem, Janet. Thus the poet's choice of words undercuts the child's sentimentality.

181.   (C)

The first line refers ostensibly to Janet's literal sleep, but by the end of the poem waking and sleeping have taken on additional meanings. Death is a sleep from which the rooster cannot be awakened. Janet's innocence is like a sleep and this experience is her awakening from that innocence.

182.   (B)

Charles Dickens and numerous other 19th century novelists published their novels in serial form in periodicals. This accounts for many of the formal elements of the novels: their construction in short, readable chapters; their complicated plots with vital information withheld from the reader; and the importance of suspense. The form was designed to hold the reader's interest from chapter to chapter while the plot unfolded.

183.   (D)

William Blake was a visionary poet. He reacted against the rationalism of the 18th century, especially against the influence of Newton and Locke. He stressed the importance of the imagination in shaping the human condition. In this he was similar to other Romantic poets. For Blake, however, the products of the imagination seemed as real, or even more real, than the material world. This was reflected in complicated personal symbolism of his poetry. He had a number of visions and he took them quite literally.

184.   (D)

"Double entendre" is a phrase meaning "twofold meaning" or "pun." Thus the editor implies that Shakespeare used the phrase "lie with" with the intention of creating ambiguity. The phrase can mean both "tell an untruth to" and "have sexual relations with." Both meanings make sense in the context.

185.   (A)

The "-ed" in "unlearned" is pronounced as an unstressed syllable. In Elizabethan English, poets exercised an option either to pronounce "-ed" as a separate syllable or to elide the "e." The "e" is elided in "untutored" (line 3) and in "suppressed" (line 8). This is determined by the meter and with the rhyme with "best". In line 4, however, the unstressed syllable is needed for the meter. The pronunciation was in transition and both forms were acceptable variations.

186.   (E)

The standard definition of a sonnet requires that the poem have fourteen lines. Shakespeare's sonnets end with a couplet, but the Italian form with a sestet is typical. Petrarch's sonnets were about love, and this was the typical subject matter of the sonnet throughout the Renaissance. Other topics were possible, however. John Donne wrote sonnets about religion, William Wordsworth about nature. Shakespeare's sonnets have three quatrains and then a couplet, but the Italian form has only two quatrains before the sestet. Wit and irony are typical of much Renaissance poetry, especially 17th century poetry. Wit and irony are not, however, essential to the genre. They are lacking, for example, in the sonnets of Romantic poets like Keats and Wordsworth.

187. (E)

The philosophical position could best be classified as nominalism, the view that abstract concepts are merely words and have no other existence. It is not stoicism, a classical philosophy that taught the patient endurance of suffering and bad fortune, and the cultivation of moral self-discipline. Stoicism is associated with Roman patriotism. Falstaff's lack of interest in honor is the antithesis of Roman stoicism. The Donatist heresy is an early variant of Christianity, according to which offices performed by heretical or corrupt clergy were deemed invalid. According to orthodox theology, the spiritual condition of the clergy is irrelevant to the efficacy of the sacrament. In any case, it is not a question with which Falstaff is concerned. According to Calvinism, the religious teachings of John Calvin, salvation is predestined by God and not determined by good works. Falstaff is not concerned with such questions. Neo-Platonism is a Renaissance variation of Plato's philosophy. While Plato taught that art was an imitation of an imatation, and thus a further step removed from the "reality" of ideal forms, neo-Platonists believed that art could mediate between ordinary experience and ideal forms. Falstaff's nominalism is directly opposed to any form of Platonism, since it denies reality to an abstraction.

188. (C)

The theory of tragedy as offering the audience a "catharsis" of emotions is presented by Aristotle in *Poetics*. Sidney in his *Defence of Poesie* argues for the superiority of poetry over history and philosophy. He is not specifically concerned with drama. Tolstoy in *What Is Art?* argues in favor of folk art, in favor of authenticity generally, and against the cultivation of highbrow art as a social affectation. He does not present a theory of tragedy per se. Freud in *The Psychopathology of Everyday Life* is concerned with slips of the tongue and lapses of memory, not with theories of tragedy. Bradley in *Shakespearean Tragedy* analyzes Shakespeare's plays, focusing particularly on characterization. He does not present a theory of tragedy based on catharsis.

189. (D)

Austen's title implies a balance between hard-headed reason and emotion. "Sensibility" refers to the refinement of emotional sensibility and it was much in vogue at the time. Austen views its excesses as a form of foolish self-indulgence. She opposes it to "sense" which thus refers to "a practical and reasonable regard for one's own self-interest."

190. (C)

These are the final lines of Keats' *Ode on a Grecian Urn*. The quotation marks imply that the final words are not spoken by the urn. If they are spoken by the poet to the urn, then "ye" refers to the urn and the final lines imply the urns' limitations. Elsewhere in the poem, however, the urn is referred to as "thou," the singular second person pronoun. Why should the poet shift from singular to plural or from informal to formal in addressing the urn? If the words are spoken either by the urn to humanity or by the poet to his readers, then the lines have a very different meaning. The lines then imply that the urn's message is the only truth we can know or need to know. The nightingale figures of course in Keats' *Ode to a Nightingale*, not this poem. Here the subject referred to by "ye" is either the urn or humanity, not a nightingale, a rose, or a woman, none of which are topics of the ode.

191. (A)

Moliere's *Tartuffe* is a satire of religious hypocrisy. Tartuffe himself is the hypocrite. The other plays are satirical but they are not directed specifically at religious hypocrisy. Jonson's *Volpone* is a satire of avarice. Wycherley's *The Country Wife* is a Restoration comedy satirizing adultery, marriage and relations between the sexes. Aristophanes' *The Clouds* is a Greek comedy satirizing Socrates, philosophy and education. Sheridan's *The Rivals* is a late 18th century comedy about, like Wycherley's play, relations between the sexes.

192. (C)

Synge spent time in western Ireland studying the dialect and the local customs in order to write *The Playboy of the Western World*. The language of the play is an Irish dialect of English. Various forms of Celtic languages still persist in Ireland, Scotland, Wales, and Brittany, but Synge wrote in English, not in Gaelic or in any other Celtic language. Old English would be the language of England about one thousand years ago. Synge was writing about modern Ireland, not old England. Thus the language of Synge's play is Irish English, a dialect of English.

193. (B)

Joseph Conrad's native language was Polish. He workd for many years as a merchant seaman. He wrote his novels in England and in

English. Dante chose his native language, Tuscan Italian, for the *Divine Comedy*, rather than writing it in Latin, the language of theology and scholarship. Thus he directed his poem toward a popular audience. Dostoevsky wrote in Russian, his native language, and Chaucer and Thackery both wrote in English, their native language.

194. (C)

Kafka, in works like *The Trial,* presents a view of the human condition as an absurd and meaningless predicament. All of the other authors wrote within the framework of cultural and philosophical assumptions that provided meaning to human experience. Virgil viewed human experience from the perspective of Roman patriotism, and classical mythology and philosophy. Dante viewed human experience from the point of view of medieval Christian theology. Tolstoy viewed human experience from the point of view of historical determinism, and Zola from the point of view of naturalism.

195. (C)

The works of Goethe provide examples of Romanticism. Writing in the 17th century, Moliere and Milton preceded Romanticism by over 100 years. Milton was a Renaissance humanist and a Puritan. Moliere was the leading author of comedies in French classic drama. Beckett and Steinbeck are 20th century authors and follow Romanticism by about 100 years. Steinbeck wrote socially-conscious realistic novels with particular concern for economic factors. Beckett wrote theater of the absurd.

196. (C)

The arrangement of poems on the page to represent objects was practiced by the 17th century author, George Herbert. For example, Herbert wrote a religous poem shaped to represent an altar, another shaped to represent wings.

197. (D)

The term "Cavalier" refers to poets associated with the royalist side in the 17th century conflict between the Puritans and the throne. Chaucer lived in the 14th century. Jonson was an early 17th century neo-classical playwright. He lived and wrote just prior to the conflict and was not directly involved in it. Milton was very much involved, but on the Puritan side. Dryden wrote in the latter part of the 17th century and tended to change with the times. Of the five, the poet who fits the definition is Richard Lovelace.

198. (E)

These four plays, written at the end of Shakespeare's career, are classified as romances. Although there are satirical elements in some of Shakespeare's works, the term "satire" has not traditionally been used for any particular group of plays. Plays designated as "histories" deal with the lives of English kings form King John to Henry VIII. Among the other plays, comedies generally end with a wedding, tragedies with a death. The romances are distinctive in that they include tragic elements of death and disaster, but they continue beyond these tragic elements to reach a happier conclusion.

199. (C)

Ben Jonson wrote many masques, but *Volpone* is not one of them. *Volpone* is a five-act satirical drama. Shakespeare included a masque as an entertainment in *The Tempest*. *As You Like It*, however, is a full-length comedy. Congreve's *The Way of the World* is a Restoration comedy, and *Everyman* is a medieval morality play. The masque was a short play, usually including music and dance, written for private entertainment at a court or household and performed by members of the household, not a professional acting troupe. Milton's *Comus* is an example.

200. (C)

These are the opening lines of Rousseau's *Confessions*. The other authors wrote about themselves, but with somewhat different purposes. St. Augustine's *Confessions* are a theological autobiography. Cellini wrote an artistic autobiography as a form of self-glorification. Pepys, in his diary, observed the daily events of 17th century London. He refers to himself with circumspect reserve. Freud discusses his own experiences and dreams from a psychoanalytical point of view.

201.　(D)

The speaker is Molly Bloom. These are the final words in the third and final section of Joyce's *Ulysses*. The section is an extended, unpunctuated, inner monologue representing Molly Bloom's steam of consciousness. This style distinguishes the text from the thoughts or expressions of any of the other heroines.

202.　(E)

These are the final lines from Archibald Macleish's *Ars Poetica*. The sentiment is typically "modern" in that it makes the work of art an end in itself, not a means to an end. The poem is viewed as an object, a material work of art, not as vehicle for transmitting a message. Elizabethan and neo-classical poetry tended to be more didactic, justifying poetry as an expression of moral doctrine. Romantic and Victorian poetry tended to view poetry as an expression of the artist, pointing beyond itself to feelings, moods, states of consciousness. While these views continue into the 20th century, the notion of the poem as an artifact is typically modern.

203.　(D)

In the course of the play the "noble sentiments" of Joseph Surface are revealed to be hypocritical states of moral platitutdes. Thus the terms "sentiment" comes to have a negative connotation by the end of the play.

204.　(C)

This sentence is from Swift's *A Modest Proposal*, a bitter satire written in response to the social and economic conditions of 18th century Ireland. Milton, Wordsworth and Tennyson did not, typically, write satire. Milton wrote epic and lyric poetry, verse drama, and numerous political and theological tracts. Wordsworth and Tennyson both wrote lyrical poetry. Chaucer wrote satire, but living in the 14th century, he wrote prior to the discovery of America. In addition, his satire was more traditional, less bitter, and he wrote in verse.

205. (C)

The principal rhetorical device in *A Modest Proposal* is irony. Swift makes an incredible proposal in order to suggest its opposite: that public and social policies should be changed to benefit the needs of the poor and the helpless. Saying one thing and meaning the opposite is a form of irony. Allegory is an extended metaphorical narrative with personifications. Simile is an explicit comparison. Litotes is understatement. Apostrophe is direct address.

206. (C)

The couplet is from the last stanza of *To a Louse: On Seeing One on a Lady's Bonnet at Church,* by Robert Burns. The language that Burns uses is Scottish English, a dialect of English spoken in Scotland, particularly in the lowlands. Old English and Middle English refer to the English spoken in England during the Middle Ages. In this case we are referring to a dialect spoken not in England, but in Scotland, and not during the Middle Ages, but at the end of the 18th century. A form of Gaelic or Celtic persists in northern Scotland, but Burns wrote in Scotch English, not Scotch Gaelic.

207. (A)

A kenning is a formulaic figure of speech used in Anglo-Saxon poetry. An example would be the expression, "whale path" for the ocean. To find such an example, one must turn of course to an Anglo-Saxon poem. Of the literary works listed, only *The Seafarer* is an Anglo-Saxon poem. *King Lear* is an Elizabethan tragedy by Shakespeare. *Samson Agonistes* is a 17th century verse drama by Milton. *Gulliver's Travels* is an 18th century satirical work by Swift. *Walden* is a collection of autobiographical essays by Thoreau documenting his retreat at Walden Pond. Poetry in Anglo-Saxon was written between the Anglo-Saxon invasion of England in the 5th century A.D. and the Norman Conquest in 1066 A.D.

208. (C)

The alternation of heroic and comic scenes is typical of Elizabethan drama and many examples can be found in the writings of William Shakespeare. Sophocles was a 5th century B.C. Athenian playwright. He wrote tragedies and did not include comic scenes in his plays. Congreve wrote Restoration comedy and did not include serious or heroic scenes. Racine wrote classic French tragedy an did not include comic scenes. Dryden followed the strict neo-classical format and did not mix comic and tragic material. Good examples from Shakespeare would be the alternation of tavern and court or battllefield scenes in *Henry IV Parts One and Two*, the gravedigger scene in *Hamlet*, the porter scene in *Macbeth,* and the scene between the nurse and Mercutio in *Romeo and Juliet.*

209.   (E)

Matthew Arnold argued that Chaucer was not of the highest stature in the poetic pantheon because he lacked "high seriousness." This argument would seem to deny that comedy could have a serious intent and thus appears to be a misreading of the satiric genre. It would also seem to reflect, on Arnold's part, a Victorian predilection for taking oneself very seriously, a vestige perhaps of Romanticism.

210.   (B)

Johnson took a somewhat begrudging view of Milton's strengths. This was typical of the 18th century neo-classical reaction against 17th century religious controversy, religous intensity, and Baroque style. Milton stood for both the Puritan theological view and the Baroque exaggeration that the 18th century rejected.

211.   (C)

T.S. Eliot judged *Hamlet* inferior to Shakespeare's *Coriolanus*. In this, Eliot was perhaps reacting against Romantic adulation of *Hamlet* as the perfect expression of intellectual angst, a play whose hero thinks too much. Eliot found the play simply muddled and inconclusive, pointlessly ambiguous, and unclear with regard to the hero's motivation. He claimed to prefer *Coriolanus*, a much simpler, clearer play, that has been generally neglected. In preferring the well-crafted play to the work that points beyond itself, Eliot exhibits a neo-classical attitude.

212.   (A)

The ascension of James I united the kingdoms of England and Scotland. Shakespeare shifted his attention from questions of Tudor legitimacy going back to 15th century English politics, to matters of

Scottish history. James based his claim to the Scottish throne back to Banquo and the opposition to the supposed usurper, Macbeth. In showing Macbeth as a villain, Shakespeare was supporting the new King of England. James also had an interest in witchcraft, making it a suitable topic for the play.

213.   (A)

The subject of this sonnet by John Milton is the massacre of the Waldenses, a Protestant sect that had separated from the Catholic church in the twelfth century. They lived principally in the Alps, along the border between France and Italy.

214.   (D)

The lines illustrate enjambment, the running over syntactically of a sentence from one line to the next without any pause of punctuation, and with the sentence, clause, or phrase ending in the middle of the next phrase. Thus there is enjambment in the first line of the poem in relative clause "whose bones/Lie scattered..." which carries over from the first verse to the second. There is not enjambment, however, in the second verse since the relative clause comes to a close at the end of the verse: "...on the Alpine mounts cold..." Lines 8-10 do not illustrate irony, since Milton is not saying one thing and meaning something else. It is not synesthesia, which is the mixing of senses. It is not litotes, which is understatement. It is not sprung rhythm, since the meter is standard iambic pentameter.

215.   (D)

Wordsworth's theme in this poem is that the experiences of the child determine the sensibilities of the adult. In particular, he felt that his love of nature was formed in childhood.

216.   (A)

By "natural piety" Wordsworth means the love and appreciation of nature. Wordsworth does not express specific theological concerns. He refers to a literal rainbow, not a symbolic one. He relates to nature directly, not as a means to an end. He does not characterize nature as mechanical, and he does worship gods and goddesses.

217. (D)

Dr. Samuel Johnson's friend and biographer was James Boswell. Their tour of Scotland and its Western Islands is described in Boswell's *Journal of a Tour to the Hebrides* published in 1784, one year after Johnson's death. The biography, *The Life of Samuel Johnson, LL.D.*, was published in 1791. This was Boswell's "great work."

218. (B)

The passage is from Hemingway's *The Old Man and the Sea*. Characteristic of Hemingway's style are the relatively short sentences with vivid, concrete images. The diction is ordinary and yet precise. The style does not call attention to itself.

219. (A)

The passage is from William Faulkner's *The Bear*. The length of the sentences and the complexity of the syntax are characteristic of Faulkner's style. Typically, there is an accumulation of words and phrases as if the author were searching for the right word, trying to express something beyond the power of words to express.

220. (E)

The passage comes at the very end of Joyce's story, *The Dead*, the last story in his collection, *Dubliners*. Although Joyce had a number of very different styles, this passage illustrated one of his great strengths: a lyrical, descriptive style that he used sparingly, but effectively.

Passage (C) is from Mark Twain's story, *The Notorious Jumping Frog of Calaveras County*. The passage illustrates Twain's use of dialect. He tells the story through the voice of a character who with the idioms and vocabulary of the frontier. Passage (D) is from Melville's *Bartleby the Scrivener*. The detailed character description and the relative formality of diction and syntax are more typical of the 19th century rather than of modern fiction.

221. (C)

Of the works listed, the one that could best be characterized as existentialist would be Sartre's *No Exit*. According to existentialism, of which Sartre is a principal exponent, the material world exists without meaning, and the meaning is provided by individual human beings in their exercise of free choice and moral responsibility. The play *No Exit* is about an imaginary afterlife in which three people are stuck in a room forever together, an inescapable damnation. The imaginary afterlife contrasts with this life, in which, Sartre implies, one is always free to leave. The works by Milton, Dante, and Marlowe would not be existentialist because, even though all three emphasize the importance of free choice, the meaning of every choice, its implications, are already determined according to theology: salvation or damnation in the afterlife. In contrast, Tolstoy's novel supports a thesis of historical determinism that tends to minimize the importance of individual choice.

222.　(A)

Several works from 14th century Middle English, including *Pearl* constitute the alliterative revival. Alliteration was the verse form of Anglo-Saxon poetry. If there was a continuing tradition down to the 14th century, then most of the intervening alliterative poetry has been lost. By 1400, and other poets were writing in rhymed iambic pentameter. At one point in the *Knight'sTale*, Chaucer uses alliteration for comic effect, suggesting that alliteration seemed at that time old-fashioned. Nevertheless, it shows a familiarity with the tradition. *Pearl, Sir Gawain and the Green Knight*, and a number of other 14th century poems combine alliteration with rhyme. As for the other works listed, *The Faerie Queene* was written in the 16th century and uses meter and rhyme throughout. *The Duchess of Malfi, Lycidas,* and *The Country Wife* were written in the 17th century. *The Duchess of Malfi* is a tragedy by Webster, and like other English Renaissance dramas, uses blank verse and prose. Milton's *Lycidas* uses rhymed iambic lines of varying length. Wycherley's *The Country Wife*, a Restoration comedy, is written in prose. None of these works uses alliteration as a verse form and none was written in the 14th century.

223.　(C)

The author is William Shakespeare. The lines are from a soliloquy by Macbeth. He is contemplating the murder of Duncan, which he and Lady Macbeth are plotting.

224.   (E)

In the context, "success" means the result or outcome of the action. This is a meaning that was current for Shakespeare, but that now is archaic and no longer in use. The results that Macbeth is referring to would apparently be additional murders, the murder of Macbeth himself perhaps, in imitation of this murder. Macbeth worries that having once set the example, he and Lady Macbeth will become the next victims. He sees a contradiciton between his plan to break the law in order to get power and his subsequent need to maintain law and order when he wants to keep power. This is one of the central themes of the play.

225.   (B)

The line is spoken by Satan in Milton's *Paradise Lost*, I, 263. It summarizes Satan's point of view, his pride, his rebellion, his ambition, his role as tyrant among the fallen angels. It is, of course, not Milton's point of view, but rather a point of view created by Milton for a principle character in his epic poem. Dr. Faustus, the hero of Marlowe's tragedy, sells his soul to the devil, but he expresses no desire to "reign in hell." In return for selling his soul, he wants to satisfy his ambitions and desires in this life here on the earth before he dies. Machiavelli was a diplomat of the Florentine Republic. He supported the republic through his work as a diplomat. After the downfall of the republic, he wrote *The Prince* describing the actions required of a tyrant in order to keep control of a city seized illegitimately. Machiavelli was one of the first to describe what rulers actually did rather than what they were supposed to do. This so offended many people that Machiavelli became associated with evil. He, himself, however was a practical diplomat with no apparent interest in theology. Shakespeare's Othello is a tragic hero consumed by jealousy. He is concerned with the faithfulness of his wife, not with the hereafter.

226.   (A)

The lines are from Matthew Arnold's *Dover Beach*.

227.   (A)

The comparison is between the withdrawing ocean wave and a general loss of religious faith.

228.   (B)

The refrain is from Poe's poem, *The Raven*.

229.   (C)

The refrain is from the song that Feste sings at the end of Shakespeare's *Twelfth Night*. The Fool in *King Lear* also sings a stanza of the song.

230.   (D)

The refrain is from Edmund Spenser's *Epithalamion*, a marriage song celebrating the poet's own marriage.

GRE

LITERATURE in ENGLISH

TEST V

THE GRADUATE RECORD EXAMINATION

LITERATURE in ENGLISH

ANSWER SHEET

1. Ⓐ Ⓑ Ⓒ Ⓓ Ⓔ	31. Ⓐ Ⓑ Ⓒ Ⓓ Ⓔ	61. Ⓐ Ⓑ Ⓒ Ⓓ Ⓔ
2. Ⓐ Ⓑ Ⓒ Ⓓ Ⓔ	32. Ⓐ Ⓑ Ⓒ Ⓓ Ⓔ	62. Ⓐ Ⓑ Ⓒ Ⓓ Ⓔ
3. Ⓐ Ⓑ Ⓒ Ⓓ Ⓔ	33. Ⓐ Ⓑ Ⓒ Ⓓ Ⓔ	63. Ⓐ Ⓑ Ⓒ Ⓓ Ⓔ
4. Ⓐ Ⓑ Ⓒ Ⓓ Ⓔ	34. Ⓐ Ⓑ Ⓒ Ⓓ Ⓔ	64. Ⓐ Ⓑ Ⓒ Ⓓ Ⓔ
5. Ⓐ Ⓑ Ⓒ Ⓓ Ⓔ	35. Ⓐ Ⓑ Ⓒ Ⓓ Ⓔ	65. Ⓐ Ⓑ Ⓒ Ⓓ Ⓔ
6. Ⓐ Ⓑ Ⓒ Ⓓ Ⓔ	36. Ⓐ Ⓑ Ⓒ Ⓓ Ⓔ	66. Ⓐ Ⓑ Ⓒ Ⓓ Ⓔ
7. Ⓐ Ⓑ Ⓒ Ⓓ Ⓔ	37. Ⓐ Ⓑ Ⓒ Ⓓ Ⓔ	67. Ⓐ Ⓑ Ⓒ Ⓓ Ⓔ
8. Ⓐ Ⓑ Ⓒ Ⓓ Ⓔ	38. Ⓐ Ⓑ Ⓒ Ⓓ Ⓔ	68. Ⓐ Ⓑ Ⓒ Ⓓ Ⓔ
9. Ⓐ Ⓑ Ⓒ Ⓓ Ⓔ	39. Ⓐ Ⓑ Ⓒ Ⓓ Ⓔ	69. Ⓐ Ⓑ Ⓒ Ⓓ Ⓔ
10. Ⓐ Ⓑ Ⓒ Ⓓ Ⓔ	40. Ⓐ Ⓑ Ⓒ Ⓓ Ⓔ	70. Ⓐ Ⓑ Ⓒ Ⓓ Ⓔ
11. Ⓐ Ⓑ Ⓒ Ⓓ Ⓔ	41. Ⓐ Ⓑ Ⓒ Ⓓ Ⓔ	71. Ⓐ Ⓑ Ⓒ Ⓓ Ⓔ
12. Ⓐ Ⓑ Ⓒ Ⓓ Ⓔ	42. Ⓐ Ⓑ Ⓒ Ⓓ Ⓔ	72. Ⓐ Ⓑ Ⓒ Ⓓ Ⓔ
13. Ⓐ Ⓑ Ⓒ Ⓓ Ⓔ	43. Ⓐ Ⓑ Ⓒ Ⓓ Ⓔ	73. Ⓐ Ⓑ Ⓒ Ⓓ Ⓔ
14. Ⓐ Ⓑ Ⓒ Ⓓ Ⓔ	44. Ⓐ Ⓑ Ⓒ Ⓓ Ⓔ	74. Ⓐ Ⓑ Ⓒ Ⓓ Ⓔ
15. Ⓐ Ⓑ Ⓒ Ⓓ Ⓔ	45. Ⓐ Ⓑ Ⓒ Ⓓ Ⓔ	75. Ⓐ Ⓑ Ⓒ Ⓓ Ⓔ
16. Ⓐ Ⓑ Ⓒ Ⓓ Ⓔ	46. Ⓐ Ⓑ Ⓒ Ⓓ Ⓔ	76. Ⓐ Ⓑ Ⓒ Ⓓ Ⓔ
17. Ⓐ Ⓑ Ⓒ Ⓓ Ⓔ	47. Ⓐ Ⓑ Ⓒ Ⓓ Ⓔ	77. Ⓐ Ⓑ Ⓒ Ⓓ Ⓔ
18. Ⓐ Ⓑ Ⓒ Ⓓ Ⓔ	48. Ⓐ Ⓑ Ⓒ Ⓓ Ⓔ	78. Ⓐ Ⓑ Ⓒ Ⓓ Ⓔ
19. Ⓐ Ⓑ Ⓒ Ⓓ Ⓔ	49. Ⓐ Ⓑ Ⓒ Ⓓ Ⓔ	79. Ⓐ Ⓑ Ⓒ Ⓓ Ⓔ
20. Ⓐ Ⓑ Ⓒ Ⓓ Ⓔ	50. Ⓐ Ⓑ Ⓒ Ⓓ Ⓔ	80. Ⓐ Ⓑ Ⓒ Ⓓ Ⓔ
21. Ⓐ Ⓑ Ⓒ Ⓓ Ⓔ	51. Ⓐ Ⓑ Ⓒ Ⓓ Ⓔ	81. Ⓐ Ⓑ Ⓒ Ⓓ Ⓔ
22. Ⓐ Ⓑ Ⓒ Ⓓ Ⓔ	52. Ⓐ Ⓑ Ⓒ Ⓓ Ⓔ	82. Ⓐ Ⓑ Ⓒ Ⓓ Ⓔ
23. Ⓐ Ⓑ Ⓒ Ⓓ Ⓔ	53. Ⓐ Ⓑ Ⓒ Ⓓ Ⓔ	83. Ⓐ Ⓑ Ⓒ Ⓓ Ⓔ
24. Ⓐ Ⓑ Ⓒ Ⓓ Ⓔ	54. Ⓐ Ⓑ Ⓒ Ⓓ Ⓔ	84. Ⓐ Ⓑ Ⓒ Ⓓ Ⓔ
25. Ⓐ Ⓑ Ⓒ Ⓓ Ⓔ	55. Ⓐ Ⓑ Ⓒ Ⓓ Ⓔ	85. Ⓐ Ⓑ Ⓒ Ⓓ Ⓔ
26. Ⓐ Ⓑ Ⓒ Ⓓ Ⓔ	56. Ⓐ Ⓑ Ⓒ Ⓓ Ⓔ	86. Ⓐ Ⓑ Ⓒ Ⓓ Ⓔ
27. Ⓐ Ⓑ Ⓒ Ⓓ Ⓔ	57. Ⓐ Ⓑ Ⓒ Ⓓ Ⓔ	87. Ⓐ Ⓑ Ⓒ Ⓓ Ⓔ
28. Ⓐ Ⓑ Ⓒ Ⓓ Ⓔ	58. Ⓐ Ⓑ Ⓒ Ⓓ Ⓔ	88. Ⓐ Ⓑ Ⓒ Ⓓ Ⓔ
29. Ⓐ Ⓑ Ⓒ Ⓓ Ⓔ	59. Ⓐ Ⓑ Ⓒ Ⓓ Ⓔ	89. Ⓐ Ⓑ Ⓒ Ⓓ Ⓔ
30. Ⓐ Ⓑ Ⓒ Ⓓ Ⓔ	60. Ⓐ Ⓑ Ⓒ Ⓓ Ⓔ	90. Ⓐ Ⓑ Ⓒ Ⓓ Ⓔ

91. Ⓐ Ⓑ Ⓒ Ⓓ Ⓔ	121. Ⓐ Ⓑ Ⓒ Ⓓ Ⓔ	151. Ⓐ Ⓑ Ⓒ Ⓓ Ⓔ
92. Ⓐ Ⓑ Ⓒ Ⓓ Ⓔ	122. Ⓐ Ⓑ Ⓒ Ⓓ Ⓔ	152. Ⓐ Ⓑ Ⓒ Ⓓ Ⓔ
93. Ⓐ Ⓑ Ⓒ Ⓓ Ⓔ	123. Ⓐ Ⓑ Ⓒ Ⓓ Ⓔ	153. Ⓐ Ⓑ Ⓒ Ⓓ Ⓔ
94. Ⓐ Ⓑ Ⓒ Ⓓ Ⓔ	124. Ⓐ Ⓑ Ⓒ Ⓓ Ⓔ	154. Ⓐ Ⓑ Ⓒ Ⓓ Ⓔ
95. Ⓐ Ⓑ Ⓒ Ⓓ Ⓔ	125. Ⓐ Ⓑ Ⓒ Ⓓ Ⓔ	155. Ⓐ Ⓑ Ⓒ Ⓓ Ⓔ
96. Ⓐ Ⓑ Ⓒ Ⓓ Ⓔ	126. Ⓐ Ⓑ Ⓒ Ⓓ Ⓔ	156. Ⓐ Ⓑ Ⓒ Ⓓ Ⓔ
97. Ⓐ Ⓑ Ⓒ Ⓓ Ⓔ	127. Ⓐ Ⓑ Ⓒ Ⓓ Ⓔ	157. Ⓐ Ⓑ Ⓒ Ⓓ Ⓔ
98. Ⓐ Ⓑ Ⓒ Ⓓ Ⓔ	128. Ⓐ Ⓑ Ⓒ Ⓓ Ⓔ	158. Ⓐ Ⓑ Ⓒ Ⓓ Ⓔ
99. Ⓐ Ⓑ Ⓒ Ⓓ Ⓔ	129. Ⓐ Ⓑ Ⓒ Ⓓ Ⓔ	159. Ⓐ Ⓑ Ⓒ Ⓓ Ⓔ
100. Ⓐ Ⓑ Ⓒ Ⓓ Ⓔ	130. Ⓐ Ⓑ Ⓒ Ⓓ Ⓔ	160. Ⓐ Ⓑ Ⓒ Ⓓ Ⓔ
101. Ⓐ Ⓑ Ⓒ Ⓓ Ⓔ	131. Ⓐ Ⓑ Ⓒ Ⓓ Ⓔ	161. Ⓐ Ⓑ Ⓒ Ⓓ Ⓔ
102. Ⓐ Ⓑ Ⓒ Ⓓ Ⓔ	132. Ⓐ Ⓑ Ⓒ Ⓓ Ⓔ	162. Ⓐ Ⓑ Ⓒ Ⓓ Ⓔ
103. Ⓐ Ⓑ Ⓒ Ⓓ Ⓔ	133. Ⓐ Ⓑ Ⓒ Ⓓ Ⓔ	163. Ⓐ Ⓑ Ⓒ Ⓓ Ⓔ
104. Ⓐ Ⓑ Ⓒ Ⓓ Ⓔ	134. Ⓐ Ⓑ Ⓒ Ⓓ Ⓔ	164. Ⓐ Ⓑ Ⓒ Ⓓ Ⓔ
105. Ⓐ Ⓑ Ⓒ Ⓓ Ⓔ	135. Ⓐ Ⓑ Ⓒ Ⓓ Ⓔ	165. Ⓐ Ⓑ Ⓒ Ⓓ Ⓔ
106. Ⓐ Ⓑ Ⓒ Ⓓ Ⓔ	136. Ⓐ Ⓑ Ⓒ Ⓓ Ⓔ	166. Ⓐ Ⓑ Ⓒ Ⓓ Ⓔ
107. Ⓐ Ⓑ Ⓒ Ⓓ Ⓔ	137. Ⓐ Ⓑ Ⓒ Ⓓ Ⓔ	167. Ⓐ Ⓑ Ⓒ Ⓓ Ⓔ
108. Ⓐ Ⓑ Ⓒ Ⓓ Ⓔ	138. Ⓐ Ⓑ Ⓒ Ⓓ Ⓔ	168. Ⓐ Ⓑ Ⓒ Ⓓ Ⓔ
109. Ⓐ Ⓑ Ⓒ Ⓓ Ⓔ	139. Ⓐ Ⓑ Ⓒ Ⓓ Ⓔ	169. Ⓐ Ⓑ Ⓒ Ⓓ Ⓔ
110. Ⓐ Ⓑ Ⓒ Ⓓ Ⓔ	140. Ⓐ Ⓑ Ⓒ Ⓓ Ⓔ	170. Ⓐ Ⓑ Ⓒ Ⓓ Ⓔ
111. Ⓐ Ⓑ Ⓒ Ⓓ Ⓔ	141. Ⓐ Ⓑ Ⓒ Ⓓ Ⓔ	171. Ⓐ Ⓑ Ⓒ Ⓓ Ⓔ
112. Ⓐ Ⓑ Ⓒ Ⓓ Ⓔ	142. Ⓐ Ⓑ Ⓒ Ⓓ Ⓔ	172. Ⓐ Ⓑ Ⓒ Ⓓ Ⓔ
113. Ⓐ Ⓑ Ⓒ Ⓓ Ⓔ	143. Ⓐ Ⓑ Ⓒ Ⓓ Ⓔ	173. Ⓐ Ⓑ Ⓒ Ⓓ Ⓔ
114. Ⓐ Ⓑ Ⓒ Ⓓ Ⓔ	144. Ⓐ Ⓑ Ⓒ Ⓓ Ⓔ	174. Ⓐ Ⓑ Ⓒ Ⓓ Ⓔ
115. Ⓐ Ⓑ Ⓒ Ⓓ Ⓔ	145. Ⓐ Ⓑ Ⓒ Ⓓ Ⓔ	175. Ⓐ Ⓑ Ⓒ Ⓓ Ⓔ
116. Ⓐ Ⓑ Ⓒ Ⓓ Ⓔ	146. Ⓐ Ⓑ Ⓒ Ⓓ Ⓔ	176. Ⓐ Ⓑ Ⓒ Ⓓ Ⓔ
117. Ⓐ Ⓑ Ⓒ Ⓓ Ⓔ	147. Ⓐ Ⓑ Ⓒ Ⓓ Ⓔ	177. Ⓐ Ⓑ Ⓒ Ⓓ Ⓔ
118. Ⓐ Ⓑ Ⓒ Ⓓ Ⓔ	148. Ⓐ Ⓑ Ⓒ Ⓓ Ⓔ	178. Ⓐ Ⓑ Ⓒ Ⓓ Ⓔ
119. Ⓐ Ⓑ Ⓒ Ⓓ Ⓔ	149. Ⓐ Ⓑ Ⓒ Ⓓ Ⓔ	179. Ⓐ Ⓑ Ⓒ Ⓓ Ⓔ
120. Ⓐ Ⓑ Ⓒ Ⓓ Ⓔ	150. Ⓐ Ⓑ Ⓒ Ⓓ Ⓔ	180. Ⓐ Ⓑ Ⓒ Ⓓ Ⓔ

181. Ⓐ Ⓑ Ⓒ Ⓓ Ⓔ
182. Ⓐ Ⓑ Ⓒ Ⓓ Ⓔ
183. Ⓐ Ⓑ Ⓒ Ⓓ Ⓔ
184. Ⓐ Ⓑ Ⓒ Ⓓ Ⓔ
185. Ⓐ Ⓑ Ⓒ Ⓓ Ⓔ
186. Ⓐ Ⓑ Ⓒ Ⓓ Ⓔ
187. Ⓐ Ⓑ Ⓒ Ⓓ Ⓔ
188. Ⓐ Ⓑ Ⓒ Ⓓ Ⓔ
189. Ⓐ Ⓑ Ⓒ Ⓓ Ⓔ
190. Ⓐ Ⓑ Ⓒ Ⓓ Ⓔ
191. Ⓐ Ⓑ Ⓒ Ⓓ Ⓔ
192. Ⓐ Ⓑ Ⓒ Ⓓ Ⓔ
193. Ⓐ Ⓑ Ⓒ Ⓓ Ⓔ
194. Ⓐ Ⓑ Ⓒ Ⓓ Ⓔ
195. Ⓐ Ⓑ Ⓒ Ⓓ Ⓔ
196. Ⓐ Ⓑ Ⓒ Ⓓ Ⓔ
197. Ⓐ Ⓑ Ⓒ Ⓓ Ⓔ

198. Ⓐ Ⓑ Ⓒ Ⓓ Ⓔ
199. Ⓐ Ⓑ Ⓒ Ⓓ Ⓔ
200. Ⓐ Ⓑ Ⓒ Ⓓ Ⓔ
201. Ⓐ Ⓑ Ⓒ Ⓓ Ⓔ
202. Ⓐ Ⓑ Ⓒ Ⓓ Ⓔ
203. Ⓐ Ⓑ Ⓒ Ⓓ Ⓔ
204. Ⓐ Ⓑ Ⓒ Ⓓ Ⓔ
205. Ⓐ Ⓑ Ⓒ Ⓓ Ⓔ
206. Ⓐ Ⓑ Ⓒ Ⓓ Ⓔ
207. Ⓐ Ⓑ Ⓒ Ⓓ Ⓔ
208. Ⓐ Ⓑ Ⓒ Ⓓ Ⓔ
209. Ⓐ Ⓑ Ⓒ Ⓓ Ⓔ
210. Ⓐ Ⓑ Ⓒ Ⓓ Ⓔ
211. Ⓐ Ⓑ Ⓒ Ⓓ Ⓔ
212. Ⓐ Ⓑ Ⓒ Ⓓ Ⓔ
213. Ⓐ Ⓑ Ⓒ Ⓓ Ⓔ
214. Ⓐ Ⓑ Ⓒ Ⓓ Ⓔ

215. Ⓐ Ⓑ Ⓒ Ⓓ Ⓔ
216. Ⓐ Ⓑ Ⓒ Ⓓ Ⓔ
217. Ⓐ Ⓑ Ⓒ Ⓓ Ⓔ
218. Ⓐ Ⓑ Ⓒ Ⓓ Ⓔ
219. Ⓐ Ⓑ Ⓒ Ⓓ Ⓔ
220. Ⓐ Ⓑ Ⓒ Ⓓ Ⓔ
221. Ⓐ Ⓑ Ⓒ Ⓓ Ⓔ
222. Ⓐ Ⓑ Ⓒ Ⓓ Ⓔ
223. Ⓐ Ⓑ Ⓒ Ⓓ Ⓔ
224. Ⓐ Ⓑ Ⓒ Ⓓ Ⓔ
225. Ⓐ Ⓑ Ⓒ Ⓓ Ⓔ
226. Ⓐ Ⓑ Ⓒ Ⓓ Ⓔ
227. Ⓐ Ⓑ Ⓒ Ⓓ Ⓔ
228. Ⓐ Ⓑ Ⓒ Ⓓ Ⓔ
229. Ⓐ Ⓑ Ⓒ Ⓓ Ⓔ
230. Ⓐ Ⓑ Ⓒ Ⓓ Ⓔ

GRE LITERATURE
IN ENGLISH
EXAM V

DIRECTIONS: Choose the best answer for each question and mark the letter of your selection on the corresponding answer sheet.

Questions 1-3 refer to the excerpts below.

1.   Which refers to Shakespeare?

2.   Which refers to Jonson?

3.   Which refers to Chaucer?

    (A) (He) does not indulge in fine sentiment; he has no bravura passages; he is ever master of himself and of his subject. The light upon his page is the light of common day.

    (B) (He) is a miserable boaster without character, with a groveling soul and an itch for writing.

    (C) He is a great lover and praiser of himself; a contemner and scorner of others; given rather to lose a friend than a jest; jealous of every word and action of those about him, especially after drink, which is one of the elements in which he liveth.

    (D) (He) was so intoxicated with the love of flattery that he sought it amongst the lowest of people, and the silliest of women; and was never so well pleased with any companions as those that worshipped him, while he insulted them.

    (E) If we wish to know the force of human genius we should read (him). If we wish to see the insignificance of human learning, we may study his commentators.

4.   "He was small in stature, with a furrowed visage, which, as yet, could hardly be termed aged. There was a remarkable intelligence in his features, as of a person who had so cultivated his mental part, that it could not fail to mould the physical to itself and become manifest by unmistakable tokens."

These two sentences describe

(A) Roger Chillingworth in *The Scarlet Letter*

(B) Roderick Usher in *Fall of the House of Usher*

(C) Natty Bumpo in *Last of the Mohegans*

(D) Jack Potter in *The Bride Comes to Yellow Sky*

(E) Giovanni in *Rappacini's Daughter*

5.   "The son of _____,
From whom this tyrant holds the due of birth,
Lives in the English court, and is received
Of the most pious Edward with such grace
That the malevolence of fortune nothing
Takes from his high respect. . ."

Which of the following correctly completes the sentence above?

(A) Gloucester   (D) Duncan

(B) Richard III   (E) Polixenes

(C) Henry IV

6.   "He lay down on a wide bunk that stretched across the end of the room. In the other end, cracker boxes were made to serve as furniture. They were grouped about the fireplace. A picture from an illustrated weekly was upon the log walls, and three rifles were paralleled on pegs. Equipments hung on handy projections, and some tin dishes lay upon a small pile of firewood."

The writing style of this passage is most characteristic of American

(A) Naturalism   (D) Romanticism

(B) Sentamentalism   (E) Modernism

(C) Rodomontadism

7.   "I celebrate myself;
       And what I assume you shall assume;
       For every atom belonging to me, as good be-
            longs to you

       I loaf and invite my soul;
       I lean and loaf at my ease, observing a blade
            of summer grass.

Song of Myself – Walt Whitman

Whitman's lines are deemed characteristic of Free Verse for all the reasons EXCEPT which of the following?

(A) An irregular, rhythmic cadence

(B) The recurrence, with variations, of significant phrases and image patterns

(C) Appearance of the poem does not interfere with established irregularity

(D) The regular use of unrhymed oxytones having assonance

(E) The lack of rhyme scheme

Questions 8 and 9

     There was never a sound beside the wood but one,
And that was my long scythe whispering to the ground.
What was it it whispered? I knew not well myself;
Perhaps it was something about the heat of the sun,
Something, perhaps about the lack of sound –
And that was why it whispered and did not speak.
It was no dream of the gift of idle hours,
Or easy gold at the hand of fay or elf:
Anything more than the truth would have seemed too weak
To the earnest love that laid the swale in rows,
Not without feeble-pointed spikes of flowers
(Pale orchises), and scared a bright green snake.
The fact is the sweetest dream that labor knows,
My long scythe whispered and left the hay to make.

8.   Which of the following best summarizes the author's concern?

(A) The secrets of nature surround us and can be revealed to anyone who will take time out and listen.

(B) One benefit of physical labor can be psychic revelation.

(C) Humans must work hard at discovering the truth: it will not come to the passive observer.

(D) The secrets of life are hinted at, yet never quite revealed.

(E) Mankind's role on Earth is to labor; to know anything beyond this is impossible.

9.   The poem is written by

(A) William Carlos Williams

(B) Robert Lowell

(C) Robert Frost

(D) Carl Sandburg

(E) William Cullen Bryant

10.   The conventional divisions of Pastoral Elegy include each of the following EXCEPT

(A) invocation of the muse.

(B) an admonition to Death.

(C) an expression of grief.

(D) a digression, usually about the church.

(E) an admission that everyone is mortal.

11.   Late in the afternoon of a chilly day in February, two
       gentlemen were sitting alone over their wine, in a well-fur-
       nished dining parlor, in the town of P_____ in Kentucky.
       There were no servants present, and the gentlemen, with chairs
       closely approaching, seemed to be discussing some subject
       with great earnestness.

       This is the first paragraph of

       (A) *The Man That Corrupted Hadleyburg*

       (B) *The Bride Comes to Yellow Sky*

       (C) *A Clean Well Lighted Place*

       (D) *Great Expectations*

       (E) *Uncle Tom's Cabin*

Questions 12-14

       How soon hath Time, the subtle thief of youth,
       Stolen on his wing my three and twentieth year!
       My hasting days fly on with full career,
       But my late spring no bud or blossom show'th.
       Perhaps my semblance might deceive the truth,
       That I to manhood am arrived so near,
       And inward ripeness doth much less appear,
       That some more timely-happy spirits endu'th.
       Yet be it less or more, or soon or slow,
       It shall be still in strictest measure even
       To that same lot, however mean or high,
       Toward which Time leads me, and the will of Heaven;
       All is, if I have grace to use it so,
       As ever in my great Taskmaster's eye.

12.   This sonnet reveals that the author wrote in conformance with
       _____models.

       (A) Shakespearean   (D) Italian

       (B) Phyrgian   (E) Romanesque

       (C) Spenserian

13. This sonnet is characterized by each of the following with the *exception* that the author

(A) avoids the final couplet.

(B) uses enclosed instead of alternating rhyme in the octave.

(C) does not make a sharp distinction between octave and sestet.

(D) does not follow a pattern of abba, abba, cdedce.

(E) alters meter and line requirements.

14. This sonnet was written by

(A) William Shakespeare   (D) Petrarch

(B) John Milton   (E) Thomas Wyatt

(C) Edmund Spenser

Questions 15-17 refer to the following excerpts from essays.

15. Which of the following is an example of an essay by Addison?

16. Which of the following is an example of an essay by Johnson?

17. Which of the following is an example of an essay by Goldsmith?

(A) As I am one of that sauntering tribe of mortals, who spend the greatest part of their time in taverns, coffee-houses, and other places of public resort, I have thereby an opportunity of observing an infinite variety of characters, which, to a person of a contemplative turn, is a much higher entertainment than a view of all the curiosities of art or nature.

(B) So far from the position holding true, that great wit (or genius, in our modern way of speaking) has a necessary alliance with insanity, the greatest wits, on the contrary, will ever be found to be the sanest writers.

(C) We are told the devil is the father of lies, and was a liar from the beginning; so that, beyond contradiction, the invention is old: and, which is more, his first Essay of it was purely political, employed in undermining the authority of his prince, and seducing a third part of the subjects from their obedience. . .

(D) I chanced to rise very early one particular morning this summer, and took a walk into the country to divert myself among the fields and meadows, while the green was new, and the flowers in their bloom.

(E) The imbecility which Berecundulus complains that in the presence of a numerous assembly freezes his faculties, is particularly incident to the studious part of mankind, whose education necessarily secludes them in their earlier years from mingled converse, till, at their dismission from schools and academies, they plunge at once into the tumult of the world, and, coming forth from the gloom of solitude, are overpowered by the blaze of public life.

Questions 18–21 refer to the following poem.

If I can stop one Heart from breaking
I shall not live in vain
If I can ease one Life the Aching
Or cool one Pain

Or help one fainting Robin
Unto his Nest again
I shall not live in Vain.

18. A most important characteristic of the poetry demonstrated here is the tendency toward

(A) an emphasis on nature.

(B) didacticism.

(C) empathy with the greater world.

(D) reclusiveness.

(E) lament for lost love.

19. The poet's use of capital first letters (exclusive of the first words of each line and "I") may be accounted for by

(A) the poet's love of hidden puzzles.

(B) personification of concepts.

(C) remnant 18th Century convention.

(D) the random quality of free verse.

(E) thematic emphasis.

20. The "Orphic" tone is related to the traditions of

(A) the 18th Century Enlightenment.

(B) American Free Thinking.

(C) Hobbesian materialism.

(D) evangelical messianism.

(E) late – Puritan literary climate.

21. The author of the poem above is

(A) Walt Whitman   (D) Ogden Nash

(B) Edna St. Vincent Millay (E) Carl Sandburg

(C) Emily Dickinson

My heart leaps up when I behold
   A rainbow in the sky:
So it was when my life began;
So is it now I am a man;
So be it when I shall grow old,
Or let me die!
The Child is the father of the Man;
And I could wish my days to be
Bound each to each by natural piety.

22. This poem illustrates a style and theme best termed

   (A) Johnsonian   (D) Wordsworthian

   (B) euphemistic   (E) Dickinsonian

   (C) Freudian

Questions 23-25

TO THE READER

This figure that thou here seest put,
   It was for gentle _____ cut;
Wherein the Graver had a strife
   with Nature, to out-doo the life:
O, could he but have drawne his wit
   As well in brasse, as he hath hit
His face; the Print would then surpasse
   All, that was ever writ in brasse.
But, since he cannot, Reader, looke
   Not on his Picture, but his Booke.

23. This famous invocation to the reader (accompanying an etching) describes

   (A) William Shakespeare   (D) John Dryden

   (B) Jonathan Swift   (E) Alexander Pope

   (C) Ben Jonson

24. The short poem was written by

   (A) William Shakespeare   (D) John Dryden

   (B) Ben Jonson   (E) Jonathan Swift

   (C) Alexander Pope

25. The purpose of the poem is to

   (A) apologize for the poor quality of the etching.

   (B) praise the author whose works follow.

   (C) divert the reader's attention from the familiar but distracting details of the author's life.

   (D) focus the reader's attention on the author's wit in the works that follow.

   (E) prepare the reader for a detailed textual analysis of the author's works.

Questions 26-28 refer to the descriptions below.

26. Which describes tragedy?

27. Which describes comedy?

28. Which describes tragi-comedy?

   (A) ... an honest or well-intended halfness; a non-performance or what is pretended to be performed, at the same time that one is giving loud pledges of performance.

   (B) It is a fog of human invention that obscures truth, and represents it in distortion.

   (C) ... they are essentially too absurd and extravagant to mention: I look upon them as a magic scene contrived to please the eyes and the ears at the expense of the understanding.

   (D) Here, a course of mirth; there, another of sadness and passion; a third of honor; and the fourth a duel. Thus, in two hours and a half we run through all the fits of Bedlam.

   (E) ... (It) ought to be a very solemn lecture, inculcating a particular Providence, and showing it plainly protecting the good, and chastising the bad, or at least the violent. ..

29. The sonnet was first introduced into England in the _____
Century by _____.

(A) 15th....Hans Holbein

(B) 17th....Bishop Percy

(C) 16th....Thomas Wyatt

(D) 14th....Earl of Surrey

(E) 17th....Shakespeare

Questions 30-33

> Of man's first disobedience, and the fruit
> Of that forbidden tree, whose mortal taste
> Brought death into the world, and all our woe,
> With loss of Eden, till one greater Man
> Restore us, and regain the blissful seat,   5
> Sing, Heavenly Muse, that on the secret top
> Of Oreb, or of Sinai, didst inspire
> That shepherd, who first taught the chosen seed
> In the beginning how the Heavens and Earth
> Rose out of Chaos; or if Sion hill   10
> Delight thee more, and Siloa's brook that flowed
> Fast by the oracle of God, I thence
> Invoke thy aid to my adventurous song,
> That with no middle flight intends to soar
> Above the Aonian mount, while it pursues   15
> Things unattempted yet in prose of rhyme.

30. These are the famous first 16 lines of

(A) *L'Allegro*   (D) *Paradise Lost*

(B) *The Song from Aglaura*   (E) *Amoretti*

(C) *De Shakespeare Nostrate*

545

31. The governing verb in this opening sentence is

(A) "restore"   (D) "sing"

(B) "taught"   (E) "invoke"

(C) "delight"

32. The style of this passage can best be described as

(A) blank verse   (D) Spenserian

(B) free verse   (E) syncretic

(C) iambic tetrameter

33. The shepherd referred to in line 8 is

(A) Jesus   (D) St. John the Baptist

(B) Paul the Apostle (E) Jeremiah the Prophet

(C) Moses

Questions 34-36

Whenever I find myself growing grim about the mouth;
whenever it is a damp, drizzly November in my soul;
whenever I find myself involuntarily pausing before coffin
warehouses and bringing up the rear of every funeral I meet;
and especially whenever my hypos get such an upper hand of
me, that it requires a strong moral principle to prevent me
from deliberately stepping into the street, and methodically
knocking people's hats off – then I account it high time
_____.

34. These well known words are spoken by

(A) Ishmael in *Moby Dick*.

(B) Bliful in *Tom Jones*.

(C) Captain M'Whirr in *Typhoon*.

(D) Samuel Johnson in *Journey To The Hebrides*.

(E) Fagin in *Oliver Twist*.

35. The word "hypo" in this selection indicates that the speaker

(A) is a drug addict.

(B) suffers spells of hyperactivity.

(C) is prone to attacks of dejection.

(D) feels he is acting hypocritically.

(E) is a hypochondriac.

36. The passage is completed with the words:

(A) ". . .pause and consider my condition."

(B) ". . .get to the sea as soon as I can."

(C) ". . .light out for the Territories."

(D) ". . .consider the words of Cato."

(E) ". . .return to the roots I was raised from."

37. The Romantic Period in English literature can be said to extend from:

(A) the publication of *Lyrical Ballads* to the death of Sir Walter Scott.

(B) the publication of *The Deserted Village* to the death of Shelley.

(C) the publication of *Biographia Literaria* to the death of Keats.

(D) the publication of *Songs of Innocence and Experience* to the death of Wordsworth.

(E) from the publication of *Ozymandias* to the death of Charles Lamb.

38. In his Preface to *Lyrical Ballads*, Wordsworth contended that the poetry he was presenting

   (A) did not represent a radical departure from previous English poetry.

   (B) should be looked upon as a revival of the tradition of the Roman poets.

   (C) could be understood as an extension of Neo-Classical poetic forms.

   (D) should be considered an experiment in adapting conversational language.

   (E) was essentially an attempt at portraying contemporary public taste.

Questions 39-40

(He) is, above all writers, at least above all modern writers, the poet of nature, the poet that holds up to his readers a faithful mirror of manners and of life. His characters are not modified by the customs of particular places, unpracticed by the rest of the world. . . they are the genuine progeny of common humanity, such as the world will always supply and observation will always find.

39. The writer referred to is

   (A) John Dryden

   (B) William Wordsworth

   (C) Robert Browning

   (D) William Shakespeare

   (E) Geoffrey Chaucer

40. The author of this passage is

   (A) James Boswell

   (B) Richard Sewall

   (C) Samuel Johnson

   (D) Samuel Pepys

   (E) Walter Raleigh

Perish the man, whoever he was, that freed me in the pastures from the cruel shackle on my feet, and saved me from death, and gave me back to life – a thankless deed! Had I died then I would not have been so sore a grief to my friends and to my own soul.

41.   These lines were spoken by

(A) Hippolytus   (D) Oedipus

(B) Charon   (E) Athena

(C) Creon

Some artists, whether by theoretical knowledge or by long practice, can represent things by imitating their shapes and colours, and others do so by the use of the voice; in the arts I have spoken of the imitation as produced by means of rhythm, language, and music, these being used either separately or in combination.

42.   The author describes artists in

(A) a predominantly Expressionistic mode.

(B) an Aristotelian ideal.

(C) a prevailing Pindaric attitude.

(D) a basically Impressionistic pattern.

(E) an Atomistic code.

43.   The marvellous should of course be represented in tragedy, but _____, where the persons acting the story are not before our eyes, may include more of the inexplicable, which is the chief element in the marvellous.

Which of the following would the author of this statement be referring to?

(A) Shakespeare's *Taming of the Shrew*

(B) Goldsmith's *She Stoops to Conquer*

(C) Ibsen's *Doll House*

(D) Homer's *Odyssey*

(E) Plutarch's *Lives of the Poets*

44. Which of the following completes the passage?

(A) Epic poetry   (D) Genteel comedy

(B) Serious drama   (E) Classical drama

(C) Melodrama

Questions 45-46

What possible motive could such a man have to deceive? His style had all the plainness and unpoetic boldness of truth. In the most straightforward way, he laid before me detailed accounts of New England witchcraft, each important item corroborated by respectable townsfolk, and, of not a few of the most surprising, he himself had been eyewitness.

45. In the passage above, Melville is

(A) berating the writer for being a hypocrite.

(B) defending the writer to his critics.

(C) facetiously illustrating the writer's deceitful intentions.

(D) describing his admiration of the writer's credentials.

(E) expressing terror at the revelation that the writer's stories must be true.

46. Melville is describing the author of

(A) *The Crucible.*

(B) *Magnalia Christi Americana.*

(C) *Sinners In The Hands of An Angry God.*

550

(D) *Murders on the Rue Morgue.*

(E) *The Inferno.*

Questions 47-49

> If the autumn would
> End!! If the sweet season,
> The late light in the tall trees would
> End! If the fragrance, the odor of
> Fallen apples, dust on the road,
> Water somewhere near, the scent of
> Water touching me; if this would end
> I could endure the absence in the night,
> The hands beyond the reach of hands, the name
> Called out and never answered with my name:
> The image seen but never seen with sight.
> I could endure this all
> If autumn ended and the cold light came.

47. An underlying contrast is presented between

    (A) images of light and of darkness.

    (B) images of coolness and of warmth.

    (C) expressions of life and of death.

    (D) sensations of contact and of loss.

    (E) impressions of fall and of winter.

48. The poet implies that

    (A) death would be preferable to his present state.

    (B) he would be more comfortable if he could not experience the everday sensations of life.

    (C) knowing more about the absent person's fate would alleviate his guilt.

    (D) only a return of his absent companion can bring happiness.

    (E) only the passage of time can heal his grief.

49.   The use of images in this poem is similar to that of

(A) William Wordsworth

(B) William Carlos Williams

(C) Walt Whitman

(D) Emily Dickinson

(E) Robert Lowell

Questions 50-51

I met the Bishop on the road
And much said he and I.
"Those breasts are flat and fallen now,
Those veins must soon be dry;
Live in a heavenly mansion,
Not in some foul sty."

"Fair and foul are near of kin,
And fair needs foul," I cried.
"My friends are gone, but that's a truth
Nor grave nor bed denied,
Learned in bodily lowliness
And in the heart's pride."

"A woman can be proud and stiff
When on love intent;
But love has pitched his mansion in
The place of excrement;
For nothing can be sole or whole
That has not been rent."

50.   The author indicates a belief in all of the following EXCEPT

(A) the paradox that wisdom may reside with fools and
        beggars.

(B) the presentation and resolution of opposites.

(C) the lack of understanding by representatives of orthodoxy.

(D) the recognition of the destructive potential of self-indul-gence.

(E) the necessity of familiarity with suffering.

51.   The poem was written by

(A) Robert Frost   (D) Edna St. Vincent Millay

(B) Robert Browning   (E) T.S. Eliot

(C) W.B. Yeats

Questions 52-54 refer to the excerpts below.

52.   Which of the following is an example of diary narration?

53.   Which of the following is an example of interior monologue?

54.   Which of the following is an example of detached autobiogra-phy?

(A) I knew it. I knew if I came to this diner, I'd draw something like this baby on my left. They've been saving him up for me for weeks. Now we've simply got to have him – his sister was so sweet to us in London: we can stick him next to Mrs. Parker – she talks enough for two.

(B) Up until I learned my lesson in a very bitter way, I never had more than one friend at a time, and my friendships, though ardent, were short.

(C) An extraordinary thing happened today. I got up rather late, and when Marva brought my boots, I asked her for the time. Hearing that ten had struck quite a while before, I dressed in a hurry.

(D) Well, I want to tell you, Mrs. Babbitt, and I know Mrs. Schmaltz heartily agrees with me, that we've never en-joyed a dinner more – that was some of the finest fried chicken I ever tasted in my life – and it certainly is a mighty great pleasure to be able to just have this quiet evening with you and George.

(E) I know what is being said about me and you can take my side or theirs, that's your own business. It's my word against Eunice's and Olivia Ann's, and it should be plain enough to anyone with two good eyes which one of us has their wits about them.

55.   In productions involving Presentational Drama

(A) actors speak directly to the audience.

(B) actors ignore the audience.

(C) actors respond to on-going cues from a director.

(D) actors explore alternate interpretations of their character with each performance.

(E) actors direct themselves.

56.   An example of a presentational play is

(A) *Ah! Wilderness!*

(B) *The Caucasian Chalk Circle*

(C) *All My Sons*

(D) *The Glass Menagerie*

(E) *Cyrano de Bergerac*

57.   The proper epic of this world is not now "Arms and the Man;" it is "Tools and the Man." All true work is religion. Admirable was that of the old monks, "Laborare est orare." "Work is worship." Older than all preached gospels was this unpreached, inarticulate, but ineradicable, forever-enduring gospel: work, and therein have well-being.

Which of the following passages was also written by the author of the passage quoted above?

(A) " Oh, captive, bound," cried the phantom; "not to know that ages of incessant labor by immortal creatures for this earth must pass into eternity before the good of which it is susceptible is all developed!"

(B) The wisdom of the scribe cometh by opportunity of leisure; and he that hath little business shall become wise. How shall he become wise that holdeth the plow? He will set his heart upon turning his furrows; and his wakefulness is to give his heifers their fodder.

(C) Then a ploughman said, Speak to us of Work.

And he answered, saying:

You work that you may keep pace with the earth and the soul of the earth.

For to be idle is to become a stranger unto the seasons, and to step out of life's procession, that marches in majesty and proud submission towards the infinite.

(D) And who art thou braggest of thy life of idleness; complacently showest thy bright gilt equipages, sumtuous cusions, appliances of folding of the hands to more sleep? Thou art an original figure in this creation. One monster there is in the world: the idle man.

(E) Man and his deed are two distinct things. Whereas a good deed should call forth approbation and a wicked deed disapprobation, the doer of the deed, whether good or wicked, always deserves respect or pity as the case may be.

58.   The first selection quoted above (beginning "The proper epic of this world") was written

(A) during the Post – Industrialization period after World War II.

(B) during the Renaissance.

(C) during the Edwardian Age.

(D) during the Industrial Revolution.

(E) during the Age of Enlightenment.

Questions 59-60

It is not that they are morally worse than other people; but they know nothing. Or, rather, it is a good deal worse than that: they know everything wrong. Put a thing on the stage for them as it is in real life, and instead of receiving it with the blank wonder of plain ignorance, they reject it with scorn as an imposture, on the ground that the real thing is known to the whole world to be quite different. Offer them Mr. Crummles's real pump and tubs, and they will denounce both as spurious on the ground that tubs have no handles, and the pump no bung-hole.

59.   The author of this passage is chastising

(A) contemporary audiences.

(B) dramatic critics.

(C) investors in theatrical productions.

(D) producers.

(E) playwrights.

60.   The author of this passage would most likely describe himself as

(A) a cynic   (D) a dramatic realist

(B) an idealist   (E) an Impressionist

(C) a satirist

Questions 61-63 refer to the excerpts below.

61.   Which is from Langland's *Piers the Plowman*?

62.   Which is from Chaucer's *The Canterbury Tales*?

63.   Which is from *Beowulf*?

(A) A fair lady, clothed in linen, came down from a castle and called me gently, saying, "My son, are you asleep? Do you see these people, moving about in such a turmoil of activity? Most people who pass through this world wish for nothing better than worldly success: the only heaven they think about is on earth."

(B) I saw the new moone late yestreen, wi' the auld moone in hir arme, and if we gang to se, master, I feir we'll cum to harme."

(C) The count of his hours to end had come, done were his days. The Danes were glad, the hard fight was over, they had their desire. Cleared was the hall, 'twas cleansed by the hero with keen heart and courage, who came from afar.

(D) But nathelees, whil I have tyme and space, er that I ferther in this tale pace, me thinketh it acordaunt to resoun to telle yow al the condicioun of each of hem, so as it seemed to me. . .

(E) O thou, wha in th Heavens dost dwell, wha, as it pleases best thysel', sends ane to heaven and ten to hell, a' for thy glory, and no for ony guid or ill they've done afore thee!

64.   From harmony, from heavenly harmony
          This universal frame began;
        When Nature underneath a heap
          Of jarring atoms lay,
          And could not heave her head,
        Her tuneful voice was heard from high:
          "Arise, ye more than dead."

In this introduction to his Ode, the poet

(A) celebrates the Classical order of nature.

(B) celebrates the life-force of nature.

(C) celebrates the power of music.

(D) celebrates the harmony between Man and Nature.

(E) celebrates the resurrection of life within nature.

Questions 65-67

Indentured long to logic and the gown.
Lean as a rake the horse on which he sat,
And he himself was anything but fat,
But rather wore a hollow look and sad.

Threadbare the little outercoat he had,   5
For he was still to get a benefice
And thoughts of worldly office were not his.

65.   The character being described by Chaucer is

       (A) the Monk   (D) the Student

       (B) the Friar   (E) the Pardoner

       (C) the Parson

66.   In line 6, the "benefice" is

       (A) a position in the church.

       (B) worldly gain.

       (C) scholarly advancement.

       (D) secular employment.

       (E) an inheritance.

67.   Chaucer here draws a parallel between

       (A) the appearance of the subject and his chances for worldly
           success.

       (B) the appearance of the horse and the subject's ambitions.

       (C) the enslaved nature of both subject and horse.

       (D) the appearance of the subject and the appearance of the
           horse.

       (E) the quality of the subject's clothes and the quality of his
           thought.

Questions 68-78. For each of the following passages, identify the
author or title of the work. Base your decision on the content and style
of each passage.

68. The unhappy man whose ravings are recorded above, was a melancholy instance of the baneful results of energies misdirected in early life, and excesses prolonged until their consequences could never be repaired. The thoughtless riot, dissipation, and debauchery of his younger days, produced fever and delirium.

(A) Fyodor Dostoevski

(D) Charles Dickens

(B) Samuel Johnson

(E) Victor Hugo

(C) Thomas Hardy

69. It was waning towards evening; there was still a faint mist, but it had cleared a little except in the damper tracts of subjacent country and along the river-courses. He thought again of Christminster, and wished, since he had come two or three miles from his aunt's house on purpose, that he could have seen for once this attractive city of which he had been told.

(A) Leo Tolstoy's *War and Peace*

(B) James Herriot's *All Creatures Great and Small*

(C) Charles Dickens *Great Expectations*

(D) Joseph Conrad's *Heart of Darkness*

(E) Thomas Hardy's *Jude the Obscure*

70. As the physician repeated these lines, a flash of intelligence seemed to revive in the invalid's eye – sunk again – again struggled, and he spoke more intelligibly than before, and in the tone of one eager to say something which he felt would escape him unless said instantly. "A question of death-bed, a question of death-bed, doctor – a reduction ex capite lecti – Withering against Wilibus – about the morbus sonticus. I pleaded the cause for the pursuer – I, and – and – Why, I shall forget my own name – I, and – he that was the wittiest and the best humoured man living –"

(A) Walter Scott's *Waverly Novels*

(B) James Fenimore Cooper's *The Spy*

(C) Marcel Proust's *Swann's Way*

(D) George Eliot's *Adam Bede*

(E) Charles Dickens' *Martin Chuzzlewit*

71.   But do not let us quarrel any more,
       No, my Lucrezia; bear with me for once:
       Sit down and all shall happen as you wish.
       Your turn your face, but does it bring your
                      heart?

(A) Dante Gabriel Rosetti

(B) Algernon Charles Swinburne

(C) William Butler Yeats

(D) Alfred Lord Tennyson

(E) Robert Browning

72.   I was called before the head matron, a tall woman, with a stolid
       face. She began taking my pedigree. "What religion?" was her
       first question. "None, I am an atheist." "Atheism is prohibited
       here. You will have to go to church." I replied that I would do
       nothing of the kind. I did not believe in anything the Church
       stood for and, not being a hypocrite, I would not attend, Be-
       sides, I came from Jewish people. Was there a synagogue?

(A) Hannah Arendt   (D) Naomi Weisstein

(B) Barbara Tuchman   (E) Betty Friedan

(C) Emma Goldman

73.   So Pete Crocker, the sheriff of Barnstable County, which was
       the whole of Cape Cod, came into the Federal Ethical Suicide
       Parlor in Hyannis one May afternoon – and he told the two six-
       foot Hostesses there that they weren't to be alarmed, but that a
       notorious nothinghead named Billy the Poet was believed
       headed for the Cape.

(A) Terkel's *Doc Graham*

(B) Vonnegut's *Welcome to the Monkey House*

(C) Steadman's *A Worker of Miracles*

(D) Robbins' *Another Roadside Attraction*

(E) Hudson's *Farnsbee South*

74. The use may be of awakening to unconverted persons in this congregation. This that you have heard is the case of every one of you that are out of Christ. That world of misery, that lake of burning brimstone is extended abroad under you. There is the dreadful pit of the glowing flames of the wrath of God; there is Hell's wide gaping mouth open; and you have nothing to stand upon, nor any thing to take hold of: there is nothing between you and Hell but the air; 'tis only the power and mere pleasure of God that holds you up.

(A) Mather   (D) Edwards

(B) Whitfield   (E) Calvin

(C) Luther

75.   FRED: You're the Devil.
LIZZIE: What?
FRED: You're the Devil.
LIZZIE: The Bible again! What's the matter with you?
FRED: Nothing. I was just kidding.
LIZZIE: Funny way to kid. Did you like it?
FRED: Like what?
LIZZIE (she mimics him, smiling): Like what? My, but you're stupid, my little lady.
FRED: Oh! Oh that? Yes, I liked it. I liked it fine. How much do you want?

(A) Edward Albee   (D) Samuel Beckett

(B) Jean-Paul Sartre   (E) Sam Shepard

(C) G.B. Shaw

76. What I said the other day about painting is true also of poetry. It is simply that one should recognize and try to express only what is excellent, and that is saying a great deal in a few words. Today I experienced something that, simply told, could be a beautiful idyl, but what is poetry, episode, and idyl? Must it always be patchwork when we participate in a revelation of nature?

(A) Goethe's *Sorrows of Young Werther*

(B) Mann's *Magic Mountain*

(C) Hesse's *Magister Ludi*

(D) Bettelheim's *Uses of Enchantment*

(E) Ruskin's *Modern Painters*

77. The first American literary essayist with an international reputation was

(A) St. John de Crevecoeur. . .*Letters from an American Farmer*

(B) Oliver Wendell Holmes. . .*The Autocrat of the Breakfast Table*

(C) H.D. Thoreau. . .*Walden*

(D) Washington Irving. . .*Sketch Book*

(E) Cotton Mather. . .*Essays To Do Good*

78. "What do you want in the way of supplies?" he asked, for he was pleased that I was staying with Lonesome Valley. "Coal bucket, erasers, chalk, windowpanes?"

"All of that and more too," I said, as John Hampton looked strangely at me. "I want two bags of lime, a water cooler with a faucet, enough paint to paint my schoolhouse, paintbrushes, hatchet, hammer, nails, hoe, rake, axe, and shovel."

"Just a minute," Mr. Staggers broke in, "who's goin' to pain the house?"

"I'm goin' to pain it," I said. "I'm going to clean that place up!"

(A) Bret Harte   (D) Jesse Stuart

(B) Mary Rawlings   (E) Frank O'Connor

(C) Willa Cather

Questions 79-80 refer to the following passage.

"My father's name being Pirrip and my Christian name, Philip,
my infant tongue could make of both names nothing more
explicit than Pip. So I called myself Pip and came to be called
Pip."

79.   These are the opening lines of:

(A) *Dombey and Son*   (D) *Great Expectations*

(B) *Hard Times*   (E) *Bleak House*

(C) *Our Mutual Friend*

80.   This passage indicates that the speaker is

(A) unsure of his lineage.

(B) somewhat frightened and over-sensitive.

(C) of limited intelligence.

(D) imitating the tone of the opening passages of Genesis.

(E) extremely egocentric.

Questions 81-82 refer to the following criticism of Wordsworth.

Wordsworth calls Voltaire dull, and surely the production of
these (referring to a brief quoted passage above) un-Voltairian lines
must have been imposed on him as a judgement. One can hear them
being quoted at a Social Science Congress; one can call up the whole
scene. A great room in one of our dismal provincial towns; dusty air and
jaded afternoon daylight; benches full of men with bald heads and
women in spectacles; an orator lifting up his face from a manuscript
written within and without to declaim these lines of Wordsworth; and
in the soul of any poor child of nature who may have wandered in

thither, an unutterable sense of lamentation, and mourning, and woe!

81. The writer of this passage criticizes Wordsworth's poetry because of its

   (A) un-Voltairian lines.

   (B) scientific system of thought.

   (C) overdone lamentations.

   (D) popular appeal.

   (E) provincial quality.

82. The author of the passage is

   (A) William Hazlitt

   (B) Samuel Taylor Coleridge

   (C) Charles Lamb

   (D) Matthew Arnold

   (E) John Ruskin

Questions 83-85 refer to the excerpts below.

83. Which excerpt was written by Wordsworth?

84. Which excerpt was written by Arnold?

85. Which excerpt was written by Browning?

   (A) O for the coming of that glorious time
   When, prizing knowledge as her noblest wealth
   And best protection, this Imperial Realm,
   While she exacts allegiance, shall admit
   An obligation, on her part, to teach
   Them who are born to serve her and obey;
   Binding herself by statute to secure,
   For all the children whom her soil maintains,
   The rudiments of letters, and inform
   The mind with moral and religious truth.

(B) I fled Him, down the nights and down the days;
          I fled Him, down the arches of the years;
     I fled Him, down the labyrinthine ways
          Of my own mind; and in the mist of tears
     I hid from Him, and under running laughter.

(C) Yes! in the sea of life enisled,
     With echoing straits between us thrown,
     Dotting the shoreless watery wild,
     We mortal millions live alone.
     The islands feel the enclasping flow,
     And then their endless bounds they know.

(D) Savage I was sitting in my house, late, lone:
          Dreary, weary with the long day's work:
     Head of me, heart of me, stupid as a stone:
          Tongue tied now, now blaspheming like a Turk;
     When in a moment, just a knock, call, cry,
          Half a pang and all a rapture, there again were we! -
     "What, and is it really you again?" quoth I:
          "I again, what else did you expect?" quoth She.

(E) The woods decay, the woods decay and fall,
     The vapors weep their bruthen to the ground,
     Man comes and tills the field and lies beneath,
     And after many a summer dies the swan.
     Me only cruel immortality
     Consumes; I wither slowly in thine arms,
     Here at the quiet limit of the world,
     A white-haired shadow roaming like a dream
     The ever-silent spaces of the East,
          Far-folded mists, and gleaming halls of morn.

Questions 86-88

I have been assured by a very knowing American of my acquaintance in London, that a young healthy child well nursed is at a year old a most delicious, nourishing, and wholesome food, whether stewed, roasted, baked, or boiled; and I make no doubt that it will equally serve in a fricassee or a ragout.

86.   The tone of this passage may best be described as

(A) factual description

(B) playful

(C) sarcastically outrageous

(D) comedically inventive

(E) cynical

87.   The reference to "a very knowing American" in this passage

(A) reflects the belief that Americans are uncivilized.

(B) underscores the preposterous nature of the author's proposition.

(C) points out the paternalistic nature of colonialism.

(D) is meant to be a statement of fact only.

(E) offers a citation from someone more experienced in what the author proposes.

88.   The author of the passage is

(A) Samuel Johnson   (D) James Boswell

(B) William Byrd   (E) Oliver Goldsmith

(C) Jonathan Swift

Questions 89-90 refer to the following.

Whoever thinks a faultless piece to see,
Thinks what ne'er was, nor is, noe e'er shall be.
In every work regard the writer's end,
Since none can compass more than they intend;
And if the means be just, the conduct true,
Applause, in spite of trivial faults, is due.

89. The poet believes that it is more important for the critic to

(A) consider the technical merits of a piece than criticize its message.

(B) consider the purpose of the piece than look for flaws in the execution.

(C) consider the effect on the readership than the impression made on the critic.

(D) consider any "trivial faults" as a natural adjunct of great works.

(E) consider the limitations of the writer when examining any technical flaws.

90. The selection was taken from

(A) Coleridge's *Biographia Literaria*

(B) Arnold's *The Function of Criticism at the Present Time*

(C) Milton's *Il Penseroso*

(D) Pope's *Essay on Criticism*

(E) Johnson's *Against Inquisitive and Perplexing Thoughts*

91. Let us just for the moment feel the pulses of Ulysses and of Miss Dorothy Richardson and M. Marcel Proust, on the earnest side of Briareus; on the other, the throb of The Shiek and Mr. Zane Grey, and, if you will, Mr. Robert Chambers and the rest. Is Ulysses in his cradle? Oh, dear! What a grey face! And Pointed Roofs, are they a gay little toy for nice little girls? Alas! You can hear the death-rattle in their throats. They can hear it themselves. They are listening to it with acute interest, trying to discover whether the intervals are minor thirds or major fourths. Which is rather infantile, really.

The author is criticizing most of all the

(A) the melodramatic quality of contemporary authors.

(B) pointless attention to meaningless novelistic detail.

567

(C) trivial nature of the popular novel.

(D) self-consciousness of the serious novel.

(E) lack of quality in contemporary literature.

Questions 92-94 refer to the descriptions below.

92. Which refers to Ibsen's *An Enemy of the People*?

93. Which refers to Wilde's *The Importance of Being Earnest*?

94. Which refers to Shaw's *Arms and the Man*?

(A) . . .it takes up the form of the "well-made"play and treats the matter with witty intelligence, so that sentiment is kept firmly in check.

(B) And for this reason we must admit that (it is) much nearer to pornography than is Boccaccio.

(C) (It) reversed the stock image of the professional soldier, showing him as a man who carries chocolate instead of ammunition and seeks to preserve his life instead of throwing it away.

(D) (It) is a fantasy revealing the sensational delights of the man in his early marriage with the young and tender bride.

(E) (It) conducts an inquiry. . .into the emerging conflict between two kinds of revolution – what might be called the traditional or conventional conception, and the new or modern conception.

Questions 95-98 refer to the following excerpts.

95. Which is a parody of Albert Camus?

96. Which is a parody of Grahame Greene?

97. Which is a parody of Willa Cather?

98. Which is a parody of Ernest Hemingway?

(A) By chance, blew up Perpigan Airport killing 3,000 people including my mother. It was a gloriously sunny day and if it hadn't been for the fact of stepping over the mutilated bodies the walk back to the boat would have been quite agreeable. I whistled to myself, thinking about the way I moved my tongue to vary the notes, and my benign disinterest stretched on to the limbless corpses that were strewn over the runway.

(B) I took a pull from the bottle. The whiskey was good. It burned my mouth and felt good and warm going down my esophagus and into my stomach. From there it was digested, and went to my kidneys and my bladder and into my intestines, and was good.

(C) I was just thinking around in my sad backyard, looking at those little drab careless starshaped clumps of crabgrass and beautiful chunks of some old bicycle crying out without words of the American Noon and half a newspaper with an ad about lotion for people with dry skins and dry souls,when my mother opened our frantic banging screen door and shouted, "Gogi Himmelman's here."

(D) I dropped off a Burlington train at Sweet Water one afternoon last fall to call on Marian Forrester. It was a lovely day. October stained the hills with quiet gold and russet, and scarlet as violent as the blood spilled not far away so many years ago along the banks of the Little Big Horn.

(E) The room was hot. Glancing round, Guy sensed that all eight of his companions were strangers to each other as well as to himself. Why had he, and they, come? What was his Lordship's motive in inviting this heterogeneous assembly to Motley Hall today?

Questions 99-101 refer to the excerpts below.

99.　In which is the "I" George Eliot's Silas Marner?

100.　In which is the "I" Thomas Hardy's Jude?

101.　In which is the "I" Stevenson's Dr. Jekyll?

(A) I have heard that in violent fevers, men, all ignorance, have
talked in ancient tongues; and that when the mystery is
probed, it turns out always that in their wholly forgotten
childhood those ancient tongues had been really spoken
in their hearing by some lofty scholars.

(B) I mean from henceforth to lead a life of extreme seclusion;
you must not be surprised, nor must you doubt my friendship, if my door is closed to you. You must suffer me to
go my own dark way. I have brought on myself a punishment and a danger that I cannot name.

(C) I am to blame – more than you think. I was quite aware that
you did not suspect till within the last meeting or two what
I was feeling about you. I admit that our meeting as
strangers prevented a sense of relationship, and that it was
a sort of subterfuge to avail myself of you. But don't you
think I deserve a little consideration for concealing my
wrong, very wrong, sentiments, since I couldn't help
having them?

(D) I am a stranger, and have been a wanderer, sorely against
my will. I have met with grievous mishaps by sea and
land, and have been long held in bonds among the hea-
then-folk.

(E) At first I'd a sor o' feeling come across me now and then,
as if you might be changed into the gold again; for some
times, turn my head which way I would, I seemed to see
the gold, and I thought I should be glad if I could feel it.

Questions 102-103.

Stick your patent name on a signboard
brother – all over – going west – young man
Tintex – Japalac – Certain-teed Overalls ads
and land sakes! under the new playbill ripped
in the guaranteed corner – see Bert Williams what?
Minstrels when you steal a chicken just
save me the wing, for if it isn't
Erie it ain't for miles around a
Mazda – and the telegraphic night coming on Thomas

102. The language of this poem is an example of

    (A) stream of consciousness

    (B) free-form

    (C) beat poetry

    (D) free association

    (E) the New York School

103. This poem was written by

    (A) E.E. Cummings   (D) T.S. Eliot

    (B) Theodore Roethke   (E) Hart Crane

    (C) Allen Ginsberg

104. In John Milton's writing two great historical movements combined into one poetic voice. These movements were

    (A) the Renaissance and Reformation

    (B) Neo-Classicism and the Renaissance

    (C) Puritanism and Utilitarianism

    (D) the Reformation and the Enlightenment

    (E) Federalism and Unitarianism

105. All of the following are Miltonian works EXCEPT

    (A) *Areopagitica*   (D) *Il Penseroso*

    (B) *Paradise Regained*   (E) *Samson Agonistes*

    (C) *Manuductio and Ministerium*

106. "Stark Romanticism" was the phrase that kept pounding through his head as he knocked on the door of Mama Paloma's, saw the slot opened and the single sloe plum that was Mama Paloma's eye scrutinizing him through the peep hole. "Oh, you again," the eye grinned at him, sliding back the bolt of the door. "The girls are all pretty busy tonight but go on up."

The author parodied is

(A) James Jones   (D) Elizabeth Kata

(B) Richard Wright   (E) Harper Lee

(C) James Baldwin

107. There is no way to count the pains we suffer. All our people are sick. There is no sword of thought which will protect us. The fruits of our famous land do not ripen. Our women cannot ease their labor pains by giving birth. One after another you can see our people speed like winged birds, faster than irresistible fire, to the shore of evening, to death. The city is dying, the deaths cannot be counted.

This is a passage from

(A) Juvenal's chronicle of the sacking of Rome.

(B) the Old Testament's description of the plagues sent against Egypt.

(C) Camus' *The Plague*.

(D) Sophocles' description of Thebes under Oedipus.

(E) the New Testament's description of Armageddon.

108. If it were done when 'tis done, then 'twere well
It were done quickly: if the assassination
Could trammel up the consequence, and catch
With his surcease success; that but this blow
Might be the be-all and the end-all here,
But here, upon this bank and shoal of time,
We'd jump the life to come.

The character speaking here is contemplating the murder of

(A) Caesar

(D) Cassius

(B) Claudius

(E) Gloucester

(C) Duncan

109. My Guide and I on that obscure road entered,
To come once more to the bright world; and taking
No thought of any rest we labored upward,
He first, I second, until I distinguished,
Through a round opening, some things of beauty
The heaven doth bear; and out of it we issued
To see above us once again the stars.

This poem is an interpretation of

(A) a near-death experience by one of Moody's subjects.

(B) the emergence out of the volcano in *Journey to the Center of the Earth.*

(C) the conversion of the Apostle Paul.

(D) the departure from Dante's *Inferno.*

(E) the classical *Orpheus in the Underworld.*

110. Neither on horseback nor seated,
But like himself, squarely on two feet,
The poet of death and lilacs
Loafs by the footpath. Even the bronze looks alive
Where it is folded like cloth. And he seems friendly.

The poet spoken about in line three is

(A) John Greenleaf Whittier

(B) William Cullen Bryant

(C) Robert Frost

(D) Walt Whitman

(E) Robert Herrick

Questions **111-112** refer to the following poem

It is not growing like a tree
In bulk, doth make man better be;
Or standing long an oak, three hundred year,
To fall a log at last, dry, bald, and sere:
A lily of a day
Is fairer far, in May,
Although it fall and die that night;
It was the plant and flower of light.
In small proportions we just beauties see,
And in short measures life may perfect be.

111.   Which of the following is the closest restatement of the poem's central theme?

(A) It is not the end that matters, but the means.

(B) Fame and success are not as important as appreciating beauty.

(C) It is how you live your life that matters, not whether you succeed.

(D) The appreciation of nature and the understanding of truth are one and the same.

(E) Perfection may be found in the small things of nature.

112.   This poem is written in

(A) the Pindaric mode

(B) the Petrarchian spirit

(C) as an Elizabethan Sonnet

(D) as an Adoration

(E) in the spirit of the Grands Rhetoriqueurs

Questions 113-114 refer to the following.

Since no man has any natural authority over his fellowmen and since force is not the source of right, conventions remain as the basis of all lawful authority among men.

There is in the State no fundamental law which cannot be revoked, not even (a) social compact; for if all citizens assembled in order to break the compact by a solemn agreement, no one can doubt that it could be quite legitimately broken.

113. The author's primary argument is

(A) anarchy is the fundamental law of human nature.

(B) civilization, as modern men know it, is superficial.

(C) there is an implied social contract between the government and those it governs.

(D) lawful authority is that which is morally right.

(E) revolutions run counter to the correct order of nature.

114. The passage was written by

(A) Thomas Jefferson

(B) Thomas Paine

(C) Karl Marx

(D) Jean Jacques Rousseau

(E) Henry David Thoreau

115. Love Virtue; she alone is free;
She can teach ye how to climb
Higher than the sphery chime:
Or, if Virtue feeble were,
Heaven itself would stoop to her.

This poem expresses

(A) the Platonic Ideal

(B) the Puritan Ideal

(C) the Zoroastrian Ideal

(D) the Deistic Ideal

(E) the Renaissance Ideal

Questions 116-118 refer to the excerpts below.

116. Which is from Hemingway's *The Short Happy Life of Francis Macomber*?

117. Which is from Steinbeck's *Tularecito*?

118. Which is from Dos Passos' *The Big Money*?

(A) The transcontinental passenger thinks contracts, profits, vacationtrips, mighty continent between Atlantic and Pacific, power, wires humming dollars, cities jammed, hills empty, the indiantrail leading into the wagonroad, the macadamed pike, the concrete skyway; trains, planes: history the billiondollar speedup,

and in the bumpy air over the desert ranges towards Las Vegas

sickens and vomits into the carton container the steak and mushrooms he ate in New York.

(B) It fell just once. For an instant they almost resembled a piece of statuary: the clinging dog, the bear, the man astride its back, working and probing the buried blade. Then they went down, pulled over backward by Boon's weight, Boon underneath. It was the bear's back which reappeared first but at once Boon was astride it again.

(C) The lightheartedness of a former time had completely faded. To their sharpened minds it was easy to conjure pictures of all kinds of incompetency and blindness and, indeed, cowardice. There was the shore of the populous land, and it was bitter and bitter to them that from it came no sign.

(D) It was neither all over nor was it beginning. It was there exactly as it happened with some parts of it indelibly emphasized and he was miserably ashamed at it. But more than shame he felt cold, hollow fear in him. The fear was still there like a cold slimy hollow in all the emptiness where once his confidence had been and it made him feel sick. It was still there with him now.

(E) Gradually, as Miss Morgan read about elves and brownies, fairies, pixies, and changelings, his interest centred and his busy pencil lay idly in his hand. Then she read about gnomes, and their lives and habits, and he dropped his pencil altogether and leaned toward the teacher to intercept her words.

Questions 119-120 refer to the following passage.

Had (he) written his own life, in conformity with the opinion which he has given, that every man's life may be best written by himself; had he employed in the preservation of his own history, that clearness of narration and elegance of language in which he has embalmed so many eminent persons, the world would probably have had the most perfect example of biography that was ever exhibited.

119. Consistent with the author's established attitude toward his subject, it is most likely that he will attribute the subject's failure to write an autobiography to

(A) his uneventful life.

(B) his inexperience in biographical forms.

(C) his lack of diligence.

(D) his belief that no one would be really interested.

(E) his egocentricity.

120. The author of this passage is referring to

(A) Benjamin Franklin   (D) Samuel Johnson

(B) Izaak Walton   (E) William Shakespeare

(C) John Milton

Questions 121-122 refer to the following selection.

> That darksome cave they enter, where they find
>   That cursed man, low sitting on the ground,
>   Musing full sadly in his sullein mind;
>   His griesie lockes, long growen, and unbound,
>   Disordred hong about his shoulder's round,   5
>   And hid his face; through which his eyne
>   Lookt deadly dull, and stared as stound;
>   His raw-bone cheekes through penurie and pine
> Were shronke into his jawes, as he did never dine.

121. The word "pine" in line 8 means

   (A) pain

   (B) a mournful look

   (C) peekedness

   (D) starvation

   (E) poverty

122. The lines were written by

   (A) Christopher Marlowe

   (B) Geoffrey Chaucer

   (C) Sir Philip Sidney

   (D) Edmund Spenser

   (E) Thomas Campion

123. The French novelist Zola did much to develop the belief in fiction that man belongs entirely in the order of nature, having no connection with a religious or spiritual world beyond nature. Man is viewed as an animal whose character and fortune are determined by heredity and environment. Zola and later writers, such as the Americans _____ and _____, try to present their subjects with an objective scientific attitude, frequently including a candor about activities and bodily functions not often found in earlier literature.

Which correctly completes the passage?

   (A) Herman Melville. . . Nathaniel Hawthorne

   (B) Frank Norris. . . James T. Farrell

(C) Sinclair Lewis. . . Willa Cather

(D) Sarah Orne Jewett. . . John Dos Passos

(E) William Dean Howells. . . Hamlin Garland

124. Of his intellectual character, the constituent and fundamental principle was good sense, a prompt and intuitive perception of consonance and propriety. He saw immediately, of his own conceptions, what was to be chosen, and what to be rejected; and, in the works of others, what was to be shunned, and what was to be copied.

In this passage, Johnson refers to

(A) Dryden   (D) Milton

(B) Pope   (E) Swift

(C) Sir Isaac Newton

125. No, I'll not weep.
I have full cause of weeping, but this heart
Shall break into a hundred thousand flaws
Or ere I'll weep. O Fool, I shall go mad!

This passage is from

(A) *The Winter's Tale*

(B) *King Lear*

(C) *A Midsummer Night's Dream*

(D) *The Tempest*

(E) *Othello*

Questions 126-128 refer to the following.

> How vainly men themselves amaze
> To win the palm, the oak, or bays
> And their incessant labors see
> Crowned from some single herb, or tree,
> Whose short and narrow-verged shade
> Does prudently their toils upbraid;
> While all flowers and all trees do close
> To weave the garlands of repose!

126. The interpretation of the word "amaze" closest to the poet's intention is

   (A) struggle

   (B) astonish

   (C) perplex

   (D) express alarm

   (E) gain an understanding

127. What are these men trying to obtain?

   (A) political power

   (B) private property

   (C) military skill

   (D) beautiful clothing

   (E) prizes in competition

128. The author of this selection is

   (A) Andrew Marvell

   (B) John Dryden

   (C) John Donne

   (D) Sir Philip Sidney

   (E) Alexander Pope

129. But since, alas! frail beauty must decay,
   Curled or uncurled, since locks will turn to gray;
   Since painted, or not painted, all shall fade,
   And she who scorns a man must die a maid;
   What then remains but well our power to use,
   And keep good humor still whate'er we lose?

The predominant poetic device in the preceding passage is

(A) irony   (D) antithesis

(B) synecdoche   (E) conceit

(C) paradox

130. Which of the following is composed in stanzas of terza rima?

(A) *To Penshurst*

(B) *Ode to the West Wind*

(C) *Troilus and Criseyde*

(D) *Astrophel and Stella*

(E) *Eve of St. Agnes*

Tragedy's experience hammers against the mystery to make a breach which would admit the whole triumphant answer. Intuition has no such potential. But there are times in the state of man when comedy has a special worth, and the present is one of them; a time when the loudest faith has been faith in a trampling materialism, when literature has been thought unrealistic which did not mark and remark our poverty and doom. Joy (of a kind) has been all on the devil's side, and one of the necessities of our time is to redeem it.

131. According to the passage, which is NOT a traditional belief that accounts for comedy's low critical estimation.

(A) Joy is often associated with evil.

(B) "Realistic" or worthwhile literature must always be concerned with "poverty and doom."

(C) In eras marked by "faith in a trampling materialism" rather than religion, comedy has no special worth.

(D) Tragedy serves a higher moral purpose than comedy.

(E) Comedy like intuition, does not penetrate the mysteries of life.

132. Only, whereas the passion for doing good is apt to be overhasty in determining what reason and the will of God say, because its turn is for acting rather than thinking, and it wants to be beginning to act; and whereas it is apt to take its own conceptions, which proceed from its own state of development and share in all the imperfections and immaturities of this, for a basis of action; what distinguishes culture is, that it is possessed by the scientific passion as well as by the passion of doing good; that it demands worthy notions of reason and the will of God, and does not readily suffer its own crude conceptions to substitute themselves for them.

The author of this passage argues that

(A) culture is distinguished by the passion of doing good.

(B) culture must be filtered through the critical notion of scientific passion.

(C) culture is subverted by deceptive reasoning.

(D) most cultures do not truly adhere to the will of God.

(E) a culture without science is destructive to its members.

Questions 133-135

133. Which of the selections was written by Cervantes?

134. Which of the selections was written by Edmund Burke?

135. Which of the selections was written by Machiavelli?

(A) Here the question arises; whether it is better to be loved than feared or feared than loved. The answer is that it would be desirable to be both but, since that is difficult, it is much safer to be feared than to be loved, if one must choose.

(B) . . . all knights cannot be courtiers, nor can all courtiers be knights-errant, nor ought they be. There must be all sorts in the world, and even though we may all be knights, there is a vast difference between one and another, for the courtiers, without leaving their chambers or the threshold of the court, roam all over the world by looking at the map, without spending a farthing and without suffering heat or cold, hunger or thirst.

(C) Terror is not always the effect of force, and an armament is not a victory. If you do not succeed, you are without resource: for conciliation failing, force remains; but, force failing, no further hope of reconciliation is left.

(D) To be liberal does not mean to understand all principles and to have none. The democratic principle is that the majority has the right to govern and that the minority has the right to criticize and oppose the majority.

(E) . . . if any shall mutiny and rise up against their commanders and officers; if any should preach or write that there ought to be no commanders nor officers because all are equal in Christ, therefore no masters nor officers, no laws nor orders, no corrections nor punishments: in such cases, whatever is pretended, the commander or commanders may judge, resist, compel, and punish such transgressors, according to their deserts and merits.

Questions 136-138 refer to the following poem.

I found a dimpled spider, fat and white,
On a white heal-all, holding up a moth
Like a white piece of rigid satin cloth –
Assorted characters of death and blight
Mixed ready to begin the morning right,   5
Like the ingredients of a witches' broth –
A snow – drop spider, a flower like a froth,
And dead wings carried like a paper kite.

What had that flower to do with being white,
The wayside blue and innocent heal-all?   10
What brought the kindred spider to that height,
Then steered the white moth thither in the night?
What but design of darkness to appall?
If design govern in a thing so small.

136. The first stanza of this poem is noted for

(A) personification.

(B) its detailed description of living forms.

(C) its attempt to compare natural objects to those of human use.

(D) the emergence of "death imagery" from the description of beautiful natural objects.

(E) its use of color in relating varied natural forms.

137. The answer posed in the last two lines of the second stanza might best be termed

(A) conditional

(B) facetious

(C) a question hidden within an answer

(D) rhetorical

(E) inquisitory

138. The author of this poem is

(A) W.H. Auden

(B) Theodore Roethke

(C) Dylan Thomas

(D) Robert Frost

(E) Wallace Stevens

Questions 139-140 refer to the following.

Meanwhile the South, rising with dabbled
        wings,
A sable cloud athwart the welkin flings,
That swilled more liquor than it could contain,
And, like a drunkard, gives it up again.

139. The governing device in this excerpt is

(A) a parallelism between the South and a bird-like creature.

(B) a metaphor between a drunk cloud and a drunkard.

(C) an allusion to Revolution in Nature.

(D) a simile, in the last line.

(E) a paradox in the inability of natural objects to become drunk.

140. This excerpt most closely resembles a famous passage in

(A) *Paradise Lost*

(B) *The Love Song of J. Alfred Prufrock*

(C) *The Tiger*

(D) *Rape of the Lock*

(E) *Stopping by Woods On a Snowy Evening*

Questions 141-144 refer to the following excerpts.

141. Which selection is from *The Greenland Sagas*?

142. Which selection is from *The History of the Dividing Line*?

143. Which selection is from *Gulliver's Travels*?

144. Which selection is from *Report of the Newfound Land of Virginia*?

(A) While we continued here, we were told that on the south shore, not far from the inlet, dwelt a marooner, that modestly called himself a hermit, though he forfeited that name by suffering a wanton female to cohabit with him.

(B) When I found myself on my feet, I looked about me, and must confess I never beheld a more entertaining prospect. The country round appeared like a continued garden, and the inclosed fields, which were generally forty foot square, resembled so many beds of flowers.

(C) . . . on both sides whereof grew most delicate and pleasant trees, bearing more rare and excellent fruits, than ever he had seen before or was able to express, and at length came to most brave and fair houses, near which he met his father that had been dead before, who gave him great charge to go back again and show his friends what good they were to do to enjoy the pleasures of that place, which when he had done he should after come again.

(D) As I walked through the wilderness of this world, I lighted on a certain place where was a Den, and I laid me down in that place to sleep; and, as I slept, I dreamed a dream.

(E) They did so, and those others rowed towards them, showing their astonishment, then came ashore. They were small, ill-favored men, and had ugly hair on their heads. They had big eyes and were broad in the cheeks. For a while they remained there, astonished, and afterwards rowed off south past the headland.

145. Within the bowels of these elements,
Where we are tortured and remain for ever.
Hewll hath no limits, nor is circumscribed
In one self place, but where we are is hell,
and where hell is, there must we ever be:

These lines are spoken by the character

(A) Mephistopheles in *Doctor Faustus*

(B) Satan in *Paradise Lost*

(C) Garcin in *No Exit*

(D) Satan in *The Inferno*

(E) John Goodwin in *The Crucible*

Questions 146-148

One of the facts that might come to light in this process is our tendency to insist, when we praise a poet, upon those aspects of his work in which he least resembles anyone else. In these aspects or parts of his work we pretend to find what is individual, what is the peculiar essence of the man. We dwell with satisfaction upon the poet's

586

difference from his predecessors, especially his immediate predecessors; we endeavour to find something that can be isolated in order to be enjoyed.

146. The "process" (line 1) to which the author of this passage is referring is

   (A) evaluating the relationship of a writer to the tradition that precedes him/her.

   (B) making an evaluation based on only the material itself.

   (C) criticizing within the limitations of the current literary period.

   (D) evaluating the personal relationship of a poet and the work.

   (E) criticizing the individual parts, not the poem itself as a whole.

147. The author most likely goes on to suggest that

   (A) looking at the individuality of an author is futile.

   (B) recognizing his individuality as part of a great tradition is beneficial.

   (C) appreciating a writer's spontaneity is what the contemporary reader calls for.

   (D) a mature writer will exhibit true individuality.

   (E) we should take little satisfaction in criticizing the writer.

148. The author of this passage is

   (A) E.M. Forster   (D) Eugene O'Neill

   (B) I.A. Richards   (E) William Faulkner

   (C) T.S. Eliot

149. What I must do is all that concerns me, not what the people think. This rule, equally arduous in actual and in intellectual life, may serve for the whole distinction between greatness and meanness.

This may be seen as a statement of

(A) the Renaissance

(B) the Non-Conformist movement

(C) the Age of Enlightenment

(D) the Golden Age of New England

(E) the Beat Era

Questions 150-151 refer to the following passage.

Now she was absolutely alone. Her father had long been dead, and his armchair lay in the attic, covered with dust and lame of one leg. She got thinner and plainer, and when people met her in the street they did not look at her as they used to, and did not smile to her; evidently her best years were over and left behind, and now a new sort of life had begun for her, which did not bear thinking about. In the evening Olenka sat in the porch, and heard the band playing and the fireworks popping in the Tivoli, but now the sound stirred no response. She looked into her yard without interest, thought of nothing, wished for nothing, and afterwards, when night came on she went to bed and dreamed of her empty yard. She ate and drank as it were unwillingly.

And what was worst of all, she had no opinons of any sort. She saw the objects about her and understood what she saw, but could not form any opinion about them, and did not know what to talk about. And how awful it is not to have any opinions! One sees a bottle, for instance, or the rain, or a peasant driving in his cart, but what the bottle is for, or the rain, or the peasant, and what is the meaning of it, one can't say, and could not even for a thousand roubles. When she had Kukin, or Pustovalov, or the veterinary surgeon, Olenka could explain everything, and give her opinion about anything you like, but now there was the same emptiness in her brain and in her heart as there was in her yard outside. And it was as harsh and as bitter as wormwood in the mouth.

150. What is the author's attitude toward Olenka?

   (A) sarcastic   (D) sympathetic

   (B) patronizing   (E) bitter

   (C) contemptuous

151. What does Chekov imply about opinions?

   (A) There is no difference between intuitive understanding and the ability to express one's ideas.

   (B) Opinions are often nothing more than a thoughtless repetition of other people.

   (C) Social oppression is often a cause of alienation from life and from knowledge.

   (D) One must contemplate "meaningful" ideas in order to formulate any kind of valid opinion.

   (E) Contact with people often causes a loss of understanding of self.

Questions 152-155 refer to the following passage.

For, while he fascinated many, there were not a few who distrusted him. He was very nearly blackballed at a West End club of which his birth and social position fully entitled him to become a member, and it was said that on one occasion, when he was brought by a friend into the smoking-room of the Churchill, the Duke of Berwick and another gentlemen got up in a market manner and went out. Curious stories became current about him after he had passed his twenty-fifth year. It was rumoured that he had been seen brawling with foreign sailors in a low den in the distant parts of Whitechapel, and that he consorted with thieves and coiners and knew the mysteries of their trade. His extraordinary absences became notorious, and, when he used to reappear again in society, men would whisper to each other in corners, or pass him with a sneer, or look at him with cold searching eyes, as though they were determined to discover his secret.

152. The individual described above is being criticized by his contemporaries for

(A) committing immoral acts.

(B) not observing the behavioral codes of his birthright.

(C) being a hypocrite.

(D) engaging in social behavior with the underclasses.

(E) attempting to engage with both classes at the same time.

153. In its fascination with "secret lives," the author of this passage is reflecting

(A) the emerging study of psychology at the beginning of the 20th Century.

(B) the rebellion against Victorian restraints through an interest in "novel experiences" during the English Decadence of the 1890's.

(C) the possibility of multiple personality as explored in the 1930's and '40's.

(D) the study of the nature of evil popular in the early to mid 1800's.

(E) the disillusionment with the upper classes as a result of the Industrial Revolution in the mid 1800's.

154. The themes of the work from which this selection is taken most closely resemble those from

(A) *Faustus*

(B) *The Scarlet Letter*

(C) *Paradise Lost*

(D) *Dr. Jekyll and Mr. Hyde*

(E) *The Old Curiosity Shop*

155. The author of this passage is

(A) Oscar Wilde   (D) Walter Pater

(B) Charles Dickens   (E) Richard Burton

(C) George Eliot

156. Dissimulation is but a faint kind of policy or wisdom; for it asketh a strong wit and a strong heart to know when to tell truth, and to do it. Therefore it is the weaker sort of politics that are the great dissemblers.

The author uses the world "politics" to mean

(A) the study of persuasion.

(B) the study of dissimulation.

(C) the use of wit in determining what is the truth.

(D) politicians.

(E) polite people.

Questions 157-158 refer to the following.

A work as "realistic" as this, filled with concrete details, many of them belonging to another age, constantly defies any translator to accomplish even his most basic task – accurate rendering of individual terms. In "Madame Bovary," children walking through the fields don't merely pull the flowers from the oats; they "pull the bell-shaped flowers from the oat stalks." The various versions of the novel already existing in English are strewn with unintentional comedy.

157. The author of this commentary is arguing for

(A) the importance of reading a work in its original language.

(B) a commitment by translators to reflect the original meaning of the work.

(C) the understanding among readers of translations that all such work is imperfect.

(D) the commitment by readers to understand the merits of another language in translation.

(E) a commitment by publishers to select for translation only those works that lend themselves to the task well.

158. The commentator feels that a perfectly "correct" translation of a phrase can be inadequate most importantly because

(A) it often appears comical.

(B) it will confuse the reader.

(C) it will likely not give a precise duplicate of the object in the original language.

(D) it may be rough and unpolished in its tone.

(E) it may fail to render an essentially symbolic meaning.

Questions 159-160 refer to the following.

They next entered the fields where roam the heroes who have fallen in battle. Here they saw many shades of Grecian and Trojan warriors. The Trojans thronged around him, and could not be satisfied with the sight. They asked the cause of his coming, and plied him with innumerable questions. But the Greeks, at the sight of his armour glittering through the murky atmosphere, recognized the hero, and filled with terror turned their backs and fled, as they used to do on the plains of Troy.

159. The character described here in "armour glittering" is

(A) Odysseus   (D) Phlegethon

(B) Aeneas   (E) Ulysses

(C) Creon

160. Shortly after this, Aeneas encounters

    (A) the Cyclops   (D) Scylla

    (B) the Sphinx   (E) the Griffin

    (C) the Hydra

Questions 161-165.

> Lullay, lullay, litel child, why weepestou so sore?
> Needes most thou weepe, it was y-yarked thee
>   yore
> Evere to live in sorwe, and siken everemore,
> As thine eldren dide er this, whil they alives wore.
> Lullay, lullay, litel child, child, lullay, lullow,   5
> Into uncouth world ycomen so art thou.
>
> Beestes and thise fowles, the fishes in the flood,
> and eech sheef alives, ymaked of boon and blood,
> Whan they cometh to the world they dooth hemself some
> sood —
> Al but the wrecche brol that is of Adames   10
>   blood.
> Lullay, lullay, litel child, to care art thou bimet:
> Thous noost nat this worldes wilde bifore thee is yset.

161. "Wrecche brol" in line 10 is best understood as meaning

    (A) unhappy brood

    (B) miserable composure

    (C) rich broth (of Adam's blood)

    (D) wretched brat

    (E) wrenching misery

162. Though the content of this stanza may seem inappropriate, it represents a

   (A) love lyric
   (B) love complaint
   (C) signature tune
   (D) lullaby
   (E) Heatho-Bardic Lay

163. According to this selection, humans differ from animals in that

   (A) only humans can find Christian salvation.

   (B) only humans can truly experience high and low points in life.

   (C) only humans are predestined to suffer.

   (D) both animals and humans live in sorrow.

   (E) animals are Biblically proscribed to serve humans.

164. "As thine eldren dide er this, whil they alives wore" (line 4) might be paraphrased

   (A) Your ancestors suffered this way too.

   (B) Suffering is the oldest thing in the world.

   (C) You will suffer more as you get older.

   (D) Parents suffer most because they witness their children's pain.

   (E) Your children will suffer just like you.

165. The implication is that the speaker is not surprised at the "litel child's" crying because

   (A) that is a natural reaction to pain, much as in the animal kingdom.

   (B) that is what the child's ancestors have had to do since the days of Adam.

(C) that is the condition of humankind because of Original Sin.

(D children are trusting by nature, and do not understand the vagaries of life.

(E) all Christians are "pilgrims" in an "uncouth world."

166. Three poets in three distant ages born,
Greece, Italy, and England did adorn.
The first in loftiness of thought surpass'd;
The next in majesty; in both, the last.
The force of nature could no further go;
To make a third, she join'd the former two.

The third poet mentioned here is

(A) Alexander Pope   (D) John Milton

(B) Christopher Marlowe   (E) Ovid

(C) John Donne

167. A noble book; all men's book! It is our first, oldest statement of the never-ending problem, – men's destiny, and God's ways with him here in this earth. And all in such free flowing outlines; grand in its sincerity, in its simplicity; in its epic melody, and repose of reconcilement.

The passage above discusses

(A) The New Testament   (D) Genesis

(B) *The Odyssey*   (E) The Book of Job

(C) *The Canterbury Tales*

168. Mrs. Mooney was a butcher's daughter. She was a woman who was quite able to keep things to herself: a determined woman. She had married her father's foreman and opened a butcher's shop near Spring Gardens. But as soon as his father-in-law was dead Mr. Mooney began to go to the devil. He drank, plundered the till, ran headlong into debt. It was no use making him take the pledge: he was sure to break out again a few days later.

(A) *Tess of the D'Urberville's*

(B) *Swann's Way*

(C) *Women in Love*

(D) *Dubliners*

(E) *Light In August*

Questions 169-170

When the friend shows his inmost heart to his friend. . . then deem me a monster, for the symbol beneath which I have lived and die! I look around me, and lo! on every visage a Black Veil.

169. The "black veil" is a metaphor for

(A) the inevitability of death.

(B) the "veil" that separates one person from another.

(C) the need to separate oneself from the sin of one's neighbors.

(D) the evil that lurked in the speaker's heart.

(E) the stained soul from Original Sin.

170. The author of this passage is also the author of

(A) *The Scarlet Letter*

(B) *Wuthering Heights*

(C) *Rip Van Winkle*

(D) *Bartleby the Scrivener*

(E) *The Pioneers*

Questions 171-172

When a deed is done for Freedom, through the broad earth's aching breast
Runs a thrill of joy prophetic, trembling on from east to west,
And the slave, where'er he cowers, feels the soul within him climb
Of a century bursts full-blossomed on the thorny stem of Time.

171. The crisis which this first stanza of a long poem addresses is

(A) the Civil War

(B) the First World War

(C) the War of 1812

(D) the Annexation of Texas

(E) the Barbary Piracy

172. The stanza is governed by

(A) awkward use of metaphor

(B) personification of geography

(C) didacticism

(D) Biblical reference

(E) grammatical parallelism

Questions 173-174

And suddenly I realized that I should have to shoot the elephant after all. The people expected it of me and I had got to do it; I could feel their two thousand wills pressing me forward, irresistibly. And it was at this moment, as I stood there with the rifle in my hands, that I first grasped the hollowness, the futility of the white man's dominion in the East. Here was I, the white man with his gun, standing in front of the unarmed native crowd - seemingly the leading actor of the piece; but in reality

I was only an absurd puppet pushed to and fro by the will of those yellow faces behind. I perceived in this moment that when the white man turns tyrant it is his own freedom that he destroys. He becomes a sort of hollow, posing dummy, the conventionalized figure of a sahib. For it is the condition of his rule that he shall spend his life in trying to impress the "natives," and so in every crisis he has got to do what the "natives" expect of him. He wears a mask, and his face grows to fit it. I had got to shoot the elephant. I had committed myself to doing it when I sent for the rifle. A sahib has got to act like a sahib.

173.   Which of the following ideas is NOT present in this passage?

   (A) Man loses his freedom in gaining control over others.

   (B) Imperialism is destructive of the oppressor.

   (C) What was initially a part in a drama can become an aspect of identity.

   (D) Man's actions are manipulated by cosmic forces beyond his control.

   (E) Imperialist rulers must behave as their subjects expect them to behave.

174.   The passage was written by

   (A) Jonathan Swift   (D) Charles Lamb

   (B) George Orwell   (E) Thomas Carlyle

   (C) E.B. White

175.   Virgil's *Eclogues* are imitations of the pastorals of

   (A) Catullus   (D) Pindar

   (B) Sappho   (E) Theocritus

   (C) Juvenal

Questions 176-177.

(Her) career has covered less ground, for she began far above Main Street. What she tried to do at the start was to imitate the superficial sophistication of Edith Wharton and Henry James — a deceptive thing, apparently realistic in essence, but actually as conventional as table manners or the professional buffooneries of a fashionable rector. She had extraordinary skill as a writer, and so her imitation was scarcely to be distinguished from the original, but in the course of time she began to be aware of its hollowness. Then she turned to first-hand representation — to pictures of the people she actually knew.

176.   The author of this passage states

(A)   that the writer was satisfied with imitation early in her career.

(B)   that the writer was inept at imitating the writing styles of others.

(C)   that the writer switched from imitation to first-hand representation.

(D)   that all of her attempts at imitation were really first-hand representation.

(E)   that she was too daring early in her career.

177.   This quote refers to

(A)   Edith Wharton   (D)   Willa Cather

(B)   Gertrude Stein   (E)   Marjorie Kinnan Rawlings

(C)   Virginia Woolf

178.   He suggested that the future citizens of his ideal republic begin their literary education with the telling of myths, rather than with mere facts or so-called rational teachings.

The "he" referred to here is

(A) Aristotle

(D) Plato

(B) Sir Thomas More

(E) Aldous Huxley

(C) Jonathan Swift

179.   "Milton! Thou should'st be living at this hour"

This is an example of

(A) a chorus

(D) an amphimacer

(B) an apostrophe

(E) an anadiplosis

(C) antistrophe

180.   "When my love swears that she is made of truth,
I do believe her, though I know she lies."

These lines from Shakespeare's Sonnet 138 are examples of

(A) synecdoche

(D) paradox

(B) ellipsis

(E) prosody

(C) pararhyme

Questions 181-183 refer to the following excerpts from autobiographical narratives.

181.   Which is by Lewis Carroll?

182.   Which is by Julian Huxley?

183.   Which is by William Blake?

(A) Certainly a large number of my early experiences had to do with natural history. I am talking now of the time we lived at old Laleham, a house on the Peperharrow Road in the Wey valley. My mother chose the name Laleham because the village of Laleham-on-Thames had been the original home of her family.

(B) "The time has come," the Walrus said,
        "To talk of many things:
     Of shoes--and ships--and sealing-wax--
        Of cabbages-- and kings--
     And why the sea is boiling hot - -
        And whether pigs have wings."

(C) The best actors in the world, either for tragedy, comedy,
     history, pastoral, pastoral-comical, historical-pastoral,
     tragical-historical, tragical-comical-historical-pastoral;
     scene individable, or poem unlimited. Seneca cannot be
     too heavy, nor Plautus too light. For the law of writ and
     the liberty, these are the only men.

(D) As I write, only six weeks after I finally turned in the novel,
     I now know what's wrong with it, which chapters lack
     conviction, where I copped out. If a book club takes it, I
     will be pleased, but only briefly, because I can remem-
     ber other club choices that were ill-advised, even embar-
     rassing.

(E) And by came an Angel who had a bright key,
     And he opened the coffins and set them all free;
     Then down a green plain leaping, laughing, they run,
     And wash in a river, and shine in the sun.

     Then naked and white, all their bags left behind,
     They rise upon clouds and sport in the wind;
     And the angel told Tom, if he'd be a good boy,
     He'd have God for his father, and never want joy.

Questions 184-189 refer to the following stanzas.

     The curfew tolls the knell of parting day,
        The lowing herd wind slowly o'er the lea,
     The plowman homeward plods his weary way,
        And leaves the world to darkness and to me.

     Now fades the glimmering landscape on the sight,   5
        And all the air a solemn stillness holds,
     Save where the beetle wheels his droning flight,
        And drowsy tinklings lull the distant folds;

Save that from yonder ivy-mantled tower
　　The moping owl does to the moon complain　　10
Of such, as wandering near her secret bower,
　　Molest her ancient solitary reign.

Beneath those rugged elms, that yew tree's shade,
　　Where heaves the turf in many a moldering heap,
Each in his narrow cell forever laid,　　　　　15
　　The rude forefathers of the hamlet sleep.

184.　In stanza three the poet implies that

　　(A)　he is going where men rarely go.

　　(B)　nature reclaims the area with the setting sun each day.

　　(C)　it is uncommon for anyone like himself to linger there.

　　(D)　through meditation he has entered a different plane.

　　(E)　he has invaded the territory of darkness.

185.　"The rude forefathers" (line 16) are

　　(A)　the buried dead.

　　(B)　the sleeping townsfolk.

　　(C)　the unappreciative past generations.

　　(D)　the tree's roots.

　　(E)　the rabbits in their den.

186.　Lines two and three are

　　(A)　dependent clauses in apposition to line one.

　　(B)　participial clauses modifying "darkness."

　　(C)　one independent and one dependent clause.

　　(D)　sentence fragments.

　　(E)　segments of a run-on sentence.

187. "Beetle wheels" is an example of

 (A) metonymy   (D) chiasmus

 (B) consonance   (E) assonance

 (C) personification

188. The poem from which the stanzas are taken is

 (A) an Ode   (D) a Pastoral

 (B) an Elegy   (E) an Eulogy

 (C) an Idyll

189. These lines were written by

 (A) Edgar Alan Poe   (D) Thomas Gray

 (B) Thomas Hariot   (E) Samuel Butler

 (C) George Crabbe

Questions 190-192 refer to the excerpts below.

190. Which is by Wilde?

191. Which is by Arnold?

192. Which is by Ruskin?

 (A) Our modern glass is exquisitely clear in its substance, true in its form, accurate in its cutting. We are proud of this. We ought to be ashamed of it. The old Venice glass was muddy, inaccurate in all its forms, and clumsily cut, if at all. And the old Venetian was justly proud of it.

 (B) On that little hill by the city of Florence, where the lovers of Giorgione are lying, it is always the solstice of noon, made so languorous by summer suns that hardly can the slim naked girl dip into the marble tank the round bubble of clear glass, and the long fingers of the lute player rest idly upon the chords.

(C) Sweetness and light evidently have to do with the bent or side in humanity which we call Hellenic. Greek intelligence has obviously for its essence the instinct for what Plato calls the true, firm, intelligible law of things; the law of light, of seeing things as they are.

(D) To him, the picture, the landscape, the engaging personal ity in life or in a book, *La Gioconda*, the hills of Carrara, Pico of Mirandola, are valuable for their virtues, as we say, in speaking of a herb, a wine, a gem; for the property each has of affecting one with a special, a unique, impression of pleasure.

(E) Or great poetry may be made without the direct use of any emotion whatever: composed out of feelings solely. Canto XV of the "Inferno" is a working up of the emotion evident in the situation; but the effect, though single as that of any work of art, is obtained by considerable complexity of detail.

193. The presence that rose thus so strangely beside the waters, is expressive of what in the ways of a thousand years men had come to desire. Hers is the head upon which all "the ends of the world are come," and the eyelids are a little weary. It is beauty wrought out from within upon the flesh, the deposit, little cell by cell, of strange thoughts and fantastic reveries and exquisite passions. Set it for a moment beside one of those white Greek goddesses or beautiful women of antiquity, and how would they be troubled by this beauty, into which the soul, with all its maladies has passed!

Walter Pater is referring here to a painting of

(A) Helen of Troy   (D) Mona Lisa

(B) The Virgin Mary   (E) Lady Godiva

(C) Joan of Arc

Questions 194-196 refer to the excerpts below.

194. Which is spoken by Browning's Fra Lippo Lippi?

195. Which is spoken by Tennyson's Ulysses?

196. Which is spoken by Coleridge's The Baron?

(A) I'll tell thee everything I can;
There's little to relate.
I saw an aged man,
A–sitting on a gate.

(B) "So careful of the type?" but no.
From scarped cliff and quarried stone
She cries, "A thousand types are gone;
I care for nothing, all shall go."

(C) I' the house that caps the corner. Boh! you were best!
Remember and tell me, the day you're hanged,
How you affected such a gullet's gripe!

(D) "Sweet maid, Lord Roland's beauteous dove,
With arms more strong, than harp or song,
Thy sire and I will crush the snake!"

(E) There lies the port; the vessel puffs her sail;
There gloom the dark, broad seas. My mariners,
Souls that have toiled, and wrought, and thought with me–

Questions 197-198

I do not believe in Belief. But this is an age of faith, and there are so many militant creeds that, in self-defense, one has to formulate a creed of one's own. Tolerance, good temper and sympathy are no longer in a world which is rent by religious and racial persecution, in a world where ignorance rules, and science, who ought to have ruled, plays the subservient pimp. Tolerance, good temper and sympathy — they are what matter really, and if the human race is not to collapse they must come to the front before long.

197. Which of the following is the best paraphrase of the passage?

(A) While it is tempting to formulate a belief, the tolerant person must avoid doing so.

(B) Tolerance, good temper and sympathy would be possible in a less militant world, but are not possible now.

(C) Science now pimps for religion, and masquerades as tolerance, good temper and sympathy.

(D) An individual is forced by a militant world to formulate his own belief.

(E) Tolerance, good temper and sympathy have never existed, yet they must, or we will face destruction.

198. The author is

(A) D.H. Lawrence   (D) Virginia Woolf

(B) Walter Pater   (E) Ralph Waldo Emerson

(C) E.M. Forster

Questions 199-203

Tears, idle tears, I know not what they mean,
Tears from the depth of some divine despair
Rise in the heart, and gather to the eyes,
In looking on the happy Autumn-fields,
And thinking of the days that are no more.   5

Fresh as the first beam glittering on a sail,
That brings our friends up from the underworld,
Sad as the last which reddens over one
That sinks with all we love below the verge;
So sad, so fresh, the days that are no more.   10

Ah, sad and strange as in dark summer dawns
The earliest pipe of half-awaken'd birds
To dying ears, when unto dying eyes
The casement slowly grows a glimmering square;
So sad, so strange, the days that are no more.   15

Dear as remember'd kisses after death,
And sweet as those by hopeless fancy feign'd
On lips that are for others; deep as love,
Deep as first love, and wild with all regret;
O Death in Life, the days that are no more.   20

199.   The poem may be classified as

(A) a prolonged metaphor

(B) a Frottola

(C) an extended simile

(D) a lengthened parallelism

(E) an allegory

200.   To the poet, "Death in Life" could best be described as

(A) a result of having lived too long.

(B) a result of having regretted too much.

(C) a result of having most of life's intense emotions in the past.

(D) a result of not being capable of experiencing intense emotion.

(E) a result of enveloping loneliness.

201.   The poet's philosophical response to life is similar to

(A) Poe's   (D) Coleridge's

(B) Swinburne's   (E) Wordsworth's

(C) Rossetti's

202.   The poem is written in

(A) mimetic verse   (D) free verse

(B) elegiac verse   (E) blank verse

(C) accentual verse

203. The poem was written by

(A) Elizabeth Barrett Browning

(B) Edward Fitzgerald

(C) John Greenleaf Whittier

(D) Alfred Lord Tennyson

(E) George Meredith

204. I impeach him in the name and by virtue of those eternal laws of justice which he has violated. I impeach him in the name of human nature itself, which he has cruelly outraged, injured and oppressed. . .

This is from a speech by

(A) Edmund Burke   (D) Daniel Webster

(B) William Pitt   (E) Martin Luther King

(C) Patrick Henry

205. Oh, Donal. . . your way's a thorny way. Your last state is worse than your first. Ah me, alas! Pain, pain ever, for ever. Like thee, Prometheus, no change, no pause, no hope. Ah, life, life, life!

The speaker here is

(A) O'Casey's Davoren

(B) Joyce's Molly Bloom

(C) Wilde's Algernon

(D) Kopit's Pete

(E) O'Neill's Paddy

Questions 206-207

Let me not, however, lose the historian in the man, nor suffer the doting recollections of age to overcome me, while dwelling with fond garrulity on the virtuous days of the patriarchs — on those sweet days of simplicity and ease, which never more will dawn on the lovely Island of Manna-hata.

206. This passage is meant to reinforce the idea that

    (A) the author is fond of relating past times.

    (B) the author is quick to admit to his prejudices.

    (C) the author dislikes verbosity.

    (D) the author has struggled to retain his subjectivity.

    (E) the author is nostalgic about his lovely island.

207. This passage is from

    (A) Cooper's *The Pioneers*

    (B) Irving's *History of New York*

    (C) Whitman's *Manna-hata*

    (D) Coleridge's *Biographia Literaria*

    (E) Hawthorne's *My Kinsman, Major Molineux*

208. Where is _____? What would I give
     To meet him now? Meet him? nay three such other,
     If they had hand in murder of our brother!
     With three? with four, with ten, nay, with as many
     As the name yields! Pray anger there be any
     Whereon to feed my just revenge, and soon!
     How shall I kill him? Hurl him 'gainst the moon,
     And break him in small portions! Give to Greece
     His brain, and every tract of earth a piece!

     Which of the following correctly completes line 1?

    (A) Antaeus   (D) Mars

    (B) Mercury   (E) Odysseus

    (C) Hercules

209. It is a truth universally acknowledged that a single man in possession of a good fortune be in want of a wife.

This is the first line of

(A) *Adam Bede*

(D) *Clarissa*

(B) *Pride and Prejudice*

(E) *Pamela*

(C) *Jane Eyre*

210. The author, _____, born in 1802, was at the age of thirty already a recognized master of the arts of poetry, drama and fiction. A political figure as well, he was banished to the Channel Island of Guernsey for opposing Louis Napoleon's coup of 1851.

This passage refers to which of the following authors?

(A) Flaubert

(D) Pontmercy

(B) Zola

(E) Hugo

(C) Gautier

211. But I have said enough. I hope you will treasure up the instructions which I have given you, and make them a guide to your feet and a light to your understanding. Build your character thoughtful and painstakingly upon these precepts, and by and by, when you have got it built, you will be surprised and gratified to see how nicely and sharply it resembles everybody else's.

This is a conclusion to a letter entitled *Advice to Youth* written by

(A) Benjamin Franklin

(D) H.D. Thoreau

(B) Samuel Clemens

(E) Laurence Sterne

(C) H.L. Mencken

Questions 212-214 refer to the following.

O, I have bought the mansion of a love,
But not possess'd it, and, though I am sold,
Not yet enjoy'd: so tedious is this day
As in the night before some festival
To an impatient child that hath new robes
And may not wear them.

212. The speaker is

(A) Portia   (D) Juliet

(B) Rosalind   (E) Desdemona

(C) Emilia

213. "Mansion of a love" is a metaphor for

(A) an emotional commitment

(B) an engagement

(C) a marriage

(D) an extra-marital affair

(E) a reawakening of love

214. In lines two and three, the speaker

(A) compares herself to a slave.

(B) refers to herself as a woman with a fine dowry.

(C) says she has not enjoyed the relationship thus far.

(D) compares herself to a commodity that can bring pleasure.

(E) refers to herself as an emotion waiting.

215. Heaven from all creatures hides the book of Fate,
All but the page prescribed, their present state:
From brutes what men, from men what spirits know:

Or who could suffer Being here below?
The lamb thy riot dooms to bleed today,
Had he thy reason, would he skip and play?

The author is

(A) Sidney

(D) Blake

(B) Milton

(E) Wordsworth

(C) Pope

216. He thought everything a discovery of his own, from moonlight to the planting of acorns and nuts by squirrels. This is a defect in his character, but one of his chief charms as a writer.

The passage above was written by

(A) Cooper about Franklin

(B) W.W. Beecher about H.W. Longfellow

(C) Thomas Fuller about Walt Whitman

(D) J.R. Lowell about Thoreau

(E) Nathanael West about Samuel Johnson

Questions 217-219. For each of the following passages, identify the author. Base your decision on the content and style of each passage.

217. Coleridge in his person was rather above the common size, inclining to the corpulent, or like Lord Hamlet, "Somewhat fat and pursy." His hair (now, alas! gray) was then black and glossy as the raven's and fell in smooth masses over his forehead. This long pendulous hair is peculiar to enthusiasts, to those whose minds tend heavenward; and is traditionally inseparable (though of a different color) from the pictures of Christ. It ought to belong, as a character, to all who preach Christ crucified, and Coleridge was at that time one of those!

(A) Thomas De Quincey

(D) Matthew Arnold

(B) William Hazlitt

(E) John Ruskin

(C) Thomas Carlyle

218. If ever mortal "wreaked his thoughts upon expression," it was Shelley. If ever poet sang – as a bird sings – earnestly – impulsively – with utter abandonment – to himself – that poet was the author of "The Sensitive Plant." Of art – beyond that which is instinctive with genius – he either had little or disdained all.

(A) Keats

(D) Poe

(B) Sheridan

(E) Trilling

(C) Faulkner

219. Homer, in point of purity, is a most blameless writer; and though he was not an enlightened man, has interspersed many great and valuable truths throughout both his poems.

(A) Oliver Goldsmith

(D) Longinus

(B) Samuel Johnson

(E) William Cowper

(C) John Sheffield

220. Which of the following is most likely to be heard at a funeral?

(A) jongleur

(D) telestich

(B) roundel

(E) flyting

(C) coronach

221. When Love with unconfined wings
Hovers within my gates,
And my divine Althea brings
To whisper at the grates;
When I lie tangled in her hair
And fettered to her eye,
The gods that wanton in the air
Know no such liberty.

Which of the following best summarizes the lines above?

(A) When I am in love, I feel liberated.

(B) When Althea is with me, even a prison can not confine my joyousness.

(C) When I am committed to a woman, love is a prison I will tolerate.

(D) Even the gods do not know what it is to be in love with a woman like Althea.

(E) I hear my love's voice even though I am imprisoned.

Questions 222-225

Blow, winds, and crack your cheeks! rage! blow!
You cataracts and hurricanes, spout
Till you have drenched our steeples, drowned the cocks!
You sulphurous and thought-executing fires,
Vaunt-couriers to oak-cleaving thunderbolts,   5
Singe my white head! And thou, all-shaking thunder,
Smite flat the thick rotundity o' the world!
Crack nature's molds, all germens spill at one,
That make ungrateful man!

222.   The speaker is addressing

    (A) winds   (D) Caliban

    (B) Macduff   (E) King Lear

    (C) wild Nature

223.   In context, "germens" (line 8) refers to

    (A) the disease that afflicts man

    (B) the seeds of discontent

    (C) the origin of ingratitude

    (D) future mankind

    (E) storm – driven rains

224. The verbs in this passage can best be characterized as

(A) descriptive   (D) action

(B) intransitive   (E) helping

(C) Anglo-Saxon

225. The speaker is

(A) Lady Macbeth   (D) Satan

(B) Lear   (E) Richard III

(C) Paulina

226. Alas, I am so faint I may not stand;
My limbs under me doth fold.
Friends, let us not turn again to this land,
Not for all the world's gold;
For into this cave must I creep
And turn to earth, and there to sleep.

The speaker of these lines is

(A) Faustus   (D) Everyman

(B) Volpone   (E) Samson

(C) Abraham

227. A fire celestial, chaste, refin'd,
Conceiv'd and kindled in the mind;
Which, having found an equal flame,
Unites, and both become the same.

These lines were written by

(A) Milton   (D) Voltaire

(B) Jonson   (E) Goldsmith

(C) Swift

615

Then we noticed that in the second pillow was the indentation of a head. One of us lifted something from it, and leaning forward, that faint and invisible dust dry and acrid in the nostrils, we saw a long strand of iron-gray hair.

228. This is the finale of

(A) *The Jilting of Granny Weatherall.*

(B) *The Necklace*

(C) *The Yellow Wallpaper*

(D) *The Snows of Kilimanjaro*

(E) *A Rose for Emily*

229. *The Sisters, Araby,* and *A Little Cloud,* are stories in

(A) Faulkner's *The Sound and the Fury*

(B) Forster's *Howard's End*

(C) Fitzgerald's *The Last Tycoon*

(D) Woolf's *Mrs. Dalloway*

(E) Joyce's *Dubliners*

230. Faustus: Why, dost thou think that Faustus shall be damned?
Mephistopheles: Ay, of necessity, for here's the scroll
     In which thou hast given thy soul to Lucifer.
Faustus: Ay, and body too; but what of that?
     Thinkst thou that Faustus is so fond to imagine
     That after this life there is any pain?
     No, these are trifles and mere old wives' tales.

Faustus implies that

(A) affection blinds a person to pain.

(B) affection cannot guard against pain in the afterlife.

(C) he does not believe there is an afterlife at all.

(D) he does not believe that the afterlife is painful.

(E) selling one's soul to the Devil is the most painful thing a person can do.

GRE LITERATURE IN ENGLISH
EXAM V

ANSWER KEY

1.	E	39.	D	77.	D
2.	C	40.	C	78.	D
3.	A	41.	D	79.	D
4.	A	42.	B	80.	B
5.	D	43.	D	81.	B
6.	A	44.	A	82.	D
7.	D	45.	E	83.	A
8.	C	46.	B	84.	C
9.	C	47.	D	85.	D
10.	B	48.	C	86.	C
11.	E	49.	B	87.	B
12.	D	50.	D	88.	C
13.	D	51.	C	89.	B
14.	B	52.	C	90.	B
15.	D	53.	A	91.	B
16.	E	54.	B	92.	E
17.	A	55.	A	93.	A
18.	D	56.	B	94.	C
19.	C	57.	D	95.	A
20.	E	58.	D	96.	E
21.	C	59.	B	97.	D
22.	D	60.	D	98.	B
23.	A	61.	A	99.	E
24.	B	62.	D	100.	C
25.	D	63.	C	101.	B
26.	E	64.	C	102.	D
27.	A	65.	D	103.	B
28.	D	66.	A	104.	A
29.	C	67.	D	105.	C
30.	D	68.	D	106.	A
31.	D	69.	E	107.	D
32.	A	70.	A	108.	C
33.	C	71.	E	109.	D
34.	A	72.	C	110.	D
35.	C	73.	B	111.	E
36.	B	74.	D	112.	A
37.	A	75.	B	113.	C
38.	D	76.	A	114.	D

GRE LITERATURE IN ENGLISH
EXAM V

115.	B	154.	D	193.	D
116.	D	155.	A	194.	C
117.	E	156.	D	195.	E
118.	A	157.	B	196.	D
119.	C	158.	E	197.	D
120.	D	159.	B	198.	C
121.	D	160.	C	199.	C
122.	D	161.	D	200.	C
123.	B	162.	D	201.	E
124.	B	163.	C	202.	E
125.	B	164.	A	203.	D
126.	C	165.	C	204.	A
127.	E	166.	D	205.	A
128.	A	167.	B	206.	D
129.	D	168.	D	207.	B
130.	B	169.	B	208.	C
131.	C	170.	A	209.	B
132.	B	171.	A	210.	E
133.	B	172.	C	211.	B
134.	C	173.	D	212.	D
135.	A	174.	B	213.	C
136.	C	175.	D	214.	D
137.	D	176.	C	215.	C
138.	D	177.	D	216.	D
139.	D	178.	D	217.	B
140.	B	179.	B	218.	D
141.	E	180.	D	219.	E
142.	A	181.	B	220.	C
143.	B	182.	A	221.	A
144.	C	183.	E	222.	A
145.	A	184.	E	223.	C
146.	A	185.	A	224.	D
147.	B	186.	E	225.	B
148.	C	187.	E	226.	D
149.	D	188.	B	227.	C
150.	D	189.	D	228.	B
151.	B	190.	B	229.	E
152.	B	191.	C	230.	D
153.	B	192.	A		

GRE LITERATURE IN ENGLISH
TEST V

DETAILED EXPLANATIONS
OF ANSWERS

1.   (E)
Hazlitt on Shakespeare

2.   (C)
William Drummond on Ben Jonson

3.   (A)
Alexander Smith on Chaucer

4.   (A)
The quote is taken from *The Scarlet Letter*, Chapter 1, and describes Roger Chillingworth.

5.   (D)
Completes the quote from *Macbeth*, Act III, Scene VI.

6.   (A)
It has often been said of Stephen Crane (from whose writing the passage is taken) that he used the devices of Impressionism to produce Naturalistic novels, which are characterized by an attempt to be accurate as well as somewhat selective in the relation of otherwise commonplace details.

7.   (D)
D defines cantar - a 15th century Spanish device in lyric composition. Regularity does not play a significant role in Free Verse - especially Whitman's.

8.   (C)
From *Mowing*, Frost states that there was "never a sound beside the wood but one," and this was the sound of man laboring. His central question, however, is: "What did it whisper?" – in other words, what is the purpose of labor and what is his place in nature's universe? The laborer is sensitive enough to know that a "hidden message" exists (it is "whispered," he can guess at it, though he "knows not well"); this knowledge alone is what gives him his sense of purpose and place. Ultimate knowledge, however, resides in the hidden processes of nature (what and how the hay "makes"). He can only appreciate the mystery.

9.   (C)
Robert Frost.

10.   (B)
The pattern for most pastoral elegies on the Classical model (from Bion's the *Lament for Bion*) does not include any admonition to Death. Rather, there is a realization of grief and an inquiry into the causes of Death. This is an important difference in posture and speaks to these poets' belief in the place of man within the universe.

11.   (E)
From Chapter 1, *In Which the Reader Is Introduced to a Man of Humanity*.

12.   (D)
This sonnet conforms more to Italian models than those of his predecessors, Shakespeare and Spenser (see next question).

13.   (D)

The author retains iambic pentameter and 14 line requirements. The others are characteristics of this sonnet, and characteristic also of some Italian forms.

14.   (B)

John Milton.

15.   (D)

From Addison's *Tulips*.

16.   (E)

From Johnson's *Of Bashfulness*.

17.   (A)

From Goldsmith's *National Prejudices*.

18.   (D)

Dickinson's poetry is known for its need to instruct (didacticism). While she has empathy for the greater world, her notorious reclusiveness intervened (as in #441: This is my letter to the World/ That never wrote to me).

19.   (C)

Writing in the middle of the 19th Century, Dickinson, like many writers, employed remnant conventions – like the capitalization of important words. This often resulted in personification, but just as often it did not.

20.   (E)

Dickinson's Biblical tone is derived from the sermons and hymns of the Amherst Church and to the late-Puritan literary climate that spawned her contemporaries Thoreau and Emerson.

21.   (C)
   If I Could Stop – #919.

22.   (D)
   Both the concentration on nature and an appreciation of the miraculous quality of the ordinary identify the sentiments in the poem as Romantic. It was written by Wordsworth in 1834.

23.   (A)
   William Shakespeare.

24.   (B)
   Ben Jonson.

25.   (D)
   While Jonson certainly praises Shakespeare in this poem, the concluding couplet underscores the pervasive message that etchings, even good ones, or biographical details (and laudatory poems, such as this one), should not be the focus of the reader's attention as he reads the First Folio (1621) collection that follows. Shakespeare's works should be attended to – more specifically, the wit which lives on within them.

26.   (E)
   From John Dennis' *The Advancement and Reformation of Modern Poetry*.

27.   (A)
   From R. W. Emerson's *Letters and Social Aims*.

28.   (D)
   From John Dryden's *Of Dramatic Poesy*.

29.   (C)
   16th Century by Thomas Wyatt.

30.   (D)
From John Milton's *Paradise Lost*.

31.   (D)
"Sing, Heavenly Muse" introduces the governing verb in the opening sentence. Urania, the muse of sacred poetry is invoked to help the poet produce his great work: his "adventurous song" that intends to "soar" above the traditional home of the muses – "the Aonian mount, Mount Helicon."

32.   (A)
Milton's passage is characterized by unrhymed iambic pentameter lines – blank verse.

33.   (C)
Moses received the Ten Commandments on Mt. Sinai (alternate name: Horeb) and interpreted it for the "chosen seed," the Hebrews.

34.   (A)
The passage is part of the opening paragraph of *Moby Dick*. In fact, the paragraph beings with the famous sentence: "Call me Ishmael."

35.   (C)
"Hypo" (or "hyps") is an old colloquialism (perhaps traced to the Greek for "under") referring to the Blue Devils, attacks of "the blues," dejection, and lowness of spirits. It also may refer to hypochondria, but the contextual meaning in this passage rules out this interpretation. The modern reader may interpret Ishmael's knocking people's hats off as playful, but again, in the context of the passage, and, indeed, the title of the chapter (*Loomings*), we see overall depression.

36.   (B)
The passage is completed in this way. As Melville says in the sentences before: "I thought I would sail about a little and see the watery part of the world. It is a way I have of driving off the spleen, and regulating the circulation." Even not knowing this, it is obvious that the

speaker desires escape from the familiar (which eliminates (E)) and his restlessness dictates action as a response (eliminating (D) and (A)). (C), of course, is taken from Twain's *Huckleberry Finn*.

37.　(A)

Coleridge and Wordsworth published *Lyrical Ballads* in 1798. Sir Walter Scott died in 1832, the same year that the Reform Bill passed Parliament, launching England into the Victorian Age.

38.　(D)

Wordsworth states: "The first volume of these poems has already been submitted to general perusal. It was published as an experiment, which I hoped might be of some use to ascertain how far, by fitting to metrical arrangement a selection of the real language of men in a state of vivid sensation, that sort of pleasure and that quantity of pleasure may be imparted, which a poet may rationally endeavor to impart."

39.　(D)

William Shakespeare.

40.　(C)

The selection is from Johnson's 1765 *Preface to Shakespeare*.

41.　(D)

From Sophocles' *Oedipus The King*.

42.　(B)

The passage is taken from Chapter 1 of Aristotle's *On the Art of Poetry*, entitled: *The Media of Poetic Imitation*. Imitation of a more fixed "ideal" is characteristic of Aristotle's teacher, Plato.

43.　(D)

Aristotle is making a direct reference to *The Odyssey*.

44. (A)

Epic poetry.

45. (E)

Melville says before this: "Cotton Mather had but amused me, upon this particular night he terrified me. A thousand times I had laughed at such stories. Old wives' fables, I thought, however entertaining. But now, how different." – From *The Apple Tree* (1856).

46. (B)

Mather's 1693 compendium, a history of New England.

47. (D)

In the first half of Archibald Macleish's poem, sensations of smell, sight, and touch (apples, light, water) are presented; in the second, loss (hands reaching out, no verbal response, ghostly memories). What is presented is the frustration of a person much in contact with his physical world, but grieving terribly over some other person's absence.

48. (C)

The poem has a modest message, even though it deals with the wrenching problem of human loss. (A) and (D) are more extreme in their possibilities; the poet only metaphorically wishes he were dead; there does not seem any real hope that the absent one will return. (B) is more the secondary message of the poem: pain in the presence of pleasure is particularly frustrating. The passage of the seasons, however, does not seem to be what he is waiting for. The poet primarily longs for the "cold light" of truth; if he only knew the explanation for the absence, the "why" behind the other's departure or death, then he might be able to endure the guilt of his survival, able to experience the sensations of life.

49. (B)

The Imagist William Carlos Williams employs similar word usage in poems such as *Paterson*.

50.   (D)

Self-indulgence, rather than being ultimately destructive, can and does lead to a truer understanding of divine love ("For nothing can be sole or whole/That has not been rent."). The word play on "sole" underscores this as well as the statement that "love has pitched his mansion in/ The place of excrement;"

51.   (C)

From *Crazy Jane Talks With the Bishop*.

52.   (C)

From Gogol's *Diary of a Madman*. Note the cataloguing of daily events.

53.   (A)

From Dorothy Parker's *But the One On the Right*. In interior monologue, the speaker is thinking to himself – the reader only overhears the speaker's thoughts.

54.   (B)

From Jean Stafford's *Bad Characters*. The content of only one sentence identifies this passage immediately – the speaker is describing her life from a distance, not only of time, but of understanding.

55.   (A)

Actors speak directly to the audience in productions involving Presentational Drama.

56.   (B)

The Caucasian Chalk Circle by Brecht.

57.   (D)

Both passages are from Thomas Carlyle's *Sartor Resartus*. (B) is a Hebrew text c. 180 B.C. (A) is from Dickens' *A Christmas Carol*. (C) is from Gibran's *Working with the Hands*. (E) is from *Mahatma Gandhi at Work*.

58.   (D)

The passage which begins "The proper epic of this world" was written during the Industrial Revolution.

59.   (B)

The passage begins: "I think very few people know how troublesome dramatic critics are."

60.   (D)

The passage is taken from G.B. Shaw's *A Dramatic Realist To His Critics*.

61.   (A)

From Langland's *Piers the Plowman*.

62.   (D)

From Chaucer's *The Canterbury Tales*.

63.   (C)

From *Beowulf*.

64.   (C)

The selection is from Dryden's *A Song o St. Cecilia's Day*. St. Cecilia is the patron saint of music. This first stanza ends: "From harmony to harmony/ Thro' all the compass of the notes it ran, / The diapason, closing full in Man."

65.   (D)
The Student, as described by Chaucer.

66.   (A)
A "benefice" is a position in the church.

67.   (D)
Both the subject and the horse are "anything but fat."

68.   (D)
From Dickens' *Pickwick Papers*.

69.   (E)
From Thomas Hardy's *Jude the Obscure*.

70.   (A)
From Walter Scott's *Waverly Novels*.

71.   (E)
From Browning's *Andrea Del Sarto*.

72.   (C)
From Emma Goldman's *In Jail*.

73.   (B)
From Vonnegut's *Welcome to the Monkey House*.

74.   (D)
From Edwards' *Sinners In The Hands Of An Angry God*.

75.   (B)
From Sartre's *The Respectful Prostitute*.

76.   (A)

From Goethe's *Sorrows of Young Werther*.

77.   (D)

Irving's collection contains essays resembling those of Addison: periodical essays which emphasize humor and satire. Irving is also credited with introducing the familiar essay to America.

78.   (D)

From Stuart's *The Thread That Runs So True*.

79.   (D)

From Dickens' *Great Expectations*.

80.   (B)

While Pip knows his lineage in general, it is only with Magwitch's help that he is able to fulfill his "great expectations." In this passage, Pip reveals the frightened and sensitive nature voice in which he describes his difficult early years.

81.   (B)

The writer says just before the cited Wordsworth poem: "Finally, the 'scientific system of thought' in Wordsworth gives us at least such poetry as this, which the devout Wordsworthian accepts –" The writer refers to this when he speaks of the poem's imagined popularity at a "Social Science Congress."

82.   (D)

From Arnold's *Wordsworth*.

83.   (A)

Note the didactic emphasis (teach/ inform/ obligation) that Arnold feels makes the poem a candidate for a "Social Science Congress."

84.   (C)
   From Arnold's *To Marguerite – Continued*. The poem emphasizes a hopeless sense of isolation felt within the mass of humanity — something not recognized in Wordsworth's "social consciousness" — which is similar to Arnold's mocking tone when describing a potential meeting of Wordsworth's "Congress."

85.   (D)
   From Browning's *The Householder*.

86.   (C)
   The use of modifiers like "very" and "most" mocks any sincerity about the subject — especially one as outrageous as cannibalism. "Fricassee" and "ragout" are almost comic in their bizarre implications. Outright sadism for its own sake has rarely been the stock and trade of great writing, so we must assume this description has a greater purpose, even if we are not familiar with the author's writing.

87.   (B)
   A common belief that American colonials were less civilized than their English counterparts is used to underscore the author's preposterous suggestion that cannibalism is a way by which Irish overpopulation might be controlled. In fact, the author implies the opposite of (A) in order to sustain his sarcastic tone: he does not take seriously the belief that Americans are uncivilized. The proposition he is making should be taken in the same sarcastic vein.

88.   (C)
   From Jonathan Swift's *A Modest Proposal*.

89.   (B)
   "Regard the writer's end" is the controlling line of thought within the passage.

90.   (B)
   From Arnold's *The Function of Criticism at the Present Time*.

91.   (B)

D.H. Lawrence in *Surgery for the Novel – Or a Bomb* claims that the serious novel is on its "death-bed": "It is self-consciousness picked into such fine bits that the bits are most of them invisible, and you have to go by smell."

92.   (E)

From a forward by Rolf Fjelde.

93.   (A)

From an introduction by Henry Popkin.

94.   (C)

From Michael Quinn's *Form and Intention.*

95.   (A)

The juxtaposition of violence and seeming indifference is the hall-mark of much of Camus' writing. Here it is exaggerated to make the speaker seem like a particularly demented human monster.

96.   (E)

Loneliness in a crowd is a Greene calling card, as well as an almost artificial questioning under the supposition that meetings such as this are necessarily suspenseful because there must be someone who has arranged it for his or her own surreptitious purposes.

97.   (D)

The obvious American setting here, the arrival by train, the attention to natural imagery, all are indications of this parody of one of America's best writers of life on the prairies.

98.   (B)

The writer who parodies Hemingway has picked up on his short sentences, "macho" references, and sometimes unnecessary biological detail. Note the almost Biblical tone, which many have criticized in Hemingway's writing.

99. (E)

The key here is the English country accent and the mention of the word "gold" – a subject central to Silas Marner.

100. (C)

There is a psychological intensity here that is characteristic of Hardy – a concentration on involved motive and conscience.

101. (B)

The sense of mystery is heightened here by the speaker's refusal to name, and the idea of "seclusion" from society goes to the heart of the famous novel – and the bifurcation of personalities about which it speaks.

102. (D)

From psychoanalysis, free association involves the seemingly haphazard recollection of associated images, from which a pattern of concern may emerge.

103. (B)

From *The Bridge.*

104. (A)

Milton is considered a Puritan writer. The revival of Greco-Roman classics in which Milton took part, was characteristic of the Renaissance, while his Puritan distrust of the Roman Catholic hierarchy and his belief in the Bible as the revealed voice of God, was characteristic of the Reformation.

105. (C)

Manuductio is a work by the American cleric, Cotton Mather.

106. (A)

From *From There to Infinity*. Note the almost breathless juxtaposition of images and the bizarre representations of ordinary objects (eg. the human eye) which create an intensity out of an everyday occurrence.

107. (D)

From *Oedipus the King*.

108. (C)

"Assassination" (line 2) would imply the killing of a powerful leader eliminating (D) and (E). Brutus did not exhibit great reservations until after Caesar's death. The constant references to time and the worry about the speaker's own fate favors choosing Macbeth over Hamlet.

109. (D)

From the closing passage of *The Inferno*.

110. (D)

From Louis Simpson's *Walt Whitman At Bear Mountain*.

111. (E)

From Jonson's *Perfection in Small Things*. Like the lily, human life is short. All things that seem permanent are, in reality, transitory. To strive for the "great" is futile. Perfection can be found in the fleeting moments of man and nature.

112. (A)

Jonson is also the author of *Ode on the Death of Sir H. Morison*, considered a fine imitation of Pinday.

113. (C)

The "solemn agreement" subjects make is the agreement to be governed. This is always the case, whether formal law admits it or not. When they no longer agree to their governance, the "social compact" is therefore legitimately broken.

114.   (D)
From *The Social Contract* by Rousseau.

115.   (B)
From the Puritan Milton's *Comus*.

116.   (D)
From Hemingway.

117.   (E)
From Steinbeck.

118.   (A)
From Dos Passos.

119.   (C)
The author states in the sentence following: "But although he at different times, in a desultory manner, committed to writing many particulars of the progress of his mind and fortunes, he never had persevering diligence enough to form them into a regular composition."

120.   (D)
The passage is taken from Boswell's *Life of Samuel Johnson*.

121.   (D)
"Raw-boned" indicates a hollow-cheeked and gaunt appearance. "Penury," of course is still indicative of poverty. The relation is clear: poverty brings on starvation – "did never dine."

122.   (D)
From Spenser's *The Faerie Queene*.

123. (B)

Norris and Farrell both contributed significantly to naturalistic fiction, the former in such novels as *McTeague*, and the latter in numerous works, including his Studs Lonigan trilogy.

124. (B)

From *Pope's Intellectual Character. Pope and Dryden Compared. Lives of the Poets.*

125. (B)

Lear speaking, II.iv.

126. (C)

Men are confused by and blinded to the simpler pleasures of life by senseless striving. They become confused rather than shocked by their behavior.

127. (E)

The palm, the oak and the bays are all awards from Classical competitions in athletics, civic merit, and poetry, respectively.

128. (A)

Andrew Marvell from *The Garden* (1681).

129. (D)

Opposing ideas are placed in grammatical parallel throughout these lines from *Rape of the Lock.*

130. (B)

Shelley's poem conforms to aba bcb cdc ded, etc.

131. (C)

Christopher Fry asserts that comedy <u>does</u> serve a special purpose in some eras, an effect that tragedy cannot duplicate.

132. (B)

Matthew Arnold in *Culture* argues that scientific passion plays a critical role in distinguishing "culture" from its imperfect imitations. It is not enough just to have the passion of doing good; without reason cultures "readily suffer (their) own crude conceptions."

133. (B)

From *Don Quixote*.

134. (C)

From *Speech On Conciliation With The Colonies*.

135. (A)

From *The Prince*.

136. (C)

In comparing the spider to a person, the moth to human clothing, and the mixture to a witches broth, the author here places the natural world he is describing within the human world of the reader's experience.

137. (D)

The answer is really rhetorical. The title of the poem is *Design*, and throughout the two stanzas there can be little doubt that the poet is saying, "Of course, there is great design in nature: let me show it to you."

138. (D)

Robert Frost.

139. (D)

This last line from Swift's *A Description of a City Shower* is a simile which compares the rain generated from the Southern clouds (in the previous lines), to the sickness of a drunkard.

140.   (B)

"When the evening is spread out against the sky/like a patient etherized upon a table;" from Eliot. Swift's simile has often been pointed to as the inspiration for Eliot's famous comparison.

141.   (E)

Erik's Saga. The passage gives every indication of describing a "discovery" of "primitive" humans – in this case the Skraelings of Vinland (Newfoundland?).

142.   (A)

The educated English prose is what would be expected of Virginia planter William Byrd – as well as his disdainful attitude toward the "hermit."

143.   (B)

Swift's prose of delight and imagination shines through here as Gulliver explores his wild and fantastical world.

144.   (C)

Captain Smith's promotional piece for settlement in the new colony rings with the same kind of hyperbole as do real estate brochures today.

145.   (A)

By Christopher Marlowe.

146.   (A)

The author is analyzing how new writers are evaluated in relationship to tradition.

147.   (B)

The author of this passage counterposes what he has said by way of criticizing the critics with the comment that "if we approach a poet without this prejudice, we shall often find that not only the best, but the most individual parts of his work may be those in which the dead poets, his ancestors, assert their immortality most vigorously."

148. (C)

From *Tradition and the Individual Talent*. Eliot's respect for tradition placed him at odds with many of his contemporaries in the 20's, when this was written.

149. (D)

This is from Emerson. The concentration here on deed, rather than simply on non-conformity, is an indicator, as is its similarity to Thoreau.

150. (D)

Chekhov's concentration on Olenka's pitiful plight ("She was absolutely alone," "how awful it is not to have any opinions") indicates a sympathetic attitude. However, he does not make Olenka a noble martyr; rather she is a wretched creature doomed to derive meaning solely through her relationships with men. Chekhov is pitying but he never respects her profound misery.

151. (B)

Clearly Olenka has an "understanding" of the world around her intuitively, but she is unable to formulate any opinion on her own. She has always been dependent on others for meaning — her father, Kukin, Pustovalov, or the veterinary surgeon. Chekhov does not imply that her social condition or her focus on the mundane is the cause of her inability to communicate. Rather, her isolation from the sources of her ideas has left her alone and opinionless.

152. (B)

The subject has violated the formal behavior required of his gentlemanly station. In the next paragraph, the author states: "For the canons of good society are, or should be, the same as the canons of art. Form is absolutely essential to it."

153. (B)

Considered a corruption of Pater's beliefs as stated in *The Renaissance,* this practice became popular in the Nineties, much to Pater's dismay.

154. (D)

While each of the works offered as choices here explores the nature of evil, *Dr. Jekyll*, written about the same time as this selection, also explores the psychological and aesthetic urges which lead some to "secret lives."

155. (A)

The passage is from *The Picture of Dorian Gray*.

156. (D)

Francis Bacon in his essay uses "politics" as a descriptive noun. Not all politicians are dissemblers, but the "weaker sort" are the greater ones.

157. (B)

Francis Steegmuller is arguing here for greater diligence from translators that to "translate a masterpiece with any justice requires an effort which parallels the author's own labor in translating his idea into adequate words."

158. (E)

The problem of attaining a meaningful translation is to retain the conceptual representation within the original language – the possible symbolism of a description for that culture – the nuances of the words, and their cojoinings. In other words, what does "children pulling up bell-shaped flowers" signify?

159. (B)

Aeneas leads the remainder of the conquered Trojans into the "Infernal Regions" in *The Adventures of Aeneas*.

160. (C)

The 50 – headed Hydra lies just inside the gates of the "judgement hall of Rhadamanthus."

161. (D)
"Of Adam's blood" is the important phrase here, indicating that the noun of which the poet speaks is a descendant and, being "wretched," could easily be followed by the description "brat" – an annoying child.

162. (D)
The rather depressing commentaries about the life the young child is embarking upon are actually common to lullabies ("Down will come baby cradle and all," etc.).

163. (C)
"Whan (animals) cometh to the world they dooth hemself som good/ Al but the wrecche brol (wretched brat) of Adames blood" Man is destined to suffer because of Original Sin.

164. (A)
Suffering is the legacy of Original Sin: we all sorrow in this world.

165. (C)
It is not that tradition or the conditions of the world dictate human misery, but that is preordained because of Adam's Fall.

166. (D)
From Dryden, 1687.

167. (B)
From Carlyle's *Heroes and Hero-Worship*, 1840.

168. (D)
Dubliners.

169.   (B)

The speaker wears a literal black veil to symbolize the isolation we all endure. Only when someone "shows his inmost heart" to another will the speaker's belief become monstrous.

170.   (A)

Nathaniel Hawthorne is author of both *The Scarlet Letter* and *The Minister's Black Veil*.

171.   (A)

References to "slave" and "Freedom" are important markers from which to identify the event for which this poem served as rallying cry.

172.   (C)

The didactic nature of this poem is evident from the first stanza, and reflects the political involvement of its author, James Russell Lowell, in *The Present Crisis*. While some elements of the other choices exist in the selection, they are not consistent throughout, and, therefore, do not govern or control the stanza.

173.   (D)

The speaker asserts that man loses his freedom when he gains control over others because he then becomes an actor, one who behaves in certain ways to live up to the expectations of those he "controls" (or rules). This role-playing can become a part of his character, an unattractive part because it is based on false notions of superiority, insincerity, and oppressive acts. Loss of freedom coupled with deterioration of character make imperialism as destructive of the oppressor as of the oppressed. The speaker does not believe that man's actions are manipulated by cosmic forces beyond his control; he can simply stop being an imperialist.

174.   (B)

The passage is from Orwell's *Shooting an Elephant*.

175.   (D)
Theocritus was a Greek pastoral poet of the third century B.C. His *Idylls,* some of which depict rustic life in Sicily, were the first pastoral poems in the literature of Greece.

176.   (C)
Mencken, here in this passage from *The Novel,* gives almost no judgmental statement – his attitude here is more the reporter. Thus, while the writer may have been aware of the hollowness of her original work, Mencken does not agree with her until the following paragraphs, wherein he praises *My Antonia* for its "accurate representation."

177.   (D)
Willa Cather.

178.   (D)
Suggested in *Republic* and commented upon by Bettleheim.

179.   (B)
By definition, a figure of speech in which there is an address to a dead or absent person. We know Milton is dead at the time of this writing because the speaker wishes he were alive.

180.   (D)
These lines, which at first appear impossible, appear on closer reading, valid – the essence of paradox. The question here: why believe a lie, especially when that lie is that the person swears she tells the truth?

181.   (B)
From *The Walrus and the Carpenter*.

182.   (A)
From *Memories*.

183. (E)

From *The Chimney Sweeper*.

184. (E)

The poet has invaded the territory of the darkness which is watched over by the moping owl. He has not entered a different plane, nor has he physically travelled. He has simply remained behind and let the passing of the day surround him by a world in which most of the living creatures of the day have left for more conventional resting places.

185. (A)

The permanent subterranean location indicates that the speaker is referring to the dead. In fact, the setting of the poem is in a graveyard.

186. (E)

Grammatically, stanza one is a run-on sentence improperly punctuated.

187. (E)

The repetition of the long "e" is a dead giveaway to this device.

188. (B)

The solemn atmosphere, the bells tolling, the fading light, and the graveyard imagery, are all indications. Certainly it is not a lovely pastoral or idyll, and, as no person is mentioned specifically, it is not a eulogy.

189. (D)

From *Elegy Written in a Country Churchyard*.

190. (B)

From *The Critic As Artist*.

191.   (C)
From *The Function of Criticism at the Present Time*.

192.   (A)
From *The Stones of Venice*.

193.   (D)
From *The Mona Lisa*.

194.   (C)
From *Fra Lippo Lippi*.

195.   (E)
From *Ulysses*.

196.   (D)
From *Christabel*.

197.   (D)
The author does not say that the three qualities have never existed, and, while he does state that the first half of the (C) statement is true, he does not state the second half. Similarly, he does not state or imply (A), and, by inference, cannot believe that the three are impossible in the contemporary world, else he would not recommend them.

198.   (C)
From *What I Believe*.

199.   (C)
Best classified as an extended simile, with "tears" being compared (using "as") to sails, dawn, kisses.

200.   (C)

The poet is certainly capable of experiencing intense emotion (witness the welling up of tears for no particular reason which is the situation in the poem). Yet, he recalls not just the people, but more especially, the intense emotions of the past, most of which cannot be repeated (eg. "first love").

201.   (E)

The reader, even today, is moved by the pain of the poet, and the suddenness with which it descended on him as he found himself reflecting on the intense emotions of the past (indeed, first there were tears, and then, recollection). In many ways this is similar to the singular "peak experience" typical of Wordsworth's Romantic philosophy.

202.   (E)

Characterized by unrhymed iambic pentameter – the medium of much reflective verse – especially in the 19th Century.

203.   (D)

Alfred Lord Tennyson from his 1847 poem.

204.   (A)

From a speech by Edmund Burke.

205.   (A)

From *Innocence and Experience*.

206.   (D)

In an artful series of clauses, the author lets the reader in on his thought process: to wit, although he is trying to be objective, he is obviously sentimentally remembering his island.

207. (B)

From Irving's *History of New York*.

208. (C)

From Jonson's *Pleasure Reconciled to Virtue*.

209. (B)

This is the famous, ironic opening sentence of Jane Austen's *Pride and Prejudice*. The implication of course is that a single woman would like a rich husband.

210. (E)

From Robinson's *Notes* to *Les Miserables*.

211. (B)

From Twain's letters.

212. (D)

The speaker is Juliet.

213. (C)

Juliet was married by Friar Laurence only two scenes before, but she has not seen Romeo since, nor consummated their new relationship. From III: ii.

214. (D)

This is particularly evident when taken in the context of the previous line, in which Juliet compares herself to a consumer.

215. (C)

Closed couplets from Pope's *An Essay on Man*, asserting that God keeps knowledge of the future from man out of mercy.

216. (D)

From J.R. Lowell's *Thoreau*.

217. (B)

Hazlitt from *My First Acquaintance with Poets*.

218. (D)

Poe from *Marginalia*.

219. (E)

Cowper from a letter to John Newton.

220. (C)

A coronach is a funeral dirge or song of lamentation. The Gaelic word means a "wailing together." The custom, common to Ireland and the Scottish Highlands, figures in various literary works, including the novels of Sir Walter Scott.

221. (A)

Althea was the Queen of Calydon in Greek mythology, therefore it is unlikely the poet is referring to the truly "divine" Queen, or to a contemporary Althea who was "divine." It seems more likely the poet is expressing the power of Love (note the capital "L," signifying the importance of the condition). This is the Lovelace poem that ends "Stone walls do not a prison make, nor iron bars a cage. . ." but again, it seems likely that Lovelace is referring to liberty in a more general sense. . . as well as the immediate one which caused him to title this: *To Althea, from Prison* (where he resided during the Civil Wars).

222. (A)

While it might at first seem as if (C) is the addressee, the speaker calls on the winds to "crack" the plans of Nature. Winds are personified, and appear to represent a greater primeval force than simply what is connoted today by "wind" as the movement of air.

223.   (C)
The speaker is asking that that which creates "ingrateful" human beings be destroyed.

224.   (D)
Blow / rage / singe / smite / spill.

225.   (B)
King Lear from III: ii.

226.   (D)
From *Everyman*.

227.   (C)
Swift's *Cadenus* and *Vanessa*.

228.   (B)
From Herrick's *His Return to London*.

229.   (E)
From Joyce's *Dubliners*.

230.   (D)
Within the context of these lines, Faustus simply asks if Mephistopheles is so foolish as to think that Faustus imagines that there will be pain in the afterlife. From Marlowe's *Faustus*.

GRE

LITERATURE in ENGLISH

TEST VI

THE GRADUATE RECORD EXAMINATION

LITERATURE in ENGLISH

ANSWER SHEET

1. Ⓐ Ⓑ Ⓒ Ⓓ Ⓔ
2. Ⓐ Ⓑ Ⓒ Ⓓ Ⓔ
3. Ⓐ Ⓑ Ⓒ Ⓓ Ⓔ
4. Ⓐ Ⓑ Ⓒ Ⓓ Ⓔ
5. Ⓐ Ⓑ Ⓒ Ⓓ Ⓔ
6. Ⓐ Ⓑ Ⓒ Ⓓ Ⓔ
7. Ⓐ Ⓑ Ⓒ Ⓓ Ⓔ
8. Ⓐ Ⓑ Ⓒ Ⓓ Ⓔ
9. Ⓐ Ⓑ Ⓒ Ⓓ Ⓔ
10. Ⓐ Ⓑ Ⓒ Ⓓ Ⓔ
11. Ⓐ Ⓑ Ⓒ Ⓓ Ⓔ
12. Ⓐ Ⓑ Ⓒ Ⓓ Ⓔ
13. Ⓐ Ⓑ Ⓒ Ⓓ Ⓔ
14. Ⓐ Ⓑ Ⓒ Ⓓ Ⓔ
15. Ⓐ Ⓑ Ⓒ Ⓓ Ⓔ
16. Ⓐ Ⓑ Ⓒ Ⓓ Ⓔ
17. Ⓐ Ⓑ Ⓒ Ⓓ Ⓔ
18. Ⓐ Ⓑ Ⓒ Ⓓ Ⓔ
19. Ⓐ Ⓑ Ⓒ Ⓓ Ⓔ
20. Ⓐ Ⓑ Ⓒ Ⓓ Ⓔ
21. Ⓐ Ⓑ Ⓒ Ⓓ Ⓔ
22. Ⓐ Ⓑ Ⓒ Ⓓ Ⓔ
23. Ⓐ Ⓑ Ⓒ Ⓓ Ⓔ
24. Ⓐ Ⓑ Ⓒ Ⓓ Ⓔ
25. Ⓐ Ⓑ Ⓒ Ⓓ Ⓔ
26. Ⓐ Ⓑ Ⓒ Ⓓ Ⓔ
27. Ⓐ Ⓑ Ⓒ Ⓓ Ⓔ
28. Ⓐ Ⓑ Ⓒ Ⓓ Ⓔ
29. Ⓐ Ⓑ Ⓒ Ⓓ Ⓔ
30. Ⓐ Ⓑ Ⓒ Ⓓ Ⓔ

31. Ⓐ Ⓑ Ⓒ Ⓓ Ⓔ
32. Ⓐ Ⓑ Ⓒ Ⓓ Ⓔ
33. Ⓐ Ⓑ Ⓒ Ⓓ Ⓔ
34. Ⓐ Ⓑ Ⓒ Ⓓ Ⓔ
35. Ⓐ Ⓑ Ⓒ Ⓓ Ⓔ
36. Ⓐ Ⓑ Ⓒ Ⓓ Ⓔ
37. Ⓐ Ⓑ Ⓒ Ⓓ Ⓔ
38. Ⓐ Ⓑ Ⓒ Ⓓ Ⓔ
39. Ⓐ Ⓑ Ⓒ Ⓓ Ⓔ
40. Ⓐ Ⓑ Ⓒ Ⓓ Ⓔ
41. Ⓐ Ⓑ Ⓒ Ⓓ Ⓔ
42. Ⓐ Ⓑ Ⓒ Ⓓ Ⓔ
43. Ⓐ Ⓑ Ⓒ Ⓓ Ⓔ
44. Ⓐ Ⓑ Ⓒ Ⓓ Ⓔ
45. Ⓐ Ⓑ Ⓒ Ⓓ Ⓔ
46. Ⓐ Ⓑ Ⓒ Ⓓ Ⓔ
47. Ⓐ Ⓑ Ⓒ Ⓓ Ⓔ
48. Ⓐ Ⓑ Ⓒ Ⓓ Ⓔ
49. Ⓐ Ⓑ Ⓒ Ⓓ Ⓔ
50. Ⓐ Ⓑ Ⓒ Ⓓ Ⓔ
51. Ⓐ Ⓑ Ⓒ Ⓓ Ⓔ
52. Ⓐ Ⓑ Ⓒ Ⓓ Ⓔ
53. Ⓐ Ⓑ Ⓒ Ⓓ Ⓔ
54. Ⓐ Ⓑ Ⓒ Ⓓ Ⓔ
55. Ⓐ Ⓑ Ⓒ Ⓓ Ⓔ
56. Ⓐ Ⓑ Ⓒ Ⓓ Ⓔ
57. Ⓐ Ⓑ Ⓒ Ⓓ Ⓔ
58. Ⓐ Ⓑ Ⓒ Ⓓ Ⓔ
59. Ⓐ Ⓑ Ⓒ Ⓓ Ⓔ
60. Ⓐ Ⓑ Ⓒ Ⓓ Ⓔ

61. Ⓐ Ⓑ Ⓒ Ⓓ Ⓔ
62. Ⓐ Ⓑ Ⓒ Ⓓ Ⓔ
63. Ⓐ Ⓑ Ⓒ Ⓓ Ⓔ
64. Ⓐ Ⓑ Ⓒ Ⓓ Ⓔ
65. Ⓐ Ⓑ Ⓒ Ⓓ Ⓔ
66. Ⓐ Ⓑ Ⓒ Ⓓ Ⓔ
67. Ⓐ Ⓑ Ⓒ Ⓓ Ⓔ
68. Ⓐ Ⓑ Ⓒ Ⓓ Ⓔ
69. Ⓐ Ⓑ Ⓒ Ⓓ Ⓔ
70. Ⓐ Ⓑ Ⓒ Ⓓ Ⓔ
71. Ⓐ Ⓑ Ⓒ Ⓓ Ⓔ
72. Ⓐ Ⓑ Ⓒ Ⓓ Ⓔ
73. Ⓐ Ⓑ Ⓒ Ⓓ Ⓔ
74. Ⓐ Ⓑ Ⓒ Ⓓ Ⓔ
75. Ⓐ Ⓑ Ⓒ Ⓓ Ⓔ
76. Ⓐ Ⓑ Ⓒ Ⓓ Ⓔ
77. Ⓐ Ⓑ Ⓒ Ⓓ Ⓔ
78. Ⓐ Ⓑ Ⓒ Ⓓ Ⓔ
79. Ⓐ Ⓑ Ⓒ Ⓓ Ⓔ
80. Ⓐ Ⓑ Ⓒ Ⓓ Ⓔ
81. Ⓐ Ⓑ Ⓒ Ⓓ Ⓔ
82. Ⓐ Ⓑ Ⓒ Ⓓ Ⓔ
83. Ⓐ Ⓑ Ⓒ Ⓓ Ⓔ
84. Ⓐ Ⓑ Ⓒ Ⓓ Ⓔ
85. Ⓐ Ⓑ Ⓒ Ⓓ Ⓔ
86. Ⓐ Ⓑ Ⓒ Ⓓ Ⓔ
87. Ⓐ Ⓑ Ⓒ Ⓓ Ⓔ
88. Ⓐ Ⓑ Ⓒ Ⓓ Ⓔ
89. Ⓐ Ⓑ Ⓒ Ⓓ Ⓔ
90. Ⓐ Ⓑ Ⓒ Ⓓ Ⓔ

91. Ⓐ Ⓑ Ⓒ Ⓓ Ⓔ	121. Ⓐ Ⓑ Ⓒ Ⓓ Ⓔ	151. Ⓐ Ⓑ Ⓒ Ⓓ Ⓔ
92. Ⓐ Ⓑ Ⓒ Ⓓ Ⓔ	122. Ⓐ Ⓑ Ⓒ Ⓓ Ⓔ	152. Ⓐ Ⓑ Ⓒ Ⓓ Ⓔ
93. Ⓐ Ⓑ Ⓒ Ⓓ Ⓔ	123. Ⓐ Ⓑ Ⓒ Ⓓ Ⓔ	153. Ⓐ Ⓑ Ⓒ Ⓓ Ⓔ
94. Ⓐ Ⓑ Ⓒ Ⓓ Ⓔ	124. Ⓐ Ⓑ Ⓒ Ⓓ Ⓔ	154. Ⓐ Ⓑ Ⓒ Ⓓ Ⓔ
95. Ⓐ Ⓑ Ⓒ Ⓓ Ⓔ	125. Ⓐ Ⓑ Ⓒ Ⓓ Ⓔ	155. Ⓐ Ⓑ Ⓒ Ⓓ Ⓔ
96. Ⓐ Ⓑ Ⓒ Ⓓ Ⓔ	126. Ⓐ Ⓑ Ⓒ Ⓓ Ⓔ	156. Ⓐ Ⓑ Ⓒ Ⓓ Ⓔ
97. Ⓐ Ⓑ Ⓒ Ⓓ Ⓔ	127. Ⓐ Ⓑ Ⓒ Ⓓ Ⓔ	157. Ⓐ Ⓑ Ⓒ Ⓓ Ⓔ
98. Ⓐ Ⓑ Ⓒ Ⓓ Ⓔ	128. Ⓐ Ⓑ Ⓒ Ⓓ Ⓔ	158. Ⓐ Ⓑ Ⓒ Ⓓ Ⓔ
99. Ⓐ Ⓑ Ⓒ Ⓓ Ⓔ	129. Ⓐ Ⓑ Ⓒ Ⓓ Ⓔ	159. Ⓐ Ⓑ Ⓒ Ⓓ Ⓔ
100. Ⓐ Ⓑ Ⓒ Ⓓ Ⓔ	130. Ⓐ Ⓑ Ⓒ Ⓓ Ⓔ	160. Ⓐ Ⓑ Ⓒ Ⓓ Ⓔ
101. Ⓐ Ⓑ Ⓒ Ⓓ Ⓔ	131. Ⓐ Ⓑ Ⓒ Ⓓ Ⓔ	161. Ⓐ Ⓑ Ⓒ Ⓓ Ⓔ
102. Ⓐ Ⓑ Ⓒ Ⓓ Ⓔ	132. Ⓐ Ⓑ Ⓒ Ⓓ Ⓔ	162. Ⓐ Ⓑ Ⓒ Ⓓ Ⓔ
103. Ⓐ Ⓑ Ⓒ Ⓓ Ⓔ	133. Ⓐ Ⓑ Ⓒ Ⓓ Ⓔ	163. Ⓐ Ⓑ Ⓒ Ⓓ Ⓔ
104. Ⓐ Ⓑ Ⓒ Ⓓ Ⓔ	134. Ⓐ Ⓑ Ⓒ Ⓓ Ⓔ	164. Ⓐ Ⓑ Ⓒ Ⓓ Ⓔ
105. Ⓐ Ⓑ Ⓒ Ⓓ Ⓔ	135. Ⓐ Ⓑ Ⓒ Ⓓ Ⓔ	165. Ⓐ Ⓑ Ⓒ Ⓓ Ⓔ
106. Ⓐ Ⓑ Ⓒ Ⓓ Ⓔ	136. Ⓐ Ⓑ Ⓒ Ⓓ Ⓔ	166. Ⓐ Ⓑ Ⓒ Ⓓ Ⓔ
107. Ⓐ Ⓑ Ⓒ Ⓓ Ⓔ	137. Ⓐ Ⓑ Ⓒ Ⓓ Ⓔ	167. Ⓐ Ⓑ Ⓒ Ⓓ Ⓔ
108. Ⓐ Ⓑ Ⓒ Ⓓ Ⓔ	138. Ⓐ Ⓑ Ⓒ Ⓓ Ⓔ	168. Ⓐ Ⓑ Ⓒ Ⓓ Ⓔ
109. Ⓐ Ⓑ Ⓒ Ⓓ Ⓔ	139. Ⓐ Ⓑ Ⓒ Ⓓ Ⓔ	169. Ⓐ Ⓑ Ⓒ Ⓓ Ⓔ
110. Ⓐ Ⓑ Ⓒ Ⓓ Ⓔ	140. Ⓐ Ⓑ Ⓒ Ⓓ Ⓔ	170. Ⓐ Ⓑ Ⓒ Ⓓ Ⓔ
111. Ⓐ Ⓑ Ⓒ Ⓓ Ⓔ	141. Ⓐ Ⓑ Ⓒ Ⓓ Ⓔ	171. Ⓐ Ⓑ Ⓒ Ⓓ Ⓔ
112. Ⓐ Ⓑ Ⓒ Ⓓ Ⓔ	142. Ⓐ Ⓑ Ⓒ Ⓓ Ⓔ	172. Ⓐ Ⓑ Ⓒ Ⓓ Ⓔ
113. Ⓐ Ⓑ Ⓒ Ⓓ Ⓔ	143. Ⓐ Ⓑ Ⓒ Ⓓ Ⓔ	173. Ⓐ Ⓑ Ⓒ Ⓓ Ⓔ
114. Ⓐ Ⓑ Ⓒ Ⓓ Ⓔ	144. Ⓐ Ⓑ Ⓒ Ⓓ Ⓔ	174. Ⓐ Ⓑ Ⓒ Ⓓ Ⓔ
115. Ⓐ Ⓑ Ⓒ Ⓓ Ⓔ	145. Ⓐ Ⓑ Ⓒ Ⓓ Ⓔ	175. Ⓐ Ⓑ Ⓒ Ⓓ Ⓔ
116. Ⓐ Ⓑ Ⓒ Ⓓ Ⓔ	146. Ⓐ Ⓑ Ⓒ Ⓓ Ⓔ	176. Ⓐ Ⓑ Ⓒ Ⓓ Ⓔ
117. Ⓐ Ⓑ Ⓒ Ⓓ Ⓔ	147. Ⓐ Ⓑ Ⓒ Ⓓ Ⓔ	177. Ⓐ Ⓑ Ⓒ Ⓓ Ⓔ
118. Ⓐ Ⓑ Ⓒ Ⓓ Ⓔ	148. Ⓐ Ⓑ Ⓒ Ⓓ Ⓔ	178. Ⓐ Ⓑ Ⓒ Ⓓ Ⓔ
119. Ⓐ Ⓑ Ⓒ Ⓓ Ⓔ	149. Ⓐ Ⓑ Ⓒ Ⓓ Ⓔ	179. Ⓐ Ⓑ Ⓒ Ⓓ Ⓔ
120. Ⓐ Ⓑ Ⓒ Ⓓ Ⓔ	150. Ⓐ Ⓑ Ⓒ Ⓓ Ⓔ	180. Ⓐ Ⓑ Ⓒ Ⓓ Ⓔ

181.	Ⓐ Ⓑ Ⓒ Ⓓ Ⓔ	198.	Ⓐ Ⓑ Ⓒ Ⓓ Ⓔ	215. Ⓐ Ⓑ Ⓒ Ⓓ Ⓔ
182.	Ⓐ Ⓑ Ⓒ Ⓓ Ⓔ	199.	Ⓐ Ⓑ Ⓒ Ⓓ Ⓔ	216. Ⓐ Ⓑ Ⓒ Ⓓ Ⓔ
183.	Ⓐ Ⓑ Ⓒ Ⓓ Ⓔ	200.	Ⓐ Ⓑ Ⓒ Ⓓ Ⓔ	217. Ⓐ Ⓑ Ⓒ Ⓓ Ⓔ
184.	Ⓐ Ⓑ Ⓒ Ⓓ Ⓔ	201.	Ⓐ Ⓑ Ⓒ Ⓓ Ⓔ	218. Ⓐ Ⓑ Ⓒ Ⓓ Ⓔ
185.	Ⓐ Ⓑ Ⓒ Ⓓ Ⓔ	202.	Ⓐ Ⓑ Ⓒ Ⓓ Ⓔ	219. Ⓐ Ⓑ Ⓒ Ⓓ Ⓔ
186.	Ⓐ Ⓑ Ⓒ Ⓓ Ⓔ	203.	Ⓐ Ⓑ Ⓒ Ⓓ Ⓔ	220. Ⓐ Ⓑ Ⓒ Ⓓ Ⓔ
187.	Ⓐ Ⓑ Ⓒ Ⓓ Ⓔ	204.	Ⓐ Ⓑ Ⓒ Ⓓ Ⓔ	221. Ⓐ Ⓑ Ⓒ Ⓓ Ⓔ
188.	Ⓐ Ⓑ Ⓒ Ⓓ Ⓔ	205.	Ⓐ Ⓑ Ⓒ Ⓓ Ⓔ	222. Ⓐ Ⓑ Ⓒ Ⓓ Ⓔ
189.	Ⓐ Ⓑ Ⓒ Ⓓ Ⓔ	206.	Ⓐ Ⓑ Ⓒ Ⓓ Ⓔ	223. Ⓐ Ⓑ Ⓒ Ⓓ Ⓔ
190.	Ⓐ Ⓑ Ⓒ Ⓓ Ⓔ	207.	Ⓐ Ⓑ Ⓒ Ⓓ Ⓔ	224. Ⓐ Ⓑ Ⓒ Ⓓ Ⓔ
191.	Ⓐ Ⓑ Ⓒ Ⓓ Ⓔ	208.	Ⓐ Ⓑ Ⓒ Ⓓ Ⓔ	225. Ⓐ Ⓑ Ⓒ Ⓓ Ⓔ
192.	Ⓐ Ⓑ Ⓒ Ⓓ Ⓔ	209.	Ⓐ Ⓑ Ⓒ Ⓓ Ⓔ	226. Ⓐ Ⓑ Ⓒ Ⓓ Ⓔ
193.	Ⓐ Ⓑ Ⓒ Ⓓ Ⓔ	210.	Ⓐ Ⓑ Ⓒ Ⓓ Ⓔ	227. Ⓐ Ⓑ Ⓒ Ⓓ Ⓔ
194.	Ⓐ Ⓑ Ⓒ Ⓓ Ⓔ	211.	Ⓐ Ⓑ Ⓒ Ⓓ Ⓔ	228. Ⓐ Ⓑ Ⓒ Ⓓ Ⓔ
195.	Ⓐ Ⓑ Ⓒ Ⓓ Ⓔ	212.	Ⓐ Ⓑ Ⓒ Ⓓ Ⓔ	229. Ⓐ Ⓑ Ⓒ Ⓓ Ⓔ
196.	Ⓐ Ⓑ Ⓒ Ⓓ Ⓔ	213.	Ⓐ Ⓑ Ⓒ Ⓓ Ⓔ	230. Ⓐ Ⓑ Ⓒ Ⓓ Ⓔ
197.	Ⓐ Ⓑ Ⓒ Ⓓ Ⓔ	214.	Ⓐ Ⓑ Ⓒ Ⓓ Ⓔ	

GRE LITERATURE
IN ENGLISH

TEST VI

DIRECTIONS: Choose the best answer for each question and mark the letter of your selection on the corresponding answer sheet.

Questions 1-3 refer to the dramatic works below.

1.   Which is a closet drama?

2.   Which is a morality play?

3.   Which is a ballad opera?

   (A) *Gammer Gurton's Needle*

   (B) Percy Bysshe Shelley, *Prometheus Unbound*

   (C) *Everyman*

   (D) Oscar Wilde, *Salome*

   (E) John Gay, *Polly*

Questions 4-6 refer to the poems below.

4.   Which is a dramatic monologue?

5.   Which is an eclogue?

6.   Which is an elegy?

   (A) the May poem from Edmund Spenser, *The Shepheardes Calender*

   (B) John Donne, *The Canonization*

(C) Wallace Stevens, *The Idea of Order at Key West*

(D) Alfred Tennyson, *In Memoriam A. H. H.*

(E) T. S. Eliot, *The Love Song of J. Alfred Prufrock*

7. William Vaughn Mody's *An Ode in Time of Hesitation* protests America's conquest of

(A) Mexico

(D) the Philippines

(B) Canada

(E) China

(C) Cuba

8. "Where there is great love, there are always miracles. The miracles of the Church seem to me to rest not so much upon faces or voices or healing power coming suddenly near to us from afar off, but upon our perceptions being made finer, so that for a moment our eyes can see and our ears can hear what there is about us always."

The speaker is

(A) Dorinda Oakley in Glasgow's *Barren Ground*

(B) Robert Jordan in Hemingway's *For Whom the Bell Tolls*

(C) Father Latour in Cather's *Death Comes for the Archbishop*

(D) Parson Adams in Fielding's *Joseph Andrews*

(E) Father Rank in Graham Greene's *The Heart of the Matter*

9.

VIVIE.   Today I know my mother better than you do.

FRANK. Heaven forbid!

VIVIE.   What do you mean?

FRA NK. Viv, theres a freemasonry among thoroughly immoral people that you know nothing of. You've too much character. That's the bond between your mother and me: that's why I know her better than you'll ever know her.

VIVIE. You are wrong: you know nothing about her. If you knew the circumstances against which my mother had to struggle-

FRANK. (adroitly finishing the sentence for her) I should know why she is what she is, shouldn't I? What difference would that make? Circumstances or no circumstances, Viv, you won't be able to stand your mother.

This excerpt is from:

(A) *The Rose Tattoo*

(B) *Mrs. Warren's Profession*

(C) *Strange Interlude*

(D) *Miss Julie*

(E) *The Playboy of the Western World*

Questions 10-12 refer to the plays below.

10. Which is an adaptation of Aeschylus' *Oresteia*?

11. Which is an adaptation of Terence's *Andria*?

12. Which has Plautus' *Menaechmi* as its source?

(A) Eugene O'Neill, *Mourning Becomes Electra*

(B) Joseph Addison, *Cato*

(C) Richard Steele, *The Conscious Lovers*

(D) Robert Sherwood, *The Road to Rome*

(E) Shakespeare, *The Comedy of Errors*

Questions 13-15 refer to the works below.

13. Which is a Quaker spiritual autobiography?

14. Which is a Puritan chronicle of Massachusetts Bay Colony?

15. Which is a Puritan autobiography that recounts the experience of spiritual conversion?

(A) John Winthrop, *Journal*

(B) Benjamin Franklin, *Autobiography*

(C) John Woolman, *Journal*

(D) William Byrd, *Secret Diary*

(E) Jonathan Edwards, *Personal Narrative*

Questions 16-19

> She dwells with Beauty--Beauty that must die;
>> And Joy, whose hand is ever at his lips
> Bidding adieu; and aching Pleasure nigh,
>> Turning to Poison while the bee-mouth sips:
> Aye, in the very temple of Delight   5
>> Veiled Melancholy has her sov'reign shrine,
>>> Though seen of none save him whose strenuous tongue
>> Can burst Joy's grape against his palate fine;
> His soul shall taste the sadness of her might,
>> And be among her cloudy trophies hung. 10

16. In line one, "She" refers to

(A) Truth   (D) Melancholy

(B) Joy   (E) Death

(C) Pleasure

17. The primary theme in this stanza is the

   (A) brevity of beauty

   (B) inevitability of death

   (C) sadness of all experience

   (D) necessity of religious faith

   (E) inextricable contrarieties of life

18. "Pleasure" is "aching" because

   (A) the speaker has been disillusioned by experience

   (B) things are transitory and turn into their opposites

   (C) melancholy is a stronger emotion than joy

   (D) the speaker lacks a "palate fine" to appreciate it

   (E) there really is no such thing as pleasure

19. The author of this stanza also wrote

   (A) *Dover Beach*

   (B) *Ode: Intimations of Immortality*

   (C) *Ode on a Grecian Urn*

   (D) *Ulysses*

   (E) *Don Juan*

Questions 20-22 refer to the poems below.

20. Which is a "translation" of a work by the Chinese poet Li Po?

21. Which is a reworking of a poem by Pierre de Ronsard?

22.   Which is an imitation of Juvenal's *Satire X* ?

   (A) Samuel Johnson, *The Vanity of Human Wishes*

   (B) Ezra Pound, *The River-Merchant's Wife: A Letter*

   (C) John Gay, *The Birth of the Squire*

   (D) Dylan Thomas, *Do Not Go Gentle into That Good Night*

   (E) W. B. Yeats, *When You are Old*

Questions 23-26

There was such speed in her little body,
And such lightness in her footfall,
It is no wonder her brown study
Astonishes us all.

Her wars were bruited in our high window.   5
We looked among orchard trees and beyond
Where she took arms against her shadow,
Or harried unto the pond

The lazy geese, like a snow cloud
Dripping their snow on the green grass,   10
Tricking and stopping, sleepy and proud,
Who cried in goose, Alas,

For the tireless heart within the little
Lady with rod that made them rise
From their noon apple-dreams and scuttle   15
Goose-fashion under the skies!

But now go the bells, and we are ready,
In one house we are sternly stopped
To say we are vexed at her brown study,
Lying so primly propped.   20

23. "Brown study" (line three) is an instance of

   (A) hyperbole

   (B) paradox

   (C) understatement

   (D) simile

   (E) litotes

24. The word in the last four lines that indicates that the speaker is not "ready" is

   (A) sternly

   (B) stopped

   (C) vexed

   (D) say

   (E) primly

25. The occasion of the poem is a

   (A) birth

   (B) christening

   (C) confirmation

   (D) wedding

   (E) funeral

26. The poet is

   (A) Robert Frost

   (B) John Greenleaf Whittier

   (C) Stephen Crane

   (D) John Crowe Ransom

   (E) Denise Levertov

Questions 27-29 refer to the works below.

27. The plot of Shaw's *Pygmalion* closely resembles an incident in which work?

28. Richardson's Lovelace in *Clarissa* is modeled on a character in which work?

29. Sir John Vanbrugh's *The Relapse* is an avowed "continuation" of (or "sequel" to) which work?

    (A) Henry Fielding, *Amelia*

    (B) Colley Cibber, *Love's Last Shift*

    (C) Tobias Smollett, *Peregrine Pickle*

    (D) Daniel Defoe, *Moll Flanders*

    (E) Nicholas Rowe, *The Fair Penitent*

Questions 30-32

A literary movement in the second half of the eighteenth century, sometimes called the Celtic Revival, focused interest on the history, mythology, and literature of the ancient Celts. The movement emphasized the primitive, remote, and mysterious. The most famous poet in the movement was _____, author of *The Bard* (1757) and *The Progress of Poesy* (1757). More controversial was _____, whose *Fingal* (1762) and *Temora* (1763) were published as translations of the poetry of the primitive Celtic bard, Ossian, but which were chiefly the "translator's" own work. The movement also produced one play, *The Fatal Discovery* (1769), by _____.

30. Which correctly completes the third sentence?

    (A) Matthew Prior   (D) Thomas Gray

    (B) Oliver Goldsmith   (E) William Collins

    (C) James Thomsom

31. Which correctly completes the fourth sentence?

(A) William Cowper

(D) Hugh Blair

(B) James Macpherson

(E) Christopher Smart

(C) George Crabbe

32. Which correctly completes the fifth sentence?

(A) John Home

(D) George Colman, the Elder

(B) Edward Moore

(E) Hugh Kelly

(C) Nicholas Rowe

Questions 33-37 refer to the works below.

33. Which uses intrusive, omniscient, third-person narration?

34. Which uses impersonal or unintrusive third-person narration?

35. Which uses a first-person narrator who is a minor participant in the story?

36. Which uses an unreliable narrator?

37. Which uses a self-conscious narrator for comic purposes?

(A) Austen, *Emma*

(B) Melville, *Moby Dick*

(C) James, *The Aspern Papers*

(D) Hemingway, *The Killers*

(E) Byron, *Don Juan*

38. The title, *Erewhon*, is an instance of

   (A) metonymy
   (B) an anagram
   (C) ambiguity
   (D) palindrome
   (E) oxymoron

39. The author of *Erewhon* also wrote

   (A) *The Time Machine*
   (B) *Hudibras*
   (C) *The Caxtons*
   (D) *Cakes and Ale*
   (E) *The Way of All Flesh*

40. Both *Lucky Jim* and *Catch-22* make use of

   (A) unreliable narrators
   (B) naturalist conventions
   (C) an anti-hero
   (D) epistolary techniques
   (E) first-person narration

Questions 41-43

   The hungry judges soon the sentence sign,
   And wretches hang that jury-men may dine.

41. These two lines provide an example of

   (A) rhyme royal
   (B) the heroic couplet
   (C) a rondeau
   (D) blank verse
   (E) an open couplet

662

42. The second line provides an instance of

    (A) antithesis   (D) oxymoron

    (B) hypallage   (E) hyperbole

    (C) synecdoche

43. The author of these lines is

    (A) John Dryden   (D) Samuel Johnson

    (B) Jonathan Swift   (E) Alexander Pope

    (C) John Milton

44. X lived as a child in Guiana, later served as a spy in Antwerp, and wrote fifteen plays (including *The Rover*, which deals with amorous adventures of English cavaliers in Naples and Madrid during Charles II's exile, and *The City Heiress*, a coarse comedy set in contemporary London) and several novels, including *Oroonoko*.

    Who is X?

    (A) Thomas Otway   (D) John Crowne

    (B) Nahum Tate   (E) Aphra Behn

    (C) Nathaniel Lee

45. Among the eighteen plays written by _____ are *The Busybody*, which contains a character whose name (Marplot) has entered the language as a term for a blundering busybody, and *A Bold Stroke for a Wife*, which contains a Quaker preacher who proves himself "the real Simon Pure," a phrase that has become proverbial.

Which correctly completes the passage?

(A) William D'Avenant   (D) Thomas Southerne

(B) Susannah Centlivre   (E) Colley Cibber

(C) George Farquhar

46. All of the following are leading novelists of the Edwardian Age EXCEPT

(A) John Galsworthy   (D) Evelyn Waugh

(B) H. G. Wells   (E) Arnold Bennett

(C) Joseph Conrad

47. All of the following are associated with *The Dial* (Boston 1840-1844) EXCEPT

(A) Ralph Waldo Emerson   (D) Henry David Thoreau

(B) Margaret Fuller   (E) Nathaniel Hawthorne

(C) Jones Very

Questions 48-50 refer to the descriptions below.

48. Which describes comedy of manners?

49. Which describes burlesque?

50. Which describes farce?

(A) Developed by Ben Jonson and George Chapman, this type of comedy focuses on characters whose conduct and dispositions are controlled by a single exaggerated trait or characteristic.

(B) As practiced by Wycherley and others, this type of comedy features witty, polished dialogue, appeals to the intellect, and examinations of the conventions of an artificial, sophisticated society.

(C) As in James Townley's *High Life Below Stairs*, this dramatic type seeks to evoke laughter through the use of improbable situations, horseplay, and coarse wit.

(D) This form of comedy is a travesty of a literary form, relies on discrepancy between subject matter and style, and employs ridiculous exaggeration to achieve its effects.

(E) This short comic type, popular in the late eighteenth century, consists of recitative and singing with orchestral accompaniment.

51. *Candide* satirizes the optimistic philosophy of

(A) Kant   (D) Bacon

(B) Leibniz   (E) Locke

(C) Descartes

Questions 52-54 refer to the poems below.

52. Which is an occasional poem?

53. Which is an *ubi sunt* poem?

54. Which is a *carpe diem* poem?

(A) Donne's *Song* (Go and catch a falling star)

(B) Lovelace's *To Althea, from Prison*

(C) Villon's *The Ballade of Dead Ladies*

(D) Herrick's *Delight in Disorder*

(E) Waller's *Song* (Go, lovely rose!)

Questions 55-57

Above the pines the moon was slowly drifting,
    The river sang below;
The dim Sierras, far beyond, uplifting
    Their minarets of snow.

55. How many lines end with feminine rhyme?

(A) none   (D) three

(B) one   (E) four

(C) two

56. How many caesuras are there in these lines?

(A) none   (D) three

(B) one   (E) four

(C) two

57. The meter of lines two and four is

(A) trochaic trimeter   (D) dactylic dimeter

(B) iambic trimeter   (E) iambic pentameter

(C) anapestic dimeter

Questions 58-60 refer to the items below.

58.   Which is an example of synecdoche?

59.   Which is an example of apostrophe?

60.   Which is an example of zeugma?

(A) using "the crown" as a term for a king

(B) "He's not the brightest man in the world."

(C) the opening line of Keats' *Ode on a Grecian Urn*: "Thou still unravished bride of quietness. . ."

(D) using "ten hands" for ten workmen

(E) "Or stain her honour, or her new brocade"

61. All of the following form part of the frontier tradition in American literature EXCEPT

(A) Sarah Orne Jewett

(B) Artemus Ward

(C) Bret Harte

(D) Caroline Kirkland

(E) Hamlin Garland

Questions 62-67

Then at dawn we came down to a temperate valley,
Wet, below the snow line, smelling of vegetation;
With a running stream and a water mill beating the darkness,
And three trees on the low sky,
And an old white horse galloped away in the meadow.   5
Then we came to a tavern with vine-leaves over the lintel,
Six hands at an open door dicing for pieces of silver,
And feet kicking the empty wineskins.
But there was no information, and so we continued
And arrived at evening, not a moment too soon   10
Finding the place; it was (you may say) satisfactory.

All this was a long time ago, I remember,
And I would do it again, but set down
This set down
This: were we led all that way for   15
Birth or Death? There was a Birth, certainly,
We had evidence and no doubt. I had seen birth and death,
But had thought they were different; this Birth was
Hard and bitter agony for us, like Death, our death.
We returned to our places, these Kingdoms,   20
But no longer at ease here, in the old dispensation,
With an alien people clutching their gods.
I should be glad of another death.

62.   The speaker is

        (A) a pagan prince

        (B) one of the three wise men

        (C) the poet himself

        (D) one of the disciples

        (E) a modern man visiting Bethlehem

63.   The images in lines 1-3 suggest

        (A) chaos   (D) renewal

        (B) hostility   (E) indifference

        (C) alienation

64.   The images in lines 4-7 can best be described as

        (A) foreshadowings of disastrous events in Christ's life and
            death.

        (B) indications of man's failure to recognize momentous
            events when they occur.

(C) allusions to significant events preceding the birth of Christ.

(D) signs of the random and trivial nature of daily life.

(E) indications of the depravity of men in general.

65. In saying "this Birth was hard and bitter agony for us, like Death, our death," (lines 18-19) the speaker means that

(A) they were able to anticipate Christ's crucifixion.

(B) the birth was a reminder of their mortality.

(C) Christ's birth destroyed their belief in their pagan religion.

(D) they experienced great hardship during their journey.

(E) the birth made them realize that all great accomplishments are accompanied by pain.

66. "Another death" in the last line refers to the death of

(A) the speaker's "alien" king

(B) the speaker

(C) Christ

(D) memory

(E) the gods of the "alien people" among whom the speaker lives

67. The poet is

(A) A. R. Ammons

(B) Richard Wilbur

(C) Ezra Pound

(D) W. B. Yeats

(E) T. S. Eliot

68. Gongorism, Marinism, and euphuism are terms for

(A) Roman rhetorical devices

(B) religious heresies

(C) schools of criticism

(D) affected writing styles

(E) philosophical movements

69. The "graveyard school" of poets includes all of the following EXCEPT

(A) Matthew Prior

(B) Thomas Parnell

(C) Robert Blair

(D) Edward Young

(E) Thomas Gray

70. All of the following wrote Gothic novels EXCEPT

(A) William Beckford

(B) Annc Radcliffc

(C) Matthew Lewis

(D) Hugh Henry Brackenridge

(E) Charles Brockden Brown

71. The author of *Tendencies in Modern American Poetry,* which states the objectives of the Imagist school of poetry, is

(A) Walt Whitman

(B) Amy Lowell

(C) Emily Dickinson

(D) Gerard Manley Hopkins

(E) Wallace Stevens

Questions 72-74 refer to the descriptions below.

72. Which is a kenning?

73. Which is litotes?

74. Which is flyting?

    (A) in Old English poetry, a boasting match between warriors; now, an exchange of verbal abuse in verse.

    (B) repetition of a line or stanza, but with an addition that furthers the story.

    (C) figurative phrase, usually a metaphorical compound, used as a synonym for a simple noun; for example, "swan-road" or "whale-road" for "sea" in *Beowulf*.

    (D) form of understatement that asserts a positive by negating its opposite; for example, "he was not afraid" when one means "he was courageous"

    (E) elegy or dirge with a single speaker.

Questions 75-77 refer to the excerpts below.

75. Which is from Katherine Mansfield's *Bliss* ?

76. Which is from Alice Walker's *Everyday Use* ?

77. Which is from Kate Chopin's *The Story of an Hour* ?

    (A) The day would proceed from this, beat by beat, without reflection, like every other day. The astronomer was still asleep, or feigning it, and she, once out of bed, had come into her own possession. Although scarcely ever out of sight of the impenetrable silence of his brow, she would be absent from him all the day in being clean, busy, kind. He was a man of other things, a dreamer. . . .That man might be each time the new arching wave, and woman the undertow that sucked him back, were things she had been told by his silence were so.

(B) The girl had taken the Ph.D. in philosophy and this left Mrs. Hopewell at a complete loss. You could say, "My daughter is a nurse," or "My daughter is a school teacher," or even, "My daughter is a chemical engineer." You could not say, "My daughter is a philosopher." That was something that had ended with the Greeks and Romans. All day Joy sat on her neck in a deep chair, reading. Sometimes she went for walks but she didn't like dogs or cats or birds or flowers or nature or nice young men. She looked at nice young men as if she could smell their stupidity.

(C) "I reckon she would," I said. "God knows I been saving 'em for long enough with nobody using 'em. I hope she will!" I didn't want to bring up how I had offered Dee (Wangero) a quilt when she went away to college. Then she had told me they were old-fashioned, out of style.

"But they're <u>priceless</u>!" she was saying now, furiously; for she has a temper. "Maggie would put them on the bed and in five years they'd be in rags. Less than that!"

"She can always make some more," I said. "Maggie knows how to quilt."

(D) Really--really--she had everything. She was young. Harry and she were as much in love as ever, and they got on together splendidly and were really good pals. She had an adorable baby. They didn't have to worry about money. They had this absolutely satisfactory house and garden. And friends--modern, thrilling friends, writers and painters and poets or people keen on social questions--just the kind of friends they wanted. And then there were books, and there was music, and she had found a wonderful little dressmaker, and they were going abroad in the summer, and their new cook made the most superb omelettes. . . .

(E) And yet she had loved him--sometimes. Often she had not. What did it matter! What could love, the unsolved mystery, count for in the face of this possession of self-assertion which she suddenly recognized as the strongest impulse of her being!

"Free! Body and soul free!" she kept whispering.

Questions 78-80 refer to the excerpts below.

78.   Which is by Henry Fielding?

79.   Which is by Joseph Addison?

80.   Which is by David Hume?

(A)   'Tis with our judgments as our watches, none
       Go just alike, yet each believes his own.
       In poets as true genius is but rare,
       True taste as seldom is the critic's share;
       Both must alike from heav'n derive their light,
       Those born to judge, as well as those to write.

(B)   "But the knowledge of nature is only half the task of a poet;
he must be acquainted likewise with all the modes of life.
. . . He must divest himself of the prejudices of his age or
country; he must consider right and wrong in their abstracted and invariable state; he must disregard present
laws and opinions, and rise to general and transcendental
truths, which will always be the same."

(C)   I shall first consider those Pleasures of the Imagination,
which arise from actual View and Survey of outward Objects: And these, I think, all proceed from the Sight of
what is Great, Uncommon, or Beautiful. There may, indeed, be something so terrible or offensive, that the
Horror or Loathsomeness of an Object may over-bear the
Pleasure which results from its Greatness, Novelty, or
Beauty; but still there will be such a Mixture of Delight in
the very Disgust it gives us, as any of these three Qualifi -
cations are most conspicuous and prevailing.

(D)   The impulse or vehemence arising from sorrow, compassion, indignation, receives a new direction from the sentiments of beauty. The latter, being the predominant
emotion, seize the whole mind, and convert the former
into themselves, at least tincture them so strongly as
totally to alter their nature. And the soul being at the
same time roused by passion and charmed by eloquence,
feels on the whole a strong movement, which is altogether delightful.

(E) From the discovery of this affectation arises the Ridicu-
lous--which always strikes the reader with surprise and
pleasure; and that in a higher and stronger degree when
the affectation arises from hypocrisy, than when from
vanity: for, to discover any one to be the exact reverse of
what he affects, is more surprising, and consequently
more ridiculous, than to find him a little deficient in the
quality he desires the reputation of.

Questions 81-83 refer to the plays below.

81.   Which is a drama of social protest that criticizes middle-class
materialism?

82.   Which is a poetic romantic tragedy?

83.   Which is an expressionistic fantasy that satirizes man's growing regimentation?

(A) Clifford Odets, *Awake and Sing*

(B) T. S. Eliot, *Murder in the Cathedral*

(C) George Henry Boker, *Francesca da Rimini*

(D) Elmer Rice, *The Adding Machine*

(E) Lillian Hellman, *The Children's Hour*

84.   T. S. Eliot's term for the disjunction of thought and feeling in
poets who think but do not feel their thoughts is

(A) discordia concors

(B) pathetic fallacy

(C) dissociation of sensibility

(D) objective correlative

(E) negative capability

85. All of the following wrote verse plays EXCEPT

(A) Lillian Hellman   (D) Christopher Fry

(B) Maxwell Anderson   (E) Stephen Phillips

(C) T. S. Eliot

86. Tennyson's lines, "The filthiest of all paintings painted well is mightier than the purest painted ill!" is a criticism of the credo of the literary movement known as

(A) aestheticism   (D) romanticism

(B) imagism   (E) surrealism

(C) naturalism

87. All of the following playwrights are significantly associated with the theater of the absurd EXCEPT

(A) Eugène Ionesco   (D) Jean Genêt

(B) Jean Anouilh   (E) Samuel Beckett

(C) Harold Pinter

88. All of the following were associated with the Abbey Theatre and with the drama of the Irish Literary Revival EXCEPT

(A) W. B. Yeats   (D) George Moore

(B) Lady Gregory   (E) Sean O'Casey

(C) J. M. Synge

Questions 89-91 refer to the excerpts below.

89. Which refers to Jonathan Edwards?

90. Which refers to Keats?

91. Which refers to Edward FitzGerald?

(A)   . . . but none can say
That Lenten fare makes Lenten thought
    Who reads your golden Eastern lay,
Than which I know no version done
    In English more divinely well;
A planet equal to the sun
    Which cast it, that large infidel
Your Omar; and your Omar drew
    Full-handed plaudits from our best
In modern letters . . .

(B) Others abide our question. Thou art free.
We ask and ask--Thou smilest and art still,
Out-topping knowledge. For the loftiest hill,
Who to the stars uncrowns his majesty.

(C) O weary Champion of the Cross, lie still:
    Sleep thou at length the all-embracing sleep;
    Long was thy sowing day, rest now and reap:
Thy fast was long, feast now thy spirit's fill.
Yea take thy fill of love, because thy will
    Chose love not in the shallows but the deep:
    Thy tides were spring tides, set against the neap
Of calmer souls: thy flood rebuked their rill.

(D) What are we in the hands of the great God?
It was in vain you set up thorn and briar
    In battle array against the fire
    And treason crackling in your blood; . . .
You play against a sickness past your cure.
How will the hands be strong? How will the heart endure?

(E) The young Endymion sleeps Endymion's sleep;
    The shepherd-boy whose tale was left half told!
    The solemn grove uplifts its shield of gold
    To the red rising moon, and loud and deep
The nightingale is singing from the steep . . .

Questions 92-94 refer to the excerpts below.

92.   Which is by Horace?

93.   Which is by Longinus?

94.   Which is by Plato?

(A) Among the chief causes of the sublime in speech, as in the structure of the human body, is the collocation of members, a single one of which if severed from another possesses in itself nothing remarkable, but all united together make a full and perfect organism.

(B) Plots are either Simple or Complex, for the actions in real life, of which the plots are an imitation, obviously show a similar distinction. An action which is one and continuous in the sense above defined, I call Simple, when the change of fortune takes place without Reversal of Intention and without Recognition.

(C) The aim of the poet is to inform or delight, or to combine together, in what he says, both pleasure and applicability to life. . . .He who combines the useful and the pleasing wins out by both instructing and delighting the reader.

(D) [The imitative poet] awakens and nourishes and strengthens the feelings and impairs the reason. As in a city when the evil are permitted to have authority and the good are put out of the way, so in the soul of man, as we maintain, the imitative poet implants an evil constitution, for he indulges the irrational nature which has no discernment of greater and less, but thinks the same thing at one time great and at another small--he is a manufacturer of images and is very far removed from the truth.

(E) Since we do not find that any one before us has treated of the science of the vernacular language, while in fact we see that this language is highly necessary for all . . . and since it is our wish to enlighten to some little extent the discernment of those who walk through the streets like blind men . . . we will endeavor, the Word aiding us from heaven, to be of service to the vernacular speech.

Questions 95-96

A variant of strong-stress meter, _____ contains feet of varying number of syllables, with the first syllable stressed in each foot. The stressed syllable may stand alone or be associated with from one to three or more light syllables.

95. Which correctly completes the passage?

(A) Alcaic verse   (D) short measure

(B) distributed stress   (E) sprung rhythm

(C) vers libre

96. Who coined the term describing this meter and wrote poetry in it?

(A) Gerard Manley Hopkins

(B) Wallace Stevens

(C) Edgar Lee Masters

(D) Vachel Lindsay

(E) William Carlos Williams

Questions 97-99 refer to the excerpts below.

97.　In which is the "I" Saul Bellow's Eugene Henderson?

98.　In which is the "I" the narrator in Ralph Ellison's *Invisible Man* ?

99.　In which is the "I" Fowler, the narrator in Graham Greene's *The Quiet American* ?

(A) Papa-Daddy woke up with this horrible yell and right there without moving an inch he tried to turn Uncle Rondo against me. I heard every word he said. Oh, he told Uncle Rondo I didn't learn to read till I was eight years old and he didn't see how in the world I ever got the mail put up at the P. O., much less read it all, and he said if Uncle Rondo could only fathom the lengths he had gone to get me that job!

(B) So before pigs ever came on my horizon, I received a deep impression from a bear. So if corporeal things are an image of the spiritual and visible objects are renderings of invisible ones, and if Smolak and I were outcasts together, two humorists before the crowd, but brothers in our souls -I enbeared by him, and he probably humanized by me--I didn't come to the pigs as a tabula rasa.

(C) Being the third son of the family, and not bred to any trade, my head began to be filled very early with rambling thoughts. My father . . . designed me for the law; but I would be satisfied with nothing but going to sea; and my inclination to this led me so strongly against the will, nay, the commands of my father, and against all the entreaties and persuasions of my mother and other friends, that there seemed to be something fatal in that propension of nature, tending directly to the life of misery which was to befall me.

(D) It goes a long way back, some twenty years. All my life I had been looking for something, and everywhere I turned someone tried to tell me what it was. I accepted their answers too, though they were often in contradiction and even self-contradictory. I was naive. I was looking for myself and asking everyone except myself questions

which I, and only I, could answer. It took me a long time
and much painful boomeranging of my expectations to
achieve a realization everyone else appears to have been
born with: That I am nobody but myself.

(E) I thought of the first day and Pyle sitting beside me at the
Continental, with his eye on the soda fountain across the
way. Everything had gone right with me since he had
died, but how I wished there existed someone to whom I
could say that I was sorry.

100. "Blue note" is an instance of

(A) syzygy   (D) synesthesia

(B) metonymy   (E) hyperbaton

(C) antithesis

101. A three-line stanza rhyming aba bcb cdc and so forth (as in
Shelley's *Ode to the West Wind*) is called

(A) Spenserian stanza   (D) ottava rima

(B) terza rima   (E) tail-end stanza

(C) rhyme royal

Questions 102-104 refer to the excerpts below.

102. Which is by Wordsworth?

103. Which is by Keats?

104. Which is by Tolstoy?

(A) Men of Genius are great as certain ethereal Chemicals
operating on the Mass of neutral intellect--but they have
not any individuality, any determined Character. . . .I am
certain of nothing but of the holiness of the Heart's affections and the truth of Imagination--What the imagination
seizes as Beauty must be truth.

(B) I hold that a long poem does not exist. I maintain that the phrase, "a long poem," is simply a flat contradiction in terms.

I need scarcely observe that a poem deserves its title only inasmuch as it excites, by elevating the soul. The value of the poem is in the ratio of this elevating excitement. But all excitements are, through a psychal necessity, transient.

(C) The Imagination then, I consider either as primary, or secondary. The primary Imagination I hold to be the living Power and prime Agent of all human Perception, and as a repetition in the finite mind of the eternal act of creation in the infinite I AM. The secondary Imagination I consider as an echo of the former, coexisting with the conscious will, yet still as identical with the primary in the <u>kind</u> of its agency, and differing only in <u>degree</u>, and in the <u>mode</u> of its operation.

(D) Art, all art, has this characteristic, that it unites people. Every art causes those to whom the artist's feeling is transmitted to unite in soul with the artist, and also with all who receive the same impression. But non-Christian art, while uniting some people together, makes that very union a cause of separation between these united people and others. . . .Christian art is only such as tends to unite all without exception.

(E) [A Poet] is a man speaking to men: a man, it is true, endowed with more lively sensibility, more enthusiasm and tenderness, who has a greater knowledge of human nature, and a more comprehensive soul, than are supposed to be common among mankind; a man pleased with his own passions and volitions, and who rejoices more than other men in the spirit of life that is in him; delighting to contemplate similar volitions and passions as manifested in the goings-on of the Universe, and habitually impelled to create them where he does not find them.

105.   All of the following are Utopias EXCEPT

(A) Francis Bacon, *New Atlantis*

(B) Edward Bellamy, *Looking Backward*

(C) William Morris, *News from Nowhere*

(D) Aldous Huxley, *Brave New World*

(E) James Hilton, *Lost Horizon*

Questions 106-110

Thou are indeed just, Lord, if I contend
With thee; but, sir, so what I plead is just.
Why do sinners' ways prosper? and why must
Disappointment all I endeavour end?
     Wert thou my enemy, O thou my friend,   5
How wouldst thou worse, I wonder, than thou dost
Defeat, thwart me? Oh, the sots and thralls of lust
Do in spare hours more thrive than I that spend,
Sir, life upon thy cause. See, banks and brakes
Now, leavèd how thick! lacèd they are again   10
With fretty chervil, look, and fresh wind shakes
Them; birds build--but not I build; no, but strain,
Time's eunuch, and not breed one work that wakes.
Mine, O thou lord of life, send my roots rain.

106.   The poem can best be described as

    (A) an Italian sonnet   (D) an Horatian ode

    (B) a Pindaric ode   (E) a Spenserian sonnet

    (C) an English sonnet

107. The speaker uses fern and chervil chiefly to

   (A) illustrate nature's indifference to man.

   (B) contrast Christian spirituality and pagan physicality.

   (C) question why morally ignoble things prosper.

   (D) contrast nature's fruitfulness and his sense of spiritual emptiness.

   (E) illustrate God's absence from the natural world.

108. "Time's eunuch" (line 13) suggests the speaker's sense of

   (A) aloofness   (D) disfigurement

   (B) despair   (E) failure

   (C) superiority

109. The speaker's tone can best be described as one of

   (A) anger   (D) desperation

   (B) depression   (E) indifference

   (C) adulation

110. The poet is

   (A) Milton   (D) Hopkins

   (B) Donne   (E) Graves

   (C) Eliot

111. "Grundyism" refers to

(A) coarseness

(B) a highly developed sense of beauty

(C) a strict sense of propriety and social convention

(D) extreme avarice

(E) an inclination toward religious rebelliousness

Questions 112-114 refer to the excerpts below.

112. Which is by Sir Joshua Reynolds?

113. Which is by Oliver Goldsmith?

114. Which is by G. E. Lessing?

(A) Imitations are of two kinds: one of nature, one of authors.
The first we call originals, and confine the term imitation
to the second. . . .Originals are, and ought to be, great
favourites, for they are great benefactors; they extend the
republic of letters, and add a new province to its dominion. Imitators only give us a sort of duplicate of what we
had, possibly much better, before; increasing the mere
drug of books, while all that makes them valuable,
knowledge and genius, are at a stand.

(B) It is true, that amusement is a great object of the theatre; and
it will be allowed, that these sentimental pieces do often
amuse us; but the question is, whether the true comedy
would not amuse us more? The question is, whether a
character supported throughout a piece with its ridicule
still attending, would not give us more delight than this
species of bastard tragedy, which only is applauded because it is new.

(C) If it be true that painting employs wholly different signs or
means of imitation from poetry,--the one using forms and
colors in space, the other articulate sounds in time,--and if
signs must unquestionably stand in convenient relation
with the thing signified, then signs arranged side by side
can represent only objects existing side by side, or whose

parts so exist, while consecutive signs can express only objects which succeed each other, or whose parts succeed each other, in time.

(D) Upon the whole, it seems to me, that the object and intention of all the arts is to supply the natural imperfection of things, and often to gratify the mind by realising and embodying what never existed but in the imagination. . . . With us, history is made to bend and conform to this great idea of art. And why? Because these arts, in their highest province, are not addressed to the gross senses, but to the desires of the mind, to that spark of di vinity which we have within.

(E) We hear it maintained by people of more gravity than understanding, that genius and taste are strictly reducible to rules, and that there is a rule for every thing. . . In art, in taste, in life, in speech you decide from feeling, and not from reason; that is, from a number of things on the mind, which impresssion is true and well-founded, though you may not be able to analyse or account for it in the several particulars.

Questions 115-117 refer to the works below.

115. Which uses Old Testament history as an allegory to satirize contemporary political events?

116. Which converts the old episodic picaresque fiction into a versified satiric form?

117. Which satirizes religious hypocrisy?

(A) La Fontaine, *Fables*

(B) Molière, *Tartuffe*

(C) Byron, *Don Juan*

(D) Swift, *Gulliver's Travels*

(E) Dryden, *Absalom and Achitophel*

118. The Scriblerus Club included all of the following EXCEPT

(A) Alexander Pope   (D) John Arbuthnot

(B) John Dryden   (E) Jonathan Swift

(C) William Congreve

119. Skeltonic verse can best be described as

(A) undignified, close to doggerel.

(B) a highly artificial form derived from French models.

(C) an attempt to emulate the plain but dignified style of the Bible.

(D) a self-conscious attempt to elevate further the epic style.

(E) an attempt to capture the natural rhythms of daily speech in verse.

120. Which of the following depends for its effects on contrasts between English and Italian culture?

(A) *Where Angels Fear to Tread*

(B) *The Longest Journey*

(C) *Howards End*

(D) *A Passage to India*

(E) *Maurice*

121. All of the following wrote works in which Arthurian legend plays a significant role EXCEPT

(A) Thomas Malory   (D) Alfred Tennyson

(B) John Milton   (E) Mark Twain

(C) John Dryden

Questions 122-124 refer to the definitions below.

122.	Which is vers de société?

123.	Which is an aubade?

124.	Which is a rubáiyát?

(A)	a lyric about dawn or a song of lovers parting at dawn

(B)	an eleven-line poem with a refrain in the fourth and eleventh lines taken from the first part of the first line; the rhyme scheme is abacbababac

(C)	a brief, graceful, genial, polished lyric, sophisticated in subject matter and tone

(D)	a collection of four-line stanzas

(E)	a short lyric, usually dealing with love or a pastoral theme and suitable to be set to music

Questions 125-127

But who can hope his lines should long
Last in a daily changing tongue?
While they are new, envy prevails;
And as that dies, our language fails.

When architects have done their part,
The matter may betray their art;
Time, if we use ill-chosen stone,
Soon brings a well-built palace down.

125.	A poet and an architect are alike in that

(A)	both seek immortality.

(B)	the talents of each can be obscured by the medium he uses.

(C)	neither is appreciated by his contemporaries.

(D)	the test of time determines the worth of each.

(E)	both are subject to artistic fads and changing taste.

687

126. The speaker's chief complaint concerns the

(A) instability of the English language.

(B) difficulty of gaining approval from a fickle public.

(C) inability of language to express complex emotions.

(D) fact that human nature is not constant from age to age.

(E) passage of time.

127. The author, who also wrote *On a Girdle* and *Go, Lovely Rose*, is

(A) Ben Jonson

(B) George Herbert

(C) John Wilmot,
Earl of Rochester

(D) Edmund Waller

(E) Thomas Traherne

Questions 128-130 refer to the titles below.

128. Which is a Künstlerroman?

129. Which is a mock epic?

130. Which is a roman à clef?

(A) Huxley, *Point Counter-Point*

(B) Tennyson, *Ulysses*

(C) Swift, *The Battle of the Books*

(D) Proust, *Remembrance of Things Past*

(E) Steinbeck, *The Grapes of Wrath*

131. "Pleasing pain" and "I burn and freeze" are examples of

(A) oxymoron

(B) verbal irony

(C) metaphysical conceit

(D) understatement

(E) intentional ambiguity

Questions 132-134 refer to the excerpts below.

132. Which is the narrator of Henry James' *The Beast in the Jungle*?

133. Which is the narrator of Ring Lardner's *Haircut*?

134. Which is the narrator of John Barth's *Lost in the Funhouse*?

(A) Personally I wouldn't never leave a person shoot a gun in the same boat I was in unless I was sure they knew somethin' about guns. Jim was a sucker to leave a new beginner have his gun, let alone a half-wit. It probably served Jim right, what he got. But still we miss him round here. He certainly was a card.

(B) One could not stand and watch very long without becoming philosophical, without beginning to deal in symbols and similes, and to hear the hog-squeal of the universe. Was it permitted to believe that there was nowhere upon the earth, or above the earth, a heaven for hogs, where they were requited for all this suffering?

(C) Philip looked away, as he sometimes looked away from the great pictures where visible forms suddenly became inadequate for the things they have shown to us. He was happy; he was assured that there was greatness in the world. There came to him an earnest desire to be good through the example of this good woman. . . . Quietly, without hysterical prayers or banging of drums, he underwent conversion. He was saved.

(D) It was a thing of the merest chance- - the turn, as he afterwards felt, of a hair, though he was indeed to live to believe that if light hadn't come to him in this particular fashion it would still have come in another. He was to live to believe this, I say, though he was not to live, I may not less definitely mention, to do much else. We allow him at any rate the benefit of the conviction, struggling up for him at the end, that, whatever might have happened or not happened, he would have come round of himself to the light.

(E) Description of physical appearance and mannerisms is one of several standard methods of characterization used by writers of fiction. It is also important to "keep the senses operating"; when a detail from one of the five senses, say visual, is "crossed" with a detail from another, say auditory, the reader's imagination is oriented to the scene, perhaps unconsciously. . . . The brown hair on Ambrose's mother's forearms gleamed in the sun like. Though right handed, she took her left arm from the seat-back to press the dashboard cigar lighter for Uncle Karl.

Questions 135-137 refer to the titles below.

135. Which satirizes Puritans?

136. Which caricatures Byron, Coleridge, and Shelley?

137. Which satirizes Thomas Shadwell?

(A) Thomas Love Peacock, *Nightmare Alley*

(B) T.S. Eliot, *The Waste Land*

(C) Samuel Butler, *Hudibras*

(D) John Dryden, *MacFlecknoe*

(E) William Wycherley, *The Country Wife*

138. Which of the following was a member of the group known as the Pre-Raphaelites?

(A) Matthew Arnold

(B) Thomas Carlyle

(C) Dante Gabriel Rossetti

(D) Robert Browning

(E) Walter Pater

Questions 139-141 refer to the excerpts below.

139. Which is spoken by Hoyden?

140. Which is spoken by Millamant?

141. Which is spoken by Mrs. Malaprop?

(A) "Oh, but, nurse, we han't considered the main thing yet. If I leave my lord, I must leave 'my lady' too: and when I rattle about the streets in my coach, they'll only say, 'There goes Mistress--Mistress--' Mistress what? What's this man's name I have married, nurse?"

(B) "I am sure I have done everything in my power since I exploded the affair! Long ago I laid my positive conjunctions on her never to think of the fellow again - -I have since laid Sir Anthony's proposition before her - - but, I'm sorry to say, she seems resolved to decline every particle that I enjoin her."

(C) "I never knew half his merit till now. He shall not go if I have power or art to detain him. I'll still preserve the character in which I stooped to conquer, but will undeceive my papa, who, perhaps, may laugh him out of his resolution."

(D) "To have my closet inviolate; to be sole empress of my tea-table, which you must never presume to approach without first asking leave. And lastly, wherever I am, you shall always knock at the door before you come in. These articles subscribed, if I continue to endure you a little longer, I may by degrees dwindle into a wife."

(E) "Well, 'tis e'en so, I have got the London disease they call love; I am sick of my husband, and for my gallant. I have heard this distemper called a fever, but methinks 'tis liker an ague, for when I think of my husband, I tremble and am in a cold sweat and have inclinations to vomit; but when I think of my gallant, dear Mr. Horner, my hot fit comes and I am all in a fever. . ."

142. All of the following regional writers are associated with the American South EXCEPT

(A) George Washington Cable

(B) Lafcadio Hearn

(C) Mary E. Wilkins Freeman

(D) Mary Noailles Murfree

(E) Joel Chandler Harris

143. "Mythopoeic" is a term applied to writers who create their own mythology or mythic framework for their work. Two mythopoeic writers are

(A) Poe and James

(B) Blake and Yeats

(C) Spenser and Melville

(D) Dryden and Johnson

(E) Milton and Wordsworth

Questions 144-146 refer to the excerpts below.

144. Which is from Nelson Algren's *The Man With the Golden Arm*?

145. Which is from Richard Wright's *Native Son*?

146. Which is from D.H. Lawrence's *The Rainbow*?

(A) He had done this. He had brought all this about. In all of his life these two murders were the most meaningful things that had ever happened to him. He was living, truly and deeply, no matter what others might think, looking at him with their blind eyes. Never had he had the chance to live out the consequences of his actions; never had his will been so free as in this night and day of fear and murder and flight.

(B) "I've seen others like him, and I believe they are very near and dear to God. He'll live on, half in, half out of the community. . . . He'll be a great favourite with the old fathers, something of a joke to the novices. Everyone will know about his drinking. . . . Then one morning, after one of his drinking bouts, he'll be picked up at the gate dying, and show by a mere flicker of the eyelid that he is conscious when they give him the last sacraments. It's not such a bad way of getting through one's life."

(C) Though he had seen not one man of them in life before, Frankie knew each man. For each was seared by that same torch whose flame had already touched himself. A torch which burned with a dark and smoldering flame from within till it dried a man of everything save a dark-charred guilt.

   The great, secret and special American guilt of owning nothing, nothing at all, in the one land where ownership and virtue are one. . . . On Skid Row even the native-born no longer felt they had been born in America. They felt they had merely emerged from the wrong side of its billboards.

(D) Her brown-gray eyes opened and looked at him. She did not know him as himself. But she knew him as the man. She looked at him as a woman in childbirth looks at the man who begot the child in her: an impersonal look, in the extreme hour, female to male. Her eyes closed again. A great scalding peace went over him, burning his heart and his entrails, passing off into the infinite.

   When her pains began afresh, tearing her, he turned aside, and could not look. But his heart in torture was at peace, his bowels were glad.

(E) His soul had arisen from the grave of boyhood, spurning her graveclothes. Yes! Yes! Yes! He would create proudly out of the freedom and power of his soul, as the great artificer whose name he bore, a living thing, new and soaring and beautiful, impalpable, imperishable.

Questions 147-150

Some village Hampden, that with dauntless breast
    The little tyrant of his fields withstood;
Some mute inglorious Milton here may rest,
    Some Cromwell, guiltless of his country's blood.

147.   The speaker uses Hampden as an example of a

    (A) petty tyrant.

    (B) man who rose to fame from humble beginnings.

    (C) man who opposed tyranny.

    (D) man who found contentment in a rural life.

    (E) man who stirred farmers to political action.

148.   The speaker cites Cromwell as an instance of a man who

    (A) gained power through violence.

    (B) has been wrongfully branded by history.

    (C) served the state selflessly.

    (D) failed to attain Milton's fame.

    (E) became powerful without shedding blood.

149.   Which of the following best expresses the sense of this stanza?

    (A) good and evil are inextricably mixed in human nature.

    (B) Even small villages contain both the morally noble and the ignoble.

    (C) The obscurity of village life is a curse that obstructs the development of heroes and poets.

    (D) Villages are a microcosm of the larger social structure.

    (E) Village conditions prevent the development of famous poets and defenders of freedom, but also prevent the development of famous tyrants and criminals.

150. This stanza is from

(A) Johnson, *The Vanity of Human Wishes*

(B) Goldsmith, *The Deserted Village*

(C) Gray, *Elegy Written in a Country Churchyard*

(D) Crabbe, *The Village*

(E) Cowper, *The Task*

151. Keats' term for Shakespeare's impersonal, objective quality and a term used later to signify an artist's ability to avoid expressing his own personality in his work is

(A) discordia concors

(B) organic form

(C) willing suspension of disbelief

(D) esemplastic power

(E) negative capability

Questions 152-154 refer to the titles below.

152. Which is a muckraking novel?

153. Which is a naturalist work?

154. Which is a novel of sentiment and sensibility?

(A) Charles Brockden Brown, *Ormond*

(B) James T. Farrell, *Studs Lonigan*

(C) James Fenimore Cooper, *The Pioneers*

(D) Upton Sinclair, *The Jungle*

(E) Hannah Webster Foster, *The Coquette*

Questions 155-157 refer to the works below.

155. Which derives its title from Virgil's *Aeneid*?

156. Which derives its title from Gray's *Elegy Written in a Country Churchyard?*

157. Which derives its title from Shakespeare's *The Tempest?*

   (A) Fitzgerald, *Tender is the Night*

   (B) Shaw, *Arms and the Man*

   (C) Huxley, *Brave New World*

   (D) Hardy, *Far From the Madding Crowd*

   (E) Forster, *Where Angels Fear to Tread*

158. A term used to describe the "error" of judging a work of art by its effects, especially its emotional effects, on the reader is

   (A) intentional fallacy   (D) expressive fallacy

   (B) bathetic fallacy   (E) affective fallacy

   (C) pathetic fallacy

159. Frederick Douglass is the author of

   (A) pastoral poetry

   (B) a slave narrative

   (C) the first American novel

   (D) numerous sermons

   (E) an early American comedy

Questions 160-161

A needless Alexandrine ends the song,
That, like a wounded snake, drags its slow length along.

160. In this couplet, Pope is satirizing

(A) the use of spondees   (D) ottava rima

(B) free verse   (E) rhyme royal

(C) the Spenserian stanza

161. The meter of an Alexandrine is

(A) trochaic pentameter   (D) iambic hexameter

(B) iambic pentameter   (E) dactylic trimeter

(C) trochaic hexameter

Questions 162-164 refer to the excerpts below.

162. Which is spoken by Paulina?

163. Which is spoken by Prospero?

164. Which is spoken by Lear?

(A)   . . .But this rough magic
I here abjure, and, when I have requir'd
Some heavenly music, which even now I do,
To work mine end upon their senses that
This airy charm is for, I'll break my staff,
Bury it certain fathoms in the earth,
And deeper than did ever plummet sound
I'll drown my book.

(B) For God's sake, let us sit upon the ground
And tell sad stories of the death of kings!
How some have been depos'd, some slain in war,
Some haunted by the ghosts they have depos'd,
Some poisoned by their wives, some sleeping kill'd--
All murdered.

(C)   I say she's dead; I'll swear't. If word nor oath
Prevail not, go and see; if you can bring
Tincture or luster in her lip, her eye,
Heat outwardly or breath within, I'll serve you
As I would do the gods. But, O thou tyrant,
Do not repent these things, for they are heavier
Than all thy woes can stir; therefore betake thee
To nothing but despair. A thousand knees,
Ten thousand years together, naked, fasting,
Upon a barren mountain, and still winter
In storm perpetual, could not move the gods
To look that way thou wert.

(D)   Come, let's away to prison.
We two will sing like birds i' th' cage.
When thou dost ask me blessing, I'll kneel down,
And ask of thee forgiveness. So we'll live,
And pray, and sing, and tell old tales, and laugh
At gilded butterflies, and hear poor rogues
Talk of court news. . .

(E) All that follow their noses are led by their eyes but blind
men, and there's not a nose among twenty but can smell
him that's stinking. Let go thy hold when a great wheel
runs down a hill, lest it break thy neck with following; but
the great one that goes upward, let him draw thee after.
When a wise man gives thee better counsel, give me mine
again.

Questions 165-167 refer to the descriptions below.

165.   Which describes John Ford's *'Tis Pity She's a Whore?*

166.   Which describes Christopher Marlowe's *Tamburlaine?*

167.   Which describes Thomas Heywood's *A Woman Killed With
Kindness?*

(A) A duke (1) poisons his wife because he is enamoured of another married woman (2); the married woman's brother (3) kills his brother and contrives the death of her (2) husband, and also kills their virtuous brother; the married woman (2) is tried for adultery and murder, the duke (1) is poisoned by his dead wife's brother, whose dependents kill the married woman (2) and her brother (3) (who earlier murdered his brother and his brother-in-law).

(B) The play's hero rises from shepherd to emperor of Persia and supreme ruler of all Asia. He conquers the Turkish emperor, placing him and his empress in a cage and taunting them until they die, vaunts himself in the play-wright's "mighty line," and defeats the Arabian king and the Soldan of Egypt, whose life he spares out of love for the Soldan's captive daughter.

(C) Pregnant by her brother, the heroine marries one of her suitors. Her brother stabs her to thwart the husband's plan of vengeance, kills the husband, and is himself killed.

(D) A husband discovers his otherwise "perfect" wife in the arms of a house-guest, and sends her to live in comfort in a remote manor-house, only prohibiting her from seeing him and her children again. The wife dies of remorse after having received forgiveness from her husband on her death-bed.

(E) The heroine, an orphan, is loved by both of the twin sons of her guardian. She secretly marries one; the other takes his twin's place during an assignation in the dark with the heroine. When the truth is discovered, the brothers kill themselves and the heroine takes poison.

168. "Mistress, I dug upon your grave

> To bury a bone, in case
> I should be hungry near this spot
> When passing on my daily trot.
> I am sorry, but I quite forgot
> It was your resting place."

This stanza is from a poem by

    (A) Thomas Lovell Beddoes

    (B) Arthur Hugh Clough

    (C) William Morris

    (D) Thomas Hardy

    (E) Edwin Muir

169. A rich, handsome, selfish, and conceited country squire is humiliated by being jilted by two prospective wives, but finally wins the hand of an intelligent but poor and shy woman who has long cherished a romantic passion for him.

This passage describes

    (A) W.M. Thackeray's *Pendennis*

    (B) Anthony Trollope's *Barchester Towers*

    (C) George Meredith's *The Egoist*

    (D) George Eliot's *Daniel Deronda*

    (E) Anne Brontë's *The Tenant of Wildfell Hall*

170. Who described her own work metaphorically as a "small square two inches of ivory?"

    (A) Jane Austin   (D) Virginia Woolf

    (B) Emily Brontë   (E) Eudora Welty

    (C) Willa Cather

Questions 171-173 refer to the poems below.

171. Which is a pastoral elegy?

172. Which is an English sonnet?

173. Which is an ode?

    (A) Marlowe, *The Passionate Shepherd to His Love*

    (B) Drayton, *Since there's no help, come let us kiss and part*

    (C) Shelley, *Adonais*

    (D) Wyatt, *He Is Not Dead That Sometimes Hath a Fall*

    (E) Dryden, *Alexander's Feast*

Questions 174-177 refer to the terms below.

174. Which would be read at a dinner honoring a living person?

175. Which would be sung at a funeral?

176. Which would be sung at a wedding?

177. Which is a ritualistic form of supplication or solemn prayer?

    (A) encomium   (D) threnody

    (B) epithalamium   (E) litany

    (C) kenning

Questions 178-180 refer to the works below.

178. Which is an exemplum?

179. Which is a fable?

180. Which is a fabliau?

    (A) Chaucer, *The Miller's Tale*

    (B) LaFontaine, *The Acorn and the Pumpkin*

    (C) *Sir Patrick Spens*

    (D) Chaucer, *The Pardoner's Tale*

    (E) Boccaccio, "Federigo's Falcon" (*Decameron*)

Questions 181-183

One day I wrote her name upon the strand,
But came the waves and washéd it away:
Agayne I wrote it with a second hand,
But came the tyde, and made my paynes his pray.
"Vayne man," sayd she, "that doest in vaine assay,   5
A mortall thing so to immortalize,
For I my selve shall lyke to this decay,
And eek my name bee wypéd out lykewize."
"Not so," quod I, "let baser things devize
To dy in dust, but you shall live by fame: 10
My verse your vertues rare shall eternize,
And in the heavens wryte your glorious name.
Where whenas death shall all the world subdew,
Our love shall live, and later life renew."

181. The primary theme of the poem is the

   (A) brevity of life

   (B) permanence of poetry

   (C) indifference of nature

   (D) immortality of true love

   (E) vanity of human wishes

182. This poem can best be described as

   (A) an Italian sonnet   (D) a narrative poem

   (B) an English sonnet   (E) a villanelle

   (C) a Spenserian sonnet

183. A poem that expresses the same theme is

   (A) Wyatt's *Whoso List to Hunt*

   (B) Herrick's *To the Virgins, to Make Much of Time*

(C) Surrey's *Alas! So All Things Now Do Hold Their Peace*

(D) Ralegh's *What Is Our Life*

(E) Shakespeare's Sonnet 55 ("Not marble, nor the gilded monuments")

Questions 184-186 refer to the novels below.

184. Which is an epistolary novel?

185. Which is a picaresque novel?

186. Which is a stream-of-consciousness novel?

(A) Le Sage, *Gil Blas*

(B) William Godwin, *Caleb Williams*

(C) Dorothy Richardson, *Pilgrimage*

(D) Tobias Smollett, *Humphrey Clinker*

(E) Willa Cather, *Death Comes for the Archbishop*

Questions 187-189 refer to the works below.

187. Which is a sentimental novel?

188. Which satirizes heroic drama?

189. Which is a comedy of manners?

(A) Sir George Etherege, *The Man of Mode*

(B) David Garrick, *The Lying Valet*

(C) Richard Cumberland, *The West Indian*

(D) John Dryden, *All for Love*

(E) George Villiers, Duke of Buckingham, *The Rehearsal*

Questions 190-193 refer to the novels below.

190.   Which is a novel of manners?

191.   Which ridicules the Gothic novel?

192.   Which is a sentimental novel (or novel of sensibility)?

193.   Which is a Bildungsroman?

    (A) Goldsmith, *The Vicar of Wakefield*

    (B) Defoe, *Moll Flanders*

    (C) Austen, *Northanger Abbey*

    (D) Burney, *Evelina*

    (E) Dickens, *David Copperfield*

Questions 194-197 refer to the plays below.

194.   Which is a domestic tragedy?

195.   Which is heroic drama?

196.   Which is a revenge tragedy?

197.   Which is a masque?

    (A) Thomas Kyd, *The Spanish Tragedy*

    (B) George Lillo, *The London Merchant*

    (C) Christopher Marlowe, *Dr. Faustus*

    (D) John Milton, *Comus*

    (E) John Dryden, *The Conquest of Granada*

198.   All of the following were part of the "Bloomsbury group"
      EXCEPT

(A) Virginia Woolf   (D) D.H. Lawrence

(B) Lytton Strachey   (E) E.M. Forster

(C) John Maynard Keynes

199. The "Melmoth" in Oscar Wilde's adopted name (Sebastian Melmoth) is taken from a romance by

(A) Nathaniel Hawthorne

(B) Robert Montgomery Bird

(C) John Bunyan

(D) Charles Robert Maturin

(E) Ann Radcliffe

Questions 200-202

Earth, receive an honored guest;
William Yeats is laid to rest:
Let the Irish vessel lie
Emptied of its poetry.

Time that is intolerant   5
Of the brave and innocent
And indifferent in a week
To a beautiful physique,

Worships language and forgives
Everyone by whom it lives;   10
Pardons cowardice, conceit
Lays its honours at their feet.

Time that with this strange excuse
Pardoned Kipling and his views,
And will pardon Paul Claudel,   15
Pardons him for writing well.

200. Time is most tolerant of those who

   (A) were brave

   (B) concealed their cowardice or conceit

   (C) had beautiful bodies

   (D) were innocent

   (E) wrote well

201. Kipling and Paul Claudel need to be "pardoned" for

   (A) failing to appreciate Yeats

   (B) their violently right-wing political views

   (C) their cowardice and conceit

   (D) their failure to write well

   (E) their intolerance of other poets

202. The poet is

   (A) A.E. Housman   (D) Dylan Thomas

   (B) Louis MacNeice   (E) Howard Nemerov

   (C) W.H. Auden

Questions 203-205 refer to the works below.

203. Which burlesques medieval romance?

204. Which parodies the style of *Paradise Lost*?

205. Which parodies *Pamela*?

   (A) Swift, *A Description of a City Shower*

   (B) John Phillips, *The Splendid Shilling*

   (C) Cervantes, *Don Quixote*

(D) Sterne, *Tristram Shandy*

(E) Fielding, *Joseph Andrews*

Questions 206-208

If wit be well described by Pope, as being "that which has been often thought, but was never before so well expressed," they certainly never attained, nor ever sought it; for they endeavoured to be singular in their thoughts, and were careless of their diction. But Pope's account of wit is undoubtedly erroneous: he depresses it below its natural dignity, and reduces it from strength of thought to happiness of language.

If by a more noble and more adequate conception that be considered as wit which is at once natural and new, that which, though not obvious, is, upon its first production, acknowledged to be just; if it be that which he that never found it wonders how he missed, to wit of this kind [they] have seldom risen. Their thoughts are often new, but seldom natural; they are not obvious, but neither are they just; and the reader, far from wondering that he missed them, wonders more frequently by what perverseness of industry they were ever found.

But wit, abstracted from its effects upon the hearer, may be more rigorously and philosophically considered as a kind of *discordia concors*; a combination of dissimilar images, or discovery of occult resemblances in things apparently unlike. Of wit, thus defined, they have more than enough. The most heterogeneous ideas are yoked by violence together; nature and art are ransacked for illustrations, comparisons, and allusions; their learning instructs, and their subtlety surprises; but the reader commonly thinks his improvement dearly bought, and, though he sometimes admires, is seldom pleased.

206. In the first sentence, "they" refers to the

(A) Restoration comic dramatists

(B) Cavalier poets

(C) New England transcendentalists

(D) metaphysical poets

(E) seventeenth-century French dramatists

207. The primary distinction between the conceptions of wit defined in the first two paragraphs concerns

(A) decorum

(B) naturalness

(C) originality

(D) universality

(E) diction

208. The definition of wit advanced in the third paragraph places primary emphasis upon

(A) properties in the work

(B) the mind of the writer

(C) the responses of the reader

(D) propriety of language

(E) universal truths

Questions 209-230. For each of the following passages, identify the author or the work. Base your decision on the content and style of each passage.

209. The king sits in Dumferling toune,
Drinking the blude-reid wine:
"O whar will I get guid sailor,
To sail this schip of mine?"

(A) *Beowulf*

(B) *Sir Gawain and the Green Knight*

(C) *Lord Randall*

(D) *Sir Patrick Spens*

(E) *Morte D'arthur*

210. Three things there be that prosper up apace
And flourish, whilst they grow asunder far,
But on a day, they meet all in one place,
And when they meet, they one another mar;
And they be these: the wood, the weed, the wag.

(A) Sir Walter Raleigh   (D) Edmund Waller

(B) Sir Thomas Wyatt   (E) William Collins

(C) Rudyard Kipling

211. A belt of straw and ivy buds,
With coral clasps and amber studs--
And if these pleasures may thee move,
Come live with me and be my love.

(A) Sir Philip Sidney   (D) Robert Herrick

(B) Andrew Marvell   (E) Lord Byron

(C) Christopher Marlowe

212. But we by a love so much refined
    That our selves know not what it is,
Inter-assuréd of the mind,
    Care less, eyes, lips, and hands to miss.

Our two souls therefore, which are one,
    Though I must go, endure not yet
A breach, but an expansion,
    Like gold to airy thinness beat.

(A) Henry Howard, Earl of Surry

(B) Thomas Campion

(C) John Donne

(D) John Milton

(E) William Shakespeare

213. What passing-bells for these who die as cattle?
Only the monstrous anger of the guns.
Only the stuttering rifles' rapid rattle
Can patter out their hasty orisons.
No mockeries for them from prayers or bells,
Nor any voice of mourning save the choirs--
The shrill, demented choirs of wailing shells;
And bugles calling for them from sad shires.

(A) Walt Whitman   (D) Siegfried Sassoon

(B) Stephen Crane   (E) Wilfred Owen

(C) E.A. Robinson

214. 'Twas mercy brought me from my Pagan land,
Taught my benighted soul to understand
That there's a God, that there's a Saviour too:
Once I redemption neither sought nor knew.

(A) Anne Bradstreet   (D) Langston Hughes

(B) Phillis Wheatley   (E) Theodore Roethke

(C) Philip Freneau

215. Away! away! for I will fly to thee,
    Not charioted by Bacchus and his pards,
But on the viewless wings of Poesy,
    Though the dull brain perplexes and retards:
Already with thee! tender is the night,
    And haply the Queen-Moon is on her throne. . .

(A) James Thomson

(B) John Keats

(C) Dante Gabriel Rossetti

710

(D) Algernon Charles Swinburne

(E) Oscar Wilde

216. That moment she was mine, mine, fair,
    Perfectly pure and good: I found
A thing to do, and all her hair
    In one long yellow string I wound
    Three times her little throat around,
And strangled her. No pain felt she;
    I am quite sure she felt no pain.

(A) Christopher Smart   (D) Elizabeth Bishop

(B) Robert Browning   (E) Hart Crane

(C) Edgar Allan Poe

217. An aged man is but a paltry thing,
A tattered coat upon a stick, unless
Soul clap its hands and sing, and louder sing
For every tatter in its mortal dress. . .

(A) Ernest Dowson

(B) D.H. Lawrence

(C) Gerard Manley Hopkins

(D) W.B. Yeats

(E) T.S. Eliot

218. For though my rhyme be ragged,
Tattered and jagged,
Rudely rain-beaten,
Rusty and moth-eaten,
If ye take well therewith,
It hath in it some pith.

(A) John Skelton   (D) Robert Burns

(B) Richard Crashaw   (E) William Blake

(C) George Crabbe

219.   . . .Hail, horrors! hail,
        Infernal world! and thou, profoundest Hell,
        Receive thy new possessor: One who brings
        A mind not to be changed by place or time.
        The mind is its own place, and in itself
        Can make a Heaven of Hell, a Hell of Heaven.

        (A) Edmund Spenser   (D) S.T. Coleridge

        (B) John Milton   (E) Robert Browning

        (C) John Dryden

220.   a salesman is an it that stinks Excuse

        Me whether it's president of the you were say
        or a jennelman name misder finger isn't
        important whether it's millions of other punks
        or just a handful absolutely doesn't
        matter and whether it's in lonjewray

        (A) Carl Sandburg   (D) E.E. Cummings

        (B) T. S. Eliot   (E) Countee Cullen

        (C) Ezra Pound

221.   Them that rule us, them slave-traders,
            Haint they cut a thunderin' swarth
        (Helped by Yankee renegaders),
            Thru the vartu o' the North!
        We begin to think it's nater
            to take sarse an' not be riled;--
        Who'd expect to see a tater
            All on eend at bein' biled?

        (A) Edward Taylor

        (B) Philip Freneau

        (C) James Russell Lowell

        (D) Frederick Douglass

        (E) Gwendolyn Brooks

222.   These beauteous forms,
Through a long absence, have not been to me
As is a landscape to a blind man's eye;
But oft, in lonely rooms, and 'mid the din
Of towns and cities, I have owed to them,
In hours of weariness, sensations sweet,
Felt in the blood, and felt along the heart;
And passing even into my purer mind,
With tranquil restoration: ...

(A) Frost   (D) Tennyson

(B) Whitman   (E) Arnold

(C) Wordsworth

223.   My aunt! my dear unmarried aunt!
     Long years have o'er her flown;
Yet still she strains the aching clasp
     That binds her virgin zone;
I know it hurts her,- - though she looks
     As cheerful as she can;
Her waist is ampler than her life,
     For life is but a span.

(A) Edward Lear

(B) John Gay

(C) Henry Wadsworth Longfellow

(D) Stevie Smith

(E) Oliver Wendell Holmes

224.   ... Check yourself, learn who it is
speaking, when you make some ultrasophisticated point, check
yourself when you find yourself gesturing like Steve
McQueen, check it out, ask in your black heart who it is you are,
and is that image black or white, you might be surprised right
out the window, whistling dixie on the way

(A) John Crowe Ransom

(B) Richard Wilbur

(C) Allen Ginsberg

(D) James Wright

(E) Imamu Amiri Baraka (LeRoi Jones)

225. Careful observers may foretell the hour
(By sure prognostics) when to dread a shower:
While rain depends, the pensive cat gives o'er
Her frolics, and pursues her tail no more.
Returning home at night, you'll find the sink
Strike your offended sense with double stink.

(A) John Wilmot, Earl of Rochester

(B) Jonathan Swift

(C) Lewis Carroll

(D) Anne Finch, Countess of Winchilsea

(E) Thomas Hardy

226. But they pulled me out of the sack,
And they stuck me together with glue.
And then I knew what to do.
I made a model of you,
A man in black with a Meinkampf look

And a love of the rack and the screw.
And I said, I do, I do.
So daddy, I'm finally through.

(A) Ezra Pound   (D) Adrienne Rich

(B) Marianne Moore   (E) Sylvia Plath

(C) Lawrence Ferlinghetti

227. Hope humbly then; with trembling pinions soar;
Wait the great teacher Death, and God adore!
What future bliss, he gives thee not to know,
But gives that hope to be thy blessing now.
Hope springs eternal in the human breast:
Man never is, but always to be blest.

   (A) Shakespeare   (D) Wordsworth

   (B) Dryden   (E) Yeats

   (C) Pope

228. That after Horror- -that 'twas us- -
That passed the mouldering Pie- -
Just as the Granite Crumb let go- -
Our Savior, by a Hair- -

   (A) Edgar Allan Poe   (D) Stephen Crane

   (B) Walt Whitman   (E) William Carlos Williams

   (C) Emily Dickinson

229. I wander through each chartered street,
Near where the chartered Thames does flow,
And mark in every face I meet
Marks of weakness, marks of woe.

   (A) Richard Lovelace   (D) Percy Bysshe Shelley

   (B) Samuel Johnson   (E) Elizabeth Barrett Browning

   (C) William Blake

230. In the dustbins, in the manure, in the cat at play,
Is the presence of God, in a sure way
He moves there. Mother, what do you say?

   (A) Stevie Smith   (D) Thom Gunn

   (B) W.D. Snodgrass   (E) H.D. (Hilda Doolittle)

   (C) Stephen Spender

GRE LITERATURE IN ENGLISH
EXAM VI

ANSWER KEY

1.	B	39.	E	77.	E
2.	C	40.	C	78.	E
3.	E	41.	B	79.	C
4.	E	42.	A	80.	D
5.	A	43.	E	81.	A
6.	D	44.	E	82.	C
7.	D	45.	B	83.	D
8.	C	46.	D	84.	C
9.	B	47.	E	85.	A
10.	A	48.	B	86.	A
11.	C	49.	D	87.	B
12.	E	50.	C	88.	D
13.	C	51.	B	89.	D
14.	A	52.	B	90.	E
15.	E	53.	C	91.	A
16.	D	54.	E	92.	C
17.	E	55.	C	93.	A
18.	B	56.	C	94.	D
19.	C	57.	B	95.	E
20.	B	58.	D	96.	A
21.	E	59.	C	97.	B
22.	A	60.	E	98.	D
23.	C	61.	A	99.	E
24.	C	62.	B	100.	D
25.	E	63.	D	101.	B
26.	D	64.	A	102.	E
27.	C	65.	C	103.	A
28.	E	66.	B	104.	D
29.	B	67.	E	105.	D
30.	D	68.	D	106.	A
31.	B	69.	A	107.	D
32.	A	70.	D	108.	E
33.	A	71.	B	109.	B
34.	D	72.	C	110.	D
35.	B	73.	D	111.	C
36.	C	74.	A	112.	D
37.	E	75.	D	113.	B
38.	B	76.	C	114.	C

GRE LITERATURE IN ENGLISH
TEST VI

ANSWER KEY

115.	E	154.	E	193.	E
116.	C	155.	B	194.	B
117.	B	156.	D	195.	E
118.	B	157.	C	196.	A
119.	A	158.	E	197.	D
120.	A	159.	B	198.	D
121.	B	160.	C	199.	D
122.	C	161.	D	200.	E
123.	A	162.	C	201.	B
124.	D	163.	A	202.	C
125.	B	164.	D	203.	C
126.	A	165.	C	204.	B
127.	D	166.	B	205.	E
128.	D	167.	D	206.	D
129.	C	168.	D	207.	C
120.	A	169.	C	208.	B
131.	A	170.	A	209.	D
132.	D	171.	C	210.	A
133.	A	172.	B	211.	C
134.	E	173.	E	212.	C
135.	C	174.	A	213.	E
136.	A	175.	D	214.	B
137.	D	176.	B	215.	B
138.	C	177.	E	216.	B
139.	A	178.	D	217.	D
140.	D	179.	B	218.	A
141.	B	180.	A	219.	B
142.	C	181.	B	220.	D
143.	B	182.	C	221.	C
144.	C	183.	E	222.	C
145.	A	184.	D	223.	E
146.	D	185.	A	224.	E
147.	C	186.	C	225.	B
148.	A	187.	C	226.	E
149.	E	188.	E	227.	C
150.	C	189.	A	228.	C
151.	E	190.	D	229.	C
152.	D	191.	C	230.	A
153.	B	192.	A		

GRE ENGLISH IN LITERATURE
TEST VI

DETAILED EXPLANATIONS
OF ANSWERS

1. (B)
Closet drama is intended to be read, not performed.

2. (C)
Morality plays are dramatized allegories of man's life, focusing especially on temptation and salvation.

3. (E)
Polly is the sequel to Gay's *The Beggar's Opera*; it uses recitative and familiar ballads for which Gay wrote new lyrics.

4. (E)
A dramatic monologue is a lyric poem with a single speaker speaking at a crucial moment.

5. (A)
An eclogue is a formal pastoral poem whose conventions derive from Theocritus' *Idylls*. *The Shepheardes Calender* contains one eclogue for each month.

6. (D)
An elegy is a formal poem presenting a sustained meditation on death or a lament for the death of a particular person.

7.   (D)

8.   (C)
Cather.

9.   (B)
By George Bernard Shaw.

10.   (A)
O'Neill.

11.   (C)
Steele.

12.   (E)
Shakespeare.

13.   (C)
Woolman.

14.   (A)
Winthrop.

15.   (E)
Edwards.

16.   (D)
"Veiled Melancholy" dwells with Beauty, and is a goddess in the very
temple of Delight.

17.   (E)

This is perhaps Keats' best-known statement of a recurrent theme in his poetry -- that opposing qualities are inextricably mixed (melancholy and joy, pleasure and pain, and so forth).

18.   (B)

Because opposing qualities are part of one another, joy turns to melancholy, pleasure to pain. Keats suggests that beauty, joy, perhaps even life, derive their value from the fact that they are transitory and are transformed into their opposites.

19.   (C)

The stanza is from Keats' *Ode on Melancholy*.

20.   (B)

Pound.

21.   (E)

Yeats' poem is a reworking of a sonnet by Ronsard. The beginnings of the two poems are very similar, but their endings differ significantly.

22.   (A)

Johnson.

23.   (C)

A "brown study" is a state of deep thought, melancholy, or reverie; here it is used to describe the girl's corpse.

24.   (C)

"Vexed" suggests "puzzled" or "baffled," indicating that he is troubled and not ready to accept her death.

25.   (E)

The occasion is the funeral of a young girl whose "tireless heart" no longer beats.

26.   (D)

The poem is Ransom's *Bells for John Whiteside's Daughter*.

27.   (C)

In the eighty-seventh chapter, Peregrine meets a sixteen-year-old beggar-girl and gradually transforms her into a lady.

28.   (E)

Lovelace is modelled on Lothario in *The Fair Penitent*.

29.   (B)

Cibber's profligate husband is transformed into a man of virtue and faithfulness. Vanbrugh retains Cibber's characters, but demonstrates that such sudden conversions are at best temporary.

30.   (D)

Both of Gray's poems are Pindaric odes and were written relatively late in his career.

31.   (B)

Macpherson gathered some genuine Gaelic verses in the Scottish Highlands, but invented much of the "Ossianic" material. The resulting controversy involved several leading literary figures.

32.   (A)

Home had helped support Macpherson's work. His play is based on an Ossianic fragment.

33.   (A)

Austen.

34.   (D)
Hemingway.

35.   (B)
Melville.

36.   (C)
James.

37.   (E)
Byron.

38.   (B)
"Erewhon" is an anagram of "nowhere."

39.   (E)
Samuel Butler (1835-1902) wrote both *Erewhon* (1872) and *The Way of All Flesh* (1903).

40.   (C)
Jim Dixon and Yossarian are examples of anti-heroes.

41.   (B)
The heroic couplet consists of two rhymed iambic pentameter lines. The couplet is "closed" (that is, it is a complete, independent statement).

42.   (A)
Antithesis is a figure of speech characterized by strongly contrasting ideas, words, or clauses. Here the opposition of contrasting ideas is reinforced by the use of a similar grammatical structure in the two parts of the sentence ("wretches" is contrasted with "jury-men" and "hang" with "dine").

43. (E)

Pope, *The Rape of the Lock*.

44. (E)

Mrs. Behn's *Oroonoko*, or *The History of the Royal Slave* is the first English philosophical novel containing dissertations on abstract subjects and the first expression of sympathy for oppressed blacks in English literature. Mrs. Behn also wrote poetry.

45. (B)

Centivre also wrote *The Wonder! a Woman Keeps a Secret* (1714), which gave Garrick one of his most successful parts.

46. (D)

The Edwardian Age refers to the period between the death of Victoria (1901) and the beginning of World War I. Waugh's work appeared later.

47. (E)

Emerson, Fuller, Very, and Thoreau all contributed to *The Dial*. Fuller was its first editor, Emerson its second. *The Dial* was a periodical that served as a mouthpiece for the New England Transcendentalists.

48. (B)

49. (D)

50. (C)

51. (B)

Voltaire satirizes Leibniz' optimism through Dr. Pangloss' belief that everything works to benefit man in this "best of all possible worlds."

52.   **(B)**

Occasional verse includes highly personal love poems addressed to a specific person; Lovelace's peom also derives from specific personal circumstances.

53.   **(C)**

"*Ubi sunt*" means "where are"; Villon's poem asks "Where are the snows of yesteryear," thus stressing the transitory nature of life.

54.   **(E)**

Waller's is a typical "seize the day" poem.

55.   **(C)**

Lines one and three end with feminine rhyme -- a two-syllable rhyme, the second of which is unstressed.

56.   **(C)**

There are two caesuras (pauses within a line), both in the third line.

57.   **(B)**

There are three iambic feet in line two and in line four.

58.   **(D)**

In synecdoche, a part of something is used to signify the whole.

59.   **(C)**

The speaker directly addresses an inanimate object.

60.   **(E)**

In zeugma, a single word ("stain") has the same grammatical relationship to two or more other words("her honour" and "her new brocade"), but has a different meaning in the two instances.

61.   (A)

Jewett is a "local-colorist," but her subject matter is Maine or New England.

62.   (B)

The speaker is one of the wise men recalling in old age the meaning of their journey to pay homage to the infant Jesus.

63.   (D)

"Dawn," "vegetation," and "running stream" all suggest renewal or rebirth.

64.   (A)

The images are foreshadowings of disaster. The "three trees on the low sky" (line 4) suggest the three crosses on Calvary and the "darkness over all the land"; the men dicing for silver suggest the silver paid to Judas for Christ's betrayal and the gambling of the soldiers for Christ's garments at the foot of the Cross; the white horse is mentioned in Revelation in passages alluding to the end of the world.

65.   (C)

The coming of Christianity makes them lose faith "the old dispensation" (the old pagan religion).

66.   (B)

The speaker's homeland is now an alien place filled with alien people and governed by a religion he no longer believes in; hence he will be glad to leave it (through death).

67.   (E)

The poem is Eliot's *Journey of the Magi*.

68. (D)
They are terms for various affected writing styles, the first named after the Spanish poet Luis de Gongóra y Argote (1561 - 1627), the second after the Italian poet Giambattista Marino (1569 - 1625), and the third after John Lyly's *Euphues* (1578,1580).

69. (A)
Prior's lively, epigrammatic verse stands in marked contrast to the long poems on death and immortality by Parnell, Blair, Gray, and Young.

70. (D)
Brackenridge's *Modern Chivalry* is a satirical novel describing American men and manners in the republic's early years.

71. (B)
Lowell.

72. (C)

73. (D)

74. (A)

75. (D)

76. (C)

77. (E)

78.   (E)

This passage is from Fielding's Preface to *Joseph Andrews*, in which he defines the "comic epic poem in prose."

79.   (C)

Addison's *The Pleasures of the Imagination* appeared in the *Spectator*, Nos. 411-421.

80.   (D)

Hume's *Of Tragedy* addresses the question of why events that give pain if witnessed in real life give pleasure in art. Hume's solution rests on the idea of the conversion of subordinate by predominant passions.

81.   (A)

Odet's play was first perfomed in 1935.

82.   (C)

The date of Boker's play is 1855.

83.   (D)

Rice's play dates from 1923.

84.   (C)

Eliot traces dissociation of sensibility in his essay *The Metaphysical Poets*.

85.   (A)

Fry and Eliot revived verse drama in England; Anderson did so in America. The success of Phillips' earlier poetic tragedy, *Paolo and Francesca* (1902), led audiences to expect a rebirth of poetry in English theater, but his subsequent work was a disappointment.

86.   (A)
Tennyson is denouncing by angry paraphrase the credo of late nineteenth-century aestheticism, "art for art's sake."

87.   (B)
Some of Anouilh's work expresses melancholy or disillusionment, but does not focus on the essential absurdity of the human condition, nor does he adopt the methods of absurdist drama.

88.   (D)
Although he played a role in the Irish Renaissance, George Moore was a novelist and short story writer, not a playwright.

89.   (D)
In this passage from *Mr. Edwards and the Spider*, Robert Lowell alludes to the text for Edward's sermon *Sinners in the Hands of an Angry God*.

90.   (E)
In *Keats*, Henry Wadsworth Longfellow identifies Keats with the hero of his poem *Endymion*.

91.   (A)
These lines are from Tennyson's tribute to his friend, *To E. FitzGerald*.

92.   (C)
Horace, in *Art of Poetry*, says the end of poetry is to both please and instruct.

93.   (A)
This is a part of Longinus' explanation, in *On the Sublime*, of what constitutes sublimity in language.

94. (D)

This passage from *The Republic* is part of Plato's explanation of why imitative poets should be excluded from his ideal state.

95. (E)

Sprung rhythm

96. (A)

Hopkins

97. (B)

Bellow

98. (D)

Ellison

99. (E)

Greene

100. (D)

Synesthesia is the description of one kind of sensation in terms of another (here, a sound in terms of a color).

101. (B)

terza rima

102. (E)

Wordsworth's definition of a poet is from the preface to the second edition of the *Lyrical Ballads*.

103. (A)

This excerpt from the *Letters* (November 22, 1817) includes both Keats' belief that the great artist must subdue his own personality, and his identification of truth with beauty.

104. (D)

In *What is Art?*, Tolstoy argues that the value of art lines in its social usefulness -- specifically, promoting the universal Christian brotherhood of man.

105. (D)

"Utopia" plays on Greek words for "no place" and "good place." The term signifies fictional works that present ideal political states and ways of life. Huxley's novel is a Dystopia ("bad place"), depicting an unpleasant imaginary world.

106. (A)

The rhyme scheme in the octave is that of the standard Petrarchan or Italian sonnet (abba abba); the sestet varies slightly from the standard rhyme scheme (cdecde or cdccdc), as is often the case in Italian sonnets.

107. (D)

Even nature, which is amoral, prospers, whereas he feels spiritually empty.

108. (E)

He calls himself "Time's eunuch" because he has not created any work that "lives" (i.e. he has "failed").

109. (B)

Hopkins' poem expresses a deep sense of depression, springing from a period that mystics call "the dark night of the soul." He has not despaired, however, and seeks God's help.

110. (D)

The poem is one of Hopkins's so-called "terrible sonnets."

111. (C)

Mrs. Grundy is the name of a character (who does not appear) in Thomas Morton's play, *Speed the Plough*. Other characters fear her judgments in matters of senseless propriety, for which she has become a symbol.

112. (D)

In *Discourse XIII*, Reynolds answers Plato by arguing that painting and the other arts do not merely imitate nature, but "correct" nature's imperfections.

113. (B)

In *An Essay on the Theatre; or, A Comparison Between Sentimental and Laughing Comedy*, Goldsmith compares sentimental comedy unfavorably with "laughing" comedy that ridicules and evokes laughter rather than tears.

114. (C)

Lessing's *Laocoon* protests the romantic tendency to obscure distinctions among the arts; in this important essay, he argues that differences in media necessarily lead to differences in effects.

115. (E)
Dryden.

116. (C)
Byron.

117. (B)
Molière.

118. (B)
The club was organized by Swift in 1714 to satirize literary incompetence. Dryden died in 1700.

119. (A)
John Skelton's verse consists of short rhymed lines of varying length. It is unconventional, "tumbling," and undignified, suited to his satirical purposes and apparently intended to offend the sensibilities of his learned peers.

120. (A)
Where Angels Fear to Tread is one of Forster's two "Italian" novels (the other is *A Room with a View*).

121. (B)
Malory's *Morte D'Arthur*, Dryden's opera libretto *King Arthur*, Tennyson's *Idylls of the King*, and Twain's *A Connecticut Yankee in King Arthur's Court* all make use of Arthurian legend. Milton contemplated an epic dealing with Arthur, but did not write one.

122. (C)

123. (A)

124. (D)

125. (B)
Language and stones are the media of the poet and the architect; both are subject to "decay" (English is analogous to "ill-chosen stone"), which obscures the artist's talent.

126. (A)

The author's complaint is that an English poet's work cannot last long because the English language, unlike Latin or Greek, changes constantly.

127. (D)

These stanzas are from Waller's *Of English Verse*.

128. (D)

A Künstlerroman ("artist-novel") portrays the development of the artist to the point at which he recognizes his artistic calling. It is a subspecies of the Bildungsroman ("novel of formation").

129. (C)

Swift's work is a mock epic in prose, satirizing various figures in the battle of the moderns and the ancients.

130. (A)

Huxley's "novel with a key" depicts well-known real people, such as D.H. Lawrence, under fictional names.

131. (A)

Oxymoron is a form of paradox that combines two terms that are contraries in ordinary usage.

132. (D)

133. (A)

134. (E)

135. (C)
Butler.

136.　(A)
Peacock.

137.　(D)
Dryden.

138.　(C)
The Pre-Raphaelites, formed about 1850, sought to return to the European art forms they believed existed before Raphael; chiefly they sought truth in nature.

139.　(A)
Hoyden's speech, which illustrates the comic amorality of the sub-plot, is from Act V of Sir John Vanburgh's *The Relapse*.

140.　(D)
Millamant's speech is part of the famous marriage contract scene in Act IV of Congreve's *The Way of the World*.

141.　(B)
Mrs. Malaprop's speech contains several instances of her "nice derangement of epitaphs" in Sheridan's *The Rivals*.

142.　(C)
Freeman's stories deal with New England.

143.　(B)
Both Blake and Yeats created elaborate mythologies as a frame for much of their poetry.

144.　(C)

145. (A)

146. (D)

147. (C)
John Hampden was a member of the Roundhead party who spoke out against royal taxes. Gray uses him as an example of someone who might oppose a tyrant.

148. (A)
Oliver Cromwell became Lord Protector of the Commonwealth after the execution of Charles I. Gray uses him as an example of the criminal who would "wade through slaughter to a throne."

149. (E)
Poverty and lack of education prevented potential Hampdens and Miltons from flowering, but also suppressed the potential Cromwells of the village.

150. (C)
Gray.

151. (E)
From his letter to George and Thomas Keats, December, 1817.

152. (D)
Sinclair's novel is an exposé of the meatpacking industry and political corruption in Chicago, and a work of socialist propaganda.

153. (B)
Farrell's trilogy embodies virtually all of the characteristics of naturalism in fiction.

154. (E)

Foster's novel is perhaps the best early American example of fiction in the mode of Samuel Richardson.

155. (B)

Shaw's title is from the opening line of *Aeneid*: "Arms and the man I sing."

156. (D)

Gray's line is "Far from the madding crowd's ignoble strife, / Their sober wishes never learned to stray."

157. (C)

The words are Miranda's, after she is introduced to people from the outside world.

158. (E)

The term was introduced by W.K. Wimsatt and M.C. Beardsley to denote "the confusion between the poem and its result (what it is and what it does)."

159. (B)

Douglass is the author of the most famous of the slave narratives, which are autobiographical accounts of the experiences of black American slaves.

160. (C)

The Spenserian stanza employs eight iambic pentameter lines followed by an Alexandrine. Here Pope describes the possible bad effects of the longer (hexameter) final line in a Spenserian stanza.

161. (D)

An Alexandrine is a line of six iambic feet.

162. (C)

Although she know that Queen Hermione is really alive, Paulina rebukes King Leontes for his jealous cruelty in Act III of *The Winter's Tale*.

163. (A)

In Act V of *The Tempest*, Prospero abjures his use of "white" magic.

164. (D)

Lear is speaking to Cordelia in Act V of *King Lear*.

165. (C)

166. (B)

167. (D)

168. (D)

The poem is Hardy's *Ah, Are You Digging on my Grave?*

169. (C)
Meredith.

170. (A)
Austen.

171. (C)

The pastoral elegy presents the mourner and the person mourned for as shepherds. The poetic form originated in ancient Greece, continued in Rome, and was practiced in England through the nineteenth century.

172. (B)
Drayton's sonnet contains three quatrains and a couplet that has an epigrammatic turn.

173. (E)
The ode is a long, serious, stylistically elevated lyric with an elaborate stanzaic structure. Like earlier Pindaric odes, Dryden's poem was written to praise something (here, the arts of poetry and music).

174. (A)
An encomium is something written to praise someone; originally, it was restricted to a poem or speech praising someone before a select group.

175. (D)
A threnody is a song of lamentation, a dirge or song of death.

176. (B)
An epithalamium is a bridal song.

177. (E)
A litany is a form of supplication, especially in difficult times (for example, Thomas Nashe, *A Litany in Time of Plague*).

178. (D)
An exemplum is a particular story told to illustrate the general text of a sermon. The Pardoner's text is "the love of money is the root of all evil."

179. (B)
A fable is a short story that illustrates a principle of human behavior or exemplifies a moral thesis. In La Fontaine's fable, a simple fellow learns from experience that God's works are good (specifically, that there is a good reason for small acorns rather than large pumpkins growing on large oaks).

180.   (A)

A fabliau is a short comic or satiric and realistic tale dealing with common people and generally focusing on the obscene or ribald, as is the case in *The Miller's Tale*.

181.   (B)

Spenser's Sonnet 75 (from his sonnet sequence *Amoretti*) expresses an ancient and traditional theme -- that poetry is capable of bestowing immortality (his verse will "eternize" her "vertues").

182.   (C)

The Spenserian sonnet, a variant of the English sonnet, links each quatrain to the next by a continuing rhyme: abab bcbc cdcd ee.

183.   (E)
Shakespeare.
184.   (D)
Humphrey Clinker (1771) consists of a series of letters among characters.

185.   (A)
Gil Blas (1715) was the most popular of French picaresque novels.

186.   (C)

Richardson sustains a stream-of-consciousness narrative throughout the twelve volumes of *Pilgrimage* (1915-1938).

187.   (C)

Cumberland's play (1771) incorporates most of the tenets of eighteenth-century sentimental doctrine.

188.   (E)
The Rehearsal (1671) satirizes the language and various extravagant aspects of heroic drama.

189. (A)

Etherege's play (1676) is among the earliest and best of the Restoration comedies of manners.

190. (D)

Burney's novel (1778) depicts the customs and conventions of eighteenth-century English society.

191. (C)

Austen satirizes the excesses and absurdities of Gothic fiction in *Northanger Abbey*.

192. (A)

Goldsmith's novel (1766) is perhaps the best fictional manifestation of eighteenth-century sentimentalism.

193. (E)

A Bildungsroman traces the maturation process of a young person.

194. (B)
Lillo.

195. (E)
Dreyden.

196. (A)
Kyd.

197. (D)
Milton.

198. (D)

Lawrence was annoyed by the apparent social complacency of most members of the Bloomsbury group.

199. (D)

Maturin's novel of terror and mystery is *Melmoth the Wanderer* (1820).

200. (E)

In this poem, time "worships language" and forgives the flaws of those who wrote well (but not the innocent, brave, or beautiful).

201. (B)

Kipling's "views" were imperialistic, and Claudel was extremely right-wing. Yeats' politics were sometimes antidemocratic and apparently supportive of dictatorship.

202. (C)

These stanzas are from Auden's *In Memory of W. B. Yeats*.

203. (C)

Cervantes subjects the forms and conventions of medieval romance to comic treatment in *Don Quixote*.

204. (B)

Phillips exaggerates the highly formal style of *Paradise Lost* and applies it to low subject matter.

205. (E)

Fielding substitutes the lusty adventures of his male hero for the tribulations of Richardson's sexually beseiged heroine.

206. (D)

The excerpt is from Samuel Johnson's *Life of Cowley*, in which he defines the wit present in metaphysical poetry.

207. (C)

Pope's description of wit as "that which has been often thought, but was never before so well expressed" does not value originality as a primary quality of wit. The "more noble and adequate" conception discussed by Johnson in the second paragraph makes originality and naturalness the two chief qualities that define wit. Pope's description also includes "naturalness." Both conceptions also stress universality (that which is widely acknowledged to be just).

208. (B)

The definition of wit Johnson proposes in the third paragraph emphasizes the psychological process or activity of mind of the poet in discovering resemblances in apparently dissimilar things. This conception of wit deemphasizes "effects upon the hearer," universality, propriety or decorum, and actual properties in the work to focus on energetic mental activity, thereby yielding a definition of wit that includes that found in metaphysical poetry.

209. (D)

These are the opening lines from the medieval popular ballad, *Sir Patrick Spens*.

210. (A)

These are the opening lines of *Sir Walter Raleigh to His Son* (ca. 1600).

211. (C)

The stanza is from *The Passionate Shepherd to His Love*.

212. (C)

These two stanzas are from *A Valediction: Forbidding Mourning*.

213.   (E)
This is the first of the two stanzas in Owen's *Anthem for Doomed Youth*.

214.   (B)
These lines are from Wheatley's *On Being Brought from Africa to America*.

215.   (B)
These lines are from *Ode to a Nightingale*.

216.   (B)
These lines are from Browning's dramatic monologue, *Porphyria's Lover*.

217.   (D)
These lines are from Yeats' *Sailing to Byzantium*.

218.   (A)
These characteristically jagged lines are from *Colin Clout*, an anti-clerical satire attacking Cardinal Wolsey.

219.   (B)
These lines from *Paradise Lost* are spoken by Satan as he bids farewell to Heaven and enters Hell.

220.   (D)
These are the opening lines from Cummings' *a salesman is an it that stinks Excuse*.

221.   (C)

   This stanza is from Lowell's *The Biglow Papers*, presented as the poetry of a young New England Yankee farmer who protests the spread of slavery.

222.   (C)

   These lines are from *Tintern Abbey*.

223.   (E)

   This is the opening stanza from Holmes' society verse *My Aunt*.

224.   (E)

   These lines are from Baraka's *Poem for Half-White College Students*.

225.   (B)

   These lines are from Swift's *A Description of a City Shower*.

226.   (E)

   These lines are from Plath's *Daddy*.

227.   (C)

   These couplets are from Epistle I of Pope's *An Essay on Man*.

228.   (C)

   This is the opening stanza from No. 286 (*The Poems of Emily Dickinson*, 3 vols., ed. T. Johnson, 1955).

229.   (C)

   This is the opening stanza from *London* in Blake's *Songs of Experience*.

230.   (A)

   These lines are from Stevie Smith's *Mother, Among the Dustbins*.